D0283465

INSIDERS' GUIDE® TO
THE FLORIDA KEYS AND KEY WEST

Help Us Keep This Guide Up to Date

Every effort has been made by the author and editors to make this guide as accurate and useful as possible. However, many things can change after a guide is published—establishments close, phone numbers change, facilities come under new management, etc.

We would love to hear from you concerning your experiences with this guide and how you feel it could be improved and be kept up to date. While we may not be able to respond to all comments and suggestions, we'll take them to heart and we'll also make certain to share them with the author. Please send your comments and suggestions to the following address:

The Globe Pequot Press
Reader Response/Editorial Department
P.O. Box 480
Guilford, CT 06437

Or you may e-mail us at:

editorial@globe-pequot.com

Thanks for your input, and happy travels!

INSIDERS' GUIDE® SERIES

Insiders' Guide®
to the Florida Keys
and Key West

SIXTH EDITION

By Victoria Shearer

Guilford, Connecticut
An imprint of The Globe Pequot Press

Maps by Brandon Ray

ISBN: 0-7627-1214-7

Manufactured in the United States of America
Sixth Edition/First Printing

Contents

Directory of Maps

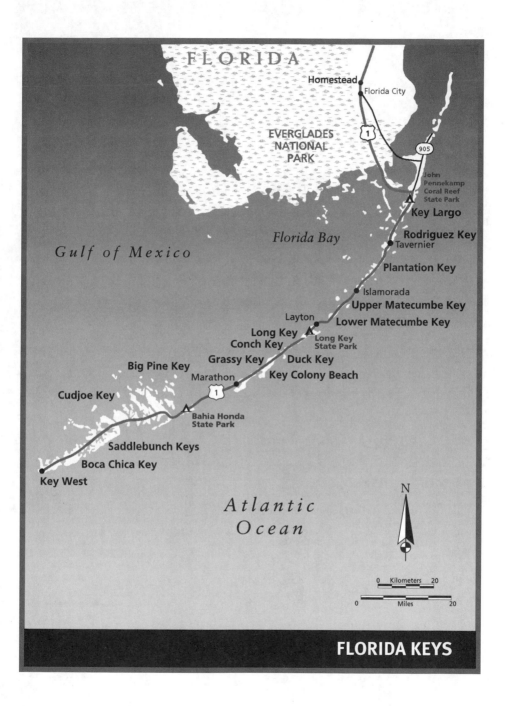

FLORIDA

Homestead
Florida City
1

EVERGLADES
NATIONAL
PARK

905

John
Pennekamp
Coral Reef
State Park
Key Largo

Florida Bay
Rodriguez Key
Tavernier

Gulf of Mexico
Plantation Key

Islamorada
Upper Matecumbe Key
Layton
Lower Matecumbe Key
Long Key
Long Key
Conch Key
State Park
Grassy Key
Duck Key
Big Pine Key
Key Colony Beach
Marathon
1
Cudjoe Key
Bahia Honda
State Park

Saddlebunch Keys
Boca Chica Key
Key West

Atlantic
Ocean

N

0   Kilometers   20

0   Miles   20

FLORIDA KEYS

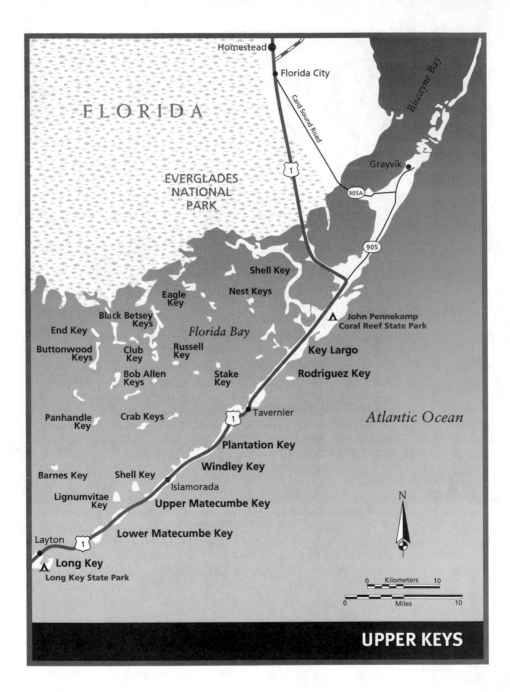

UPPER KEYS

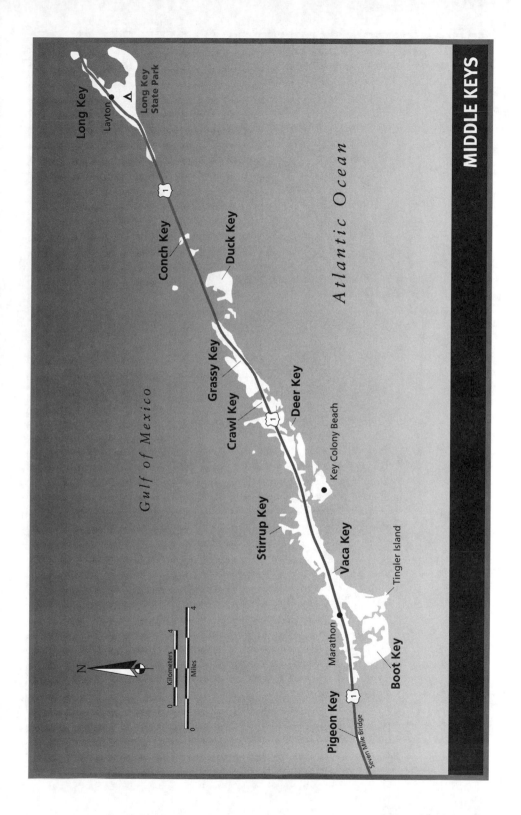

MIDDLE KEYS

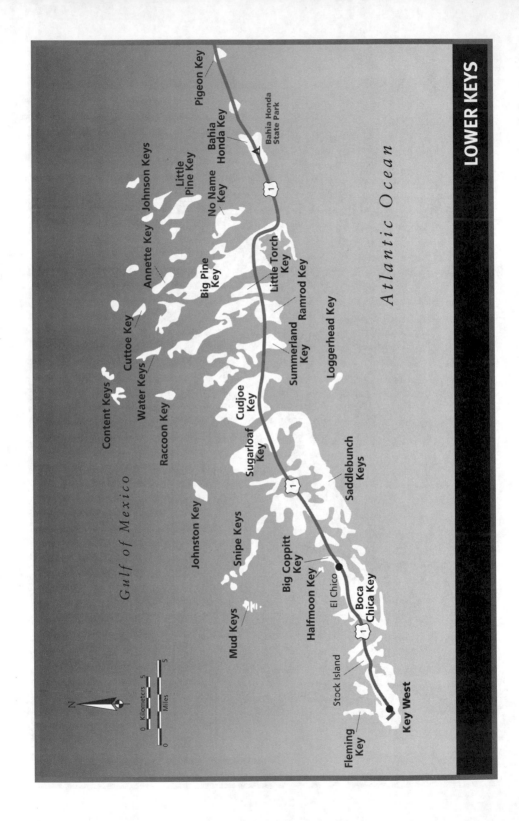

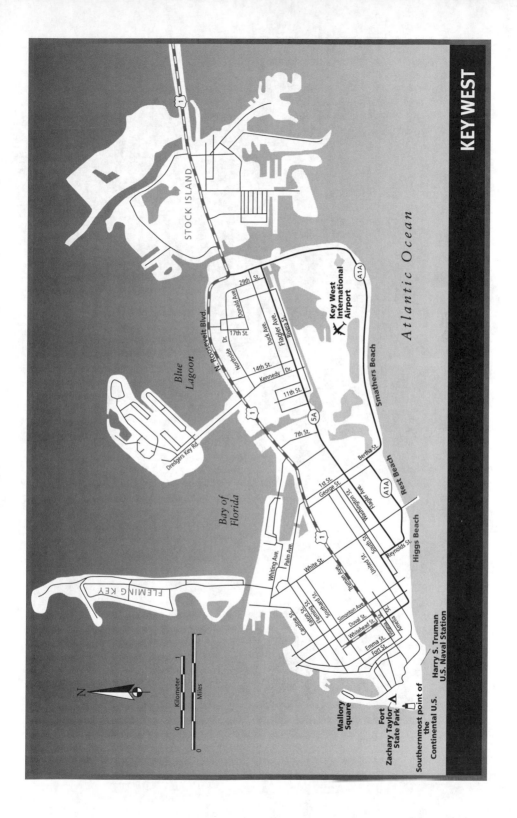

KEY WEST

In the Florida Keys we justifiably lay claim to the most spectacular sunsets in the universe.

Acknowledgments

The Beatles said it all when they crooned, "I get by with a little help from my friends," and mine rank right up there on the Top 40. To my best friend and life partner, my husband, Bob, thank you for undying patience, encouragement, and support from the first edition right through this 6th update. And my gratitude for translating a lifetime of Florida Keys angling experience for me so that we can all catch the magic of the sport. To my dear friends Wayne and Mary Moccia, thank you for sharing your expansive knowledge of the Keys' cruising waters and for divulging your secret hideaways and favorite dive locations. And a special thanks to Mary, who shared her newfound love of photography with Insiders everywhere for this edition. Your shots are fantastic! To Barbara and Dick Marlin, thanks for all the good camping tips. To James and Frankie Hankins, Joe Winter, and John and Louise Skidmore, thanks for the fishing photo ops and the many Insider angling and lobstering tips. To the Lunch Bunch—which grows larger and more dedicated every year—culinary medals of the year to you all for *still* visiting the restaurants of my choice and critiquing your food. To John Ghee, Dick Adler, and the Everglades houseboat gang, thanks for the green flash, the sunset scale, and years of giggles. To my many friends on Duck Key—you know who you are—thank you for all the unsolicited tips and Insider info that you continue to send my way, and, most importantly, for never failing to ask, "How's it going?" I am truly blessed. My appreciation to my Insiders' Guide editor, Erika Serviss, and to the folks at Globe Pequot Press. And finally, love to my all-grown-up children and their spouses—Kristen, John, Brian, and Lisa—and to my mothers, June and Ann, for their enduringly patient understanding of my deadline-oriented lifestyle. And love and kisses to the lights of my life, my grandchildren Bethany, Bobby, and Christopher. Good job, Insiders. Thanks for the memories.

Preface

Forget the black-and-white world you leave behind. When you arrive in the Florida Keys, life suddenly turns to Technicolor, and it doesn't take a twister to lead you to the lush Emerald City of Oz. Settle yourself in. Take Toto along, too.

Nowhere else on earth is there an Eden such as ours, where all are admitted freely and via so many varied means. Ours is the land of dreamers, doers, and do-si-doers, of train makers, treasure trovers, and time-honored tranquillity. There are no munchkins along the yellow brick road that unites each of our magical isles and then appends us to the mainland. In the Florida Keys, everyone and everything is larger than life.

Look closely, and the enigmatic view from afar becomes as lucid as the crystalline waters of the Atlantic Ocean and the Gulf of Mexico that envelop us. From coconut palms to cormorants, you'll see that we are more than the Duval Street party scene in Key West. We are angelfish and anemones, gorgonians and groupers, lobsters and lizard-fish, sponges and stone crabs. We're a thriving city of marine creatures commuting daily from North America's only barrier reef, approximately 6 miles offshore, to sweeping underwater meadows of turtlegrass nearshore where we forage and feed.

By day, we are the golden sun that rises over the ocean, glows brightly and then, in ardent shades of red, dips ever-so-gently beneath the Gulf horizon. As darkness enfolds the Florida Keys, we are the cornucopia of stars that seem to gleam more brilliantly here in our endless skies than anywhere else.

We are a necklace of tiny, pearl islands tenuously strung together by 42 majestic bridges and the dream of one man, Henry Morrison Flagler. We're divers and diesel mechanics, anglers and archaeologists, sailors and salvagers, cruisers and commercial fishermen, boaters and bartenders, gunk-holers and guides, restaurateurs and real estate agents, hoteliers and hostesses. And our heart is in the sea.

In countless ways we are history. We're the ghosts of Spanish conquistadors, Native American Calusas, Bahamian fishermen, and Cuban cigar makers. We're the bones of ships smashed so soundly against the reef that we forever rest in a watery, offshore grave-yard. We're pirates, smugglers, wreckers, spongers, and turtlers. We've built boats, light-houses, and wharfs—even a bat tower. We've survived without fresh water and in hurricane gales, amid clouds of mosquitoes and through Indian massacres. We're no strangers to courage.

We are hardwood hammocks, tropical pinelands, and mangrove islets. Unique in the universe, we are diminutive Key deer, sour Key limes, and endangered Key Largo woodrats. We are nesting great white herons, communal white pelicans, and showy roseate spoonbills. Creatures great and small, we are bonefish and billfish, sharks and stingrays, sea turtles, manatees, and dolphins. And, because we vigilantly guard our copi-ous treasures, we are The Florida Keys Wild Bird Center, Reef Relief, The Turtle Hospi-tal, The Nature Conservancy, and Bay Watch. At last we have a brain.

We are the 81,000 full- and part-time Florida Keys citizens: men, women, and chil-dren of all races, religions, and sexual preferences. Rich, poor, and somewhere in between, each of us sports similar T-shirts, shorts, and sunglasses. We bear genuine, unpretentious smiles, seeking little more than the harmony needed to fully render a place called Paradise.

Whether you mistakenly believe that you lack a heart...a brain...the nerve...you're sure to unearth it all along with a deeply enriched spirit, on your journey through the mysteries, rich history, and legends of the Florida Keys. Experience all the marvels of this awe-inspiring Oz. You'll never want to click your ruby slippers, sandals, or bare feet—or board a plane, boat, or automobile longing for home. One visit is, after all, what led so very many of us to become Insiders. Welcome to this side of the rainbow. We are the Florida Keys.

Superlatives fall short when describing Little Palm Island because this resort, a tiny slice of Paradise, soars off the charts. PHOTO: LITTLE PALM ISLAND

Bananas, with colorful flower heralding the prolific stand, grow well in the Florida Keys' subtropic climate. PHOTO: VICTORIA SHEARER

How to Use This Book

Here at the southernmost tip of the continental United States, the serpentine Overseas Highway fuses many of our 800-plus islands with ligaments of vaulted bridges and concrete connective tissue.

Ours is a marriage of land and sea. To merely introduce you to the topside society of the Florida Keys would neglect the flamboyant and fascinating communities living below. This guide lifts the curtain, bringing the many facets of our watery stage to life. We treat you to our unique geology and colorful history. We introduce you to the flora and fauna of the habitats of our tropical ecosystem. And we take you where you may have never been before—fishing, diving, and boating in our waters.

We'll help you sate your appetite with listings of restaurants, seafood markets, and specialty food shops. We'll show you where the action is with the rundown on attractions, recreation sites, festivals and special events, and nightlife of the Keys. We'll offer myriad alternatives for you to rest your weary head: hotels, motels, inns, guesthouses, and condominiums; campgrounds; even resort marinas and anchoring-out spots for your motor or sailing yacht. Landlubber or seafarer, everything you need to know is in *The Insiders' Guide to the Florida Keys and Key West*.

To navigate this book, begin with the assumption you are traveling "down the Keys," that is, from Key Largo to Key West. We have organized our information by descending mile marker. Mile markers are those small green signs with white numbers you'll see posted at the sides of the Overseas Highway (U.S. Hwy. 1). We have designated mile marker addresses as either oceanside (on your left as you travel down the Keys) or bayside (on your right as you go toward Key West). At Key West, which is MM 0, locations are stated using street names.

Most chapters have three parts. A general preface to the subject matter acquaints you with aspects of the topic common to all areas of the Florida Keys. This is followed by specifics for the Upper Keys (MM 106 on Key Largo to MM 70 on Long Key), Middle Keys (MM 70 to MM 39 on Ohio Key) and the Lower Keys (MM 39 to Stock Island). The final section will give you the scoop on Stock Island and Key West, the entrance to which is actually about MM 3, although such appellations are not used in Key West.

When making phone calls from outside the area, note that the area code in the Florida Keys is 305. The Florida Keys is divided into calling areas, or scopes. You may call within a scope by using only seven digits. To dial Florida Keys numbers outside a calling scope you will need to first dial 1-305 and then the seven digits. Such calls made with BellSouth service, as well as some calls made to area code 305 in Miami, incur a flat 25 cents rate, regardless of how long you talk. Calls with other carriers, such as MCI or AT&T, may be charged differently.

The following calling scopes require only seven-digit numbers:

Key West—from Key West to Sugarloaf Key.
Sugarloaf Key—from Big Pine Key to Key West.
Big Pine Key—from Marathon to Sugarloaf Key.
Marathon—from Big Pine Key to Islamorada.
Islamorada—from Key Largo to Marathon.
Key Largo—from Islamorada to North Key Largo.
North Key Largo—to Key Largo.

Throughout all the chapters we have sprinkled Insiders' Tips, extracted from those in the know with a little arm-twisting. You'll find enlightening Close-ups chock-full of information on everything from a recipe for Key lime pie to how to make yellowtail chum balls. And, just so you will be sure to understand the language, we have included a glossary of Keys-speak.

You hold in your hand a passport to the Florida Keys. We help you hit the road, explore the sea, and speak the language of the natives. Locals call this Paradise. Judge for yourself.

Keys-Speak Glossary

backcountry—shallow seagrass meadows and mangrove islet waters of Florida Bay

bayside—anything on the opposite coast from the Atlantic; i.e. Florida Bay in the Upper Keys, the Gulf of Mexico in the Middle and Lower Keys

bight—a body of water bounded by a bend or curve in the shore; several are found in Key West

bluewater—deep, offshore waters of the Atlantic Ocean

chickee—an open-sided, thatched-roof hut commonly found near the water's edge that is used as shelter from the sun

Conch—a descendant of the original Bahamians that settled the Keys; a person born in the Florida Keys

freshwater Conch—a person who has lived in the Florida Keys for at least seven years

conch—meat of a marine mollusk used in chowder and fritters; once a staple in the diet of early Conchs and Keys-dwelling Native Americans, now an endangered species that may not be harvested in the Keys

Croakies—band for securing sunglasses around your head so they don't fall overboard

'cuda—slang for barracuda

flats—shallow, nearshore waters of the Atlantic

gunk-hole—to explore the shallow, nearshore waters and mangrove islets in a shallow draft craft in search of bird life and marine species

hammock—an elevated piece of bedrock covered with a hardwood tropical forest; also a woven lounger strung between two palm trees

oceanside—anything on the Atlantic coast of the Keys

Paradise—The Florida Keys

The Rock—Slang for the Florida Keys, usually uttered by locals heading for the mainland to vacation, shop, or party, i.e., "I need to get off the Rock."

Gateway to the Keys

The rural areas of Homestead and Florida City, home to alligators, airboat rides, agriculture, and achievement, are known as the Gateway to the Florida Keys.

Residents of these two south Miami-Dade County cities are courageous and industrious individuals, continuously demonstrating resilience in the wake of peril. To date, four mighty hurricanes have altered their region's history. Andrew, the most recent, roared across South Florida in August 1992 with 150 mph winds, causing some $30 billion in damage and leaving an estimated 160,000 homeless. Almost immediately, the residents of south Miami-Dade County resolved to rejuvenate their community, and they have remarkably succeeded.

Today, with two of nature's most splendid showpieces and the opening of the multi-million-dollar motorsports complex in November 1995, Homestead and Florida City draw more than a million tourists each year. Riveted by the glory of Everglades and Biscayne National Parks and the thrill of NASCAR racing, visitors find ample reason to pause at "The Gateway" before continuing on to the Florida Keys and Key West.

First settled by the Tequesta and Calusa Indian tribes some 11,000 years ago, south Miami-Dade County was later inhabited by Creeks and Muskogees, or Seminoles (meaning "separatists"). In 1830, many Seminoles were forced west to Oklahoma along the Trail of Tears. Those who remained in south Miami-Dade either lost their lives or barely managed to endure the tragic Seminole Wars. Ultimately, survivors found refuge within the area now designated as Everglades National Park. Their descendants continue to reside there.

Had it not been for the Florida Keys and Key West—and Henry Flagler's effort to extend the Florida East Coast Railroad to this country's southernmost city—Homestead and Florida City might not be what they are today. Railway officials laid out a town toward the end of the mainland, workers settled in, and a station house and water plant were built. These workers recommended naming the town Homestead, and Flagler approved. He sent a tomato farmer to the area south of Homestead, and the town founded by this farmer became known as Detroit. Engineer William Krome directed construction of the railway, and Krome Avenue, which parallels U.S. Highway 1 through the two cities, was named for him.

The marl lands (marl is calcitic mud beneath the water of the Everglades) near Detroit had already spurred a growth in farming. Portions of the Everglades had been drained, crops were harvested and, at last, the railroad station provided a means of shipping produce north. When the railway to Key West was completed in 1912, it provided easier access to the Florida Keys and a means of receiving fresh water. Property values in this new agricultural community began to skyrocket. In 1914, residents of Detroit incorporated and renamed their new city Florida City. Ten years later, the residents of Homestead incorporated their city. In 1926, a powerful hurricane prompted an exodus of many area residents, and the great Labor Day hurricane of 1935 came along and destroyed Flagler's Key West extension of the railway (see our Historical Evolution chapter).

The "Gateway" population dwindled.

It wasn't until 1942 that Homestead and Florida City began to experience a rebirth. The Army Air Corps established Homestead Army Air Field as a training base on the site of what had been a county-owned airfield used by Pan American Ferries Inc., and it became one of the largest military installations in the nation. Home to approximately 25,000 military personnel, civilian employees, and dependents as well as its own hospital, bank, post office, library, nursery, preschool, barber shops, and more, the field eventually became an official military base, pumping $450 million annually into the local economy.

Following World War II and yet another hurricane in 1945, the base closed, reopened, and then closed again. In 1979, the Pentagon transferred 25 percent of its military personnel from south Miami-Dade to other bases, and retail businesses and housing in Homestead and Florida City suffered immeasurably. Later, the facility reopened as a tactical air command and training base, but it never again funneled the amount of money into these communities it once did. In the early '90s, heavy damage during Hurricane Andrew and federal government budget cuts leveled a knock-out punch to the once robust base.

The south Miami-Dade County economy today relies heavily on agriculture. Fruits and vegetables for many tables throughout the United States are grown in this area, and nurseries and landscaping operations are big business here.

One word describes the Florida Keys—Paradise. PHOTO: VICTORIA SHEARER

Historical Evolution

The saga of the Keys, like the livelihoods of its inhabitants, tethers itself first, foremost, and forever to the sea. Our fragile strand of coral beads, which arcs southwest from the U.S. mainland to within 100 miles of Cuba, has endured for eons at the mercy of the elements. Nature determined, more than humans ever did, the course of our history. That is, until one man accomplished what natural forces could not: he connected the islands to each other and to the mainland United States.

We will chronicle the Florida Keys, therefore, as a manmade triptych, highlighting the eras before, during, and after Henry Flagler's Florida East Coast Railroad Extension refashioned the subsequent history of the region.

Prologue

Native Americans and the Spanish

The earliest recorded evidence of a Native American population in the Keys is estimated to be around A.D. 800, when maritime Indians populated the islands. Kitchen middens, or mounds of fish and sea-turtle bones and conch shells, can be found throughout the Keys. Archaeologists believe that although ancient villages may have existed thousands of years before this time, the rising sea level of the present Holocene Epoch (see our Paradise Found chapter) has buried these settlements beneath the ocean.

Historians cannot agree on which tribes of Native Americans inhabited the Florida Keys in the ensuing centuries. The Tequestas, Calusas, Matecumbes, Caribbean Island tribes, and Seminoles from the mainland are all mentioned, although no archaeological evidence is conclusive. Widely accepted, however, is the notion that the Native Americans were seafarers by necessity and initially friendly to the white men they encountered.

Ponce de Leon garnered the credit for naming the Florida Keys *Los Martires* in 1513 during his exploration of the Gulf of Mexico. Legend maintains that the string of rock islands looked to him like suffering martyrs from his vantage point at sea. The Spanish took interest in the Native Americans of *Los Martires* in the centuries that followed, but had no desire to seize their rocky islands. Priests from Havana attempted to convert the Native Americans to Catholicism. This was not an attempt to save their souls but to teach them to be friendly to the crews of the Spanish ships and to hate the French and English, Spain's enemies who also were attempting to explore the New World. Spain's overriding interest in the Florida Keys at this time simply was to protect their fleet of treasure ships voyaging past its shores en route from Mexico and Cuba to the mother country.

The Gulf Stream: Treasure Highway

Long before the Overseas Highway became the main road of the Florida Keys, another highway controlled the islands' destiny: the great, blue river-in-the-Atlantic—the Gulf Stream. (The warm water of the Gulf Stream, the temperature of which varies greatly from surrounding waters, flows in a northerly direction between the Keys and Cuba, up the northeast coast of the United States and then turns toward the east where it crosses the Atlantic Ocean to the European continent.) Conquistadors, explorers, and adventurers capitalized on the pulsing clockwise current (2 to 4 knots) to carry them swiftly back to Europe, where they unloaded the harvested riches of the New World at the feet of greedy monarchs.

The Spanish were the first to send their treasure-laden ships on this precarious route past our island chain, which is protected from the ocean's fury by a barrier coral reef (see our Diving and Snorkeling chapter). The Gulf Stream, which is not a definitive channel, winds an uneven course about 45 miles wide just outside the reef. Bad weather or bad judgment dashed the hopes, dreams, and cargo of hundreds of ships against this unforgiving coral graveyard.

It was the Native Americans who initially took advantage of this unexpected shipwrecked bounty, but salvaging became big business in the Keys with the arrival of the Bahamian Conchs (see "Wrecking Industry" in this chapter). The passing ships inspired piracy from many nations, particularly the English who lurked in the cuts and channels between the islands waiting to raid the ships' caches of gold and silver.

The Native Americans learned the ways of the Europeans, trading with the Spanish in Havana by means of large oceangoing canoes, pirating English ships, and free-diving to salvage the cargo of their wrecked vessels. Falling ill with the white man's diseases greatly reduced Native American numbers. In 1763 Spain gave Florida to England in exchange for Cuba. At this time, the last of the indigenous Native American families fled to Havana, fearing retribution for the cruelty they had heaped upon the British sailors found dashed upon the reef and stranded.

The Bahamians

By the early 1700s, a group of white settlers from the Bahamas had begun active trading with Havana. Their ancestors, religious dissenters from England, had originally settled on Eleuthera and the Great Abaco Islands in the Bahamas in the 1600s. Experienced seamen and fishermen, these Bahamians harvested the waters of the Florida Keys, selling their catch in Havana. (Many believe the word "key" is derived from the English word

"cay," which in turn is a corruption of the Spanish "cayo," all meaning "island.") The Keys were considered the pantry of Havana, for our waters supplied Cuba with green-turtle meat, conch, fish, and crawfish. The Bahamians traded their catch for knives, rope, spices, and other much-needed supplies, which they took back to the Bahamas.

When the English took over Florida in 1763, they proclaimed the waters near the Florida Keys off-limits to residents of the Bahamas, which upset the trade balance between the Bahamas and Havana. This inconvenience was short-lived, however, because Spain regained Florida in 1783, and trade between the Bahamas and Cuba returned to normal. There was some settlement of the Keys by the English during this interval, but colonization of Key West did not begin in earnest until 1821, when Spain ceded Florida to the United States. Before 1821 Key West was just a watering stop for ships traveling the Gulf Stream route from the Gulf to the Atlantic.

A new edict insisting that only U.S. residents could engage in the now lucrative wrecking operations off the Florida Keys spurred many Bahamian families to emigrate to the settlement of Key West. Many dismantled their entire houses and transported them to our southernmost city (see the Architecture Close-up in our Attractions chapter). Some settlers were freed black slaves, dumped throughout the Bahamian islands by the English as they were released from captured slave traders. Ship owners and captains of merchant ships moved to Key West to be close to the trade lanes.

British Bahamians were known as Conchs for three legendary reasons: First, a prolific amount of conch flourished in the waters of the Bahamas, and the meat from the conical shells was a staple in the Bahamian diet. Second, it is believed that as a means of early communication, the Bahamian islanders blew into queen conch shells, creating a distinctive wailing cry that could be heard a great distance. Third, during the American Revolution of 1776, Tory sympathizers escaped to the Bahamas, where they supposedly said, "We'd rather eat conchs than go to war." Only descendants of the original settlers may legitimately be called Conchs, although today the word generally refers to anyone born in the Florida Keys.

Key West

A time-honored story persists that warring tribes of mainland Seminoles and island Calusas had one final battle on the southernmost island of our chain of keys. Spanish conquistadors purportedly found the island strewn with bleached bones of the Native Americans and called the key *Cayo Hueso*, (pronounced KY-o WAY-so) or "island of bones." Bahamian settlers pronounced the Spanish name as Key West.

Settled long before the other keys in the chain, Key West was very much a maritime frontier town by the 1820s, booming with sea-driven industries. Ships sailing out of Key West Harbor set across the Florida Straits to Havana, their holds filled with the fish, sea turtles, and sponges harvested along the length of the Keys. A lively fishing trade with Cuba continued into the 1870s. The melting pot of Key West included seamen from many cultures: black Bahamians, West Indian

During the Second Seminole War Indian Key was attacked and burned by Seminole Indians. Today, Indian Key is a state historical site. PHOTO: MARY MOCCIA

Once the railhead of Flagler's East Coast Railway Extension, the Seven Mile Bridge is now a modern highway linking Marathon and the Lower Keys. PHOTO: FLORIDA KEYS & KEY WEST TDC

blacks, Spanish Cubans, and white Bahamians of English descent.

Key West was incorporated in 1828. Within 10 years it was the largest and wealthiest city in the territory of Florida, even though it could only be reached by ship, a geographic fact of life that continued until Henry Flagler's Florida East Coast Railroad Extension was finished in 1912. But it was the very waters isolating Key West from the rest of the world that contributed to its wealth.

Piracy

When the United States gained possession of Florida and the Florida Keys in 1821, the island of Key West took on a strategic importance as a U.S. naval base. Lt. Matthew Perry, who was assigned to secure the island for the United States, deemed Key West a safe, convenient, and extensive harbor. It became the base of operations to fight the piracy that ravaged the trading vessels traveling the Gulf Stream superhighway and those heading through the Gulf of Mexico to New Orleans. English, French, and Dutch buccaneers had threatened the Spanish treasure galleons in the eighteenth century. In the early days of the 1800s, Spanish pirates, based mainly in Cuba, hid among the islands of the Keys and preyed on all nations, especially the United States. Using schooners with centerboards that drew only 4 to 5 feet of water, the pirate ships dipped in and out of the shallow cuts and channels to avoid capture.

In 1830 Commodore David Porter was sent to Key West to head up an anti-piracy fleet and wipe out the sea-jacking from the region. Commandeering barge-style vessels equipped with oars, Porter and his crews were able to follow the sea dogs into the shallow waters and overtake them. After 1830 the area was safe from banditry once again.

The Wrecking Industry

Whereas the Gulf Stream was once the sea highway carrying Spanish treasure galleons back to Europe, in the eighteenth and nineteenth centuries the route was traversed in the opposite direction. Trading vessels sailed from New England ports to the French and British islands of the West Indies and the Antilles, hugging the shoreward edge of the Gulf Stream so as not to have to run against its strong northerly currents. They often ran aground on the reef, giving birth to a lucrative wrecking industry that salvaged silks, satins, lace, leather, crystal, china, silver, furniture, wine, whiskey, and more.

After the United States took possession of Florida in 1821, Key West became an official wrecking and salvage station for the federal government, which sought to regulate and cash in on the lucrative trade that until this time was going to Nassau or Havana. Salvage masters had to get a license from a district court judge, proving that they and their salvage vessels were free of fraud. By 1854 wrecking was a widely practiced profession in the Keys. Fleets of schooners patrolled the Keys from Biscayne to the Dry Tortugas. First

Insiders' Tip

Widows' walks atop Key West buildings—long said to be the spots where lonely sea captains' wives watched for their husbands' arrivals—were actually the lookout spots from which islanders awaited sightings of shipwrecks in the waters off the reef. "Wreck ashore," was heralded when a ship went aground, inciting a frenzy of people to the wharf to watch the wreckers race to the floundering ship.

Exhibits at the Key West Shipwreck Historeum recall the days when wrecking was the southernmost city's chief industry. PHOTO: JANET WARE

they would assist the shipwrecked sailors, then try to save the ship (there was no Coast Guard in those days).

Unlike early unregulated times, the wreckers couldn't just lay claim to the ship's cargo for themselves. They were paid off in shares of the bounty. During peak wrecking years, 1850 to 1860, nearly one ship per week hit the reefs, some with cargo valued in the millions of dollars.

Although by 1826 some of the reefs along the length of the Keys were marked by lighthouses or light ships, most remained treacherous and claimed many cargoes, particularly in the Upper Keys where the Gulf Stream meanders close to the reef. Stories have endured throughout the years that some of the more enterprising and unscrupulous wreckers even changed or removed navigational markers or flashed lights in imitation of a light ship to lure an unsuspecting vessel to its demise on a shallow shoal so they could salvage the cargo. The construction of additional lighthouses along the reef in the mid-1800s improved navigation to the

point that the wrecking industry gradually faded away by the end of the nineteenth century.

Sponging

Sponging developed quickly in the Keys after the area became part of the United States, maturing into a commercially important industry by 1850.

Sponge harvesting initially was accomplished from a dinghy: One man sculled while the other looked through a glass-bottomed bucket. The spotter held a long pole with a small, three-pronged rake on one end used to impale the sponge and bring it into the boat. On shore, the sponges were laid on the ground to dry in the sun so that the living animal within would dehydrate and die. The sponges then were soaked for a week and pounded on a rock or beaten with a stick to remove a blackish covering. Cleaned of weeds, washed, and hung to dry in bunches, the sponges were displayed for sale.

Cubans, Greeks, and Conchs harvested the sponges as fast and furiously as they could, with little regard for how the supply would be maintained, and it inevitably began to diminish. The Greeks began diving deeper waters for the sponges, much in demand on the world market by 1900, and eventually moved to Florida's west coast at Tarpon Springs, where the sponging was more bountiful.

By 1940 a blight wiped out all but about 10 percent of the Keys' sponge population. Although sponges again grow in our waters, commercial sponging is no longer a viable industry as synthetic sponges have absorbed the market.

Cubans and the Cigar Industry

Cuba, closer to Key West than Miami is, has always played a role in the historical evolution of the Keys. Cuban fishermen long frequented the bountiful Keys waters, and in the nineteenth century Cuban émigrés brought new life and new industry to Key West. William H. Wall built a small cigar factory in the 1830s on Key West's Front Street. It was not until a year after the Cuban Revolution of 1868, when a prominent Cuban by the name of Señor Vicente Martinez Ybor moved his cigar-making factory to Key West from Havana, that the new era of cigar manufacturing began in earnest.

E.H. Gato and a dozen or so other cigar-making companies followed Ybor. And an influx of Cuban immigrant cigar workers "washed ashore," joining the melting pot in Key West. Tobacco arrived in bales from Havana, and production grew until factories numbered 161, catapulting Key West to the rank of cigar-making capital of the United States. Though the manufacturers moved their businesses to Key West to escape high Cuban tariffs and the cigar-makers union, the unions reestablished themselves in Key West by 1879, and troubles began anew.

The industry continued to flourish in Key West until its peak in 1890, when the city of Tampa offered the cigar manufacturers lower taxes if they would move to the Gulf Coast swamplands, an area now called Ybor City. With this incentive, the cigar-making industry left the Keys, but many of the Cuban people stayed, creating a steady Latin influence on Key West that has endured to this day.

The Salt Industry

Early settlers of Key West and Duck Key manufactured sea salt beginning in the 1830s, using natural salt-pond basins on both islands. Salt was essential for preserving food in those days because there was no refrigeration. Cut off from tidal circulation except during storms, the salt ponds were flooded with seawater and then allowed to evaporate. The resulting salt crystals were harvested.

Capricious weather often flooded the salt ponds with fresh water, ruining the salty "crop." By 1876 the salt industry no longer existed in the Keys. The destructive forces of repeated hurricanes made the industry economically unfeasible.

Homesteading the Keys

Bahamians also homesteaded other Keys in the early nineteenth century, settling in small family groups to farm the thin soil. Familiar with cultivating the unique

Insiders' Tip

During Prohibition in the 1920s, rum running became a cottage industry in the Florida Keys. Runners secured liquor in Cuba or the Bahamas, staying in international waters out of U.S. jurisdiction, while small boats spirited the drink in the dead of night back to shore. They hid the contraband in the mangroves (see our Paradise Found chapter).

land of limestone islands, the Bahamians worked at farming pineapples, Key limes, and sapodillas, called "sours and dillies."

Many believe Indian Key was the first real settlement in the Upper Keys. By 1834 it had docks, a post office, shops, and a mansion belonging to the island's owner, Jacob Housman. It became the governmental seat of Dade County for a time, but attacks from mainland Native Americans proved an insurmountable problem for this little key (see our Attractions chapter). Through the ensuing decades, Bahamian farmers homesteaded on Key Vaca, Upper Matecumbe, Newport (Key Largo), Tavernier, and Planter. By 1891 the area that is now Harry Harris Park in Key Largo had a post office, school, church, and five farms (see our Recreation chapter).

The census on any of these keys varied widely over the course of the century, and little is known as to why. For instance, Key Vaca had 200 settlers in 1840, according to Dr. Perrine of Indian Key, but by 1866, a U.S. census revealed an unexplained population of zero for Key Vaca.

Flagler's Folly: The Florida East Coast Railroad Extension

The dream of one man changed the isolation of the Florida Keys for all time. Native New Yorker Henry Flagler, born in 1830 and educated only to the 8th grade, established the Standard Oil Company with John D. Rockefeller in 1870 and became a wealthy, well-respected businessman. In 1885 he purchased a short-line railroad between Jacksonville and St. Augustine and began extending the rails southward toward Miami, then only a small settlement.

Flagler's vision of his railroad project went beyond Miami, however. He wanted to connect the mainland with the deep port of Key West, a booming city of more than 10,000 people, in anticipation of the growing shipping commerce he thought

would be generated by the opening of the Panama Canal in the early years of the twentieth century. He may even have set his sights on eventually connecting Key West with Cuba.

By 1904, the railroad extended to Homestead, at the gateway to the Keys. The year 1905 saw the commencement of what many perceived as an old man's folly: a railroad constructed across 128 miles of rock islands and open water, under the most non-idyllic conditions imaginable, by men and materials that had to be imported from all over the world. Steamships brought fabricated steel from Pennsylvania, and cement from Germany and Belgium was used to create concrete supports below the water line. Cement for above-water concrete came from New York state; sand and gravel, from the Chesapeake; crushed rock, from the Hudson Valley; timbers and pilings, from Florida and Georgia; and provisions, from Chicago. Barges carried fresh water from Miami to the construction sites. Nothing was indigenous to the Keys except the mosquitoes and the sand flies.

By 1908 the first segment, from Homestead to Marathon, was completed, and Marathon became a boomtown. Ships brought their cargoes of Cuban pineapples and limes here, where they were loaded onto railway cars and sent north.

FLORIDA EAST COAST RAILWAY CO. FLAGLER SYSTEM DAILY SCHEDULE EASTERN STANDARD TIME			
PM			**AM**
0:05	Lv.	New York Ar.	6:45
:35	Lv.	Washington Ar.	1:05
5:25	Lv.	Savannah Ar.	10:57
0:00	Lv.	Jacksonville Ar.	7:15
0:50	Ar.	St. Augustine Lv.	6:20
2:05	Ar.	Daytona Beach Lv.	4:56
2:30	Ar.	New Smyrna Lv.	4:30
3:40	Ar.	Fort Pierce Lv.	1:25
5:00	Ar.	West Palm Beach Lv.	11:55
6:13	Ar.	Fort Lauderdale Lv.	10:38
6:28	Ar.	Hollywood Lv.	10:27
7:00	Ar.	Miami Lv.	5:00
2:20	Lv.	Key West Ar.	3:45
6:20	Ar.	Havana Lv.	9:45
THE HAVANA SPECIAL			

Thanks to the vision of Henry Flagler, you could once take a train from New York to Key West and connect with the ferry to Havana. PHOTO: JANET WARE

(The railroad turnaround was at the present site of Knight's Key campground.) Railroad workers used Pigeon Key (see our Attractions chapter) as a base for further railway construction.

The 7-mile "water gap" between Marathon and Bahia Honda took some engineering prowess to overcome, and the completion of the project was severely hampered by several devastating hurricanes in 1909 and 1910. But on January 22, 1912, Henry Flagler—by then age 82—finally rode his dream from Homestead to Key West. He traveled across 42 stretches of sea, over 17 miles of concrete viaducts and concrete-and-steel bridges, and over 20 miles of filled causeways, ultimately traversing 128 miles from island to island to the fruition of his vision. He entered Key West that day a hero. He died the following year probably never knowing that his flight of fancy changed the course of the Florida Keys forever.

Flagler's railroad, called the Key West Extension, made Key West America's largest deepwater port on the Atlantic Coast south of Norfolk, Virginia. Trade with the Caribbean increased, and Key West flourished for 23 years, recovering from the loss of the sponge and cigar industries.

The railroad stop on Key Largo was called Tavernier, and it developed into a trading center for the Upper Keys. Pineapple farming faltered in Key Largo and Plantation Key from a combination of tapping out the nourishment in the thin soil and market competition from the shiploads of Cuban pineapples transported by railway car from the docks of Key West to the mainland. The railroad company built a fishing camp on Long Key that attracted sportfishing aficionados from all over, including writer Zane Grey, a camp regular. Real estate boomed for a time, as people came to the Keys to homestead. The Florida East Coast Railroad Company completed construction of Key West's first official tourist hotel, the Casa Marina, in 1921. La Concha was built in 1928.

In 1923 Monroe County appropriated funds to construct a road paralleling the railroad. The bumpy rock road crossed Card Sound with a long area of fill and a wooden bridge. Half a dozen humpback bridges crossed the creeks and cuts on Key Largo. Extending the length of Key Largo, the road continued over Plantation Key, Windley Key, and Upper Matecumbe. At the southern end of our island chain, a narrow, 32-mile road connected Key West with No Name Key off Big Pine Key. A car ferry service provided the waterway link between the two sections of roadway by 1930, which traversed what we now call the Upper and Lower Keys.

Still, the journey across this 128-mile stretch from Homestead to Key West proved a rugged, dusty, insect-ridden, costly, all-day affair, and tourism did not flourish as hoped and expected. Fresh water remained a coveted, scarce resource in the Florida Keys. Cisterns saved the funneled rainwater, which was parsimoniously meted out. Salt water was used whenever possible, and wash days were also always bath days. This was hardly a tourist mecca.

The Great Depression delivered a near-fatal blow to the Florida Keys with a one-two punch. The cigar industry had moved to Tampa, sponging went to Tarpon Springs, and lighthouses had put an end to wrecking long before. The population of Key West dropped from 22,000 to 12,000. By 1934, 80 percent of the city's residents relied on government assistance. The Federal Emergency Relief Administration stepped in and commenced development and promotion of Key West as a magnet for increased tourism in the Keys.

To that end, developers began building bridges to connect the Middle Keys to each other and to the two sections of finished roadway. A "bonus army" of World War I veterans was employed to accomplish this momentous task. However, in 1935 Mother Nature reasserted her authority and once again charted the destiny of our islands. On Labor Day, what today we would call a Category Five hurricane hit the Upper and Middle Keys, destroying much of Flagler's Railroad. Hundreds of lives were lost when the 17-foot storm surge hit the bridge-building crew working on a bridge at Islamorada.

Because of mismanagement and lack of foreign freight heading northward from Cuban and Caribbean ports, the railroad was already in receivership. The railroad chose not to rebuild, citing financial difficulties. By this time, it had become cheaper to haul cargo by truck than by train. The county's Overseas Road and Toll Commission purchased the right of way from the Florida East Coast Railroad and converted the single-track railway trestles, which remained intact after the hurricane, into two-lane bridges for automobiles. The highway from Homestead to Key West opened for traffic in 1938.

Epilogue

In the late 1930s, the U.S. Navy, stationed in Key West, began construction of an 18-inch pipeline that carried fresh water from wells in Homestead to Key West. The naval presence in Key West grew with the beginning of World War II, when antisubmarine patrols began surveillance of surrounding waters. The Navy also improved the highway to better accommodate the transfer of supplies for its military installation. The Card Sound Road was bypassed. The new road, which followed the old railroad bed, now is known as the "18-mile stretch." By 1942, the Keys enjoyed fresh water and electricity service, and the Overseas Highway (U.S. Highway 1) officially opened in 1944, ushering in a new era of development that continues to this day.

After World War II, the Florida Keys became more and more popular as a sportfishing destination, and fishing camps dotted the shores from the Upper Keys to Key West. Still a rather remote, primitive spot to visit, the Florida Keys nevertheless continued to evolve into a desirable tourist terminus, and Key West burgeoned as a port of call. Also contributing to Key West's rebirth was the discovery of pink gold: shrimp. Fishermen who had caught a shark in the waters between Key West and the Dry Tortugas found the fish's stomach filled with large pink shrimp. This led to the discovery of a bountiful shrimping area off the Tortugas, and the "Key West Pinks" shrimping industry spawned in the Florida Keys. It is still a viable occupation as far up the Keys as Marathon.

From 1978 to 1983 the old rail-bed conversion bridges were retired. Modern concrete structures, some four lanes wide, now span our waters. Most mind-boggling as an engineering feat is the seemingly endless Seven Mile Bridge, which connects the once insurmountable watery gap between Marathon and Bahia Honda Key. Many of the old bridges have been recycled as fishing piers, but others still stand, abandoned and obsolete alongside their successors, crumbling reminders of the Keys' not-so-distant past.

By the 1980s the Florida Keys had emerged as a tourist-driven economy.

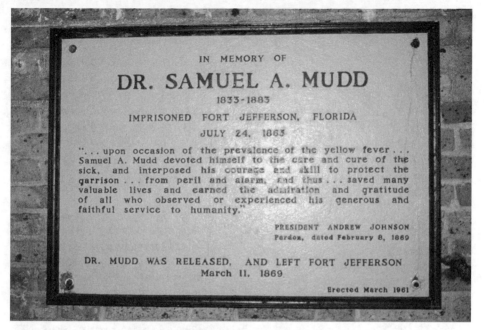

Samuel Mudd, who treated John Wilkes Booth after he shot President Lincoln, was imprisoned at Fort Jefferson in the Dry Tortugas. PHOTO: WAYNE MOCCIA

Tourism remains the major industry of the Keys today, with fishing, scuba diving, boating, and the attractions of Key West topping the list of popular agendas.

Of growing concern with the dawn of the twenty-first century is the effect the influx of visitors will ultimately have on the delicate balance of habitats within the tropical ecosystem of the Florida Keys (see our Paradise Found chapter). The jury is still out. Will man or Mother Nature determine the postscript for Paradise?

The Military in Key West

The position of Key West on the Straits of Florida allowed protection of American sea commerce in any war in the Western Hemisphere because vessels heading to all Gulf ports historically had to go through here. During the Civil War, more ships were stationed in Key West than in any other port in the United States, and historians feel the result of the war may have been different if the island had not been occupied by Union forces. Even though most of Key West was sympathetic to the Confederacy, Union forces stationed at Key West's Fort Taylor and at Fort Jefferson in the Dry Tortugas were considered essential in the capture of the Confederate blockade runners heading for Southern ports from Havana. Key West remained in the hands of the federal government for the entire war.

The forts acted as coaling stations during this conflict and were so employed again in the Spanish-American War (1898), when every available vessel was again dispatched to Key West along with a flotilla of newspaper boats filled with war correspondents. The USS *Maine* made Key West home port before she met her demise in Cuba in this conflict.

During World War I, with protection of the Panama Canal of paramount importance, the U.S. government stationed a submarine and naval aviation training base in our southernmost city. The base expanded in World War II, when blimps scouted for German U-boats preying on tankers and freighters in the shipping lanes off the Florida Keys. A mine field (removed in 1944) was planted north and west of Smith Shoal, and it also claimed four non-German vessels that accidentally entered the area (see Key West dive sites in our Diving and Snorkeling chapter). Today, a U.S. Naval Air Station is still maintained in Key West at Boca Chica.

Rafts to Freedom

With the onset of the Cuban Revolution in 1959, when Fidel Castro took over that country, large numbers of Cubans chose to immigrate to the United States, and many settled in the Florida Keys. In spring of 1980 Castro allowed an unprecedented 125,000 people to leave Cuba en masse. Called the Mariel Boat Lift, the immigrants landed in Key West from April through September of that year. Many continued on to Miami, where they settled in Little Havana.

Cuban refugees have continued to escape Castro's brand of communism on small homemade rafts, drifting to our shores. In the mid '90s, the U.S./Cuban immigration policy changed. Political asylum is no longer a guaranteed option for these immigrants, even if they triumph over the suppression of their homeland

Insiders' Tip

There is a historic reason behind the recipe for our classic Key lime pie, in which only the pie crust is baked. The filling of eggs, fresh Key lime juice, sugar, and sweetened milk "cooked" by the chemical action of the lime juice. No refrigeration was available in the early days of the Keys settlements, and this pie did not require it. (See our Restaurants chapter for an authentic recipe for Key lime pie.)

and the turbulence of their sea voyage. They must reach land undetected by U.S. authorities in order to stay here.

Paradise Found

Make no mistake, the sea is in charge here and always has been.

About 100,000 years ago during the Sangamon Interglacial period of the Pleistocene Epoch, the Florida Keys flourished under the waters of the Atlantic Ocean as a string of living coral patch reefs at the edge of the continental shelf. Deposits of oöids (small calcareous spheres resembling fish roe) accumulated on the lower portion of the reef. Sea level was some 25 feet higher than it is today. But with the onset of the last glacial period, the Wisconsin, the oceans receded and the sea dropped more than 150 feet.

The reef emerged as a landmass, exposing the corals and oöids to the atmosphere, rain, and pounding surf. The onslaught of the elements killed the corals, and the fossil remnants cemented themselves together, creating coral bedrock. This bedrock, called Key Largo limestone, now comprises the basis of the Upper and Middle Keys from Soldier Key near Miami to Big Pine Key. When the waters receded, the oöids compacted into rock called oölite. Now referred to as Miami Oölite, this rock forms the foundation of the Lower Keys and Key West, cut through by tidal channels from the Gulf of Mexico to the Florida Straits. At the lowest sea level of the Wisconsin period, Florida Bay and Hawk Channel unfolded as dry land.

About 15,000 years ago the climate began to warm and sea levels rose again. This present interglacial period is called the Holocene Epoch. As the sea once again claimed portions of the coral bedrock, living corals attached themselves to the limestone and began to grow anew. These growths now form the living coral reef tract that is presently submerged 4 to 5 miles offshore, extending from Fowey Rocks to the Dry Tortugas (see our Diving and Snorkeling chapter). The higher elevations of bedrock became isolated above sea level, a sparkling chain of islands dividing the seas.

Throughout the ages, the fluctuation of the sea has determined the fate of the coral islands we call the Florida Keys and will dictate its future as well. Put into simple perspective, sea level has been rising for the past 15,000 years, and the rate appears to be increasing due to the long-range effects of global warming. Just imagine: A 6-foot rise in sea level would eliminate all of the Lower and Middle Keys except Key West. The Upper Keys, being somewhat higher, would escape extinction for a time. But if sea level increases by 15 feet, the string of islands known as the Florida Keys will be reduced to a couple of tiny islets, and the majority of Paradise will be lost once again to the sea.

To be in the Florida Keys is to become one with nature, for the Keys offer unparalleled opportunities to be in direct daily contact with her substantial bounty. You'll know what we mean the moment you crest the first of the 42 bridges now spanning our islands and feel the vast power of the surrounding seas. Gaze down on our string of coral pearls from the air and you'll see that the Keys look insignificant juxtaposed against the encompassing Atlantic Ocean and Gulf of Mexico.

Insiders' Guides to other locales will introduce you to the lay of the land. But to gain an understanding of our world, which we reverently refer to as Paradise, you must be forearmed with the scope of our waters, for all things revolve around the sea here. We will acquaint you with our climate, weather, and the multiple interrelated habitats of our tropical ecosystem—the only such ecosystem in the continental United States.

The word "tropical" generally refers to plants and animals living in the latitudes between the Tropic of Cancer in the Northern Hemisphere and the Tropic of Capricorn in the Southern Hemisphere. The Florida Keys are somewhat north of the Tropic of Cancer, but the warming influence of the nearby Gulf Stream assures us the benefits of a tropical climate. Our natural flora grows nowhere else in North America, and the combination of our eight interrelated habitats and the creatures dwelling therein are truly unique. Come, join us for a sneak preview of Paradise. We're one of a kind—here, there, or anywhere.

Habitats of the Florida Keys

The Land

Hardwood Hammocks

When the coral reef emerged from the sea eons ago and calcified into limestone bedrock, floating debris accumulated on it, decomposed, and gradually evolved into a thin layer of soil. Seeds from the hardwood forests of the Yucatan, Honduras, Nicaragua, South America, and the Caribbean Islands were carried to the Florida Keys by the winds of hurricanes, the currents of the Gulf Stream, migrating birds, and eventually even by humans. Thus, the vegetation of the Florida Keys is more common to the tropical Caribbean Basin than to the adjoining temperate areas of mainland Florida.

Found throughout the Keys, these West Indian tropical hardwood hammocks nurture highly diverse communities of rare flora and fauna—more than 200 species—some found nowhere else in the United States. The hammocks (originally an Indian word meaning "shady place") also shelter a variety of endangered species.

Most of the hardwood hammocks of the Keys were cleared years ago to supply the wood for ship and home building and to clear the land for planting pineapples or citrus as a commercial venture. But several good examples of West Indian hardwood hammocks still flourish in the Keys. The largest contiguous hammock in the continental United States is on North Key Largo. Known as the Key Largo Hammock State Botanical Site, it encompasses 2,700 acres. You will find a virgin hardwood hammock on Lignumvitae Key, which is preserved as a state botanical site. You can access the island only by boat. State park naturalists offer guided tours of the hammock. The Crane Point hammock in Marathon offers self-guided tours (see our Attractions chapter). You'll find other stands of hardwood hammocks sprinkled throughout the Keys.

A hardwood hammock has a layered structure much like other forests, with a tall overstory, a midstory, and an understory. Many of the trees and plants will be unfamiliar to you, and some carry with them a colorful past. In the next paragraphs we describe four of our hammocks' more infamous residents: lignum vitae, gumbo limbo, Jamaica dogwood, and poisonwood trees.

Probably the most sought-after tree in the virgin hammock was the lignum vitae (Latin for "wood of life"). It is so valuable, heavily harvested, and slow-growing that it now tops the endangered list. Most visible today sprinkled throughout the hardwood hammock on Lignumvitae Key, the tree has a resin content of 30 percent. The wood cannot be kiln-dried or glued because of the gum content of this resin, called guaiac gum. Lignum vitae was used in the hinges and locks on the Erie Canal, which have been functioning now for more than 100 years. Mythical tales surround the tree: Old texts suggest lignum vitae, often called the "holy wood," was the tree referred to in the Biblical Garden of Eden and was used to fashion the holy grail.

Bold and brazen, the gumbo limbo trees, often reaching 40 feet, cop the moniker "tourist trees" because their reddish, peeling bark brings to mind sunburned visitors to our islands. The tree hides a checkered past. In early times, settlers stripped off a piece of bark from the

Poling a shallow-draft flatsboat is the best way to see the creatures dwelling beneath the water's surface.
PHOTO: VICTORIA SHEARER

gumbo limbo, revealing the tree's gluelike oozing sap. When birds landed on this particular branch, they stuck tight and could not fly away. Gathered by the human predators, the birds were sold for 5 cents each to the Cuban cigar industry for the entertainment of the cigar rollers. Florida law forbids this practice of bird capture today. On a more respectable note, the resin from the gumbo limbo was once used in the manufacture of varnish.

Also contributing to antics on the wrong side of the law is the Jamaica dogwood tree, called the fish poison tree. The roots, twigs, leaves, and gray-green scaly bark were used to stupefy fish and aid in their capture. When ground into a sawdust chum and placed in the shoreline waters, the vegetation emitted a chemical similar to an invertebrate poison that paralyzed the gills of the fish, affected their air bladders, and caused them to float to the surface where they were easily harvested.

Belonging to the same family as poison ivy, the poisonwood tree masquerades as a beautiful, harmless canopy but contains a poisonous sap that causes severe dermatitis in humans. Native Americans of the Keys would tie their captives beneath the foliage of the 30-foot poisonwood tree. When it rained, the fresh water passing through the leaves carried the urushiol oils with every drop, causing a raging rash and slow torture.

Beneath the wide awning of the overstory, the smaller trees of the midstory flourish with less drama. Many of the trees bear fruits favored by the feathered tenants of the hardwood hammock habitat.

A dense understory of plants, shrubs, and vines adapts to the shady conditions on the hammock floor. And wildflowers must reach for the sky under the shady foliage top hat of the hammock, often turning into creeping vines.

The Key Largo wood rat, an endangered species that looks more like a big-eared Disney mouse than a London sewer rat, joins the Key raccoon, the Key cotton mouse, opossums, gray squirrels and an assortment of migratory birds amid the flora of the hammocks. This 16-inch-long rodent, found only in the hammocks of North Key Largo, has been dubbed a "pack rat," because it likes to collect empty shells, aluminum pop-top tabs, and the colorful rings from plastic milk bottles.

The Pinelands

Pinelands in the Lower Florida Keys differ from the vast forests you may have seen in other areas of the United States. Adapting to growing conditions atop Miami Oölite with limited fresh water, the tall, spindly trees are small in girth and sparsely foliated. Primarily found on Big Pine Key, these South Florida slash pines mingle with an understory of silver palms and brittle thatch palms, both of which are rare outside the Keys and protected under the Preservation of the Native Flora of Florida Act. Among the 7,500 protected acres in the Lower Keys, other pinelands grace No Name Key, Little Pine Key, Cudjoe Key, Sugarloaf Key, and Summerland Key.

The most famous pineland resident in the Lower Keys is undoubtedly the Key deer, a subspecies of the Virginia white-tailed deer, found nowhere else in the world. These tiny deer, each about the size of a large dog, attempt to coexist with human inhabitants who have taken over much of the unpreserved woodlands of the Lower Keys. However, the diminutive animals frequently venture out of the woods and onto the Overseas Highway, where they are often struck and killed by vehicles. For that reason, speed limits through Big Pine Key are reduced (45 mph daylight, 35 mph nighttime) and strictly enforced by law enforcement officials.

In 1957 the National Key Deer Refuge was established in Big Pine Key to ensure a sheltered natural habitat for the endangered species. About 800 Key deer exist in the Lower Keys today. The Key deer feed on red and black mangroves, thatch palms, and a variety of native berries. While they can tolerate small quantities of salt in brackish water, fresh water is essential to their survival. No official records

Insiders' Tip

Do not feed the Key deer. Deer accustomed to being hand-fed lose their natural fear of humans and venture into areas that put them at risk, such as busy highways and residential subdivisions.

document the origin of the Key deer in the Florida Keys, but it is widely believed they migrated from the mainland as white-tailed deer when the seas receded in the Wisconsin Glacial Period. When sea level rose again during the present interglacial epoch, the deer were trapped in their pineland habitat. Over time their diminutive stature evolved as an adaptation to their sparsely vegetated environment.

The Shoreline

Mangrove Habitats

Called the island builders, mangroves comprise the predominant shoreline plant community of the Florida Keys, protecting the land mass from erosion. Able to establish itself on the coral underwater bedrock or in the sand, the mangrove's root structure traps, holds, and stabilizes sediments. Over time the infant mangrove habitats establish small islets such as those you'll see peppering Florida Bay and the oceanside nearshore waters. Mangrove habitats bordering the Keys filter upland runoff, maintaining the water quality of our seas.

The leaf litter that falls from the red mangroves decomposes in the tangle of its prop roots, forming a critical base in the food chain that supports the myriad species of the marine community inhabiting shoreline waters. Important as a breeding ground and nursery for juvenile spiny lobster, pink shrimp, snook, mullet, tar-

Look up to spot an osprey nest, for they are constructed on the very pinnacles of trees and telephone poles.
PHOTO: MARY MOCCIA

pon, and mangrove snapper, the mangroves also shelter these sea creatures from their predators. (See our Diving and Snorkeling chapter and our Fishing chapter for more on the fascinating underwater creatures living here.)

Great rookeries of wading and shore birds roost and nest on the canopy of broad leaves of the mangrove habitats, creating a virtual aviary in every uninhabited islet (see the Gunk-holing Close-up in this chapter for our bird-watching primer). Three kinds of mangroves thrive in the Florida Keys. The distinctive high-arching prop roots of the red mangrove enable the plants to exchange gases and absorb oxygen from the seawater. Long, pencil-like seedpods, called propagules, develop during the summer and drop off the mangroves in the autumn, floating upright hither and yon with the tides. Eventually snagged on a branch or caught against a rock, the seedling establishes itself by growing prop roots, and a key is born.

The black mangrove, with dark, scaly bark, grows in the high-tide zone. The white mangrove, smallest of the three species, looks like a shrub with broad, flat, oval leaves and grows above the high-tide line along with stands of buttonwood trees.

Sand Beach Habitats

Most of the islands of the Florida Keys have a limestone rock shoreline, but Long Key, Bahia Honda Key, and small portions of the shoreline of Lower Matecumbe have beaches of sand consisting not of quartz but of tiny fossils. These minuscule remains of calcareous, lime-secreting marine plants and animals are broken down by wave action upon the sea bottom. Only keys that have a break in the offshore reef line or are near a deep tidal channel receive enough sediment to build a natural beach. Fronted in most cases by beds of seagrass, the Keys beaches always have a "weed line" on shore made up of remnants of turtle grass, manatee grass, or sargassum weed washed up with the tide.

The natural beaches of the Keys don't have sand dunes but rather more bermlike mounds. Sea oats grow in the sand, helping to hold the particles together. State law mandates that you may not pick sea oats at any time.

Gunk-holing

Rachel Carson may have said it all in *The Edge of the Sea*: "I doubt that anyone can travel the length of the Florida Keys without having communicated to his mind a sense of the uniqueness of this land of sky and water and scattered mangrove-covered islands."

Nowhere will you be more aware of our quintessence than when you are gunk-holing. Here in the Florida Keys, gunk-holing simply means slipping off land in a small dinghy, canoe, sea kayak, or shallow-draft skiff equipped with a push pole and tranquilly gliding through our shallow, inshore, mangrove-lined waters in search of sightings of indigenous birds and aquatic creatures.

Though the dedication to spotting feathered friends may be referred to as birding or bird-watching in some areas of the country, here in the Keys another arena of fascinating marine creatures presents itself in the shallow waters of our flats. You can easily gunk-hole on your own without a guide, or you can sign up for a guided eco-tour (see our Recreation chapter).

Hundreds of virgin mangrove islets sprinkle the inshore waters of the inhabited Keys, often serving as giant rookeries for shorebirds and wading birds who are attracted to the abundant chow wagon beneath the surface of the water. Look to our Recreation chapter for information on renting a kayak, canoe, or small skiff. See our Attractions chapter for descriptions of the wildlife refuges of the Florida Keys, many of which encompass myriad out-islands. And most importantly, read on for a primer of the most frequently encountered species on a gunk-holing expedition in our tropical ecosystem.

Nature's Aviary

When gunk-holing around the mangrove islets in search of wild bird life, be sensitive to the presence of nesting birds. Do not anchor within 200 feet of an island, and keep noise to a minimum so as not to frighten the birds. If you do happen to flush a bird from its nest, move away from the nest area so that the bird will swiftly return to guard its young.

Here are several species you can expect to spot:

Brown Pelican—Some say the brown pelican's mouth can hold more than its stomach can, but this common resident of the Florida Keys will push this theory to the limit given half a chance. The brown pelican will dive from 20 to 30 feet above the sea, entering the water like a competing Olympian and scoring with a freshly caught fish every time. You'll see these cute, personality-packed fish-beggars everywhere, especially hanging out at fishing marinas. Look for them on their favorite gravity-defying perches atop mangroves or feathery Australian pines.

American White Pelican—With a wingspan of 10 feet, the white pelican is more than a bird of a different color. These winter visitors to the Florida Keys (they are frequently spotted in Montana in the summer months) live a much different lifestyle than their brown cousins. Completely white except for black-tipped wings and long yellow beaks, white pelicans live together in flocks in the uninhabited wild of the backcountry keys. The white pelicans, far from the panhandling ways of the browns,

White pelicans live in flocks of 500 or more, and are cooperative feeders who herd fish into an ever-narrowing circle.

PHOTO: MARY MOCCIA

are cooperative feeders, congregating as a team on the water's surface and herding fish into an ever-narrowing circle where the group will dine. Look for white pelicans at Little Arsnicker or Sandy Keys in the Upper Keys backcountry.

Cormorant—Cormorants by the thousands inhabit rookeries in the mangroves of the unpeopled islands. These large-bodied, hook-billed black birds, consummate fish-catchers all, will launch themselves in attempted flight at the first inkling of an approaching gunk-holer, often hitting the water in a brief belly-flop before gaining momentum to become airborne. Like the lesser-seen anhinga, or water turkey (more prevalent in the Everglades), the cormorant's plumage becomes waterlogged, which facilitates diving and swimming skills in its endless search for fish. You'll often see the birds perched on poles and buoy markers, wings outstretched in a drying maneuver. Cormorants swim with only their necks and heads visible above the water.

Snowy Egrets and Great Egrets—Plume hunters nearly eradicated the egret population at the turn of the nineteenth century, for the birds' magnificent snow-white aigrettes were high fashion in the millinery industry. The egrets achieve their feathery plumage only in breeding season, so it was easy for the hunters to kill the birds in their nests. Both snowy and great egrets thrive once again in the Florida Keys. Distinguished from their cousins, the great white herons, which also grace the shorelines of the Keys, the white egrets have black legs with yellow feet and black bills. Though both egrets display magnificent white plumage, the snowy egret is about half the size of the great egret.

Great White Heron—Formerly considered a separate species from the great blue heron encountered in many parts of the United States, what we commonly call the great white heron is actually the white "morph," or color phase, of the great blue. Found only in the tropical ecosystem, this large white heron, more than 4-feet tall, is not as fearful of humans as other species, and is often seen in backyards and other inhabited areas. You'll be able to tell a great white heron from a great egret because the heron has long yellow legs and a yellow beak. The heron still-hunts for its food: Standing stiffly at full-alert, the heron stalks a prey of fish, frogs, or lizards; it then stabs the prey with its beak, flips the prize whole into its narrow throat, and swallows it in one long neck-expanding gulp. Herons and egrets build their lofty stick nests atop the mangroves of remote rookery keys.

Roseate Spoonbill—A rare sighting in the Florida Keys, the roseate spoonbill, or pink curlew, is more common in the upper Florida Bay near Flamingo in Everglades National Park. Like the great white heron and egret, it also was slaughtered to near extinction in the early 1900s for its brilliant pink plumage, which was used for ladies' hats. The roseate spoonbill moves its large spatulate bill from side to side under water in the shallows, searching for minnows and small aquatic creatures. This distinctive bird is costumed like a vaudeville dancer—pink body accented by an orange tail, a bare greenish head, bright-red shoulder and chest patches, and a black-ringed neck.

White Ibis—Common in the Florida Keys, the white-plumed ibis bears black-tipped wings, most apparent when spread in flight, a distinctive scarlet, down-curved bill, and red legs. You'll often see young ibises, which are brown, in a flock of their white brethren, searching for aquatic insects, crabs, shrimp, and small snakes. The ibis was once worshiped in Egypt as a bird-headed god, and the pharaohs were buried alongside a mummified ibis. Killing an ibis for any other purpose was an offense punishable by death.

Osprey—The high platform-topped poles you may see along the Overseas Highway have been erected for the osprey, which builds its bulky nest atop, laying three eggs out of harm's way each breeding season. Look up when trying to spot these fish-eating birds in the wild as well, for their nests will be constructed on the very pinnacles of the trees. Resembling a bald eagle, the osprey can be distinguished by a black streak behind each eye.

Magnificent Frigatebird—The graceful, effortless flight of the frigatebird, or man-o-war bird, often heralds fish below, for this coastal forager is constantly on the lookout for finned pleasures. Often known to harass other sea birds until they drop their catch, the piratical frigatebird catches the spoils midair. Having a wingspan greater than 7 feet, the frigatebird inflates its throat sac and floats on air currents, its deeply forked, scissorlike tail a distinctive sight.

The fish-eating osprey can be distinguished from the bald eagle by the black streak behind each eye. PHOTO: MARY MOCCIA

American Bald Eagle—Once endangered nearly to the point of extinction, the American bald eagles have made a recovery all across the United States due to preservation efforts. Look for the bald eagle's distinctive white head and tail high in the mangroves of uninhabited keys in Florida Bay, where they build their nests. Fish dominates their diet, and it is not uncommon for the bald eagle to steal the catch of a neighboring osprey.

Nature's Aquarium

As you gunk-hole through our shallow seagrass, mud, sand, and hardbottom habitats surrounding mangrove areas of our uninhabited keys, you may observe life below the surface of the water. Be sure to wear polarized sunglasses and proceed in a shallow-draft craft.

Starfish—Commonly adorning the sandy bottom areas or seagrass meadows of the shallow waters are the cushion sea stars, often referred to as starfish. These heavy-bodied, orange-brown creatures with five thick, starlike arms don't look alive, but they are.

Sponges—See "Hardbottom Habitats" in this chapter for a description of the sponges you'll see growing on the sea floor.

Stingray—This unusual creature, shaped like a diamond or disk, often lies motionless on the ocean bottom, partially buried in the sand. The ray has eyes and breathing holes on its topside, with its mouth positioned on the under side to feed off the sea floor. When frightened, the stingray will swim away, its huge, winglike fins flapping in gentle undulation.

Horseshoe Crab—You'll quickly spot the distinctive spikelike tail and smooth, horseshoe-shaped body shell of this 300-million-year-old species as the crab forages the seagrass habitat for algal organisms.

Sea Turtle—Keep a close lookout for the small head of the giant sea turtle as it pops out of the water for a breath of air. Loggerheads can remain submerged for as long as three hours. Green turtles, once commonplace here but overharvested for use in soup, for steaks, in cosmetic oils, and for leather, are rarely encountered today. The sea turtles' front appendages have evolved into flippers.

Manatee—On a lucky day, you may catch a rare glimpse of the timid West Indian manatee, or sea cow, a docile aquatic mammal that likes to graze on the turtle-grass flats. The brownish-gray manatee has armlike flippers, a broad, spoonlike tail, and an adorable wrinkled face. It can grow to 15-feet long, weighing-in at nearly a ton. Protected as an endangered species, the manatee often rolls on the water's surface for air and cannot swim rapidly enough to avoid collision with oncoming boaters, a constant source of peril. (See Insiders' Tip in this chapter for regulatory information.)

Bottle-Nosed Dolphin—A more frequent sight on a gunk-holing excursion is that of the bottle-nosed dolphins, which you probably remember as the "Flipper" performers of marine parks. Seen in free-swimming pods in open waters, the graceful dolphins undulate through the waves with rhythmic regularity, and are sometimes curious enough to approach your boat.

Fish of the Flats—Alert attention to underwater movements in the seagrass of the flats may net you a sighting of a baby black-tip or bonnethead shark, a nurse shark, barracuda, bonefish, and more. See The Flats section of our Fishing chapter for descriptions of the finned treasures lurking beneath the shallows.

A shark sighting is a common occurrence while gunk-holing.
PHOTO: MARY MOCCIA

Seagrass Habitats

In the shallow nearshore waters of the ocean or Florida Bay, sediments build up on the limestone bedrock sea bottom, supporting a variety of seagrasses that perform an integral function in our tropical ecosystem. Seagrasses grow entirely under water, one of the few flowering plants to do so. Most prevalent of the seagrasses in the Florida Keys are the sweeping meadows of turtle grass, which have interlocking root systems that burrow as deep as 5 feet into the sediment. The wide, flat blades, often more than 12 inches long, break the force of the waves and slow current velocity.

The turtle grass traps marine sediments and silt carried in and out on the tides, allowing them to settle to the bottom. This natural filtration system clarifies the water and enhances coral growth in the nearby reef habitat. The sunken pastures of turtle grass and the less-abundant shoal grass and manatee grass, which have rounded leaves and weaker root systems, become very dense, providing food and shelter for marine life at all levels of the food chain. (See our Fishing chapter for more on the species dwelling within.)

More than 80 species of resident and migratory coastal birds forage the seagrasses, feeding on fish and invertebrates of the habitat (see the Gunk-holing Close-up in this chapter for our bird-watching primer).

Boat propellers and personal watercraft can easily scar the shallow turtle grass meadows, effectively destroying that portion of the habitat. These scars do not heal over because the seagrass will not grow back. The drastic reduction in fresh water from the Everglades also threatens the seagrass habitat, for it is believed to have contributed to the seagrass die-off in Florida Bay. Because of its pivotal position among the habitats, ill health of the turtle grass meadows will ultimately affect the entire Florida Keys ecosystem.

Hardbottom Habitats

Wave action and tidal currents sweep the limestone bedrock of the nearshore sea-bottom habitats nearly clean, permitting no sediment buildup. Algae, sponges, gorgonian corals, and stony corals attach themselves directly to the bedrock. The most common sponge you will see from your small skiff or while snorkeling in these waters is the loggerhead sponge, a barrel-shaped sponge easily identified by the dark holes in its upper surface.

Snapping shrimp often make their homes within the sponges; they make a popping sound with their large snapping claw to repel predators.

More seaward of the nearshore waters, colonies of soft corals dominate the underwater hardbottom landscape. A feathery fairyland blooms like a backstage theater costume room.

Tentacled anemones also call the hardbottom habitat home and peacefully coexist with conchs and tulip snails, the spiral-striped spindle-shaped mollusks. The much sought-after stone crabs and juvenile spiny lobsters try to stay out of sight here (see our Diving and Snorkeling chapter). Boat wakes, anchor damage, and collection of sea creatures by divers and snorkelers threaten the hardbottom habitats.

Coral Reef

Extending 200 miles, from Fowey Rocks near Miami to the Dry Tortugas, our living coral reef habitat—the only one in the

Insiders' Tip

Don't feed gulls, pelicans, or shorebirds. They are more likely to become entangled in fishing line if they learn that anglers are a source of fresh fish food.

The oystercatcher is a rare sighting in the Florida Keys. PHOTO: MARY MOCCIA

continental United States—is a national treasure. The reef, composed of the limestone remains of colonies of individual animals called polyps, plays host to an unbelievable assortment of marine creatures, fish, and vegetation (see our Diving and Snorkeling chapter and our Fishing chapter). The coral reef habitat, together with the mangrove and seagrass habitats, is the breeding ground for 70 percent of the commercial fishing industry's catch.

This wave-resistant barrier, which protects the seagrass meadows from erosion and heavy sedimentation, is particularly beautiful off the Upper Keys. The landmass of Key Largo shields the coral habitat from changing water temperatures and sediments that emanate from Florida Bay through the tidal channels of the Middle and Lower Keys. Though it rigidly protects the shoreline of the Florida Keys from tropical storms, the coral reef itself is a fragile habitat. Field studies since 1984 have indicated some coral die-off and the sometimes-fatal bleaching or discoloration of the corals in select areas of the Keys' barrier reef. Excessive nutrients in the water due to land-based pollution will degrade water quality and foster the growth of algal blooms, which screen the sunlight, robbing the coral of the oxygen that is necessary for healthy development.

Humans constitute one of the reef's most destructive threats. Anchor damage, boat groundings, and snorkelers and divers touching, collecting, or stepping on the delicate organisms can cause injury and certain death to the reef.

Bare Mud and Sand Bottom Habitats

Along the barrier reef, skeletons of reef plants and animals form areas of open, bare-sand sea bottom, inhabited by species of algae, sea urchins, snails, clams, and worms that serve as the food train for visiting starfish, conch, and finfish. Similar belts or patches of bare-mud bottom habitats, both oceanside and in Florida Bay, support a like assemblage of marine creatures. Joining this group are burrowing shrimp, whose tunneled dwellings leave telltale mounds in the mud.

Weather and Climate

The mild tropical climate of the Florida Keys has no equal in the United States.

Sunrise, Sunset

In the Florida Keys we justifiably lay claim to the most spectacular sun awakenings and finales in the universe. Anglers rise early enough to witness the brilliant fireball burn its way out of the ocean, its igneous shafts dramatically piercing the clouds overhead. Divers relish the midday sun's intense rays, which light up the ocean waters like a torch, illuminating the colorful corals below. Sunbathers lie prone on pool decks and manmade beaches, soaking the solar rays, storing up some much-needed vitamin D.

But our sunsets take center stage in the twilight hours. Both visitors and residents jockey for an unobstructed vantage point from which to watch the smoldering orange ball ooze into the sea like a sphere of molten lava. Flotillas of small boats drift anchorless in the Gulf waters . . . waiting. Travelers pull their autos off the Overseas Highway and stand at the water's edge, their awestruck attention riveted on the setting sun. Key West even has a daily sunset celebration ceremony at Mallory Square, complete with fire-eaters, jugglers, and Keys buskers of every shape and description.

If you are vigilant, you may see the green flash, a brilliant, emerald-colored spark of light that occasionally appears just as the sun melts into the sea. The rare sighting lasts only a second or less and has inspired legends the world over. According to Usha Lee McFarling of the *Boston Globe*, "The green color results from the refraction, or bending, that sunlight undergoes as it passes through the thick layers of atmosphere

Rate our famous sunset with the Ghee Whiz sunset rating scale. PHOTO: MARY MOCCIA

Every sunset rates a celebration in the Keys. PHOTO: MARY MOCCIA

near the horizon. Blue and green wavelengths of light are refracted the most, just like in a prism, so the setting sun appears to have a very thin blue-green fringe on its top edge. This fringe is hidden by the glare from the rest of the sun until all but the last of the sun's rim is blocked by the horizon."

In the Florida Keys the sun sets over the Gulf of Mexico. The day must be clear, and the sun must meet the horizon through a cloudless sky to see the green flash.

Although sighting a green flash is a singular phenomenon akin to spotting a comet or a shooting star, every sunset is reason for celebration in the Florida Keys. So allow us to share with you our little-known and much guarded 10-point secret rating scale for the ceremonial Keys sunset watch:

The Ghee-Whiz Sunset Rating Chart

Score five points if the sun sets at all because that means you are alive.

Add:

one point for pre-glow (reflection of sun and streaks across the water).

one point if you see the bottom of the sun touch the horizon.

one point if the top of the sun touches the horizon.

one point for an afterglow (the sky turns pastel colors).

one point for the company you keep while you are watching the sunset.

Score a bonus point if a sailboat, bird, or cloud moves in front of the sun as it sets. Sighting of the green flash is an automatic 10.

A rare sighting in the Florida Keys, the roseate spoonbill is more common in upper Florida Bay near Flamingo in Everglades National Park. PHOTO: MARY MOCCIA

Neither frost, nor ice, nor sleet, nor snow visits our islands. In fact, Key West is the only city in the continental United States below the frost line.

Temperature

The proximity of the Keys to the Gulf Stream in the Straits of Florida and the tempering effects of the Gulf of Mexico guarantee that average winter temperatures vary little more than 14 degrees from those of the summer months. Average year-round temperature is about 75 degrees. Cold, dry air moving down from the north in the winter is greatly modified by the Gulf waters over which it passes. And southeasterly trade winds and fresh sea breezes keep summer temperatures from ever reaching the triple-digit inferno experienced by the Florida mainland. The water and land heat and cool at different rates, creating thermal currents that air-condition the Keys.

Rainfall

The Florida Keys experiences two seasons: wet and dry. From November through April, the sun shines abundantly and less than 25 percent of the year's precipitation falls, usually associated with a cold front in the dead of winter. May through October is the rainy season, when nearly three-quarters of our annual rainfall occurs during brief daily showers or thunderstorms. But these percentages are deceiving; our climate is really quite dry. Average rainfall in the winter is less than 2 inches a month; summer months see closer to 4 to 5 inches of rain.

Hurricanes

The piper must be paid for this idyllic climate, and hurricanes have always been a key ingredient in our tropical mix. The potentially deadly weather systems move westerly off the African coast during hurricane season (officially June 1 to November 30 but most prevalent in August and September) and generally turn northward near the Lesser Antilles islands, often heading our way.

Hurricanes have been harassing visitors to our shores for centuries. In 1622, at least five ships of the Spanish *Tierra Firma* Fleet wrecked as a result of a hurricane west of the Dry Tortugas. One of the most famous of these ships, the *Atocha*, was discovered and salvaged just over a decade ago by Mel Fisher (see Mel Fisher Museum in our Attractions chapter). The New Spain Armada suffered a fatal blow by a hurricane in 1733, when 17 of 21 galleons struck the reefs of the Upper Keys, spewing treasure cargo amid the coral.

Key West suffered a devastating hurricane in 1835, but the hurricane of 1846 is considered the city's most severe. Key West residents pluckily rebuilt after these hurricanes and through the repeated hammerings of 1909, 1910, 1914, and 1919. On Labor Day 1935, a Category Five hurricane tore through the Upper Keys and Lower Matecumbe, totally destroying the area, including Flagler's Florida East Coast Railroad. Five hundred people lost their lives in the high winds and 7-foot tidal surge in Lower Matecumbe alone. Experts estimate that the Labor Day hurricane packed winds of between 200 and 250 miles per hour. By comparison, Hurricane Andrew's winds, which hit the Miami area in 1992, peaked at an intensity of 175 miles per hour.

On August 29, 1960, an African storm caused an airplane crash near Dakar, Senegal, Africa, killing 63 people. Three days later this storm system was officially named Donna by the National Hurricane Center, which was formed in 1955 in Miami. By September 9, Donna's eye, which stretched 21 miles wide, passed over the region, bringing horrendous winds that effectively leveled the area from Marathon to Lower Matecumbe. Tides in Marathon were more than 9 feet high, and the surge in Upper Matecumbe topped 13 feet. Tea Table Bridge washed out; the freshwater pipeline broke in six places, and electricity was out. Donna ranks among the most destructive storms in U.S. history.

Two hurricanes hammered the Florida Keys in recent years. Hurricane Georges, a strong Category Two hurricane with sustained winds of 105 mph, wreaked havoc from the Middle Keys to Key West on September 25, 1998. The massive cleanup and repair effort took residents nearly a year, but courtesy of *La Niña*, a wet summer in 1999 restored most of the lost foliage to its former glory. Then on October 15, 1999, Hurricane Irene battered the Keys with 75 mph winds and dumped 10- to 20 inches of rain on the still recovering islands.

Visitors to the Florida Keys during hurricane season should heed official warnings to evacuate our islands in the event of a potential hurricane. Because we have only one main artery linking our islands to the mainland (the Overseas Highway) it takes 22 to 26 hours of crawling, bumper-to-bumper traffic to clear residents and visitors out of the Florida Keys. Officials warn that storm-watching during a hurricane is not a diversion to be considered here. A sizable hurricane will cut all services in the Keys and communications to the outside world.

Protectors of Paradise

The natural wonders that make up the Florida Keys have good friends in the following organizations, which oversee efforts to protect the region's environment as best they can.

Florida Keys National Marine Sanctuary

In 1990, President George Bush signed into law the Florida Keys National Marine Sanctuary and Protection Act, designed to protect our spectacular marine ecosystem. The resulting Florida Keys National Marine Sanctuary encompasses 2,800 square nautical miles, incorporating within its boundaries the previously formed Key Largo National Marine Sanctuary (1975)

Insiders' Tip
Help us preserve this fragile environment that we regard as Paradise. Please respect our environmental laws during your visit.

and the Looe Key National Marine Sanctuary (1981). The Florida Keys National Marine Sanctuary engulfs all of the Florida Keys, including the Marquesas Keys and the Dry Tortugas, and surrounding waters. In an effort to provide a secure habitat for the marine flora and fauna that make the Florida Keys so special, the Protection Act immediately prohibited oil drilling within the sanctuary and created an "area to be avoided" (ATBA) for large ships in our waters.

Ecologists hope that the access restrictions and activity regulations in select areas of the Florida Keys National Marine Sanctuary will help protect sensitive areas of the ecosystem. Furthermore, professionals feel that, with minimal human contact, areas of high ecological importance will evolve naturally and those areas representing a variety of habitats will be sustained. This zoning program will be monitored for revision every five years. (See our Boating chapter for more information on specific regulations and restrictions.) For more information, call the Florida Keys National Marine Sanctuary offices at (305) 743-2437 or log on to www.fknms.nos.noaa.gov.

The Nature Conservancy of the Florida Keys

The Nature Conservancy established a Florida Keys program in 1987 to protect the health and extraordinary diversity of our tropical ecosystem. This nonprofit conservation group states its mission as: "dedicated to preserving plants, animals, and natural communities that represent the diversity of life on Earth by protecting the lands and waters they need to survive." To date it has helped preserve more than 6,000 acres in the Keys.

The Conservancy is working to preserve the coral reef and Florida Bay, the rock pinelands of Big Pine Key, and the tropical hardwood hammocks of North Key Largo. To engage people in caring for our precious lands and waters, the Conservancy operates the Volunteer Stewardship Exchange. Among their volunteer programs are GreenSweep, Florida Bay Watch, and Sea Stewards.

GreenSweep, a non-native plant control and native plant restoration program, teaches volunteers about the damage invasive exotics cause to our native habitats. The volunteers help in the effective removal of the exotics and help restore native plants to the environment.

Volunteers to Florida Bay Watch collect water samples that provide support for scientists who are working to understand the complex ecology of Florida Bay. Scientists at Florida International University and University of Miami utilize this water quality data.

Sea Stewards are trained volunteers who monitor no-take areas within the Florida Keys National Marine Sanctuary. These divers visit designated sites several times a year to observe reef health, measure changes, and collect data on damselfish and sea urchin populations.

For more information about The Nature Conservancy, to visit a preserve, or to become a member, call the Conservancy's Florida Keys program office at (305) 296-3880. To learn more about volunteering, call the Conservancy's Volunteer Stewardship Exchange in Marathon at (305) 289-9060. The Conservancy's website is www.tncflorida.org.

Reef Relief

Reef Relief, a Key West-based nonprofit group of volunteers founded in 1986, works toward the preservation and protection of the coral reef habitat of the Florida Keys. The group has installed more than 100 mooring buoys, which, when used properly, eliminate anchor damage at the reef. The Florida Keys National Marine Sanctuary maintains the mooring buoys.

Another part of Reef Relief's mission is public awareness and education regarding the living coral reef habitat. To this end, each year the organization sponsors a cleanup campaign that attracts hundreds of volunteers. They comb shorelines and out-islands and dive the reef, collecting trash and storm-driven debris. For more information, contact Reef Relief Environmental Education Center, 201 William Street, Key West, (305) 294-3100, www.reefrelief.org.

The Turtle Hospital

The grounds of the Hidden Harbor Motel—MM 48.5, Bayside, Marathon (see our Accommodations chapter)—shelter the famed Turtle Hospital, a turtle rapid-care center and recovery room run as a labor of love by Richie Moretti since 1984. The reptilian effort, which is financially supported in total by the income generated from Hidden Harbor Motel, has drawn the attention and cooperation of the University of Florida.

Local veterinarians volunteer their time, often performing complicated turtle surgery on fibro-papilloma tumors, impactions and shell fractures caused by hit-and-run boating injuries. After surgery, the turtles are moved to the recovery room, the property's original saltwater pool.

More than 5,000 school children visit the Turtle Hospital every year, learning about the fascinating reptilian order Chelonia. Moretti does not allow the public access to the Turtle Hospital. However, guests at Hidden Harbor are among the privileged few invited to tour the turtle recovery room at will, often assisting with a rescue at sea or a dash in the Turtle Hospital ambulance.

Reef Environmental Education Foundation

A sort of Audubon Society for fish, the Reef Environmental Education Foundation's mission is "To educate, enlist, and enable divers and non-divers alike to become active stewards in the conservation of coral reefs and other marine habitats." To that end, the foundation offers

educational programs and informational seminars for divers and snorkelers on the wonders of our coral reef as well as those in the waters of North and South America and the Caribbean. The foundation also maintains an on-going data collection program, whereby underwater aficionados record what types of marine life they see, where these creatures are spotted, and how many of each species are seen. Each summer, the Great American Fish Count, from July 1 to July 14, focuses particular attention on this program, with a series of educational seminars that prepare volunteer divers and snorkelers for undersea survey excursions with local Keys dive shops. For more information, contact the Reef Environmental Education Foundation, MM 106, Bayside, Key Largo, (305) 451-0312, or check out their website: www.reef.org.

You'll often see bottle-nosed dolphins in free-swimming pods in open waters. PHOTO: SUZANNE TOBEY

Getting Here, Getting Around

You are headed for the Florida Keys. Whether you travel by land, by sea, or by air, you must conform to some strict, uncompromising standards that your travel agent may have neglected to tell you.

"Ha!" you say.

"Ah, but true," say we.

First, remove your socks. You won't need them here. Don your shorts. They are de rigueur. Slip on those shades. How else can you see? And reset your watch. The pace is slower here; you're on Keys time now.

Things really are different here. Our single main street stretches 126 miles—from Florida City to Key West—and dead-ends at the sea. Our 42 bridges span the kissing waters of the Atlantic Ocean and the Gulf of Mexico, from Key Largo to Key West. And our Keys communities resound as distinctively as the ivories of a piano (see our Key West section in this chapter for information on transportation options in that city).

So come on down. We're playing your song.

The Florida Keys

By Air

Commercial Flights

Florida Keys Marathon Airport
MM 52 Bayside
Marathon, FL
(305) 743–2155, (305) 289–6060
www.floridakeysairport.com

The Florida Keys Marathon Airport is a FAA-certified facility that makes Flagler's railway journey seem a bad dream. The $7.5 million, 20,000-square-foot building opened in February 1995. The tropical architecture in the structure and the utilization of the talents of local artists in its interior design led the Federal Department of Transportation and the National Endowment for the Arts to award Florida Keys Marathon Airport the 1995 Design for Transportation Award. Don't miss the ceiling fans fashioned from fishing rods and strung canvas.

Unfortunately, this modern, state-of-the-art operation now offers no option of flying directly to the middle of the Keys. Until May 2000, American Eagle operated regularly scheduled flights between Marathon and Miami. Since they ceased operation here, Vintage Props and Jets and Florida Air have come and gone. Airport management is seeking more carriers.

Avis, Budget, and Enterprise rental cars are available at the airport. Make

Insiders' Tip

Make **your** airline reservations into the Key West airport as early as possible. During the peak tourist season, Christmas through Easter, last-minute flight availability into the Keys is rare.

reservations for a vehicle in advance whenever possible (see our By Land section in this chapter). Taxis stand by in front of the airport awaiting each flight.

Other Commercial Options
Miami International Airport
LeJeune Road
Miami, FL
(305) 876–7000

An international airport offering flights on most major airline carriers, Miami International Airport is accessible from either Interstate 95 or Florida's Turnpike via Florida Highway 836 and LeJeune Road. You can rent a car (see the listing in this chapter for 800 numbers) and drive the distance to the Keys. Miami to Key Largo is approximately 60 miles; to Islamorada, 80 miles; to Marathon, 115 miles; to Big Pine, 130 miles; to Key West, 160 miles.

Fort Lauderdale-Hollywood
International Airport
Interstate 595-East
Fort Lauderdale, FL
(954) 359–1200

Smaller than Miami International, this airport off Interstate 595 offers fewer flight options but is hassle-free compared to Miami's. To drive to the Keys from Fort Lauderdale-Hollywood International Airport, follow signs to Florida's Turnpike via Interstate 595. Driving from the Fort Lauderdale-Hollywood International Airport will add about 45 more minutes to your total trip.

Private Aircraft

Paradise Aviation
MM 52 Bayside
Marathon, FL
(305) 743–4222
Pilots: ARINC 131.45

Paradise Aviation is a flight-based operation at the east end of the Florida Keys Marathon Airport runway. If you wish to land your private aircraft or jet in Marathon, call Marathon UNICOM on

Insiders' Tip

Directions from Miami International Airport via Florida's Turnpike: Take LeJeune Road south to FL Hwy. 836 W. As you approach the ramp for FL Hwy. 836 W., get in the right-hand lane. Be aware, however, that a frontage-road access just before the FL Hwy. 836 W. sign and arrow often lures confused first-timers into turning too soon. The ramp is actually just after the FL Hwy. 836 W. sign and arrow. Follow FL Hwy. 836 W. to Florida's Turnpike South, Homestead. Continue on Florida's Turnpike until it ends in Florida City at U.S. Hwy. 1. Continue south on U.S. Hwy. 1 to the Keys.

frequency 122.8. Paradise Aviation will issue a wind and a runway advisory. After you land, they will contact you by tail number and advise you where to tie down. No landing fee is charged, but it will cost you from $10 to $25 to tie down at Paradise Aviation for the night, depending on the size of your aircraft. Paradise Aviation offers both 100 low-lead (LL) fuel and Jet A fuel. Jet charter service is available to most locations.

Grantair Service Inc.
MM 52 Bayside
Marathon, FL
(305) 743–1995

Located at the west end of Florida Keys Marathon Airport, Grantair Service Inc. is a flight-based operation that caters to general aviation and light aircraft. It

Fort Jefferson in the Dry Tortugas is the end of the line in the Florida Keys. PHOTO: WAYNE MOCCIA

offers a maintenance facility on premises and sells 100 low-lead fuel. Tie downs cost $10 per night or $90 per month. You can earn a single or twin engine, sea plane, or instrument license at Grantair's flight school, then rent either a Cessna 152, a Cessna 177, or one of three Cessna 172s. Grantair also offers sightseeing tours of the Middle Keys and the reef.

By Sea

Visit the Florida Keys as the pirates and buccaneers did before you—by sea. Revel in the beauty of these sea pearls, strung together by the wisp of the Overseas Highway. Your perspective of the Keys will be different when viewed from our waters. Navigate your motor or sailing craft through the Intracoastal Waterway, which extends from Miami through Card Sound and Barnes Sound and down the length of the Keys in the Florida Bay/Gulf of Mexico. Or parallel the oceanside shores following Hawk Channel, a well-marked route protected by the reef. For comprehensive information on arriving and vacationing on your pleasure craft, see our Cruising chapter.

By Land

The Overseas Highway tethers our islands to the mainland like a long umbilical cord. Addresses along this common main street are issued by mile markers, designated as MM. Commencing with MM 126 in Florida City and culminating with MM 0 in Key West, small green markers with white numbers are posted every mile.

The Overseas Highway actually curves and drifts toward the southwest, rendering it all but impossible to refer to directions as "north to here" or "south to there." Here in the Keys everything is grounded by a mile marker, and you'll note that we orient most of the addresses we give in this book by mile marker.

As you head toward Key West, mile marker numbers descend in order. Any

The Seven Mile Bridge traverses the once-impassable "water gap." PHOTO: FLORIDA KEYS & KEY WEST TDC

place on the right side of the road bordering Florida Bay or the Gulf of Mexico is referred to as bayside. The opposite side of the road, bordering the Atlantic Ocean, is therefore called oceanside. So, addresses on the Overseas Highway will usually be referred to by both mile marker number and a bayside or oceanside distinction.

The old saying, "All roads lead to the sea," could very well have been written about the Keys. The occasional side street you might encounter on one of our wider islands—such as Key Largo, Marathon, or Big Pine Key—will terminate at the bay, the Gulf, or the ocean after only a few blocks.

One dangerous stretch of road calls for diligence from drivers. From Florida City at MM 126 to Key Largo at MM 106, a two-lane, 20-mile section of U.S. Highway 1 monotonously rolls through barren-looking sawgrass prairie. This paved purgatory is statistically so treacherous that government leaders are considering having the road widened to four lanes. Be patient and cautious. Although brief passing lanes are interspersed throughout the stretch, the flat, straight road incites reckless, lead-footed, or impatient drivers to pass slower-moving vehicles.

Rental Cars

Public transportation in the Keys (except for Key West) is practically nil. You really need a car to get around. Most rental car companies are based in Marathon. Some pick up and deliver vehicles. Reserve your automobile before you arrive in the Keys—availability in peak seasons is often limited—at one of the following agencies:

Avis Rent A Car
MM 52 Bayside
Florida Keys Marathon Airport
(305) 743–5428, (800) 331–1212
www.avis.com

Avis offers pickup and delivery in Marathon from Coco Plum to the Seven Mile Bridge only.

Budget Car & Truck Rental
MM 52 Bayside
Florida Keys Marathon Airport
(305) 743–3998, (800) 527–0700
www.budget.com

Budget picks up and delivers within Marathon only.

Enterprise Rent-A-Car
MM 100.2 Oceanside
Key Largo, FL
(305) 451–3998, (800) 736–8222
MM 52 Bayside
Florida Keys Marathon Airport
(305) 289–7630, (800) 736–8222
www.erac.com

Enterprise has locations serving the Keys from top to bottom, including Key West (see subsequent listing). The Key Largo office offers pickup of vehicles from Key Largo to MM 70, Fiesta Key. The Marathon Enterprise office is in the Florida Keys Marathon Airport terminal. This office will pick up your rental car as far up the Keys as MM 70 or as far down the Keys as Little Palm Island.

Taxi Service

If you don't have your own automobile or haven't rented a car for the duration of your visit, you may find yourself in need of ground transportation within the Keys. Be aware that the fare could get pricey (sometimes approaching the cost of a daily rental vehicle), especially if you are traveling any distance. But if you need a lift call one of the following:

In the Upper Keys, Key Largo Cabs, (305) 451–9700, (305) 852–8888, or Mom's Taxi, (305) 852–7999, (305) 852–8888.

In the Middle Keys (Marathon), try Action Taxi, (305) 743–6800, or Cheapo Taxi, (305) 743–7420, (305) 872–0377.

In the Lower Keys, you can call Courtesy Transportation, (305) 872–9314, or All Keys Transport, (305) 872–0577, (305) 289–7575.

Limousine and Airport Shuttle Service

In the event you are stranded without transportation to either of the mainland

> ## Insiders' Tip
>
> Card Sound Road (County Rte. 905A) forks off U.S. Hwy. 1 just south of Florida City and provides an alternative to the sometimes dangerous primary route to the Keys. The picturesque, less-traveled road (also two lanes with no passing lane) traverses a toll bridge ($1) that passes between Card Sound and Barnes Sound. This route will put you north of Key Largo, near the Ocean Reef Club. At the T-junction with County Rte. 905, turn right and follow the road until it merges with U.S. Hwy. 1 (Overseas Highway) in Key Largo.

airports, alternative transportation is available.

Go Tours Airport Shuttle
MM 53 Oceanside
Marathon, FL
(305) 743–8446, (800) 689–3304

This airport shuttle operates 24 hours a day, seven days a week, transporting travelers from anywhere in the Keys to Miami International or Fort Lauderdale-Hollywood International Airport. Based in mid Marathon, across from Burger King, Go Tours picks up customers at all Keys resorts as well as private homes. Following are examples of daytime fares to Miami International: from Key Largo or Islamorada, $49.90; from Marathon, $59.90; from Big Pine or Key West, $69.90. Nighttime fares will be higher. Call for reservations 24 to 48 hours in advance. Go Tours also offers bus charters and island tour packages.

Luxury Limousine of the Florida Keys, Inc.
Ocean Reef
North Key Largo, FL
(305) 367–2329, (305) 664–0601,
(800) 664–0124

Four super-stretch limos seating up to 10 passengers, smaller limos, Lincoln towncars, minivans, and a 27-passenger bus are available from Luxury Limousine for private transportation anywhere between Key West and West Palm Beach. Price is quoted per trip, one way. For example, limo transportation from Key West to Miami International Airport is about $300; from the Middle Keys, $175; Upper Keys, $125. Prices vary with other options. Advance reservations are required. All prices are for private transportation, based on one to three people and do not include gratuity.

Bus Service

Greyhound Bus Lines
Adam Arnold Annex
Key West International Airport
3535 S. Roosevelt Boulevard
Key West, FL
(305) 296–9072, (800) 410–5397 (tri-county),
(800) 231–2222 (nationwide)
www.greyhound.com

Greyhound bridges the gap in mass ground transit from Key West to Miami and beyond. Greyhound departs the Key West depot, which is housed in the Adam Arnold Annex at the airport, usually four times a day, seven days a week, bound for Miami International Airport, the Miami Amtrack Station, and downtown Miami, with convenient connections for the Tri-Rail system. (Schedules vary during the off season.) Four of the Greyhound stops in the Keys sell tickets: Big Pine Motel, Big Pine, MM 30.7 Bayside; Chamber of Commerce, MM 53 Bayside, Marathon (tickets only, pickup spot is at Florida Keys Marathon Airport, MM 52); Burger King, Islamorada, MM 83.5 Oceanside; and Howard Johnson Hotel, Key Largo, MM 102 Bayside.

Additional boarding locations are sprinkled along the Overseas Highway, marked by signs with the Greyhound logo. They are at the corner of Virginia and Simonton Streets (in Key West); Boca Chica, MM 7; Big Coppitt, MM 10.6; Sugar Loaf, MM 17; Cudjoe Key, MM 22; Ramrod Key, MM 27.8; Florida Keys Marathon Airport, MM 52; Layton, MM 69; Islamorada, MM 82.5; and Tavernier, MM 92. The bus also stops at MM 126 in Florida City.

The trip will take 4 hours, 15 minutes from Key West to Miami International by Greyhound Bus. Fares to Miami International Airport depend on embarking and disembarking sites. For example, the fare per person from Key West is about $32 one way, $62 round trip. Discounts are offered for multiple riders. Commuter rates are also available. Fares are slightly higher on weekends. Special offers apply. Greyhound schedules and fares are subject to change. Be sure to confirm your specific travel arrangements when purchasing tickets.

Key West

Key West, the southernmost point in the continental United States, slumbers closer to Havana than it does to Miami—when it sleeps, that is, which is not all that often. In Keys-speak, this is where the action is.

Although nearly 25,000 people make Key West their home, this island still retains a small-town charm. The quaint Old Town area remains essentially a charming, foliage-canopied grid of streets lined with gingerbread-trimmed frame structures that evoke a succession of bygone eras and a cache of simmering secrets. This area, by the way, boasts the largest collection of frame structures in a National Register Historic District of any city in Florida—nearly 3,000—and some architectural elements that are found nowhere else in the world.

The Mid Town area is predominantly residential. New Town takes in the shopping centers and fast food and hotel chains along N. Roosevelt Boulevard on the Gulf side and across the island to the airport and beaches along S. Roosevelt Boulevard on the Atlantic side.

Old Town, destination of choice for most visitors to Key West, is accessed from the Overseas Highway by either N. Roosevelt Boulevard (U.S. Highway 1) to Truman Avenue or S. Roosevelt Boulevard (A1A) along the beach to White Street. From White Street, Southard Street runs one way toward the heart of Old Town. Fleming Street is one way leading the opposite direction.

Old Town is anchored by Duval Street, which has been dubbed the longest street in the world because it runs from the Atlantic to the Gulf of Mexico. It is actually only a little more than a mile long. Although finding your way around Key West is not difficult, the narrow, often one-way streets—combined with a proliferation of tourist-driven rental cars and scooters in peak seasons—can make driving around this island both frustrating and time-consuming. Old Town is best explored on foot or by bicycle.

Key West provides public bus service and several other unique modes of transportation, which we describe in this section.

By Air

Commercial Flights

Key West International Airport
3491 S. Roosevelt Boulevard
Key West, FL
(305) 296–5439

Although Key West is the Florida destination of choice for thousands of visitors each year, do not expect to arrive here via commercial jetliner. Air service to this island in the sun is of the commuter variety. The planes are small, and flights are often overbooked during peak seasons, especially in January and February, so be sure to arrive early to check in for your flight.

If you are meeting a flight, short-term metered parking is available (25 cents per 15 minutes, with a one hour limit). You

Insiders' Tip

The official website for the Florida Keys is www.fla-keys.com. You can also find information at these sites: www.thefloridakeys.com and www.fabulousvacations.com.

may also park in the long-term lot at 50 cents for the first hour, then 50 cents each additional half hour with a $4 maximum per day. Weekly rates are available.

Avis, Budget, Dollar, and Hertz rental cars are available at the airport terminal; Alamo and Enterprise are just a courtesy call away (see subsequent listings in our Rental Cars section). Whenever possible, make reservations for your vehicle in advance. Taxis stand by in front of the airport awaiting each flight and many hotels offer complimentary shuttle service.

Commercial flights into and out of Key West are provided by the following airlines:

American Eagle (American Airlines, 800-433-7300, www.aa.com): American Eagle offers connecting service to a multitude of American Airlines flights via Miami.

Cape Air (305-293-0603, 800-352-0714, www.flycapeair.com): Cape Air provides scheduled service between Key West and Fort Lauderdale as well as southwest Florida airports in Naples and Fort Myers.

Delta Air Lines (800-221-1212, www.delta.com): Comair, the Delta Connection, offers service between Key West and Orlando. In Orlando, you can pick up any number of connecting flights on Delta Airlines.

Continental Connection, operated by Gulfstream International Airlines, (305-294-1421, 800-525-0280, domestic; 800-231-0856, international): Gulfstream provides feeder service to Key West for both Continental Airlines and United Airlines.

Flights from Key West connect through Miami, Tampa, and Fort Lauderdale.

USAir Express, (800–428–4322, www.usair.com): USAir Express offers flights from Key West to Miami, Tampa, and Orlando, where you can connect with many USAir—and, in some cases, even British Airways—flights.

Private Aircraft

Island City Flying Service
3471 S. Roosevelt Boulevard
Key West, FL
(305) 296–5422

Island City Flying Service is a flight-based operation at the Key West International Airport. If you want to land your private aircraft or jet in Key West, call Island City UNICOM on frequency 122.95. There is no reserved parking—you may take any available space you see on the ramp. No landing fee is charged, but daily parking and overnight tie-down fees are assessed depending on the size of your aircraft: $10 for single engine; $15 for twin; $45 for turbo. The daily parking fee is waived with a fuel purchase.

Island City Flying Service offers both 100 low-lead (LL) fuel and Jet A fuel and rents life vests and life rafts as required by law for flying to the Bahamas or the Caribbean. Flight instruction is available.

By Sea

Long a bustling port, Key West harbor is still busy—full of commercial traffic, tourist-filled tour boats, and visiting cruise ships. If you choose to navigate your motor or sailing craft to Key West from the Atlantic, come in through the main ship channel, which is marked "S.E. Channel" on the charts. From the Gulf take the N.W. Channel until it intersects with the main ship channel. You can anchor out in protected areas of the harbor or put into one of the comprehensive Key West marinas (see our Cruising chapter).

By Land

Rental Cars

Most of the nationally advertised names in the rental car business maintain locations in Key West. Several have lots at the airport, and many will even pick up and deliver your rental vehicle directly to your hotel. Inquire when you make your reservation. And speaking of reservations, it is always wise to phone ahead to reserve your car, especially during peak travel periods.

The following companies offer rental vehicles:

Alamo Rent A Car, 2516 N. Roosevelt Blvd., (305) 294–6675, (800) 327–9633.

Avis Rent A Car, Key West International Airport, 3491 S. Roosevelt Blvd., (305) 296–8744, (800) 831–2847.

Budget Car & Truck Rental, Key West International Airport, 3495 S. Roosevelt Boulevard, (305) 294–8868, (800) 527–0700.

Dollar Rent A Car, Key West International Airport, 3491 S. Roosevelt Blvd., (305) 296–9921, (800) 800–4000.

Enterprise Rent-A-Car, 2834 N. Roosevelt Blvd., (305) 292–0220, (800) 325–8007.

Hertz Rent A Car, Key West International Airport, 3491 S. Roosevelt Blvd., (305) 294–1039, (800) 654–3131.

In most cases, you will need a credit card to rent a car from any of the nationally advertised rental car agencies listed above. However, the following locally owned and operated auto rental agencies will accept cash: Island Auto Rentals, 5300 U.S. Hwy. 1, Stock Island, (305) 295–7368, (305) 289–7368; and Tropical Rent-A-Car, at 1300 Duval St., (305) 294–8136, www.tropicalrentacar.com.

One final word about rental cars: The island of Key West is only eight square miles in size and thanks to the ready availability of taxicabs and shuttle services, you really don't need a car to get around it. In fact, you may be better off without wheels. Our streets are narrow and almost always

Insiders' Tip

In addition to (800), the Keys now uses (888) and (877) to designate a toll-free telephone number.

See our Keys section for comprehensive information on schedules for Greyhound bus service to Miami International Airport. Buses make multiple stops between Key West and the top of the Keys. The fare per person from Key West to Miami International is about $32 one way, $62 round trip. Schedules and fares are subject to change so be sure to confirm your travel arrangements when purchasing tickets.

congested with a combination of cars, vans, delivery vehicles, scooters, buses, Conch Trains, trolleys, and bicycles. Not only is parking expensive and often not readily available in the historic district, if you plan to party hardy on Duval, you'd be better off letting someone else do the driving.

Taxi and Limousine Service

Taxis are plentiful, reliable, and relatively inexpensive in Key West. You will find several at the airport awaiting each flight. Or, you can call one of the following companies directly for door-to-door service: A Airport Cab Company (305-292-1111); Five 6's Cab Company, (305-296-6666, 305-294-5678, www.keywesttaxi.com); or Friendly Cab Company, (305-292-0000 or 305-295-5555).

Limousine companies offer a variety of services. Some will take you all the way to Miami if you like, and others cater specifically to groups. Prices and services vary so call around and compare. The following options are available to Key West visitors: Airport Limousine Van Service (305-294-5678); or try Eggs Transport, Inc. (305-294-0190, 888-707-8166); also Go Tours (305-743-9876, 800-689-3304); Island Coaches (305-296-4800, 800-539-7386); and Luxury Limousine of the Florida Keys (305-664-0601, 800-664-0124).

Bus Service

Greyhound Bus Lines
Adam Arnold Annex
Key West International Airport
3535 S. Roosevelt Boulevard
Key West, FL
(305) 296–9072, (800) 296–9072 (tri-county),
(800) 231–2222 (nationwide)

City of Key West Department of Transportation
627 Palm Avenue
Key West, FL
(305) 292–8160

Public transport city buses, many of which are brightly decorated with the works of local artists, circle the island of Key West several times a day along four color-coded routes. Buses on the blue and red routes travel clockwise while buses on the orange and green routes run counterclockwise. Signs at all of the bus stops sport colored dots to indicate the routes they serve.

Buses on all routes travel to Old Town as well as to the hospital on Stock Island and to the shopping plazas along N. Roosevelt Boulevard (U.S. Hwy. 1) in New Town. However, only the green and blue routes serve the airport, Smathers Beach, and other stops along S. Roosevelt Boulevard (Rte. A1A). The orange and red routes, which traverse the interior of the island along Flagler Avenue, serve Key West High School. The red and blue routes are the only ones to serve Bahama Village via Emma and Angela Streets.

Although this may sound confusing, the buses in Key West are actually quite easy to use as long as you keep one basic rule in mind: if you took the blue route to your destination, take the green route home; red route out, orange route home. And if all else fails, just take the same route to and from your destination. Remember that this is an island where the buses traverse in a great big circle. You simply cannot get lost if you stay on a particular bus since it will eventually return to the stop where you boarded it. If you are in doubt about a particular route, ask the bus driver before boarding or call the Key West Department of Transportation (KWDOT) for directions.

On weekdays, bus service starts as early as 6:05 A.M. and continues until 11:27 P.M.; on weekends and holidays, the hours may be shorter and the stops less frequent depending on the route. The green route, for example, operates Monday through Friday only. Buses on each route make their complete rounds once an hour. At any given stop, however, you can expect a bus to appear, going one direction or the other, every half-hour throughout the day. A complete timetable and route map is available from KWDOT.

The fare is 75 cents for adults. Children younger than 5 ride free with a paying adult. Senior citizens pay 35 cents, but they must first obtain an identification card for $2 at the KWDOT office (see address above). Students also may ride for 35 cents if they display their school ID card upon boarding. The bus drivers do not carry change so you must have exact fare. Monthly passes may be purchased from the bus driver or at the KWDOT office.

Alternative Transportation

Trolley Tour

Old Town Trolley Tours of Key West
Key West Welcome Center
3840 N. Roosevelt Boulevard
Key West, FL
(305) 296–6688
www.trolleytours.com

Listen to a narrative of historic Key West on this continuous loop tour, learning as you go. Although this transportation option is promoted and sold as a 90-minute tour, you can hop on and off the trolley as many times per day as you wish. It's one hassle-free way to shop, dine, or take in the myriad attractions Key West has to offer.

You can park your car free at the Key West Welcome Center where you can also buy tickets and board the trolley. Daytrip-pers will find the Welcome Center readily accessible upon entry into Key West. Bear right and follow the signs for U.S. Hwy. 1. The Welcome Center is on the left side of the road. Park your car, then grab a trolley and let your conductor spirit you around Key West. You can disembark at Mallory Square, Key West Hand Print Fashions & Fabrics, Holiday Inn La Concha, Angela Street Depot (corner of Angela and Duval), Fairfield Inn, Ramada Inn, Radisson Key West, Key West Welcome Center, Key Ambassador, Sheraton Suites, Wyndham Casa Marina, and the Southernmost Point Trolley Stop. Trolleys stop at each location every 30 minutes.

Cost of the trolley tour is $19 per day for adults and teens, $10 for children ages 4 through 12. Children 3 and younger ride free.

Note: The Conch Trains that you see chugging around town are bona fide touring vehicles; you cannot get on and off a Conch Train at will. See our Attractions chapter for further information on this and other tours.

Shuttle Services

Bone Island Shuttle
Various locations around Key West
(305) 293–8710

On an island with too many cars and not enough places to put them, the idea of a shuttle service specifically designed to cart tourists from one end to the other is such a no-brainer we wonder why someone didn't think of it sooner. At just $7 for a full day of unlimited transportation, Bone Island Shuttle provides an inexpensive, worry-free way to get around Key West—several times a day if you like.

These easy-to-spot vehicles—hand-painted with tropical designs by local artists—operate from 9 A.M. to 10 P.M., seven days a week along two routes. Shuttles on the red route travel in a clockwise direction around the island; shuttles on the blue route travel counterclockwise. On any given day, there are always at least four, and sometimes six, Bone Island Shuttles in operation between the tourist attractions in Old Town and the hotels/motels in New Town. A shuttle going one way or the other stops at least every 15 minutes at the Key West Welcome Center, Quality Inn, Sheraton Suites, Wyndham Casa Marina, Key West Historic Seaport, Mallory Square, Bahama Market, Fairfield Inn, Ramada Inn, and Radisson Key West. Route maps and schedules are available at the Key West Chamber of Commerce, Mallory Square, and in brochure racks all across the island.

Individual shuttle tickets may be purchased at the Key West Welcome Center, 3840 N. Roosevelt Blvd., from Trolley and Conch Train ticket vendors, at several Old Town attractions, or from the concierge/front desk staff at any of the hotel stops. Group charters are available too.

Pedal Cabs

Hail a pedal cab if you'd like an Old World–type transport around Key West. These bicycle-driven, open-air, two-seater passenger carts weave in and out of traffic on Duval Street and in the surrounding historic district. Your pedal-pumping guide will point out the sights for $1 per minute, with discounts generally given for journeys of 30 minutes or more. Be sure to negotiate the price before you set off so there won't be any surprises on either side.

Just like a taxicab, your pedal-cab can transport you to a destination that you specify. However, most pedal-cab drivers are also willing to do any kind of tour you like—tours of restaurants, bars, historic sites and architectural wanderings. Pedal-cabs make regular journeys up and down Duval Street; the best way to secure a ride is to simply flag one down. But if you can't hail a pedal-cab, feel free to call Perfect Pedicab at (305) 292-0077 to reserve a vehicle.

Bicycles, Mopeds, Scooters, and Electric Cars

Key West is the perfect place to explore by bicycle or moped, although we wouldn't recommend riding in the Mallory Square/lower Duval Street area or along N. Roo-sevelt Boulevard, which are heavily congested with people, automobiles, and delivery trucks. Many places rent a choice of either mopeds or bicycles by the hour, day, overnight, or week. Some rentals provide a backpack, and some may include a helmet in the rental price. Expect to pay between $5 and $10, depending on the type of bike and the length of your rental period (see our Recreation chapter).

Mopeds or scooters swing a wider range, varying from $10 to $30 per day. Some companies consider a daily moped rental to be 24 hours; others cap the day at eight hours. Inquire when you call. Some moped rental agencies even rent double scooters that seat two; it is illegal to carry a passenger on any other kind. The following Key West companies rent a full range of vehicles—bicycles, mopeds, and/or scooters: Adventure Scooter & Bicycle Rentals, 2900 N. Roosevelt Blvd. (and six other locations), (305) 293-9933; The Bicycle Center, 523 Truman Ave., (305) 294-4556; Moped Hospital, 601 Truman Ave., (305) 296-3344; Pirate Scooter, 401 Southard St., (305) 295-0000; Scooter Safari, 3706 N. Roosevelt Blvd., (305) 294-4420; and Tropical Scooters, 1300 Duval Street, (305) 294-8136.

The newest additions to the Key West self-propelled transportation scene are the Key West Cruisers, 1111 Eaton St., (305) 294-4724, (888) 800-8802. These egg-shaped electric vehicles are eerily quiet and understandably slow. They seat two or four, have no doors, and top out at 25 mph, making them ideal for an island where the speed limits never go above 35. You can rent a Key West Cruiser for a half-day, full-day, or overnight. Expect to pay $90 to $200 depending on the size of your vehicle and the length of time you rent it.

A few words of caution about two-wheeled transportation: Bicycle, moped, and scooter riders are subject to the same traffic laws as those who operate four-wheeled vehicles. That means you must have lights at night, obey all traffic signals and signs, stay off the sidewalks, and travel in the correct direction on one-way

Scooters are a popular mode of transportation along the streets of Key West for tourists and locals alike.

PHOTO: JANET WARE

streets. Keep in mind, too, that you operate these vehicles at your own risk. In a collision with a car, a scooter or moped almost always loses. If you wreck your rental scooter, you will be personally liable for the damages. The rental agents are not required to offer insurance. They are, however, required to provide instruction and to offer helmets. Even so, the hospital emergency room on Stock Island sees an average of two scooter accidents per day. And that doesn't account for the drivers who simply pick themselves up off the street and carry on. Words to the wise: Be careful!

Foot Power

Strolling Key West is a great way to work off the pounds you'll be packing on by grazing the tempting kiosks, juice bars, ice-cream shops, restaurants, and, of course, bars of Key West. The sidewalk-lined streets in Old Town often front little-known lanes where unusual shops or galleries hide beneath ancient foliage. You'll miss these—and much of the mystery and charm of this southernmost city—if you don't get out of your car and walk a bit.

You can explore on your own or take advantage of one of the many guided tours that are available (see our Attractions chapter for several options). Perhaps the best-documented, self-guided walking tour of Key West has been compiled by Sharon Wells. Her *Walking & Biking Guide to Historic Key West* is free for the asking at the Key West Chamber of Commerce (open 8:30 A.M. to 5 P.M. daily) at Mallory Square. You can also find copies at several shops around town. Wells guides you along 10 routes, identifying the buildings of architectural or historical significance you will pass along the way.

While at the Chamber, you may also want to pick up a copy of the Pelican Path map/brochure. Originated by the Old Island Restoration Foundation, the Pelican Path is a self-guided walking tour that takes you past some of Key West's most historically and architecturally significant buildings.

Parking

Ask any local if there's a downside to living in Paradise and he or she will almost always complain about parking. There are simply too many cars in Old Town Key West and too few places to put them. And because the permanent population of this tiny island keeps growing and most visitors either arrive by car or rent a vehicle when they get here, the parking problem isn't going away any time soon.

Patrons of the shops and restaurants in Duval Square (1075 Duval Street) will find free parking available in an adjacent lot accessed from Simonton Street. Free parking for patrons of some Duval Street restaurants, shops, and bars may also be available in designated lots off either Whitehead or Simonton Streets, both of which run parallel to Duval. Metered curbside parking is, of course, available on several downtown streets, including Duval, Whitehead, and Simonton, as well as along most of the streets that intersect them. Special curbside parking areas are designated for scooters and mopeds; do not leave vehicles on the sidewalk.

In the past, tourists who wanted to avoid feeding meters and didn't mind a little extra walk could simply secure a free curbside parking spot in the many residential Old Town neighborhoods several blocks off Duval. No more. In an effort to appease Key West residents who complained about having to park several blocks from their homes because tourists had taken their curbside spots, the city of Key West inaugurated a resident parking program in early 1998. We're sorry to say it's not very visitor-friendly.

Here's how parking in residential Old Town works: Curbside spots along many Old Town streets have been ruled off with white paint and marked with the large yellow letters "RP." In order to park your vehicle in one of these spots, your car must display either a Monroe County license plate or a residential parking permit (available for $5 from the City of Key West with proof of residence).

If you park in one of the "RP" spaces and your car does not show the proper proof of residence, you may return to find it gone. Your "illegally parked" vehicle will have likely been towed to the city's impound lot on Stock Island. To retrieve it, you will have to have cash (about $75)—no checks or credit cards are accepted.

However, if you want to be right in the thick of things, you will either have to feed a meter or pay to park in a lot. The meters cost $1 per hour, and they run until midnight daily, including Sundays and holidays. Meter maids (and men) regularly patrol the streets of Key West, and $20 tickets are liberally distributed. All-day parking is available for more reasonable prices at several privately owned lots on either side of Duval Street; watch for the lot attendants holding cardboard signs. You might also consider one of the convenient parking facilities described below.

In all cases, we recommend that you lock your car and either carry your valuables or stow them out of sight, preferably before you park. Key West is a relatively safe place. However, leaving your video camera in plain view on the front seat of your rental car or stuffing your purse into the trunk just as you leave your car unattended is an open invitation to thievery.

Keep in mind that none of the parking lots described below accepts RVs, nor are you allowed to park your RV on a public street in Key West. During the day, you may park your vehicle on Barracuda Pier at Garrison Bight, off N. Roosevelt Boulevard, or on the bridle path across from Smathers Beach on S. Roosevelt Boulevard. Do not park in any of the beachside spaces at Smathers, however; S. Roosevelt is considered a city street, and your vehicle may be towed. After 11 P.M., you must park your RV on private property, in a licensed RV park or campground. For additional information about RV parking in Key West, call (305) 292-PARK.

Whatever kind of vehicle you drive, be sure to park only in designated areas, pay attention to the signs, and never, never block a driveway or park alongside a yellow curb. If the sign says that unauthorized vehicles will be towed, believe it. And tempting as those empty spots in the post office lot on Whitehead Street may be, don't even think about leaving your car in one all day. They are for post office customers only. After 5 P.M., however, the post office lot becomes a public parking lot and you may park your vehicle here for a fee.

Caroline Street Parking Lot
Corner of Caroline and Margaret Streets
Key West, FL
(305) 293–8309

Adjacent to the attractions at Key West's Historic Seaport, this open-air lot offers full-day parking for $10. If you just need to run a quick errand, you can park here for $1.50 per hour. The lot is accessible 24 hours to cars, motorcycles, and scooters only; no RVs, trailers, or buses permitted.

Hilton Parking Garage
231 Front Street
Key West, FL
(305) 296–9296

At the end of Front Street, just past the lobby entrance to the Hilton Hotel, this public parking garage can accommodate 400 cars and offers 24-hour security. Rates are $2.50 per hour ($24 maximum). Sorry, no trailers, bikes, scooters, or motorcycles are allowed here.

Mallory Square Parking Lot
Corner of Wall and Front Streets
Key West, FL
(305) 292–8158

This parking lot abuts the cruise ship dock off Wall Street in the Mallory Square area and is convenient to all the west-end attractions and the sunset celebration. Over the years, it has, however, been reduced in size to accommodate the enlarged and improved Mallory Square so parking space is limited. Rates run $2 per hour, day and night. The lot is open from 8 A.M. until midnight. Cars, motorcycles, small trucks, and vans are welcome; campers, RVs, buses, and trailers are not.

Old Town Parking Garage
Key West Park N' Ride
300 Grinnell Street
Key West, FL
(305) 293–6426

The award-winning Old Town Parking Garage offers you the chance to find one of 250 covered parking spaces at a reasonable rate any time, day or night. Cars, small trucks, and motorcycles are welcome here. For $1.25 an hour ($8 maximum), you can park and then ride one of the shuttles to the downtown area several blocks away. There is no extra charge for the shuttle when you show your ticket; a shuttle ride will cost 50 cents per person without the ticket. If your stay will be long-term, choose the monthly rate of $50, plus tax.

Restaurants

Price-Code Key

Our price-code rating reflects the cost of entrees for two, without cocktails, appetizers, wine, dessert, tax, and tip.

$	Less than $25
$$	$25 to $40
$$$	$41 to $60
$$$	More than $60

Surrounded by water, the Florida Keys yields a bounty that easily could qualify as the eighth wonder of the world. We confidently can boast that nowhere else in the continental United States—oh, why not say it, the universe even—will you find fresher, more innovatively prepared fish and seafood than in our restaurants.

Be sure to sample our special natural resources, served any way you like. We import a few raw materials in the feather and flesh categories as well, so your palate will be truly well rounded. (For preparing your own fare, see our Seafood Markets and Specialty Foods chapter.)

Enjoy the relaxed atmosphere of our restaurants, where even the most upscale dining carries a laid-back apparel code. Be it a roadside cafe or a resort dining room, you need dress no more formally than "Keys casual," typically an ensemble of shirt and shorts, shoes, or sandals. Men may leave their sports jackets at home, and don't even think about bringing a suit to the Keys unless it is the swimming variety. The same code applies to women as well; we don't discriminate here. The occasional restaurant, such as Cheeca Lodge or Little Palm Island affords you the chance to dress up a bit more if you like—long slacks for the gentlemen, perhaps an island-style dress for the ladies. But the choice is yours. As we keep saying, "Things really are different down here."

The appearance of a restaurant's decor doesn't hold to the strict expectations of other parts of the country either. You'll find that the most unassuming hole-in-the-wall cafe, diner, or bistro may serve the best food in town. Don't drive by. Some of our culinary treasures are hidden away off the beaten track. We'll help you find them.

You may find our specialties, from fish to fowl, a trifle confusing. We will translate the Keys-speak. Join us on a culinary tour of the Florida Keys, where the sea meets the land with a gustatory bang and nary a whimper. We have organized the restaurants of the Keys from Key Largo to Big Coppitt Key by descending mile marker and have located them as oceanside or bayside. In the Key West section, we offer a cuisine-oriented arrangement with restaurants listed alphabetically.

Free on-site parking is available at virtually all our recommended establishments in the Upper, Middle, and Lower Keys. However, most restaurants in Key West do not have on-site parking. Most restaurants suggest that you make reservations, especially during the high season. Those that do not take reservations will be noted.

Many restaurants serve limited alcoholic beverages. You may infer that unless we specify that an establishment offers a full-service bar—usually the larger restaurants or resort facilities—only beer and wine will be served.

Accessibility for the physically challenged varies greatly in restaurants throughout the Keys. While many of our establishments are ground level and some second-story locations within large resorts may have elevators, steps sometimes must be negotiated and some bathrooms may be too tiny to accommodate a wheelchair. If this is of particular concern to you, be sure to call the restaurants to see exactly what arrangements might be made to fit your needs.

Unless otherwise specified, you may assume that our recommended restaurants are air-conditioned. Those that provide outdoor seating or accessibility by sea will be highlighted. Children are generally welcome in Florida Keys restaurants. The odd exceptions or age restrictions will be stated.

The dollar sign price code indicated in each restaurant listing will help you gauge the cost of your dining experience. Each code category is based on dinner for two, without starters, dessert, alcoholic beverages, tax, or tip. Some of our restaurants include soup or a house salad with an entree; at others, entrees are strictly à la carte. Most of our restaurants accept major credit cards but rarely a personal check. If plastic is not acknowledged, we alert you in advance so you won't be caught short of cash.

The Florida Keys

Upper Keys

Crack'd Conch
MM 105 Oceanside
Key Largo, FL
(305) 451–0732
$$

Inside this 1930s white Conch house, trimmed in bright lime green and lavender, is some of the tastiest seafood in all the Florida Keys. Wallpapered with business cards, the Crack'd Conch has been operated by the Peterson family since the 1970s . . . from all appearances with a hearty sense of humor as well as talent in the kitchen. They note on the menu: "This establishment is run by a very close staff and family . . . close to broke, close to insanity, and close to killing each other!"

The conch chowder is loaded with conch and fresh vegetables and packs a bit of a spicy punch; conch salad contains just enough tangy juice to give it the right kick. The seafood combo basket, consisting of shrimp, cracked conch, and fried fish, is a hefty enough portion to feed two. Fried 'gator tails—not a local catch of the day in the Keys—are a popular appetizer and dinner. Crack'd Conch features more than 100 different types of beers.

The restaurant is open for lunch and dinner every day except Wednesday. Reservations are not accepted. In addition to cash, traveler's checks, or credit cards, Crack'd Conch gladly will accept "gold, pirate treasure, or the keys to expensive sports cars" as payment for your dining adventure.

Italian Fisherman
MM 104 Bayside
Key Largo, FL
(305) 451–4471
www.keysdining.com/italianfisherman
$$

Guarding the entry to this Italian seafood establishment is La Pescatore, the Italian fisherman, behind which you will find an open dining room filled with white Italianate tables—candlelit in the evening—overlooking Blackwater Sound and the restaurant's docks. Ceiling fans enhance the coastal breezes.

Specializing in southern-style Italian cooking, the Italian Fisherman offers pastas, pizzas, sandwiches, and salads at reasonable prices, but you can also dine on steak, veal, chicken, or seafood platters. The specialty of the house is Linguine Marechiaro, a cioppino-style combination of scallops, shrimp, mussels, and cubed catch of the day served in a white wine, olive oil, and marinara sauce over linguine.

Every Friday night, the Italian Fisherman serves a sumptuous seafood buffet.

Spacious and open to sweeping views of Florida Bay by day, the Italian Fisherman offers spectacular sunset vistas as well. Its dock is brightly lit at night, and patrons head there to feed an abundance of visiting catfish. The Italian Fisherman has a full-service tiki bar. The restaurant is open every day for lunch and dinner and is accessible by boat.

Sundowners on the Bay
MM 104 Bayside
Key Largo, FL
(305) 451–4502
$$

One of Key Largo's most popular places to enjoy the sunset, this open and airy—yet cozy and intimate—establishment overlooks the azure expanse of Blackwater Sound. On the light side, Harvey's Fish Sandwich—fried or broiled fresh fish, topped with American cheese and tomatoes, then grilled on whole grain bread—tops the specialty list. If you prefer a more elaborate meal, the Surf and Turf and the Seafood and Steak Kabobs draw raves, and Shrimp Alfredo rates as a particular favorite among diners. The Friday night all-you-can-eat fish fry is also popular.

All tables are set with fresh flowers for evening dining. A large bar, adjoining the indoor dining area, is available for dinner service as well, and busy evenings tend to run on the loud side. The patio and deck afford more privacy. Sundowners offers a full bar and is open for lunch and dinner. Reservations are recommended. The restaurant is accessible by boat.

Señor Frijoles
MM 103.9 Bayside
Key Largo, FL
(305) 451–1592
$

Don your sombrero for a taste of Mexico by the sea—Keys style. Señor Frijoles nestles on Florida Bay next to Sundowners and offers the usual popular Tex-Mex fare, such as Burritos Supreme; a burrito, taco, and cheese enchilada combo; and quesadillas, as well as some jazzed up Conch Republic versions, such as Grilled Shrimp and Pineapple Pizza and Enchiladas del Mer, which are filled with shrimp, crabmeat, and fish in a red sauce.

You don't have to look for Jimmy Buffett to find Margaritaville. Señor Frijoles offers five different margaritas as well as a potpourri of other tropical libations and Mexican beers with which you can toast the fabulous Keys sunset. Señor Frijoles is accessible by boat and open for lunch and dinner daily.

Gus' Grille
MM 103.8 Bayside
Marriott Key Largo Bay Beach Resort
Key Largo, FL
(305) 453–0000
www.marriottkeylargo.com/restaurants
$$

Gus' seafood-inspired menu mixes Asian, Latin American, and traditional American cuisine to create a style referred to by the chef as Floribbean. Dinner specialties such as grilled dolphin served with Asian mango and papaya salsa and exotic greens tossed with a jalapeño vinaigrette dressing and a side of fried rice noodles or yellowtail snapper with an almond crust, topped with avocado, orange, and chive sweet-butter sauce are very popular. Food is prepared before your eyes in an open kitchen, an upmarket grill-style presentation reminiscent of a tony trattoria.

Unobstructed views of the Florida Bay and the famous Keys sunset are available from virtually every seat in the house. Booths line the window walls of the light and airy dining room; outdoor patio dining is also available.

Open daily for breakfast, lunch, and dinner, Gus' has wheelchair-accessible facilities and an elevator. You can dock your boat at the Marriott while you enjoy your meal at Gus', but reservations for both slips and tables are recommended.

Num Thai Restaurant & Sushi Bar
MM 103.2 Bayside
Key Largo, FL
(305) 451–5955
$$

If your taste for Asian food hovers around Thailand or Japan, Num Thai can offer you the best of both worlds: spicy Thai curries and noodle dishes or sushi, sashimi, and traditional Japanese dishes. The restaurant basks in the glow of deep-teal colored walls covered with Asian accents. Three tatami tables, which seat two to four people, complement the wood laminate tables peppering the interior. A sushi bar affords one and all the opportunity to watch the masters at work. Japanese offerings include temaki, cone-shaped hand rolls; hosomaki, medium rolls cut into bite-size pieces; a wide assortment of sushi, by the piece or in dinner combos; and tempura. Or, enjoy Thai satays; spicy beef salad; seafood, chicken, or beef curries; or Volcano Jumbo Shrimp, grilled and fired with chili sauce. Pad Thai proves to be a hefty portion.

Open for lunch Monday through Friday and dinner every day, Num Thai accepts reservations for parties of more than five. American and Oriental beers, wine, plum wine, and sake all are offered.

The Quay Key Largo
MM 102.5 Bayside
Key Largo, FL
(305) 451–0943
www.quayrest.com
$$$

You can spend the entire day at The Quay Key Largo . . . literally. Perched on Florida Bay, the restaurant guarantees every patron in the main dining room a view of the water. Diners also are invited to enjoy the swimming pool, watersports, or boat excursions.

Head to The Quay's casual venue, the Dockside Grille, for light fare such as burgers and fish sandwiches. This outdoor facility is open for both lunch and dinner and offers happy hour drink specials. The main dining room of The Quay—open for dinner only—features candlelit tables surrounded by tropical flowers, plants, and trees. Both have full bars. In the dining room, you can enjoy steak, pasta, and seafood specialties, such as Bouillabaisse, Blackened Swordfish with fruit chutney, or the ultra-rich Stuffed Baked Yellowtail, which is stuffed with crabmeat imperial, baked, then topped with two grilled shrimp and béarnaise sauce.

The Quay is accessible by boat. Reservations are recommended for the main dining room. Early-bird specials are served in the main dining room from 4 to 6 P.M. The Quay and Dockside Grill are open daily.

The Fish House
MM 102.4 Oceanside
Key Largo, FL
(305) 451–4665, (888) 451–4665
www.fishhouse.com
$$

The scent of freshly prepared seafood lures patrons into this campy nautical establishment, which is bedecked with fish nets, mounted fish, buoys, and twinkling fish lights. Seafood is the name of the game here, and the food doesn't disappoint. The chef offers three special seafood presentations each day in addition to an extensive menu that also features a few choices for carnivores. One of the most popular Fish House dishes is Fish Matecumbe, a drop-dead combination of fresh catch of the day sautéed and topped with tomatoes, shallots, capers, fresh basil, olive oil, and lemon juice. The exquisite combination is melt-in-your mouth lovely.

Decadent desserts are offered at The Gift House, a dessert and coffee bar situated in a separate building next door connected by a brick path. Choose from such yummies as Chocolate Nemesis, Caramel Apple Grammy, or Chocolate Raspberry Bash as you browse the Keysy gift items displayed within (see our Shopping chapter).

The Fish House is open for lunch and dinner daily. Reservations are not accepted.

Upper Crust Pizza
MM 101.6 Oceanside
Key Largo, FL
(305) 451–4188
$

Long a favorite pizza restaurant in Marathon, Upper Crust moved up the Keys, now winning raves in Key Largo. You can build your own thick-crust pizza with an array of ingredients, but the House Deluxe is a combination you won't want to miss—pepperoni, sausage, mushroom, green pepper, onion, black olives, and extra cheese. Upper Crust also serves pasta and subs and offers daily specials that are difficult to pass up.

Upper Crust is open daily for lunch and dinner.

Makoto Japanese Restaurant
MM 101.6 Oceanside
Key Largo, FL
(305) 451–7083
$$

Behind the incongruous screaming yellow awning, a touch of the Orient awaits your taste buds. At this Japanese restaurant you can dine in the hibachi room, where chefs will cook teppanyaki selections before your nose. Or, sit in the traditional dining room and enjoy sukiyaki, tempura, teriyaki, katsu, and noodle dishes.

If sushi or sashimi are your fancy, belly-up to the sushi bar, where you can order selections a la carte, as a dinner or in special combinations. Makoto's selection of beer and wine includes American and Japanese favorites along with sake and plum wine.

The restaurant serves lunch and dinner daily except Wednesday. Reservations for large parties are suggested.

Tower of Pizza
MM 100.5 Bayside
Key Largo, FL
(305) 451–1461, (305) 451–3754
$
MM 81.5 Bayside
Islamorada, FL
(305) 664–8216, (305) 664–8246
$

Antipasto, Greek salad, minestrone, and a potpourri of great pasta dishes vie with fantastic pizza at both Tower of Pizza establishments. Sauces and dough here are homemade, and cheeses are fresh. Locals particularly like the Sicilian-style pie, but you can build your own from a long list of tantalizing ingredients. Delivery is free with a minimum order.

Both Towers are open every day for lunch and dinner.

Frank Keys Cafe
MM 100.2 Oceanside
Key Largo, FL
(305) 453–0310
$$$

For fine Florida Keys dining, Frank Keys Cafe, off the main highway amid burgeoning foliage and somewhat tricky to uncover, is well worth a couple of trips around the block. Situated in a natural hardwood hammock, the restaurant was built in 1994, designed as a replica of a Victorian Conch-style home—peachy-pink stucco with a white wraparound porch and lots of gingerbread trim. Both on the veranda and in the dimly lit pastel interior dining room, the tables are appointed with white linen cloths, fresh flowers, and flickering candles. Ceiling fans revolve overhead. Despite the traffic sounds on the nearby Overseas Highway, outdoor dining is romantic because lush tropical gardens surround Frank Keys Cafe.

The specialties here are steaks, seafood, rack of lamb, and imaginative pasta dishes. Wowing the palate are specials such as filet mignon served on a bed of spinach with portobello mushrooms, brandy sauce, and mashed-potato accents or pistachio-encrusted grouper with black bean salsa.

Frank Keys Cafe is open daily, except Tuesdays, for dinner only. To find Frank Keys Cafe, look for the large sign with white lights on the Overseas Highway and turn toward the ocean.

Coconuts Restaurant & Lounge
MM 100 Oceanside
Marina del Mar Resort
528 Caribbean Drive
Key Largo, FL
(305) 453–9794
www.coconutsrestaurant.com
$$

This vibrant outdoor restaurant, cornered between Key Largo Harbor and the swimming pool of Marina del Mar Resort & Marina, offers fine cuisine and lively after-hours entertainment. Ceiling fans cool patrons, who enthusiastically devour Coconuts' many specialties: Large portobello mushrooms stuffed with crabmeat and topped with béarnaise sauce teases the palate as a tasty starter. Turkey breast filled with roasted red peppers and spinach with pesto mayonnaise proves to be Coconuts' most popular sandwich. Yellowtail Largo Style, a signature dish, finds yellowtail snapper sautéed with artichoke hearts, shrimp, and capers in a lemon-white wine sauce.

After dinner, head for Coconuts' indoor nightclub and dance the night away or sit back and enjoy the live entertainment (see our Nightlife chapter). The establishment has a full bar and offers weekday happy hours from 5 to 7 P.M. Coconuts is accessible by boat. Reservations are accepted for parties of more than nine. To reach Coconuts, head toward the ocean on Laguna at MM 100; the restaurant is about a quarter-mile in on the left.

Calypso's
MM 99.5 Oceanside
1 Seagate Boulevard
Key Largo, FL
(305) 451–0600
$, no credit cards

Nattily situated dockside at Ocean Bay Marina, Calypso's offers fresh fish—right off the boat two times daily—and a primo setting right on the water. Seafood rules here, and you can find a great fish sandwich, she-crab soup, crabmeat quesadilla, cracked conch, and some nonpiscatory choices if you want a light meal. The chef turns out some interesting combos in the evenings as well, offering a handful of daily specials. An on-the-menu favorite, Serrano Cream, features the chef's homemade pepper sauce over grilled catch of the day.

To find Calypso's, turn toward the ocean on Ocean Bay Drive and continue about a half-mile; the restaurant is on the left, on the corner of Seagate Boulevard. Calypso's picks up the beat on Monday and Wednesday evenings with live entertainment.

Snook's Bayside Restaurant
MM 99.9 Bayside
Key Largo, FL
(305) 453–3799
www.snooks.com
$$$

Exquisitely nestled amid towering palms at the very edge of Florida Bay, Snook's secrets itself away down a narrow, winding driveway off the Overseas Highway. Virtually every seat in the house affords a view of the water, be it from the elegant pink, teal, and white indoor dining room—fronted by a glass window wall—or on the patio deck suspended over the bay. Expect linen cloths and napkins, fresh flowers, and candlelight—not always an ambiance found accompanying great food in the Keys. And great food it is.

Snook's signature fish, yellowtail snapper, is seared in oregano with shrimp, tomato, almonds, and Pernod, for one popular specialty. You'll find Seafood Dieppoise a rich combination of shrimp, scallops, and mussels in a lobster cream sauce. Carnivores will find Angus beef here, and chicken lovers appreciate Snook's Hazelnut Chicken, which is prepared with a delectable Frangelico orange-thyme sauce.

Snook's pastry chef prepares all breads and desserts, which challenge the waistline with decadence. Two full bars are on premises, one sporting a pounded copper top, and an extensive wine list includes more than 175 selections from all over the world.

Snook's offers live entertainment nightly in season and on weekends during the off-season. The restaurant is open for lunch and dinner Monday through Saturday; brunch is served on Sundays. Snook's is accessible by boat.

Cafe Largo
MM 99.5 Bayside
Key Largo, FL
(305) 451–4885
$$

Bistro tables atop terra-cotta tile floors at this Italian trattoria evoke a continental flair, the interior punctuated with a swirl of stark white, hunter green, and peach and wall murals featuring local scenery.

House specialties include a vast array of pasta, chicken, veal, and eggplant dishes as well as Angus beef and individual hand-tossed pizzas. Fresh fish and seafood offerings round out the diverse menu.

The restaurant has a full bar. It is open every day for dinner only.

Bayside Grille
MM 99.5 Bayside
Key Largo, FL
(305) 451–3380
$$

Situated at the end of a winding drive behind Cafe Largo and perched on the very edge of Florida Bay, Bayside Grille commands one of the most premier waterfront vistas in the Keys. Small, casual, and bistro-ish, the open-air Bayside Grille sports a dozen or so tables, fronted by pocketing glass doors, enabling all diners to drink in the shimmering blue sea while partaking of a palate-tingling selection of offerings. Garlic mussels join forces with clams casino, fried calamari, and Cajun clams as appetizers. Seafood reigns here, but landlubbers will also find a good selection of beef, chicken, and lamb entrees.

Bayside offers libations from a full bar. The restaurant serves lunch and dinner daily and provides live entertainment Friday and Saturday nights in season.

Harriette's
MM 95.7 Bayside
Key Largo, FL
(305) 852–8689
$, no credit cards

This popular roadside diner-style restaurant offers reasonably priced home-style meals in a simple setting. Tables and chairs surround counter dining; local arts and crafts on consignment provide the decor.

Harriette's specialty? Ensuring that no guest leaves the restaurant hungry. Open only for breakfast and lunch, Harriette's serves filling omelets, oversize homemade biscuits with sausage gravy, burgers, and hot and cold sandwiches. The restaurant caters primarily to a repeat local crowd, so lunch specials change daily. Look for comfort food at Harriette's: meat loaf, pork chops, stuffed peppers, roast pork, and chicken and dumplings.

Harriette's is open seven days a week from 6 A.M. to 2 P.M. Reservations are not accepted.

Snapper's Waterfront Saloon & Raw Bar
MM 94.5 Oceanside
139 Seaside Avenue
Key Largo, FL
(305) 852–5956
www.thefloridakeys.com/snappers
$$

The best part of Snapper's is sitting out on the deck near the water overlooking Snapper's Marina . . . next to the food, that is, which is Old Florida and Bahamian cuisine at its best. You can graze on blackened dolphin fingers, nut-encrusted baked brie with strawberry sauce, or Dominican-style chicken wings (marinated in rum and jalapeño peppers and served with a sweet yet hot chili sauce). Or for a "reel meal," choose selections from the Florida Keys piscatory pantry: Try Onion Encrusted Yellowtail or Grouper Roulade. Key Largo Crab Cakes are a specialty of the house. Snapper's offers an extensive raw bar as well as sandwiches, burgers, and a few selections for landlubbers. On Sunday they serve a champagne jazz brunch from 10 A.M. to 2 P.M.

Weekends feature live entertainment. The restaurant is accessible by boat. Reservations are accepted.

The Copper Kettle
MM 91.8 Oceanside
Tavernier, FL
(305) 852–4113
www.tavernierhotel.com
$

Margaret Thompson, owner of the historic Tavernier Hotel (see our Accommodations chapter), offers a dining room with an English country ambiance—lace curtains, floral drapes, an antique hutch, and an intimate bar. Thompson herself painted the artwork that lines the walls.

Dine inside or out in the backyard garden. The menu features local cuisine that combines Thompson's European background with her newfound island home. You'll find traditional fish and chips along with more innovative offerings such as grilled yellowfin tuna, blue-crab cakes, or chicken piccata. The island conch chowder at Copper Kettle marries New England–style and Caribbean-style chowders, creating a unique, tasty concoction.

The Copper Kettle is open for breakfast, lunch, and dinner. Reservations are recommended on weekends.

The Frog and the Fly Cafe
MM 91.2 Bayside
Tavernier Towne Shopping Center
Tavernier, FL
(305) 852–8584
$

It's just a little hole in the wall, but the taste sensations are mighty at The Frog and the Fly Cafe. You'll enjoy creative omelettes, soups, and salads as well as fabulous wraps, panini's, and gourmet sandwiches. The fat-free sandwich, a combination of curried chicken salad with raisins, cilantro, celery, Bermuda onions, and mango chutney on homemade honey wheat bread, will convince you that healthy eating can be habit forming. Also a coffee bar, Frog and Fly whips up mean fruit smoothies and veggie juices, such as the "Accelerator"—carrots, ginger, celery, parsley, cucumber, and spirulina. On second thought . . . try an iced mochaccino.

The Frog and the Fly Cafe is open Monday through Saturday at 7 A.M. They close at 5 P.M. on Mondays and Saturdays, the rest of the week at 6 P.M.

Old Tavernier Restaurant
MM 90.3 Oceanside
Tavernier, FL
(305) 852–6012
$$

One of the Upper Keys' most popular establishments, the Old Tavernier marries the Mediterranean and the Caribbean with a continental flair to create a singular cuisine.

Diners enjoy traditional Italian pasta favorites such as pasta primavera, angel hair marinara, baked ziti, fettuccine Alfredo, or eggplant, chicken, and veal parmigiana. Or, they can opt for a culinary adventure with yellowtail Provençale (pan-sautéed and served with fresh tomatoes, button mushrooms, scallions, garlic, white wine/lemon butter sauce, and fresh basil); cioppino (fresh seafood stewed in a zesty tomato sauce with white wine and served over fettuccine); grill-seared Greek rack of lamb rubbed with kosher salt and oregano in a lemon glaze; or yellowtail snapper with a toasted almond-banana-berry-rum glaze.

Guests have the option of dining indoors—where white linen tablecloths are aglow with candles and watercolor sailboat scenes dot the walls—or outdoors on a balcony overlooking a narrow canal. Old Tavernier has a full bar and is open daily for dinner only. The restaurant is accessible by boat.

Craig's Restaurant
MM 90.1 Bayside
Tavernier, FL
(305) 852–9424
$$

A 1977 graduate of the Culinary Institute in Hyde Park, New York, chef/owner Craig Belcher opened his namesake establishment in 1981 with his signature sandwich, which he bills "World Famous Fish Sandwich."

A simply appointed, diner-style restaurant with an all-day menu, Craig's tries to sate every palate, be it down-home or gourmet. Specialties of the chef include Fish Tropical (grouper or dolphin sautéed with bananas, pineapples, oranges, and strawberries and topped with sliced almonds) and Fish Seminole (baked grouper or dolphin with sautéed shrimp and mushrooms, scallops, scallions, tomatoes, and hearts of palm in lemon-butter sauce). The Jon Chicken Sandwich, a grilled chicken breast with Dijon mustard, Cajun seasoning, melted cheese, grilled onions, grilled mushrooms, and bacon, puts a little pep in the ubiquitous poulet.

Open seven days a week, Craig's does not accept reservations.

Marker 88
MM 88 Bayside
Islamorada, FL
(305) 852–9315, (305) 852–5503
www.marker88restaurant.com
$$$

An Islamorada culinary landmark for decades, Marker 88 combines bayside ambiance with innovative preparation of the Keys' freshest bounty. Established in 1978 by German-born, Swiss-trained André Mueller, Marker 88 is popular with presidents—such as George H.W. Bush—and local patrons alike.

Marker 88's cuisine is legendary. Signature dishes include Fish Rangoon, a sautéed catch of the day served with banana, papaya, pineapple, mango, currant jelly, and cinnamon butter, and Filet Mignon Rossini, a filet broiled and topped with goose liver pâté and laced with bordelaise sauce.

Dessert is no less lavish. Key Lime Baked Alaska towers with layers of ice cream and Key lime filling encased in meringue.

As sophisticated as the Marker 88 cuisine may be, decor here is charmingly rustic: Wood tables are made of hatch covers lifted from boats. Tiffany lighting provides a soothing romantic setting, and views of Florida Bay abound. Marker 88 is surrounded by heavy tropical vegetation and rambling docks, and a deck laden with wood outdoor tables and chairs provides the perfect setting for a pre-dinner sunset libation or a starlit after-dinner drink.

This boat-accessible restaurant maintains a full bar and is open for dinner every day except Monday. Reservations are recommended.

Smuggler's Cove
MM 85.5 Bayside
Islamorada, FL
(305) 664–5564, (800) 864–4363
www.thefloridakeys.com/smugglerscove
$

If you want to find a good place to eat, ask a local. Smuggler's Cove, a local's favorite in Islamorada, puts on no pretensions. What they do put on, however, is a great fish sandwich that draws raves, even from visitors coming from as far away as Massachusetts. What Smuggler's lacks in decor and ambiance, they make up for in taste.

Horizon Restaurant & Lounge
MM 84 Oceanside
Holiday Isle Resorts
Islamorada, FL
(305) 664–2321
www.holidayisle.com
$$

Holiday Isle is always hopping, and Horizon lets you see it all from a gull's eye perch. The restaurant's sixth-floor interior is completely surrounded by windows, offering sweeping views of the Atlantic Ocean and the percolating partying going on below. Among Horizon's seafood specialties are Yellowtail Almondine, sautéed snapper filets with a toasted almond amaretto sauce, and Onion Crusted Dolphin, which is encased in an onion crust and served with warm sundried tomato vinaigrette. You'll find a selection of meats, poultry, soups, specialty salads, and pastas, as well as a "lite bites menu," which is served in the lounge from 2 P.M. to closing. Live music is offered on weekends.

Open for breakfast, lunch, and dinner every day but Wednesday, Horizon has a full bar and an extensive wine list. The restaurant is accessible by boat.

Bentley's Restaurant
MM 82.8 Oceanside
Islamorada, FL
(305) 664–9094
www.keysdining.com/bentleys
$$

At Bentley's Restaurant, the names of the dishes will intrigue your mind and ignite your taste buds. And the portions guarantee that you don't go home hungry. Try the house specialty, Outtahand Lobster, a steamed lobster topped with sautéed shrimp, scallops, mushrooms, scallions, spinach, cashews, and lemon caper butter sauce. It's outrageous. Equally creative, Dolphin in the Weeds nets you baked mahi-mahi over creamed spinach with shrimp, crab, and artichoke heart stuffing.

Bentley's raw bar is popular with the happy-hour crowd (see our Nightlife chapter). The restaurant is open daily for dinner.

Lorelei Restaurant, Cabana Bar, and Grand Slam Lounge
MM 82 Bayside
Islamorada, FL
(305) 664–4656
www.keysdining.com/lorelei
$$$, restaurant; $, bar and lounge

The legend of Lorelei—a nymph of the Rhine—maintains that her sweet, lyrical singing lured sailors to shipwreck on a rock. Today's Lorelei lures you to a primo perch on the very edge of the Florida Bay, where you'll relish breakfast, lunch, or dinner daily as well as those other munching hours in between. Come by boat, if you like, because the Lorelei also maintains a marina where you'll be able to rub shoulders with some of the Keys' renowned fishing guides.

The Cabana Bar breaks the day starting at 7 A.M., then serves a casual lunch menu from 11 A.M. until 9 P.M. The air-conditioned Lorelei Restaurant's expansive seafood-inspired menu makes a gustatory decision a difficult task. The shrimp or the catch of the day can be enjoyed six different ways. Or mix it up with a combination platter of shrimp, fish, scallops, conch, and crab cakes. Landlubbers are accommodated with steak, chicken, and pasta offerings.

The Lorelei Restaurant is open daily for dinner. Early bird specials are offered from 5 to 6 P.M. In addition to the Cabana Bar, the air-conditioned Grand Slam Lounge serves lunch until 3 P.M. Reservations are not taken at the Cabana Bar.

Atlantic's Edge
MM 82 Oceanside
Cheeca Lodge,
Islamorada, FL
(305) 664–4651
www.cheeca.com
$$$

Chef Dawn Sieber, a University of Miami alumna who obtained her culinary degree in Maryland, has been with Cheeca Lodge since 1988 (see Accommodations). So successful is Sieber that she was invited to act as a guest chef for Julia Child's 80th birthday bash in Boston. Sieber's specialties are renowned: spicy orange shrimp with passionfire, dark rum, cilantro black bean fritter, and cilantro oil; Florida snapper pan-seared with an onion crust and served over braised Roma tomatoes and baby artichoke hearts in a warm balsamic vinaigrette sauce; and dolphin baked in filo and served with sautéed spinach in a balsamic glaze.

The Cheeca children's menu is the result of consultations with local Plantation Key elementary school children; it includes all their favorites, such as pizza, chicken fingers, fish fingers, popcorn shrimp, even a child-size filet mignon. A dessert highlight is "The Dirt Cup"—chocolate pudding with crumbled Oreo cookies topped with a candy gummy worm.

The indoor dining atmosphere at Atlantic's Edge features casual elegance—linen tablecloths, crystal goblets, and bud vases—highlighted by a panoramic view of the Atlantic through floor-to-ceiling glass walls.

Atlantic's Edge is open for dinner nightly, offering libations from a full bar.

Squid Row
MM 81.9 Oceanside
Islamorada, FL
(305) 664–9865
www.keysdining.com/squidrow
$–$$

This unassuming roadside diner will surprise you. The food is good, portions are hearty, and the prices are reasonable.

You'll find an extensive array of appetizer offerings such as a Conch chowder, called Bahamian Borscht, which is loaded with conch. A number of the seafood dishes are fried, but you can also find sautéed fish, such as Catch of the Day Almondine, which is coated with breadcrumbs and sliced almonds and served with Key lime butter. Landlubbers can expect to find a selection of beef, chicken, and pasta dishes.

Homemade desserts include such yummy concoctions as Jeanne's Tollhouse Pie a la Mode and Lupe's Key Lime Pie. Squid Row is open daily, except Wednesday, for lunch and dinner.

Manny & Isa's Kitchen
MM 81.6 Oceanside
Islamorada, FL
(305) 664–5019
$

Cuban cooking at its finest is the treat in store for you in Manny & Isa's Kitchen, the tiny, unassuming, one-room restaurant on the old U.S. Highway 1 in Islamorada. You'll find traditional favorites such as picadillo and ropa vieja, palomilla steak, and black beans and rice, but you can enjoy steaks, chicken, and chops here, too. A specialty of the house is lobster or shrimp enchilado, bite-size pieces of seafood served in a hot or delicate Spanish sauce. The special Cuban dinner, Spanish paella (minimum two people), requires advance notice. Isa's secret-recipe salad dressing is always a hit.

The pièce de résistance here is Manny's Key lime pie. Residents come from as far as Marathon to pick up one of these famous meringue-laden treats, which are usually out of the oven by 11 A.M. Visitors have been known to carry Manny's creations by airplane all the way back to New York City. Manny was kind enough to share his secret recipe with us, so whether you go back to Tucson, Tulsa, or Timbuktu, you'll always be able to have an Insiders' taste of the Keys (see Manny's Key Lime Pie recipe in this chapter).

Manny's Authentic Key Lime Pie

This is a recipe for the best Key lime pie in the Florida Keys, say Insiders whose taste buds have thoroughly researched the subject. Our thanks to Manny, from Manny & Isa's Kitchen in Islamorada (see our listing in this chapter) for sharing his trade secrets with us.

    1 14-ounce can Eagle Brand condensed milk
    4 large eggs or 6 medium eggs
    4 ounces Key lime juice
    1 piecrust, baked and cooled
    ½ cup sugar
    ¼ teaspoon cream of tartar

Separate egg yolks and put aside whites to make meringue. Slightly beat yolks; add condensed milk and mix together. Add Key lime juice and mix again. Pour into baked, cooled piecrust. (If you are using fresh Key lime juice, the pie will set without refrigerating. If you are using bottled Key lime juice, you must refrigerate the pie until set.) To make meringue, beat egg whites until medium peaks form. Add cream of tartar and continue to beat. Add sugar slowly and continue beating until the mixture is stiff. Preheat the oven to 375 degrees. Spread the meringue over the pie, sealing it to the crust. Bake until meringue is golden brown. Refrigerate Key lime pie until cold. Serve to applause.

Manny & Isa's is open every day except Tuesday for lunch and dinner.

Morada Bay
MM 81.6 Bayside
Islamorada, FL
(305) 664-0604
$$

Leading the Purple Isle's lineup, Morada Bay restaurant in Islamorada delivers a tapas-style selection of eclectic dishes in the most seductive of atmospheres. From the bark-chip parking lot, past a huge copper urn filled with bougainvillea petals, to the cobblestone brick entrance under a thatched roof canopy—Morada Bay neglects no detail of ambiance. Pastel beach tables and low Adirondack-style chairs pepper a wide expanse of sandy beach (imported from the Bahamas) that fronts the gentle waters of Florida Bay. Curving palms and tiki torches complete the outdoor illusion. The white Key West–style restaurant building itself sparkles with raspberry shutters and periwinkle trim. Design detailing on light fixtures, wall sconces, and artistic renderings is exquisite. Funky painted pine tables sit outdoors under a canopy and inside beneath a vaulted whitewashed ceiling.

You'll be happy to know the food at Morada Bay is as imaginatively designed as the decor. Caribbean kabobs of beef or chicken with a jerked rum glaze, tuna tartar, stuffed Anaheim chili, Thai ribs, and to-die-for mussels shine from the tapas menu. The four designer salad creations—Mediterranean, Sunshine, Morada Bay, and Caesar—tempt even the most ardent meat-and-potatoes lover. If you prefer a traditional dining entree instead of the wonderful array of light noshes, any of Morada Bay's fresh fish selections—all imaginatively prepared—will more than satisfy your taste for the sea. The special shrimp entree, served with basmati rice, is "to die for." Morada Bay finishes you off with some calorie-loaded ammunition. Save room for dessert if you are able. Morada Bay is open for lunch and dinner daily.

Pierre's Restaurant at Morada Bay
MM 81.6 Bayside
Islamorada, FL
(305) 664–3225
$$$$

At Pierre's, the sophisticated stepsister of Morada Bay, you'll enjoy innovative cuisine with a South Beach–style touch of class. Sharing the same beach, sunset, and ambiance with the more casual Morada Bay, Pierre's is the place to go for a romantic, deep-pocket dining experience. Flickering candlelight and comfy leather sofas greet you in the downstairs lounge area for pre-dinner libations, and a covered porch welcomes you to sit a spell upon cushioned wicker chairs and watch the famed Keys sunset. Walk up the sweeping curved staircase, however, and your dining adventure begins. The decor, tropically British Colonial, is elegant yet casual. Dine indoors or out on the covered porch.

The culinary stars shine with such signature dishes as Lotus-root-crusted Yellowtail, Thai Curry Seared Snapper, and a constantly changing rota of the chef's creative offerings. Pierre's is open every evening for dinner.

Islamorada Fish Company
MM 81.5 Bayside
Islamorada, FL
(305) 664–9271, (800) 258–2559
www.ifcstonecrab.com
$$

Islamorada Fish Company, primarily a seafood market that opens at 8 A.M. also serves lunch and dinner daily until 9 P.M. Eat indoors at the Island Conch House Eatery or outside under umbrella tables that perch on a peninsula jutting into Florida Bay. Renowned for fish and stone crabs so fresh they almost jump out of the

water and onto your plate, Islamorada Fish Company's restaurant is so popular that it is not unusual to wait an hour or more for a table. But don't worry. The restaurant abuts World Wide Sportsman's cavernous sports emporium, so you can browse your wait away or sit in a rocking chair on the store's porch, look at the sunset, and wait for your name to be called. This is the perfect place for a light, casual meal on a fine day. (See our Seafood Markets and Specialty Foods chapter for more information.)

Green Turtle Inn
MM 81.5 Oceanside
Islamorada, FL
(305) 664–9031
www.keysdining.com/greenturtle
$$

Generations of Keys vacationers have flocked to the Green Turtle Inn since its inception in 1947, for this place is a historic landmark, both officially and in the hearts—and stomachs—of all who have eaten here. Until a few years ago, the Green Turtle Cannery and Seafood Market operated across the Overseas Highway. But, unlike yesteryear, today the turtle steak and chowder served at the Green Turtle Inn comes from tortoise meat imported from Nicaragua and the Cayman Islands; our sea turtles are endangered and illegal to harvest.

The menu at the darkly lit Green Turtle is extensive, and the chef creates nightly specials as well. You'll find a great conch chowder and cracked conch here as well as fresh, fresh fish, as you might expect. A traditional catch-of-the-day favorite is prepared a la Roxie (named after one of the original owners)—broiled and covered with tomatoes and onions. Landlubbers can order steak, chops, chicken, or prime rib. If you're adventuresome, try Turtle Steak, which is sautéed and topped with peppercorn sauce, or Alligator Steak, which is served "Green Turtle Style" with spinach soufflé, crabmeat, and hollandaise sauce. The Green Turtle is open for lunch and dinner daily except Monday.

Dino's of Islamorada Ristorante Italiano
MM 81 Oceanside
Islamorada, FL
(305) 664–0727
$, family dining; $$, fine dining

Dino's covers all culinary bases with dual restaurants: Both are distinctively designed, both authentically Italian, both under one roof.

The family dining side of Dino's is an upscale pizza parlor, offering individual brick-oven gourmet pies topped with an inspiring array of ingredients as well as an array of pasta dishes, salads, and sandwiches.

When the mood hits to dine in style, try the fine dining room at Dino's where you'll find linen tablecloths, china and crystal settings, sprays of fresh flowers, and live operatic music. Complimentary garlic knots and tomato bruschetta start the meal here. The entree selection is extensive, ranging from an assortment of traditional preparations for pasta, seafood, poultry, and veal to some truly unusual combinations such as the signature dish Salmone Fantasia—a melt-in-your-mouth salmon creation made with vodka, cream, and grapefruit juice. And just when you think you can't possibly put away any more food, around comes the dessert cart, loaded with diet busters.

Both dining rooms are open every night for dinner; the family dining room also serves lunch. You can order from the fine dining menu while seated in the family dining room if you like, the perfect solution for supping with your kids.

Uncle's Restaurant
MM 80.9 Oceanside
Islamorada, FL
(305) 664–4402
www.keysdining.com/uncles
$$$

Mexican tiles, ceiling fans, stained glass, candlelit tables, soft music, and original paintings of Keys flora and fauna set the stage for fine dining at Uncle's. And if you'd prefer to sit under the stars, Uncle's will accommodate you, for it also serves dinner at tables sprinkled on an outdoor deck.

Uncle's cuisine sparkles with a decidedly Mediterranean flair. Seafood selections abound and you'll find a number of tasty veal choices. Specialties of the house include a hefty Veal Loin Chop, Rack of Lamb with Port Wine Demi-glace, and Teriyaki Marinated Chargrilled Tuna with Wasabi Aioli.

Uncle's offers a full bar and is open daily, except Sunday, for dinner only. They will happily cook your catch for a fraction of the normal dinner price.

Lazy Days Oceanfront Bar & Seafood Grill
MM 79.9 Oceanside
Islamorada, FL
(305) 664–5256
$$

Lazy Days provides the ideal setting for kicking back, gazing over the sparkling blue Atlantic, and dining on a revolving selection of seafood offerings. The elevated plantation-style building with turquoise roof, French doors, and wraparound balcony is, indeed, designed for lazy days, for it perches directly on the shoreline of the ocean. During the winter season all doors are open, and Bahama fans circulate the fresh ocean air inside and out. Brass hangings and rich tropical foliage enhance the dining room.

Seafood aficionados will love Lazy Days signature dishes: Caribbean Bouillabaisse or Dolphin with Tropical Fruit Salsa, which is served with a mango rum sauce, and Mediterranean Dolphin, which is finished with roasted shallots, garlic,

Fresh seafood can be enjoyed at some seafood markets, or take the catch of the day home and cook it yourself. PHOTO: JAMES DILORETO

shiitake mushrooms, Roma tomatoes, and fresh basil.

Lazy Days serves lunch and dinner. The restaurant is closed Mondays and Tuesdays. Lazy Days is accessible to boats with a 2- to 3-foot draft.

Papa Joe's Landmark Restaurant
MM 79.7 Bayside
Islamorada, FL
(305) 664–8109
$$

Built in 1937, Papa Joe's is a historic landmark and the site of Islamorada's very first fishing tournament. The restaurant has a no-nonsense, no-frills ambiance that is perennially popular with visiting anglers and locals alike.

Papa Joe's specializes in lobster and catches of the day. Try Yellowtail Maria, which is coated with crushed pecans and served over roasted pepper chipotle. If you've had a lucky day fishing, Papa Joe's will cook your catch any way you like it. Steaks, prime rib, chicken, and veal dishes are available for carnivores.

Open daily for lunch and dinner, Papa Joe's is accessible by boat and features an on-premises marina. The restaurant maintains a full bar. A waiting list takes the place of reservations; when you call, you're put at the top of the waiting list.

Little Italy
MM 68.5 Bayside
Layton
Long Key, FL
(305) 664–4472
$$

If good, hearty Italian cooking is what you're after, Little Italy rates a hearty molto buono. This family-style restaurant offers an extensive menu of pasta, veal, chicken, and seafood dishes and a selection of steaks for red meat lovers. Favored by locals who appreciate the huge portions, Little Italy garners particular accolades for its Veal Parmesan, Linguine with Red Clam Sauce, and Mermaid's Delight, a savory concoction of scallops layered with crabmeat stuffing topped with shrimp, mushrooms, butter, and sherry and finished with a light cream sauce.

Little Italy is open for breakfast, lunch, and dinner seven days a week. It offers libations from a full-service bar.

Middle Keys

WatersEdge
MM 61 Oceanside
Hawk's Cay Resort
Duck Key, FL
(305) 743–7000
www.hawkscay.com
$$$

Flanking Hawk's Cay Marina, WatersEdge, which was completely remodeled in 1999, provides the option of dining on the casual open-air porch or indoors in air-conditioned comfort in the Caribbean-style dining room or in the low-lit Truman Bar. Nightly specials center on fresh local fish prepared many ways, and the stuffed Florida lobster—stuffed with shrimp, scallops, and crabmeat—is one of the best you'll find in the Keys. Barbecued ribs and Yellowfin Tuna Caesar are other perennial favorites. All dinner entrees include the soup and salad bar, which rates as a meal in itself. WatersEdge serves dinner nightly. If you plan to come by boat, be sure to call the marina in advance to secure a slip (see our Cruising chapter).

The Wreck & Galley Grill and Sports Bar
MM 59 Bayside
Grassy Key, FL
(305) 743–8282
$–$$

Nautically decked out with photos of some of the dive wrecks in the Keys, Wreck & Galley Grill ranks as a topnotch Middle Keys watering hole. Buffalo wings here—billed as the largest in the Keys—live up to their hype. Burgers are made from Black Angus beef, and Jamaican jerked chicken and grilled or blackened fish sandwiches have won raves from the locals. This is the perfect place for a beer and a bite.

Grassy Key Dairy Bar
MM 58.5 Oceanside
Grassy Key, FL
(305) 743–3816
$$

Gone are the two giant ice cream cones along the oceanside of the Overseas Highway in Grassy Key that for decades marked the spot of an unpretentious dining treasure favored by locals and visitors alike: the Dairy Bar, a.k.a. Grassy Key D.B. But, not to worry, the Dairy Bar still serves up some of the best "vittles" in the Middle Keys.

Once actually a dairy bar serving ice cream creations, the Dairy Bar's extensive menu reflects the considerable self-taught culinary talents of owners/chefs Johnny and George Eigner. Their renditions of Yellowtail Almondine, Wasabi Dolphin, and Lobster Marsala are legendary, and the reasonably priced filet mignon melts in your mouth. Tuesday night is Mexican night, when the brothers cook with a south-of-the-border flair, and Saturdays often feature chicken and dumplings. October is always German Oktoberfest month, when the chefs—who hail from Wisconsin—bring on the sausages, Wiener schnitzel, and kraut. All seasons find Johnny and George developing new creations and taste sensations for a changing rota of tempting daily specials.

Grassy Key Dairy Bar serves lunch and dinner Tuesday through Saturday. The Dairy Bar is closed for the month of September.

Hideaway Café
MM 58 Oceanside
Rainbow Bend Resort
Grassy Key, FL
(305) 289–1554, (800) 929–1505
www.hideawaycafe.com
$$$–$$$$

The only thing rivaling the direct ocean vistas at Hideaway Café is the cuisine. Sure to please the gourmand, the Hideaway also will intrigue the diner who likes to pig out: the Hideaway Rib Steak is large enough to serve a family of four. Other favorites include the whole roasted duck, seafood or beef Wellington, rack of lamb, and the Hideaway Seafood Special, which contains catch of the day, shrimp, scallops, and shellfish in scampi sauce.

Hideaway Café is open daily for lunch and dinner. The service is "relaxed," so plan to drink in the view along with your libations.

Smuggler's Landing
400 Key Colony Beach Causeway
Key Colony Beach, FL
(305) 289–0141
$–$$

Perched on the canal waters of Key Colony Beach, Smuggler's Landing offers casual dining on picnic and patio tables and great food. Winner of the Gourmet Diners Society of N.A. "Golden Fork Award" in 2001, Smuggler's Landing's primarily seafood-laden menu runs the gamut from raw bar to really tasty entrees. Specialties of the house include Grouper Gratinee, which is grouper sautéed with mushrooms in a sherry cream sauce and smothered in cheese; Seafood Salad, made with fresh dolphin, grouper, tuna, shrimp, and scallops; or Smuggler's Stuffed Grouper, which is topped with crabmeat stuffing and artichoke hearts.

Of course you can get fish sandwiches, fried seafood baskets, burgers, steak, or chicken. Ribs come with a bourbon, jalapeño barbecue sauce.

You can motor up to Smuggler's dock, tie up, and enjoy your repast. Smugglers is open daily for lunch and dinner.

Key Colony Inn
MM 54 Oceanside
700 West Ocean Drive
Key Colony Beach, FL
(305) 743–0100
$$

The Key Colony Inn is a favorite dining haunt of residents and visitors alike. Besides the varied menu selections—75 entrees—of Italian-style pasta, veal, and chicken dishes, Key Colony Inn offers innovative presentations of Florida Keys seafood, steaks, and interesting daily specials. Diners agree, portions here are large, and you'll get a lot of bang for your buck.

If dinner conversation is important, request a corner table, which may be a bit quieter, because ceiling acoustics in Key Colony Inn do not filter the noise of a room full of chattering diners. Or, if the weather is fine, and it usually is, sit outside on the covered veranda. The restaurant features a full-service bar. Key Colony Inn is open for lunch and dinner daily. This place is always packed, lunch or dinner. Reservations are suggested all year long.

The Quay
MM 54 Bayside
Marathon, FL
(305) 289–1810
$$$

Three cavernous air-conditioned dining rooms and an outdoor palm-speckled patio bustle with diners, for the perpetually popular Quay packs them in. The Quay has snagged a prime piece of waterfront aside the Gulf of Mexico so sunsets and starlight create a romantic ambiance here.

The restaurant sports an eight-page menu, and you can find fish, seafood, pasta, and a good offering of hooved selections prepared in many different ways. You'll even find alligator or frogs' legs on this diverse menu. The tropical drinks are fun too: Sample a Marathon Yellow Bird or a Hemingway's Paradise from the selections offered at its full-service bar.

The Quay draws a good-size early-bird crowd from 4 to 6 P.M. You can come here by boat and dock at the Quay pier if you like. The Quay serves lunch and dinner daily.

The Island Tiki Bar & Restaurant
MM 54 Bayside
Marathon, FL
(305) 743–4191
www.keysdining.com/theisland
$–$$

Perched on a narrow spit of land, jutting out into the Gulf of Mexico, The Island provides one of the most scenic sunset spots in the Middle Keys and some dog-gone great food to boot. Whether you feel like a margarita and some nachos, a grilled grouper sandwich, a bowl of conch chowder, or a more substantial meal, The Island doesn't disappoint. Try the chef's salad; unlike its ubiquitous cousins elsewhere, this one is loaded with shrimp, grilled chicken, faux crab, and two types of shredded cheese. Not a cold cut in sight. Or, choose a more tantalizing dinner entree from the offerings of lobster, steak, catch of the day, or one of the chef's creative specials.

Tables are of the picnic or patio varieties, super casual. Kids love playing in the open-air terrain. You can come to The Island in a shallow draft boat and dock alongside the restaurant. The Island is open for lunch and dinner daily.

Don Pedro Restaurant
MM 53.5 Oceanside
Marathon, FL
(305) 743–5247
www.keysdirectory.com/donpedros
$

Savor the fine cuisine of our neighbor to the south, Cuba, at Don Pedro's. Specialties at this storefront cafe include a tasty whole-fried yellowtail snapper, ropa vieja, churrasco, and Argentinian steak. All the especialidades Cubanas are served with yellow rice, black beans, sweet plantains (a member of the banana family), and Cuban bread. Top off your meal with a traditional Cuban dessert, such as flan de leche or arroz con leche. Be sure to select cafe con leche when you order coffee, because Cuban coffee is very strong, like espresso. Don Pedro's also serves home-made sangria.

Don Pedro's serves lunch and dinner Monday through Saturday. All menu prices include sales tax.

Leigh Ann's Coffee House
MM 52 Oceanside
Marathon, FL
(305) 743–2001
$

This popular coffeehouse is quaintly closeted in a pale peach-and-white Key West–style building on the Overseas Highway. With French doors flung open wide, tile floors, tropical plants, and an eclectic array of rustic furniture and Keys art, this is coffeehouse a la Keys. Chic, clean, and packed with personality, Leigh Ann's food is pretty good, too. Homemade soups rival sandwiches on bagels, croissants, and sub rolls. Specials are made in small batches to ensure freshness. You can get an upscale pizza and a selection of salads as well. And don't forget the coffee. Choose among cappucino, mocha coolers, muddy mocha, or macchiato.

During the winter months Leigh Ann's is open for dinner six nights a week. Tuesday is spaghetti night, and it's pizza on Thursdays. Other specialty nights feature poetry readings and music jam sessions. This is a happening place!

Wooden Spoon
MM 51 Oceanside
Marathon, FL
(305) 743–7469
$

Start your day with freshly squeezed orange juice at the Wooden Spoon, one of Marathon's most popular breakfast spots. This small cafe bustles with good service and good cheer. Besides an extensive menu of normal breakfast fare, you'll find omelets 11 different ways (with egg substitutes if you like), blueberry or banana pancakes, corned beef hash, and polish sausage.

During the winter season it is not unusual to see a line out front awaiting entry to the Wooden Spoon for breakfast, as it doesn't take reservations. The restaurant also is open daily. From 5 A.M. to 2 P.M., the Wooden Spoon serves breakfast and lunch; dinner is served from 2 to 10 P.M.

Shucker's Raw Bar & Grill
MM 50.5 Bayside
Marathon, FL
(305) 743-8686
www.keysdining.com/shuckers
$

Shucker's moved their popular eatery to an Overseas Highway location in 2000, but the large menu still is Keys eclectic, offering everything from burgers, conch chowder, and grilled fish sandwiches to full dinners with a bevy of seafood, beef, chicken, or pasta dishes. Some menu offerings, like the chef's salad, mirror those of Shucker's sister restaurant, The Island (see separate listing in this chapter).

The spacious restaurant, with vaulted ceilings, pale yellow walls, and green carpeting, creates an indoor island feeling. You'll find a great kid's menu, and the little ones are served a coloring book and crayons to occupy themselves during the wait for their meal.

This is a good choice for lunch or a light dinner with the family. Shuckers is open daily. Happy hour is from 3 to 5 P.M.

Village Cafe
MM 50.5 Bayside
Gulfside Village
Marathon, FL
(305) 743-9090
$-$$

Generous portions and tasty Italian pasta and pizza entrees distinguish the extensive menu of the Village Cafe, a bustling place at breakfast, lunch, or dinner.

Murals of scenes from Venice to Rome grace the walls of this trattoria, a vision of white-latticed simplicity. Village Cafe offers separate smoking and nonsmoking dining rooms, as well as a posh service bar offering a complete selection of libations. The outstanding pizza at the Village shines amid a number of perennial pasta favorites: ziti with broccoli, blue crab with spaghetti in red sauce, penne with fresh tomato and basil, and gnocchi. You'll find the traditional Italian renditions for veal, chicken, and seafood, as well as a changing rota of daily specials.

Village Cafe is open for all three meals from Monday through Saturday. Sundays it serves a breakfast buffet until 2 P.M. and then reopens at 5 P.M. for a dinner buffet. You'll find entertainment and dancing here on the weekends.

53rd Street Dock & Deli
MM 50.3 Oceanside
71 53rd Street
Marathon, FL
(305) 743-0500
$

Though this tiny restaurant/delicatessen does actually sit alongside a Marathon canal, it isn't vital to maintaining its quirky island charm. The brightly painted interior re-creates the dockside experience—in air-conditioned indoor comfort. You really need to visually take in all the decorative details here before you ever glance at the menu. The floor of Dock & Deli is painted as a dock, with sharks and manatees swimming alongside. Twinkling lights ornament artificial palm trees. Tables, chairs, and accent furniture are eclectically painted, and bright buoys and Caribbean dolls hang over the edge of an actual boat that is suspended from the ceiling. Local art adorns the walls, and there's even a mermaid on the back door.

Once you're sated with funky island ambiance, order salad, soup, or a sandwich, such as a Cuban Press, Muffellata, or Richie's Rubin, along with a side or two. The portions are enormous. You may want to sample a few selections and share.

And save room for ice cream; it's the old-fashioned kind. The Dock & Deli is open Monday through Saturday from 7:30 A.M. until 3 P.M.

Herbie's
MM 50 Bayside
Marathon, FL
(305) 743–6373
$–$$, no credit cards

Ask anyone; Herbie's is classic Keys. This roadhouse-style watering hole—two simple rooms and a porch with a large bar area and picnic tables—attracts a loyal contingent of locals and snowbirds alike. The conch chowder here is outstanding—packed with conch and chunks of potato. You can order fried shrimp, clam, oyster, or fish baskets or platters, or opt for burgers, dogs, and conch or fish sandwiches. Dinner specials are surprisingly sophisticated, and portions are generous. Herbie's will also cook your catch if you've had a lucky day on the water.

Wednesday is Hump Day at Herbie's, and the joint is jumping from 6 to 10 P.M. with music and dancing and $1 drafts. Herbie's is open for lunch and dinner daily during high season. Herbie's is closed Sundays in the off season. The restaurant is not air-conditioned and does not accept reservations.

Gary's Pub & Billiards
MM 49.6 Oceanside
Marathon, FL
(305) 743–0622
$

A cavernous mahogany-paneled pub with high ceilings and lots of atmosphere, Gary's sports a potpourri of billiard tables, darts, computer card games, video games, a mile-long bar, and smattering of tables. Sounds like the recipe for a bubba bar, but it isn't. The atmosphere is upscale and trendy and the clientele, respectable.

Gary's chicken wings are legendary (Thursday night is wing night), and the burgers and sandwiches are great, too. This is a great place to come after a movie or to shoot some pool.

Barracuda Grill
MM 49.5 Bayside
Marathon, FL
(305) 743–3314
www.barracudagrill.com
$$–$$$

Imaginative preparation and presentation showcase the entrees at the Barracuda Grill, a small, lively bistro in the heart of Marathon. Chef/owners Jan and Lance Hill invest their considerable talents in an exquisite selection of culinary offerings, assuring that Barracuda Grill retains its coveted place in the hearts—and tummies—of locals and visitors alike. Tantalizing repeat stars of the menu are the char-grilled veal chops, roasted rack of lamb with a sauté of portobello mushrooms, and the stellar Bahamian conch cakes, which are served with a Key lime-honey-mustard sauce. The broth of the littleneck clams appetizer is so tasty it fairly dictates that you mop it up with lots of bread. And Jack's Really Red Hot Calamari—named after the Hill's son Jack—packs a popular wallop thanks to a healthy dose of Barracuda's secret hot sauce. A changing menu of the chefs' creative interpretations rivals the old favorites.

Barracuda's is open for dinner Monday through Saturday. Reservations are not taken. This popular spot fills up quickly, especially in high season, so come early if you don't want to wait for a table.

Takara
MM 49.5 Bayside
Marathon, FL
(305) 743–0505
$$

Nimble fingers at this Japanese restaurant and sushi bar fashion sushi and a wide assortment of sashimi. Here in the Florida Keys you are assured that the raw fish is fresh, right off the boat. If you prefer your food cooked, Takara creates a tasty teriyaki or tempura, ranging from chicken or steak to lobster or salmon.

Takara is open for lunch Monday through Friday and dinner seven days a week during the season but is closed on Sundays during the summer.

The Stuffed Pig
MM 49 Bayside
Marathon, FL
(305) 743–4059
$, no credit cards

During high season mornings, you'll see a line of hungry diners outdoors reading newspapers and patiently awaiting admittance to the inner sanctum of The Stuffed Pig. This popular cafe packs 'em in for hearty country breakfasts. Try the Pig's Breakfast: two eggs, two pancakes, two sausages, two slices of bacon, potatoes, and toast. Or a Pig's Omelet, a four-egg wonder with the works. You'll find grits-and-grunts, which includes fish, two eggs, potatoes, and toast, and, of course, country-fried steak or gravy and biscuits. If you adhere to less porcine standards, the veggie-and-egg-substitute omelet will hold the cholesterol. The Stuffed Pig also serves lunch.

The Stuffed Pig is open seven days a week at the crack of dawn (5 A.M.; an hour later on Sunday). No reservations are accepted.

Annette's Lobster & Steak House
MM 49 Bayside
Marathon, FL
(305) 743–5516
$$

An extensive menu and hearty portions distinguish this Marathon steak and seafood restaurant. Annette's sports a nautical decor with dark paneling, wooden plank floors, and memorabilia from the sea. The restaurant offers a smoking and a nonsmoking room, which are separated by a huge salad bar. You'll enjoy choosing from the vast selection of pastas, steaks, seafood, and, of course, lots of lobster. Signature dishes include

Horseradish Grouper and an 18- to 20-ounce Cowboy Steak, which is an Angus bone-in ribeye. Annette's will also cook your catch for you.

Libations from the full bar include creative tropical rum concoctions, such as a Raspberry Rita or a Bushwacker. Annette's places dessert selections on the menu's first page, so you are sure to be tempted and forewarned to save room.

Annette's Lobster & Steak House is open daily for lunch and dinner.

Angler's
MM 48.5 Bayside
Faro Blanco Marine Resort Bayside
Marathon, FL
(305) 743–9018
$–$$

This percolating lounge atop the swimming pool deck at Faro Blanco Resort serves a delightfully laid-back lunch inside or out. Besides a bar-menu selection of burgers, grilled fish sandwiches, salads, soups, and self-avowed "mishmash," lunch and dinner mean chef's specials such as Sautéed Yellowtail with Fruit Salsa or Blackened Dolphin with Spinach Ravioli.

Angler's, featuring a full-service bar, is open seven days a week and serves lunch until 3 P.M., dinner until 9:30 P.M. The beat at Angler's often picks up in the evening with live entertainment.

Latigo Dinner Cruise
MM 47.5 Oceanside
Marathon Marina
11th Street
Marathon, FL
(305) 289–1066
www.latigo.net
$$$$

Cruise into the sunset aboard a 56-foot power yacht for a private dinner cruise in our sparkling waters. Ken and Val Waine, your hosts aboard the *Latigo*, pamper you with attention down to the last detail. You'll enjoy hors d'oeuvres such as cheese pinwheels, artichoke dip, or smoked salmon canapés and sip your choice of beer, wine, or chilled champagne while you watch the famed Florida Keys sunset from a comfortable location in sheltered waters.

Then the Waines will prepare and serve your dinner entrees, usually a choice of filet mignon, grilled dolphin with garlic butter, or mesquite-grilled, boneless chicken breast. Your meal will include salad, bread, mixed vegetable, and rice pilaf or a baked potato. And you'll top off the evening with coffee and dessert.

Latigo takes only private parties on their four-hour dinner cruise, so whether you are a couple or a group of friends, you'll not be thrown together with strangers.

For ultimate pampering, you may also book the yacht for a private bed-and-breakfast cruise, which includes the sunset dinner; an evening's lodging in the master stateroom, anchored out; full or continental breakfast; and a morning snorkeling excursion to the reef. The bed and breakfast cruise is $220 per person. (See our Accommodations chapter.)

Porky's Bayside
MM 47.5 Bayside
Marathon, FL
(305) 289–2065
$, no credit cards

You wouldn't guess to look at Porky's from the Overseas Highway, but this tiny open-air restaurant offers casual, waterfront dining. On a canal inlet across from a picturesque setting of lobster traps stacked on the commercial fishing docks, Porky's is known for great barbecue . . . among other things. Touted as "Swinin'

and Dinin'," Porky's is decked out with skull-and-crossbones banners and lobster buoys hanging from the ceiling.

Porky's serves lunch and dinner every day beginning at 11 A.M. Only reservations for large parties are accepted. Porky's will treat you to a free sunset cruise to Fanny Key and the Seven Mile Bridge aboard a pontoon boat; availability is first-come, first-served.

Lower Keys

Montego Bay Food and Spirits
MM 30.2 Bayside
Big Pine Key, FL
(305) 872–3009
$$

A welcome addition to the restaurants of Big Pine Key, Montego Bay offers a taste of the islands in a cozy atmosphere. Grab a casual lunch of soup, salads, or sandwiches or come for dinner when you can choose from an extensive menu of steaks, ribs, veal, pasta, chicken, and seafood dishes. Opt for the Stuffed Shrimp or Seafood Alfredo specials if they are offered. Montego Bay is open seven days a week. Reservations are only necessary if you have a large party.

No Name Pub
MM 31 Bayside
N. Watson Boulevard
Big Pine Key, FL
(305) 872–9115
$

This funky, one-of-a-kind establishment bills itself as "a nice place . . . if you can find it." And you might not find it without a little Insider knowledge. The No Name Pub—a pale yellow building with teal trim that looks like a house in a residential neighborhood—is topped with a small sign declaring its beginnings in 1936. And N. Watson Boulevard is off the beaten track too. Turn right at the traffic light at MM 31 in Big Pine (the only light from Marathon to Stock Island) onto Key Deer Boulevard. Proceed to Watson Boulevard and take another right. At the fork in the road, bear left heading toward No Name Key. Go over a humpback bridge and past a residential subdivision. Just before the No Name Bridge over Bogie Channel, the pub will be on your left, all but hidden under a canopy of large trees.

Although the pizza is a star culinary attraction at No Name Pub, the decor and local Keys characters distinguish it from other pizza establishments. The interior is literally wallpapered with dollar bills autographed by diners of years past. Be sure to scope out the bar stools; no two of them stand at the same height. Those that are too short for the bar have four-by-four blocks of wood nailed to the bottoms of their legs. The management brags: "Friendly people, lousy service, great food!"

The famous pizza is deep dish and arrives at your picnic table steaming hot; let it cool a bit to avoid burning your palate. You'll taste a jolt of oregano, and the cheese is so thick it will drip down your chin with every bite. Yummm!

No Name Pub is open seven days a week for lunch and dinner from lunchtime until "whenever."

The Sandbar
MM 28.5 Bayside
183 Barry Avenue
Little Torch Key, FL
(305) 872–9989
$

Perched 14-feet-high on stilts overlooking Big Pine Channel, the multi-windowed, pavilion-style Sandbar serves as a gathering place as well as a restaurant. An all-day, all-night bar menu runs the gamut: fried conch and calamari; quesadillas, lobster bites, and stuffed jalapeños; Maryland-style crab cakes; and dinner entrees such as fresh catch-of-the day, coconut shrimp, oysters, stone crab, steaks, and pasta.

Each month The Sandbar celebrates with a Full Moon Party, when the pace picks up with live entertainment. The Sandbar serves lunch and dinner and does not take reservations. The Sandbar is easily accessible by boat.

Little Palm Island
MM 28.5 Oceanside
Little Torch Key, FL
(305) 872–2551
www.littlepalmisland.com
$$$$

Dining at Little Palm Island is pure magic . . . romance with a capital R. You step into a fairy tale the moment you check in at the mainland substation on Little Torch Key to await one of the Grand Craft launches. *The Truman* or *Miss Margaret* will spirit you to the island. The 15-minute boat ride to Little Palm Island simply heightens the anticipation. As you arrive at the island's dock, you'll spot the Great House nestled amid towering coconut palms. Once a rustic, fishing camp retreat, the Great House now houses Little Palm Island's world-renowned restaurant.

You may dine beneath the stars under a palm tree, at water's edge alongside the beach, on the outside wood deck, in the covered open-air porch, or indoors in air-conditioned comfort. Wherever you choose to partake of Little Palm's gourmet repast, you will be pampered with exquisite food and unobtrusive service. Chef Adam Votaw fuses French and Asian cuisine, treating guests to an ever-changing menu of Floribbean offerings. Insiders know this translates into the meal of a lifetime.

Little Palm Island accepts a limited number of reservations from the general public for lunch and dinner daily. Sundays a tropical buffet-style brunch from 11:30 A.M. to 2:30 P.M. replaces the luncheon offerings. Call well in advance to secure a booking.

Little Palm offers libations from a full-service bar and maintains an extensive wine list. The launch leaves the Little Torch Key substation for luncheon dining at 11:30 A.M., 12:30, and 1:30 P.M.; for dinner at 6:30 and 8:30 P.M. You will be seated immediately upon disembarking. You may come to Little Palm Island on your own boat, but be sure to make slip reservations in advance (see our Cruising chapter). Children must be 16 or older to dine at Little Palm Island.

Boondocks
MM 27.5 Bayside
Ramrod Key, FL
(305) 872–4094
$

The appearance of this happening place can be deceiving from the Overseas Highway. The expansive, open-air informal restaurant/bar that is Boondocks sits under a massive, thatched roof surrounded by palm trees. A casual, nosh-style menu ranges from steamed shrimp and clams on the half shell to conch fritters and chowder, hot wings, and fried oysters. You'll find the de rigueur burgers and dogs plus some innovative toppings for garden salads and imaginative presentations for the catch of the day. The Maryland-style crab cakes are particularly good.

Boondocks is open for lunch and dinner daily and does not accept reservations.

Monte's Restaurant and Fish Market
MM 25 Bayside
Summerland Key, FL
(305) 745–3731
$, no credit cards

Don't let the picnic tables and paper plates fool you. Insiders know that Monte's is a great place for fresh fish in the Lower Keys. The small open-air restaurant area adjoins the seafood market (see our Seafood Markets and Specialty Foods chapter) and is almost always packed, with long lines outside. During the season you have the best chance of securing a table quickly between 2 and 4 P.M.

You can overdose on the plethora of difficult-to-resist seafood selections: oysters, clams, mussels, Louisiana crawfish, shrimp, Florida lobster, stone crab claws, conch, or locally caught fish, prepared grilled or fried. Try the super seafood basket, where you'll get a taste of them all. Top off your meal with a Key lime tart.

Monte's is open seven days a week for lunch and dinner. No reservations are accepted.

Raimondo's Ristorante Italiano
MM 21 Oceanside
457 Drost Drive
Cudjoe Gardens
Cudjoe Key, FL
(305) 745–9999
$$

The striking forest-green-and-white color scheme of Raimondo's sets the stage for a fine Italian-style dining experience. From the green swags softening the windows to the ribboned green-and-white tile on the floors, the light, airy feeling reverberates throughout the restaurant and out onto a dining patio amid palms and scheffleras.

Decor aside, the food makes the biggest splash at Raimondo's. This is Italian cuisine at it finest. The extensive menu features imaginative variations of classic veal, chicken, and seafood dishes as well as some stellar pasta creations. The chef concocts enticing specials nightly.

Raimondo's Ristorante Italiano is open for dinner seven days a week. To find Raimondo's, turn at the Sheriff's Substation at MM 21 on the Overseas Highway.

Mangrove Mama's Restaurant
MM 20 Bayside
Sugarloaf Key, FL
(305) 745–3030
$$

Everyone agrees Mangrove Mama's is special. This brightly hued Caribbean-style roadhouse offers a rustic old garden in the back where you can nosh or dine amid the banana trees. The old chairs are painted in a barrage of drizzled primary colors; ceramic fish sculptures adorn the walls. Bright tropical tablecloths cover the simple tables, and painted buoys hang from the trees and suspend from the rafters.

You'll find shrimp and seafood get special treatment—scampi, tempura, stuffed with crabmeat, barbecued on a skewer, or rolled in coconut and deep fried. Ribs are spicy, and scallops, chicken, steaks, and fresh fish march to a different drummer here, too.

The restaurant serves lunch and dinner daily and brunch on Saturday and

Sunday. Indoor dining is air-conditioned. In addition to a full-service bar, Mangrove Mama's has an extensive wine list.

Geiger Key Pub, Grill, and Marina
MM 10.5
Big Coppitt Key, FL
(305) 294–1230
$

This open-air combination marina, restaurant, and bar bills itself as being "on the back side of Paradise." No kidding. It is located about 12 miles east of Key West on Geiger Key, which is accessible from Big Coppitt Key. Follow the Overseas Highway to Boca Chica Road. Turn toward the ocean at the Circle K, then follow the road for about a quarter mile to Geiger Road and turn left.

In addition to a great view of the mangrove islands and bay waters that surround them, Geiger Key serves up a full breakfast menu, plus hot and cold appetizers, soups, sandwiches, seafood, and steaks. But the real highlights are the weekend specials. The Friday night steak and grilled fish dinner includes a twice-baked potato and roll; the Saturday night Cuban pork roast feast is complete with black beans, yellow rice, corn on the cob, and cole slaw; Sunday evenings present a lip-smacking, all-you-can-eat barbecue that includes chicken, ribs, baked beans, cole slaw, and cornbread.

Come by boat or car and be prepared to have a great time. The friendly cooks, waitresses, and bartenders will make sure of it. Geiger Key is open daily for breakfast, lunch, and dinner. Beer and wine are available, and on weekends, you can listen to local bands.

Bobalu's Southern Café
MM 10 Bayside
Big Coppitt Key, FL
(305) 296–1664
$

Appearances can be deceiving. Bobalu's may look a little shabby on the outside, but the food and portions are anything but. The cuisine at Bobalu's is homestyle, hearty, and Southern. The menu includes entrees like pot roast, pork chops, and authentic fried chicken. Side dishes include sweet potatoes, okra, and turnip greens. The mashed potatoes are the made-from-scratch kind, and desserts like blackberry cobbler and bread pudding will take you back to the days when families sat down together over Sunday dinner. The restaurant itself is a family affair—run by dad Bob and mom Lu with all the kids helping out. It's family-priced, too, with most entrees under $10.

Even though it's located 10 miles outside of Key West, Bobalu's is famous enough to garner intense loyalty in many locals who willingly make the drive. Key West's favorite native son Jimmy Buffett has been known to dine here on occasion; he even mentioned this place in his book *Where is Joe Merchant?*

If inexpensive, stick-to-your-ribs food is what you're looking for, then look no more—you have come home. Bobalu's is open daily for lunch and dinner.

Key West

Some have called Key West the most successful melting pot in the United States. And no wonder. The southernmost city has a vibrant spirit that sparkles nowhere more brilliantly than in its cuisine. With restaurants as diverse and creative as a miniature Manhattan, Key West reflects the enduring ethnic traditions of generations past as well as the cutting-edge composition and presentation you would expect to find in major cosmopolitan cities worldwide. Add to all this gustatory wonder a dash of plain old Key West party and pizzazz, and you have a combination that is difficult to beat—anywhere! You can graze the sidewalk cafes of Duval Street or drink and nosh at Key West's panoply of saloons. Sit beneath a canopy of poinciana trees to sample the upscale, up-to-the-minute cuisine or eat your way around the world without ever leaving our eight-square-mile island.

But while it's tough to find a bad meal in Key West, it isn't tough to find an expensive one. When it comes to dining out, our small town leans toward big-city prices. Even a simple hamburger can be costly here. But hey—you're on vacation. Just sit back, relax, and enjoy!

Whatever your pleasure, remember this is still the Keys. Dress code is always Keys casual; just make sure you wear a shirt and shoes with your shorts, and you're dressed for any occasion.

Key West has more than 150 restaurants, some say the most per capita in the United States. Many line the famed Duval Street; others are tucked away down tree-lined alleys or in unassuming residential-looking buildings. We will not highlight the national restaurant chains, most of which are in the newer sections of Key West along N. Roosevelt Boulevard, because you are probably already familiar with their offerings. But we will assist you in finding those treasures known to locals—Insiders who keep their collective culinary finger on the pulse of the restaurant scene in Key West.

Our restaurants, like our people, defy easy classification. But we have divided the establishments into four categories to help you choose your dining preference: Key West Classics, those inimitable restaurants that the locals love and you won't want to miss; Surf and Turf, primarily casually presented, simply prepared red meat and/or seafood; Island Eclectic, upscale gourmet dining of the modern-American or new-American cuisine genre, created with a tropical flair; and The Melting Pot, a potpourri of diverse ethnic offerings that spirit your taste buds to the far corners of the globe—The Americas, South of the Border, The Continent, The Far East, and The Islands. Restaurants are listed in alphabetical order in each category.

You will find that reservation policies vary in Key West. The more upscale the restaurant, the more likely you will need a reservation, especially in high season. If it's something you need to consider, we mention the restaurant's reservation policy in its description.

Unlike many restaurants in the rest of the Keys, most of those in Key West have full-service bars. We will highlight the ones that serve beer and wine only. On-site parking is a rarity among our recommended restaurants, most of which are in Old Town where land is at a premium. In most cases you will need to park curbside on one of Key West's side streets or in a municipal or private lot (see our Getting Here, Getting Around chapter).

Unless stated otherwise, you may assume that restaurants are air-conditioned. Major credit cards and traveler's checks are widely accepted, but personal checks are not. And there is no restriction as to children dining in most establishments. Because restaurants in Key West's Old Town are often situated in nineteenth-century frame buildings that were formerly houses, accessibility for the physically challenged varies greatly. Sometimes steps must be negotiated, some bathrooms may be too tiny to accommodate a wheelchair, and separate nonsmoking sections may not always be available. If any of these anomalies is of particular concern to you, be sure to call the establishment to see exactly what arrangements might be made to fit your needs.

Our price code mirrors that of the rest of the Florida Keys and is based upon dinner for two, without starters, dessert, alcoholic beverages, tax, or tip.

Price-Code Key

$ . . . . Less than $25
$$ . . . . $25 to $40
$$$ . . . . $41 to $60
$$$$ . . . . More than $60

Key West Classics

A & B Lobster House
700 Front Street
Key West, FL
(305) 294–5880
www.ab-lobsterhouse.com
$$

A & B Lobster House, named for its original owners Alonzo and Berlin, is considered a Key West institution among seafood connoisseurs. Situated beside the water at the foot of Front Street, A & B offers a sumptuous selection of seafood as well as terrific views of the yachts moored at the Key West Historic Seaport.

In addition to Maine and Florida lobster, the classic menu includes traditional oyster and clam stews as well as pan roasts which are prepared by slow roasting oysters, clams, mussels and lobsters, then adding them to a broth of fresh herbs and vegetables with a touch of cream and sherry. Steaks and pasta dishes are also available.

Dine inside or outside; in either case, reservations are suggested. After dinner, retire to Berlin's Bar to sample the fine selection of cigars and after-dinner drinks.

A & B Lobster House is open daily from 6 P.M.; Berlin's opens at 5:30 P.M. for pre-dinner cocktails.

Alonzo's Oyster Bar
700 Front Street (downstairs)
Key West, FL
(305) 294–5880
www.alonzos-oysterbar.com
$–$$

If you like oysters, Alonzo's is the place to go. You can order them up raw, on the half shell, baked, or batter dipped and fried. This casual seaside eatery, situated downstairs from A & B Lobster House, also serves freshly shucked clams, lobster, conch, mussels, and a variety of dishes made with the native shrimp known as "Key West pinks." If you're in the mood for a seafood soup beside chowder, try a bowl of the white clam chili. It's plenty filling but not as rich as its creamier cousin.

Alonzo's is open daily from 11 A.M. to 11 P.M. There's plenty of indoor and outdoor seating; reservations are not necessary.

Blue Heaven
305 Petronia Street
Key West, FL
(305) 296–8666
www.blueheavenkw.com
$$

The word is out without so much as a cock's crow: Blue Heaven—at various times a bordello, a pool hall, a railroad water tower, a cockfighting arena, a boxing ring (frequented by Papa Hemingway himself), and an ice cream parlor—is now a popular restaurant at the corner of Petronia and Thomas Streets. Owned by brothers Richard and Dan Hatch, this throwback to the hippie era offers Caribbean and vegetarian cuisine in an unhampered island setting. Situated in historic Bahama Village, Blue Heaven's ambiance is as legendary as its cuisine. Roosters, hens, and chicks strut all around the picnic tables that fill Blue Heaven's backyard; so do the resident kitties. Jimmy Buffett's 1995 song, "Blue Heaven Rendezvous," was inspired by this diamond in the rough.

Indeed the magic is alive and well at Blue Heaven, where patrons enjoy specialties such as jerk chicken, Caribbean shrimp, and locally caught seafood entrees. Vegetable roulade is a light and pleasing appetizer, and burgers are made with tofu, no beef. Sunday brunch at Blue Heaven, with diverse preparations of eggs, waffles, and pancakes—including the famous beer-batter and pecan varieties—draws crowds that line themselves up

Blue Heaven's ambiance is as legendary as its cuisine: Roosters, hens, and chicks strut around the picnic tables that fill the restaurant's backyard. PHOTO: FLORIDA KEYS & KEY WEST TDC

'round the corner. Shrimp and grits are a highlight of brunch.

This is a place where kids are actually encouraged to run around and play; there's even a rope for them to swing on.

Although Blue Heaven once served only beer and wine, the restaurant now has a full liquor license. The mimosas made with fresh-squeezed orange juice are a breakfast favorite. Blue Heaven is open daily for breakfast, lunch, and dinner. Reservations are not accepted so expect to encounter a wait.

BO's Fish Wagon
801 Caroline Street
Key West, FL
(305) 294–9272
$

Almost any restaurant in Key West can make you a fish sandwich, but no one can make you a fish sandwich like Buddy Owen. He starts with Cuban bread, then piles the fresh fish and grilled onions so high, we dare you to try and get your mouth around it.

Belly up to the counter and place your order for a fish sandwich grilled (yellowtail) or fried (grouper); add sides like fries or onion rings only if you're really hungry. The portions here are huge. The menu also features squid rings (what every other restaurant in town politely calls calamari), fish and chips, the ubiquitous conch fritters, burgers, and hot dogs. To quench your thirst, select from bottle or draft beer, wine by the glass (plastic that is), sodas, or Key limeade.

While you're waiting for your sandwich to be delivered to your table, take a look around. The decor here can only be called Key West eclectic—fishing nets, lobster traps, a muffler shop sign, even an old pick-up truck abound.

Camille's Restaurant
703½ Duval Street
Key West, FL
(305) 296–4811
www.camilleskeywest.com
$–$$

Ask Key West residents where you should eat, especially for breakfast, and they'll send you to Camille's. The menu at this eclectic local favorite features a wide array of gourmet breakfast, lunch, and dinner specials, and the reasonably priced menu changes daily and nightly. Stone crab clawmeat cakes are grilled and served with spiced rum–mango sauce. Full rack of lamb is a hefty portion of seven to eight pieces, grilled and cooked to order, then served with garlic-oregano marinade or raspberry coulis. Weekend breakfast at Camille's is a particular treat, with pecan waffles fluffy and sweet, and as many as five styles of eggs Benedict. Sample Black Angus filet mignon or Norwegian smoked salmon. And for lunch, the homemade chicken salad sandwich is always a delicious choice.

In the People's Choice Awards sponsored annually by WKRY Key 93.5 FM, Camille's almost always garners Best Breakfast, Best Lunch, and Best Dining on a Budget. The restaurant is owned by Denise Chelekis, who is the former catering manager to Donald Trump, and

Denise's husband, Michael, once a sound system director for Atlantic City's Golden Nugget Casino. Camille's serves only the freshest ingredients.

Beer and wine are offered, and the ambiance is so friendly that tourists are treated like locals. At Camille's, you'll find patrons so moved by Beatles songs on the CD player that they often join in a rendition of "I Wanna Hold Your Hand." Camille's, which has seating for 42, does not accept reservations; expect a wait—especially for breakfast. Camille's is open every day for breakfast and lunch; dinner is served Tuesday through Saturday.

Captain Runaground Harvey's Floating Restaurant
Garrison Bight City Marina
Key West, FL
(305) 296–9907
www.strandlopersportfishing.com/runagrounds
$

You say you want to eat beside the water? Why not eat on the water? This double-decker barge-turned-restaurant is docked beside N. Roosevelt Boulevard at the Garrison Bight City Marina.

It's an informal place, serving mostly burgers, soups, sandwiches, and baskets of fried calamari, clam strips, and fish and chips. Sip your favorite cocktail from the full-service bar while you enjoy a light breeze off the water, watch the fishing charters return, and listen to the tourists talk about the "one that got away."

Captain Runaground's is open daily for breakfast, lunch, and dinner. And we do mean open. This is a boat, folks. On a rainy day, you will get wet here.

The Deli Restaurant
531 Truman Avenue
Key West, FL
(305) 294–1464
$

Enter through the double portals of The Deli Restaurant, each of which sports a giant seahorse-shaped window, and you will be welcomed home.

This family-run restaurant has been greeting Key West locals with good cheer and affordable home-style cookin' since 1950. The Deli Restaurant received a face-lift in 1995, when more windows were added. Established by John and Joan Bernreuter as a corner delicatessen where Aunt Mamie and John's grandmother, Poppy, made the salads, The Deli Restaurant today serves up generations of vintage Conch dishes under the supervision of Bobby Bernreuter. His daughter Patty is in charge of baking the pies and keeping track of the orders and paperwork.

Try roast turkey (the real thing) or fried chicken, franks and beans or sugar-cured ham, roast beef or pork. You'll find Key West shrimp or yellowtail grilled or fried and conch chowder made from the secret family recipe. Allow some room for dessert, because Toll House cookie pie, apple crumb pie, or sweet potato pie are sure to bring on a wave of nostalgia.

The Deli Restaurant is open daily from 7:20 A.M. to 10 P.M. Beer and wine are available. The Deli Restaurant does not take reservations.

Dennis Pharmacy
1229 Simonton Street
Key West, FL
(305) 294-1577
$

This no-nonsense establishment is reputedly the restaurant that inspired Jimmy Buffett's song "Cheeseburger in Paradise." To the left of its entrance is a pharmacy; to its right, an old-fashioned, brightly lit lunchroom with two horseshoe-shaped counters and white metal tables and chairs with turquoise vinyl upholstery.

To add a homier feel to the place, owners Emilio and David Alea have added tablecloths. This facility, which sits on the site of a former grocery store, was converted in 1962 to a pharmacy with a soda fountain and sandwich counter. In the 1970s the Aleas expanded the menu to include full meals.

Hearty, homestyle cuisine is the star here. Dennis Pharmacy specializes in American food with a Latin flair. On the regular menu are breaded steaks and pork chops, fried shrimp, sandwiches, and burgers. The palomino steak and grilled chicken and dolphin sandwiches are particularly popular, and daily specials include ropa vieja, roast pork, roast chicken, corned beef and cabbage, meat loaf, and Spanish beef stew. Homemade soups are offered each day; chili is served once a week. Beer, wine, and soft drinks are available, as is a real, old-fashioned, thick, and flavorful chocolate malt.

Dennis Pharmacy is open seven days a week for breakfast, lunch, and early dinner. Off-street parking is available, and reservations are not accepted.

Harpoon Harry's
832 Caroline Street
Key West, FL
(305) 294-8744
$

Harpooned and hanging from the ceilings of this hometown-style diner is everything—including the kitchen sink. Across from Key West Historic Seaport, on the site of what was a small hospital turned barber shop, Harpoon Harry's combines Tiffany lighting fixtures with old roller skates, sleds, and carousel horses. Framed advertisements recall the days of Lucky Strike cigarettes, Mennen Toilet Powder, knee-highs, and antique cars. The restaurant's movie star wall boasts Elvis, Sophia, and Lucy and Desi. A case contains a collection of Mickey Mouse glasses, which are probably worth a fortune. It is, in fact, this original decor that drew The Travel Channel to Harpoon Harry's in 1995. Restaurateur Ronald Heck is the creative genius responsible for it. The owner of Michigan's Lighthouse Inn, Heck informed his Midwestern employees and patrons of the interior design plans he had for his new establishment, and they came bearing all sorts of amusements.

The luncheon menu at Harpoon Harry's is much less eccentric than the decor: meat loaf or roast turkey with mashed potatoes, breaded veal cutlets, homemade chicken pot pie, and melt-in-your-mouth roasted pork chops with gravy. Breakfast is highlighted by Harry's Special: eggs, sausage, bacon, ham, toast and jelly served with home fries or grits. Two counters and booths and tables are available. Beer is the alcoholic beverage of the house.

Harpoon Harry's is open daily for breakfast and lunch. It closes at 2 P.M. Reservations are not accepted.

Hog's Breath Saloon
400 Front Street
Key West, FL
(305) 296–4222
www.hogsbreath.com
$

The name of this establishment may not be appealing, but its fish sandwiches—blackened or grilled with lemon—are. They're served up by the ton. Built to resemble an authentic surfer bar, Hog's Breath features lots of wood, including an African mahogany bar at which some guests are fortunate enough to land a seat. Mounted fish and surfboards hang from the walls, along with active water-related photographs. Not surprisingly, owner Jerry Dorminy of Alabama is a watersports enthusiast. He originally established a Hog's Breath Saloon in Fort Walton Beach, Florida, in 1976, as a place where he and his friends could retreat after a day of fishing and sailing.

In 1988 Dorminy opened Hog's Breath Key West. Here, nautical charts of Caribbean waters are lacquered into wood tables, and patrons dine indoors or outside on a brick patio from which large trees sprout. In addition to the fish sandwich, Hog's Breath's smoked fish dolphin dip and raw bar with oysters, shrimp, and stone crabs (in season) are extremely popular.

The restaurant's full-service bar features the medium-bodied Hog's Breath beer, brewed in the Midwest and now served at all four of Dorminy's locations, including those in Cancun and New Orleans. In case you were wondering, the name of the joint comes from an old say-ing of Dorminy's grandmother, that "hog's breath is better than no breath at all."

The restaurant is open for lunch and dinner, and live bands play folk rock, rock, blues, and jazz throughout the day and evening. Reservations are not accepted.

Jimmy Buffett's Margaritaville Cafe
500 Duval Street
Key West, FL
(305) 292–1435
www.margaritaville.com/keywest
$

Lunch really could last forever at Jimmy Buffett's Margaritaville Cafe, and patrons who steer here quite often remain throughout much of the day, regardless of whether or not they have amended their carnivorous habits. Margaritas are de rigueur, but bartenders also serve up the performer's personal favorite: a Cajun martini infusion of Smirnoff vodka and potent jalapeño and Scotch bonnet peppers. "Parrothead" and other island music sounds in the background, and decorations include oversize props from stage settings of Buffett tours, including stuffed iguanas from "Off to See the Lizard," a mock-up version of his seaplane, a flying goose, and a big warm bun and a huge hunk of meat. The fixin's—lettuce and tomato, Heinz-57 and French fried potatoes—are not forgotten.

In 1985, Buffett opened a store at the city's Land's End Village. Two years later he decided that he also wanted a cafe, and he opened this establishment in the heart of downtown Key West. The casual and friendly Margaritaville, he feels, combines his great love for music and food, both of which satisfy the soul. He has since opened cafes in New Orleans and Orlando.

Specialties of the house include Cheeseburgers in Paradise, fresh fish platters, sandwiches, and fried Key West shrimp baskets.

Margaritaville is open for lunch and dinner daily. Live music is offered nightly, beginning at 10:30 P.M. Reservations are not accepted, but those on the waiting list may shop for souvenirs in Buffett's adjacent store.

Kelly's Caribbean Bar & Grill
301 Whitehead Street
Key West, FL
(305) 293–8484
www.kellyskeywest.com
$$

Actress Kelly McGillis and her husband Fred Tillman own this Caribbean restaurant on the site of the original Pan American World Airways offices. In 1927, Pan Am launched its first international air service from Key West, when mail was flown from the island's Meacham Field to Havana. The following year, Pan Am began providing passenger service to Havana.

A display of early photographs and memorabilia of Pan Am service from Key West line the elegant violet and blue library room on the first floor. Clever decorating details fit the theme. When you dine in the front room of the first floor, you settle your tail feathers into old airplane seats, some of which offer views of a triangular bar designed to resemble the wing of a plane. Ceiling fans in the first-floor lounge (known as the Crash Room Bar) are miniature reproductions of an airplane motor.

Outdoor dining is available on a stone patio with gardens. On the second floor, Kelly's Clipper Club Lounge invites patrons to relax in an open-air gazebo-style setting.

Among the house specialties here are jambalaya, Bouillabise' Caribbean, and Camarones Curcacao, grilled shrimp first marinated in coconut mile, lime juice, ginger, and teriyaki.

Kelly's Caribbean Bar & Grill also is home to the Southernmost Brewery, which whips up an all-natural selection including Key West Golden Ale, Havana Red Ale, Southern Clipper wheat beer, and Black Bart's Root Beer.

The restaurant is open for lunch and dinner seven days a week. Reservations are accepted for parties of more than six. Key West hotel guests receive preferred seating.

McGillis and Tillman have opened two more Kelly's in Key West: Kelly's Key West, 314 Duval Street (305-292-0092) serves a tapas menu and offers late night entertainment. Kelly's Beach Club, 1405 Duval Street, (305) 295-6550, on the beach, offers drinks and dining, inside and out. You can even reserve your own beach chair here.

Lobo's Grill
#5 Key Lime Square
Key West, FL
(305) 296–5303
$, no credit cards

Lobo's is where locals love to lunch. The menu includes burgers, nachos, quesadillas, and salads. But the real stand-outs are the roll-up sandwiches—a mix of meats, cheeses, fresh veggies, and spreads tucked tightly, then rolled, in a giant flour tortilla. Choose from selections like the French Twist—a tasty mix of honey-baked ham, brie, tomato, cucumber, scallions, and honey mustard—or Thanksgiving—a combination of turkey breast, stuffing, cranberry sauce, onions, lettuce, and basil mayo.

You can eat in or take out; call ahead for quick pick-up or free delivery in Old Town. Lobo's is generally open daily for lunch and early dinner (before 6 P.M.), but keep in mind that hours may vary depending on the season.

Paradise Cafe
1000 Eaton Street
Key West, FL
(305) 296–5001
$, no credit cards

The sign outside reads "home of the island legend monster sandwich." Indeed. It would be tough to find a bigger, better sandwich anywhere in Key West. Choose from 15 lunchtime varieties—everything from ham and cheese, sliced turkey and hot Italian beef to chicken salad, tuna salad and BBQ pork—all made to order on Cuban bread with the fixin's you select. Paradise Cafe also serves up breakfast sandwiches—hearty combinations of egg, cheese, ham and/or steak, on Cuban bread, of course.

Nothing on the menu here costs more than $5.50. Eat in, take out, or phone ahead for delivery. Paradise Cafe is open Monday through Saturday for breakfast and lunch.

Pepe's Cafe & Steak House
806 Caroline Street
Key West, FL
(305) 294–7192
$$

Billed as the "Eldest Eating House in the Florida Keys, established 1909," Pepe's is as beloved to Conchs and Key Westers as the Mallory Square sunset celebration. In the old commercial waterfront area of Old Town, Pepe's touts its Apalachicola Bay oysters, when available, as among its specialties: raw, baked, Florentine, Mexican, or Rudi-style. But you will find a bit of the hoof available at Pepe's as well: New York strip steaks at 8, 12, and 15 ounces, filet mignon, pork chops, even barbecue. And Pepe's burgers sound as intriguing as they taste: White Collar Burger, Blue Collar Burger, Slit Ray Burger, and patty melt. Be sure to try a margarita here (the lime juice is squeezed fresh) and, for dessert, the brownie pie, served warm with ice cream—ask for Cuban coffee flavor instead of vanilla. Mmmmm! Pepe's serves early (mainly breakfast, 6:30 A.M. to noon), late (primarily dinner, after 4:30 P.M. to closing) and in between, predominantly oysters, soups, and sandwiches.

One thing is for certain, no matter when you visit Pepe's, you will not leave hungry. And don't forget: Pepe's gives free pickles to pregnant women! The restaurant is open every day. Patio dining is also available. Reservations are not accepted.

Turtle Kraals Waterfront Seafood Grill and Bar
1 Land's End Village
Key West, FL
(305) 294–26400
www.turtlekraals.com
$–$$

Offering Southwestern food with a definite seafood influence, Turtle Kraals occupies the site of a former turtle cannery, thus the name which essentially means "turtle pen." Turtle Kraals has an immense affection for wildlife, which is evidenced by the large saltwater enclosure behind the restaurant, where many kinds of injured sea life recover. Lobster Chili Rellenos—lobster stuffed poblano peppers, crispy fried and served with tomatillo sauce, sour cream, yellow rice, and black beans—is just one of the many Spanish-inspired seafood offerings. Turtle Kraals offers a huge selection of beer, and a full bar is available as well. Turtle Kraals is open daily for lunch and dinner. The upstairs Tower Bar, adjoining the restaurant, overlooks the marina and offers a great view of the sunset.

Surf and Turf

Commodore Waterfront Steakhouse
700 Front Street at Key West Historic Seaport
Key West, FL
(305) 294–9191
$$$

Tables covered in white linen are surrounded by mahogany paneling, brick walls, and lush greenery. Ceiling fans gently whirl. Window walls look out onto the charming harbor of Key West Historic Seaport. The Commodore exudes the elegance of a fine ship, and the establishment offers some topnotch meat and seafood to match the refined ambiance.

Signature dishes abound. Oysters Commodore are lightly breaded, flash fried, and topped with remoulade. The New York Steak Roquefort is a prime New York sirloin strip topped with melted

Insiders' Tip
Want to sample the fish you caught today? Many Keys restaurants will be happy to prepare your catch—along with some side dishes, like potatoes, corn on the cob, and coleslaw. Phone around for availability and prices.

Roquefort cheese. The broiled veal chop is thick and served in its own juices. Steamed mussels are lightly steamed in white wine, garlic, and ginger.

Commodore Waterfront Steakhouse serves dinner nightly. Free parking is available at A & B Marina.

Conch Republic Seafood Company
631 Greene Street
Key West, FL
(305) 294-4403
www.conchrepublicseafood.com
$$

From the look of this place—with its old wooden railings, weathered tin roof, and lazy, wobbly ceiling fans—you'd swear it had been in Key West for decades. Not so. The Conch Republic Seafood Company opened for business in the newly renovated Key West Historic Seaport in 1999.

As you've no doubt surmised, the menu here is heavy on seafood. Entrees include grilled or fried Key West "pinks" (shrimp), grilled tuna steak, Bahamian-style cracked conch, and pan-seared grouper fillet. For starters, try a bowl of Callaloo soup—a blend of island greens and crabmeat in a spicy lobster stock.

The full-service, 80-seat bar boasts one of the best rum selections around—more than 80 varieties are available, along with 25 kinds of beer. The full menu is available daily from noon until 11 P.M. Live music is offered nightly.

Reservations are not necessary and you need not ask for a waterfront table. Every seat has an open-air view of the harbor action. And if that's not enough to keep you occupied while you wait for your food, check out the 80-foot aquarium stocked with local seafood that is the centerpiece of the restaurant.

Crabby Dicks' Seafood Restaurant and Lounge
712 Duval Street (upstairs)
Key West, FL
(305) 294-7229
$-$$

Note the apostrophe placement in the name of this restaurant—it refers to the two owners, Dick Cami and Richard First. Though they were newcomers to Key West when they opened this establishment in 1996, they are no newcomers to the restaurant business. Cami was owner of the famed Peppermint Lounge in New York City.

The specialty here is—you guessed it—seafood. The menu boasts everything from crab legs to catfish to fresh shucked oysters and clams. The prices are reasonable (a dozen oysters will set you back just $3.88), sauces are made from scratch, and the portions are plentiful.

In addition to some of the freshest seafood on the island, Crabby Dicks' has a couple of other things going for it, too. You get a great view from the second story veranda overlooking the 700 block of Duval Street and there is ample free parking for diners behind the restaurant.

Crabby Dicks' is open daily from 11:30 A.M. to 10 P.M. The daily Happy Hour is from 4 to 7 P.M. Happy Hour features $1 drafts.

Duffy's Steak & Lobster House
Corner of Simonton Street and Truman Avenue
Key West, FL
(305) 296-4900
$$

The beginnings of this structure date back to the late 1890s, but it wasn't until 1948 that the building actually became Duffy's Tavern. Today, the interior has been updated with deep-green paint and the original glass block set off by neon lighting. Bulky wood booths, a wood floor, and high ceilings lend a rustic atmosphere. The entertainment is found through abundant windows, for Duffy's proves ideal for people watching.

Owned by Timothy Ryan, proprietor of Cafe des Artistes (see separate restaurant listing in this chapter) next door, Duffy's specializes in prime rib, steaks, and lobster. All dishes are simply prepared and served with a salad, freshly baked bread, and a choice of potato. Daily specials, such as angel hair pasta with Gulf shrimp in a brochette or chicken San Bernardino, a breaded breast of chicken sautéed and covered in eggplant and mozzarella in a tomato-basil sauce, satisfy more intricate taste buds.

Lunch and dinner are served here daily. Reservations are not accepted.

Half Shell Raw Bar
231 Margaret Street
Key West, FL
(305) 294–7496
www.halfshell-rawbar.com
$$

When Half Shell Raw Bar's owners opened this seafood establishment in 1980, they dotted the all-wood walls with amusing license plates. Today, these same walls are literally covered with plates donated by customers, and many a spare is stored out of view.

Always consistent at Half Shell Raw Bar is its fresh seafood served on the casual, open-air waterfront. Located in Land's End Village at the Historic Key West Seaport, the restaurant is known for its oysters, clams, crabs, and local seafood simply prepared, reasonably priced, and served with plastic silverware on paper plates at picnic tables. Half Shell carries stone crabs in season and Maine lobster. Its full bar offers beer, wine, and frozen drinks.

Patrons may opt for outdoor dining on either a waterfront deck or a patio. Reservations are accepted for parties of more than six. Half Shell Raw Bar is open daily for lunch and dinner. Off-street parking is abundant.

Martha's Steaks & Seafood
3591 S. Roosevelt Boulevard
Key West, FL
(305) 294–3466
www.marthas-benihana.com
$$$

The panoramic vista of the Atlantic Ocean is but a precursor to the aged, certified Black Angus beef and fresh native seafood starring nightly at Martha's. Prime rib is a specialty of the house, joining a stellar array of steaks, calves liver, lamb tenderloin, and roast duck entrees.

You'll find Yellowtail Grenoblaise, Blackened Swordfish, and Nut-crusted Grouper among the selections. Florida lobster and stone crabs in season round out the menu. Enjoy fancy island drinks while you listen to nightly piano music.

Once a bowling alley, Martha's, which has the same owners as Benihana's next door (see separate listing elsewhere in this chapter), offers early-bird specials for entrees ordered between 5:30 and 6 P.M. Reservations are suggested in all seasons. Martha's is open for dinner seven days a week.

Michaels
532 Margaret Street
Key West, FL
(305) 295–1300
www.michaelskeywest.com
$$$

Tucked away in a quiet Old Town neighborhood several blocks off Duval, this casual yet elegant little gem of a restaurant would be easy to miss, but we urge you not to. Since January 1997, owners Melanie and Michael Wilson have been serving up some of the best food on the island.

Michael, the former corporate chef for the Chicago-based Morton's Steakhouses, knows how to cook a piece of beef. His prime rib is flown in fresh via Federal Express from Allen Brothers in Chicago and his Filet al Forno, rubbed with roasted garlic and Roquefort, has garnered rave reviews and numerous awards. The menu also includes seafood and pasta specialties; for theatregoers, a specially priced, two-course dinner is offered nightly. No matter which entree you select, be sure to

Insiders' Tip
Some Key West restaurants offer a discount to locals upon proof of residency.

save room for dessert. The Chocolate Volcano is a house specialty—it erupts at the touch of your fork!

Martini drinkers will appreciate the wide selection of vodkas and olives—they're stuffed with everything from the traditional pimientos to blue cheese, anchovies, and prosciutto. And if martinis aren't your forte, there are plenty of other liquors to choose from as well as a wide selection of fine wines.

Michaels is open nightly from 5:30 P.M. Reservations are recommended for both indoor and outdoor seating.

Rusty Anchor Restaurant
MM 5 Oceanside
5510 Third Avenue
Stock Island, FL
(305) 294–5369
www.rustyanchorseafood.com
$$

Weigh anchor for a satisfying seafood meal at the Rusty Anchor, a casual seafood haven for the piscatorially inclined. You won't find fresher fish and seafood anywhere, for in the back of the Rusty Anchor is a commercial seafood market that supplies many of Key West's restaurants. The fish, lobsters, shrimp, and stone crab claws are delivered right from the boat (see our Seafood Markets and Specialty Foods chapter). The restaurant exudes a casual nautical atmosphere punctuated by rope-edged tables, wood buoys, nautical art prints, and photographs of the fishing fleets of old Key West. A 400-plus pound marlin is mounted at one end of the dining room, and a couple of 15-pound lobsters grace the other walls.

Lunch and dinner are simply prepared. The saltwater fish is caught daily in the Key West area and generally is served broiled or fried. Try the teriyaki-grilled tuna sandwich on Cuban bread if it is offered as a special. You can nosh on conch fritters or slurp chowder, peel steamed shrimp, or nibble a salad. If seafood is not your favorite, Rusty Anchor also serves burgers, steaks, and ribs. Food is presented picnic-style on plastic plates, drinks in plastic cups, and beer out of the can.

Open Monday through Saturday, the Rusty Anchor does not require reservations. It's a great place to bring the kids.

Seven Fish
632 Olivia Street
Key West, FL
(305) 296–2777
$$

Don't be fooled by the name. Although the seafood here is excellent, this restaurant, which is located at the corner of Olivia and Elizabeth Streets, has much more to recommend it. In addition to the freshest fish, the menu includes grilled chicken, meat loaf with mashed potatoes, and a New York strip steak cooked the way you like it and served with roasted red skins on the side. Salads—three-cheese Caesar or mixed greens with balsamic vinegar, roasted red pepper, and goat cheese—are available in two sizes. And for an additional charge, you can add grilled chicken or a crab cake to your greens if you like.

The environment at Seven Fish is cozy and friendly, the food flavorful and inexpensive. Nothing on the menu here tops $20. On the downside, Seven Fish is small—go early or you may have to wait—and the tables are quite close together. But don't worry about inhaling any second-hand smoke from the table next door: Seven Fish is smoke free; there isn't an ashtray in the place. The restaurant is open nightly 6 to 10 P.M. except Tuesdays. That's when the staff goes fishing. Reservations are recommended.

Island Eclectic

Alice's at La Te Da
1125 Duval Street
Key West, FL
(305) 296–6706
$$$

"Eclectic" means to select from various doctrines, methods, and styles, and Alice's rightly bills itself as "eclectic cuisine" with a menu you won't find anywhere else.

Alice's creations have earned her awards . . . and rightfully so. Her breakfast menu features the likes of a magic mushroom and goat cheese omelet created from shiitake and porcini mushrooms and Sonoma County goat cheese. Luncheon choices include a Monte Cristo sandwich that is beyond even the heartiest appetite. Dinner offerings range from macadamia-coconut-crusted shrimp with honey wasabi to Dijon-herb-crusted rack of New Zealand lamb with a port, pear, and mint demi glace. And to cap it off, Alice makes a cappuccino bread pudding that is beyond delicious.

Relocated from the corner of Duval and Amelia Streets to La-Te-Da, Alice's is open daily for breakfast, lunch, and dinner. Reservations are strongly recommended.

Bagatelle
115 Duval Street
Key West, FL
(305) 296–6609
$$$

Incongruous amid the tourist trappings of lower Duval, Bagatelle sits reservedly amid the fray, adding a touch of class to the surroundings. Situated on two floors of a gracious old Key West home, Bagatelle serves fresh local ingredients with island inventiveness. Try the grilled Portobello mushroom or the Bahamian conch steak for something different. Or allow a salad made with hearts of palm or escargot Martinique to foreshadow grilled fresh tuna or snapper Rangoon, which is served with tropical fruit.

Wraparound balconies on both levels afford outdoor dining, or you may choose to dine indoors where the decor favors that of a first-rate art gallery. Bagatelle is a premier spot from which to view the Fantasy Fest parade (see our Annual Events chapter). An extravagant seafood buffet is offered that evening, and a dinner reservation secures you a seat for the entire night. You receive a Bagatelle wristband so you may come and go as you like, partying the night away on Duval Street. Reservations for the evening of Fantasy Fest should be made well in advance of the event, even up to a year.

Bagatelle serves lunch and dinner daily. Reservations are suggested for dinner in all seasons at this popular restaurant, but at least a day in advance in high season.

Cafe Marquesa
600 Fleming Street
Key West, FL
(305) 292–1244, (800) 869–4631
www.cafemarquesa.com
$$$

Golden walls covered with paintings, pastel tile floors, large mirrors, and a panoramic country-kitchen mural set the scene for one of the finest dining encounters in Key West. Long a front-runner in the panoply of establishments plying to please your palate, Cafe Marquesa remains a consistent winner.

Gracing the white linen tablecloths is an eclectic assortment of innovative dishes. Specialties of the house include: Peppercorn Dusted Seared Yellowfin Tuna, Feta and Pine Nut Encrusted Rack of Lamb, and Grilled, Marinated Key West Shrimp.

Cafe Marquesa, reminiscent of a European brasserie, is a nonsmoking restaurant. Reservations are highly recommended in all seasons. Cafe Marquesa serves dinner nightly.

Cafe Solé
1029 Southard Street
Key West, FL
(305) 294–0230
www.cafesole.com
$$

This charming little restaurant sits out of the way of the hustle and bustle of downtown Key West, so you might have a little trouble finding it. If you find Southard Street, you are halfway there; just wander the wrong way up Southard until you come to Frances Street. Look to the left and you will see this great little French-Caribbean eatery offering gourmet seafood, lamb, and even ostrich.

The most popular dishes here are probably the seafood ones, like grouper Romanesco, with a sauce consisting of tomatoes, hazelnuts, roasted red peppers, and garlic. Cafe Solé only seats 60 diners, so reservations are highly recommended. The cafe is open for dinner only, starting at 6 P.M., and is closed on Wednesdays.

Latitudes Beach Cafe
Sunset Key
245 Front Street
(305) 292–5394
$$$

When you think of dining seaside somewhere on a secluded island, this is the kind of place that comes to mind. Just five minutes across the water from the hustle and bustle of Mallory Square, Latitudes might just as well be half a world away. It is that peaceful, that serene. And, as near as we can tell, still largely undiscovered. Granted, it takes some planning to get here. You have to make a reservation, and you have to board a boat. But if what you seek is a quiet evening escape from the craziness of Key West, dinner at Latitudes on Sunset Key is well worth the effort.

The cuisine here could best be described as eclectic. Dinner entrees include the likes of pan-seared Chilean sea bass, coconut and macadamia encrusted grouper, Key lime chicken piccata, and beef tenderloin with Gorgonzola scallion butter and a marinated Portobello mushroom. Latitudes also serves breakfast and lunch. A full bar offers exotic frozen island drinks as well as beer and wine.

Sunset Key is a private island, half of which is devoted to guest cottages, the other to pricey waterfront homes (see our Accommodations and Real Estate chapters for additional information). Island access is thus largely limited to residents. Launches for Sunset Key leave regularly throughout the day from the pier at the Hilton Resort and Marina on Front Street. If you are not living or staying on the island, you must make a reservation for your meal at Latitudes with the Hilton concierge to secure a boarding pass.

Insiders' Tip

Conch fritters, made from imported conch (harvesting this shellfish in our waters is not permitted), are seasoned with garlic and spices and then deep-fried. They do not resemble true Southern fritters you may have encountered elsewhere.

Louie's Backyard
700 Waddell Avenue
Key West, FL
(305) 294–10610
www.louiesbackyard.com
$$$$

An enduring favorite among locals and visitors alike, Louie's Backyard combines island manor house ambiance with cutting-edge cuisine. And though the exquisitely prepared, complex combination of ingredients that marks Louie's is often imitated elsewhere in Key West, this restaurant continues to shine. A sweeping veranda, for outdoor dining, overlooks Louie's "backyard," which is actually a prime piece of Atlantic oceanfront property. Indoors, the pale lavender-blue walls showcase the finely appointed tables. In the '70s this spot was a favorite with next-door neighbor Jimmy Buffett, who often played for his supper.

Dinner entrees span the globe, with fresh local seafood garnering center stage. An equally innovative cuisine is offered on the lunch menu for half the price of evening dining. Try lunch menu offerings such as Bahamian Conch Chowder with bird-pepper hot sauce, Spicy Fried Chicken Salad with a citrus-sesame-peanut dressing, or Stacked Duck Enchilada with green chili sauce and roasted corn. Dinner offerings include Sautéed Key West Shrimp with a saffron noodle cake; Grilled Spice-rubbed Loin of Venison with apples, onions, and juniper berries; or Florida Lobster Braised in truffle butter. Top off lunch or dinner with the truly decadent Burnt Honey Mousse or Chocolate Banana Crème Caramel.

Louie's Backyard serves lunch and dinner daily, except from Labor Day to Columbus Day, when it's open for dinner only. Reservations are recommended in all seasons but especially in winter and on weekends. The Afterdeck outdoor oceanside bar is open all day and into the wee hours (see our Nightlife chapter).

Mangoes
700 Duval Street
Key West, FL
(305) 292–4606
www.mangoeskeywest.com
$$

Patrons enjoy one of the best views of Duval Street at Mangoes, where fresh Caribbean-style seafood is served in an outdoor, corner cafe setting of white umbrella-covered tables. Indoor dining is equally sophisticated, with candlelight and fresh flowers on every table and original artwork lining the walls.

Open daily for lunch, dinner, and late-night pizza (15 varieties cooked in a wood-fired oven), Mangoes' specialties include pan-seared yellowtail snapper with passion fruit, on the sweet side, and a lobster, scallops, and shrimp dish known as Gueddengo, served with a slightly spicy tomato sauce. Reservations are accepted during peak season for parties of more than five.

Rooftop Cafe
310 Front Street
Key West, FL
(305) 294–2042
$$$

High amid the treetops, Rooftop Cafe looks down on the tourist mecca along Front Street near Mallory Square. And although the restaurant bustles with dining activity, the atmosphere remains unhurried and removed from the fray. Diners may sit on a second-floor balcony, which extends on two sides of the building, under the canopy of ancient leafy trees. Inside, ceiling fans mounted on the white vaulted ceiling gently move the air about the open-air, pavilion-style dining room. Philodendron trails from overhead and dwarf bougainvillea trees dot the floor. Oilcloth in a modern-art barrage of primary colors covers the tables.

The cuisine, innovative in both composition and presentation, combines local piscatory resources with an international flair. Dinner creations have included: Sautéed Pepper Tiger Tuna, a tuna steak with black pepper and sesame seeds served with soy-wasabi sauce and mung sprouts; Savory Shrimps, Key West pinks marinated in shallots, herbs, and oil, then grilled and served on roasted corn and fennel risotto; Shellfish Lasagna, a chef's selection of seafood under a blanket of lemon-pepper pasta served on a lobster and oregano coulis. Luncheon selections transcend the norm as well. Rooftop Cafe is open daily for breakfast, lunch, and dinner. Reservations are strongly suggested for dinner in all seasons, especially at sunset.

Square One
1075 Duval Street
Key West, FL
(305) 296–4300
www.squareonerestaurant.com
$$$

Enjoy a touch of class and a bit of craziness, Manhattan-style, at Square One, a casually sophisticated uptown bistro in Duval Square. Two enormous tropical floral murals flank the walls, offsetting the highly polished wood of other areas. The green carpet is mirrored in the green-rimmed chargers, which sit upon white linen tablecloths in the rich-looking dining room.

Diners are treated to light piano music as they sample Square One's considerable creative offerings. You may wish to try these signature dishes: Roast Rack of Lamb, seasoned with whole grain mustard, honey shallot confit, and minted bordelaise sauce or Sautéed Sea Scallops served on a bed of poached spinach with a light mustard cream sauce. And there is always a chef's choice pasta selection and other daily specialties.

Square One offers the option of outdoor dining in the tree-lined courtyard. Ample free parking is available in the adjoining lot accessed from Simonton Street. Square One serves dinner nightly, 365 days a year. Reservations are always highly recommended.

Melting Pot

The Americas

Garden Cafe
310 Duval Street
Key West, FL
(305) 294-2991
$, American

Jewelry makers, glass blowers, and artists surround visitors to the Garden Cafe, which offers exclusively outdoor seating on an elevated concrete platform. Views include busy Duval Street or more private and shady courtyard gardens. Situated next to the Porter mansion, circa 1880s, this establishment serves one of Key West's biggest and best burgers. Also on the menu is a wide variety of homemade vegetarian fare, including Caesar salads, sautéed veggies with or without brown rice, vegetable soups, and a garden veggie burger. Tropical and Asian chicken salads satisfy light meat eaters, and specials such as a grilled organic tofu sandwich with roasted peppers are offered daily. Homemade ice cream and brownies are dessert options . . . if you have the room. Portions here are plentiful.

Garden Cafe is open daily for breakfast, lunch, and dinner; Mondays the restaurant closes early, about 7 P.M. Beer, wine, and frozen margaritas, daiquiris, and piña coladas are available. Reservations are not accepted.

Iguana Cafe
425 Greene Street
Key West, FL
(305) 296-6420
$, American

Iguana is not on the menu at this 24-hour eatery, but alligator sure is. You can have it as a burger or in chowder or fritters. You'll also find traditional burgers and a wide array of sandwiches.

The owners—Jim and Cathy Cowan—are a couple of transplanted Texans who bought the cafe on a whim and turned it into a profitable business. In the process, they also acquired a mascot. Mr. Iggy is the resident (real) iguana and CEO.

Seating is available inside or out on the patio, but the real treat is to grab one of the street-side barstools and watch the late night revelers stumble out of Captain Tony's Saloon across the street.

This is one of the few places in Key West where you can get late-night food. The full menu, including breakfast, is served seven days a week, 24 hours a day.

Meteor Smokehouse
404 Southard Street
Key West, FL
(305) 294-5602
www.keywest.com/themenu/meteor
$$, American

Nestled tight against the Green Parrot Bar, one of Key West's oldest and most popular watering holes (see our Nightlife chapter), this unassuming eatery is easy to find—just follow the enticing smell of hickory-smoked meats sizzling on the island's only authentic pit barbecue.

Meteor specializes in ribs—the Memphis-style, dry-rubbed, baby-back variety and St. Louis-style spare ribs, to be exact—as well as pulled pork and Texas beef brisket, all smoked low and slow for 16 hours. Opt for a platter if you're especially hungry—you get the meat, plus a cornbread muffin and two sides—or just have a sandwich if you're not. And be sure to ask for plenty of napkins. These ribs are the lip-smackin', mouth-watering, and up-to-your-elbows-in-barbecue-sauce kind.

If you'd rather not eat in, phone ahead and carry out. Either way, the full menu is available daily, except Sundays, from 5 P.M. to 2 A.M. Lunch is served in season. Free parking for diners is available next door.

Mo's Restaurant
1116 White Street
Key West, FL
(305) 296–8955
$, no credit cards, French-Canadian

Locals know that for good, modestly priced food, Mo's is the place to go. In fact, originally the restaurant was called Mo's to Go, for it sold only take-out items. Now the small (fewer than 30 seats), white clapboard eatery offers an interesting menu with a strong French influence. Run by a French-Canadian brother-sister team, Mo's seafood lasagna, variety of quiches, and casseroles and garlic- and spinach-stuffed leg of lamb receive raves from regulars and critics alike. Look for the smilin' moustached garlic that denotes Mo's Restaurant. It foretells of palate pleasers to come.

Mo's serves beer, wine, and homemade sangria. The restaurant serves lunch and dinner from 11 A.M. onward, Tuesday through Saturday during the season; it is closed in summer. Reservations are not accepted.

Our Place & Co.
1900 Flagler Avenue (corner of Bertha Street)
Key West, FL
(305) 292–4002
$, American

> ## Insiders' Tip
>
> Remember, the dolphin you see offered on the menu is not the cute bottle-nosed variety that cavorts in our seas. You will be ordering dolphin fish, commonly marketed outside the Keys as mahi-mahi.

That $22 pepper-crusted tuna steak with wasabi sauce you saw on a menu downtown might be fine for a special occasion. But for steady fare, locals want reasonable prices and comfort foods—the very kinds that are offered at Our Place.

This is the kind of restaurant you come to after a hard day's work to kick back with your friends. It's short on atmosphere but long on the kind of stick-to-your-ribs cooking that would make Mom proud. Specialties of the house include meat loaf and mashed potatoes, pot roast with vegetables, beef tips over noodles, and chicken pot pie. There's always a catch of the day and fresh, hot soup on the menu, too. Portions here are generous (half portions are available, by the way) and the prices are right. Most entrees cost less than $10. You'll want to save room for dessert, of course—the peach cobbler is a must.

Our Place caters primarily to locals, which is one reason it's open late. Servers, bartenders, and taxi drivers can pick up a full meal on their way home as late as 3 A.M.

PT's Late Night Bar and Grill
920 Caroline Street
Key West, FL
(305) 296–4245
$, American

PT's (short for Paul Tripp, the owner) is a friendly neighborhood grill that lives up to its motto—"large plates, small prices."

With few exceptions, everything here is priced under $10 and the portions are ample.

Choose from all-American favorites like meat loaf, Yankee pot roast, smothered pork chops, and country-fried steak. Or chow down on a plate of fajitas. The choices include steak, chicken, shrimp, and veggie, or combination thereof. Salads and sandwiches appease lighter appetites, too.

The full menu is served until 3 A.M. nightly; the bar remains open until 4 A.M.

South of the Border

B's Restaurant
1500 Bertha Street
Key West, FL
(305) 296–3140
$, no credit cards, Cuban

Hola, and welcome to the simple home-style restaurant of Cuban émigré Bertha Cubria, affectionately known as "B." For more than 15 years, Señora B has been doling out generous portions of roast pork, fresh fillet of grouper, and grilled top sirloin steak, each served either with beans, rice, and plantains or French fries and salad.

B's Restaurant is open daily for breakfast, lunch, and dinner. It offers beer, wine, and soft drinks in smoking and nonsmoking rooms with dark, paneled walls and red tablecloths.

Beware that "B" also stands for busy, and reservations are accepted only for parties of more than five. Off-street parking is available.

Chico's Cantina
MM 4.5 Oceanside
Stock Island, FL
(305) 296–4714
www.chicoscantina.com
$$, Mexican

Sit among giant cacti, Mexican tapestries, and a selection of south-of-the-border folk art at Chico's Cantina, a perennial favorite for Mexican cuisine. This small cantina—only 12 tables—knocks itself out with the freshest ingredients fashioned into off-the-charts homemade Mexican dishes. The food at Chico's is not your ordinary Mexican fare. Complimentary salsa is prepared with fresh tomatoes, onions, and peppers, creating the perfect balance between sweet and sassy. The salsa is so popular among locals that the restaurant sells the stuff in bulk. The sizzling fajitas—with a choice of vegetarian, chicken, beef, chicken-and-beef combo, shrimp, or shrimp-and-beef combo—are accompanied by fresh vegetables, cooked just until crispy. And the Fish Adobado, grilled in corn husks, packs just the right spicy zing. Daily specials usually highlight local seafood such as yellowtail snapper.

Chile peppers rule the roost at Chico's Cantina. Not only is their subtle presence notable in the cuisine, but their icons appear on the curtains, as lights around the windows, even on ceramic pots. Chico's serves the same menu for both lunch and dinner. It's open every day except Monday. Beer and wine are served; take-out is available.

El Meson de Pepe
410 Wall Street
Key West, FL
(305) 295–2620
$$, Cuban

Just when you thought Key West could not possibly support another Cuban restaurant, along came this one and it is almost always humming with activity. Part of the reason may have to do with its location. Situated just off Mallory Square, El Meson de Pepe draws a large post-sunset crowd. A salsa band plays nightly as the sun sinks into the Gulf of Mexico, which adds to the festive and welcoming atmosphere.

Look for Cuban-Conch classics on the menu—mollete a la pancho, Cuban bread stuffed with picadillo, a spicy combination of ground beef, capers, raisins, olives, and seasonings and ropa vieja, a traditional Cuban dish of shredded beef sautéed with tomatoes. Quench your thirst with a mojito—a rum concoction made with mint and sugar syrup that is similar to a mint julep.

The coffee shop here opens at 8 A.M. Lunch is served from 11 A.M. until 3 P.M. and dinner is available from 3 until 10 P.M. Indoor and outdoor seating is available. Large groups are welcome and reservations are appreciated but rarely necessary.

El Siboney
900 Catherine Street
Key West, FL
(305) 296–4184
$, no credit cards, Cuban

A cascade of bilingual chatter washes over the enthusiastic diners at El Siboney restaurant, an informal restaurant specializing in Cuban cuisine. The words *El Siboney* refer to a Cuban Indian, and artwork depicting the El Siboney adorns the white walls of the restaurant. Red vinyl covers the simple cafe chairs, and your cutlery is served in a white paper bag. The food is top drawer all the way, though. Hot, buttery Cuban bread is immediately whisked to your table, and then begins the difficult decision of which taste-tempting delicacy to order. Portions are enormous at El Siboney; the same menu is offered at lunch or dinner.

We recommend one of the combination platters, especially if trying Cuban cuisine is a new experience for you: A platter of roast pork, black beans, yellow rice, and cassava is served heaped with raw onions. The pork melts in the mouth. Or try the roast pork accompanied with yucca and tamale; sounds similar, tastes totally different. You'll find myriad Cuban twists with beef, including the popular ropa vieja (shredded beef) and boliche (Cuban pot roast). Crab, shrimp, and chicken all get the wonderful Cuban garlic treatment, and you can choose paella for two persons. You can order an array of sandwiches or sides of tamale, yucca, black beans, plantanos, and tostones. Wash it all down with homemade sangria, beer, or house wines, and try rice pudding, flan, or natilla for dessert if you have room.

El Siboney is closed on Sundays.

Jose's Cantina
800 White Street
Key West, FL
(305) 296–4366
$, Cuban

Step inside this little neighborhood diner and you might believe you'd just walked in from the streets of Havana. The owners are Cuban and so are most of the customers. But even if you don't speak Spanish, you're sure to receive a hearty *bienvenida* (welcome) here. The menus are in English, the waitstaff is bilingual, and the food is plentiful, delicious, and cheap.

Jose's has one of the best Cuban mixes on the island—that's a sandwich combination of ham and shredded pork on Cuban bread with lettuce, tomato, mayo, mustard, onions, and pickles. The dinners—Cuban variations on chicken, pork, and beef—come with the traditional black beans, yellow rice, and plantains. Beer, wine, and homemade sangria are available.

Jose's is open for breakfast, lunch, and dinner, 365 days a year—yes, even Christmas. This restaurant is very small and, judging from the lack of parking spaces in the surrounding neighborhood at 8 A.M., high noon, and 7 P.M., quite popular. To avoid the congestion, plan to arrive a little ahead or well after peak dining periods. Reservations are not accepted.

The Continent

Abbondanza
1208 Simonton Street
Key West, FL
(305) 292–1199
$, Italian

At last, a place to enjoy casual Italian fare in Old Town. The specialty here is pasta, of course, in a variety of shapes and with sauces that range from marinara to Alfredo. You'll also find main dishes like chicken Marsala and veal Parmesan, plus daily specials.

The food is quite tasty, the atmosphere is comfortable, and you're sure to discover that this restaurant lives up to its name, which is Italian for "plenty."

Abbondanza is a choice place to have dinner for two or a crowd. There is a full bar and the menu selections are more reasonably priced than some other Italian restaurants in town. Do bring your appetite—the portions are huge.

Abbondanza is open daily for lunch and dinner. No reservations are accepted.

Antonia's Restaurant
615 Duval Street
Key West, FL
(305) 294–6565
$$, Italian

Stroll by this Northern Italian restaurant on any afternoon, and you can watch pasta in the making along the marble window-front table. Stringy mozzarella also is made fresh on-premises. Established in 1979 and named for owner Antonia Berto, Antonia's burned to the ground 16 years later as a result of arson, along with a string of neighboring buildings. After 10 months, the restaurant reopened, displaying the same elegant wood floors and walls, upholstered benches, candlelit tables, recessed lighting, and small wood bar. Equally spectacular is Antonia's food prepared by Berto's husband, chef Phillip Smith—particularly the grilled fillet of beef tenderloin Rossini, served with mushrooms, brandy, and cream; the pan-seared yellowtail braised with watercress, endive, radicchio, and white wine; and the linguine Cousteau with a variety of shellfish and fresh tomatoes.

Virtually all the restaurant's veal dishes are popular, and even with all these spectacular entrees, patrons simply cannot pass up the homemade desserts. Tiramisu features layers of lady fingers dipped in espresso, filled with rich mascarpone cheese sauce, and topped with grated dark Belgian chocolate. Antonia's flourless chocolate-and-walnut tart is topped with warm chocolate sauce and whipped cream, and Tuscany's well-known grandmother's torte is a baked pastry cream served with toasted almonds. Crème brûlée is always a taste tempter, and this dessert's specials are made with chocolate and mocha. *Bellisimo!*

Antonia's maintains an extensive Northern Italian and American wine list. The restaurant is open daily for dinner only.

Banana Cafe
1211 Duval Street
Key West, FL
(305) 294–7227
$$$, French

Settle into this quiet open-air bistro, and choose from more than 40 breakfast and lunch crepes. The exterior of Banana Cafe resembles a quaint Caribbean cottage; the airy interior says "French bistro," with pinkish pine wood, artistic black-and-white photography, ceiling fans, and a small piano bar. Dining also is offered on the front balcony or along the side on a wood deck shaded by large tropical trees.

Thin, pancake-like crepes are stuffed with veggies, fish, and meat, and they are designated either sweet or savory. The most desirable crepe among patrons is the ratatouille, overflowing with sautéed eggplant, zucchini, peppers, extra-virgin olive oil, and garlic and topped with a fried egg sunny-side up. Also on the menu are salads, sandwiches, and daily specials.

Dinner also is served throughout the winter season. Meals are complemented by soft drinks, beer, and a nice selection of wines. Reservations are recommended, particularly on weekends. Live jazz is offered here on Thursday nights.

Cafe des Artistes
1007 Simonton Street
Key West, FL
(305) 294–7100
$$$$, French

This enduring tropical French establishment has won awards and accolades from *Gourmet*, *Bon Appetit* and *Wine Spectator* magazines, and the recognition is well-deserved. At Cafe des Artistes, Chef Andrew Berman's creativity culminates in such delicacies as Lobster with Passion Fruit Sauce and Raspberry Duck, and Shrimp in Pumpkin Broth. One of his finest treasures is Yellowtail Atocha, snapper sautéed in tarragon butter with shrimp and scallops. Specials are available nightly.

Each of two dining rooms has a distinctive character. Exquisite as the food, the decor at Cafe des Artistes features wainscoting, lace curtains, subdued lighting, and local acrylic, watercolor, and oil paintings. Fresh flowers decorate every table.

Dining is available seasonally on the outdoor patio. This establishment's extensive wine list features some of the best of the vineyards of France and California. Cafe des Artistes is open every day for dinner. Reservations are recommended.

Finnegan's Wake Irish Pub & Eatery
320 Grinnell Street
Key West, FL
(305) 293–0222
www.keywestirish.com
$, Irish

No need to kiss the Blarney stone at Finnegan's Wake, whose staff guarantees this is one wake you won't want to miss. This Irish pub and eatery sails your spirit across the Big Pond, as you toast the legend of the miraculous resurrection of mythical Tim Finnegan. Try authentic Irish fare: bangers and mash (sausages and mashed potatoes, to those of you not

Insiders' Tip

You will need to make dinner reservations during high season and holiday weekends. Our popular restaurants attract hungry crowds.

wearing the green), shepherd's pie, corned beef and cabbage, Mrs. Finnegan's Irish Stew, potato pancakes, or the Dublin Pot Pie. The lip-smacking lovely Irish potato-leek soup, a house specialty, is thick and chunky and served with grated cheddar, chopped scallions, and bacon. And be sure to try a black and tan—half Guinness, half lager—or a pint of bottled cider.

Like any good Irish wake, the merriment goes on all day and into the wee hours. Finnegan's Wake is open from lunchtime until 4 A.M. (serving dinner until 10:30 P.M., bar menu until 3 A.M.). Patio dining is available. Reservations will be honored at Finnegan's Wake but usually are not necessary. Wednesday through Saturday enjoy live Irish music.

La Trattoria
524 Duval Street
Key West, FL
(305) 296–1075
www.latrattoriakeywest.com
$$, Italian

This upscale SoHo-style New York bistro rates as a Key West treasure. A romantic taste of old Italy favored by locals, visitors, and Keys residents from as far away as Key Largo, La Trattoria redefines the traditional pasta, veal, chicken, lamb, and seafood dishes of the mother country. The sophisticated decor—linen cloths top intimate tables encircled with black lacquer-style chairs—belies the fact that you are a stone's throw from the sidewalks of busy Duval Street.

Try Agnello alla Grigflia (lamb with rosemary) or Spaghetti alla Pescat, topped with a bounty of seafood. Penne all Arabbiata delivers a bit of a bite, and Rigatoni al Ragù does not disappoint. The insalata mista will transport your taste buds to Venice for sure. And don't forget dessert—the tiramisu is to die for here. La Trattoria serves dinner nightly.

Reservations are suggested, especially in high season. After dinner, retire to Virgilio's, the charming little cocktail lounge with live music just around the corner.

Mangia Mangia
900 Southard Street
(305) 294-2469
Key West, FL
www.mangia-mangia.com
$$, Italian

Off the main drag but definitely on the right track is the pasta lovers' nirvana, Mangia Mangia. Meaning "eat, eat" in Italian, Mangia Mangia bestows a passel of homemade fresh pasta (made daily on the premises) and finely seasoned sauces that would excite even Marco Polo's palate. The paneled interior of the storefront trattoria at the corner of Southard and Margaret Streets showcases Caribbean-style artwork.

The chefs work their macaroni magic in plain view. You can always order the basic sauces—marinara, Alfredo, pesto, and seafood—but, for something out of the ordinary, try picadillo pasta (black bean pasta shells with a Cuban-inspired sauce). The daily specials will prove difficult to pass up.

Mangia Mangia does not allow smoking inside the air-conditioned restaurant. Diners wishing to smoke may sit in a brick patio area outside, where the tables are surrounded by palm trees. Mangia Mangia serves dinner daily. The restaurant does not take reservations; plan to arrive before 7 P.M. to avoid a wait. You can enjoy selections from Mangia Mangia's extensive wine list. Beer also is served.

Martin's Cafe Restaurant
416 Appleroth Lane
Key West, FL
(305) 296-1183
www.keywest.com/themenu/martins
$$, German

Put on your lederhosen, for Martin's treats you to German cuisine with an island flair. Tucked a few steps off the 500 block of Duval Street on Applerouth Lane, Martin's expansive menu all but guarantees *guten appetit*. Begin with Pilze a la Martin, toasted bread rounds topped with sautéed mushrooms and herb garlic butter. You'll find classic German dishes such as pepper steak, sauerbraten with spaetzle and red cabbage, and Wiener schnitzel, but Martin's also prepares island seafood creations *a la deutsch*. Grouper Dijon arrives on a bed of champagne kraut with rosemary potatoes. Sea Scallops Wunderbar is baked with spinach encased in puff pastry and is served with a Riesling sauce. Choose from a large selection of fine German wines and beers.

Martin's Cafe Restaurant serves dinner nightly and offers Sunday brunch. Reservations are suggested.

The Far East

Benihana Japanese Steaks and Seafood
3591 S. Roosevelt Boulevard
Key West, FL
(305) 294-6400
www.marthas-benihana.com
$$$, Japanese

If ever you have been to Benihana, you know that this is not the place for a quiet, romantic evening at a corner table.

Rather, tepan chefs entertain as many as eight guests per table with skillful cooking on grill-like tables and salt-and-pepper sideshows. Tepan training at Benihana takes three to six months, depending upon each chef's ability to "cook a table." Chefs come from a variety of backgrounds and offer different antics. Some are, like Benihana founder Rocky Aoki, more entertaining than others. This particular establishment does not offer sushi. Privately owned, it features the standard beef and seafood combination dinners amid original Japanese artwork and oceanfront views. The snapper at Benihana is locally caught (calamari, shrimp, lobster, and scallops are imported).

Dinner is served nightly.

Dim Sum
613 Duval Street
Key West, FL
(305) 294–6230
www.wedeliverkeywest.com/dim
$$, Chinese

Head through an alley off Duval Street, and you will be pleasantly surprised by the interior architecture of Dim Sum: all white walls with etched-wood window trims, sconces dimly aglow, Bali batik tables with candles and fresh flowers, and framed photographs that recount the owner's travels to Asia. Dim Sum's a la carte menu carries these travels into the tummy with specialties such as Duck in Chinese Black Bean Sauce, whole-fried yellowtail snapper and coconut shrimp in red curry sauce. The signature dish here is Dragon Hot Noodles, stir-fried noodles combined with vegetables and fish and spiced with a fiery pepper sauce. Daily specials may include grilled salmon in red curry sauce or fish tempura over mixed greens with sliced avocado and tomato with a miso mustard sauce.

Open daily for dinner only, Dim Sum serves beer and wine. Off-street parking is available behind the building. Reservations are recommended during the high season.

Dynasty Chinese Restaurant
918 Duval Street
Key West, FL
(305) 294–2943
$, Chinese

Red, black, and white colors dominate the interior of this traditional Szechwan and Cantonese restaurant. One of four establishments throughout the country owned by the Chow family of Hong Kong, Dynasty has been serving Key West since 1990. Spicy dishes such as Kung Pao Chicken and Szechwan Shrimp, Chicken, and Lobster are most in demand. More mild offerings include Honey-garlic Chicken and Peking Duck served with thin pancakes for wrapping and sauces for dipping. Daily combination specials, such as Grouper Fillet with Szechwan Sauce, come with steamed rice and vegetables, a choice of soup, and an egg roll.

Outdoor dining is offered on a patio surrounded by plants and palms, and music from the Orient sounds from speakers. Dynasty serves beer and wine and is open nightly for dinner. Reservations are recommended.

Kyushu Japanese Restaurant
921 Truman Avenue
Key West, FL
(305) 294–2995
$$, Japanese

Take off your shoes! Kyushu provides an authentic Japanese dining experience in tatami rooms, or individual low-to-the-ground tables and benches secluded by bamboo screens. As a courtesy, your Asian waitress removes her slippers in unison with you. The open entranceway at Kyushu takes patrons out of Key West and into an exotic garden with a bridged pond and views of royal poinciana trees. Hand-painted Japanese sheets stretch from floor to ceiling, and saltwater aquariums, fresh flowers, and Japanese paintings of geisha women are found throughout. Crepe-paper box lights add soft lighting.

The menu includes sashimi, sushi rolls, tempura, katsu, and stir-fry and teriyaki dishes. An extensive selection of sushi—including eel, conch, octopus, yellowtail, tuna, and snapper—is most popular, and patrons are offered the option of dining at the informal sushi bar.

The full-service bar features sake and plum wine, along with Japanese beers such as Sapporo, Kirin, and Asahi. Off-street parking is available at the restaurant lot on Packer Street. Reservations are recommended during high season; Kyushu is open for lunch Monday through Saturday and for dinner seven nights a week.

Origami Japanese Restaurant
1075 Duval Street
Key West, FL
(305) 294–0092
$$, Japanese

The stark, white decor of Origami provides a backdrop for the brightly colored tropical fish adorning the walls. And like the Japanese art of folding paper into decorative or representational forms—origami—the restaurant fashions fresh, local seafood into exquisite sushi and sashimi. Rumor has it that the dragon roll must not be missed. Origami also offers traditional Japanese cuisine, such as teriyaki, chicken katsu, steak yakiniku, and tempura.

Sit at the cafe-style tables or at the sushi bar and watch the masters at work. Origami is situated in Duval Square. Free parking is available in the adjoining lot off Simonton Street. Origami is open for dinner every day except Sunday. From December through May it is open for lunch, too. Smoking is not permitted inside, but smokers may sit in Origami's lovely outdoor seating area. Beer, wine, and sake are served. Reservations are suggested in high season.

Siam House
829 Simonton Street
Key West, FL
(305) 292–0302
www.wedeliverkeywest.com
$$, Thai

Owner Suriya Siripant of Bangkok has combined imported sculptures, woodwork, and paintings from Thailand with

Insiders' Tip
If you're in the mood for take-out, check the menus posted on www.wedeliverkeywest.com.

genuine Thai food. His luncheon buffet, offered along with menu fare each day but Sunday, features a selection of six items including curry and sautéed beef, chicken, and pork, noodles, and fried rice. Specialties such as curry lobster and roast duck are offered in a variety of spice levels.

Reservations at Siam House are recommended during high season. The restaurant serves beer and wine. Siam House is open for dinner nightly.

Thai Cuisine
513 Greene Street
Key West, FL
(305) 294–9424
$, Thai

Screaming banana-yellow walls bathe the tiny interior of Thai Cuisine with a cheerful glow. And the salubrious cuisine of Thailand tingles your palate with the afterglow of Thai curries. Thai curry is a fiery Southeast Asian stew that's not even a kissing cousin to the bland Indian-style powder we Americans associate with the moniker. Thai curry is actually a cooking method, not an ingredient. Together with spices, herbs, and aromatic vegetables, hot chile peppers are ground into a dry paste that infuses Thai curries with heat and passion. At the same time, coconut milk, fish sauce, sugar, and kaffir lime leaves—ubiquitous to every variation of Thai red and green curry—confuse the palate with a riot of sweet and sour sensory stimuli.

For another traditional delight, try Pad Thai, spicy rice noodles sautéed with shrimp, chicken, egg, ground peanuts, scallions, and bean sprouts. The portions are enormous. Enjoy a selection of Thai and Japanese beers, house wines, plum wine, and sake. Outdoor seating is available in the evening. Thai Cuisine serves lunch Monday through Friday and is open for dinner every night. Take-out is available, and Thai Cuisine offers free delivery in Key West.

The Islands

Bahama Mama's Kitchen
324 Petronia Street
Key West, FL
(305) 294-3355
www.keywest.com/themenu/bahamamamas
$, Bahamian

If it's island food and atmosphere you seek, you can't get any more authentic than Bahama Mama's Kitchen. Owner Cory Sweeting is a fourth generation Bahamian on both sides. For a logo, he chose a drawing of his Grandma Sweeting wielding a wooden spoon (most of the recipes have come from her kitchen) and for location, he picked the Key West neighborhood known as Bahama Village.

The menu here is limited but tasty. Conch is the obvious seafood choice, but you'll also find grouper, shrimp, and red snapper. The lamb chops are blackened and the chicken is curried with ginger. Dinners come with two sides—choose from the likes of hushpuppies, plantains, collard greens, pigeon peas, and rice. You can even opt for a veggie platter that includes three sides, enough to appease an average appetite, for a reasonable $7.50.

Bahama Mama's serves breakfast most weekdays beginning at 9 A.M. Lunch and dinner are available from 11 A.M. to 1 A.M. Reservations are not necessary.

Coco Palms, Jamaican Me Hungry
300 Front Street
Key West, FL
(305) 296-0046
www.keywestfoods.com
$, Jamaican

Jerk cuisine appears on lots of Key West menus these days, but Coco Palms has the real thing—authentic Jamaican-style jerk with just the right blend of flavors and seasonings. No wonder. Owner/chef Warren Lemard was born and raised in Montego Bay. He specializes in homemade island fare that includes blackened fish, jerk chicken and pork, and curried shrimp, lobster, chicken, and even goat. Wife Abby makes the desserts—yummy tropical ice creams and her signature rum cake.

Just like the island of Jamaica, Coco Palms is laid back and unpretentious. It's a family operation and you will be treated like just one more member. The restaurant can also be tough to spot. But if you stand on Front Street with your back to the Conch Train ticket booth and look up, you're sure to spot the sign on the second floor across the way.

Coco Palms is open daily for lunch and dinner. The restaurant does not have its own parking lot, but if you park your car at the Hilton garage a block away, your ticket will be validated for the time you are in the restaurant.

Paco's Hukilau
1990 N. Roosevelt Boulevard
Key West, FL
(305) 296-7277
www.keywest.com/themenu/pacoshukilau
$$, Hawaiian

Hukilau is Hawaiian for a feast consisting mainly of seafood. And that's exactly what you'll get here. Start with a frosty fruit daiquiri or a mai tai and a puu-puu platter for two—a tasty conglomeration of barbecued ribs, beef tips, chicken strips, tempura shrimp, potstickers, vegetables, and egg rolls you grill on your tabletop hibachi. But do save room for the main course. Hukilau features a mouthwatering selection of seafood—tuna steak, cracked conch, mahi-mahi, grouper, and coconut shrimp—prepared with a tropical twist. Prime rib, steaks, and Polynesian-style barbecued ribs are also on the menu.

After dinner, stick around for the entertainment. Coffee Butler, with his smoky voice and distinctive keyboarding style, always draws a crowd around the piano.

Florida lobster is among the perennial favorites at Keys' seafood markets and restaurants.

Seafood Markets and Specialty Foods

Here in the Florida Keys, we think our fish is pretty special. It's certainly the freshest—sometimes only minutes from line to linen. Its pedigree is elite; most species are not marketed outside South Florida. And the abounding variety of innovative culinary presentations is astounding. Visitors to the Florida Keys, accustomed back home to choosing among cod, halibut, haddock, swordfish or tuna, are often overwhelmed when confronted with the bountiful selections from our underwater treasure trove.

When you stop at one of our many seafood markets, you will undoubtedly meet the three royal families of our tropical waters: snapper, grouper, and dolphin. The famed yellowtail or the equally desirous mangrove or mutton snapper most often represents the moist, sweet snapper dynasty. The firm, mild-flavored grouper clan, members of the sea bass family, competes in popularity with the large-flaked and sweetly moist dolphin fish (not to be confused with the porpoise dolphin, which is a mammal).

You won't want to miss our Florida lobster, a delicacy any way you look at it (see Diving for Lobster in the Diving and Snorkeling chapter). And, if you have never tasted a stone crab claw, you are in for a treat (see the Close-up in this chapter).

To round out your palate, we have provided you with a rundown of delicatessens and shops selling specialty foods. If you're eating in tonight or tomorrow, you'll want to know what we know: the out-of-the-way shops that help you make Martha Stewart look like an also-ran.

We have listed our recommended seafood markets and specialty food shops by mile marker (MM) from the top of the Keys in Key Largo to Big Coppitt in the Lower Keys and Stock Island at the gateway to Key West. Key West businesses are listed in alphabetical order.

Most places remain open until at least 5 P.M., with the exception of bakeries, which usually open early and close in the early afternoon. During high season, December through April, many of these markets and stores extend their hours. The off-season often brings abbreviated hours, so you may want to call before you shop.

Upper Keys

Dockside Cakes Bakery & Deli
MM 103 Bayside
Key Largo, FL
(305) 451–7060

You won't lose any weight indulging here, but it's definitely worth it. All cakes, breads, pastries, muffins, and bagels are made on the premises, and they taste as good as they smell. Enjoy a potpourri of deli sandwiches or freshly brewed specialty coffees, too. Dockside Cakes also caters deli and breakfast platters.

The Fish House Restaurant
& Seafood Market
MM 102.4 Oceanside
Key Largo, FL
(305) 451–4665, (888) 451–4665
www.fishhouse.com

Primarily a seafood restaurant (see our Restaurants chapter), The Fish House also offers fresh catch of the day from their small seafood market so that you can be the chef of the day if you like. You'll find just-off-the-boat local favorites such as snapper, dolphin, and grouper, as well as other seasonally caught species.

Key Largo Fisheries
MM 99.5 Oceanside
1313 Ocean Bay Drive
Key Largo, FL
(305) 451–3782, (800) 432–4358

The family-run Key Largo Fisheries ships wholesale to hundreds of clients throughout the country and also offers retail sales at their Key Largo store and via overnight delivery. At Key Largo Fisheries, customers will find choice seafood, including snapper, grouper, shrimp, and, in season, Florida lobster and stone crab claws. Conch here is imported from the Bahamas and the Turks and Caicos Islands.

Remedy's Health Foods
MM 99.5 Oceanside
Key Largo, FL
(305) 451–2160

If your idea of a pick-me-up requires vitamins, herbs, and healthful foods, you'll find all this plus berries, dried fruit-and-nut mixes, and more at this health food store. The shop stocks food supplements, herb cheese, and protein supplements as well as a wide range of natural products for face and body—soaps, shampoos, conditioners, toothpaste, moisturizers, and face creams.

Chad's Deli & Bakery
MM 92.3 Bayside
Tavernier, FL
(305) 853–5566

Fresh, bright, and clean, Chad's offers a mouth-watering assortment of pastries and breads as well as custom sandwiches, salads, and soups. Coca-Cola memorabilia adorns the deli's walls. And judging from the volume of hungry locals popping in for a bite, Chad's special brand of chow satisfies the palate and keeps 'em coming back for more. Chad's closes at 3 P.M.

Sunshine Supermarket
MM 91.8 Oceanside
Tavernier, FL
(305) 852–7216

There isn't a Tavernier resident who doesn't know about the rotisserie chicken and

> ## Insiders' Tip
> Shucked oysters are plump and have a natural creamy color and clear liquid. There should be no more than 10 percent liquid, by weight, when shucked oysters are purchased in a container.

Cubano bread here. Family owned and operated, Sunshine Supermarket offers some tasty Cuban specialties as well: roast pork, ribs, yellow rice, and black beans and rice, all at reasonable prices. The pork is marinated in mojo sauce—a Cuban concoction of oil, vinegar, garlic, and other spices. It is available for chicken as well, upon request, and you can buy it by the bottle here.

The Garden Cafe
MM 86.7 Bayside at the Rain Barrel
Islamorada, FL
(305) 852–6499

For those locals long-addicted to Jose Palomino's famed vegetarian wraps at the Garden Gourmet in Marathon and for all visitors to the Keys, good news! Jose and wife Teddy Thompson have moved up the Keys to the Rain Barrel complex, where they now run The Garden Cafe. You'll love your veggies even more with the creative selection of salads, sandwiches, and wraps. And you'll find smoothies, fresh-squeezed juices, coffees, and ice teas as well.

Henry's Bakery & Gourmet Pizza Shop
MM 82.8 Oceanside
Islamorada, FL
(305) 664–4030

Ummmm. It is tough to pick out a pizza from Henry's—the choices are so unusual and palate pleasing. How about saltimbocca pizza? Or California Bird, a concoction of avocado, turkey, tomatoes, onions and mozzarella? Or Sublime Pie—I'm not kidding—shrimp or Florida lobster with roasted bell peppers and sundried tomatoes. Just in case pizza doesn't float your boat, pick from a large selection of salads, sandwiches, pastas, and soups. Eat in or take out. Free delivery is offered from mile marker 74 to mile marker 88 with a minimum order of $8.

Islamorada Restaurant and Bakery
MM 81.6 Bayside
Islamorada, FL
(305) 664–8363

The banner out front proclaims, "Best Buns in Town," and these oversize cinnamon rolls live up to the hype. Topped with cream-cheese icing, the buns are undoubtedly one of the local favorites. Also available are "gooey" or sticky buns, bagels, muffins, scones, and croissants. As you might imagine, this restaurant is a wildly popular Islamorada breakfast spot.

Islamorada Fish Company
MM 81.5 Bayside
Islamorada, FL
(305) 664–9271, (800) 258–2559
www.ifcstonecrab.com

This Islamorada legend operates out of a state-of-the-art, 5,000-square-foot facility in the totally renovated former Green Turtle Cannery building next door to the Islamorada Fish Company's original location. Ten thousand pounds of super-fresh fish and seafood find their way through the cutting rooms here, much displayed in a showy 31-foot display case. Everything is temperature controlled at Islamorada Fish Company, so the fish stays extra fresh. You can watch the cutters in action from a glassed-in cutting room.

You'll find all the local favorites, such as dolphin, Florida lobster, grouper, snapper, swordfish, stone crab claws, blue crab, Key West pink shrimp, and tuna. Conch here is offered either ground or in steaks and is flown in from the Turks and Caicos Islands. Sea and bay scallops come from Boston, oysters from Apalachicola, and the market carries clams and mussels. You can liven things up with their extensive selection of hot sauces.

If you prefer to dine in this charming seafood market ambiance, the store has a full-service restaurant (see our Restaurants chapter). Its fried grouper sandwich is an award winner.

The Trading Post
MM 81.5 Bayside
Islamorada, FL
(305) 664–2571

This is definitely Islamorada's "super" market. Here you'll discover super grocery selections, super-good deli items, a super meat market, super wine offerings, and super hours. The Trading Post is open 24 hours a day, seven days a week! The store also offers customized catering.

Middle Keys

Nichols Seafood of Conch Key Inc.
MM 63 Bayside
Conch Key, FL
(305) 289–0900

Nichols Seafood is a family affair. The Nichols family offers a large selection of fresh whole yellowtail, and fillets of grouper and dolphin are usually available. You'll also find lobsters and stone crab claws in season. For something different, try their smoked fish and seafood.

Duck Key Emporium
MM 61 Oceanside
794 Duck Key Drive,
Duck Key, FL
(305) 743–2299

Whether you want breakfast or sandwiches to take on your fishing charter or you need to stock up on provisions for your motor or sailing yacht anchored at neighboring Hawk's Cay Marina, the Duck Key Emporium delicatessen can fit the bill. Or, you can enjoy your repast outdoors: an expansive deck out back features umbrella-shaded tables with a tranquil view of the boat basin of Duck Key Marina. The deli features salads and home-cooked take-out dinner entrees, which change daily. Catering for private functions is also available.

Big Betsy is a sculptural reminder of that cagey crustacean, the Florida lobster, popular with divers and gourmets in the Keys. PHOTO: MARY MOCCIA

Captain's Three
MM 54 Oceanside
Coco Plum Drive
Marathon, FL
(305) 289–1131

Captain's Three maintains its own fishing, crabbing, and lobstering crews, guaranteeing the freshest catches of the day. The shop always has plenty of Key West shrimp. The staff will special-order oysters and cherrystone clams for you with advance notice. Be sure to try the homemade cocktail sauce. Captain's Three is closed May through August.

Island City Fish Market & Eatery
MM 53 Oceanside
Marathon, FL
(305) 743–9196, (888) 662–4822
www.floridalobster.com

Stop in at Island City for shrimp, stone crab, conch, and catch of the day, which you can buy whole or filleted. This is also the place to find fresh mussels and clams

in the Middle Keys. The market will ship a taste of our islands home for you if you like. Or, pop into the adjoining eatery for a fry-up—fish, oysters, clams, calamari, shrimp, even conch fritters. If you've had a successful day of fishing our waters, Island City Fish will cook your catch for you.

Produce Express
MM 52.5 Oceanside
Marathon, FL
(305) 743–9131

Sweet, ripe fruits and veggies at bargain prices distinguish Produce Express. You'll always find great tomatoes, melons, pineapples, eggplants, and sugar snap peas, as well as mixed baby greens and baby spinach, hydro-washed and ready to toss. Berry offerings are vine ripened and succulent. For those who like to "put up" their produce by canning or making jam, Produce Express offers specials on overly ripe veggies and fruits.

Food for Thought
MM 51 Bayside
Gulfside Village
Marathon, FL
(305) 743-3297

If you are in the market for health food products, you'll find them tucked in Food for Thought, a shop that is also half bookstore. It carries wheat-free, fat-free, and sugar-free staples, organic foods, vitamins, and homeopathic remedies. Pick up your favorite novel or magazine in the book section to treat your mind as well.

Marathon Liquors & Deli
MM 49.5 Oceanside
Marathon, FL
(305) 743-6350

Probably stocking the mostly wide-ranging selection of wines and spirits in the Middle Keys, Marathon Liquors & Deli tempts the palate as well. You can choose from an array of deli-sandwich features or prepared salads and entrée items, guaranteed to keep you out of the kitchen. You'll find fresh baked goods, gourmet food items, and a limited selection of fresh produce.

The Garden Gourmet
MM 49.5 Oceanside
Marathon Plaza
Marathon, FL
(305) 289-9425

The garden palate pleasers we've loved for years still wow tastebuds all over Marathon. Garden Gourmet—once owned by Teddy Thompson, who, along with her husband Jose Palomino, has opened the Garden Cafe up the Keys (see listing in this chapter)—is now under the direction of daughter Lynn Thompson. Lynn offers a wide range of cappuccinos, lattes, and flavored coffees as well as fresh tropical fruit smoothies and fresh-squeezed orange juice. You'll enjoy a healthy lunch with one of the enduringly popular garden rolls or tuna bites, or be a bit more decadent and indulge in a Cuban sandwich, a custom-created deli-style sandwich, or a Greek salad. Top it all off with yummy

pastries, which, along with a wide selection of fresh breads, are baked on the premises.

Lower Keys

Good Food Conspiracy
MM 30 Oceanside
Big Pine Key, FL
(305) 872-3945

A full assortment of health foods, homeopathic remedies, vitamins, organic poultry, and organically grown produce is offered at the Good Food Conspiracy. If you browse the shelves you'll find interesting specialty foods as well. Part of the Conspiracy is a juice and sandwich bar, which features an "outgoing menu" of healthy selections.

Monte's Restaurant and Fish Market
MM 25 Bayside
Summerland Key, FL
(305) 745-3731

Locals in the Lower Keys love Monte's for fresh seafood. Besides local snapper,

Insiders' Tip

Conch (pronounced "konk") meat is taken from the inside of the conch shell and served fried, in breaded fritters, as a ceviche (cold salad), or in chowder. Harvesting this mollusk in Florida waters is illegal. Therefore, most seafood markets import conch from the Turks and Caicos Islands. Firmer in texture than that from most other waters, conch from Turks and Caicos waters is some of the best in the world.

grouper, and dolphin, you can find imported Caicos conch (tenderized or ground steaks) and spicy Louisiana crayfish. Monte's will ship any of its inventory for you overnight or ice it for the rest of your journey up or down the Keys. You may eat a selection of Monte's seafood bounty in the adjoining restaurant if you wish (see our Restaurants chapter).

E Fish and Seafood
MM 22.5 Oceanside
Cudjoe Key, FL
(305) 745–3887

Shelves and shelves of marinades and seafood sauces will inspire you to try your culinary skills in a new creation when you stop in at E Fish. The very complete fish and seafood selection lets you choose between the usual Keys finfish (grouper, snapper, and dolphin) and golden crab, stone crab claws, lobsters, blue crabs, oysters, and mussels.

Nut House Corporation of Key West
MM 10 Bayside
Big Coppitt Key, FL
(305) 292–8688, (800) 240–5864
www.keywestnuthouse.com

You can really mix it up with the nuts at this little shop full of handcrafted baskets, kitschy kernels, and crunchy munchies. The Nut House will concoct gift creations for all your friends, pulling together any number of shop specialties. With a hand-painted parrot bowl or hand-carved wooden tray from Bali as a base, select your favorite nuts: Duval Crawl, Heming-

way Bar Mix, Wreckers Mix, or Key West Trail Mix, to name a few. Mix in some Key Lime Taffy, Keys Krunch, Flamingo Fruit Mix, and a few Fantasy Balls, and you've about got all the fruits and nuts on your Christmas list covered. The Nut House also offers bath and body gift baskets, candles, jewelry, glassware, and other interesting gift items.

Key West

The Blond Giraffe
629 Duval Street
Key West, FL
Key Lime Pie Factory
1209 Truman Avenue
(888) 432–6283
www.blondgiraffe.com

Key lime pie is indigenous to the Florida Keys. Ask any local and they'll be happy to tell you their favorite recipe. Rating right up there at the top of the list is the superb blend of flavors offered by the Key Lime Pie Factory and sold on Duval Street at the Blond Giraffe. The super-tart custard filling and sweet, fluffy meringue sit upon a sinfully rich yet delicate pastry crust, reminiscent of an English butter cookie. This recipe won the 1989 Key West Key Lime Pie Festival. You can order pies and have them shipped anywhere in the U.S. from Blond Giraffe's website.

Cafe Europa
1075 Duval Street
Duval Square
Key West, FL
(305) 294–3443
www.keywest.com/themenu/cafeeuropa

A little taste of the continent awaits you at this charming cafe, where you will most likely overhear several foreign languages from the customers seated at the outdoor tables. Offering mostly German fare and bakery products, Cafe Europa is open for breakfast, lunch, and dinner. But it will probably be the baked goods that lure you in. The smell of croissants, Linzer tortes, apple strudel, Danish pastries, cookies, and assorted breads fresh from the oven is sure to attract your attention any time of day. For foot-weary travelers, this cafe offers a bonus—free parking. The entrance to the lot is off Simonton Street.

Caribbean Deli
1220½ Simonton Street
Key West, FL
(305) 294–6312
www.keywest.com/themenu/caribdeli

Not only does this neighborhood deli have great food, it has that small-town, soda-fountain kind of feel that makes you just want to hang out for awhile. The deli, which is open only from 9 A.M. to 2 P.M. and 5 P.M. to 9 P.M., has daily lunch and dinner specials, but you can't go wrong with any of the regular menu items either. Try our favorites—the gumbo with jalapeño peppers and cornbread for the authentic "'Nawlins" muffuletta sandwich. The muffelata comes on a large Italian loaf roll piled with honey ham, mortadella, salami, provolone, and olive salad. The deli is the home of Mick's Spicy Caribe Beans. The beans, which are pickled and packaged by one of the deli's owners, are used in Bloody Marys at many Key West bars. Ask for a sample.

The Coffee Beanery
420 Front Street
Key West, FL
(305) 293–7662

If you wake up and smell the coffee, it just might be coming from the direction of Front Street. This attractive little shop, with limited indoor seating, is tucked just around the corner from Duval in the First Union Bank building. Here, you can buy your coffee by the cup or the pound. In addition to the hot, fresh-brewed kind, this shop stocks a variety of coffee beans with prices averaging around $13 a pound. These are whole bean coffees, but if you don't have your own grinder, the folks here will be glad to do the honors. On a hot day, the frozen coffees are big-sellers. Try the Caribbean iceberg—a delectable frozen concoction of coffee, toasted almonds, chocolate, and caramel syrup with cream and sugar.

The Coffee and Tea House of Key West
1218 Duval Street
Key West, FL
(305) 295–0788

One look at the broad porch and big, shaded yard will have you stepping inside for your coffee, then back out to sip it. Select from a plain old cup of joe or treat yourself to a latte, con leche, espresso, cappuccino, iced mocha, or fresh-brewed iced or hot tea in a variety of flavors. And how about a fresh-baked muffin, croissant, bagel, or slice of Key lime pie to accompany that beverage? Mmmm . . . now grab a seat outside. Sit a spell and watch the world go by.

Cole's Peace Artisan Breads
930-A Eaton Street
Key West, FL
(305) 292–6511
www.colespeace.com

This tiny little slice of Old World artistry could well be dubbed the bakery-that-the-people-saved. In June 1999, Cole's Peace announced that it would be closing due to lack of interest. Hah! In a town like Key West, a statement like that is considered a challenge and the orders began pouring in—at a steady enough rate, it seems, to keep this European-style bakery alive and thriving. Bread is the specialty here, but not just any bread, mind you. These are artisan loaves—each one based on an Old World recipe, handcrafted and baked

> ## Insiders' Tip
> The similar taste and texture of filleted and skinned snapper makes it difficult to differentiate between species. You will only know for sure what kind of snapper you are buying if you see the whole fish and identify characteristic markings.

Florida Stone Crab Claws

Now, you Yankees can brag about your blue crabs, and you West Coasters may boast of Dungeness. But here in the Florida Keys we crow about crab claws like none other—those of the Florida stone crabs.

The stone crabs, large nonswimming crabs found in deep holes and under rocks in the waters surrounding the Keys, have the unusual ability to release their legs or pincers if caught or when experiencing extreme changes in temperature. The separation always occurs at one of the joints to protect the crab from further injury. What is particularly unique about this situation is that the stone crab regenerates the severed appendage, a feat it can accomplish three or four times during its lifetime.

The stone crab's two claws serve distinct purposes: The largest claw, or crusher, is used to hold food and fight predators. The smaller claw, known as the ripper, acts as a scissors for cutting food.

The crabs are harvested commercially in the Florida Keys with baited traps. One or both of the crab's claws are removed (it greatly improves the crab's chances of survival if only one claw is taken). The forearm must measure at least 2¾ inches to harvest it legally. The live stone crabs must then be returned to the water, where in 18 months a new claw will have grown to legal size. It is illegal in the state of Florida to harvest whole stone crabs. They are one of our precious resources.

A stone crab claw has a hard, heavy porcelain-like shell with a black-tipped pincer. Seafood markets sell stone crab claws fully cooked. When cooked, the meat inside the shell is sweet and firm-textured. A mild sweet odor indicates freshness.

The shells must be cracked before serving. If you plan to eat your stone crab claws within an hour of purchase, have the seafood market crack them for you. It is not recommended that you crack the claws until you are ready to eat them. If you crack the claws yourself, lightly tap the crockery-like shells with a hammer, a small wooden mallet (available at seafood markets), or the back of a tablespoon. The shells also will crack like a fine china teacup if you hit one claw against the other. Pick the meat from the shell using a small cocktail fork and serve with mustard sauce (cold claws) or with clarified butter (re-steamed claws).

Stone crab claws are in season from October 15 until May 15. They do not freeze particularly well, but most seafood markets listed in this chapter will ship iced, fresh stone crab claws anywhere in the United States.

from scratch. All of the mixing, kneading, rising, shaping, and baking are done right on the premises, and every loaf, from sourdough to focaccia, is a work of art. The stock changes daily and with the season. You're apt to find pumpernickel in winter or whole grain laced with mangoes when the fruits are ripe. Housed in the old Salgado Brothers' Market at the corner of Eaton and Grinnell, the bakery is easy to find. The good smells wafting from the open doors are sure to lure you in.

The Cook's Bazaar
516 Fleming Street
Key West, FL
(305) 296–6656

Tucked amid an eclectic display of gourmet cooking accessories, barrels of exotic coffee beans from all over the world tickle your olfactory nerve in this compact shop. Unusual teas, candies, oils, chutneys, and mustards tempt the connoisseur, but the best find is Lighthouse Gourmet Flamingo and Palm Pasta—dried pasta shaped as pink flamingos and green palm trees. Only in the Keys!

Croissants de France
816 Duval Street
Key West, FL
(305) 294–2624
www.keywest.com/themenu/croissants defrance

If you repressed the calorie count, you could sit here all morning and evening munching French creations and watching the characters stroll Duval. Fifteen types of croissants—cream cheese, coconut, feta, spinach, and others—join forces with chocolate eclairs, Key lime mousse, and a family of rich pastries. A wide selection of crunchy French breads provides a conscience salvo. The adjoining cafe serves breakfast and lunch, but you can sip cappuccino from the espresso bar anytime.

Damn Good Food To-Go
700 Front Street
Key West, FL
(305) 294–0011

It's 4 A.M. The bars on Duval Street just called it quits, but your appetite won't. Where can you go for a bite to eat . . . or better yet have that bite delivered right to your door? Damn Good Food To-Go, that's where. This always-open, never closed, eat-in, take-it-out, have-it-come-to-you emporium has everything you need to appease your late-night munchies. You can get breakfast from midnight to 11 A.M., plus hot or cold sandwiches, soups, salads, burgers, dogs, and rotisserie chicken the rest of the time. You can even satisfy your sweet tooth with a slice of New York–style cheesecake or a wedge of chocolate suicide layer cake. It's all good and all prepared fresh from recipes the owners have collected across the country. Delivery is free to Old Town, but you'll need to spend at least $15 minimum for a free delivery to New Town.

Fausto's Food Palace
522 Fleming Street
Key West, FL
(305) 296–5663
1105 White Street
Key West, FL
(305) 294–5221
www.keywest.com/themenu/faustos

"Not just a grocery, a social center" reads the slogan in the ads for this gourmet food emporium, which has been serving Key West since 1926. The Fleming Street site is its largest and oldest. Here, in addition to the usual bread, milk, produce, canned goods, and kitchen staples, you will find fresh local seafood, premium meats and poultry, and more than 700 varieties of wine as well as Beluga caviar, pates, rare cheeses, and desserts. A sushi chef is on duty every day and party platters are available with as little as one-hour's notice. The deli counter is especially busy at noontime when the folks who work downtown line up for their daily ration of hot soup, fresh-made sandwiches, and specials like homemade meatloaf and mashed potatoes, Cuban pork, or black beans and rice. The White Street site is more like a neighborhood grocery, with a smaller deli counter and a more limited selection of produce, bread, frozen foods, and canned goods.

Felice, Italian Gourmet
1101 Truman Avenue
Key West, FL
(305) 296–1886

If you want to feel as though you are in a fine food store in Italy, don't miss this delight! The charming corner building is large, airy, and reminiscent of the corner groceries you might find in Venice, Florence, or Rome. Your senses alert you immediately as to what your taste buds are about to experience. Selections include sandwiches (served on a custom-made "Felice" hoagie), homemade salads, soups, hot pasta or meat entrees, and desserts. You can also buy pizza by the slice—the real Italian kind with thin crust and more cheese than tomato sauce—imported cold meats, cheeses, and desserts. In true trattoria style, Felice offers daily specials, too. The folks here will also cater a party or prepare a yummy gift basket to your specifications.

5 Brothers
930 Southard Street
Key West, FL
(305) 296–5205

If you're headed downtown along Southard Street any weekday morning between 7:30 and 8, expect to encounter a traffic jam at the corner of Grinnell Street. It's just the locals pulling over to pick up their "fix" at 5 Brothers. This is where Key West goes for bucchi, that tiny cup of industrial-strength Cuban coffee that satisfies your caffeine habit with a single swig and gets your juices flowing. This tiny corner grocery also makes a mean Cuban mix—that's a combination ham/pork/salami/swiss/lettuce/pickle sandwich served on Cuban bread—and great conch chowder (Fridays only). For you early birds, 5 Brothers opens at 6 A.M. (closed Sundays).

Flamingo Crossing
1107 Duval Street
Key West, FL
(305) 296–6124

A favorite with locals and visitors alike, Flamingo Crossing is the place to pause for refreshment as you make your way up and down Duval. Fresh homemade ice cream is the business here, and it's the closest thing to Italian gelato this side of the Mediterranean. You can choose from such flavors as Cuban coffee, raspberry cappuccino, coconut, piña colada, Key lime, passion fruit, or green tea, among others. Or try the ice cream—called guanabana/sour sop—two names for the same tasty, delicate fruit. Flamingo Crossing also makes its own sorbet and yogurt. If you're just in the mood for a thirst quencher, try a Key limeade. This tangy concoction will gear you up for a walk all the way from the Gulf to the Atlantic.

Flora & Flipp on Fleming
811 Fleming Street
Key West, FL
(305) 296–1050

Don't be fooled by appearances. This unassuming little neighborhood deli attracts everyone from the movers and shakers of Key West to tourists who just happen on it. Why? Because the folks at Flora and Flipp really know how to make a sandwich. There's a special concoction on the menu each day, but you can enjoy a perennial favorite, the Very Veggie, anytime. The sandwich has avocado, tomato, leaf lettuce, daikon, watercress, beets, and red onion with tamari dressing on Cuban bread; it's presented like a gift—wrapped in floral wrapping paper and topped with a candy kiss. To give your repast the respect it deserves, walk one block up Fleming toward Duval to the brick patio garden beside the pale pink Monroe County Public Library and sit on a park bench under the palms.

Goldman's Bagel Deli
2796 N. Roosevelt Boulevard
Overseas Market
Key West, FL
(305) 294-3354
www.keywest.com/themenu/goldmans

If not for the palm trees outside the door of this full-service restaurant/deli in the Overseas Market, you'd swear you just walked in from the streets of New York or Chicago. Here, the hot corned beef and pastrami sandwiches are sliced thin and piled high in traditional deli style, the bagels are baked fresh daily and the cans of Dr. Brown's black cherry and cream sodas are icy cold. You can carry out such delicacies as chopped liver, potato knishes, smoked whitefish, and kosher franks, along with the bagels and an array of flavored cream cheeses sold by the pound. Try our favorite—the everything bagel "schmeered" with smoked-salmon cream cheese. Breakfast and lunch are served at tables along one side and at the counter. Deli platters and catering are also available.

Grand Vin
1107 Duval Street
Key West, FL
(305) 296-1020

When you find that your feet can't possibly carry you to one more T-shirt shop or gallery along upper Duval, step into Grand Vin for a bit of chat and a chance to sample from the best selection of wines in the Florida Keys. Grab a seat at the bar or on the veranda overlooking Duval Street and let master sommelier Sean McConnell help you select from his daily menu of wines by the glass or full bottles (no corkage fee). If a particular wine, port, or champagne, suits your fancy, you can take it home by the bottle or the case.

Heavenly Ham
925 Toppino Drive
Key West, FL
(305) 292-6444
www.keywest.com/themenu/ham

Off North Roosevelt just past Searstown and First State Bank, Heavenly Ham has a misleading name. Inside the unimposing exterior lies a store that looks just the way you would love your pantry to look. Exotic breads, crackers, pasta, platters, gift tins, gourmet vinegars, sauces of all kinds, and baked goods fill this airy country store. More than 60 kinds of whole-bean coffees fill your senses with their aroma. And then there are the meats: whole hams, rib eye, filet mignon, turkey, and roast beef are among the choices. Luckily, Heavenly Ham does double time as a deli. Let these folks prepare a platter full of appetizers, a whole country dinner, or just a box lunch order for you. You'll be glad you did.

Independent Fisheries
6475-F Second Street
Stock Island, FL
(305) 292-7785

This wholesale fish and seafood operation maintains a small retail counter in the warehouse area of Stock Island. You'll find a selection of fresh locally caught fish, Key West shrimp, stone crab claws, and Florida lobster tails.

Java Lounge
622 Green Street
Key West, FL
(305) 296-7877

Serving terrific roasted coffee, fresh juices, baked goodies, teas, and granitas, Java Lounge is a great place for lunches that are not your run of the mill. With its true coffeehouse ambience Java Lounge has won numerous awards from the National Academy of Restaurant Evaluation as the Best Coffee in Key West.

Key West Candy Company
810 Duval Street
Key West, FL
(305) 293–8508

Become a kid again—or become your kid's sweet-tooth fairy—with a visit to this old-fashioned candy store. All those wonderful little candies of every shape, size, and color sit in covered bins just waiting for copious consumption. Make your selection from chocolates to Gummi Bears to Jelly-Bellies and beyond. Sold by the piece or the pound, these treats will take you back in time. Key West Candy Company will ship anywhere in the United States, so your friends and family back home can nourish their sweet teeth as well.

Key West Key Lime Pie Company
701 Caroline Street
Key West, FL
(305) 294–6567

Key lime pie, a Florida Keys tradition, is the primary business at this Old Town company, established in 1985. Each handmade, 9-inch pie (also sold by the slice) is frozen, literally melting in your mouth, bite by bite. The company will ship the pies anywhere in the continental United States overnight or provide you with a frozen travel pack, so you can take a pie on the road with you or back home by airplane. If a fork isn't your style, how about Key lime pie on a stick, dipped in

dark chocolate? Messy to eat, but oh-so-yummy.

Key West Key Lime Shoppe
200 Elizabeth Street
Key West, FL
(305) 296–0806, (800) 376–0806

Key lime yourself into a state of ecstasy at this little store on the corner of Elizabeth and Greene Streets. Everything inside is made with Key lime juice, including oils, cookies, candy kisses, salad dressings, juice concentrate, pie filling, and sweets of all sorts. You'll also find Key lime soaps and lotions here. And be sure to look outside for the authentic Key lime tree—the source of all this pleasure and a rarity these days in the Florida Keys.

La Dichosa Bakery
1206 White Street
Key West, FL
(305) 296–6188

If you've had anything on Cuban bread anywhere in Key West, chances are that bread came from this bakery. La Dichosa supplies just about all of Key West's restaurants with these long loaves of flat, flavorful, crusty bread. But that's not all you'll find here. The cases are filled with all kinds of baked goodies—cupcakes, eclairs, napoleons, and chocolate chip cookies so buttery rich they crumble at the touch. La Dichosa also makes wedding cakes. You can even grab a con leche or bucchi to complement your sweet treat. Sit inside or take it to go.

Mattheessen and Magilner's Candy Kitchen
419 Duval Street
Key West, FL
(305) 296–8014

No tourist destination is complete without at least one fudge shop. In Key West, you'll find more than your fill of this melt-in-your-mouth confection at this Duval Street emporium. Traditional chocolate is always a favorite, of course, but the Key lime and maple/pecan varieties are equally tasty and sinful. If you happen to miss this shop as you wend your way down Duval toward the Gulf, do not despair. There's a second, albeit slightly smaller, Mattheessen's inside Clinton Square Market, 291 Front St., near Mallory Square. The fudge is just as rich and creamy there.

Millie's Sundries
425 Front Street
Key West, FL
(305) 294-6877

A little bit of merry olde England comes to Key West at Millie's Sundries. As you might have guessed, the owner is a transplant from the United Kingdom. In addition to the usual convenience store stock of necessities like M&Ms, cigarettes and aspirin, you'll find an amazing array of products from the other side of the Pond—pork pies, steak and kidney pies, shortbread, biscuits, bangers, Cadbury Fingers, crisps (we know them as potato chips), toffee and plum puddings. Here, too, are traditional Christmas crackers—not the edible variety, but the pull-apart kind filled with tiny surprises that are used to decorate English holiday tables. Millie's is set back from the street a bit but easy to spot. Just look for the Union Jack.

Natural Food Market
107 Simonton Street
Key West, FL
(305) 296-3800

This bright, airy market is loaded with organically grown produce, vitamins, herbs, nutritional supplements and personal care products aimed at helping you live a healthier lifestyle. Shop for gourmet sandwiches, salads, and smoothies at the deli and browse the racks in the front of the store for books and magazines devoted to healthy eating and homeopathic remedies. This Natural Food Market is one of three in South Florida. The others are on the mainland in south Miami-Dade County and on South Beach in Miami Beach.

Peppers of Key West
602 Greene Street
Key West, FL
(305) 295-9333, (800) 597-2823
www.peppersofkeywest.com

Peppers, where chili peppers are the name of the game, bills itself as "the hottest spot on the island." More than 300 varieties of hot sauces already grace the shelves and more arrive from all over every day. Peppers always has a basket of chips and a few open bottles at the front counter so you can have a taste, if you dare. In addition, the folks here will open any bottle in the store if you ask for a sample. Try our favorite—Tahiti Joe's Garlic Hot Sauce—or get a bottle of the bestselling Ring of Fire Hot Sauce. You'll find Key West S.O.B. hot sauces here as well as oils, vinegars, and prepared sauces like pad Thai and sweet-and-sour ginger. Chili pepper memorabilia of all kinds decorate this upbeat shop—even Christmas lights! And be sure to look around the neighborhood for the chili pepper car. It belongs to one of the owners and can usually be found parked near the shop.

Pierogi Market Place
706 White Street
Key West, FL
(305) 292-0464

You'd expect to find a Cuban or Caribbean deli this far south, but a Polish market? At first glance, this tiny grocery seems a bit out of place in the southernmost city until you stop to consider that the second largest ethnic group in Key West these days hails from Eastern Europe. For the many Poles, Czechs, and Romanians who, like the owner of this shop, have come to Key West for jobs in the tourist industry, the Pierogi Market Place is a welcome slice of home. The shelves are brimming with the foods they remember from childhood—black sausage, Crakovia pickles, green tomato salad, herring, and, of course, pierogi—those tasty little dumplings filled with potato, cheese, meat or fruit. There's also a selection of Polish films, books, magazines, and candy.

Rusty Anchor Fisheries
5510 Third Avenue
Stock Island, FL
(305) 296–2893

Where's the fish? A little Insider help is needed to negotiate for fish at this place, known to locals as having the freshest at the best prices. The fish market is directly behind Rusty Anchor Restaurant, which is on Fifth Avenue (see our Restaurants chapter), although no sign on Third Avenue indicates the fishmonger's presence. Your safest bet is to enter the restaurant and look for brown double doors at the far end of the room. Exit through these portals, and you will find yourself outside, directly in front of a fish-cleaning building. Find out about the catch of the day, and then it's "Let's make a deal!" Rusty Anchor is known for some of the best prices on jumbo stone crab claws and colossal shrimp ("under 15s"). Alternately, but not as much fun, you can call and get the daily fish report by telephone.

Sippin' Coffee House
424 Eaton Street
Key West, FL
(305) 293–0555

Long before Internet cafes became popular, Sippin' had already opened its doors on Eaton Street with an offer many Key Westers could not refuse: sip a cup of coffee while checking e-mail or chatting online. And although more and more locals have their own Internet connections these days, they still come to Sippin' for coffee, conversation, and pastries. This is no slick little Starbucks clone. This is a true, blue coffeehouse, Key West style. The couches are a little bit lumpy, the tables sometimes wobble, and the chairs don't always match. But the coffee is hot, the muffins are fresh, and you're welcome to sit as long as you like. If you didn't bring a book, don't worry. There are books and magazines aplenty to choose from, plus

> ### Insiders' Tip
> The skin of the grouper is tough, so the fish does not lend itself to cooking whole or as an unskinned fillet. The most important factor to note when buying grouper is the size of the natural fillet. As the fish grows older and larger, its flesh may get tougher and less flavorful. Giants such as the Warsaw grouper (300 to 750 pounds) usually end up as chowder. Those 25 to 50 pounds are best cut up in fingers and fried. Look for grouper in the 2- to 20- pound range for all other preparations.

you and your friends can even grab one of the many board games available here and while away an afternoon.

Stock Island Lobster Co.
6639 Maloney Avenue
Stock Island, FL
(305) 296–5844

This wholesale fishery and lobstering operation doesn't have a showcase retail shop, but it will sell to the general public. Call for prices and availability of the catch of the day (sold as whole fish only), stone crab claws, and whole Florida lobsters in season.

Sugar Apple Natural Foods
917 Simonton Street
Key West, FL
(305) 292–0043

A longtime favorite of health-conscious Key Westers, Sugar Apple stocks organic and hard-to-find groceries, vitamins, beauty aids, homeopathic remedies, books, and herbs. A juice bar and deli serve up sandwiches, smoothies, specials, and teas. Therapeutic ball chimes are among the most popular items sold here.

Waterfront Market
201 William Street
Key West, FL
(305) 296–0778
www.keywest.com/themenu/waterfront
market

The serious cooking aficionado and the robust eater will have a ball in this market, now located on the Caroline Street side of the Historic Keywest Seaport. Browsing the shelves reminds us of perusing an international library. All the weird, difficult-to-find ingredients for Japanese, Thai, Chinese, or even Middle Eastern dishes dress the shelves here, often scrutinized by Key West's top professional chefs. A dried-bean emporium showcases bins of baby limas, black beans, pintos, and even black-eyed peas. A similar rice case offers sushi rice, hard red, winter wheat, and bulgur (and those are just the ones we recognize).

Besides a complete fish market, bakery, deli, coffee-bean center, and produce counter, this market stocks some of the best bottled fat-free dressings and marinades we've found anywhere, even off the Rock. Be sure to stop at the juice bar to drink your vitamins before you leave.

Nightlife

In the Florida Keys, what to do after our famous sunsets is a choice as individualistic as our residents and visitors.

But for those revelers who like to party until the wee hours, we take you on a club crawl, tavern tromp, saloon slog—call it what you like. Come promenade our pubs, bars, and nightclubs from Key Largo to Key West, our southernmost city where a night on the town redefines the cliché.

As a general rule, bars are open later the farther down in the Keys you go, with many establishments in Key West open until 4 A.M. Taverns and pubs in the Upper and Middle Keys are more likely to close between midnight and 2 A.M.

We encourage you to have fun and enjoy our casual Keys pubs, but keep in mind that the DUI limit here is .08, less than some other states. Remember, too, that driving-under-the-influence laws apply to all vehicles—scooters and bikes included. So if you drink, don't drive. Or pedal. Take a cab or take along a designated driver.

You'll find the majority of these places open seven nights a week. Exceptions are noted. Remember, however, that hours and entertainment may vary depending on the season or whim of the owners. To avoid disappointment, it is always best to phone ahead.

Upper Keys

Caribbean Club
MM 104 Bayside
Key Largo, FL
(305) 451–9970

Bogie and Bacall discovered each other at the Caribbean Club in the 1948 film classic *Key Largo*. What you'll find today is a dark, brooding bar where the barely visible walls are loaded with movie memorabilia. Caribbean Club offers live music Friday, Saturday, and Sunday; it's open every night. Designated drivers receive free soft drinks.

Breezer's Tiki Bar
MM 103.8 Bayside
Marriott Key Largo Bay Beach Resort
Key Largo, FL
(305) 453–0000
www.marriottkeylargo.com

Breezer's is an elegant, elevated gazebo-sheltered bar overlooking the showy property and wondrous waters of the Marriott Key Largo Bay Beach Resort. This fantasy island setting provides the perfect backdrop for the accompanying live island-style music on Fridays and Saturdays. Having a drink here is soothing to the soul.

Coconuts Restaurant & Lounge
MM 100 Oceanside
Marina del Mar Resort & Marina
528 Caribbean Drive
Key Largo, FL
(305) 453–9794
www.coconutsrestaurant.com

A perennial nightclub favorite with a percolating dance floor, Coconuts has theme nights that keep 'em coming: Monday, disco night; Tuesday, blues; Wednesday, ladies' night, with free drinks to all females from 9 to 11 P.M.; Thursday, Friday, and Saturday, live top-40 dance bands; and Sunday, karaoke. See our Restaurants chapter for dining options here.

Holiday Inn Key Largo
MM 100 Oceanside
Key Largo, FL
(305) 451–2121
www.holidayinnkeylargo.com

Insiders' Tip

For the latest listing of which bands are playing where in Key West, check Paradise, the entertainment section in Thursday's edition of *The Key West Citizen*. Free copies of Paradise are available throughout the Keys at hotels, restaurants, and wherever newspapers are sold.

You'll discover a couple of options at the Holiday Inn Key Largo. Bogie's Cafe has a piano lounge where you can enjoy the tinkling of the ivories. Picking up the pace a bit with live music Thursday through Saturday, a mix of reggae, rock, and bop attracts an equal mingling of locals and tourists to the outdoor tiki bar.

Snappers Waterfront Saloon & Raw Bar
MM 94.5 Oceanside
Key Largo, FL
(305) 852-5956
www.thefloridakeys.com/snappers

Snappers oozes Keys atmosphere, especially on the cypress-and-palm-frond chickees on the outside waterside deck. Menu items are innovative (see our Restaurants chapter), and patrons enjoy live entertainment on the weekends.

Hog Heaven Sports Bar
MM 85.3 Oceanside
Islamorada, FL
(305) 664-9669
www.keysdining.com/hogheaven

The congenial outdoor saloon of Hog Heaven Sports Bar sits unassumingly on the waterfront. You can consume yourself with televised sports, talk with the locals, or head to the point, where a chickee yields seclusion that may foster romance.

As you might expect, the pork here is heavenly.

Holiday Isle Resorts & Marina
MM 84 Oceanside
Islamorada, FL
(305) 664-2321
www.holidayisle.com

No two ways about it: Ask anyone where the action is around here and, day or night, the answer undoubtedly will be: Holiday Isle. With two beaches and a number of outdoor restaurants and bars, Holiday Isle buzzes with activity. You can nosh at the Wreck Bar, Raw Bar, Beach Bar, or Bimini Treats, enjoy steel drums at Kokomo's, or drink a tall, cool one at the Tiki Bar. Come evening, live music at the Tiki Bar raises the adrenaline and dancers gyrate until the wee hours. Holiday Isle often hosts weekend special events ranging from charity luaus to bikini and body-building contests to Fourth of July fireworks and Halloween costume parties (see our Annual Events chapter).

Lorelei Cabana Bar
MM 82 Bayside
Islamorada, FL
(305) 664-4338
www.florida-keys.fl.us/lorelei

Winning "The People's Choice Award" for the best view of the sunset seven years running, Lorelei's outdoor Cabana Bar offers live entertainment seven nights a week, beginning at sunset and continuing by starlight. The bar is a laid-back, waterside watering hole and lunch spot all day long, and the views of Florida Bay cannot be beat. See our Restaurants chapter for dining options here.

Bentley's Raw Bar
MM 82.8 Oceanside
Islamorada, FL
(305) 664-9094
www.keysdining.com/bentleys

The upstairs bar at Bentley's Restaurant is small and intimate but usually bustling with a happy-hour crowd and those waiting for a table at this popular eatery (see

After the Beach Boys released the song "Kokomo," travelers to the Florida Keys looked all over for the fictitious place. Holiday Isle provided for their needs. PHOTO: JAMES DILORETO

our Restaurants chapter). Noshing on fresh raw bar offerings brings to mind an after-work Manhattan crowd, but there isn't a power suit or necktie in sight.

Woody's Saloon & Restaurant
MM 82 Bayside
Islamorada, FL
(305) 664-4335
www.keysdining.com/woodys
Woody's hand-tossed, Chicago-style pizza is great, but this saloon's claim to fame just has to be its regular entertainment offering: Big Dick and the Extenders. A suggestive play on words, Big Dick is most certainly a tall man, and his schtick—making rude fun of members of the audience—makes Howard Stern look like a choir boy. The Extenders do play some music, but the audience-participation dirty joke contest allows Dick, who wears a very big top hat, to sharpen his barbs. Sit in the back unless you have a thick skin or a penchant for verbal abuse. Oh, and having said that, there is always a line waiting outside for the privilege of admission to Woody's.

Middle Keys

Truman's at WatersEdge
MM 61 Oceanside
Hawk's Cay Resort & Marina
Duck Key, FL
(305) 743-7000
www.hawkscay.com
An intimate dance floor heats up the action with live entertainment during high season, but all year long this watering hole, just off the Hawk's Cay Marina, finds guides, island residents, and hotel guests trading fish stories. The bar area is adjacent to the popular family-style restaurant, the WatersEdge (see our Restaurants chapter).

Dockside Lounge
MM 53 Oceanside
35 Sombrero Road
Sombrero Marina
Marathon, FL
(305) 743-0000
The dock rocks during Sunday night jam sessions, when bands from throughout

Florida showcase their talents. This laid-back, open-air harborside lounge is a hub for Boot Key live-aboards who ride dinghies to shore and park their bicycles and cars nearby. Live entertainment is offered nightly at Dockside.

Gary's Pub & Billiards
MM 49 Oceanside
Marathon, FL
(305) 743-0622

Gary's took over the nightlife scene in Marathon with a quick eight ball in the corner pocket. This billiard parlor cum public house draws a diverse crowd, all happy to partake of libations aside the long mahogany bar, shoot pool, or OD on sporting events televised simultaneously on all of Gary's 25 television screens. Hot hors d'oeuvres are offered during happy hour. An electronic sobriety test can tell whether or not you should take a taxi home.

Angler's Lounge
MM 48 Bayside
Faro Blanco Resort & Marina
Marathon, FL
(305) 743-9018

Live entertainment on Thursday, Friday, and Saturday nights sets the stage at Angler's, a popular nightspot amid the Faro Blanco Resort. Situated topside, adjacent to the resort's swimming pool, Angler's concocts island drinks such as the Pink Cadillac, Mud Ball, and Goombay Smash. (See our Restaurants chapter for Angler's restaurant offerings.)

Lower Keys

No Name Pub
MM 31 Bayside
N. Watson Boulevard
Big Pine Key, FL
(305) 872-9115

Wallpapered with dollar bills and full of good cheer and local color, No Name Pub is a must-do, night or day. (See our Restaurants chapter for menu offerings

and directions.) Off the beaten path about as far as you can go in Big Pine, this small saloon sports a funky bar and a pool table.

The Sandbar
MM 28.5 Bayside
Barry Avenue
Little Torch Key, FL
(305) 872-9989

High on stilt legs above the Big Pine Channel of the Gulf, The Sandbar's pavilion-like interior beckons Lower Keys wassailers. Party bashes celebrating the full moon, Valentine's Day, the Kentucky Derby and more compete with myriad pool tables and an enormous bar. An all-day, all-night menu will satisfy any hunger pangs (see our Restaurants chapter).

Boondocks
MM 27.5 Bayside
Ramrod Key, FL
(305) 872-4094

This open-air, thatched-roof gathering place, surrounded by copious plantings of coconut palms and cooled by Bahama fans, offers a light-bite menu from lunchtime to bedtime. Built in 1989 by Miccosukee Indians, who specialize in palm thatching, the casual bar bursts with activity: televised sports, billiards, and horseshoes. On Wednesday evenings outdoor live entertainment draws a crowd of locals to the starlit dance floor. Boondocks serves beer and wine only.

The evenings heat up at Truman's Bar at Hawk's Cay Resort. PHOTO: HAWK'S CAY RESORT

Key West

Renowned for its nightlife, Key West boasts of having more bars per capita than anywhere else in the United States. With many of the establishments open seven days a week until 4 A.M. this tiny island lives up to its slightly eccentric reputation. An age-old tradition in Key West is called the "Duval Crawl"—a sampling of libations from all the nightspots on Duval Street, until the only means of moving is to crawl.

In this section, we recommend a road map for such a crawl. We start at the Atlantic end of Duval Street, where the pubs are more sparsely located, and move toward the Gulf of Mexico, where the kegs flow freely. **Note:** We do not recommend trying to take in every establishment listed here in one night, but if you do, please take a taxi when you finish (see our Getting Here, Getting Around chapter).

Of course, not all the bars in Key West are on Duval Street. We have also included a section called Local Favorites—Key West classics that are a little more off the beaten

path but definitely worth checking out. Cheers!

The Quintessential Duval Crawl

801 Bourbon Bar
801 Duval Street
Key West, FL
(305) 294-4737

With a clientele consisting of primarily gay patrons and tourists, the 801 offers a first-floor bar with billiards. A second floor offers live entertainment with drag shows nightly, beginning at 11 P.M.; if you've never seen a drag show, you may be pleasantly surprised. The professionally choreographed productions here are loads of fun.

Bourbon Street Pub
730 Duval Street
Key West, FL
(305) 296-1992

Live entertainment at the predominantly gay Bourbon Street includes bands, drag shows, comedians, and, on weekends, male dancers. Key West's only VJ plays tunes, mixing videos with songs for dancing. The emphasis here is on high-energy dance music. Happy hour is noon to 8 P.M. daily, and Friday is the Drag Your Ass to Bourbon Street party, when all bartenders dress in drag and the bar sees its largest crowd of the week.

Diva's
711 Duval Street
Key West, FL
(305) 292–8500

There's never a cover charge at Diva's, Key West's most popular dance club, where the music is loud and the action doesn't really get started until well past 10 P.M. The club attracts a varied clientele but is largely frequented by gay revelers. Happy hour runs from noon to 8 P.M. Stop in for a drink and be sure to stay for the show—drag queens strut their stuff on stage here nightly.

Green Parrot
601 Whitehead Street
Key West, FL
(305) 294–6133

Not exactly on Duval Street, but close enough and so quintessentially Key West, the Green Parrot rates a stop on any Duval Crawl. Frequented primarily by locals, this eclectic bar is housed in an 1890s-era building a half-block off Duval, down Southard Street. Walls are adorned with unusual oversize portraits and a wall mural of the Garden of Eden. Weekends feature local and national bands playing blues and zydeco, and the large dance floor is usually crowded. The bar also sports video games, billiard tables, darts, a pinball machine, and a jukebox. And if you're hungry, the Meteor Smokehouse next door has great ribs (see our Restaurants chapter).

Virgilio's
524 Duval Street
Key West, FL
(305) 296–8118

This classy little New York–style bar is not really on Duval; it's actually situated on Applerouth Lane, just around the corner from La Trattoria, one of Key West's best Italian eateries (see our Restaurants chapter). Martinis and their cousins—Gibsons, Manhattans, and Cosmopolitans—are the specialty here. Grab a seat at the bar or in one of the overstuffed easy chairs while you sip your cocktail and listen to live light jazz and contemporary music from some of Key West's finest musical talent.

Mulcahy's Tavern
509½ Duval Street
Key West, FL
(305) 295–8797

Stop in at this watering hole, popular with locals, for a little taste of Dublin on Duval. Guinness is the drink of choice here, and on the menu you'll find plenty of mouthwatering Irish fare. Live bands play on Friday and Saturday nights.

Jimmy Buffett's Margaritaville Cafe
500 Duval Street
Key West, FL
(305) 292–1435
www.margaritaville.com/keywest

Yes, the big man himself does play here once in a while, as do some of the Coral Reefers and bands that have opened for Jimmy on tour. Props from past concerts decorate the walls and ceiling. Beginning at 10:30 each night and continuing well into the wee hours, a variety of bands and solo artists perform everything from rock 'n' roll to reggae to rhythm and blues. Margaritas are just one of the many frozen drinks offered at the air-conditioned yet open-air bar. You can nosh on a

> ### Insiders' Tip
> Nightlife needn't involve a bar at all. Some of our best nighttime activities can be found on stage. Read our Arts and Culture chapter for live theater offerings.

Insiders' Tip

If you plan to imbibe, be sure to carry ID. Anyone who looks under 30 will likely be carded, especially in Key West, where underage spring breakers try their best each year to circumvent the law. (They rarely succeed, by the way.)

"cheeseburger in Paradise" with all the fixin's or pick up some Buffett clothing, recordings, books, and memorabilia at the shop next door (see our Restaurants and Shopping chapters).

Celebrities at La Concha Hotel
430 Duval Street
Key West, FL
(305) 296–2991
www.laconchakeywest.com

With its art deco styling and classic glassware, this glitzy, ground-floor hotel bar has a 1920s New York feel. But when the doors are open onto bustling Duval, you'll know you're definitely in twenty-first century Key West. Grab a spot at the bar or at one of the linen-covered cocktail tables for the nightly keyboard entertainment. And for a glimpse of 1920s Key West, be sure to check out the aged black-and-white photos and framed *Life* magazine covers hanging around the lounge and along the wall leading to the hotel lobby.

Hard Rock Cafe
313 Duval Street
Key West, FL
(305) 293–0230
www.hardrock.com

A world-renowned classic, Hard Rock Cafe joined the Conch Republic in the summer of 1996. Situated in a renovated,

three-story, Conch-style house on Duval Street, Hard Rock Cafe Key West celebrates historic Key West, the preservation of the Florida Keys' fragile environment and, of course, rock 'n' roll. This 235-seat Hard Rock is open seven days a week and serves up all-American fare.

Fat Tuesday
305 Duval Street
Key West, FL
(305) 296–9373

Stop in at Fat Tuesday and choose from one of 26 flavors of frozen drinks, including Margaritas, piña coladas, and 190-octane rumrunners. Our favorite is the Pain in the Ass, a combination piña colada and rumrunner. The motto here is "One daiquiri, two daiquiri, three daiquiri, floor," and you can even buy a T-shirt that says it.

Oak Beach Inn
227 Duval Street
Key West, FL
(305) 296–4545
www.oakbeachinn.com

New Yorkers have been flocking to the Oak Beach Inn on Long Island for more than 32 years to sip on the specialty of the house—Long Island Iced Tea. This potent concoction of clear liquors, sour lemonade, and cola looks like ordinary iced tea, but packs a much more powerful punch. Now, if Long Islanders want to order that signature drink from the original source, they'll have to come to Key West to do so. Oak Beach Inn—OBI for short—has relocated to the southernmost city. Housed in the historic old Fogarty House (formerly

Insiders' Tip

Many Florida Keys watering holes have a happy hour, which often coincides with the sunset celebration.

Hooters) on the corner of Duval and Caroline, OBI features live music seven nights a week. A full menu of sandwiches and appetizers is available until midnight (burgers and hot dogs until 4 A.M. on weekends). Two bars serve up Long Island Iced Teas (and much more) well into the wee hours.

Bull and Whistle
224 Duval Street
Key West, FL
(305) 296–4545
www.thebullandwhistle.com

This local favorite is actually three bars in one. The Bull is downstairs and features live music in an open-air setting. The Whistle is upstairs and offers pool and video games, along with a great view of Duval Street from the balcony. The Garden of Eden, on the very top, has a great view of Key West . . . and more. It's the only clothing-optional roof garden in town.

Rumrunners/Hideaway/Upstarez/
Channel Zero
218 Duval Street
Key West, FL
(305) 294–1017

This entertainment complex has something for everyone. Rumrunners offers reggae nightly; the Hideaway presents live alternative rock; Upstarez features live adult entertainment; and Channel Zero caters to the classic rock crowd.

Durty Harry's/Rick's/Angelina's Pizzeria/
Red Garter Saloon
208 Duval Street
Key West, FL

Owner Mark Rossi offers four nightspots in one complex. Durty Harry's Bar (305–296–5513) features acoustic guitars and karaoke in the first-floor sports bar setting. Rick's Bar (305–296–4890) is an all-mirror, second-floor discotheque. Angelina's Pizzeria (305–296–3600) satisfies late-night cravings and the Red Garter Saloon (305–296–4964) is a mirror-and-brass adult club. Pick your pleasure.

Captain Tony's Saloon
428 Greene Street
Key West, FL
(305) 294–1838

Just a half-block off Duval, this watering hole is the site of Key West's first hanging tree, still in evidence inside the bar. Captain Tony's is the original location of Sloppy Joe's. Once owned by Capt. Tony Tarracino, a friend of Jimmy Buffett and a former Key West mayor, the saloon features walls concealed by undies and business cards. Live entertainment is offered nightly.

Captain Tony's Saloon is the original Sloppy Joe's. It is also home to Key West's hanging tree and the bar where Jimmy Buffet got his musical start.
PHOTO: JANET WARE

Sloppy Joe's Bar
201 Duval Street
Key West, FL
(305) 294–5717
www.sloppyjoes.com

It's no wonder this was Hemingway's favorite watering hole. The upbeat atmosphere of Sloppy Joe's is contagious. The bar opened in 1933 on the site of what is now Captain Tony's Saloon. In 1937 it moved to its current location. Some say that Hemingway did some writing in the back rooms of the bar and kept a few of his manuscripts locked up here. Photos of Hemingway line the walls. Live entertainment is offered from noon to 2 A.M. daily. Among the brews offered here is Sloppy Joe's beer, which is actually made by Coors. A gift shop sells T-shirts, boxer shorts, hats, and other souvenirs with the Sloppy Joe's logo.

Around the corner and upstairs, you'll find Sloppy Joe's Speak Easy, an intimate little cigar bar where the specialty of the house is a chilled martini and a more genteel atmosphere. The Speak Easy is open most afternoons and every night until 4 A.M. Look for the entrance on Greene Street, between Sloppy Joe's Food and Sloppy Joe's Bar.

Hog's Breath Saloon
400 Front Street
Key West, FL
(305) 292–2032
www.hogsbreath.com

"The Hog," as locals know this place, features an open-air mahogany bar surrounded by watersports-related memorabilia, including mounted fish and surfboards. You can try the medium-bodied Hog's Breath beer and sample one of the saloon's famed fish sandwiches. The restaurant (see our Restaurants chapter) is open for lunch and dinner. Live bands play rock, folk rock, blues, and jazz throughout the day and well into the evening. You can purchase T-shirts, hats, and sundry other items emblazoned with the saloon's slogan: "Hog's Breath is better than no breath at all."

> ## Insiders' Tip
> Don't drink and drive. Always have a designated driver.

Pier House Resort
1 Duval Street
Key West, FL
(305) 296–4600
www.pierhouse.com

Pier House offers a little something for everyone. The view of the famous Key West sunset is beautiful from the Havana Docks bar and the intimate Beach Club Bar has great entertainment nightly. If you like things a little quieter, settle in and enjoy the piano bar in the dimly lit Wine Galley. The tiny Chart Room Bar, which is filled with peanut shells, is a favorite hangout with the locals.

Local Favorites

The Afterdeck Bar at Louie's Backyard
700 Waddell Avenue
Key West, FL
(305) 294–1061

The deck is large and right on the water. And we do mean right on the water. One false step, a few cocktails too many and…splash! Service is friendly and courteous, and the setting is exactly what you were thinking of when you first thought of coming to the Florida Keys. The adjoining restaurant is one of Key West's finest (see our Restaurants chapter under Louie's Backyard).

Atlantic Shores Resort
510 South Street
Key West, FL
(305) 296–2491

The weekly tea dance at Atlantic Shores—Key West's own version of Miami's South Beach–style art deco joints—draws Sunday night party-goers in droves. A poolside disc jockey plays dance tunes, and a wait staff serves cocktails. The pool area at Atlantic Shores is clothing-optional and tends to be mostly frequented by gays. On Thursday nights, Atlantic Shores also shows artistic independent and foreign films not found at the big cinemas as well as some popular recent flicks you may have missed; call for details.

Finnegan's Wake Irish Pub & Eatery
320 Grinnell Street
Key West, FL
(305) 293–0222
www.keywestirish.com

Exactly like a good Irish public house ought to be, Finnegan's keeps the merriment going until nearly dawn (4 A.M.) and is among a mere handful of Key West establishments serving food into the wee hours (see our Restaurants chapter). You're sure to find your Guinness here, and you can even down a Black and Tan. Order one and the barkeep will think you just returned from the Emerald Isle. Enjoy live Irish music Wednesday through Saturday and karaoke on Tuesdays and Wednesdays.

Flagler's Steakhouse and Lounge
Sun Sun Pavilions and Raw Bar
Wyndham Casa Marina Resort
and Beach House
1500 Reynolds Street
Key West, FL
(305) 296–3535
www.wyndham.com/casamarinaresort

Live music kicks off nightly beginning around 9 P.M. in the lounge of the Flagler Steakhouse. The Monday night jam sessions are especially popular.

Tucked next to the ocean on the grounds of the Casa Marina, the Sun Sun Pavilions and Raw Bar isn't really a raw bar (unless you count peel-and-eat shrimp). It is, however, a great place to sip a cocktail beside the sea. In addition to one of the best piña coladas on the island, you'll find a friendly staff and tasty entrees like blackened mahi-mahi Caesar salad and a cheeseburger with all the fixin's. Sporting events like Monday night football, the Super-

Bowl, and the NCAA Final Four bring out big-screen TVs and a good-size crowd for a burger buffet and drink specials.

Key West Bar and Grill and
Down Under Sports Bar
1970 N. Roosevelt Boulevard
Key West, FL
(305) 294–1057, (305) 294–1970

This is two bars in one. Upstairs is the Key West Bar and Grill, where you can order a tasty, fresh-grilled fish sandwich and a beer. Downstairs is Down Under, the "bar with balls." Free pool and popcorn draw the locals back time and again.

PT's Late Night Bar & Grill
920 Caroline Street
Key West, FL
(305) 296–4245

This local gathering spot offers billiards, darts, trivia games, and the opportunity to catch up with friends over a variety of homestyle meals or drinks. The pot roast here is legendary. Televised sports provide most of the entertainment, but live bands do occasionally perform.

Schooner Wharf Bar
202 William Street
Key West, FL
(305) 292–9520
www.schoonerwharf.com

Dockside at the Historic Key West Seaport is the open-air, thatched-palm Schooner Wharf, which bills itself as "the last little bit of old Key West." The place offers outdoor thatched-umbrella tables, a covered bar, grill, and indoor games, including billiards and darts. Live jazz, rhythm and blues, and island music are featured each Thursday through Saturday night. Wednesday at the Wharf is ladies' night.

Stick and Stein Sports Rock Cafe
Key Plaza Shopping Center
2922 N. Roosevelt Boulevard
Key West, FL
(305) 296–3352

With pool tables galore, air hockey, darts, and video and pinball games, Stick and

winning large Lotto ticket ever sold in the Florida Keys (worth $6.8 million) came from Stick and Stein in 1997.

Turtle Kraals Waterfront Seafood Grill and Bar
1 Lands End Village
Key West, FL
(305) 294–2640
www.turtlekraals.com

Stein earns its reputation as the biggest sports bar in Key West. Watch the game of your choice on one of 70 TV screens (yes, you read that right!), or just hunker down for a drink at one of the four bars. If your appetite beckons, satisfy it with some classic bar food like chicken wings or peel-and-eat shrimp. By the way, in addition to the most TVs anywhere around, Stick and Stein has another claim to fame. The only

The lounge portion of this turtle cannery-turned-restaurant rocks throughout the evening, offering live entertainment (in season) and billiard tables in an open-air, waterfront setting (see our Restaurants chapter). Turtle Kraals' full bar is known for its frozen margaritas, microbrewed beers, and imported beers on tap. For a great view of the wharf, climb up to TK's upstairs bar. It opens daily at 3 P.M.

The Keys are a great place for a honeymoon—or even a second honeymoon. PHOTO: VICTORIA SHEARER

Accommodations

Price-Code Key

$ .... $55 to $99
$$ .... $100 to $150
$$$ .... $151 to $250
$$$$ .... $251 and higher

From luxury resorts to little-known hideaways, the Florida Keys' myriad accommodations suit every vacation fantasy and budget.

What began in the 1930s as a small assortment of fishing camps experienced a renaissance after World War II ended. Henry Flagler's railroad and the creation of the Overseas Highway had made our islands more accessible, but residents still relied on cisterns for fresh water until water lines were installed to service the Key West naval base during World War II. The availability of fresh water made our region a more civilized and desirable vacation destination, and, by the 1950s and 1960s when motoring became a popular means of travel, hotels and motels sprang up all over our islands.

Location and Amenities

Like our Conchs—those of us born in the Keys—and Keys characters—those of us who were not—accommodations in the Florida Keys are highly individualistic. Most are situated on the Florida Bay, the Gulf of Mexico, or the Atlantic Ocean. We commonly refer to the Atlantic as "oceanside." For simplicity's sake in this chapter, we refer to the bayside and gulfside as "bayside."

You can enjoy swimming and watersports in either the bay or the ocean. Expect to find our coastline waters calmer than those you may have encountered in the rest of South Florida. The waters of the Gulf of Mexico and Florida Bay cover shallow seagrass flats, and the barrier reef, some 4 to 5 miles offshore in the Atlantic, breaks the surf, thereby keeping waters inside the reef from 1 to 3 feet most of the time. The oceanside coastline is also fronted with shallow flats in places. The interruption of wave action by the coral reef dictates that the Florida Keys does not have an abundance of natural beaches. Most of our beaches are made with imported sand and are unsupervised.

Oceanside accommodations offer exotic sunrises and proximity to dive sites, oceanside flats, and bluewater locations for sportfishing. Water access is generally deeper on the oceanside than in the bay, affording boaters and sailors more options. Bayside lodgings can boast of our spectacular Keys sunsets, which sink into the placid skinny waters of the Gulf like a meltdown of molten lava. Some hotels, motels, resorts, and inns sit alongside inland canals or marina basins, and many of our waterfront facilities are accessible by boat.

Many of our small mom-and-pop lodgings you will see lining the Overseas Highway were primarily built in the 1950s and 1960s as fishing camps. These facilities offer basic, affordable rooms and efficiencies, some with screened patios. Mom-and-pop motels often draw cost-conscious families, last-minute travelers, anglers, and scuba divers—those active, outdoorsy types seeking nothing more than a bed and a shower. These motels have a high return rate.

Also individually owned, but often with more expansive waterfront properties and recreational amenities, are facilities that offer a potpourri of accommodation options, ranging from sleeping rooms to watersports, fishing charters and dive excursions. Some offer optional conference rooms or a variety of travel/sport packages. Couples often opt for romantic weddings and honeymoons amid our tropical breezes, lush foliage, crystal seas, and magnificent sunsets.

And when spring break rolls around, college students throughout the country flood our hotels, beaches, tiki bars, and nightspots.

Whether the accommodations are large, small, or somewhere in-between, all of our guest properties exude a casual, barefoot ambiance. To one degree or another, all bestow the uninterrupted escape for which the Florida Keys has always been known.

Rate Information

Rate structures for Keys lodgings vary nearly as much as the accommodations themselves, but you can draw a few generalizations. Rates fluctuate by season and depend largely upon the size of the accommodation and its proximity to the water.

High season (December through April) supports the highest rates. High-season rates usually prevail during sport lobster season in July (a near-holiday in the Keys; see our Diving chapter), Fantasy Fest in the autumn (our southernmost decadent version of Mardi Gras; see our Annual Events chapter), and most national holiday weekends. You must make reservations well in advance of your visit during any of these times. Many facilities fully book available accommodations one year in advance for high season and the holidays.

A second season commences in May and continues through the summer months, attracting vacationers seeking to escape the steamy heat of the rest of Florida and the deep South. Rates during this period are generally slightly less than high season.

Low season is September and October, bringing a saving of about 20 percent off high-season rates. Some facilities maintain low-season rates into November as well.

efficiencies to multiple-bedroom apartments, often within one diverse property. Many sleeping rooms provide mini refrigerators and have balconies, while efficiencies offer abbreviated kitchens as well. Suites, villas, and cottages will allow you the space to spread out a bit and to cook a meal or two "at home" when the mood hits. They usually have a sleeper sofa in the living space and a full kitchen. These accommodations often maintain freshwater swimming pools, hot tubs, and guest laundry facilities. If they don't offer on-premises watersports, these recreational activities are almost always located nearby. Since all of these properties have evolved over the decades with a multitude of owners, ask whether your accommodations have been updated recently. Most owners renovate when the budget allows, so some rooms or cottages may be more desirable than others.

Our large comprehensive resorts offer all the amenities of a mom-and-pop facility and then some. From fitness to childcare centers and concierge to room services, these hotels cater to families and honeymooners, business travelers and sports enthusiasts, power players and movie stars. You'll find tennis courts and

Rates for motel or sleeping rooms, which typically hold two double beds, are based on single or double occupancy. Additional guests are charged a supplementary fee, but motels impose a maximum occupancy for each room.

Children younger than 13 frequently are permitted to stay for free when accompanied by an adult. Cribs and cots often are provided at no charge or at a minimal additional cost.

Condominiums, villas, and cottages generally establish a weekly rate per unit, but many also offer a three- or four-night package as well, which is priced per night.

Accommodations of like stature will command differing prices, depending upon how close they are to the waterfront and what kind of view they offer. If you prefer accommodations overlooking the bay or ocean, ask for a bayfront or ocean-front room. Sometimes waterfront means a canal or lagoon. Be sure to query. Water view does not necessarily mean that your room will be on or facing the water, but as a general rule, water view is less expensive and provides at least a glimpse of the bay or ocean. Garden views and non-waterfront accommodations, often just a short walk to water's edge, are priced even lower.

We suggest you shop around for exact daily or weekly rates and vacancies. Be sure to ask if the facility offers any discounted rates. Sometimes you can luck into a short-term discount or sport package that will be just what you are seeking.

In all cases, rates are expressed for the high season. Prices for motel or sleeping room facilities are figured on a double-occupancy average rate per night. Villas, efficiencies, and condominium units, which generally establish rates per unit rather than per person, will be quoted as such. And even though these units traditionally are rented by the week, we have computed our code on an average daily rate so that you can compare apples with apples.

It is not uncommon to find accommodations that run the gamut of several price code categories all at the same place. The code will indicate if you can expect a range of space and pocketbook possibilities. (Accommodations in Key West generally are more expensive than the rest of the Keys, therefore we have established a separate pricing key for Key West accommodations.)

Price codes are figured without additional fees, such as room service and calls, and without the 11.5 percent room tax. Our recommended accommodations accept major credit cards unless otherwise specified.

Reservation and Cancellation Policies

Typically, you confirm your room by holding it with a major credit card. If you do not have a major credit card, you may often hold a room with an advance check or money order. The balance—always paid with a credit card, traveler's checks, or cash—will be collected either upon check-in or check-out. Be aware that cancellation policies vary.

If you do not cancel your room within a property's specified advance time, you will likely be charged a sizable fee whether or not you arrive. And when you pay for a room when you check-in, most facilities do not provide refunds or credits if you pay for more days than you are able to stay.

During high season and special events, our facilities almost always are full. You might benefit from a no-show on a walk-in basis late at night, but we suggest reserving and confirming dates, accommodations, and prices three to six months in advance. More desirable facilities fill up more rapidly, and special events sometimes require one-year advance planning.

To avoid potential complications, be sure to inquire about all details of your accommodations when making reservations and confirmations. Obtain a confirmation number and the full name of the person who takes your reservation.

If you are planning to arrive at one of our resort marinas by sailing or motor

These floating houseboats redefine "room with a view." PHOTO: FLORIDA KEYS & KEY WEST TDC

yacht, be sure to read our Cruising chapter first. Dockage space for transient cruisers is at a premium at these desirable establishments and is often booked a year in advance during high season. Be sure to ascertain water depth and size restrictions of the marina before you venture here in your vessel. Many of our recommended accommodations offer marina facilities where you may bring your own trailered boat and, for a small daily fee, secure dockage of your craft for the duration of your stay. The boat basins of these facilities are usually not as deep as the resort marinas that accommodate large vessels and therefore are more suitable for shallow-draft boats. Those accommodations offering accessibility by boat have been noted throughout.

Check-in time typically is after 2 P.M., and check-out is between 10 and 11 A.M. Some facilities levy an extra charge if you occupy your room after check-out time. But, in some cases, the management is prepared to keep your luggage safe while you soak in a few extra rays before catching that flight home. They may even have a room designated for you to shower and change before you leave. It is always better

to inquire than to ignore posted check-out times.

In this chapter, we escort you through some of the Florida Keys' more outstanding facilities. Our selections are based on attributes of rooms, service, location, property and/or overall ambiance. Listed by descending mile marker number beginning with Key Largo in the Upper Keys and heading down the Keys to Big Coppitt, these facilities encompass a wide assortment of styles and rates. We have included directions for those establishments located off the Overseas Highway that may be difficult to find. In the Key West section, we switch to alphabetical order; we also provide a separate section of inns and guest houses in our southernmost city, with a corresponding pricing code for those accommodations.

The Florida Keys

Upper Keys

At the top of the Keys, Key Largo, home of John Pennekamp Coral Reef State Park, bustles with an energetic crowd of divers and snorkelers in all seasons. The orientation here is definitely geared toward the underwater treasures of the coral reef that lies just 4 miles offshore. Many motels and resorts in this area offer diving and snorkeling packages.

The settlement of Tavernier snuggles between Key Largo and Islamorada. This quiet area is known for its historic qualities. Dubbed the Sportfishing Capital of the World, Islamorada stretches from Plantation Key at mile marker 90 to Lower Matecumbe Key at mile marker 73. This village of islands, incorporated in 1998, is renowned for its contingent of talented gamefishing guides (see our Fishing chapter) and prestigious fishing tournaments.

The Upper Keys pulsates with tiki bars and watering holes as well as an array of fine restaurants (see our Restaurants and Nightlife chapters). Party animals head for a popular nearby spot known as Holiday Isle. Excursions to historic Indian Key and Lignumvitae Key and visits to Theater of the Sea, which offers dolphin and sea mammal shows and allows guests to swim with the dolphins, rate high on the list of things to do for families and sports enthusiasts alike (see our Attractions chapter).

Kelly's on the Bay
MM 104.2 Bayside
Key Largo, FL
(305) 451–1622, (800) 226–0415
www.kellysonthebay.com
$–$$$

Well-known as a dedicated dive resort, Kelly's is a 1950s-style island-Caribbean motel. Constantly updated, the 34 rooms feature tile floors, bright window treatments, wicker furnishings, and eclectic wall hangings. All rooms have mini refrigerators, and efficiencies feature stoves and sinks.

Part of the Kelly's operation is Aqua Nuts Dive Center. Two 42-foot dive boats transport guests to underwater sites within John Pennekamp Coral Reef State Park (see our Diving and Snorkeling chapter). Guests enjoy Kelly's heated pool, situated to take full advantage of the

Insiders' Tip

Consult these websites for more lodging information: www.thefloridakeys.com and www.fabulousvacations.com.

spectacular sunsets over Florida Bay. Complimentary kayaks are available to explore a small adjacent cove.

Kelly's provides a complimentary full "divers" breakfast to all guests. These facilities are boat-accessible.

Amy Slate's Amoray Dive Resort
MM 104.2 Bayside
Key Largo, FL
(305) 451–3595, (800) 426–6729
www.amoray.com
$$–$$$

About 80 percent of the guests at Amy Slate's Amoray Dive Resort are divers. An eclectic collection of plantation-style villas springs to life daily as the undersea enthusiasts rustle about, eager to embark on the resort's 45-foot Amoray Diver for the half-hour ride to John Pennekamp Coral Reef State Park (see our Diving and Snorkeling chapter).

Amy Slate's Amoray owes its name in part to *People* magazine. The publication sent a writer to Key Largo to cover an Amy Slate underwater wedding "crashed" by a moray eel, and thus coined the term "That's Amoray."

The rooms here are named after tropical fish. Varying in size, amenities, and price, the rooms range from the standard motel variety to small apartments with full kitchens. The accommodations all have ceiling fans and feature tile floors, queen-size beds, and day beds. Two-story, two-bedroom, two-bath duplexes accommodate as many as eight guests; they offer full kitchens and screened porches with personal hammocks. Some accommodations afford partial water views.

A pool and hot tub front Florida Bay, and a bayfront sun deck and small sandy area at the water's edge sport a picnic table, barbecue grill, and hammock, allowing for swimming, snorkeling, and fishing. Continental breakfast is included in the room rate. Boat slips are available.

Marriott Key Largo Bay Beach Resort
MM 103.8 Bayside
Key Largo, FL
(305) 453–0000, (800) 932–9332
www.marriottkeylargo.com
$$$–$$$$

Bayside sunset views and a primo location near John Pennekamp Coral Reef State Park mark only two of a multitude of pluses at the Marriott Key Largo Bay Beach Resort. The 153 hotel rooms of this Key West–style resort vary in view (bayview and deluxe bayview cost more), but all include a room safe, minibar, pay-per-view in addition to free cable television, hair dryer, coffeemaker, iron, and ironing board. All but 20 have patios.

Rooms are equipped with voice mail and a data port. For more spacious quarters but more dearly priced, 23 suites—1,000 square feet apiece—have a full kitchen, a full bathroom, a queen-size sleeper sofa in the living room, and two bedrooms, one with a king-size bed and one with two doubles. Wraparound patios provide panoramic views of Florida Bay and its famed sunsets. For the royal treatment, the resort also offers one 1,400-square-foot penthouse suite, which, in addition to the amenities of the other suites, features a Roman tub in the master bedroom as well as a bath-and-a-half.

Treat yourself to libation or dining at one of Marriott Key Largo Bay's restaurants or bars—Gus' Grille (see our Restaurants chapter); Breezer's Tiki Bar & Grille (see our Nightlife chapter); or Flipper's Pool Bar, aside the pool, hot tub, and beach area. The beat heats up on weekend evenings with late-night live entertainment at Gus' After Dark nightclub.

The resort also features a fitness area with state-of-the-art equipment and offers a full-service complete day spa as well as therapeutic sea-breeze-kissed massage in a private open-air tiki hut. A nine-hole "putting challenge" golf course, "hot clock" basketball, table bowling, Ping-Pong, horseshoes, and Velcro target toss stand ready to amuse you. Marriott Key Largo Bay Beach Resort also has a tennis court. A boutique shop in the lobby called By the Way will lure the shopaholics. It's A Dive provides on-premises watersports selections ranging from diving, snorkeling, parasailing, and glass-bottom boat excursions to boat or personal watercraft rentals.

Fishing charters can be booked through the hotel as well. Guests receive unlimited passage aboard the SunCruz casino ship (see our Recreation chapter). Boat dockage is available for guests' vessels at no extra charge. Marriott also offers a full activities program for children ages 5 to 15.

Largo Lodge
MM 101.7 Bayside
Key Largo, FL
(305) 451–0424, (800) 468–4378
www.largolodge.com
$$

A secluded, romantic, rain forest setting greets you at this old-island-style adults-only hideaway. At Largo Lodge, a collection of three rustic duplex cottages is nestled among lush, tropical gardens overflowing with bromeliads, orchids, and trickling water fountains. A quiet and spacious sandy pier faces the waters of Florida Bay, where you can relax and read, swim, picnic, or simply worship the sun. And you may meet one of the wild bird contingents that frequents the premises.

Each one of the lodge's six ground-level concrete block–style units features one bedroom, a living/dining combination, full kitchen, terrazzo floors with area rugs, open-beamed cathedral ceilings with fans, and French doors opening to spacious screened patios. Bedrooms feature two queen beds; some units have sleeper sofas, and rollaway beds are provided. The private, tiled baths are small but functional. Maximum capacity in each unit is four occupants.

Largo Lodge's owner, Harriet Stokes, collects ceramic memorabilia from the 1940s and 1950s, which you'll see decorating the rooms. Boat dockage is available, but you should launch your boat at a public ramp (see our Boating chapter) and bring it around to Largo Lodge, because the lush tropical plantings make it difficult to maneuver a trailer.

Marina Del Mar Resort and Marina
MM 100 Oceanside
527 Caribbean Drive
Key Largo, FL
(305) 451–4107, (800) 451–3483
www.marinadelmarkeylargo.com
$$–$$$$
Marina Del Mar Bayside Resort
MM 99.5 Bayside
Key Largo, FL
(305) 451–4450, (800) 242–5229
www.marinadelmarbayside.com
$$–$$$$

Two expansive Marina Del Mar facilities serve two distinct sets of travelers.

The West Indies–style Marina Del Mar Bayside Resort, set back from the Overseas Highway, overlooks the Florida Bay and attracts those seeking a private beach, sunset views, and backcountry fishing. The bayside facility also offers a freshwater swimming pool, sun deck, and volleyball court.

The contemporary Marina Del Mar Resort and Marina, on a quiet, dead-end street along an ocean-fed canal and boat basin, draws an active boating, fishing, and diving crowd.

The rooms of both facilities are bright and modern with tile floors, ceiling fans, white wicker furnishings, and bold tropical accents and feature king-size beds or two doubles. Some also have whirlpool tubs, complete kitchens, and private waterfront balconies. All are equipped with ironing boards and irons. Both facilities offer complimentary continental breakfast and room service; restaurants and attractions are nearby.

Guests at either hotel may take advantage of the unique properties and services of both facilities. Deep-sea charter fishing boats are docked behind the Resort and Marina. This hotel also maintains two tennis courts and a small fitness room with Nautilus equipment.

Overlooking the Resort and Marina's heated freshwater swimming pool, complete with brick sun deck and hot tub, is Coconuts, a casual indoor/outdoor restaurant (see our Restaurants and Nightlife chapters). Coconuts features a raw bar and serves lunch and dinner throughout the week; the place heats up with live entertainment nightly.

The resort's marina attracts long-term and transient cruisers (see our Cruising chapter). A snorkeling excursion vessel and a glass-bottom tour boat, which both offer daily trips to the coral reefs, are berthed here as well. Next door are Club Nautico powerboat rentals and a full service dive center that offers resort and open-water diving instruction and certification.

Port Largo Villas
MM 100 Oceanside
417 Bahia Avenue
Key Largo, FL
(305) 451–4847
www.portlargovillas.com
$$$

This upscale timeshare resort offers nightly and weekly rentals with all the comforts of home. Each of Port Largo's six buildings contains four units, two on the first floor and two on the second. All are spacious two-bedroom, two-bathroom villas with more than 1,500 square feet of living space and wraparound patios or decks.

Features include large, full kitchens with washer/dryers, master baths with whirlpool tubs, and ceiling fans. Furnishings mix dark wood, bamboo, and wicker with pastel floral prints. With a queen-size bed in the master bedroom, two singles in the second bedroom, and two sleeper-sofas in the living room, each unit accommodates as many as six guests.

Port Largo's extensive, manicured property offers two swimming pools, volleyball, basketball, table tennis, shuffleboard, and croquet. Tennis, dining, and entertainment are available at the adjacent Marina Del Mar Resort and Marina (see directions in an earlier listing), and diving, snorkeling, fishing, and boating excursions are nearby. A $20-per-day surcharge is added to all rates during major holiday periods. Port Largo Villas is located on a canal, not direct oceanfront, but is accessible by boat.

Holiday Inn Key Largo Resort and Marina
MM 99.7 Oceanside
Key Largo, FL
(305) 451–2121, (800) 843–5397
www.HolidayInnKeyLargo.com
$$–$$$$

If action is what you seek on your vacation, the 132-room Holiday Inn, situated on a busy boat basin, bustles with activity from dawn until dark. You'll find charters for snorkeling, diving, fishing, sunset cruises, and sailing excursions and even a Las Vegas–style gambling boat emanating from the docks that run between the Holiday and its sister hotel, the Ramada Ltd. (see separate listing). Together they compose the Key Largo Resorts.

Bogie's Cafe offers indoor or outdoor dining for breakfast, lunch or dinner. The tiki bar serves light fare all day while live music percolates poolside on weekend evenings. You'll find a small "marketessen" in the lobby for sandwiches, pastries, juice, soda, and bottled water.

Rooms at the Holiday Inn face lush tropical gardens or the harbor, and the colorful appointments in each room reflect the flora that flourishes outside the tinted glass doors. Rooms feature modern bathrooms, king-size beds, floor-to-ceiling beveled mirrors, and great vacation amenities such as coffeemakers, hair dryers, mini refrigerators, ironing boards and irons, cable TV with HBO guest choice movies, and voice mail.

Palm trees, frangipani, and bougainvillea weave a foliage trail between the two heated pools and the hot tub, and chickees and tropical waterfalls pepper the property. Docked canalside at the Holiday Inn are two famous boats: the original *African Queen* from the legendary movie of the same name and the *Thayer IV* from the motion picture *On Golden Pond*.

The Holiday Inn maintains a fitness room, children's playground, and a changing rota of children's activities. Guests receive complimentary passes for the casino cruise.

Ramada Key Largo Resort and Marina
MM 99.7 Oceanside
Key Largo, FL
(305) 451–3939, (800) 843–5397
www.RamadaKeyLargo.com
$$–$$$$

Sister hotel to the Holiday Inn, the Ramada exudes a quieter, more laid-back ambiance. Reciprocal privileges exist between the two facilities, so guests may enjoy dining at or room service from Bogie's Cafe as well as all the chartered action.

The 88 rooms and five Jacuzzi suites of this boutique hotel have all the same amenities as the Holiday Inn (see the previous listing) and are decorated in island rattan. The spacious rooms have king-size, queen-size, or two double beds; some also have sleeper sofas. Each room opens onto a private patio or balcony. The king suites feature two bathrooms, two televisions, and a Jacuzzi bath as well as a shower and a private sun deck. The Ramada wraps around a small, private kidney-shaped swimming pool. All room rates include a complimentary continental breakfast and tickets for the casino cruise.

Sunset Cove Motel
MM 99.5 Bayside
Key Largo, FL
(305) 451–0705
www.digitalpark.com/suncove
$–$$

Concrete camels, elephants, lions, tigers, and leopards lurk on the grounds of the Sunset Cove Motel, incongruously poised between the nine scattered sleeping rooms and the 10 freestanding cottages. Don't worry, they are only life-size painted statues of the African beasts, remnants of a former owner's travels and hobbies.

All the units at Sunset Cove are individually decorated, most still sporting '50s and '60s decor and furnishings, and offer a variety of bedding options, tile floors, and dated but clean, functional private baths. The cottages also have full kitchens. Each unit showcases wall murals of exotic flora and fauna, painted by area artists.

Down at the waterfront on Florida Bay, you'll enjoy free use of paddleboats, canoes, and kayaks. The beach is peppered with lounge chairs and barbecue grills if your idea of recreation is more reclined. A large thatched chickee with a stone waterfall in the middle of the property creates an island ambiance. Guests are welcome to use Sunset Cove's boat ramp, and boat dockage for vessels up to 20 feet in length is available at no extra charge. Maid service is not available; fresh towels must be obtained at the office. Sunset Cove does not have a swimming pool.

Hungry Pelican Motel
MM 99.3 Bayside
Key Largo, FL
(305) 451–3576
$

Murals of manatees, pelicans, and wading birds decorate the outside walls of the one-story buildings at Hungry Pelican, which are linked by masses of bougainvillea. The motel's 20 clean, basic units are grouped two to four in a building. A variety of bedding options is available. Each unit is air-conditioned, has a small refrigerator, private bathroom with a shower, and tile floors. Some have kitchens as well. The duplex unit by the water features two queen-size beds and screened porch on one side and one queen-size bed, a kitchen, and screened porch on the other. These units are more expensive and cannot be connected.

Situated on Florida Bay, Hungry Pelican has two fishing piers. You'll be able to swim or snorkel between the piers, but the facility does not have a swimming pool. You may launch your boat from Hungry Pelican's boat ramp, and dockage for small boats is free for guests. Use of a paddleboat and canoe is complimentary. Continental breakfast is offered daily. The property sports a large chickee for lounging, and barbecue pits are scattered about.

Kona Kai Resort
MM 97.8 Bayside
Key Largo, FL
(305) 852–7200, (800) 365–7829
www.konakairesort.com
$$$–$$$$

Lost in a cluster of mom-and-pop motels toward the southern end of Key Largo sits a truly intimate, adults-only gem known as Kona Kai. Owners/operators Joe and Ronnie Harris have created a small, quiet tropical resort hermitage, sure to dissolve your city cares. Near the facility's tennis court, the owners have planted an exotic tropical fruit garden of lichees, guava, starfruit, sapote, Florida pistachios, jackfruit, and more. Guests are free to help themselves to samplings of the tropical fruits.

Gardens throughout the 2-acre property of winding walkways showcase 20 varieties of palm trees, 30 varieties of hibiscus, 30 species of bromeliads, plus heliconia and birds-of-paradise. The owners collect and plant rare and endangered species of flora. An orchid shadehouse features 150 species of exotic blooms. The gardens were featured on HGTV's "Secret Garden Show" in 2001.

An elevated freshwater swimming pool and a hot tub are accented by a magnificent circular staircase and paver-stone deck, as well as a thatched-palm chickee; a glass-block wall shelters a saltwater pond with a waterfall. Lounge chairs, picnic tables, barbecue grills, a hammock, and a fiberglass Ping-Pong table sit close to Kona Kai's white sand beach, which is guarded by a stone alligator. You'll be able to snorkel, swim, and fish off a platform at the end of a dock, and a paddleboat, kayak, and other water "toys" are available free of charge.

Kona Kai's 11 cottage-style suites and guest rooms have been completely renovated in the mid '90s with flair and style, and attention to every detail. All units feature double-, queen-, or king-size beds. Suites have ceiling fans, tile baths and floors, glass-block showers, antiques, CD players and VCRs, and eclectic design accents. Many also have full-size sofa/ sleeper futons, and some units have full kitchens complete with Noritake china and matching flatware. Those without kitchens have small refrigerators and coffeemakers. Each room is named after a tropical fruit. Just look for the corresponding icon on the tile under the outside lantern to your room. Keeping with this theme, the Harrises place fruit-scented soaps, shampoos, and skin lotion in each bathroom. Rooms, some of which are connected, offer either courtyard or full waterfront views. Kona Kai is a nonsmoking establishment.

A small, lovely fine art gallery on the property exhibits the work of South Florida artists such as Clyde Butcher (see our Arts and Culture chapter). Many of the original paintings from the gallery are hung in the individual guest suites as well and can be purchased. An outdoor dive station with rinse and soak tanks, an outdoor shower, and open-air lattice lockers are just down the walkway. Kona Kai can accommodate five boats with up to a 2-foot draft.

Westin Beach Resort Key Largo
MM 97 Bayside
Key Largo, FL
(305) 852–5553, (800) 539–5274
www.keylargoresort.com
$$$–$$$$

The Westin Beach Resort Key Largo sparkles with $4 million in renovations, which were completed in March 1998. Orchids, bromeliads, towering palms, and gas torches set the stage for tropical

---

Insiders' Tip

Those little beige-colored chameleonlike lizards you see everywhere in the Keys won't harm you. In fact, these critters—called geckos—actually perform a public service. A gecko in the house is considered good luck because it voraciously eats insects—some even larger than its own head!

---

ambiance in this four-story, tin-roofed enclave, painted in shades of beige and featuring walls of windows. The three-story open lobby showcases a Mexican-tile floor, mahogany and rattan furnishings, a coral encased elevator, and open-air walkways.

Probably the most unique aspect of the Westin Beach Resort is its 2,000-foot boardwalk nature trail, which stretches virtually the full length of the hotel through a protected hardwood hammock. In one direction, hikers may head for a lighted gazebo area and dock for views of the sunset. Or, they may hike through mangroves and view environmentally protected exotic flora and fauna. The predominant species of trees in the hammock are labeled and guests receive an annotated map so that they might further enjoy the nature trail.

In the resort's pool area, which is tucked amid the hardwood hammock, water cascades into the resort's family and adult-only pools over mounds of bougainvillea-lined coral rock. Colorful mural-covered walls surround a large hot tub. A nearby bar and grill provide creative gustatory comforts. Bayside, the Westin boasts an intimate sandy beach, a waterside tiki bar/grill, and a dive and watersports concession (see our Recreation chapter).

The Westin Beach Resort Key Largo provides fitness facilities, a gift boutique, a full-service unisex salon, two lighted tennis courts, and a game room. The resort offers several on-premises dining options: Cafe Key Largo serves breakfast, lunch, and dinner; Treetops offers fine evening dining from its third-floor perch amid the leafy tops of giant gumbo limbo trees; and Parrots Lounge provides libations at its tapas bar daily. Don't miss the Sunday champagne brunch on the cafe balcony overlooking the bay.

The 200 guest accommodations include standard and standard-deluxe bay-view, island-view, or trail-view rooms and Jacuzzi suites. All rooms have full marble baths, safes, and refreshment centers. Standard rooms are comfortably sized with a choice of one king-size bed or two queen-size beds, and each features a sleeper sofa. Double the size of a standard room, the Jacuzzi suite features a wet bar, mini refrigerator, queen-size sleeper sofa, and long, private balconies with sweeping waterfront views. A partition divides the living and sleeping areas, where a large Jacuzzi tub, dressing room, and connecting bathroom invite guests to pamper themselves.

The Westin Beach Resort Key Largo's Fun Factory offers full-day hiking, swimming, and arts and crafts programs for child guests (see our Kidstuff chapter). And boaters will enjoy the 21-slip docking facilities at no extra charge.

Ocean Pointe Suite Resort
MM 92.5 Oceanside
500 Burton Drive
Tavernier, FL
(305) 853–3000, (800) 882–9464
www.thefloridakeys.com/oceanpointe
$$$

Directly on the Atlantic Ocean, this tropical contemporary three-story, all-suite stilt condominium complex boasts 240 units with gingerbread-trimmed balconies facing the water. Suites at Ocean Pointe are individually owned and decorated, but, for the most part, expect to find tropical prints with wicker and rattan furnishings.

The spacious one- and two-bedroom units (two full baths) feature whirlpool tubs, complete kitchens with microwave and coffeemaker, washer and dryer, living rooms with sleeper sofas, and private balconies.

Just outside your door are nature walks, private beach, large heated swimming pool, barbecue grills, picnic areas, and lighted tennis courts. The 70-acre property also has a playground, a boat ramp, and a marina.

If you feel like a light bite, head for the outdoor cabana club. Kayak and canoe rentals also are available.

To reach Ocean Pointe, head toward the ocean at Burton Drive (mile marker 92.5) where signs lead to Harry Harris Park. Follow Burton Drive about a quarter-mile, turn right into the Ocean Pointe complex and pass the guardhouse. Signs will guide you to the manager's office.

Bay Breeze Motel
MM 92.5 Bayside
160 Sterling Road
Tavernier, FL
(305) 852–5248, (800) 937–5650
www.baybreezemotel.com
$$

Bay Breeze Motel enjoys 3 acres of primo bayfront property, planted with palms and bougainvillea and featuring a large beach area peppered with chaise lounges and barbecue grills, Adirondack beach chairs, and hammocks. Unique to this property is a special feature of Florida Bay called the "deep hole," where depths drop dramatically to 20 feet right off shore. A coral rock ledge shelters lobsters and starfish and a regiment of sergeant-major fish, who keep company with mangrove snappers and parrotfish. This assortment of marine life as well as a sunken Haitian raft makes for dynamic snorkeling.

The Bay Breeze Motel offers 15 units, all with full kitchens or kitchenettes, for self-catering convenience, and hardwood or tile floors. The units are tropically furnished with colorful upholstered rattan and wicker. The three Caribbean suites, which have kitchenettes with microwave and small refrigerator and private decks, are closest to the beach.

The Caribbean cottages are a little further back from the water and enjoy views of either the heated swimming pool or Florida Bay. Each cottage has a full kitchen, living room, and separate bedroom with a king-size canopy bed. One-bedroom efficiencies are housed in a two-story, motel-style building toward the back of the property. Each unit has a full kitchen, living room with futon, and a separate bedroom with a king or twin beds.

Bay Breeze maintains two boat ramps and a 100-foot dock. Boat dockage and use of the boat ramp is available to guests at no extra charge.

Guests enjoy complimentary use of a rowboat and paddleboat during their stay. To find Bay Breeze Motel, turn onto Sterling Road at mile marker 92.5 and proceed toward Florida Bay.

Tavernier Hotel
MM 91.8 Oceanside
Tavernier, FL
(305) 852–4131, (800) 515–4131
www.tavernierhotel.com
$

Gracing Tavernier since 1928, the historic building now sheltering the Tavernier Hotel withstood the ravages of the hurricane of 1935 (see our Historical Evolution chapter). The pale-pink building contains 17 simple sleeping rooms. A variety of bedding options is offered, but all rooms are decorated in hot pinks and pastels and sport lacy curtains and comforters, exuding an English bed and breakfast ambiance that reflects the owner's British roots.

The reasonably priced accommodations here are basic but spiffy; each unit features cable television and a small refrigerator. The facility also provides a small fitness center and a laundry. A hot tub nestles amid lush greenery out back. The popular Copper Kettle Restaurant, next door and under the same ownership as the hotel (see our Restaurants chapter), provides breakfast, lunch, and dinner a stone's throw from the hotel.

Lookout Lodge Resort
MM 87.7 Bayside
Islamorada, FL
(305) 852–9915, (800) 870–1772
www.lookoutlodge.com
$–$$

Situated next to Marker 88, one of the Upper Keys' most distinguished restaurants (see our Restaurants chapter), Lookout Lodge is a clean, modestly priced motel of Spanish-influenced architecture. The resort's nine basic rooms—featuring a decidedly '60s decor and amenities—come in four styles: studios with one double and one twin-size bed; studios with two double beds and a patio; and one- and two-bedroom suites. Suites each include a queen-size sleeper sofa. Cribs, side rails, and rollaway beds are provided at no additional cost. All suites have kitchenettes, tile floors and baths, voice-mail telephones, and ceiling fans. Three afford full water views. A limited number of small pets are allowed.

Steps lead from the resort's raised man-made beach to the bay for swimming and snorkeling. The property features gas grills, picnic tables, a thatched-palm chickee, and lounge chairs, but no swimming pool. Dock space, available at an additional fee, is limited and must be reserved in advance. A dive/snorkel boat on premises takes guests to the reef.

Two weeks' advance cancellation is required.

Tropical Reef Resort
MM 84.9 Oceanside
Islamorada, FL
(305) 664–8881, (800) 887–3373
www.fabulousvacations.com/tropicalreef
$–$$$$

Here is an eclectic tropical mix that thoroughly captivates children and adults alike. Thatched chickees line the oceanfront beach, the grounds are peppered with playground equipment, and three pools (one just for kids) dot the property.

Divergent accommodations offering a full gamut of bedding options in a pot-pourri of vintage buildings range from economy motel rooms to penthouse suites overlooking the ocean. Children younger than 13 stay free, and cribs and rollaway beds are available.

Outdoor facilities and activities abound at Tropical Reef Resort. In addition to the three pools, the resort has its own basketball court, two shuffleboard courts, and two hot tubs. A dive shop is on premises. Tropical Reef has a boat ramp, and trailer space can be secured for a fee.

Pelican Cove Resort
MM 84.5 Oceanside
Islamorada, FL
(305) 664–4435, (800) 445–4690
www.pcove.com
$$$–$$$$

Perched aside the Atlantic Ocean, Pelican Cove Resort—constructed in concrete with a tin roof and Bahamian shutters—ensures an ocean view from almost every room.

The resort offers a choice of accommodations ranging from standard rooms with one or two queen-size beds, mini refrigerators and coffeemakers, to efficiencies and one-bedroom hot tub suites, each with its own balcony. Efficiencies and suites have full modern kitchens with curved breakfast bars and either two queen-size beds or a queen-size bed and sleeper sofa. Some hotel rooms and suites connect, and all units feature tropically inspired furnishings.

Behind the resort, steps connect the raised man-made beach to the ocean, where dredging for a once used quarry has caused waters to run 30 feet deep. A fresh-water swimming pool with sun deck, outdoor cabana bar and cafe, poolside hot tub, volleyball net, playground, and watersports concession all front the beach.

Complimentary coffee and juice are offered in Pelican Cove's office 24 hours a day and a complimentary continental breakfast is served daily. Children younger than 17 stay free at Pelican Cove. Sandbox toys for children are available in the office.

Limited boat dockage is available to guests at an additional fee. Reservations must be made in advance.

Holiday Isle Resorts
MM 84 Oceanside
Islamorada, FL
(305) 664–2321, (800) 327–7070
www.holidayisle.com
$–$$$$

Holiday Isle is a bustling, happening place (see our Cruising, Restaurants, Nightlife, and Annual Events chapters). Holiday Isle is a pulsating entertainment complex favored by Generations X,Y,Z—a mass of indoor and outdoor restaurants, boardwalk shopping, thatched-palm chickees, white-sand beaches, and a full-service marina with a charter fishing fleet and watersports facilities.

Four separate hotel facilities, offering a wide range of bedding options, operate under the Holiday Isle umbrella: Howard Johnson's and Holiday Isle are on premises; El Capitan and Harbor Lights Motel are a short distance away. Rooms within the Howard Johnson and Holiday Isle hotels are similar, but Holiday Isle offers direct oceanfront views and spacious suites. El Capitan, a small cottage-style complex to the north of HoJo, is a collection of quiet beachfront wood-paneled cottages with full kitchens and sliding glass doors. The Harbor Lights offers 11 sleeping rooms and 22 efficiencies that sport kitchenettes. Prices and amenities vary greatly among the four facilities so be sure to inquire when you book your stay.

Chesapeake Resort
MM 83.4 Oceanside
Islamorada, FL
(305) 664–4662, (800) 338–3395
www.fabulousvacations.com/chesapeake
$$–$$$$

The elegant Chesapeake Resort hugs the Atlantic on 6½ acres of lushly landscaped grounds. This pristine three-story, 65-unit resort sports two heated pools, a hot tub, tennis courts, on-site laundry facilities, and an outdoor gym as well as a 700-foot sunning beach and a saltwater lagoon.

Accommodations are offered in a variety of styles, from the garden-view standard to villas and oceanfront suites. All are exquisitely adorned pastels, pickled bamboo, and faux-stone furnishings and have tile floors. Some connecting rooms combine to provide 1,000 square feet of living space. Suites and villas offer full kitchens and have balconies or screened porches.

The higher-priced units also feature whirlpool bathtubs, king-size beds, queen-size living room sleepers, two televisions, and wet bars. The one- and two-bedroom suites even have a Jacuzzi in the bedroom.

Fishing, snorkeling, diving, and parasailing excursions can be booked on premises as well as sunset cruises. You can rent kayaks and powerboats of up to 33 feet. Chesapeake also provides a boat ramp and boat dockage.

Chesapeake provides a playground for children, who can stay for free if they are younger than 13.

Casa Morada
MM 82.2 Bayside,
136 Madeira Road
Islamorada, FL
(305) 664–0044, (800) 881–3030
www.casamorada.com
$$–$$$

Tucked on the shores of Florida Bay, out of the fray of U.S. Hwy. 1 on a residential street, this all-suites hotel exudes the charm of a Mediterranean villa. The 16 suites, each uniquely different, have private terraces or semi-private gardens overlooking the water and are decorated with a mixture of wrought iron and mahogany furniture, which is exclusively created for Casa Morada at the owner's Mexican factory. Unusual memorabilia from all over the world accents the rooms. And amazingly, most of the furnishings are for sale. Rooms have cable TV, phones with modum ports, refrigerators, electric kettle

coffee/tea set-up, electronic safes, and hair-dryers.

Opened at the end of 2000, the 2-acre property showcases lush tropical gardens. Cross a small, circa-1950 bridge to a private island and you'll find a swimming pool and marina with boat ramp, where you can dock you boat (prior arrangement required). At Casa Morada you'll find a floating sundeck, barbeque facilities, and a tiki gazebo with a comfy hammock.

To find Casa Morada, turn in at the Lorelei Restaurant sign and follow Madeira Road into a quiet, residential neighborhood.

Cheeca Lodge
MM 82 Oceanside
Islamorada, FL
(305) 664–4651, (800) 327–2888
www.cheeca.com
$$$$

Majestically sprawling amid 27 manicured, tropical acres with more than 1,100 feet of beachfront, Cheeca Lodge creates a vacation enclave you may never want to leave. Follow the winding drive through splashes of bougainvillea beneath towering coconut palms, stroll across the courtyard between an avenue of date palms, and enter an island lobby alive with tropical birds, bromeliads, and potted palms. This elegant main building, tiled with Key Largo limestone and peppered with stone pillars, houses the famed Atlantic's Edge Restaurant as well as the casually laid-back Ocean Terrace Grill. The Light Tackle Lounge, which offers cocktails and light fare, is wallpapered with photos of celebrity anglers, including former President George H. W. Bush, for Cheeca hosts many a prestigious fishing tournament in the Florida Keys (see our Fishing chapter).

All 203 spacious guest rooms and one- or two-bedroom suites sport tropical themes and colors that reflect the sun and the sea of the Florida Keys. The units are furnished with bamboo and wicker furniture as well as comfortable armchairs with ottomans. All units feature ceiling fans,

Line-up for relaxation at Cheeca Lodge in Islamorada. PHOTO: CHEECA LODGE

minibars, and televisions with videocassette players. Tennis Villas, Golf Villas, Lake Villas, and Ocean Villas also offer full kitchens.

Five hot tubs are sprinkled around the property, tucked privately amid lush tropical foliage. Many rooms have balconies that over look the ocean or across the grounds of the resort; some units have screened porches.

Focused on fishing, families, and the environment, Cheeca Lodge offers an overflowing cache of recreational options. A saltwater lagoon is stocked with tropical fish for easy on-site snorkeling. A fishing pier juts out into the ocean where guests can dock boats with up to a 3-foot draft or just drop a line and try their luck. Two pools grace the premises, a freshwater option to the sand beach and seductively salty Atlantic.

Guests enjoy Cheeca's par 3, nine-hole golf course, designed by Jack Nicklaus, and six Hard-tru tennis courts. Nature trails wind throughout the property. Cheeca also maintains a full-service dive center, Caribbean Water Sports (see our Recreation chapter), and offers water toys such as Hobie Cats and Hobie Waves.

The state-of-the-art luxury Avanyu Spa was completed in 2001. This 5,000-square-foot health spa and fitness center, whose name means "plumed water serpent," features four massage therapy rooms, two facial rooms, one wet treatment room for mud wraps, and a 1,200-square-foot, mirrored exercise room. You'll also find both a men's and a women's steam room here.

The award-winning children's club, Camp Cheeca, keeps the kids happily occupied with specially designed, environmentally inspired activities (see our Kidstuff chapter).

The Moorings Village Resort
MM 81.5 Oceanside
123 Beach Road
Islamorada, FL
(305) 664–4708
www.themooringsvillage.com
$$$–$$$$

The Florida Keys may be Paradise, but The Moorings Village is utopia. Eighteen cottages and homes are peppered throughout 18 acres of a former oceanfront coconut plantation; hammocks laze between majestic palms; winding, floral-draped trails emit the essence of gardenia; and canoes and skiffs dot the 1,100-foot white-sand beach as if guests simply washed ashore. The exquisitely elegant Moorings Village maintains a low, laid-back profile, creating an inimitable tropical ambiance not readily found in the Florida Keys.

Cottages range from one to three bedrooms with one to $3\frac{1}{2}$ baths. The four original cottages, which have been completely renovated, date to the 1930s; newer buildings were completed in 1992. All are white with Bahamian shutters and trimmed in bright Caribbean colors. The cottages, which are named after some of Islamorada's pioneers, feature complete kitchens, telephone and television, and bathrooms with hand painted tiles. Most units have plantation-style porches as well as washers and dryers. The newer cottages offer luxurious soaking tubs and oversize shower stalls.

Guests enjoy use of sailboards and kayaks, a 25-meter lap pool, and tennis court. Barbecue grills, a volleyball net, thatched-roof gazebo and citrus trees are sprinkled about the lush bougainvillea-bedecked grounds. Pristine and private, The Moorings Village rates as one of the best-kept secrets in the Keys.

Kon-Tiki Resort
MM 81.2 Bayside
Islamorada, FL
(305) 664–4702
www.thefloridakeys.com/kontiki
$–$$$

Kon-Tiki's pebbled walkways, private patios, and cottages consistently attract anglers and families alike. The resort's quiet, U-shaped property boasts a shuffleboard court, a chickee, pier, private beach on Florida Bay, park benches, and a brick barbecue. The primary attraction here, though, is the saltwater pond stocked with all sorts of tropical fish. Guests are invited to don snorkel and mask and take an underwater look-see.

Accommodations feature bright, clean, and comfortable motel units, fully equipped efficiencies and one-bedroom apartments, most of which have private patios or screened porches. Two-bedroom, two-bath apartments and three-bedroom, three-bath villas, priced according to size, accommodate as many as six.

Kon-Tiki offers a freshwater heated pool and a boat ramp and dockage for vessels up to 24 feet long at no extra charge.

Hampton Inn & Suites
MM 80 Oceanside
Islamorada, FL
(305) 664–0073, (800) 426–7866
www.hamptoninnfloridakeys.com
$$$–$$$$

The Hampton Inn & Suites, constructed in 1997, adds a touch of class to the Atlantic shores. Situated directly at ocean's edge, the hotel offers 59 suites, 16 standard rooms, and four wheelchair-accessible rooms with vistas of our endless sparkling sea.

Suites feature one or two bedrooms, one or two baths, sleeper sofas in the living rooms, and full kitchens (coffee and popcorn are supplied every day). Satellite television with HBO and pay-per-view movies entertains in each unit; suites have two televisions, which are equipped with VCRs. The fresh furnishings of the Hampton Inn reflect island ambiance with fabrics of pastels and teal amid light rattan.

The common lobby area of the Hampton sports a fishing theme—giant mounted dolphin, wahoo, and tarpon; carved wood piscatory reliefs; bronze game-fish sculptures. Tables and comfy chairs flank a keystone fireplace, which is more decorative than functional, given the balmy Keys weather. A complimentary continental breakfast buffet is served here daily.

Outside, guests enjoy a heated pool and spa, tiki bar and palm-laden, sandy sunning area. A dock jutting out into the Atlantic affords boat dockage for small vessels, but be aware that depths fall to a scant 18 inches at low tide. You'll find a complete selection of watersports on premises, including snorkel or dive excursions, parasailing, and fishing charters.

The popular Outback Steak House (305–664-3344) also is on the premises.

Breezy Palms Resort
MM 80 Oceanside
Islamorada, FL
(305) 664–2361
www.breezypalms.com
$–$$$

Quaint coral buildings with turquoise doors and trim, shake roofs, and screened porches mark Breezy Palms Resort, a cozy place nestled on 320 feet of oceanfront. The brightly wallpapered motel rooms, efficiencies, apartments, and cottages are clean, spacious, and well-appointed, featuring rattan furniture and colorful island floral prints.

Chickees and copious coconut palms pepper the property, which sits directly on the Atlantic Ocean and sports a sandy beach as well as a freshwater pool. A brick barbecue, picnic table, and volleyball net add to the amenities; dockage is available for an additional fee. No straight inboards or personal watercraft, such as Jet Skis or Waverunners, are permitted.

Breezy Palms is accessible by boat. Children younger than 13 stay free.

Matecumbe Resort
MM 76.3 Oceanside
Islamorada, FL
(305) 664–8801
$$

The sprawling Matecumbe Resort—32 fully equipped apartments in four two-story buildings—provides the perfect family vacation setup. The reasonably priced units, which are constantly updated, range from one- or two-bedrooms to efficiencies and all have complete kitchens. A range of bedding options is available (doubles, queens, kings), and most baths have been modernized with fresh tile and appointments. Units vary in decor and layout, but all sport tropical pastels and have some sort of eat-in dining arrangement. Televisions with cable hookup are standard.

The grounds feature a heated freshwater pool and a man-made beach adorned with chaise lounges and chickees. A sand volleyball court, horseshoes, and shuffleboard provide adult entertainment while two children's play areas beckon the kiddies. The expanses of mature trees and curving coconut palms are peppered with grills and picnic tables.

Matecumbe Resort offers the use of its boat ramp to guests and provides free boat dockage as well as boat rentals.

White Gate Court
MM 76 Bayside
Islamorada, FL
(305) 664–4136, (800) 645–4283
www.whitegatecourt.com
$$–$$$

A touch of understated European elegance marks the restored villas and bungalows at White Gate Court, situated on 3 acres abutting the placid Gulf of Mexico. These 1940s-era Conch cottages survived the hurricane of 1961 and decades of neglect before receiving tender loving care from owner Suzanne Orias DeCargnelli, a native of Hungary who spent many years in South America. Painted cheerful yellow and white inside and out, the seven private units—completed in 1997—exude a rustic Old World charm. Spacious interiors feature rough-plastered walls; fresh tile and lightly stained wood-plank floors; fully equipped, stylistically European white kitchens; and sparkling modern bathrooms. Beds are covered with exquisite individualized quilts. All units have covered porches and outdoor tables and chairs. Some even feature rope hammocks.

White iron gates guard this tropical hermitage, fronting a long, narrow driveway lined with palm trees, oleanders, and white coach lamps. Lounge chairs pepper a 200-foot white sand beach where guests enjoy swimming and snorkeling in the sandy-bottom Gulf; White Gate Court does not have a pool. A finger dock stretches into the water for fishing, and tiki torches and barbecue grills are available for an evening cookout. A guest laundry also is provided. Pets and children are welcome.

Tropic Aire Resort Motel
MM 75.8 Bayside
Islamorada, FL
(305) 664–4989
$–$$

If there is any question as to why this small motel promotes itself as "Almost Heaven," the reason becomes apparent with one step inside the rooms: many are painted stark white with white tile, white wicker, and white wood-beamed ceilings. The motel makes a fine choice for those who enjoy clean, relaxed comfort at a value.

Don't let this facility's understated exterior mislead you: one- and two-story adjacent units come in an assortment of styles and sizes and overlook a parklike setting of picnic tables, grills, and large shade trees. A volleyball court and a coral barbecue grill sit near the man-made beach and swim area.

Tropic Aire has a lighted fishing pier and fish-cleaning station. It is accessible by boat.

Topsider Resort
MM 75.5 Bayside
Islamorada, FL
(305) 664–8031, (800) 262–9874
www.baysidekeys.com
$$$

The 20 octagonal, elevated time-share villas at Topsider Resort flank a wood boardwalk that marches from the secluded parking lot to the crystalline waters of the Gulf of Mexico. Ablaze with gumbo limbos, crotons, and bougainvillea, the grounds of the Topsider effect a rain forest mystique, even though the resort itself is right off the Overseas Highway.

Units are identical in layout. Each features two bedrooms, two baths, a dining area, living room, and full kitchen. Ceiling fans, washer and dryer, and ground-level storage are standard.

Guests at Topsider Resort enjoy an elevated pool and spa, a tennis court, children's swings and slides, grills, picnic tables, and bayfront wood lounges for sunning on the sandy lagoonside beach.

Insiders' Tip
For child-friendly resorts at a glance, see our Kidstuff chapter.

Free boat dockage is available on Topsider's long pier. Minimum stay here is three nights, but most guests opt for a week's sabbatical.

Coral Bay Resort
MM 75.6 Bayside
Islamorada, FL
(305) 664–5568
www.thecoralbayresort.com
$$–$$$$

Renovated in 1997, Coral Bay Resort's three motel rooms, eleven efficiencies, and two villa suites are secreted away in white-trimmed, pastel pink, air-conditioned Conch-style cottages, each with a lazy-days front porch. A painted icon distinguishes each unit, creating a virtual school of tropical fish.

The fresh interior furnishings sparkle with light furniture, pastel fabrics, and tile floors. A selection of South Florida art adorns the walls, supplied by an Orlando art gallery. A variety of bedding options is available. The efficiencies feature full kitchens, and each villa suite also provides a living area with a sleeper sofa.

You'll enjoy Coral Bay's heated pool as well as the sandy beach on the Gulf of Mexico that is peppered with lounges and chickees. Fishing and snorkeling in the 14-foot-deep saltwater tidal pool are excellent. The pier itself has built-in seating and a fish-cleaning station. Guests can dock their own vessels for free or use the resort's paddleboat for exploration. Waters beyond the dock are illuminated at night so the seaside fun doesn't have to end at sunset.

One thing that hasn't changed at Coral Bay is the lush tropical ambiance created by mature plantings of yesteryear.

You'll find a bougainvillea two stories high, and palms and indigenous hardwood trees pepper the property. The casual elegance of this resort, coupled with Coral Bay's dedication to the carefree simplicity of "the Keys the way they used to be," ensures a relaxing holiday.

Caloosa Cove
Resort Condominium
MM 73.8 Oceanside
Islamorada, FL
(305) 664–8811
www.caloosacove.com
$$$

An irregularly shaped condominium complex set apart from civilization on a large parcel of prime oceanfront property, Caloosa Cove offers 30 spacious, light and bright efficiencies and one-bedroom suites. Suites offer eat-in kitchens, spacious bedrooms, and living rooms with sofa beds. Each efficiency is a large one-room unit with an eat-in kitchen, queen-size bed, and loveseat. All are decorated with tropical rattans and pastels. A covered deck that looks directly at the Atlantic fronts every unit.

Caloosa Cove's large irregular-shaped pool, surrounded by extensive decking and thatched-palm chickees, sits directly on the ocean's edge, affording endless vistas of the beyond. The grounds encompassing the coral-laden exterior of Caloosa Cove burgeon with mature tropical plantings.

Activities and amenities on condo premises include shuffleboard and basketball courts, a barbecue area, lighted tennis courts, a full-service marina, fishing charters, and boat and bicycle rentals. The nearby Safari Lounge serves your choice of cocktails.

Middle Keys

The Middle Keys, known locally as the "heart of the Keys," stretch from the Long Key Bridge to the Seven Mile Bridge. Long, Conch, Duck, and Grassy Keys lead the way to the string of bridge-connected islands known as the incorporated city of Marathon.

Basing your accommodations in the Middle Keys offers some distinct advantages. The barrier reef sheltering the prolific fishing waters of the Atlantic supports a plethora of marine life and harbors a number of primo shipwrecks for divers (see our Diving and Snorkeling chapter). Fishing in the Middle Keys rivals that of the famed Islamorada, a well-kept secret. From flats to backcountry, bluewater to bridges, you won't hear too many tales of the "one that got away" here (see our Fishing chapter).

Marathon offers two golf courses: the nine-hole Key Colony Beach public course and the 18-hole private Sombrero Country Club. Sombrero honors reciprocal privileges from other golf clubs in the United States (see our Recreation chapter). Active, ongoing tennis programs with drills, round-robins, and lessons are available at Hawk's Cay Resort on Duck Key and at Sombrero Resort (a separate facility from the Sombrero Country Club) in Marathon to all players regardless of where they are staying.

Marathon has a movie theater, too (cinemas are few and far between in the Keys). This quirky little theater, which shows first-run movies that change weekly, seats viewers in movable, swivel barrel chairs that surround small round tables designed to hold your popcorn and soda. (See our Recreation chapter for details of golf, tennis, movie theaters, and more.)

The Dolphin Research Center on Grassy Key is a must-do regardless of where your accommodations might be. And, in Marathon, Crane Point will captivate the whole family, as will historic Pigeon Key, at the end of a length of the old Seven Mile Bridge accessed at mile marker 47 (see our Attractions chapter). Sombrero Beach in Marathon, a very nice man-made public beach, provides endless ocean vistas to all.

Needless to say, like the rest of the Keys, this whole area is packed with recreational water options from party fishing boats and glass-bottom reef excursions to personal watercraft and sea kayak rentals. Parasailing and ultralight rides are available here as well (see our Recreation chapter).

The pace is less tiki-bar frenetic here than in the Upper Keys. The sidewalk rolls up at a relatively early hour. But this area will appeal to families with children as well as serious anglers and divers who, after a day on or under the water, relish a relaxing dinner at one of the many top-notch restaurants and then a nocturnal refueling of energy for whatever tomorrow may bring.

Lime Tree Bay Resort
MM 68.5 Bayside
Layton
Long Key, FL
(305) 664–4740, (800) 723–4519
www.limetreebayresort.com
$$–$$$

Wiggle your toes as you laze in one of the string hammocks tied among the copious palms surrounding Lime Tree Bay Resort. Perched on the shores of Florida Bay, this resort—which features a variety of overnight options—tucks chickees and lounge chairs amid lush tropical vegetation so that your escape from the workaday world is complete. An elevated freshwater pool and heated hot tub extend over a wood boardwalk at water's edge. Accommodations range from waterfront motel-style rooms and efficiencies to one- and two-bedroom apartments. Rooms have been renovated over the years, but span the decor of several decades. If a recently updated room is your desire, be sure to inquire.

Pier 68, next door, offers watersports, including diving, snorkeling, and sunset excursions as well as boat and personal watercraft rentals (see our Recreation chapter). Guests may dock their own boats at no extra charge (up to 28 feet, 3-foot draft at low tide), but Lime Tree Bay has no boat ramp, so boats must be launched at nearby Seabird Marina near Fiesta Key. Shuffleboard, a horseshoe pit,

and one tennis court stand ready in case you feel like a little exercise. Children younger than 8 stay free. Two restaurants are adjacent to the property.

Conch Key Cottages
MM 62.3 Oceanside
Walker's Island, FL
(305) 289–1377, (800) 330–1577
www.conchkeycottages.com
$$–$$$$

Step back in time as you drive across the narrow causeway from the Overseas Highway into Keys past. Lovingly restored beyond their former grandeur, the pastel, gingerbread-trimmed Conch Key Cottages—like an upended basket of Easter eggs—reflect the upbeat, zany personalities of owners Wayne Byrnes and Ron Wilson. Each cottage—bright, fresh, and full of crisp, tropical cottons—is as unique as the conch shells for which they're named.

The wood-paneled Coquina, resting at water's edge, provides king-size beds in each of its two voluminous bedrooms. A walled patio with a hot tub and gas grill maximizes your privacy, and the sizable well-equipped kitchen might even entice you to cook during your holiday. The largest cottage, the King's Crown, is about 1,200 square feet of living space, with a king-size bed in one bedroom and two queen-size beds in the other, plus a living room, dining room, kitchen and 1½ baths. The Whelk, Queen, and Fighting Conch cottages each fringe the living/dining/kitchen combo room with a queen-size bedroom, one bathroom, and a massive, screened porch overlooking a primo bonefish flat. These one-bedroom oceanfront units received full facelifts in 1998, complete with new kitchens and baths. The honeymoon cottage, the Baby Conch, miniaturizes the features of the others, but the custom-painted lamps and specially made furnishings mirror the details of its more capacious relatives.

Periwinkle, Seahorse, and Horse Conch cottages were constructed in 1997. Grabbing a coveted ocean view, these two-bedroom, two-bath units feature full kitchens, living and dining areas, two cable televisions (one with VCR), and every amenity imaginable for a luxurious vacation stay.

A small freshwater swimming pool nestles amid towering palms, and several varieties of bananas hang at the ready for guest consumption. Plantings reflect the owners' philosophy of growing old-fashioned vegetation that attracts birds and butterflies.

Conch Key Cottages maintains a boat ramp and marina that can accommodate an 8-foot draft. Guests may dock their vessels at no extra charge. So you are sure to bring those freshly caught snappers to the table, there is a fish-cleaning station complete with water and electricity.

Hawk's Cay Resort
MM 61 Oceanside
Duck Key, FL
(305) 743–7000, (888) 443–6393
www.hawkscay.com
$$$–$$$$

Step through the pink portico of Hawk's Cay to the strains of a disembodied steel drum. A pith-helmeted doorman sporting a riotously colored shirt bids you welcome. Mount the steps to the tiled veranda, its Bahama fans slowly stirring the subtropical air over the wicker settees. Pass into the palm-filled lobby and out the other side to...the West Indies? Like Alice passing through the looking glass, you will adjust your perspective, slow down, kick back, and recharge your batteries at this rambling Caribbean-style resort. Gracious yet low key, opulent but subdued, Hawk's Cay's 60-acre facility encompasses one of the five islands of the Duck Key configuration.

Accommodations in the hotel building include standard rooms with two full-size beds; captain's suites, each with a king-size bed and a sleeper sofa in a separate seating area; and large penthouse suites with two bedrooms, 1½ baths, a living room, dining room, and private rooftop sun deck with hot tub. All rooms have balconies, mini refrigerators, and coffeemakers.

The Villas at Hawk's Cay—completed in 1999 and 2000—offer guests the option of self-contained vacation homes. These two-story, Key West–style abodes all offer full kitchens, living rooms, covered porches, washers and dryers, ceiling fans, and televisions with VCRs. The Bungalow units feature two bedrooms and 1½ baths. Conch villas have two bedrooms and two baths. The more spacious Cottages offer two bedrooms, a den, and 2½ baths. The 18 older Marina Villas each have two bedrooms and two baths. All are individually owned and decorated with tropical Keys furnishings.

Unique to this Keys property is the saltwater lagoon, belted by a man-made, sandy beach, which borders the canal entrance to Hawk's Cay Marina boat basin (see our Cruising chapter).

When you've had enough of doing nothing at all—lazing around the lagoon, the freshwater family or adults-only pools or the hot tub—check out the diversions. Observe the ongoing dolphin discovery program at Dolphin Connection (see our Attractions chapter). Take the glass-bottom Osprey's morning boat trip or afternoon snorkeling trip. Book a fishing or diving charter or a sunset sailing cruise. Sign up for parasailing, fly-fishing school, or sailing instruction, or rent a sea kayak for a self-guided eco-tour through the backcountry waters (see our Fishing, Recreation, Boating, and Paradise Found chapters). Work out at the Indies Club recreation and fitness center. Or swing your racket in the tennis garden, participating in lessons, round-robins, or just whacking returns at the ball machine.

The four popular restaurants on premises whet any appetite: Palm Terrace for breakfast; Cantina for poolside light bites; Porto Cayo for eclectic Italian; and the WatersEdge for steaks and seafood (see our Restaurants chapter). Children fare equally well at Hawk's Cay. The Little Pirates and Island Adventure Clubs guarantee that Mom, Dad, and the kids all find a holiday wonderland (see our Kidstuff chapter).

The villas at Hawk's Cay offer guests the option of self-contained vacation homes. PHOTO: HAWK'S CAY RESORT

Rainbow Bend Resort
MM 57.7 Oceanside
Grassy Key, FL
(305) 289–1505, (800) 929–1505
www.rainbowbend.com
$$–$$$

Fire up a 15-foot motorboat and head for the flats, for at Rainbow Bend each day of your stay entitles you to four free boating hours. If you'd rather silently glide across the water, a sailboat awaits. Or try a kayak, spyak (a kayak with a glass bottom), or paddleboat. Stretched across $2\frac{1}{2}$ acres of palm-speckled oceanfront beach, Rainbow Bend presents a mixed bag of accommodations, ranging from large sleeping rooms and efficiencies to oceanfront one- and two-bedroom suites, all with varying decor that spans the decades.

Relax under chickees on the lounges and Adirondack chairs that pepper the beach. If fresh water appeals to you, dip into the large pool and hot tub that edge the property. A long, wood pier extends into the shallow ocean waters, where you can drop a line or dock your own small watercraft for the duration of your stay.

Or climb the giant wooden beach tower for a sweeping view across the Atlantic.

Small pets are allowed for an additional fee.

The Hideaway Restaurant, which overlooks the beach, offers lunch and dinner. A complimentary full breakfast is served here each morning.

Grassy Key Beach Motel & Resort
MM 58.2 Oceanside
Grassy Key, FL
(305) 743–0533
www.thekeysresort.com
$$$

Literally wedged on a narrow strip of land between the Atlantic and U.S. Hwy. 1, Grassy Key Beach Motel and Resort, completed at the end of 2000, offers an upclose ocean vista across a 200-foot, white sandy beach.

All 10 units enjoy the spectacular ocean views as well as private covered parking. The units, which surround a freshwater swimming pool, come in two plans—the 1,000-square-foot Dolphin and the 1,200-square-foot Manatee. Both styles feature two bedrooms, one bath, and fully equipped kitchens that include refrigerator, self-cleaning oven, microwave oven, and all the cooking utensils and linens you could ever need. Laundry facilities are on site. The living room has a sleeper sofa.

So, although their nightly rate puts them in our three dollar-signs Price Code Range, each unit at Grassy Key Beach Motel & Resort accommodates a maximum of six people, making this new addition to the Grassy Key strip of lodgings a good value.

White Sands Inn
MM 57.6 Oceanside
Grassy Key, FL
(305) 743–5285
www.whitesandsinn.com
$–$$$

Hugging a prime piece of direct ocean frontage on Grassy Key, White Sands Inn was lovingly refurbished in 1999. The pale pink and white inn houses seven one-room units—four efficiencies and three sleeping rooms—and the Tree Top Terrace suite, which has two bedrooms with two singles and a king-size bed, living room, full kitchen, and a private deck. The other units have tile floors and remodeled bathrooms, two queen-size beds, and crisp bedding. The rooms are air-conditioned, and some sport ceiling fans as well. Efficiencies feature fully equipped kitchens, but even the sleeping rooms are fitted with mini refrigerators, coffeemakers, and microwaves so you can self-cater if you wish.

The White Sands Inn nestles amid towering coconut palms at water's edge, where sparkling white imported sand forms a beach. Grills are available, and a large picnic table rests under a thatched chickee. The ambiance at this intimate hideaway is casual and friendly.

A long curved pier stretches out into the ocean, where two kayaks, a rowboat, and a paddleboat are docked for free usage by guests. At low tide, the nearshore waters abutting the inn recedes, forming a natural sandy beach. You can walk for miles along the sandy flats. And rumor has it that bonefish lurk at the edge of the flat.

Royal Plum Condominiums
MM 54.5 Oceanside
133 Coco Plum Drive
Marathon, FL
(305) 289–1102
$$–$$$

Sitting directly on a 200-foot private beach on the ocean, this property looks like a piece of the Caribbean. The spacious, well-appointed units with one, two, or three bedrooms offer full kitchens and all linens. All overlook either the subtropical gardens or the heated swimming pool flanking the Atlantic. If you get restless soaking up the sun and surf, play tennis on Royal Plum's regulation court.

Reservations require a one-week minimum stay.

Cocoplum Beach and Tennis Club
MM 54.5 Oceanside
109 Coco Plum Drive
Marathon, FL
(305) 743–0240, (800) 228–1587
www.cocoplum.com
$$$–$$$$

If you want quiet, quiet, quiet, find the illusive Cocoplum Beach and Tennis Club. Hidden among 53 varieties of palm trees and other tropical plantings, the pod of 20 three-story, art deco–colored "mushrooms" bestows a true island ambiance. The endless ocean stretches to tomorrow, ribboned in a blue-to-green prism.

Each octagonal villa—ringed with sliding doors to a wraparound deck and screened porch—houses two bedrooms, two baths, and a family room with sleeper sofa, wet bar, two TVs, VCR, two telephones, and an answering machine. Each unit has a dining room and a full-size kitchen, complete with a microwave oven, blender, and coffeemaker. Guests enjoy use of a private utility room and washer and dryer on the lower level of each unit. In 1998 all units were updated with new carpeting and drapes.

Cocoplum Beach and Tennis Club has planted a fruit-and-spice park that sports 10 varieties of banana trees, 16 types of citrus, and four kinds of Key limes. Guests are invited to freely pick any of the ripe fruit and enjoy the tastes of the topics.

Loll by the illusion-edge swimming pool, which was built in 1999 and surrounded by paver-stone decking. Or pop into one of the blue cabanas sprinkled about the sandy beach area that now is much larger than it was, thanks to 1998's Hurricane Georges. The hot tub awaits your tired muscles after a few hours of spirited tennis or beach volleyball. Or just fold yourself into one of the many secluded hammocks and take a snooze.

Reservations require a three-night minimum and a full week for Christmas and New Year's. Prices vary by proximity to the ocean.

Sea Isle Condominiums
MM 54 Oceanside
1101 W. Ocean Drive
Key Colony Beach, FL
(305) 743–0173
$$

The sandy beach and ocean views distinguish this 24-unit condo resort. Three tri-level, white buildings, one behind another, line Sea Isle's narrow strip of Key Colony Beach. Built in the late '60s and individually owned and decorated, the furnishings of these spacious two-bedroom, two-bath apartments swing widely between styles of ensuing decades. Many were freshened with new ceilings, carpeting, air conditioners, and appliances in 1998 and 1999.

Nevertheless, all necessities for a sun-filled, fun-filled vacation are provided: a freshwater heated swimming pool, shuffleboard, gas grills and picnic tables, lounge chairs, and chickees. Stroll down Key Colony's "condo lane" to the public golf course and tennis courts or head into Marathon for a selection of boating, fishing and diving activities (see chapters devoted to those subjects).

Reservations require a one-week minimum stay.

Continental Inn
MM 54 Oceanside
1121 W. Ocean Drive
Key Colony Beach, FL
(305) 289–0101, (800) 833–5397
www.thefloridakeys.com/continentalinn
$$–$$$

Don your mask, fins, and snorkel because a small, rocky formation at the edge of Continental Inn's beach supports an aquarium of marine life. Located on the coveted sandy stretch of Key Colony Beach, this condominium resort, with its white stone balustrade, looks faintly Mediterranean. Gulls and terns dart about the three oceanfront chickees as guests drink in the limitless vistas of the Atlantic.

These individually owned, simply decorated, one-bedroom efficiencies flank a large, heated swimming pool. A small kitchen/dining/sitting area adjoins each bedroom and bathroom unit. Two, two-bedroom apartments, each of which has a full living room with a sofa and a full eat-in kitchen, provide more spacious quarters for up to four people.

You can play the links at the nearby public golf course, head for the tennis courts, or take your kids to a nice playground (see our Recreation chapter). No boats or trailers are allowed.

Key Colony Beach Motel
MM 54 Oceanside
441 E. Ocean Drive
Key Colony Beach, FL
(305) 289–0411
$

Sitting proudly beside the ocean in Key Colony Beach—often called "condo row"—the modest Key Colony Beach Motel provides simply furnished rooms, each featuring two double beds and a refrigerator, and a primo location. A lovely, palm-lined, sandy beach fronts this two-story white motel, which also has a heated swimming pool that was finished in 1999. All you need here is a towel, some sunscreen, and a good book.

The 20 three-story, self-contained units at Cocoplum Beach and Tennis Club resemble a pod of mushrooms. PHOTO: COCOPLUM BEACH AND TENNIS CLUB

Bonefish Bay Motel
MM 53.5 Oceanside
Marathon, FL
(305) 289–0565, (800) 336–0565
www.bonefishbay.com
$–$$

Offering a range of homey accommodations from sleeping rooms with two double beds to one-bedroom apartments, Bonefish Bay's guests enjoy the added luxury of the motel's boat ramp and canalside dockage (3-foot draft) at no extra charge. The motel's location just above Vaca Cut ensures easy boat access to our ocean waters.

In 1997 the caretaker's residence was converted into two efficiency units and two large apartments. The efficiencies feature two double beds, private bath, and kitchenette. Each apartment has one bedroom, a full kitchen, living and dining areas, and a private bath. The apartments can be connected if desired.

A mature landscape of coconut palms frames the raised-deck swimming pool. Painted white with screaming yellow trim, Bonefish Bay began its days as a 1950s fishing camp. Guests are treated to free use of bicycles.

The Bonefish Bay office sells bait and tackle as well as basic boating supplies for the convenience of their guests.

Holiday Inn & Marina
MM 54 Oceanside
Marathon, FL
(305) 289–0222, (800) 224–5053
www.spottswood.com/holidayinn
$$–$$$

Taken over by Spottswood Corporation after the last two devastating hurricanes and totally remodeled and revamped, the Marathon Holiday Inn—opened in 2001—features 134 freshly decorated guest rooms with the usual Holiday Inn amenities. You'll find minibars, coffeemakers, cable TV, hair dryers, in-room safe, and phones with voice mail.

Outside, you can enjoy the freshwater swimming pool and kiddie pool or rent a boat, personal watercraft, or a bicycle. The Marathon Holiday Inn is located on a cut that leads from the Atlantic to the Gulf of Mexico.

Coral Lagoon Resort
MM 53.5 Oceanside
Marathon, FL
(305) 289–0121
$$

The 18 duplex-cottage efficiencies of Coral Lagoon Resort—swaddled in trailing purple and red bougainvillea—flank a quiet, dead-end, deep-water canal. Each unit opens onto a private, canal-side wooden deck, where you can lounge in a hammock strung between the posts of your own private canvas-covered chickee. Dock your boat (up to 30 feet) at the palm-lined bulkhead in front of your room for easy access out Vaca Cut to the ocean.

The units vary in size, but each one features a compact living room, dining area, and kitchen as well as a king-size bed or two twins. Most have a sleeper sofa. Each duplex shares a barbecue grill. Many units received new ceramic tile floors in 1998.

Complimentary use of tennis rackets, fishing equipment and a built-in wall safe add an extra touch of hospitality.

Seascape Ocean Resort
MM 51 Oceanside
1075 76th Street
Marathon, FL
(305) 743–6455, (800) 332–7327
www.floridakeys.net/seascape
$$–$$$

Seascape Ocean Resort is a 5-acre oceanfront resort reminiscent of a small exclusive European country-house hotel. Built as a stone-faced private home in 1953, Seascape offers nine exquisite units uniquely reflecting the talents of the owners, Sara and Bill Stites.

Sara, an artist whose canvas-filled studio intrigues her guests, has painted stylized tropical fish on the headboards of each bed. African prints dominate the custom-made bedding, and her colossal modern-art creations grace the walls. Books featuring Bill's photography casually adorn the arty common room, where morning will greet you with a buffet of specialty coffees, tropical fruits, and freshly baked muffins. Each evening at 6 P.M., complimentary wine and hors d'oeuvres magically appear as Brazilian or Hawaiian slide-guitar music softly whispers through the room.

You will notice small, gracious touches everywhere: a seashell basket of vanilla bean soap, almond lotion, and shampoo in each bathroom; thick, luxurious towels; fresh fruit and flowers in every room; and a backyard herb garden for the guests' use.

Seascape has several efficiency units, and, although the other rooms are not equipped with full kitchens, all have small refrigerators. Gas grills, outdoor tables and chairs nest in the shaded gardens in case you care to stay in and cook your own dinner. Purple passionflowers bloom along the white picket fence surrounding the gated swimming pool that hugs the ocean edge.

You can even arrive at Seascape by boat. A deep channel leads to the U-shaped bulkhead that accommodates crafts drawing up to 4 feet. Enjoy exploring the saltwater flats in one of Seascape's complimentary kayaks.

To find Seascape Ocean Resort, turn on 76th Street toward the ocean and follow the signs.

Seahorse Motel
MM 51 Bayside
Marathon, FL
(305) 743–6571, (800) 874–1115
www.floridakeys.net/seahorse
$

You can't miss the hot-pink doors and trim of the Seahorse Motel, a roadside lodging offering perky, clean, affordable accommodations to cost-conscious travelers. The 40 basic motel-style rooms sport two double beds; some also have sleeper sofas and mini refrigerators. Efficiency units have full kitchens. A plugged canal borders the back of the property affording dockage for your boat for an additional fee. Rooms with sliding-glass doors open onto canalside patios or overlook the central swimming pool and play-

Each evening complimentary wine and hors d'oeuvres magically appear in the common room at Seascape Resort. PHOTO: SEASCAPE/BILL STITES

ground. Gas grills and picnic tables are scattered about the premises.

The Reef Resort
MM 50.5 Bayside
Marathon, FL
(305) 743–7900, (800) 327–4836
www.thereefresort.com
$$–$$$

As you drive through Marathon, you may spot what looks like a cluster of beige spaceships hugging Florida Bay. No, the aliens have not landed. These 22 octagonal villas, suspended on "landing" shaft stilts, actually provide a luxurious Keys getaway.

Each villa features the same floor plan—two bedrooms, two baths, a full kitchen, and living room with sleeper sofa. The open ceiling vaults around a spoked, central fulcrum. Each unit has a washer and dryer. Lushly landscaped grounds surrounding the two tennis courts belie the fact that The Reef Resort borders the Overseas Highway.

Bicycles, canoes, paddleboats, and rowboats are available at no extra charge for guests who can tear themselves away from the freshwater pool. Picnic tables, grills, and chickees on the waterfront inspire a cookout at sunset. The Reef Resort's marina offers dockage for your boat of 25 feet or less (5-foot draft at low tide).

Minimum stay at the Reef Resort is three nights.

Sombrero Resort & Lighthouse Marina
MM 50 Oceanside
19 Sombrero Boulevard
Marathon, FL
(305) 743–2250, (800) 433–8660
www.sombreroresort.com
$$–$$$

Flanking Boot Key Harbor and an adjoining inland canal, Sombrero Resort & Lighthouse Marina offers efficiencies and condominium accommodations with all the amenities of a resort. Though not on the ocean, this destination resort, located in the heart of Marathon between the Overseas Highway and the oceanfront Sombrero Beach, allows you to be within steps of all the action, yet bathed in a laidback and relaxing atmosphere.

The 123 suites are situated in two three-story, white buildings with covered parking beneath (first-come, first-served). A typical one-bedroom condominium is light, bright, modern, and clean, featuring a living room with sleeper sofa, dining area, kitchen, bedroom with a king-size bed, and a full bathroom with shower. Some units have two double beds. Connecting doors may be opened between units if desired. Rooms received a complete facelift in the late '90s, sporting fresh paint, furnishings, and carpeting.

A keystone deck surrounds the large swimming pool, complete with tiki bar for that mid-afternoon tropical libation. A game room, also poolside, will amuse the kids with billiards, table soccer, and video arcade games. You'll be able to improve your tennis on the four lighted courts under the expert tutelage of Tim Wonderlin. Lessons, round-robins, and group drills are scheduled on a regular basis. Complimentary morning coffee is served daily in the lobby.

Sombrero Resort maintains a marina and a boat ramp. Guests may launch their boats at Sombrero's ramp and secure dockage at one of the slips for an additional fee per day based on availability. Boats and trailers may be kept in the parking lot. Lighthouse of Blues, a restaurant and bar on premises, is open nightly.

Banana Bay Resort & Marina
MM 49.5 Bayside
Marathon, FL
(305) 743–3500, (800) 226–2621
www.bananabay.com
$$–$$$

Ozzie and Harriet, two blue-crowned conures, raucously squawk from their screened aviary as you register at Banana Bay, the Caribbean plantation-style resort tucked on 10 acres aside Florida Bay. The two residential areas—Island House and Marina Bay House—are decked out in the prerequisite Keys teals and peaches. The spacious rooms feature upscale island-style rattan furnishings and Bahama shutters. The grounds are ancient:

gnarled trunks of massive royal poinciana trees, 20-foot traveler's palms, and mature bird-of-paradise plants. And don't miss the bananas, 15 varieties tucked between towering schefferas and gumbo limbos, papayas, and staggering banyan trees. A resident hawk makes regular passes at the small goldfish pond, hoping for an unsuspecting appetizer.

Don't let this quiet island charm fool you. There is plenty to do besides loll by the L-shaped swimming pool or soak in the hot tub. Banana Bay offers an on-premises playland: tennis, parasailing, sea kayaking, sailboarding, or rentals of personal watercraft, sailboats, and powerboats from Rick's Watercraft Rentals.

Just when you think you can't take any more, Safari Charters sets off from Banana Bay's marina dock for a sunset champagne cruise (see our Recreation chapters) or takes off for the reef for a day of diving or snorkeling. The sand-floored tiki bar, which looks out over the Gulf of Mexico, bumps and grinds with live entertainment on weekends. Banana Cabana Restaurant, on premises, is conveniently open for lunch and dinner daily. A complimentary continental buffet breaks the day poolside each morning.

Banana Bay offers popular island wedding packages, including a choice of romantic settings for the ceremony. For Banana Bay Sailing School, refer to our Boating chapter.

For a complete getaway, opt to rent Banana Bay's private offshore island, "Pretty Joe Rock." Rented by the week, the island—which is only a few hundred yards from the resort's marina—features its own two-bedroom, two-bathroom cottage. This is the perfect place to become a castaway in style.

Marathon Key Beach Club
MM 49.5 Bayside
Marathon, FL
(305) 743–6522
www.floridakeys.com/marathonkeybeach
club
$$$

All the comforts of home await you at the Marathon Key Beach Club. Each of these 1,300-square-foot timeshare condominiums features two bedrooms, two baths, a living room with queen-size sleeper sofa, dining alcove, a complete kitchen, and washer and dryer. A screened porch off the living room nestles in a canopy of mature trees on the shores of Florida Bay.

Gas grills and picnic tables are sprinkled throughout the property. Guests at Marathon Key Beach Club share all the facilities of the adjoining Banana Bay Resort (see separate listing in this chapter), including pool, hot tub, tennis, marina, sandy beach, sunset tiki bar, and Banana Cabana Restaurant.

Marathon Key Beach Club rents by the week.

The Blackfin Resort
MM 49.5 Bayside
Marathon, FL
(305) 743–2393, (800) 548–5397
www.blackfinresort.com
$–$$$

The Blackfin Resort received tender loving refurbishment in 1997, the 35 units now sporting freshened paint, carpeting, and bedspreads and drapes in tropical florals. Accommodations fall into a number of comfortable, affordable configurations: doubles, each of which features a queen-size bed and small sitting area; singles, which are smaller rooms than the doubles, but still are equipped with queen-size beds; and king rooms, which have king-size beds and loveseats. Some mini refrigerators are available for these rooms.

Blackfin Resort also offers six cozy single efficiencies, queen-size bedrooms with kitchenettes that are comfortable for two adults; two large efficiencies, each of which features a big kitchen, dining area, and two queen-size beds; and one very large two-bedroom apartment, a 1,600-square-foot unit that offers a separate kitchen and dining room, two baths, and a porch.

The Blackfin Resort sits upon 4½ acres abutting the Gulf of Mexico. The grounds are peppered with poinciana, gumbo limbo, and strangler fig trees and curving coconut palms. Stone paths wind through gardens of tropical flora. On a remote point of land at the end of the marina marked by a miniature lighthouse, guests enjoy a 600-foot, man-made, sandy beach sprinkled with lounge chairs, picnic tables, barbecue grills, and a thatched chickee. A freshwater pool overlooks the Gulf. The placid waters of the Gulf shelter a potpourri of tropical fish, a virtual aquarium for anglers and snorkelers.

A large marina accommodates guests' vessels at an additional charge. The resort lies just 2 nautical miles from the Seven Mile Bridge for easy access to the Atlantic for fishing or diving. Benches and a fish cleaning station at the marina are well-utilized by anglers. Personal watercraft and kayak rentals are available on premises. Also on the premises are Hurricane Grille restaurant and a jazz/blues bar with live entertainment.

Crystal Bay Resort
MM 49 Bayside
Marathon, FL
(305) 289–8089, (888) 289–8089
www.crystalbayresort.com
$–$$

The best kept new secret in Marathon is hereby out of the bag! Situated in the heart of the city on the Gulf of Mexico, Crystal Bay Resort offers a primo location and reasonably priced lodging in newly remodeled Conch-style bungalows. Jack and Veronica Leggett, who bought the property in 1999, have lovingly reincarnated the buildings into bright, light, modern accommodations, the likes of which are unusual to find in the Middle Keys. Renovations were completed in 2001.

Crystal Bay Resort has 27 units, which include spacious sleeping rooms, efficiencies, a studio, and a full apartment. The bungalows and guest rooms, with many bedding configurations, are a vision of whites and pastels and feature tile floors, new or updated baths and kitchens, and stenciled walls.

Dotted with hammocks, coach lights, and a gazebo, the grounds stretch from the Overseas Highway back to the placid waters of the Gulf. Children enjoy an extensive sandbox play yard complete with state-of-the-art, climb-upon equipment. Adults like the picnic area, which is peppered with brick barbecue grills. And, everyone loves the free-form swimming pool and waterfall. Equipped with fiber-optic lighting, the waters change colors in the evening, creating a kaleidoscopic effect that carries on where the spectacular sunset left off.

Chaise lounges and chickees are sprinkled about the water's edge, and a small marina basin allows easy access to explore surrounding waters. Guests may launch their boats here; dockage is an extra fee. A fishing pier, complete with cleaning station, juts offshore.

Hidden Harbor Motel
MM 48.5 Bayside
Marathon, FL
(305) 743–5376, (800) 362–3495
www.thefloridakeys.com/hiddenharbor
$$

If you're looking for a clean and simple room plus boat dockage and a spectacular view of the bayside sunset, this is the place. The 21 reasonably priced rooms of Hidden Harbor offer five different floor plans and bedding options, but each features a full bath and a small refrigerator.

The Honeymoon Cottage, a one-bedroom hideaway near the Gulf, features a full kitchen, living room, and bath. Decorated in island rattan and tropical florals, the cottage requires a three-night minimum.

Guests enjoy a freshwater swimming pool. Hidden Harbor maintains a video rental facility on premises. Boat dock and ramp are available for an additional charge. And, no fishing license is required to fish from the motel's jetty.

Hidden within this unassuming motel property, far from the madding crowd percolating up and down the Overseas Highway, nurtures a special secret: Hidden Harbor is also the home of the renowned Turtle Hospital. Guests at the motel are among the privileged few invited to tour the hospital, where they are treated to a slide show about the turtle recovery program. Registered guests can watch as volunteers feed the turtles and dispense their medications at the saltwater turtle recovery room. (See our Paradise Found chapter.)

Blue Waters Motel
MM 48.5 Bayside
Marathon, FL
(305) 743–4832,
(800) 222–4832 (reservations only)
www.thefloridakeys.com/bluewaters
$–$$

You'll enjoy a Mediterranean feeling here at Blue Waters Motel, for the white stucco buildings, gray tile roofs, and bright, turquoise-blue doors evoke visions of Greece. Two banks of motel units, some with efficiency kitchens, flank the parking lot. The rooms feature two double beds or a king-size bed. Rooms were renovated with new tile floors in 1997.

A raised swimming pool affords a view of a small boat basin on the Gulf where guests may dock their boats for a small additional charge per day.

Faro Blanco Marine Resort
MM 48.5 Bayside
Marathon, FL
(305) 743–9018, (800) 759–3276
www.spottswood.com/faroblanco
$–$$$$

Straddling the Overseas Highway, Faro Blanco Marine Resort fronts both the Atlantic and the Gulf of Mexico with a potpourri of lodging alternatives. Purchased by Spottswood Corporation in 2000, Faro Blanco underwent extensive renovations throughout 2001. The hotel now offers lodging in 16 individually owned two- and three-bedroom condominiums (each 2,000 square feet) in "the towers" as well as in the Conch cottages that originally graced this property.

Faro Blanco also offers some more unusual lodging options. Perhaps the most recognized lighthouse in the Middle Keys, Faro Blanco's working navigational structure lights up the oceanside marina. Its five-story tower has been remodeled into two suites. One two-bedroom suite is on the second floor, the other encompasses the top three floors. Both units are accessed by a winding staircase.

At Faro Blanco Bayside you'll find nine newly renovated "floating staterooms," actually two-story barges permanently moored to floating docks. The houseboats have two guest rooms on each floor.

An Olympic-size swimming pool adjoins Angler's (see our Restaurants chapter), which purrs at lunch and dinner and pulses the night away with entertainment and dancing. Kelsey's Restaurant has remained closed during the renovations.

Hampton Inn & Suites
MM 48 Bayside
Marathon, FL
(305) 743–9009, (800) 426–7866
www.keyshampton.com
$$–$$$

A welcome addition to the hotel lineup in Marathon, opened March 2000, Hampton Inn & Suites hugs the Gulf of Mexico. The spacious rooms and suites are decked out in bright tropical hues. One-bedroom suites feature two queen-size beds, a kitchenette, one bath, and a living room with sleeper sofa. Sleeping rooms mirror the bedroom and bathroom portion of the suites. All units have private balconies, most with at least a glimpse of the pool or the Gulf. Cable television with free movies is standard in all guest rooms.

Continental breakfast is served in the expansive lobby, which dramatically soars three stories high with a beamed, vaulted ceiling and walls of windows. Guests enjoy a heated swimming pool, where a gulfside tiki bar provides libations and light noshing fare. The facility boasts a physical fitness center.

Boat dockage is available at an additional charge, but vessels must be launched from the 33rd Street public boat ramp. An on-premises watersports center offers parasailing, Waverunner and boat rentals, eco-tours, and daily reef trips.

Latigo Bed and Breakfast Cruise
MM 47.5 Oceanside
11th Street
Marathon Marina
Marathon, FL
(305) 289–1066, (800) 897–4886
www.latigo.net
$$$$

Sample the lifestyle of the rich and famous aboard the 56-foot yacht *Latigo,* where captains Ken and Val Waine will pamper you and spirit you away for a bed-and-breakfast cruise or a multi-day sojourn into "the beyond." The *Latigo* features a spacious main salon, a king-size master bedroom aft, and a double and two singles forward; it carries a maximum of six passengers. You'll enjoy gourmet repasts prepared by Val in the galley.

Prices range from $220 per person for an overnight bed-and-breakfast cruise to a $6,900 flat rate for four people per week. The Waines will customize a charter for you anywhere in the Florida Keys, the Dry Tortugas, the Florida West Coast, or the Bahamas for a rate of $950 per day for two or $1200 per day for four. The Waines also cater to sunset wedding ceremonies and bed-and-breakfast weddings. (See our

Restaurants chapter for information on *Latigo*'s dinner and sunset cruises.)

To find the yacht, turn on 11th Street toward the ocean at mile marker 47.5. Drive past Shucker's restaurant and look for slip 73 on the right.

Lower Keys

The Lower Keys, sleepier and less densely populated than the Middle or Upper Keys, distinguish themselves with acres and acres of shallow-water turtle grass flats and copious uninhabited mangrove out-islands. This is a gunk-holing bonanza. The Lower Keys are surrounded by the Great White Heron National Wildlife Refuge, a large area in the Gulf of Mexico encompassing tiny keys from East Bahia Honda Key to the Content Keys to Cayo Agua and the Bay Keys. Big Pine Key is the home of the National Key Deer Refuge, a preserved area of wilderness sheltering our diminutive Key deer.

Fishing is outstanding here, though ocean access is more limited. The Lower Keys can also boast of the Looe Key National Marine Sanctuary, one of the best snorkeling and diving reefs in the world. (See our Paradise Found and Diving chapters for details.)

Accommodations are scattered throughout the Lower Keys, where campgrounds tend to predominate (see our Campgrounds chapter if you'd like to camp in the area). Most of the accommodations here started as fishing camps decades ago and have been updated to varying degrees. Several wonderful bed-and-breakfast inns are tucked away on a little-known oceanfront road, offering seclusion, privacy, and limitless vistas of the sea.

Crowning the assets of Lower Keys accommodations is Little Palm Island, a premier resort that rules in a class by itself. Whatever your lodging choice in the sanctuaries of the Lower Keys, your close proximity to Key West more than makes up for any tourist attractions or nightlife that may be lacking here.

Barnacle Bed & Breakfast
1557 Long Beach Drive
Big Pine Key, FL
(305) 872-3298, (800) 465-9100
www.thebarnacle.net
$-$$

Isolated from the clot of autos percolating down the Overseas Highway toward Key West, the Barnacle Bed & Breakfast lolls on a serene stretch of beach on an elbow of oölite extending into the Atlantic. Constructed as three rotated, star-shaped levels, the Barnacle is a study in contradictions.

The generous Tarpon and Dolphin rooms on the second level, with two queen-size beds per room, open to a foliage-filled atrium that houses the hot tub. Comfortably furnished with ceiling fans, a sofa, television, table, and chairs, the atrium serves as a common room. Guests meet here each morning for a complimentary breakfast buffet. The Blue Heron cottage perches in an outbuilding, its stained-glass windows lending a romantic perspective. Both the Blue Heron and the Ocean room (which nearly rests on the sand) have kitchens, living rooms, private entrances, and patios.

A circular stairway crawls to the crow's nest, where you can recline on lounge chairs to soak up the sun. Or perhaps you'd like to roll into one of the many hammocks strung between palms around the property.

Guests enjoy use of a catamaran, a paddleboat, bicycles, snorkeling gear, and barbecue grills. Children younger than 16 are not permitted. Smoking is permitted only outside the guest rooms.

Finding Long Beach Road is a little tricky: turn left at Big Pine Fishing Lodge, mile marker 33, oceanside, and proceed about 2 miles.

Casa Grande Bed & Breakfast
MM 33 Oceanside
1619 Long Beach Drive
Big Pine Key, FL
(305) 872-2878
www.floridakeys.net/casagrande
$$

The architecture of this mission-style hacienda harkens back to the roots of the Spanish conquistadors who once settled in the Keys. The second of a trio of bed and breakfast inns along oceanfront Long Beach Drive, Casa Grande exudes a reserved, almost mystical, charm. Owner Kathleen Threlkeld recycled the foyer light fixture and stained glass from a demolished church in New York City; from Maryland she salvaged the clanking old mission bell on the red tile roof.

All three airy bedrooms with combination louvered and paneled doors feature both Bahama fans and individually controlled central air conditioning. Queen-size beds and private baths grace the nicely appointed rooms, and each is equipped with a small refrigerator, television, and sofa. You can watch television by the seldom-needed fireplace in the common room or hop into the hot tub on the deck. Bicycles, sailboarding, kayaks, and snorkeling equipment afford you a little exercise if you are between books. The hostess serves a full breakfast at 8:30 A.M. daily in the garden patio.

If you'd like to bring your boat, Casa Grande's canal will accommodate craft up to 26 feet in length. Children are not allowed at Casa Grande. There is a two-night minimum and reservations are essential.

To find Long Beach Road, turn left at Big Pine Fishing Lodge, mile marker 33, oceanside, and proceed about 2 miles.

Deer Run Bed & Breakfast
MM 33 Oceanside
Long Beach Drive
Big Pine Key, FL
(305) 872–2015
www.floridakeys.net/deer
$$, no credit cards

The diminutive Key deer really do have the run of this Florida cracker-style home, for they stroll the grounds like boarded guests. Owner Sue Abbott met the herd years ago when she first bought the property, and they've remained fast friends ever since. Staying at Deer Run is akin to vacationing in a nature preserve. Self-proclaimed the "Mother Teresa of wildlife," Abbott hand-raises macaws, and at least a half dozen cackle in a wild cacophony around the property.

If you love animals and eccentricity, the three diverse units at Deer Run emanate a homey folksy appeal. Two of the three rooms have a private entry and bath. A king-size bed fills the lower level oceanfront room, which sports a large screened porch. A small, affordable room-without-a-view is accessed from the side yard. And in the upper level of the main house, a queen-size bed distinguishes the oceanfront third bedroom. Bathroom facilities are the conventional hallway variety.

The peaceful beach, only 50 feet beyond a raised hot tub, fronts a productive bonefish flat. After you've visited with the animals, wade out and spot a tailing fish. Breakfast is served on the verandah, overlooking the ocean.

Deer Run caters to adults. Smoking is not permitted. A three-night minimum is required on holidays. Payment must be made in cash or traveler's checks. To find Long Beach Road, turn left at Big Pine Fishing Lodge, mile marker 33, oceanside, and proceed about 2 miles.

Parmer's Resort
MM 28.5 Bayside
565 Barry Avenue
Little Torch Key, FL
(305) 872–2157
www.parmersplace.com
$–$$$

Originally a fishing camp in the 1930s, Parmer's Resort is something of an institution in the Lower Keys. The 43 units in 13 buildings sprinkled over the 5-acre property have copped the monikers of the fish, birds, and flora populating the Florida Keys.

From the Grunt, Hibiscus, and Flamingo to the Permit, Spoonbill, and Jasmine, the homey '60s-style units differ widely in both size and amenities. Small, medium and large motel rooms, standard and small efficiencies, cottages and one- and two-bedroom apartments, are all clean and simple.

Fronting Big Pine Channel, Parmer's offers boat dockage at a small additional fee, but there is no beach. A free-form swimming pool anchors the center of the property. You'll need to use a pay phone to call the office, and you must pick up after yourself or pay a fee for maid service. But you can always stoke up the barbie, because Parmer's loans small gas grills to cook your catch of the day. A complimentary continental breakfast is served daily.

Dolphin Resort & Marina
MM 28.5 Oceanside
Little Torch Key, FL
(305) 872-2685, (800) 553-0308
www.dolphinresort.com
$–$$$

If snorkeling, diving, fishing, and boating top your agenda of must-do activities, consider staying in the bustling Dolphin Resort & Marina. Canals border two sides of the peninsular marina, and an almost-a-beach shoreline on Newfound Harbor forms the third. A variety of diverse suites, in pastel Bahamian-style bungalows, speckle the property, most featuring two bedrooms, one bath, a completely equipped kitchen, a living area, and a screened porch or patio. The units were renovated with fresh paint and tile floors and all new kitchens in 1999.

Rent a motor boat for a day or half-day and explore the neighboring waters (see our Boating chapter). Marina staff are very helpful in plotting a waterway route to rookery out-islands and sand spits. A bait store, fuel dock, and ship's store cater your provisioning needs.

Little Palm Island
MM 28.5 Oceanside
Little Torch Key, FL
(305) 872-2524, (800) 343-8567
www.littlepalmisland.com
$$$$

Superlatives fall short when describing Little Palm Island because this tiny slice of Paradise soars off the charts. An exquisite resort encapsulated on its own 5-acre island 3 miles offshore from Little Torch Key, Little Palm is the centerpiece of the jeweled necklace of the Florida Keys. And like all really fine gems, a stay here carries a hefty price tag. But, if you just won the lottery, gave your final answer on *Who Wants to be a Millionaire*, or simply want to splurge on the experience of a lifetime, read on.

Fifteen elevated, thatched-roof bungalows, reminiscent of the South Pacific, shelter Little Palm's privileged guests. The one-bedroom suites (two under each thatch) are exquisitely designed in three predominant themes: Indonesian, Polynesian, and British Colonial. But no matter what the ambiance, you will be pampered with opulence. The villas each have an elegant yet cozy sitting room, complete with a stocked minibar. The bedroom's king-size bed is romantically draped in mosquito netting. A Guatemalan lounger, and a polished wicker- and rattan-writing desk adorn the room. A lavish dressing room with vanity and a luxurious terra-cotta-tile bathroom sporting an indoor whirlpool and privately fenced outdoor shower complete the suite. To top it all off, add optional massages, facials, pedicures, manicures, and body treatments, either in your suite or in the Island Spa.

The island restores your soul as well. Television sets, telephones, and alarm clocks are banned, ensuring your escape from reality. Curving coconut palms and flourishing flora pepper the grounds surrounding the villas. At Little Palm Island, you can elevate doing nothing at all to an art form. The unhurried pace encourages serious lounging aside the free-form pool, atop the crystal sand beach, or enveloped in a two-person hammock. You'll find a life-size chess set (the pieces are lighter than they look) nestled between the bungalows and a peaceful, meditative Zen garden secreted away deep within the island. If the sun is too much for you, stop in at the 600-volume reading library, find a good book, and sit a spell.

When you've unwound at last and you're ready to function vertically once

Little Palm is more like the South Seas than South Florida. PHOTO: LITTLE PALM ISLAND

again, the island offers a cornucopia of diversions. Play with Little Palm's complimentary toys—surf bikes, day sailers, kayaks, canoes, a Hobie Cat, and snorkeling and fishing equipment. Rent a pontoon boat or a nifty Sun-Kat motorized lounge chair and gunk-hole around the surrounding miniature mangrove islets. Dive Looe Key National Marine Sanctuary or hire a backcountry guide and fish for tarpon, permit, or bonefish. Head offshore with a sportfishing captain and catch that marlin. And if you are really adventurous

(and your pocketbook is limitless), Little Palm will shuttle you to a deserted island by seaplane for a tropical tryst.

Access to Little Palm Island is provided from its mainland substation at Little Torch Key. A pair of Grand Craft launches—The *Truman* and *Miss Margaret*—ferry you and your worldly possessions to this very civilized outpost. Meals are taken in the outstanding gourmet dining room (see our Restaurants chapter). Choose one of three dining plans while on the island: The Modified American Plan (most popular option) provides a choice of any two meals per day; the Full American Plan supplies breakfast, lunch and dinner; the European plan allows guests to order a la carte.

Once a fishing camp called Little Munson Island, this quiet hermitage has hosted the nation's movers and shakers, such as presidents Roosevelt, Truman, Kennedy, and Nixon. Little Palm Island still attracts a tony clientele. Such notables as Al and Tipper Gore and Joan Lunden, formerly of *Good Morning America*, found the lifestyle irresistible.

A Relais & Chateau property, Little Palm Island and its restaurant garner myriad awards and accolades from rating services and publications all over the world, consistently ranking in the top 10. But Insiders know Little Palm Island is No. 1 in the Florida Keys. (Children younger than 16 are not permitted.)

Caribbean Village
MM 10.7 Bayside
Big Coppitt Key, FL
(305) 296–9542
www.keysdirectory.com/caribbean
$–$$

Each evening, tiny ground lights illuminate the white-trimmed pastel clapboards of the Key West–style Caribbean Village. Basic, clean, and inexpensive, Caribbean Village offers 32 units that range from a sleeping room with an outside bathroom to rooms with private baths in two floating houseboats. Some feature an efficiency kitchen in addition to a sleeping room and bath and have a metal spiral staircase that can connect the lower quarters to another unit above.

Only 6 miles from Key West, Caribbean Village offers the best of both worlds: it is close to the action of Key West at a fraction of our southernmost city's lodging prices. Prices at Caribbean Village do go up during special event weekends in Key West.

Key West

Price-Code Key

$	$100 to $150
$$	$151 to $200
$$$	$201 to $300
$$$$	$301 and higher

This diverse, charming, historic city is considered one of the nation's top travel destinations. Key West's accommodations range from the comfort of a standard motel room to the luxury of a private suite in a historic inn. In this section, we escort you through a variety of facilities. Our selections are based on attributes of rooms, service, location and overall ambiance. All facilities have air conditioning, cable television, and telephones unless stated otherwise.

Daily rates for the high-season (mid-to late December through early to mid-April) for double-occupancy are categorized in the Price Code. Because many facilities offer a variety of accommodations within one property, we have provided a range, the first to indicate the rate for a typical room and the second for more complex units, such as apartments and suites. Prices indicated in the key do not include the 11.5 percent room tax, room service, or added fees for phone calls, rollaway bed, crib rentals, and other incidentals. In most cases, an additional per-person charge is levied when occupancy exceeds two. Off-season rates are typically lower, and in some cases dramatically less.

Off-street parking is usually available for guesthouses at about $5 per day.

Motels, Hotels, and Resorts

Motels often cater to families, Europeans, last-minute travelers, spring breakers, and active, outdoorsy types. Count celebrities among those who enjoy our full-service resorts. While filming the movie *True Lies* in the Florida Keys, Arnold Schwarzenegger chose The Pier House; *Good Morning America* host Charles Gibson and former co-host Joan Lunden stayed at the Key West Hyatt. Couples often opt for romantic weddings and honeymoons at hotels that offer tropical breezes, lush foliage, crystal seas, and magnificent sunsets. And when spring break rolls around, college students throughout the country head for Key West's less expensive hotels, motels, and chains.

Hotels, motels, and resorts on this island tend to be so pricey that it is difficult to find a room for less than $100 during the high season (mid- to late December through early to mid-April). During Fantasy Fest (see our Annual Events chapter) in October and Christmas week, rates jump even higher.

Some chains and individually owned motels along N. Roosevelt Boulevard offer waterfront accommodations. Those accommodations near the city's shopping centers and fast food restaurants in New Town are somewhat removed from the charm of the city's historic district, the hustle and bustle of Duval Street, and public beaches.

Motels

Blue Marlin Resort Motel
1320 Simonton Street
Key West, FL
(305) 294-2585, (800) 523-1698
www.bluemarlinmotel.com
$-$$

With its reasonable rates, heated swimming pool, and off-street parking spaces that allow you to pull the car fairly close to your door, the Blue Marlin is a good choice for families that want to be near the action but don't want to pay dearly for the privilege. This two-story, pink cement-block structure is not luxurious, but the 54 rooms—all of which overlook the pool—are carpeted, clean, bright, and spacious. All rooms come equipped with a refrigerator; ten have kitchenettes.

The best thing about the Blue Marlin, perhaps, is its location. It's tucked just a block off Duval Street on the Atlantic side of the island. The Southernmost Point and South Beach are about three blocks away; other downtown attractions like the Hemingway House, Key West Lighthouse, and even Mallory Square (on the Gulf side of the island) are within a reasonable walking distance. There's no restaurant on premises, but several reasonably priced eateries, including a 24-hour Denny's, and a convenience store are located nearby.

No more than four people may occupy a room here. No cots are available.

Best Western Hibiscus Motel
1313 Simonton Street
Key West, FL
(305) 294-3763, (800) 972-5100
$-$$

As Best Westerns go, this independently owned affiliate is small and understated. It is also one of few chains or franchises within Key West's historic Old Town. Of concrete-block construction, the Hibiscus has 61 units, including standard rooms and five one-bedroom efficiencies.

Standard rooms are relatively large with two queen-size beds, while efficiencies offer separate bedrooms and kitchens. Decor is bright and clean and features wood furnishings, carpeting, and coordinating wallpaper and bedspread patterns. All units overlook either the motel's heated swimming pool and hot tub or the street and a variety of palms. Bicycles are available for rent, and cribs cost an additional $5 per night.

Four people can share a room at the given rate. Breakfast is included.

Blue Lagoon
3101 N. Roosevelt Boulevard
Key West, FL
(305) 296-1043
www.floridakeys.net/bluelagoon
$-$$

Most of the 72 rooms in this one- and two-story complex are furnished either with one queen-size or two double beds; six have king-size beds. First-floor rooms have tile floors, and upstairs rooms are carpeted. Cedar furnishings and walls provide a rustic appeal. Some rooms offer full water views.

Blue Lagoon has a swimming pool and a cement sun deck facing the Gulf, and along the motel's small beach are watersport rentals for personal watercraft, fishing boats, parasailing, and pontoon boats. You can even take an ultralight airplane ride from here. Parking is outside your door. Rates are based on double occupancy, with each additional guest costing $10 per night. Cots also cost an additional $10 per night.

Comfort Inn at Key West
3824 N. Roosevelt Boulevard
Key West, FL
(305) 294–3773, (800) 228–5150
$–$$

Guests at the two-story Comfort Inn have a choice of 100 rooms housed in three buildings. Options include a room with two double beds or a few larger rooms with king-size beds. The rooms are carpeted and have comfortable furnishings; rollaways are provided upon request to a limited number of rooms. Smoking and nonsmoking rooms are available, as are wheelchair-accessible facilities.

The motel is less than a half-mile from the Stock Island Bridge and is across the street from the Gulf of Mexico. Rooms face either the pool or the parking lot. Those on the second floor share a common balcony.

The motel offers complimentary continental breakfast and maintains a large outdoor swimming pool surrounded by concrete decking. Scooter rentals are on-premises, and public transportation is available. Complimentary hot and cold beverages are served in the lobby throughout the day. Children younger than 17 stay free. Comfort Inn proprietors also own the Radisson Key West (see listing in this section) next door, where a poolside tiki bar, 24-hour restaurant, and coin-operated laundry are available.

Fairfield Inn by Marriott
2400 N. Roosevelt Boulevard
Key West, FL
(305) 296–5700, (800) 228–2800
www.fairfieldinn.com/eywfi
$–$$

Fairfield Inn's easygoing prices and comfortable, well-kept facilities make this one of Key West's popular choices with vacationers. The motel offers 100 standard rooms and 32 suites throughout three two-story buildings. Standard rooms primarily are furnished with two double beds; suites with varying amenities, including kitchens or kitchenettes and king-size beds, are other options.

Fairfield Inn offers contemporary furnishings and attractive decor, two swimming pools, gas grills, a tiki bar, volleyball court, and guest laundry facilities. A separate concessionaire offers on-premises scooter rentals.

Complimentary continental breakfast is offered daily, and covered parking spaces are available. The inn has smoking and nonsmoking rooms.

Radisson Hotel Key West
3820 N. Roosevelt Boulevard
Key West, FL
(305) 294–5511, (800) 333–3333
www.floridakeys.net/radisson
$–$$

Next door to the Comfort Inn (see listing in this section) is the six-story Radisson Hotel Key West (formerly Econo Lodge), offering 145 rooms with two double beds or a king-size bed. Suites and efficiencies also are available. When the hotel became a Radisson in 1999, all of the rooms underwent extensive renovation. Decorated in the traditional tropical style—pastel prints and white walls—they feature refrigerators, coffeemakers, and hair dryers. All of the rooms overlook either the Gulf of Mexico or the swimming pool.

On premises at the Radisson are an outdoor swimming pool, a lobby bar, a tiki bar by the pool, and a 24-hour coin-operated laundry. A 24-hour Denny's is conveniently located next door. There is plenty of parking, but public transportation is easily accessed from here, too. In addition, front desk personnel will assist you with sightseeing and sporting excursions.

Wheelchair-accessible facilities and smoking and nonsmoking rooms are available.

South Beach Oceanfront Motel
508 South Street
Key West, FL
(305) 296–5611, (800) 354–4455
www.oldtownresorts.com/southbeach.htm
$–$$$

So you want to stay right on the beach? This property offers an affordable way to do just that.

Built in the 1950s and renovated in 1992, this two-story, 47-unit motel sits on a peninsula overlooking the water. As waterfront properties go, it provides an incredible value, with 90 percent of its rooms offering a full ocean view. Carpeted rooms appointed in florals and pastels primarily feature king-size and double beds, and all rooms have safes. Balconies overlook the beachfront bay from six rooms, and three of these have kitchenettes. Rooms with a balcony or full ocean view command a higher price.

South Beach also has an Olympic-size swimming pool, a tanning pier leading to the Atlantic, and an on-site dive shop. The motel offers limited parking, but its owners and managers also operate the Southernmost Motel (see listing in this section), which provides additional spaces.

Southernmost Motel in the USA
1319 Duval Street
Key West, FL
(305) 296–6577, (800) 354–4455
www.oldtownresorts.com/southernmost1.htm
$–$$

Gingerbread architectural detail and native flora all come together at Southernmost Motel, reminding visitors that they have reached an eclectic city on an island. Situated just across from South Beach, Southernmost's six buildings are surrounded by ample parking and are trimmed with exotic plants, flowers, and trees. One of the motel's two swimming pools sits in the center of the parking lot, concealed by lush greenery and a wall. The courtyard features the main pool, surrounded by decking, and a hot tub. Each pool has its own outdoor tiki bar.

Rooms have either two double beds or a king- or queen-size bed; some rooms include sleeper sofas. A large room with two double beds and a kitchen serves as the facility's one and only efficiency. Some rooms have private balconies.

Scooter and bicycle rentals and concierge services are available. The tiki bars serve light bites for breakfast and lunch. Southernmost Motel is wheelchair-accessible and offers smoking and nonsmoking rooms.

Hotels

Best Western Key Ambassador Resort
3755 S. Roosevelt Boulevard
Key West, FL
(305) 296–3500, (800) 432–4315
www.keyambassador.com
$$

The Best Western Key Ambassador Resort consists of a cluster of two-story buildings scattered over seven acres of profuse tropical gardens punctuated by palm trees and hibiscus across from the Atlantic Ocean. Every room has a private balcony and all 100 units have pleasant views of the garden, the harbor, the pool, or the ocean.

Rooms are decorated in "Key West tropical"—light wood furnishings and floral bedspreads and drapes—and the walls are hung with the works of local artists. Floors are a combination of tile and pastel carpeting, and guests have a choice of two double beds or a king-size bed. Each unit is equipped with mini refrigerator.

Central to Best Western Key Ambassador and overlooking the ocean is an elevated (heated in winter) swimming pool with a sun deck. A small bar and grill sits beside it. For do-it-yourselfers, a cookout area offers barbecue grills and outdoor tables and chairs. Other amenities include guest laundry facilities and a daily complimentary continental breakfast.

From Best Western Key Ambassador it's a 10-minute walk to Smathers Beach and 2 miles to historic Old Town. Scooter rentals are available next door or the front desk staff can arrange for a trolley tour. Pets are not permitted here.

Hampton Inn Key West
2801 N. Roosevelt Boulevard
Key West, FL
(305) 294–2917, (800) 960–3054
www.hamptoninnkeywest.com
$–$$

The L-shaped design of Hampton Inn Key West provides bay-view rooms in back of the building; gulf-view and garden-view rooms are also available. All 159 rooms are carpeted, with king-size beds or two double beds and all-wood decor. All rooms are the same size with the exception of the one-bedroom, hot-tub suite, which has a king-size bed, two televisions, a stereo system, a mini refrigerator, a sleeper sofa, and an oversize bath with glass-block shower.

The swimming pool and hot tub are open 24 hours a day, and lunch and full outdoor bar service is provided in a nearby tiki hut. Hampton Inn's gazebo overlooks the bay, providing a quiet alternative to Mallory Square for sunset viewing. Parking spaces under the hotel are available, and a full parking lot is in front of the building.

Also on-premises are a gift shop and personal watercraft, bicycle, and scooter rentals. A complimentary continental breakfast buffet, including toast, muffins, and cereals, is offered daily in the lobby. Local telephone calls are free, and guests may request discount passes to a nearby fitness facility.

At the Hampton Inn Key West, rates vary according to the room's view and the size of the bed you select. Rooms with king-size beds are slightly more expensive than those with double beds. Weekend rates, too, are higher. Rates are assigned on a per-room basis, however, so rooms with two doubles sleep as many as four, while rooms with king-size beds can accommodate as many as three.

Rollaways cost $15 per day and mini refrigerators cost $10 per day; use of cribs is free. Hampton Inn also maintains designated pet rooms, with guests paying $20 per night per pet. The Hampton Inn guarantees guest satisfaction; if you're not satisfied, your night's stay is free.

Holiday Inn La Concha
430 Duval Street
Key West, FL
(305) 296–2991, (800) 465–4329
www.laconchakeywest.com
$$–$$$

If you truly want to stay where the action is, you can't do better than this. Not only is the La Concha the tallest building on the island of Key West, it is situated smack dab in the center of the busy Duval Street scene.

Originally opened to great fanfare in 1926, the La Concha has, over the years, played host to a wide variety of guests, including royalty, presidents, and Pulitzer Prize winning authors. Hemingway mentions it in one of his novels and Tennessee Williams completed the award-winning play *A Streetcar Named Desire* while in residence here.

Like the island itself, the La Concha has weathered many changes and undergone numerous facelifts. Today, its 150 guest rooms and 10 suites have a casual yet elegant feel. Each is furnished in 1920s style, with wicker chairs, poster beds, floral bedspreads, lace curtains, and period antiques. Many rooms overlook either the never-ending parade of activity on Duval Street or the pool terrace. The spacious pool, set amidst lush island foliage, features a multi-level sun deck and tiki bar serving snacks and tropical libations.

The hotel's Celebrities Restaurant, which opens directly onto Duval Street, serves breakfast, lunch, and dinner; and features nightly entertainment. There are two gift shops on property, as well as bicycle and scooter rental and concierge service. The Old Town Trolley stops at the door of the La Concha and the island's favorite haunted attraction, Ghost Tours of Key West, leaves nightly from the lobby (see our Attractions chapter).

This hotel's most notable feature, perhaps, is its 7th-floor wraparound observation deck. The Top of the La Concha offers not only a birds-eye perspective on downtown Key West, it is one of the best places in town to view the sunset. You're well away from the craziness down at Mallory Square and while you're drinking in all that beauty, you can be drinking a cocktail, cold beer, or soda as well. A small bar at the Top is open limited hours around sunset each evening.

Pegasus International Hotel
501 Southard Street (corner of Duval)
Key West, FL
(305) 294–9323, (800) 397–8148
www.pegasuskeywest.com
$–$$

Located on a busy corner in the heart of downtown Key West, Pegasus International Hotel is reminiscent of Miami's famed South Beach district. This pink stucco structure claims to be the only art deco property in the Florida Keys.

Pegasus offers 30 rooms with various bedding combinations, including two doubles, a queen, or king. The rooms are tastefully appointed in tropical decor. Rates are reasonable, especially considering the hotel's prime location, which is within easy walking distance of Mallory Square and the restaurants/bars on lower Duval Street, plus the fact that parking is free.

Amenities here include a swimming pool, hot tub, and sun deck, all located on the second floor and all overlooking bustling Duval Street. There are no on-premise food outlets at Pegasus; however, several restaurants are conveniently located within a block or two. There is a deli next door and Dunkin' Donuts right across the street. Also nearby—a dive shop, several T-shirt shops, and a video rental store.

Pelican Landing Resort & Marina
915 Eisenhower Drive
Key West, FL
(305) 293–9730, (800) 527–8108
$–$$$$

You've found your home away from home in the inconspicuous gulf-side Pelican Landing, a concrete-block condominium and marina complex with an on-site manager. Among the 32 units, guests are offered a choice of standard rooms with two double beds or one-, two-, or three-bedroom suites. All accommodations are decorated according to the taste of their individual owners.

Suites have balconies overlooking the marina, and those on the fourth (top) floor are duplex-style with either loft bedrooms or two enclosed, second-story bedrooms. Large sliding glass doors with vertical blinds lead to furnished balconies, and all suites have washer/dryers. Suites have king-size beds in the master bedroom, two double beds in the second and third bedrooms, and queen-size sleeper sofas. Some suites have hot tubs. A one-bedroom penthouse suite is among the most romantic.

Pelican Landing's heated swimming pool is surrounded by a sun deck. Gas barbecue grills and a fish-cleaning station are available for guests. The facility is boat-accessible by powerboat only because a fixed bridge offers only an 18-foot clearance. All guests have off-street parking. Charter fishing boats are just across the dock.

Full-Service Resorts

Banana Bay Resort
2319 N. Roosevelt Boulevard
Key West, FL
(305) 296–6925, (800) 226–2621
www.bananabay.com
$–$$$

This exclusively adult complex is a little gem of a resort tucked tight against the Key West Yacht Club on the right-hand

Many couples honeymoon in the Keys, where romance lingers around every palm tree and in every lagoon. PHOTO: HAWK'S CAY RESORT

side of N. Roosevelt as you head toward Old Town Key West. A sister property to the Banana Bay Resort in Marathon (see listing elsewhere in this chapter), Banana Bay–Key West offers similar amenities and value.

The rooms are configured in three styles. The standard guest room has either one king-size bed with canopy or two double beds. Mini-suites feature a queen bed, bath, and kitchenette. One-bedroom suites have a private bedroom with queen bed, bath, living area with a pullout sleeper sofa, and a kitchenette. The roomier suites are rented out on a weekly basis; all other accommodations have daily rates. Only some rooms have ocean

views, but all have patio-style verandas. Each comes equipped with a wet bar, refrigerator, ceiling fans, coffeemaker, and hair dryer. A complimentary continental breakfast is served daily.

From the Roosevelt Boulevard side, Banana Bay looks rather unimpressive. The grounds, however, are spacious enough to include a pool, small sandy beach, whirlpool, mini–fitness center, wedding gazebo, and tiki bar. Boat rentals, eco-sailing trips, flats fishing adventures, and twice-daily snorkeling cruises to the reef leave from here. There is plenty of free parking and, for a small fee, you can catch the shuttle service that departs every 30 minutes for downtown Key West. Dockage for boats up to 24 feet is available at an additional cost.

Pets are not permitted here, nor are children under the age of 16. Rates are based on double occupancy. Additional adults sharing the room must pay an additional per-person fee per night.

Grand Key Resort
3990 S. Roosevelt Boulevard
Key West, FL
(305) 293–1818, (888) 310–1540
www.grandkeyresort.com
$$$–$$$$

Just when locals thought the island of Key West could simply not support one more hotel, along comes this new luxury resort. Grand Key Resort boasts 216 guest rooms in a variety of configurations, from connected double queen rooms to luxurious suites. The property is tucked between two condominium complexes on the north side of the island, not far from Key West International Airport. Rooms overlook the parking lot on one side and the salt ponds that border the airport on the other; if you're lucky enough to be on one of the upper floors, you might have a pretty decent view of the Atlantic Ocean and Smathers Beach in the distance.

Everything at Grand Key is, of course, brand spanking clean and bright. All of the rooms are appointed in the casually elegant tropical style that has become the hallmark of upscale hotels in Key West. All of them feature a full complement of guest amenities, including minibars, coffeemakers, hair dryers, in-room safes, ceiling fans, bathrobes, Sony PlayStations and cable TV with HBO, and in-room movies. A focal point in the lobby is the 25,000-gallon aquarium that stretches from floor to ceiling and is filled with the kind of colorful fish you would likely see in their natural habitat on a trip to the reef.

The Palm Haven Restaurant, which overlooks the pool at the far end of the lobby, serves island fare. Snacks and tropical libations are available at an open-air bar positioned poolside. A large deck and plenty of white rocking chairs beckon sun worshipers.

An on-premise gift shop, meeting facilities, and concierge services are available. Children are welcome here. In fact, those under 18 stay free with parents and nature-based programs are being planned to keep them entertained.

Hyatt Key West
601 Front Street
Key West, FL
(305) 296–9900, (800) 554–9288
www.hyatt.com
$$$–$$$$

Fronting on the Gulf of Mexico, the five-story Hyatt Key West is a three-building, 120-unit complex of standard rooms, junior suites, and standard suites, all with sliding glass doors and private balconies. Rooms overlook the city, pool, or Gulf of Mexico.

Fully carpeted except for tile entranceways, standard rooms generally face the city and have one king-size or two double beds, fully-stocked minibars, hair dryers, coffeemakers, irons, and ironing boards. Some have ceiling fans, and bathrobes are provided upon request. A variety of suites feature panoramic views of the Gulf.

Junior suites (L-shaped with a small sitting area and no dividing walls) and standard suites (one-bedroom units with a door separating the bedroom from the living area) are all fully tiled and boast the same amenities as standard rooms. Junior suites also have whirlpool tubs. Furnishings all are primarily light oak accented by wicker and rattan; bed coverings and draperies are in tropical prints. Wall hangings feature colorful local and Caribbean scenes.

Hyatt has an outdoor swimming pool and hot tub, two restaurants, a small health club, two dive boats, a charter fishing boat, and a 68-foot sailing yacht for afternoon snorkeling and early evening sunset sails. Also available are watersport rentals, scooter and bike rentals, and the hotel has a small private beach.

A three-tier sun deck overlooks the beach, and the resort's own Nick's Bar & Grill is a great place to enjoy the sunset. Concierge, room service, and laundry valet are available, as is a resident masseuse, who will provide a massage in your room at an additional cost.

The Hyatt has smoking and nonsmoking rooms and wheelchair-accessible facilities. Children younger than 18 stay free. Pets are prohibited. The resort offers special packages throughout the year, so inquire when you call to make reservations. Rates are based on double occupancy, each additional person is charged an additional fee per night.

Key West Hilton Resort and Marina
245 Front Street
Key West, FL
(305) 294–4000, (800) 445–8667
www.keywestresort.hilton.com
$$$–$$$$

Opened in winter 1996, the bayfront Hilton was designed so all rooms provide views of either the pool, the bay, or the marina (see our Cruising chapter) and its surrounding waters. Guests here also are provided launch service to a relatively secluded public beach at Sunset Key (see separate listing).

The two buildings that make up the Key West Hilton have 178 rooms; one structure has only nonsmoking rooms. The three-story building overlooks the marina; the other, a four-story structure, sits adjacent to Mallory Square (see our Attractions chapter). Situated in historic Old Town near the old Custom House (see our Attractions chapter), the Hilton and its grounds are surrounded by brick walkways. Sliding glass doors framed by wooden shutters open onto private terraces. Textured interior walls boast sconces; floors feature stone tiles. Bleached oak and stone furnishings and handpainted walls welcome visitors to the hotel lobby.

On premises are a swimming pool, hot tub, and sun deck area, fitness facilities, a restaurant offering indoor and outdoor dining, and a sunset deck and lounge. Meeting space is available for large groups.

Ocean Key Resort
Zero Duval Street
Key West, FL
(305) 296–7701, (800) 328–9815
www.oceankey.com
$$$–$$$$

Part of the Noble House family of resorts, Ocean Key House is a large resort with an intimate flavor. From their rooms and balconies, Ocean Key guests can see the water, our famous sunsets, and offbeat Mallory Square entertainers, all without the hassle of crowds.

Among the 100 units in this five-story resort are guest rooms and one- and two-bedroom, two-bath suites furnished with laminated wood and other lightweight furnishings. Ceiling fans are standard. Standard guest rooms all feature tiled floors and one queen-size bed, plus a queen-size pullout sofa in the sitting area. Kitchens and living rooms in all suites are tiled, and bedrooms are carpeted. Other features include oversize baths and private hot tubs, kitchens, living rooms with sleeper sofas, and private balconies.

One-bedroom suites have a king-size bed. Two-bedroom units have a king-size bed in the master bedroom and a queen-size bed in the second bedroom. Penthouse suites, the most expensive units in the facility, feature full kitchens with microwaves and washers and dryers.

On premises are three bars, a swimming pool, deli and raw bar, and a marina with fishing, snorkeling, dive charter boats, and a glass-bottom tour boat. A highlight of Ocean Key Resort is its sunset pier overlooking both the harbor and Mallory Square (see our Attractions chapter). Other amenities include valet laundry, room service, and concierge service. The hotel honors requests for nonsmoking rooms. Children younger than 12 stay free when accompanied by an adult. Pets are not allowed. Ocean Key Resort does not provide cots. Cribs are provided free upon request.

Pier House Resort & Caribbean Spa
One Duval Street
Key West, FL
(305) 296–4600, (800) 327–8340
www.pierhouse.com
$$$–$$$$

Portions of the Pier House are on the grounds of Key West's former Porter Dock Company and Aeromarine Airways Inc., two companies that played significant roles in the city's illustrious shipping days. The Pier House offers 126 luxurious, tropically appointed standard rooms with one king-size bed or two double beds and 16 suites. All have views of the Gulf, the swimming pool, or the city.

Rooms overlooking the pool and the Gulf have sliding glass doors and private balconies, and those facing the water may look out on topless sunbathers along a portion of the resort's private beach. Standard in all rooms are minibars, coffeemakers, and hair dryers. A magnificent owner's suite is now available. Lush tropical foliage and brick paving surround the swimming pool and outdoor hot tub. The resort's beach and a secluded island glisten in the distance.

The Pier House is noted for its full-service spa, which offers fitness facilities, facials, massages, and hair and nail care. Room service is available and a concierge will arrange for additional needs. The hotel features two restaurants, a beachside snack bar, and several bars, including the Chart Room, Wine Galley, and Havana Docks sunset deck.

Off-street parking is abundant. Rates are based on double occupancy; each additional person is charged an additional fee per night. Children younger than 17 stay free when accompanied by an adult. Pets are not permitted.

Sheraton Suites Key West
2001 S. Roosevelt Boulevard
Key West, FL
(305) 292–9800, (800) 452–3224
www.sheratonkeywest.com
$$$–$$$$

Situated across from Smathers Beach, the Conch-style, three-story, 180-unit Shera-ton is a luxurious all-suite facility built around an expansive concrete sun deck and a swimming pool. The roomy (550 square feet) suites here are decorated in relaxing tropical teals, peaches, and lavenders and are furnished in colorful wicker.

Walls feature bright Caribbean-colored borders; floors are carpeted, and rooms are furnished with refrigerators and wet bars, minibars, microwaves, and coffeemakers. Most offer king-size beds and whirlpool tubs, and those facing the pool and ocean have sliding glass doors leading to furnished balconies. Suites have irons and ironing boards, built-in hair dryers, and two televisions—one in the bedroom and another in the living room. Central courtyard gardens feature a mix of palms and flowering plants.

The Beach House restaurant offers breakfast, lunch, and dinner poolside or indoors. A hot tub by the pool accommodates eight, and lounge chairs and pool towels are provided. Sheraton Suites offers guests complimentary shuttle service to and from Key West International Airport as well as hourly transportation to Mallory Square (see our Attractions chapter) between 10 A.M. and 10 P.M.

The staff at the guest activities desk will assist you in planning fishing and diving excursions, restaurant bookings, and more. On the premises are a fitness center, 1,100 square feet of banquet meeting space, and a gift shop. Guest laundry facilities are available, and off-street parking is plentiful.

Sunset Key Guest Cottages
245 Front Street
Key West, FL
(305) 292–5300, (888) 477–7786
www.sunsetkeycottages.hilton.com
$$$–$$$$

Billed as the ultimate island hideaway, the guest cottages at Sunset Key are an extension of the Key West Hilton Resort and Marina, tucked away directly across the harbor from the main hotel, overlooking Mallory Square. Access is strictly by private launch, which operates 24 hours a day between Sunset Key and the Hilton marina.

Nestled amid swaying palms and lush flowering hibiscus, the cottages offer an opportunity to truly get away from the hustle and bustle of Duval Street, yet still enjoy the heart of Key West. You may come and go from Sunset Key at will, of course, but you truly never have to leave at all. The emphasis here is on privacy and service; if whatever you require is not on the island, rest assured that it can be delivered post-haste from Key West.

Cottages feature a beachfront, ocean view or garden view, with beachfront being the most expensive. Rates are structured on a per-cottage basis and up to six guests may share a single cottage. Interiors feature separate living and dining areas and bedrooms with either double or king-size beds; every bedroom has its own bath stocked with hair dryer, bathrobes, and plush, oversize towels. The decor has a distinctly Caribbean flavor—ceramic tile floors, pastel accents, ceiling fans, and comfortable, casual, whitewashed furnishings. Every cottage features a CD player, state-of-the-art stereo system, and VCR.

Airy living rooms open onto private verandas, and kitchens are fully stocked with select foods and beverages and the requisite utensils for preparing and serving your own meals. Each has a microwave/convection oven, coffeemaker, toaster, refrigerator, and dishwasher. Guests will find a limited selection of groceries at the island outpost market; however, grocery delivery service from Key West is also offered for more extensive orders. If you'd prefer to leave the cooking to someone else, simply walk a few steps to the full-service gourmet restaurant, Latitudes (see our Restaurants chapter), or arrange for a private chef to prepare a meal in your own kitchen. Room service is also available and a complimentary breakfast basket of muffins and freshly squeezed orange juice is delivered daily, along with the newspaper, to your doorstep.

In addition to a white sandy beach, the island features a freshwater pool, hot tub, two tennis courts, and a health club. No cars are permitted on Sunset Key. However, parking is available in the Key West Hilton garage.

Reservations for specific cottage assignments are accepted but not guaranteed; cottages are assigned on a first-come, first-served basis upon arrival. All cottages are nonsmoking, and pets are not allowed. Guests must be older than 25 unless accompanied by an adult. Children younger than 18 stay free with parents or grandparents.

Wyndham Casa Marina Resort and Beach House
1500 Reynolds Street
Key West, FL
(305) 296–3535, (800) 626–0777
www.wyndham.com/casamarinaresort
$$$–$$$$

Construction of the Casa Marina Hotel dates back to 1918, after railroad magnate Henry Flagler had envisioned a resort hotel for wealthy snowbirds. Made of poured concrete and featuring walls 12 to 22 inches thick, the hotel has hosted many prominent guests, including professional baseball legend Lou Gehrig and President Harry Truman.

The original structure is one of three buildings that now make up the resort, and its Old World–style lobby is lined with old photos of Flagler, Gehrig, Truman, and others. Lobby walls, floors, and columns are made of Dade County pine, and an expansive mahogany front desk with marble top accommodates seven check-in terminals.

The Casa Marina's three- and four-story buildings are set on the Atlantic Ocean, offering a total of 311 standard rooms and suites. Rates increase from the standard non-ocean view to the standard ocean view and from non-ocean view suites to ocean-view suites. Standard rooms hold two double beds or one king-size bed. Each suite has a king-size bed in the bedroom and a double sleeper sofa in the living room. All suites have sliding glass doors and private balconies. Floors are carpeted, and rooms have stocked minibars, cotton robes, hair dryers, irons, and ironing boards. Suites also have two televisions, mini refrigerators, and ceiling fans.

Two restaurants, one inside, the other outdoors beside the beach, serve everything from burgers, salads, and sandwiches to steaks and seafood. The Casa's Sunday brunch, which is served on the terrace overlooking the ocean, is legendary. The Casa Marina also has two swimming pools, one of which is lap-size and the other designated for, but not restricted to, children. Both pools and a hot tub are surrounded by a concrete sun deck with ramps leading to the resort's private beach, the largest such beach in Key West. The pools and hot tub are open 24 hours. During the day, poolside concierge service is available with complimentary fresh fruit and frozen "drinks of the day" from the poolside tiki bar.

A concession stand rents scooters, bicycles, personal watercraft, and Hobie Cats. Parasailing, sunset cruises, and fishing, snorkeling, and diving excursions can also be arranged through this concession. On the premises is a fitness facility with dry or wet sauna, and masseuse services are offered on a large lawn beneath magnificent palm trees or in the privacy of your room.

Three hard-surface tennis courts on the property are lighted, and equipment and lessons are available. The Casa Marina offers concierge services, valet laundry, and complimentary shuttle service to and from Key West International Airport. On slow evenings, the shuttle provides free transportation downtown; more often, a taxi company provides this same service at a discounted rate.

Room service operates nightly until 2 A.M. Smoking and nonsmoking rooms are available, and cribs and cots are free.

Casa Marina rates are structured on a per-room basis, so as many as five guests can share the cost. Children younger than 19 stay free when accompanied by an adult. The Casa Marina offers organized activities for children; most are free of charge (see our Kidstuff chapter). The resort is wheelchair-accessible, and off-street parking is provided at no charge.

Wyndham Reach Resort
1435 Simonton Street
Key West, FL
(305) 296–5000, (800) 874–4118
www.reachresort.com
$$$–$$$$

Splendor by the sea is what visitors to the Wyndham Reach Resort will discover. The resort boasts the only natural sand beach on the island of Key West. A gracious ambiance and a friendly front desk staff await every guest.

All 150 rooms within the resort feature Spanish-tile floors and soothing tones of cream, purple, teal, yellow, and orange, combining a Caribbean twist with Southwestern appeal. Standard rooms, junior suites, and one-bedroom executive suites offer either island or ocean views. Standard rooms have either one queen-size bed or two double beds, and those with queen-size beds also have queen-size sleeper sofas.

Junior suites are large, L-shape studios with queen- or king-size beds and queen-size sleeper sofas. King-size beds and pull-out sleeper sofas are standard in all executive suites. Each room at the Reach Resort has a ceiling fan, private balcony, wet bar, minibar, hair dryer, terry-cloth robes, iron/ironing board, and coffeemaker.

The resort has an outdoor swimming pool, hot tub, and full watersports concession for rafts, parasailing, personal watercraft rentals, and more. The Sand Bar, a casual poolside bar and restaurant, provides full service from 7 A.M. to 9 P.M. New in 2001, Shula's On The Beach, a Don Shula steakhouse, serves prime Angus beef. The restaurant is filled with sepia-toned pictures of Shula's career and showcases Wilson footballs signed by Shula.

An on-premises gift shop carries a wide variety of items, and a salon offers haircuts, colorings, facials, and body wraps. Enjoy a massage beneath an outdoor gazebo or in the privacy of your

Sand, sun, and a hammock for two—it doesn't get any better than this. PHOTO: COCOPLUM RESORT

room, or head for the fitness center with sauna and steam room.

Room service, valet laundry service, and concierge services are available, along with complimentary transportation to and from Key West International Airport.

Tennis facilities at the neighboring Wyndham Casa Marina Resort and Beach House are open to all guests, as are the Casa's magnificent beach and two pools

(see separate listing). Use of rollaways and cribs are free, and children younger than 13 stay free. Rates are based on double occupancy. Each additional person is charged an extra fee per night. Pets are not allowed. Please note: RV campers will not fit under the resort's enclosed parking garage. Smoking and nonsmoking rooms and wheelchair-accessible facilities are provided upon request.

Bed and Breakfasts, Inns, and Guesthouses

Key West's Conch-style mansions and captains' and cigar-workers' homes date back to the 1800s, and many have been marvelously restored to accommodate a thriving tourist industry. Close to 100 intimate hideaways are tucked along the streets, avenues, and lanes of Key West's Old Town, and these charming, romantic inns, bed and breakfasts, and guesthouses provide a sense of history, tranquility, and intimacy within the active city.

The inns, which are within walking distance of Duval Street, offer spacious rooms that often showcase high ceilings, fine antiques and reproductions, and ornate woodwork. Renovations have brought about modern amenities: private baths, air conditioning, telephones, and cable television with remote control. In some cases, guest rooms may share bathroom facilities in the European tradition.

You'll find few waterfront or water-view guesthouse accommodations. Rather, rooms enjoy tranquil garden views or views of the often active, ever-changing streetfront. French doors tend to lead to private verandas with picket fences overlooking lush courtyards where deluxe continental breakfasts, full breakfasts, and afternoon cocktails frequently are served beside tranquil swimming pools, goldfish ponds, or hot tubs. Some guesthouses provide passes that allow use of beach, spa, and fitness facilities at some of the island's full-service resorts.

Ideal for those seeking a quiet escape accessible to restaurants, bars, theater, and watersports, these facilities are run by gracious innkeepers who pay careful regard to detail: Fresh flowers, terry-cloth robes, and other amenities often are provided in each room, cottage, and suite; continental breakfast and sometimes even afternoon cocktails are included in the price of the accommodation.

Key West welcomes diversity, and some guesthouses cater primarily or exclusively to gay travelers. Others are considered all-welcome or gay-friendly. In a separate section at the end of this chapter, we highlight primarily and exclusively gay retreats, many of which maintain clothing-optional policies. Some straight guesthouses and inns also have begun to incorporate a clothing-optional policy. But unlike gay accommodations—where if you disapprove of the policy you shouldn't stay there—heterosexual guesthouses may require clothing upon complaint.

Rates quoted by inns typically are based on double occupancy, and additional guests pay anywhere from $10 to $50 extra per night. Rooms do have a maximum capacity. Inquire about this and all other details when you call to make reservations. If you are certain you'll need full telephone service in your room, check, too, to determine if your service is designed both for call-ins and call-outs.

Pets tend to be more welcome in Key West guesthouses than in hotels or other accommodations throughout the Florida Keys and Key West, but be sure to ask when making your reservation. Where pets are permitted, a flat fee or refundable deposit may be required.

As a rule of thumb, guesthouses are for adults only. If a particular property welcomes children, we'll tell you. Otherwise, you may assume that you should either leave the kids at home or look elsewhere in this chapter for kid-friendly accommodations.

The city's high season is typically December through April, and room rates are even higher—with minimum stays required—during special events and holidays. If you come to Key West for Fantasy Fest in October or during Christmas week in December, the minimum stay may be set at six to seven nights. If you plan to be in Key West at either of these times, you should call and reserve your room at least six months to a year in advance.

And last but not least, the accommodations cited below are only a sampling of what is currently available in Key West. At last count, the Key West phone book had listings for close to 100 guesthouses and inns. We have done our best to provide a representative sampling. For a complete list of accommodations, contact the Key West Information Center at (305) 292-5000 or the Key West Chamber of Commerce at (305) 294-2587 or (800) 527-8539.

Ambrosia House Tropical Lodging,
Ambrosia Too
615/618 Fleming Street
Key West, FL
(305) 296–9838, (800) 585–9838
www.ambrosiakeywest.com,
www.flemingstreetinn.com
$$–$$$

As its name implies, Ambrosia is like a deliciously flavored tropical oasis. This delightful bed-and-breakfast compound is really a combination of two properties—the original Ambrosia guesthouse on one side of Fleming Street and the former Fleming Street Inn, now dubbed Ambrosia Too, on the other.

The compound consists of six carefully restored buildings nestled among lush tropical landscaping and clear, cool ponds. Located in the heart of Old Town Key West, just a block and a half off Duval, Ambrosia is convenient to shopping, restaurants, and nightlife. The accommodations include suites, townhouses, and a stand-alone cottage. Townhouses have full living rooms, complete kitchens, and spiral staircases leading to master suites with vaulted ceilings and private decks. The cottage, which overlooks a dip pool, is a perfect family retreat; it has two bedrooms, two baths, a living room, and full kitchen. Honeymoon suites have four-poster canopy beds and in-room Jacuzzis.

All rooms and suites feature individual entrances with French doors opening onto private verandas, patios, or gardens. The walls are adorned with the original works of Key West artists, the beds are dressed in designer linens. Guest amenities include refrigerators, coffeemakers, portable phones, computer modems, ceiling fans, and cable TV. Large sunning areas, a lap pool, and hot tub are also available.

Ambrosia welcomes kids, but pets are not permitted.

Andrews Inn
Zero Whalton Lane
Key West, FL
(305) 294–7730, (888) 263–7393
www.andrewsinn.com
$$–$$$

You might have to search a bit to find this place, but once you do, we guarantee you won't want to leave. After a day at the beach or a night on Duval, this tiny inn offers a welcome little slice of tranquility that is tough to beat. Andrews Inn is practically in Hemingway's backyard. You'll find it tucked behind his former house—the only thing that separates the two is a brick wall—on a shaded narrow lane between Duval and Whitehead Streets.

Guest rooms here are named for settings in Hemingway's books, like Paris and Pamplona. They all have vaulted ceilings, a queen- or king-size bed, remote control TV, phones, and private bath. Just outside your door, you'll find a lush tropical garden and comfortable lounge chairs situated around a cool, refreshing pool. You're assured of privacy here all right, but we should warn you about the neighbors because you're almost certain to have a visit from at least one of them. A representative from that gang of six-toed cats that reside next door at the Hemingway House is likely to wander over to say hello.

Andrews Inn offers a complimentary champagne continental breakfast each morning and cocktails by the pool every afternoon. If you're lucky and you're able to snag one of the inn's limited off-street parking spaces, you can just abandon your car for the full length of your stay. Andrews Inn is within easy walking distance of most Key West restaurants, bars, and attractions.

The Artist House
534 Eaton Street
Key West, FL
(305) 296–3977, (800) 582–7882
www.artisthousekeywest.com
$–$$$

With the addition of guest suites a block away from the original property, Artist House now offers accommodations at two levels—in a charming turn-of-the-century Victorian mansion and in modern, tastefully appointed guest suites. The one you choose is a matter of personal taste.

What the Artist House Guest Villas might lack in old-world charm, they more than make up for by being exceptionally bright and roomy. Each of the six suites includes a fully equipped kitchen with microwave, stove, and refrigerator and a separate bedroom with a queen-size bed and cable TV. Private sun decks, a heated swimming pool, and a reserved parking space for each guest round out the amenities.

Accommodations in the old house do not sparkle like those in the villas, but all are quite charming and spacious, with 14-foot-high ceilings, private baths, and ceiling fans. Rooms have various antique furnishings and wallpaper patterns and large windows with lace curtains. The parlor suite on the first floor features a four-poster, queen-size bed and has a sitting area with Chippendale couch and Oriental rugs over wood floors. The Turret Suite, on the second floor, offers a dressing room and a winding staircase that leads to a cupola, or circular, loft-style room with daybed. Four of the six guest rooms have working fireplaces, and three have claw-foot tubs.

Legend has it that this 1890 Victorian mansion, formerly the home of Key West painter Eugene Otto, is haunted by the ghost of Otto's deceased wife, whose burial place in the Key West cemetery lacks a tombstone. Some guests claim they have seen Mrs. Otto on a winding staircase in a room on the second floor.

If you'd care to learn more about this somewhat peculiar family, you will find Eugene Otto's paintings on display at the East Martello Museum. At the Key West cemetery (see our Attractions chapter), the former artist's tombstone is surrounded by those of his pet Yorkshire terriers.

Ironically, pets are not allowed at the Artist House or Villas these days. However, children 10 and older are permitted.

Authors of Key West Guesthouse
725 White Street
Key West, FL
(305) 294–7381, (800) 898–6909
www.authors-keywest.com
$–$$$

Visiting writers to Key West often select this private three-building compound as their outpost. Each has his or her favorite room, and each room is named after one of Key West's legendary authors, such as Ernest Hemingway or Tennessee Williams. Look for memorabilia on the author of your choice.

The main two-story, eight-room house is tucked neatly behind a cement wall. Lined with lush tropical foliage, it boasts a two-sided sun deck. Two poolside Conch houses, built around the turn of the nineteenth century, are available for rent; these one-bedroom homes feature queen-size beds and full kitchens. Both have small private porches.

Rooms within the main house are equally diverse, offering views of the street, the sun deck, or the gardens.

Continental breakfast is served daily in the lounge or by the swimming pool. The inn provides off-street parking, and bicycles are available for rent. Pets are not permitted. Children 13 and older are allowed. Note that the entrance to Authors is on Petronia Street.

Banana's Foster Bed and Breakfast
537 Caroline Street
Key West, FL
(305) 294–9061, (800) 653–4888
www.bananasfoster.com
$$–$$$$

Foster Meagher, a talented interior designer who restored the Alexander Graham Bell home in Washington, D.C., considers himself bananas—and he is proud of this fact, hence the unusual name for this two-story, 1880s, Conch-style mansion he restored in 1994.

Banana's Foster offers six rooms in an intimate and elegant setting. All feature exposed and restored Dade County pine, queen- or king-size beds, eighteenth- and nineteenth-century antiques, and private baths. Two rooms are accessed through the main house; the remainder have private entrances. For ultimate luxury, splurge on the two-bedroom Banana suite, with private veranda, stereo system, compact-disc player, VCR, and refrigerator. A cottage behind the main house features a room with a king-size bed and a queen-size bed. The room opens to the brick courtyard patio and garden surrounding an oversize hot tub.

The inn serves a continental breakfast each morning and a wine and relaxation hour before guests venture out to Mallory Square (see our Attractions chapter). Guests may not bring pets.

The Banyan Resort
323 Whitehead Street
Key West, FL
(305) 296–7786, (800) 853–9937
www.banyanresort.com
$$$–$$$$

The Banyan Resort is a collection of eight beautifully preserved and refurbished Conch-style homes, five of which are listed on the National Register of Historic Places. One of these buildings formerly served as a cigar factory.

Homes boast 38 contemporary studios, suites, and duplexes, with full kitchens. Some units have been sold as condominiums; others are available as timeshares and guest accommodations. Studios are least expensive, and rates increase with size: one bedroom, one bath; two bedrooms, one bath; and two bedrooms, two baths. All accommodations have French doors leading to private patios and verandas that overlook award-winning gardens. Included among the gardens are jasmine, frangipani, hibiscus, ixora, rare orchids, palm and fruit trees, and two magnificent 200-year-old banyan trees. Bicycle rentals are available on the premises.

> ## Insiders' Tip
> Dade County pine is a dense, termite-resistant species of the slash pine family. The unusual amount of resin in the wood makes it very hard and heavy, unlike most pines. It was a popular lumber source in the early years of the Keys. A drawback: it's extremely difficult to drive a nail through Dade County pine.

Children, with restrictions, are permitted; pets are not allowed. Limited off-street parking is available at an additional charge.

Blue Parrot Inn
916 Elizabeth Street
Key West, FL
(305) 296–0033, (800) 231–2473
www.blueparrotinn.com
$–$$

Built in 1884 with wood pegs that are more hurricane-friendly than nails, the Blue Parrot Inn offers 10 rooms—seven in the main house and three in a servant's quarters-turned-cottage. Rooms vary in size, number of beds, and decor. The only blue parrot in residence here is a stuffed one; however, the cats you'll see wandering the grounds are very much alive.

A large Irish room with two double beds features Celtic prints and green accessories; the pink flamingo room, with a queen-size bed, is flocked with feathers and photographs of the famed Floridian birds. Still others remain true to this guesthouse's name through parrot-print bedspreads. All rooms have phones and most have mini refrigerators.

Out back, a heated swimming pool surrounded by extensive decking sets the scene for a leisurely continental breakfast consisting of fresh fruit, bagels, English muffins, and home-baked quiche or fruit breads served every morning. A tremendous staghorn fern strung along branches of a gumbo limbo tree makes a magnificent garden centerpiece.

The atmosphere at the Blue Parrot is friendly and intimate, but sorry, pets are not permitted and guests must be at least 16 years of age. The Inn is wheelchair-accessible. Curbside parking is free; off-street parking is available for an extra charge.

Center Court Historic Inn & Cottages
915 Center Street
Key West, FL
(305) 296–9292, (800) 797–8787
www.centercourtkw.com
$–$$$$

Center Court is a fine example of the historic preservation for which Key West is so justly famous. Nestled on a quiet, inconspicuous lane just a half-block from Duval Street, the main guesthouse, constructed in 1874, is surrounded by a collection of former cigar-maker cottages. Owner/operator Naomi Van Steelandt enrolled in construction courses so she could carry out the restoration, which won two Historic Preservation Awards of Excellence in 1994.

Walls are pastel-colored and feature original local art. Guest rooms are cozy and sleep two to six. Rooms are stocked with beach bags, beach towels, and other goodies. Each cottage has its own bright and cheerful personality, as well as a fully stocked kitchen, barbecue grill, and private hot tub.

The main building houses a spacious, airy breakfast room; dining takes place out on the back porch overlooking a freshwater swimming pool, spa, and exercise pavilion. Two cottages are set beside a lily pond. A spiral staircase alongside one of these cottages leads to a clothing-optional sun deck. Breakfast is complimentary for guests in rooms; cottage guests have the facilities to fix their own.

Children are allowed in the cottages and suites. Pets are permitted for an additional fee per night.

Van Steelandt also performs and coordinates weddings and makes honeymoon arrangements. For information, call her at the numbers shown above.

Chelsea House
707 Truman Avenue
Key West, FL
(305) 296–2211, (800) 845–8859
www.chelseahousekw.com
$$–$$$$

Built in 1870 for a British ship captain who hauled tobacco from Havana and later became the first general manager of Duval Street's La Concha Hotel, Chelsea House was later converted to a guesthouse by the captain's grieving widow to provide lodging to Key West's military visitors. Later, Chelsea House became an apartment complex. In 1985, massive renovations included the addition of private baths throughout and the conversion of the carriage house into guest accommodations.

The Conch-style mansion serves as the main guesthouse. And with the addition of a pool house, garden rooms, and suites building, the total number of units now stands at 19. Each has 10-foot-high ceilings and individualized decor. Guest rooms in the main house feature hardwood floors and heavy mahogany and oak period-antique furnishings. Pool house rooms open directly onto the sun deck and the garden rooms feature raised decks with rocking chairs for lounging. All rooms are furnished with antiques and feature private baths, ceiling fans, refrigerators, and complimentary bath amenities. Some have private or shared porches, oversize tubs, and cathedral ceilings.

Unlike The Red Rooster (Chelsea House's more casual sister hotel, described later in this chapter), this is co-owner Jim Durbin's showpiece, boasting four-poster beds and armoires plus nightly turndowns and fresh pool towels.

A full acre of property, shared with the neighboring Red Rooster, is likely the largest of all of Key West's guesthouse properties. Here, a private garden with massive palms and flowering plants forms an L-shaped alcove visible from the windows, French doors, and balconies of some rooms in the main house. Every room at Chelsea House either has a balcony or opens onto the pool area.

A daily continental breakfast is served in an enclosed poolside cafe, and clothing is optional on a secluded elevated sun deck. Also available for topless lounging at this adults-only inn are the gardens, deck, pool, and cabana areas. Off-street parking provides a space for every guest.

With prior approval, pets are accepted.

The Conch House Heritage Inn
625 Truman Avenue
Key West, FL
(305) 293–0020, (800) 207–5806
www.conchhouse.com
$–$$$

Since the 1800s, this historic two-story estate has been passed on from generation to generation. The owners are Sam Holland, Jr. and his mother, Francine Delaney Holland. She is the great-granddaughter of Cuban émigré Carlos Recio, a close friend of Cuban revolutionary Jose Marti.

The inn is listed on the National Register of Historic Places and was restored in 1993 to combine Old World decor with modern amenities. The five bedrooms in the main house feature high ceilings, wood shutters, wraparound porches, and picket fences. A poolside cottage offers three guest rooms decorated with Caribbean prints and wicker. Guests may have their continental breakfast in the dining room or on the veranda.

Neither pets nor children are permitted at the inn.

> ## Insiders' Tip
>
> Do you notice a malodorous smell as you travel along certain mangrove-lined stretches of the Overseas Highway? Leaf litter that remains caught in the prop roots of the red mangroves decomposes into sediment that often forms into peat. When the peat is exposed to the sun at low tide, its sulfur content oxidizes and a rotten egg smell is noticeable.

Cuban Club Suites
1102 Duval Street
Key West, FL
(305) 296–0466, (800) 432–4849
$$–$$$$
La Casa De Luces
422 Amelia Street
Key West, FL
(305) 296–3993, (800) 432–4849
www.keywestcubanclub.com
$–$$$

Both Cuban Club Suites and La Casa De Luces share guest check-in and lobby facilities on Amelia Street, but Cuban Club Suites is actually in a separate building at 1102 Duval Street. These two-story luxury suites are condominiums occupying second and third floors above boutique shops that are open to the public.

A large living area, full kitchen, bath, and bedroom with a queen-size bed occupy the main level of the two-bedroom suites. An oversize loft area above the main level is furnished either with a queen- or king-size bed and features a second bath and a small private sunning deck. One-bedroom suites have a large living area, full kitchen, and half-bath on the first floor; the second-floor loft has a queen-size bed, full bath, and small sunning deck. All suites have washer/dryers and are furnished primarily with light wicker furnishings or heavy wood furnishings accented by antique reproductions.

At the less exclusive La Casa De Luces (Spanish translation: house of lights) are eight units ranging from two small rooms sharing a bath to large garden suites with king-size bed, living room, washer/dryer, and full kitchen. Most rooms are furnished with lightweight wicker furnishings and tropical prints; all have exterior access via private verandas.

Complimentary continental breakfast is delivered to guest rooms each morning, and within the La Casa De Luces lobby is a small museum illustrating the rich Cuban history of both buildings. Neither facility has a swimming pool, but guests are provided passes to a nearby resort.

Off-street parking is available. Families are welcome. Dogs are permitted if management is notified at the time the reservation is made.

Curry Mansion Inn
511 Caroline Street
Key West, FL
(305) 294–5349, (800) 253–3466
www.currymansion.com
$$–$$$

Curry Mansion Inn's chief claim to fame is its location on the grounds of the estate that once belonged to the Currys, Florida's first home-grown millionaire family. Situated on Caroline Street, just a few steps off Duval, the 22-room mansion was begun by William Curry in 1855 and completed by his son Milton in 1899. Innkeepers Al and Edith Amsterdam purchased the property in 1975. Curry Mansion is today a museum, housing a selection of turn-of-the-nineteenth-century furnishings and memorabilia from Key West's heyday as the richest city in America (see our Attractions chapter). It is also the centerpiece for a guesthouse that is consistently rated among the best in Key West.

Guests at the Curry Mansion Inn do not actually stay in the mansion; they do, however, have full access to it. Guest accommodations consist instead of 28 rooms adjacent to the mansion, most of which open onto a pool and all of which are surrounded by the lush foliage that characterizes the Curry estate. All of the rooms feature wicker furnishings, antiques, and ceiling fans; the beds are draped in handmade quilts. Modern amenities include private baths, wet bars, small refrigerators, air conditioning, cable television, and telephones.

A complimentary breakfast buffet is offered poolside each morning; complimentary cocktails are served each evening from 5 until 7. The Inn's heated pool and hot tub are open 24 hours. Ask about beach privileges at nearby oceanfront resorts; Curry Mansion Inn has agreements with several.

A particularly appealing feature of this guesthouse is its location—right in the heart of downtown Key West. The restaurants, bars, shops, and other Duval Street attractions are just steps away; parking is plentiful. Pets are not permitted.

Cypress House
601 Caroline Street
Key West, FL
(305) 294–6969, (800) 525–2488
www.cypresshousekw.com
$–$$$

The 40-foot heated lap pool surrounded by lush tropical gardens on the grounds of this 100-year-old mansion is among the largest at any of Key West's inns. The New England–style, three-story home, constructed of cypress, is listed on the National Register of Historic Places and is a noted attraction along the Conch train tourist route (see our Attractions chapter).

Rebuilt in the wake of the fire of 1886 that consumed much of Key West, the facility was originally owned by Richard Moore Kemp, a shipbuilder and naturalist credited for the discovery of the ridley turtle (now known as the Kemp ridley turtle). Twenty years after Kemp built his own home, he added another house to the property for his daughter and son-in-law, a pioneer Key West sponger.

Connected by a wooden fire escape, the two homes share a sun deck. Rooms throughout the structures feature 12-foot-high ceilings and wood floors with area rugs. In-room telephones allow for outside calling, and most rooms have queen-size beds and ceiling fans. Six of 16 rooms have private baths, one of which is a whopping 14 square feet. A hand-painted floral ceiling border accents one room, and all are furnished with period antiques.

Porches on the first and second floor are accessible to guests. A breakfast buffet featuring home-baked goods is served poolside, as is a nightly complimentary cocktail hour with beer, wine, and snacks.

Formerly an exclusively gay guest-house, Cypress is now an all-welcome, adults-only facility. Pets are not permitted, but you are invited to pet the resident dog and cat in case you miss your own.

Douglas House
419 Amelia Street
Key West, FL
(305) 294–5269, (800) 833–0372
www.douglashouse.com
$$–$$$

Douglas House is a collection of six Victorian homes, four of which are more than 100 years old. Each house contains two to five spacious units for a combined total of 15.

Standard rooms and one-bedroom suites are furnished with a queen-size bed or two double beds; suites have a full kitchen. All units have private baths and outdoor entrances, and each unit is furnished differently. Some are carpeted with standard wood furnishings; others have hardwood floors and wicker furnishings. Suites have French doors opening to a private deck, patio, or balcony. Some suites have loft-style bedrooms.

Within the compound are two swimming pools and a hot tub surrounded by gardens. Continental breakfast is served poolside each morning, and coffee perks throughout the day.

Pets are permitted. Children younger than 12 are not allowed during the high season.

Duval House
815 Duval Street
Key West, FL
(305) 294–1666, (800) 223–8825
www.duvalhousekeywest.com
$$–$$$$

This two-story inn may be set on busy Duval Street, but its pigeon plums, banyans, heliconia, and hibiscus successfully guard it from intrusion. Lounge poolside amid traveler's palms and light jazz music, linger on a shady hammock, or chat with others in a gazebo by the fishpond. The inn's breakfast room maintains a library of books, board games, magazines and newspapers, and a weather chart listing temperatures throughout the world.

In the 1880s, Duval House was inhabited by cigar workers. Today, the 30 standard and deluxe rooms and apartments are furnished with English antiques, white wicker, and wooden French doors. All are air-conditioned. Locally made frangipani soap is placed in each bathroom.

Most rooms have color television, and some feature elegant poster beds and private porches. All except the two apartments and two front rooms look out onto the gardens.

If you visit Duval House, look for Mush, the resident cat, who receives letters from former guests all over the world.

Eaton Lodge
511 Eaton Street
Key West, FL
(305) 292–2170, (800) 294–2170
www.eatonlodge.com
$–$$$

Built in 1886, the treasure that is Eaton Lodge was owned by one of Key West's first physicians, Dr. William Warren. His wife, Genevieve, founded the Key West Garden Club. Notice her intricate designs for the home's diverse courtyard, which features a fountain, fishpond, Spanish lime tree, jacaranda, and more.

Present owners Carolyn and Stephen West have painted the inn's shutters to match the lavender jacaranda and have preserved all historic appointments within the home's interior, adding a courtyard hot tub.

Eaton Lodge's main house served as both home and office for Dr. Warren. Its elegant living room features Oriental and Turkish carpets over wood floors, a Venetian glass chandelier and an antique fireplace, and bookshelves pose as inconspicuous doors to divide the living room and kitchen.

All 16 rooms and suites, including those within the William Skelton House next door, vary in size, decor, and view. The carriage house at the rear of the home provides two-story, garden-view accommodations that connect to create duplexes.

With their high ceilings and original moldings, rooms and suites in the main house feature eighteenth-century furnishings (the Recuperating Room), two antique brass beds (the Operating Room), picket-fence porches and private terraces (the Anniversary and Sunset rooms). The unique Sunset Room has a raised bathroom and a terrace that sides a three-story cistern.

Look for the manager's apartment, which has a tree growing out of its bathroom and through the roof. All rooms feature watercolor and oil paintings by local artists and wood plank or parquet flooring with area carpets.

The three-bedroom, two-bath William Skelton House is typically rented in its entirety, and its pool is shared by all Eaton Lodge guests. Homemade tropical breads and fresh fruits are served on the patio each morning, and an open-bar afternoon break is offered on the brick patio.

There are a number of exotic caged birds on the property, so Kuma, the inn's docile Akita, is the only pet allowed. Smoking is prohibited at Eaton Lodge.

Eden House
1015 Fleming Street
Key West, FL
(305) 296–6868, (800) 533–5397
www.edenhouse.com
$–$$$

For years Eden House was known as a no-frills, low-budget hangout for writers, intellectuals, and Europeans. Over the past few years, owner Mike Eden has added several enhancements.

When producers of the movie *Criss Cross* scouted Key West locations, they opted for this facility. With the enhancements, the c. 1924 building was too polished for the film's needs. They "roughed it up" a bit cosmetically and sent Goldie Hawn here to portray the movie's main character. Rest assured, once the film was completed, Eden House was quickly restored to its vintage art deco grandeur.

Constructed of wood and concrete, the facility categorizes units by luxury rooms and efficiencies (two of them have sleeping lofts); private rooms and efficiencies with bath or shower; semiprivate rooms with shared baths; and European rooms with double or twin-size beds, a sink, and a bath and shower in the hall. Most other units feature queen-size beds. Prices descend respectively.

Accommodations are decorated in light, subdued colors and tropical prints and furnished with a mix of wicker and rattan. Many units have French doors leading to porches and decks near the center of the facility, where gardens surround a swimming pool, hot tub, and gazebo.

Children are permitted, but pets are not. Bicycle rentals are available and guests are treated to a cold drink at check-in. Be sure to check out the new elevated sun deck and hammock area, but tread softly. Those tanning bodies are likely to be sound asleep.

Eden House is a smoke-free facility.

Insiders' Tip

See our Healthcare chapter for listings of veterinarians who will board your pet.

The Frances Street Bottle Inn
535 Frances Street
Key West, FL
(305) 294–8530, (800) 294–8530
www.bottleinn.com
$–$$

Tucked away in a quiet residential neighborhood on the edge of Old Town, this charming inn takes its name from the owner's collection of antique bottles and cobalt blue glassware displayed in every window and along several interior shelves. The trim, white frame structure, once a corner grocery store and boarding house, has a unique place in recent Key West history, too. It was the set for the Meteor newspaper office in the short-lived television series Key West.

The atmosphere here is quiet and intimate. The Bottle Inn has just seven guest rooms, each with private bath, air-conditioning, and color television. White wicker chairs line a gracious porch across the front of the house, and in the lush tropical gardens, a complimentary continental breakfast is served each morning under the poinciana trees. Concierge service is available. Although the grounds are too small to allow for a pool, there is a hot tub.

If you're looking for a guesthouse experience well removed from Duval, yet still within walking distance of most Old Town attractions, you'll find excellent value here.

The Gardens Hotel
526 Angela Street
Key West, FL
(305) 294–2661, (800) 526–2664
www.gardenshotel.com
$$$$

In 1930 the late Key West resident Peggy Mills began collecting various species of orchids from Japan, Bali, and other exotic parts of the world. As neighboring homes were placed on the market, Mills would purchase and level them, adding to her garden until it encompassed a full city block.

Before she passed away, the Mills garden became public, gaining the attention of botanists worldwide and national magazines. These gardens have been restored to much of their original splendor by Bill and Corrina Hettinger, owners and operators of The Gardens Hotel, a member of Small Luxury Hotels of the World.

A complex of five guesthouses and a carriage house, the hotel offers 17 units, including two two-bedroom suites set around a tiki bar, swimming pool, hot tub, fountain, and a winding path of bougainvillea, orange jasmine, palm, mango, breadfruit trees, and more. The architecture is classic, and rooms are furnished with mahogany reproductions from Holland and floral chintz.

InStyle magazine once described The Gardens Hotel as being like a secluded European inn. Famous guests here have included actors George Clooney and Mickey Rourke and singer k. d. lang.

Floors are hardwood, bathrooms marble with whirlpool tubs, and telephones, and walls are decorated with original Key West scenes painted by equestrian Peter Williams. All rooms have garden views, and fountains throughout the grounds enhance the sense of tranquillity. Each room has a television, coffeemaker, mini-bar, and private porch. All except the historic rooms and the master suite have separate entrances and private porches.

Heron House
512 Simonton Street
Key West, FL
(305) 294–9227, (888) 861–9066
www.heronhouse.com
$$–$$$$

Centered around a 35-foot swimming pool, decorated with a mosaic of a heron, and a Chicago brick patio and sun deck, every one of the 23 rooms at the Heron House features unique woodwork and stained glass created by local artists.

Platform-style oak beds are hand-crafted, and all accommodations have French doors leading to private porches or balconies overlooking the English-style country gardens. This historic facility was built prior to the turn of the nineteenth century. It offers basic, upper-standard and deluxe rooms. All are spacious with incredibly high ceilings and double, queen- or king-size beds. Deluxe rooms and junior suites have wet bars, futon sitting areas, and mini refrigerators. Coffee is served in the breezeway. A private sun deck is clothing-optional.

Heron House accepts children older than 15.

Island City House Hotel
411 William Street
Key West, FL
(305) 294–5702, (800) 634–8230
www.islandcityhouse.com
$$–$$$

At Island City House, two 1880s homes and a cypress wood house designed to resemble a cigar factory encompass an Old World–style enclave lined with brick walkways and lush tropical gardens. Wood decking surrounds the hot tub and swimming pool tucked neatly at one end of the compound; the swimming pool has a tiled alligator motif at bottom.

Central to Island City House is its charming courtyard patio, where antique iron benches and bistro-style tables are set around a fountain and fishpond. This is the setting for the daily continental breakfast.

Island City House itself is a Conch-style mansion originally built for a wealthy merchant family. Here, guests choose from 12 one- and two-bedroom parlor suites with kitchens and antiques that provide a New England maritime feel. The Arch House, the only carriage house in Key West, maintains six studio and two-bedroom suites decorated with casual furnishings of rattan and wicker. At the Cigar House, built on a cistern and the former site of a cigar factory, spacious suites feature plantation-style decor that combines antique furnishings with wicker and rattan. The homes have hardwood floors throughout, and many rooms feature French doors leading to private patios and decks.

Children are permitted; those under 12 stay free. Pets are not allowed. Bicycle rentals are available on premises and a complimentary breakfast is served in the garden each morning.

Key West Bed & Breakfast
415 William Street
Key West, FL
(305) 296–7274, (800) 438–6155
www.keywestbandb.com
$–$$$

When strong winds blow through the city of Key West, you can feel the three-story Key West Bed & Breakfast move with them, for this 1890 home was built by shipbuilders skilled in crafting structures able to weather any storm. Step inside from the front porch and you likely will be greeted by Dave, the inn's resident golden retriever.

With the exception of one suite, all of the inn's eight guest rooms feature a mix of bright colors, elegant Victorian furnishings, exposed Dade County pine, and 13-foot ceilings. Most have queen-size beds, and third-floor suites in the dormered attic offer a choice of two magnificent views. The back suite has French doors leading to a private deck and is decorated in more muted tones because it gathers color from the backyard's flowering trees, including a wild orchid tree that produces rich purple flowers. The suite at the front of the house is noted for its 5-foot arched Palladian window, which provides a view of the sunset above the city's rooftops and trees.

Continental breakfast, including fresh baked goods and freshly squeezed orange juice, is served outdoors, where tables and chairs line the backyard wood deck. All rooms are air-conditioned, and most have ceiling fans. The inn has no televisions or telephones except for a community telephone to which all guests are provided access.

Owner Jodi Carlson is an artist who weaves, and her bright yarns provide added color to the inn's community room where magazines, Florida Keys–related books, and an extensive compact disc collection and player are available to guests. Two of the inn's four porches are furnished with a swing and double hammock, and the oversize backyard hot tub is also used as a dip pool. Pets are prohibited.

La Mer Hotel
506 South Street
Key West, FL
(305) 296–5611, (800) 354–4455
$$$–$$$$
Dewey House
1319 Duval Street
Key West, FL
(305) 296–5611, (800) 354–4455
www.oldtownresorts.com/lamerdewey.htm
$$$$

La Mer and Dewey House are Key West's only oceanfront bed and breakfasts. They have the same owner, but they are marketed as individual luxury getaways with distinctly different names and ambiance.

La Mer is actually a turn-of-the-century Conch house with 11 rooms decorated with wicker furnishings and light, tropical prints. Most rooms, which feature king- or queen-size beds and private baths, also offer a private balcony or patio. One room has two twin beds; some rooms have sleeper sofas.

If this is not luxurious enough for your taste, the eight-room Dewey House offers decor in rich greens and golds with heavy draperies, fine antiques, whirlpool bathtubs, and French doors leading to private balconies and patios. Named for its original owner, philosopher and educator John Dewey, the house is joined to La Mer by a lush tropical garden.

Rooms at both facilities have high ceilings with ceiling fans, mini-bars, and Italian marble bathrooms with built-in hair dryers. Rooms have king- or queen-size beds, and some have fully equipped kitchenettes with microwaves.

In addition to a deluxe continental breakfast of freshly baked breads and coffeecakes, plus croissants, English muffins, and fresh fruits, the inn serves tea, crumpets, fresh fruits, and cheeses at 4:30 P.M. daily. *USA Today* is delivered to the door of each guest room. An 8-square-foot hot tub is set among beautifully landscaped gardens, and La Mer and Dewey House guests are allowed access to pool facilities at their owner's Southernmost and South Beach Oceanfront motels. Pets are not permitted.

The Lightbourn Inn
907 Truman Avenue
Key West, FL
(305) 296–5152, (800) 352–6011
www.lightbourn.com
$$

Owners/operators Kelly Summers and Scott Fuhriman have drawn upon sojourns in Europe and Asia in decorating rooms in their classic Conch-style mansion, which is listed on the National Register of Historic Places.

All 10 guest rooms within the Lightbourn Inn feature antiques, Key West wicker, and signed celebrity memorabilia. A complimentary breakfast, including hot entrees, is one of the inn's most popular features. Wine is served on the deck during wine hour while an outdoor jukebox plays your favorite tunes, and three levels of private decking overlook the clothing-optional pool area.

Because the owners reside on the property, holidays always include home-away-from-home celebrations.

The Marquesa Hotel
600 Fleming Street
Key West, FL
(305) 292–1919, (800) 869–4631
www.marquesa.com
$$$–$$$$

This cluster of homes dates back to the 1880s. Each standard room, deluxe room, junior suite, standard suite, and terrace suite is furnished with ceiling fans and an eclectic collection of antique English and West Indian reproductions that evoke the ambiance of an exquisite English plantation.

Accommodations are spacious, with oversize marble baths. Many rooms feature French doors and private porches overlooking two pools and the garden. At the east end of the garden, brick steps accented by a fountain lead to a newer building of complementary architecture.

Breakfast (available for a nominal fee) includes a feast of baked goods fresh from the oven of the highly praised Cafe Marquesa (see our Restaurants chapter).

The Palms Hotel
820 White Street
Key West, FL
(305) 294–3146, (800) 558–9374
www.palmshotelkeywest.com
$$–$$$

Completely restored in 1995, the main Conch-style house with its wraparound porches was built in 1889. It features Caribbean influences and is listed on the National Register of Historic Places. In the 1970s, the hotel added an L-shaped structure built in a complementary style, around a large heated swimming pool.

All 20 rooms are painted in pastels and furnished with wicker and Caribbean-style decor; rooms in the main house have separate access to the porch. Most have queen- or king-size beds or two double beds. Some floors are carpeted, some are tiled, and several rooms in the main house feature all-wood flooring. Private entrances, private baths, and ceiling fans are standard.

For a real Old World–style getaway, ask for the mini-suite with turret, where a king-size bed is surrounded by windows and walls of exposed Dade County pine, and the downstairs living area features hardwood floors. This suite can be connected to a guest room with queen-size bed to accommodate larger parties.

A deluxe continental breakfast is served each morning at the full-service poolside tiki bar, and the large heated swimming pool is open around the clock.

The Palms has a small parking lot on the street directly behind the hotel; on-street parking is also available. Children are permitted; pets are allowed with advance approval.

The Paradise Inn
819 Simonton Street
Key West, FL
(305) 293–8007, (800) 888–9648
www.theparadiseinn.com
$$$$

Style and distinction mark the 15 suites and three cottages of the Paradise Inn. Two of the three cottages are refurbished Conch houses; the rest are recently built two-story buildings of coordinating architecture.

Painted white with Caribbean-blue Bahamian shutters, all units have high ceilings, large marble baths, natural oak flooring, and unique window dressings that combine stagecoach and handkerchief valances with wood mini-blinds. French doors lead to outdoor porches in all but one cottage, and the interior decor features distressed pine, botanical prints, and pale shades of tan. Rooms have queen- and king-size wrought iron and California sleigh beds.

The inn's diverse gardens, designed by award-winning landscape architect Raymond Jungles of Coral Gables, feature Barbados cherry and avocado trees and bromeliads. Even the swimming pool and hot tub, separated by a lily pond, evoke luxury.

Children are permitted; pets are not. A complimentary breakfast is served in the lobby; room service is available from the Thai restaurant next door.

Pilot House Guesthouse
414 Simonton Street
Key West, FL
(305) 293–6600, (800) 648–3780
www.pilothousekeywest.com
$$–$$$

Restored in 1991, this 100-year-old Conch-style home provides rooms and suites that mix antique furnishings with functional pieces and tropical rattan prints.

Once a three-bedroom home, the floor plan has been altered so the first-floor library and dining room now accommodate a guest room and two two-bedroom suites. Suites on the second floor are furnished with its original family in mind.

Built by the late Julius Otto, son of a prominent Key West surgeon, the 3,000-square-foot mansion served as a winter retreat. Julius' brother Eugene inherited The Artist House (see listing in this chapter) around the corner, and the yards of the two Otto homes almost back each other. Here in the gracious Pilot House, curved archways lead from one room to another, and moldings are massive but not overpowering.

Frangipani and royal poinciana trees thrive in the yard, and a gumbo limbo grows through the roof of what is known as this facility's spa building. Set along the brick-patio backyard is a Spanish-style stucco cabana building that offers six suites with queen- and king-size beds, full kitchens, and in-room hot tubs. Furnishings in the cabana are contemporary white wicker amidst adobe-colored walls. Mirrors are abundant, and 6-square-foot open showers have sleek European-style showerheads jutting from the ceilings.

Passageways rather than doors create privacy for each area of these suites, and all entrances face the swimming pool.

Most rooms in the main house have balconies but are accessed through a formal entrance, and all rooms have kitchenettes, ceiling fans, and private baths. The inn does not provide breakfast, but restaurants are nearby. All guests are encouraged to carry on at their own pace.

The backyard swimming pool, at 15 feet by 30 feet, is larger than most in Key West, and an in-ground spa for 12 is sheltered from the sun by a tin roof with lattice and the aforementioned gumbo limbo tree that grows through the roof.

Clothing here is optional. Pets are prohibited, and no off-street parking is provided.

The Red Rooster Inn
709 Truman Avenue
Key West, FL
(305) 296–6558, (800) 845–0825
www.redroosterinn.com
$–$$

Built in 1870 by the Delgato family, The Red Rooster is considered Truman Avenue's oldest house. At the time, the street was called Hard Rock Road. It later became Division Street and during the 1950s Truman era received the name Truman Avenue.

In the early twentieth century, this private house was converted to apartments to house the U.S. Coast Guard; then it was converted to provide casual, low-end guest accommodations. Left to disrepair, the home was purchased by Jim Durbin and Gary Williams, owners of the exclusive Chelsea House next door (see listing in this chapter), and renamed The Red Rooster. Colorful stories about the home tell of a scandalous past, including illicit use by prostitutes and drug dealers. According to local legend, Mrs. Delgato murdered her husband and buried him beneath a concrete porch along the front of the building.

The 18 carpeted rooms, all with private, renovated bathrooms, exude an eclectic flavor, and all but one of the rooms are accessible via exterior doors. Most have queen-size beds, and some are incredibly spacious, with fireplaces and French doors leading to a front veranda. Others are small but cozy.

This reasonably priced, liberal adult guesthouse shares a yard and outdoor facilities with The Chelsea House, and clothing is optional in designated outdoor areas. A coffee bar at the entrance doubles as space for the desk clerk and evokes a European atmosphere. Continental breakfast is served here daily. Impromptu cocktail hours provide a party-like atmosphere.

Pets are welcome; children are not.

Simonton Court Historic Inn and Cottages
320 Simonton Street
Key West, FL
(305) 294–6386, (800) 944–2687
www.simontoncourt.com
$$–$$$$

Situated on 2 acres of property that once boasted a cigar factory, Simonton Court offers 10 varied structures with equally varied accommodations. The inn's four outdoor swimming pools once served as cisterns. Simonton Court's original building is a Victorianesque mansion with maritime influences including a widow's walk. Built by a judge in the late 1880s and known as "the mansion," it now houses the most luxurious rooms and suites on the property.

Some of Simonton Court's guest rooms are furnished in period antiques and have green marble bathrooms and large terraces; others offer Caribbean-style decor. One has a spa tub and includes the widow's walk.

A two-story clapboard building with porches, once the actual cigar factory, is now known as the "inn." Within the inn today are nine rustic old Key West–style rooms paneled with Dade County pine and featuring high ceilings and heavily shuttered windows. When closed, the shutters effectively bar the heat. Rooms here range from basic units with king-size beds to a triplex with kitchen, bedroom, and living and dining area. All rooms at the inn have hardwood floors and private baths.

On the "rustic" side are Simonton Court's two-story cottages. Decorated with antique bamboo furnishings and brightly colored handmade fabrics, interiors are bright and airy. The first floor of each cottage has a kitchenette with microwave (no oven) and a queen- or king-size bed. Attic-style lofts with skylights are furnished with two double beds.

Still another building, known as the Manor House suite, offers a spacious two-bedroom complex with full kitchen and living room and a private outdoor pool. Simonton Court's two-story townhouse is extremely plush, decorated in Grand Floribbean–style antiques and white linens. The first floor has a living room, a bedroom with queen-size bed, a private patio, and a bath with shower. A similar floor plan upstairs is enhanced by vaulted ceilings, skylights, and a spa tub. Both floors have separate entrances via a private balcony or brick patio so that only half the townhouse can be rented if desired. Townhouse guests enjoy their own semiprivate swimming pool.

Simonton Court's tropically landscaped gardens, antique brick pathways, swimming pools, and hot tub all come aglow at night, when lighting emphasizes all the right places.

Pets and children are not permitted. An expanded continental breakfast is served poolside daily. Inn and townhouse guests who visit during high season are greeted by a complimentary bottle of wine and treated to a nightly turndown.

Southernmost Point Guesthouse
1327 Duval Street
Key West, FL
(305) 294–0715
www.southernmostpoint.com
$$–$$$

Throughout Key West, you will discover all kinds of things dubbed "the southernmost"—a southernmost hockey rink and Southernmost Motel, for instance. The Southernmost Point Guesthouse, across from the Southernmost House, is a showy, three-story, Conch-style mansion built in 1885 for E.H. Gato Jr., son of Key West's first cigar manufacturer.

The home is notable for its wraparound porches and private balconies, some of which afford partial ocean or garden views. Rooms come in varying sizes,

Insiders' Tip

The following Florida Keys chambers of commerce can provide information about most area accommodations: Key Largo, MM 106 Bayside, (305) 451-1414, (800) 822-1088, www.keylargo.org; Islamorada, MM 82.5 Bayside, (305) 664-4503, (800) 322-5397, www.islamoradachamber.com; Marathon, MM 53.5 Bayside, (305) 743-5417, (800) 262-7284, www.floridakeysmarathon.com; Lower Keys, MM 31, Oceanside, (305) 872-2411, (800) 872-3722, www.lowerkeyschamber.com; Key West, Mallory Square, (305) 294-2587, (800) 648-6269, www.fla-keys.com.

tropical gardens of banana, coconut palm, breadfruit, and mango trees.

Continental breakfast includes fresh-baked goods and cold cuts, cheeses, and boiled eggs. Children younger than 12 and accompanied by an adult stay free, and guests with pets are charged an additional nominal fee per night. Rollaway beds are available, and cribs are complimentary. Other thoughtful amenities include wine, mints, and fresh flowers placed in each room prior to a guest's arrival.

Speakeasy Inn
1117 Duval Street
Key West, FL
(305) 296–2680, (800) 217–4884
$–$$$

Casa 325
325 Duval Street
Key West, FL
(305) 292–0070, (800) 227–2325
www.keywestcigar.com/innspage
$$–$$$

The Speakeasy, a turn-of-the-nineteenth-century inn offers spacious rooms in its main Duval Street house plus three spacious suites in a back-alley building along Amelia Street. The original building was the home of Raul Vasquez, a cigar selector at the Gato cigar factory whose true passion was rumrunning between Key West and Cuba.

The newer building, built as a residence for the owner's stepdaughter, offers what is referred to as the Gallery Suite, considered to be the best offering in the house. The large, apartment-size unit has a queen-size bed and sleeper sofa and features beamed ceilings, hardwood floors, track lighting, and patio doors leading to a private deck and yard. This and other rooms at Speakeasy also are appointed with private, tiled baths, refrigerators, wetbars, and ceiling fans.

First-floor rooms feature queen-size beds and private patios. Those on the second floor offer queen- or full-size beds but lack a wet bar. And room No. 2 in the main house features an elegant claw-foot bathtub.

but all have private entrances, private baths, and ceiling fans. The Ernest Hemingway suite is a deluxe, two double-bed efficiency designed with a jungle-like theme in honor of the legendary author's ardor for hunting, but most rooms are furnished either with queen-size or double beds and antiques with a tropical flair.

Some rooms have kitchenettes, and the largest of all is the two-bedroom master suite with queen-size bed in the master bedroom, with a pullout sleeper sofa, and a private balcony that offers a partial view of the Southernmost Point (see our Attractions chapter). Suite No. 6 is a duplex that comprises portions of the home's second and third floors, and suite No. 5 features a king-size bed and a private porch with a swing.

All guests are given a key to the hot tub (large enough for 12 people). Lounge chairs are provided amid the guesthouse's

Casa 325 offers one- and two-bedroom suites in a vintage Victorian building that has been recently restored and decorated in a tropical island theme. Suites feature queen-size beds, kitchenettes with refrigerators, microwave, and wet bar, and ceiling fans. A center courtyard—completed in 2001—showcases gardens and a swimming pool.

Limited passes to the Wyndham Reach Resort pool, spa, and fitness facilities are provided on a first-come, first-served basis. Children and small pets are allowed; large pets must be kept in kennel carriers.

Travelers Palm Tropical Suites
815 Catherine Street
Key West, FL
(305) 294–9560, (800) 294–9560
www.travelerspalm.com
$$–$$$$

This secluded little retreat tucked inside a lovely walled tropical garden takes its name from the surrounding foliage. As you step inside the gate, you will find yourself beneath the huge leaves of the largest stand of traveler's palms on the island. Look around. See the whimsical works of art peeking out from behind the greenery? And doesn't that hammock strung between two palms and framed by flowering hibiscus and bougainvillea just make you want to stretch out and while away the afternoon?

Each of the five suites you'll find here is unique. The decor is eclectic; rattan furnishings and tropical prints reflect a casual island lifestyle. All suites have a full-size refrigerator and kitchenette, plus private courtyards with grills, hammocks, and picnic tables; two have private decks. There's a heated pool and hot tub, too.

Children are welcome here; they will enjoy the small playground. Dogs under 20 pounds also are welcome for a small additional fee.

Traveler's Palm offers additional rooms in their bed and breakfasts on White Street and Newton Street.

The Watson House
525 Simonton Street
Key West, FL
(305) 294–6712, (800) 621–9405
www.keywestparadise.com/watsonhs
$$$–$$$$

Though modified, the original portions of this two-story, three-room Bahamian-influenced Conch house were built in the mid-1800s. A detached kitchen with connecting breezeway has been enclosed and extensions added to the home.

Named for the home's original owners, William and Susan Watson, this guesthouse features three suites, each decorated in a distinctive style. Tastefully appointed with lots of lace and white Ralph Lauren wicker furnishings, the Susan Suite evokes a feminine, turn-of-the-century feeling. The William Suite has a four-poster, queen-size bed and items reminiscent of a ship captain's bunk. The William and Susan suites feature wainscoting and period hand-silkscreened wallpapers and, when combined to form the Watson Suite, become a two-bedroom/two-bath unit. A third suite, referred to as the Cabana Suite, is really a fully equipped home that features a light and airy tropical decor and a triple set of French doors leading to the pool.

All suites have ceiling fans and telephones with private numbers. A heated, two-tiered backyard pool creates a centerpiece waterfall effect for lush tropical gardens and a hot tub. Continental breakfast is catered to each room, and limited off-street parking is available. Pets and children are not permitted.

Weatherstation Inn
57 Front Street
Key West, FL
(305) 294–7277, (800) 815–2707
www.weatherstationinn.com
$$–$$$$

Nestled deep within one of Key West's premier residential communities, Weatherstation Inn could easily be considered one of this town's best-kept secrets in luxury guesthouse accommodations. Guests here are just two blocks off bustling Duval Street, but they'd never know it. Rarely does any sound intrude.

Opened in 1997, this two-story, eight-room guesthouse sits on the grounds of the Old Navy Yard inside the gated Truman Annex compound and just down the street from Harry Truman's Little White House. The beach at Fort Zachary Taylor is a short walk away (see our Attractions chapter). Motorized access is limited to the residents of the Annex, and so within these gates, life is always quiet and serene.

With its glistening hardwood floors and elegant island furnishings, the Inn calls to mind the plantation homes of days gone by in the British and Dutch West Indies. The balconies and decks overlook lush tropical landscaping, and from the second-floor rooms guests can catch an occasional glimpse of the cruise ships arriving in the harbor just beyond. Amenities here include a heated pool, concierge service, and complimentary continental breakfast. Pets are not allowed.

Westwinds Guesthouse
914 Eaton Street
Key West, FL
(305) 296-4440, (800) 788-4150
$-$$$$

This complex encompasses a 22-room, two-story New England–style home, two-story Conch houses, and poolside cottages. The majority of guests are couples. Room decor is wicker throughout, with queen-size beds in suites, private entrances to the cottages and Conch houses, and some furnished private and shared porches.

All rooms provide a feel of tropic ambiance, painted in various shades of pastels, with ceiling fans and carpeted floors. Some rooms in the main house share a bath. Suites include one-bedroom cottage and Conch units with kitchenettes and kitchenless accommodations that sleep several guests.

In back of the compound, brick walkways wind through gardens of hibiscus, bromeliads, and other flowers and shrubs, and the kidney-shaped swimming pool with waterfall is sizeable. Continental breakfast is served poolside.

Children younger than 12 are not permitted, nor are pets.

Whispers Bed & Breakfast Inn
409 William Street
Key West, FL
(305) 294-5969, (800) 856-7444
www.whispersbb.com
$-$$

This house was one of a few spared by the great 1886 fire that consumed most of Key West. All seven guest rooms within this Bahamian-influenced home have their own personalities. They are furnished with four-poster iron beds, canopy beds, spindle sleigh beds, sleeping lofts, and claw-foot tubs.

The most masculine decor of all is in the third-floor Captain's Hideaway, which boasts peak ceilings, photos of shipwrecks, and nautical memorabilia. The room has a queen-size iron bed and shares a bathroom with the old-fashioned room known as Grandma's Attic, which has both a queen and a twin bed. Kitty Cat's Meow, with its Key West cat motif, is the smallest room in the house—so small, in fact, that it couldn't be named the Cat's Meow.

All rooms have ceiling fans, hardwood floors, and Oriental rugs. A community phone for guests' use is available in the kitchen.

A unique full gourmet breakfast is served daily along the brick patio in the Whispers garden, and menu items have included grilled cheesecakes with peach papaya and mango sauce and omelets filled with snowpeas, carrots, fresh rosemary, scallions, and water chestnuts.

Also in the yard is a hot tub, fishpond, and sun deck. Guests are provided passes for beach, spa, and fitness facilities at nearby full-service resorts. Whispers' owners boast that their guesthouse is within walking distance of Duval Street and within crawling distance back.

Some pets and children are permitted; call for details.

William Anthony House
613 Caroline Street
Key West, FL
(305) 294–2887, (800) 613–2276
www.floridakeys.net/williamanthony
$–$$

Four luxury suites and two guest rooms are the draw at this charming, renovated historic inn just a half block off Duval Street. Amenities in the Ramon Navarro Guest Suites—named for a former owner of the house—include sitting and dining areas, private baths, kitchenettes, air conditioning and heating, cable TV, and phones. However, it's not the phones that will draw you into the aura of idyllic retreat, but the spa, pond, deck, and delightful gardens. One room is wheelchair accessible.

The inn offers a complimentary continental breakfast and wine at social hour. Pets are not allowed. While you're here, be sure to check out nearby Mallory Square for a superlative Key West sunset (see our Attractions chapter).

Gay Guesthouses

Alexander's Guesthouse
1118 Fleming Street
Key West, FL
(305) 294–9919, (800) 654–9919
www.alexghouse.com
$–$$$

The main three-story building of Alexander's, a Conch-style design, was built around the turn of the last century and has since been renovated. Two additional two-story Conch houses combine for a total of 17 guest rooms. This guesthouse, which attracts both gay men and women, is gay owned and operated, and has received the Editor's Choice Award in the guesthouse category from *Out and About* magazine for six years running.

The rooms at Alexander's are relatively basic, equipped with queen-size beds. All rooms have private baths, and two share shower facilities. Deluxe rooms, some with private porches and patios, have king-size beds. For larger accommodations, opt for a more luxurious suite with king-size bed and queen-size sleeper sofa. Some rooms feature hardwood floors, while others are completely carpeted. Throughout the inn, eclectic local art mixes with poster prints. Many units offer VCRs.

A highlight is the cobalt blue, tiled swimming pool surrounded by lush tropical flora. Second- and third-level tanning decks are clothing-optional. An expanded continental breakfast is served by the pool each morning; wine and cheese are offered every evening. Pets are not permitted.

Atlantic Shores Resort
510 South Street
Key West, FL
(305) 296–2491, (800) 598–6988
www.atlanticshoresresort.com
$–$$

Atlantic Shores bills itself as an adult alternative resort. It's not exclusively gay, but then it's not what you would call straight either. Atlantic Shores is somewhere in between. If you choose to stay here, you will almost assuredly find it quite an experience . . . no matter which way your sexual preferences lean.

Situated at the end of Simonton Street, on the oceanside of Key West, the Shores boasts 72 rooms. The decor is not particularly remarkable, but the accommodations are always clean and quite affordable; they also fill up fast. If you have your heart set on staying here at a particular time, it would be best to book early. This is one popular place.

If not the accommodations, then what draws people to Atlantic Shores? The clothing-optional pool, for starters. This is where locals and visitors alike flock on sunny afternoons to work on "real tans"—the kind that aren't defined by lines. They come to see and be seen, to meet and mingle—sans suits—while they sip frozen drinks and munch on standard fare like burgers, grilled chicken, and fries from the Pool Bar and Grill.

Regular events such as the Sunday night tea dances and Cinema Shores (Thursday night movies by the sea) really bring in the locals. So does Diner Shores, a full-service restaurant offering breakfast, lunch, and late-night munchies.

Big Ruby's Guesthouse
409 Applerouth Lane
Key West, FL
(305) 296–2323, (800) 477–7829
www.bigrubys.com
$$–$$$$

Formerly the home of a sea captain, the main guesthouse at Big Ruby's, like its two additional on-premise structures, is New England–style clapboard architecture on the outside with contemporary styling on the inside.

Seventeen rooms of varying sizes and décor feature clean lines, hardwood floors, and Simmons Beautyrest mattresses in a variety of sizes. Refrigerators, ceiling fans, robes, and beach towels are standard in all rooms.

Four resident miniature dachshunds roam the premises of this exclusively gay male and female property, and all three buildings share a clothing-optional sunning yard and swimming pool. An outdoor rain-forest shower amid the vines allows for rinsing before and after swimming, and a bike rack provides a secured space for those utilizing a two-wheeler as a primary means of transportation.

Continental and full cooked-to-order breakfasts are served poolside as are wine and juice in the early evening. Big Ruby's is set back about 20 feet from the narrow, one-way lane through which it is accessed, and all three buildings are surrounded by orchids and bougainvillea. Balconies on the third floor are set amid the trees, and the grounds are so lush that the second-floor porch does not even allow a view of the street.

Limited off-street parking is provided on a first-come, first-served basis. Pets are not permitted.

Coral Tree Inn and Oasis Guesthouse
822 and 823 Fleming Street
Key West, FL
(305) 296–2131, (800) 362–7477
www.oasiskeywest.com
$$–$$$

With its Main, Lopez, and Margaret Houses, the Oasis offers 20 guest rooms on three fronts that share a yard: The Main house faces Fleming Street; Lopez House faces Lopez Lane, and Margaret House looks toward Margaret Street. Guests at the facility, which caters to gay men, check in at Main on Fleming.

Oasis offers a range of accommodations, including standard rooms with one queen-size bed or two double beds, poolside rooms with queen-size beds and living rooms, and a penthouse on the second, and top, floor of Margaret House. All rooms feature updated furnishings and custom drapes and matching bedspreads in tropical or paisley prints. Some rooms have baths with whirlpool tubs; still others share a bath. The pool and the sun deck surrounding it are clothing-optional.

Also owned by Oasis proprietors is Coral Tree Inn across the street. When purchased in 1993 this 11-room facility was merely a shell. With all-new fixtures, Coral Tree is now designed as a European-style, gay male guesthouse—smaller, more intimate, and upscale. Rooms here feature a queen-size or two double beds. They have porches and balconies facing either the pool or Fleming. Penthouse suites are on the third floor.

The clothing-optional Coral Tree Inn has a 24-man hot tub and sunning area, and guests here and at Oasis share facilities.

Both establishments are known for hospitality. A bottle of wine welcomes guests upon arrival; continental breakfast is served each morning. Tropical cocktails are offered by the pool each afternoon, and wine and hot hors d'oeuvres are served in the evening. Pets are not permitted at either location.

Equator Resort
818 Fleming Street
Key West, FL
(305) 294–7775, (800) 278–4552
www.equatorresort.com
$$–$$$

Opened in 1998, Equator Resort is one of the more recent additions to Key West's gay guesthouse scene. The building that houses this state-of-the-art, all-male resort looks as though it might have been around for awhile, but it is new. It was simply designed to blend with the surrounding structures in this Old Town neighborhood. When it came to guest rooms, the architects opted for upscale with no attempts at conserving space. All 18 rooms are bright and spacious, each featuring Mediterranean tile floors, incredibly comfortable beds, in-room refrigerators, genuinely ample closets, and plenty of walking-around space. Some have special luxuries like wet bars and two-man whirlpool bathtubs.

Common areas are equally well appointed, with a clothing-optional pool, eight-man outdoor whirlpool, lush tropical gardens, a sun deck, and outdoor covered patio.

A complimentary full breakfast is served daily; complimentary cocktails and snacks are offered every evening except Sunday. All guest rooms are nonsmoking; however, most of them open directly to private decks or balconies where smoking is permitted.

Pearl's Rainbow
525 United Street
Key West, FL
(305) 292–1450, (800) 749–6696
www.rainbowhousekeywest.com
$–$$$

Lesbian owned and operated, Pearl's Rainbow is one of only a handful of exclusively female resorts in Key West. Men, children, and pets are not permitted here.

Expanded in 1998 to incorporate the property next door, which had been The Pines, a gay male guesthouse, Pearl's Rainbow now includes two clothing-optional swimming pools, two hot tubs, and 38 guest rooms.

All standard guest rooms at Rainbow House feature queen-size beds, private baths, color TV, air-conditioning, and ceiling fans. The priciest accommodation is a deluxe poolside suite consisting of a king bedroom, private bath, and separate living room with big-screen TV.

Pearl's Rainbow is located a half-block off Duval on the oceanside of the island. Shops, bars, and restaurants are within a reasonable walking distance.

Hostels

Hostelling International Key West
718 South Street
Key West, FL
(305) 296–5719
www.keywesthostel.com
$

If you want to save money on accommodations in Key West, one very inexpensive option is Hostelling International Key West. The facility has 10 air-conditioned, dormitory-style rooms with bunk beds and separate baths. The hostel accommodates as many as 92 guests for as little as $18.50 per night (nonmembers pay $3 more) and is near Old Town and beaches along the Atlantic.

Ten motel rooms at the Sea Shell Motel—the hostel's affiliate in the same building—each have two double beds, a private bath, and a mini refrigerator. Each room sleeps four, and rates are between $50 and $125 per night, depending upon the season. A common kitchen is open to all hostel and motel guests for food preparation between the hours of 8 A.M. and 9 P.M., and a common dining area is in the courtyard. Those who prefer to have their meals served pay a mere $2 for breakfast and $2 for dinner. Laundry facilities and lockers are available within this wood structure.

Popular with Europeans, students, and adventurous adults, the Hostelling International Key West, like other hostels worldwide, provides travelers with low-cost, friendly accommodations and an ideal means of meeting a diverse group of individuals. Bicycle rentals and snorkeling, scuba, and sunset excursions (see our Recreation and Diving and Snorkeling chapters) all are offered at rates that are discounted as much as 20 percent.

The hostel is open 24 hours a day. Reservations should be made at least one week in advance. No dorm reservations are accepted in March.

Vacation Rentals and Real Estate

Most snowbirds and full-time residents of the Florida Keys (except for the native-born Conchs) first rented homes, condominiums, or mobile homes while on vacation in Paradise. Seduced by our ocean breezes, beguiling sunshine, percolating waters, and sensational sunsets, we all decided to buy a piece of the rock. Throughout the Florida Keys, rentals primarily are classified as short-term and long-term. Short-term rental agreements range from a weekend to six months; anything exceeding six months is considered a long-term rental. However, to preserve the integrity of our residential communities, the Monroe County Planning Commission has prohibited short-term rentals of 30 days or less throughout residential areas of unincorporated Monroe County. Incorporated areas such as Islamorada, Layton, Key Colony Beach, Marathon, and Key West can opt for differing regulations. The bottom line for vacationers is this: Fewer short-term rental options are currently available in the Florida Keys, and the competition is fierce for those that are. The best advice we can offer in this ever-changing environment is to work through a rental agent who knows what's legally available and always book your accommodation early.

Unlike long-term tenants, short-term tenants are required by the State of Florida to pay an 11.5 percent sales tax. Generally not incorporated into the price quoted for short-term rentals, this tax includes the same tourist bed tax charged by hotels, motels, inns, and resorts for maintaining, advertising, and promoting our facilities and attractions. Quotes for short-term rentals do, however, typically include furnishings and utilities, with the exception of long-distance phone calls.

The Role of Real Estate Agents

Real estate agents handle most short-term rental properties. The exceptions are condominiums that act as hotels and employ on-site managers (see our Accommodations chapter) and homeowners who market rentals on their own. Because of changes in laws as indicated above, the latter choice is becoming more and more scarce.

Depending upon its size and specialty, an agency that handles rentals may list anywhere between 10 and 200-plus short-term rental options. Most large agencies employ sales associates who specialize in short-term rentals. Except for Key West, where agents handle much of the entire island, Florida Keys agents typically specialize within the region of their office (see the Real Estate Companies section in this chapter).

Finding a rental property through an agency has its advantages. Rental agencies almost always offer descriptions and photographs of available properties and advice on the best option for your needs and desires. Most of them, in fact, maintain websites, which allow you to peruse the options at your leisure and, in most cases, actually see the property you are booking. Agents ensure that a home is clean and that its grounds are maintained. If appliances such as air-conditioning units or televisions require repair, most real estate agents are on call to solve the problem. Agents also frequently handle additional rental needs, such as cribs, rollaway beds, VCRs, office equipment, even boats.

In order to manage short-term rentals for stays of fewer than 30 days, real estate agencies and/or property owners and managers of condominium complexes must be licensed by the State of Florida. Units rented for fewer than 30 days are considered resort dwellings, and agents and/or owners and managers must therefore abide by a Florida statute that applies to hotels and restaurants. Depending upon the category of accommodation (condominium or single-family home, for instance), safety and health standards set by this statute may require fire extinguishers, electric smoke detectors in sleeping areas, mattress covers on all beds, and deadbolt locks on doors.

Seasonal Rates

As Old Man Winter rolls around, travelers flock to the Florida Keys seeking respite from cold and snow. Referred to locally as "snowbirds," these visitors drive rental rates up between the months of December and April, the high season.

Summertime is when diving is typically best (see our Diving and Snorkeling chapter). It's also the time of year when residents throughout Florida head to the Keys for the relief of the ocean breezes. However, the rest of the mass market moves back home, so rents may be a bit lower than high season during the months of May through August.

September through November is relatively quiet, tourism-wise, because autumn is the prime season for hurricanes in the Florida Keys. However, you'll find rental prices typically reduced 20 to 25 percent, and, as long as you keep a watchful eye on the forecasts, you'll be able to enjoy relatively uncrowded streets, shops, and attraction.

Minimum Stays

Most short-term tenants rent a home or condominium in the Florida Keys for a week to three or four months. The bulk of the short-term rental market consists of two-week vacationers, but our islands are also popular with northern residents and retirees who retreat here for the winter. Virtually no private homes are available for rent on a daily basis, and only a few condominium complexes—those with on-site managers that act as hotels—offer this option (see our Accommodations chapter).

Throughout the year, the minimum condominium stay is typically three days and for a rental home, it's at least a week. During holidays, such as Christmas and Easter, and special events, including lobster season and Fantasy Fest, minimum stays range from four days to two weeks. Individual property owners establish these policies. Inquire of your rental agent or property owner/manager.

Options and Restrictions

Owners designate their rental properties as smoking or nonsmoking. The number of nonsmoking properties is growing.

Children are generally welcome, but some condominium complexes restrict the number of children allowed in a single unit. One adult-only facility, Silver Shores, a mobile home park in Key Largo catering to senior citizens, exists in the Florida Keys.

Condominiums typically do not allow pets, but some single-family homes and mobile home parks do accept them. An additional security deposit or a fee (sometimes both) is often required. The fee covers the cost of spraying the home for fleas, which ensures accommodations free of pesky insects. Tending to pets outside the rental facility, however, is the owner's responsibility, and fleas can be abundant on hot and humid days.

Reservations and Payment Options

Naturally, the most desirable rental properties tend to book the earliest, and many tenants book the same home for the same weeks year after year. To achieve the greatest selection of rentals, we suggest that you reserve at least six months to a year in advance. During holidays, the demand for short-term rentals can exhaust the supply. If you plan to travel to the Florida Keys during the high season (December through April) and holidays (especially Christmas week or during Fantasy Fest), you would be wise to reserve one to two years in advance.

Payment options vary according to how far in advance you book and when you check in. Typically, an initial deposit of 10 to 25 percent of the total rental cost, made with a personal check or a credit card, will hold a unit. If you book a rental unit one year in advance, you frequently can opt for an installment plan. The balance typically is paid 30 to 60 days prior to your arrival. Some agents allow you to pay with cash or credit card upon arrival, provided that you check in during office hours, which vary from agency to agency. Ask about these specifics when you call.

When you book a unit, your real estate agent will mail you a lease application and reservation agreement that must be completed and returned with a rental deposit. Reservation agreements will list the address and telephone number of the property so you can notify family and friends accordingly.

Security Deposits

Your rental agreement holds you responsible for any damage to the dwelling and its contents. Security deposits provide the homeowner with added protection and a means of paying any telephone charges not billed to your credit card. As a general rule, count on supplying 50 to 75 percent of one week's rent (slightly more for a monthly rental). Security deposits on large homes with expensive furnishings can be much higher.

If you have opted for an installment plan, you will pay the security deposit with your final payment when you check in. The deposit often is returned in the mail

two weeks to one month after your departure, or after the homeowner's telephone bill is received and a damage assessment completed.

Cancellation Policies

Homeowners set monetary penalties for cancellations anywhere between 30 days in advance of reservations, with a nominal cancellation fee for administrative services, to 60 days in advance, with a full refund. Don't assume that an impending hurricane or other emergency beyond your control will warrant a refund of your payment. In such cases, some homeowners may be generous in providing full or partial refunds or offering credit toward accommodations at a future date—but don't bank on it. Generally, you forfeit your deposit when weather emergencies cancel your vacation plans.

Refund policies are negotiated between the tenant, real estate agency, and property owner and usually are not included in lease agreements. Many real estate agencies sell trip insurance, whereby a third party will refund the full cost of a vacation rental for which you have paid a portion but not used. These policies typically cost 5 percent of the total dollars at risk.

The Florida Keys

Owning a parcel of Paradise in the Florida Keys can be summed up in two words: very expensive. Real estate prices in the Florida Keys depend largely upon access to the water. Direct oceanfront or bayfront property garners the highest prices, followed by property on a canal with an ocean or bay view, and by property on a canal with access to the ocean or bay. Other areas, such as Ocean Reef, Duck Key, and Sunset Key, have special features that make homes desirable—such as gated security, golf courses, swimming pools, strict building covenants, and other community amenities—and owning a home there is pricey, indeed.

Some relief in the cost of owning a Keys home is available for certain owners in the form of a homestead exemption. In Florida, this exemption allows $25,000 of the assessed value of a house purchased as a primary residence to be exempt from property tax. Real estate taxes in Monroe County are based on a millage rate that changes annually with the county budget, and are some of the highest in the state. In addition, besides homeowner's insurance, homeowners must factor in the cost of windstorm and flood insurance to guard against our ever-threatening hurricanes.

Those of us who have chosen to live in the Florida Keys think the price of Paradise is worth it. To assist you in your search for a piece of the rock, we provide you with a general overview of the communities of the Florida Keys, as well as the types of homes you'll encounter in our neighborhoods. At the end of the chapter, we include listings of real estate professionals who can assist you in finding a rental property or a home of your own. Look to our Key West section of this chapter for vacation rental and real estate information in our southernmost city.

Community Overviews

Upper Keys

Key Largo

Key Largo is popular with divers interested in the abundant reefs within John Pennekamp Coral Reef State Park and the Florida Keys National Marine Sanctuary. And, because Key Largo is within 20 miles of the mainland, property here often is in great demand by weekday commuters and South Floridians purchasing weekend retreats. In real estate terms, Key Largo generally includes the exclusive, members-only Ocean Reef subdivision at the extreme northeast edge and encompasses all land southwest to Tavernier.

Ocean Reef

A luxury subdivision in North Key Largo, Ocean Reef is a private, all-inclusive gated community of large single-family homes, condominiums, and town houses. Properties here attract buyers seeking privacy, exclusivity, and the opportunity to fish, dive, snorkel, swim, shop, and dine out without ever leaving the complex. This community has three golf courses, a marina, and other amenities open only to residents.

Tavernier

Toward the southern end of Key Largo is Tavernier, one of the Florida Keys' oldest settlements. Some Tavernier homes date back to the early farming settlements at the turn of the last century. Plantation Key (its northern end also maintains a Tavernier postal designation) has a wide range of real estate opportunities, with single-family subdivisions primarily bayside. The Snake Creek Drawbridge makes Plantation Key an ideal homesite for owners of large yachts and sailboats.

Islamorada

Islamorada, which was incorporated in 1998, stretches from Plantation Key to Lower Matecumbe. Lot sizes in Islamorada typically are larger than those in other areas of the Florida Keys, a factor intended to attract builders of large, impressive homes. Upper Matecumbe Key is the heart of Islamorada, commercially developed but with homes tucked along the waterfront in quiet residential areas.

Lower Matecumbe Key is Islamorada's predominantly residential island, with a bike path, tennis club, and private beach.

Layton

The late Del Layton, a Miami grocery store owner, developed tiny Layton into a subdivision in the 1950s. Later, he incorporated it as the Florida Keys smallest city. Except for several oceanfront homes, all single-family residences in Layton are on oceanside canals, with the nearby Channel 5 Bridge allowing access to the bay. Fifteen miles from Marathon and Islamorada, Layton is largely a community of retirees, with a population of approximately 250.

Middle Keys

Duck Key

Duck Key is composed of five islands connected by white Venetian-style bridges. A series of flow-through canals encircle each island, ensuring that nearly half the homes or lots offer canalfront dockage or open-water views. The uniquely situated islands allow direct access to both the ocean and the Gulf of Mexico. The Duck Key Property Owners Association, an active group, maintains rights of way and public area plantings, has established distinctive signage, and sponsors myriad social events throughout the year. Residents pay a small out-of-pocket tax to employ a private security firm to supplement county services. Hawk's Cay Resort is on the first island, Indies Island, which

is zoned differently than the rest. The other four islands—Center, Plantation, Harbour, and Yacht Club—are designated for single-family residential housing only. All homes must be of CBS construction.

Grassy Key

Grassy Key, a sleepy, rural island with a few oceanfront bungalow courts and several restaurants, is distanced from Marathon by preservation lands. With no canals on Grassy Key, there is no pricing middle ground. The area has single-family homes on dry lots or waterfront estates along the Gulf of Mexico and the Atlantic. Grassy Key is now a part of incorporated Marathon.

Key Colony Beach

Incorporated in 1957, Key Colony Beach— a 285-acre peninsular finger surrounded by incorporated Marathon—developed its property with a row of condominiums directly on the Atlantic and single family homes built on a series of canals. Key Colony Beach employs its own police and enforces its own signage and zoning ordinances. Accessed by a causeway from U.S. Hwy. 1, Key Colony Beach has a post office and a few small shops and restaurants.

Marathon

Marathon was heavily developed in the 1950s, when dredging was relatively commonplace. This area probably has more canals and waterways—and thus more canalfront properties—than any other

Duck Key is made up of five islands connected with Venetian-style bridges. PHOTO: HAWK'S CAY RESORT

region of Monroe County; however, with no active zoning ordinances for all these years, in some neighborhoods it is not uncommon to find a rundown mobile home situated next to an upscale canal-front dwelling. Marathon was incorporated in 1999 and now has its own mayor and city commission, as well as the ability to levy citywide property taxes. Marathon is the commercial hub of the Florida Keys, featuring supermarkets, a movie theater, Home Deport, Office Depot, K-Mart, and other shops and restaurants.

Lower Keys

Big Pine Key

This rural, semi-isolated island has acres of open space and limited development potential. Home to the National Key Deer Refuge, this island is popular with many Key West and Marathon workday commuters. This area probably offers the best value for the money in affordable housing.

Little Torch and Ramrod Keys

Little Torch Key and Ramrod Key have a rural feeling, with homes on both the Atlantic and the Gulf of Mexico as well as on dry lots. These communities aren't far from Key West.

Summerland, Cudjoe, and Sugarloaf Keys

Heading closer to Key West and into the more exclusive subdivisions of Summerland, Cudjoe, and Sugarloaf Keys, you'll find luxurious properties. Summerland features a number of waterfront homes, along with a small airstrip that allows residents to park their private airplanes directly beneath their homes.

Baypoint, Shark Key, Big Coppitt, and Key Haven

Shark Key is a gated community developed with strict architectural guidelines. Large open-water lots on Shark Key are beautifully landscaped, and houses set on them typically are very expensive. Bay-

point, Big Coppitt, and Key Haven are in demand for their convenient location only minutes from Key West.

Kinds of Properties

Condominiums

Condominiums are scattered throughout the Upper and Middle Keys, and many homebuyers find them a low-maintenance way to keep up a part-time residence. For full-time residents, condos commonly offer amenities not always available in a single-family home, such as swimming pools, fitness facilities, saunas, hot tubs, boat dockage, and covered parking. Condos also are likely to have more affordable water views than single-family homes.

During our peak tourist season (generally December through April), condominiums often are teeming with activity, affording residents the opportunity to meet renters from across the country. When the low season rolls around and occupancy typically drops to 30 percent or less at any given time, full-time residents have the facilities nearly all to themselves. If you plan to become a full-time Florida Keys resident in a condominium, be sure to check on whether the complex you have your eye on maintains an active rental program. You may not enjoy living alongside transient residents.

What you'll pay for a condo depends on the size of the unit, its location, and its view. You also need to factor monthly

> ### Insiders' Tip
> If you rent a condominium unit anywhere in the Florida Keys, remember the water-to-wallet ratio: The closer the accommodation is to the water, the higher the rental price is likely to be.

maintenance fees into the overall cost; these increase with unit sizes and cover maintenance of the common area, a reserve account for future major repairs, and insurance for damage by flood, wind, storm, peril, and salt air.

Mobile Homes

First the good news: A mobile home is the least expensive real estate you can buy in the Florida Keys. The bad news? Most vulnerable to hurricane damage, mobile homes are the first properties ordered for evacuation during severe-storm watches in the Florida Keys. Zoning ordinances restrict mobile homes to specific communities. Fortunately, the Keys have several mobile home subdivisions and communities, many of them on desirable waterfront land.

Often the least expensive mobile homes are those that have existed in residential subdivisions since before zoning ordinances were established. These mobile homes, which have individual septic tanks, lack the recreational and service-oriented amenities typically offered in mobile-home communities here.

Buyers who purchase property in a mobile home community pay more but frequently enjoy a clubhouse atmosphere complete with a swimming pool, shuffleboard court, boat ramp, dockage, on-site manager, sewage treatment, and a convenience store. The price of any mobile home increases with a concrete or wood-frame addition—an elevated Florida room, built-up gravel roof, poured concrete slab, and other features.

Single-Family Homes

Dry-lot homes—those not fronting a water view or canal—are the least expensive single-family home option in the Keys. Canalfront homes generally sell for much more, with homes on the open water usually topping a million dollars. Because many real estate purchases here are made by boaters, homes that sit closer to a bridge—providing access to both the ocean and the bay—sell more quickly.

Since 1975, the county has required that most homes be constructed of concrete block, be positioned on stilts, and have hurricane shutters. Nonconforming structures built before the 1975 ordinance took effect have been grandfathered, but, if 50 percent or more of the dollar value of a nonconforming use structure is destroyed and requires rebuilding, new zoning laws and building restrictions apply.

Much of a buyer's decision to purchase a home in the Florida Keys depends upon the structure's ability to withstand a hurricane. Concrete block–style (CBS) homes are considered more solid than those made of wood. Most are elevated on stilts to avoid potential flooding. CBS stilt homes typically cost more than ground level CBS homes of comparable sizes. CBS homes typically command higher prices than all-wood frame structures.

A large percentage of Lower Keys homes are factory-built, wood-frame modulars. Because they are constructed under controlled circumstances and designed to withstand 135-mile-per-hour winds, some homeowners believe they're stronger than wood-frame homes built on site.

If you are considering buying a home in the Florida Keys, landscaping also may influence your decision. Some buyers prefer intricate vegetation, which requires costly irrigation, while others want low-maintenance pearock and xeriscaping (landscaping using indigenous plantings that require no irrigation).

Real Estate Companies

Though all of Florida Keys agents share a multiple listing service (MLS) with properties available throughout Monroe County, each agency tends to specialize in its own territory. We describe some of the largest agencies for sales and rentals in the sections that follow. This is not meant to be a comprehensive listing by any means. For a complete list, consult the Yellow Pages for the appropriate communities, or pick up copies of the many real estate

Finding your place in the sun could mean owning a piece of Paradise. PHOTO: VICTORIA SHEARER

guides available free of charge at supermarkets and other locations throughout Monroe County. See our Key West section for real estate companies in that city.

Upper Keys

Loveland Rentals
MM 103.2 Bayside
Key Largo, FL
(305) 451–5055, (800) 454–5263
www.lovelandrentals.com

Loveland's primary focus is on vacation rentals, particularly in Key Largo and Tavernier.

Prudential Keyside Properties
31 Ocean Reef Drive
Suite A 101
Key Largo, FL
(305) 367–2336, (800) 692–7653
91951 Overseas Highway, Tavernier
MM 91.5 Oceanside
Key Largo, FL
(305) 853–1100, (800) 663–9955
www.floridakeys-realestate.com

Prudential Keyside Properties covers the Florida Keys from the top of Key Largo (Ocean Reef) to Key West. Located in the

private Ocean Reef Community, the North Key Largo office focuses exclusively on "the Reef." The Tavernier office covers both residential and commercial properties from Key Largo to Marathon. Both the Old Town and New Town offices of Prudential Knight Keyside Properties in Key West cover real estate from Key West to Marathon (see our Key West section of this chapter for a separate listing).

Century 21 Keysearch Realty
Tradewinds Shopping Plaza
MM 101.9 Oceanside
Key Largo, FL
(305) 451–2912, (800) 210–6246
MM 91.8 Bayside
Tavernier, FL
(305) 852–5595, (800) 850–7740
MM 86 Bayside
Islamorada, FL
(305) 664–4637, (800) 541–5019
www.centurykey.com

With three offices in the Upper Keys, onsite rental offices in Landings of Largo and Buttonwood Bay condominium complexes in Key Largo, and offices all the way to Key West, Century 21 Keysearch

Realty has the vacation home rental market covered.

Coldwell Banker Schmitt Real Estate Co.
MM 100 Bayside
Key Largo, FL
(305) 451–4422, (877) 289–0035
MM 91.9 Bayside
Tavernier, FL
(305) 852–9901, (800) 207–4160
MM 82.2 Oceanside
Islamorada, FL
(305) 664–4470, (800) 207–4160
www.realestatefloridakeys.com

Coldwell Banker Schmitt covers the Florida Keys real estate sales and rental market from one end of U.S. Hwy. 1 to the other. In addition to these three offices, which serve the Upper Keys, the firm also maintains offices in Marathon, Big Pine, and Key West (see separate listings below).

The Rental Store (Marr Properties Inc.)
MM 99.9 Bayside
Key Largo, FL
(305) 451–3879, (800) 585–0584
www.therentalstore.net

As a real estate agency, Marr Properties dates back to 1965. This division, which handles vacation rentals exclusively, specializes in properties from Key Largo to Islamorada.

American Caribbean Real Estate Inc.
MM 81.8 Bayside
Islamorada, FL
Sales: (305) 664–4966,
Rentals: (305) 664–5152
MM 52 Oceanside
Marathon, FL
(305) 743–7636, (800) 940–7636
www.acresales.com

American Caribbean specializes in Middle Keys sales and rental properties, from Islamorada to Marathon.

Freewheeler Realty
MM 85.9 Bayside
Islamorada, FL
(305)664–4444, (305) 664–2075 (rentals)
www.freewheeler-realty.com

Freewheeler deals in property management and sales and is a primary rental agent for The Palms of Islamorada and Summer Sea condominiums.

Middle Keys

Duck Key Realty
MM 61 Oceanside
796 Duck Key Drive
Duck Key, FL
(305) 743–5360
www.duckkey.com

Duck Key Realty handles sales and rentals in Duck Key and Marathon.

Keys Island Realty
MM 53.5 Oceanside
309 Key Colony Beach Causeway
Key Colony Beach, FL
(305) 289–1744, (800) 874–3798
www.flkeys.com

Check here for Marathon area sales and rentals, especially in Key Colony Beach.

Coldwell Banker Schmitt Real Estate
MM 52.5 Bayside
Marathon, FL
(305) 743–5181, (800) 366–5181
MM 30.5 Oceanside
Big Pine Key, FL
(305) 872–3050, (800) 488–3050
www.realestatefloridakeys.com

Sales and vacation rentals in the Middle Keys are the focus at these two offices of a firm that covers the real estate market

> ## Insiders' Tip
> For details about our recycling program and obtaining a recycling bin, call (305) 296-8297. Aluminum and metal cans, glass bottles and jars, plastic containers, and newspapers are recyclable.

from one end of the Keys to the other (see other listings in this section).

The Waterfront Specialist
MM 54 Oceanside
Marathon, FL
(305) 743–0644, (800) 342–6398
www.waterfrontspecialists.com

Despite its name, this agency can direct you to sales and rental opportunities both on and off the water.

Century 21 Keysearch Realty
MM 54 Bayside
Marathon, FL
(305) 743–3377, (800) 451–4899
www.centurykey.com

Century 21 Keysearch serves the Middle Keys from Islamorada to Big Pine. Although the primary focus is on residential sales, vacation and long-term rentals are available here, too.

All-Pro Real Estate
MM 50 Bayside
Marathon, FL
(305) 743–8333, (800) 766–3235
www.allpro-realestate.com

Established in 1990, All-Pro has a good handle on the Marathon sales and vacation rental market.

RE/MAX Keys to the Keys
MM 49.5 Bayside
Marathon, FL
(305) 743–2300, (800) 743–2301
www.wilkinsonteam.com

Agents handle sales and rental properties from Long Key to Big Coppitt.

Lower Keys

Latitude 24 Real Estate Inc.
MM 31.3 Bayside
Big Pine Key, FL
(305) 872–2800
www.latitude24.com

Latitude 24 specializes in sales and vacation rentals in Big Pine, Torch, Ramrod, Summerland, Cudjoe, and Saddle Bunch Keys.

> ## Insiders' Tip
> Recent changes in the laws concerning transient rental properties in the Florida Keys and Key West have significantly reduced the number of single-family homes available for short-term rental. To ensure the widest choice of accommodations, book early.

Century 21 PRO-Realty
MM 30.5 Bayside
Big Pine Key, FL
(305) 872–2296, (800) 637–7621
MM 22 Oceanside
Cudjoe Key, FL
(305) 745–3340
MM 17 Bayside
Sugarloaf Key, FL
(305) 745–1856, (800) 745–8610
www.c21pro.com

With three offices in the Lower Keys, Century 21 PRO-Realty helps find the right property to rent or buy between Big Pine and Sugarloaf.

Raymond Real Estate/Realty World
MM 30.5 Oceanside
Big Pine Key, FL
(305) 872–9116, (800) 747–4206
www.raymondrealtyflkeys.com

Established in 1981, this agency knows the Big Pine real estate market.

ERA Lower Keys Realty
MM 30 Oceanside
Big Pine Key, FL
(305) 872–2258, (800) 859–7642
www.eralowerkeysrealty.com

This establishment deals with sales and rentals in the Lower Keys.

**Century 21 Keysearch Realty/
Greg O'Berry Inc.
MM 30 Oceanside
Big Pine Key, FL
(305) 872–3052, (800) 741–6263
www.oberry.com, www.centurykey.com**

Part of the Keysearch Realty group, this office specializes in sales and rentals in Big Pine.

**ActionKeys Realty, Inc.
MM 25 Oceanside
Summerland Key, FL
(305) 745–1323, (800) 874–1323
www.actionkeysrealty.com**

In addition to residential sales throughout the Lower Keys, this agency also handles vacation rentals, primarily on Summerland, Ramrod, and Little Torch Keys.

Key West

Despite the fact that Key West is heavily developed, with both old and new homes on generally small lots throughout the city, real estate agents report that the demand for homes far outstrips the island's supply. Also, while waterfront property is a prime attraction for home-buyers throughout the rest of the Florida Keys, it is rarely found in Key West, because commercial development lines all waterfront areas. Nevertheless, real estate in the southernmost city is expensive.

The island of Key West is an incorporated city governed by local elected representatives as well as by Monroe County. Consequently, the property tax structure here includes both city and county government expenses. Key West has its own land-use plan with zoning ordinances, permitting units, density requirements, and building height and setback minimums. Within the historic district of Old Town, another layer of control and review exists. The five-member Historical Architecture Review Commission (HARC) reviews applications for improvements and new construction. Established in 1986, HARC works to ensure the integrity of the historic district.

Key West offers a selection of styles in single-family homes, town houses, and condominiums. (See the Architecture closeup in our Attractions chapter.) The island has few mobile home parks, and the only mobile home communities here are small and hidden away. There are also several on Stock Island.

Town houses, typically adjoining structures with a common wall, allow homeowners to own the ground beneath them. The center of the common wall is the dividing line, and party wall agreements determine who maintains responsibility in cases of repair or destruction.

If you wish to purchase beachfront housing, owning a condominium is without a doubt the way to go. Along the south side of Key West are several relatively new, multi-story beachfront condominiums with elevators, enclosed parking, pools, tennis courts, and hot tubs. Units range in size from one bedroom, one bath to three or four bedrooms and two or three baths. Only a few units have waterfront or partial water views, however.

Insiders' Tip

In the past, many nonresidents have purchased second homes in the Florida Keys with the intention of renting them out part of the year to vacationers. If that is your intention, too, beware. Rules concerning transient rentals, particularly in Key West, have been altered recently, so be sure to check the latest ordinances for your area before signing on that dotted line.

Mansions and cottages share the same neighborhood in Key West. Most are painted a glistening white, but some remain weathered and worn. PHOTO: JANET WARE

The majority of single-family homes in Key West are in areas known as Old Town, Mid Town, and New Town, and real estate agents further break two of these regions into "old" and "new" Old Town and "old" and "new" New Town. Boundaries are roughly established, with some overflow, and within all Key West areas you'll discover a diverse array of properties dating between the early 1800s to the late 1900s.

Convenience to the water or to touristy Duval Street is not usually a factor in the cost of Key West property. Rather, prices generally depend on the size and condition of the house, its lot, and its location. The island itself is only 2 miles long by 4 miles wide, so beaches and harbors are never far away. Some homebuyers seek property as far from the busy roadways and attractions as possible.

Community Profiles

Old Town

Settled in the early to late 1800s and the early 1900s, Old Town is characterized by large wood-frame houses of distinctive architectural styles (see our Architecture closeup in our Attractions chapter). Typi-

cally built by shipbuilders and carpenters for New England sea captains, many of these homes feature Bahamian and New England influences and high ceilings. Several historic district homes are now exquisite guesthouses (see our Accommodations chapter).

In addition to its obvious aesthetic qualities, Old Town is desirable because it is within walking distance of just about everything Key West has to offer, including shops, restaurants, nightlife, and galleries. Among the community's residents are a large number of artists and writers. Toward the southern end of Whitehead Street and west of Duval on Petronia Street, about a block from the Ernest Hemingway Home and Museum, lies Bahama Village. This community now is undergoing gentrification as homebuyers purchase and renovate existing properties here.

One of Key West's more recent developments in Old Town is Truman Annex, where private homes, town houses, and condominiums all boast features of Key West's distinctive architecture. This self-contained development once was an extension of the island's Bahama Village section and later a portion of the Key West naval base.

Truman Annex was constructed and renovated according to a unified plan reminiscent of Old Town but with more green space and winding streets. Because of the charm that this gated development exhibits, even the hubbub created by large cruise ships entering the nearby harbor does not affect its pricey real estate values. Condominiums in the Harbour Place complex of Truman Annex are almost directly on the water and start at nearly a half-million dollars. Single family homes are in the multimillion-dollar price range.

Mid Town and New Town

Stretching from White Street all the way east to Kennedy Boulevard, Mid Town boasts a mix of wood-frame and concrete-block ground-level homes built in the late 1950s and 1960s. New Town, developed a bit later, spreads out along North Roosevelt Boulevard, and is largely commercial on its perimeter.

Recently completed in the Mid Town area is Roosevelt Annex, a gated community of 25 single-family homes and town houses fronting the Gulf of Mexico on the former county fairgrounds along N. Roosevelt Boulevard. Billed as the last developable site in Key West with open water views, Roosevelt Annex was constructed by the developer of Truman Annex and the Key West Golf Club.

The Key West Golf Club community, on Stock Island, looks a lot like Truman Annex. Here, single-family homes, town houses, and condominiums display elements of Conch-style architecture. Each residence overlooks the Florida Keys' only 18-hole public golf course, along with surrounding lakes and ponds. If you are not in the market to buy at this time, a variety of long-term rental options is available. All residents have free access to tennis courts, nature walks, several swimming pools, and, of course, golf.

Sunset Key

If you would truly like to live on a secluded island—but not too far from civilization—consider a home on Sunset Key. Formerly known as Tank Island (the Navy once stored its fuel in huge tanks here), Sunset Key is just a stone's throw across the harbor from Mallory Square. About half of the island is devoted to guest cottages and a beachfront restaurant/bar operated by the Hilton Marina and Resort (see our Accommodations and Restaurants chapters); the rest is reserved for single-family homes. Homesites start at nearly half a million dollars. In addition to fabulous open-water sunset views, homeowners on Sunset Key enjoy such amenities as a health club, pool, tennis courts, and putting green. Their cars, however, must remain behind at the Hilton parking garage on Key West; only golf carts and bicycles are permitted on Sunset Key. Regular ferry service is available from the Hilton Marina.

Real Estate Companies

We describe some of the largest Key West agencies for sales and rentals in this section. However, this is not meant to be a comprehensive listing. For a complete list, consult the Yellow Pages.

Insiders' Tip

Be sure to ask about parking when making your reservation for a rental property in Key West. On some Old Town streets, cars bearing non-Monroe County plates may be ticketed or towed.

Accommodations Key West
Century 21 Keysearch Realty/
Greg O'Berry Inc.
701 Caroline Street
Key West, FL
(305) 294–6637, (800) 741–6263
www.oberry.com, www.centurykey.com

Century 21 Keysearch Realty deals with real estate sales in our southernmost city. The separate Accommodations Key West division handles Key West vacation rentals.

Bascom Grooms Real Estate
1110 Truman Avenue
Key West, FL
(305) 295–7511, (888) 565–7150
www.keywesthomes.cc

In addition to residential sales, this agency also handles commercial properties and vacation rentals.

Beach Club Brokers Inc.
1304 Simonton Street
Key West, FL
(305) 294–8433, (800) 545–9655
www.kwreal.com

Specializing in residential sales, Beach Club Brokers also maintains an office at La Brisa Condominiums. They have a separate rental division, Rent Key West Vacations Inc. (see below).

Key West Realty Inc.
1109 Duval Street
Key West, FL
(305) 294–3064, (800) 652–5131
www.keysrealty.com

In addition to real estate sales, this agency is very heavily into the rental business with a wide variety of vacation options.

Olde Island Realty Inc.
525 Simonton Street
Key West, FL
(305) 292–7997, (800) 621–9405
www.oldeisland.com

Olde Island has an extensive list of rentals, including large homes. They also handle real estate sales.

Preferred Properties of Key West, Inc.
525 Southard Street
Key West, FL
(305) 294–3040, (800) 462–5937
www.realkeywest.com

This agency offers residential and commercial property sales as well as vacation rentals, investment properties, and long-term property management.

Prudential Knight-Keyside Properties
336 Duval Street
Key West, FL
(305) 294–5155, (800) 843–9276
3332 N. Roosevelt Boulevard
Key West, FL
(305) 294–4949, (877) 294–4949
www.floridakeys-realestate.com,
www.pruknight.com

A part of the quartet of Prudential Keyside Properties offices, Prudential Knight concentrates sales efforts on properties from Key West to Marathon. The Key West site handles rental listings.

The Real Estate Company of Key West Inc.
701 Simonton Street
Key West, FL
(305) 296–0111
www.oldkeywest.com

Specializing in sales and rentals of upscale residential properties, the staff

Gingers bloom prolifically in Florida Keys' gardens. PHOTO: VICTORIA SHEARER

here includes a full-time property manager who oversees luxury vacation rentals ranging from cottages to multi-bedroom estates.

Rent Key West Vacations Inc.
1107 Truman Avenue
Key West, FL
(305) 294–0990, (800) 833–7368
www.rentkeywest.com

A division of Beach Club Brokers Inc., this agency handles rentals exclusively. Rent Key West offers extensive listings, with properties ranging from studio apartments to four-bedroom homes.

Sara Cook Inc.
905 Truman Avenue
Key West, FL
(305) 294–8491
www.scireal.com

This agency has an extensive listing of both short- and long-term rental options as well as properties for sale.

Truman Annex Real Estate Company Inc.
201 Front Street
Building 45
Key West, FL
(305) 292–1881, (800) 884–7368
www.trumanannex.com

Don't let the name fool you. Truman Annex Real Estate Company has been listing and selling property all over Key West—not just in Truman Annex—for more than 10 years. The primary focus here is, however, on the sales of Truman Annex properties as well as those in the Key West Golf Club and Roosevelt Annex communities. A separate division handles rentals of the three developments.

Campgrounds

Price-Code Key

Our listings rate campgrounds according to a four-symbol price key, representing average site cost per night during the high season.

$ . . . . $20 to $40
$$ . . . . $41 to $60
$$$ . . . . $61 to $80
$$$$ . . . . More than $81

Close your eyes and concentrate on this vision: The turquoise waters shimmer like a '57 T-bird. The sun melts like orange sherbet on a hot summer day. The stars sparkle like a gilded mosaic.

Jimmy Buffett has nothing on you when you are camping in the Florida Keys.

Whether you enjoy pitching a tent or traveling with a self-contained motor home, the campgrounds of the Keys offer a reasonably priced alternative to motels and resort accommodations. However, you will find that camping rates in the Florida Keys are generally much higher than in other areas of the United States. But all our recommended campgrounds have water access, and many are perched at the edge of the Atlantic or the Gulf of Mexico.

A wide range of amenities distinguishes each campground, but one thing is certain: If you wish to camp in the Keys during January, February, or March—those winter months when the folks up North are dusting off their snow boots—you must reserve your site a year in advance. The Keys have a second high season in the summer months, when Floridians locked into triple-digit temperatures head south to our cooling trade winds and warm, placid waters. During sport lobster season, the last consecutive Wednesday and Thursday of July, it is standing room only in the Keys.

We have listed our recommended campgrounds and RV parks by descending mile marker beginning in Key Largo and ending at Stock Island. Key West devotes its land use to mega-hotels and quaint guesthouses, presenting a dearth of recommendable campgrounds. If you think you might fancy a really unusual camping experience, be sure to see "Camping in the Beyond" in this chapter for information on camping in the Dry Tortugas National Park or Everglades National Park.

You may assume that all our inclusions maintain good paved interior roads, clean restrooms and showers, laundry facilities and 20- and 30-amp electrical service. Most campgrounds accept pets if they are kept on a leash at all times and walked only in designated areas and never on the beach. Exceptions will be noted. Most campgrounds enforce a quiet time from 10 or 11 P.M. until 7 A.M. the next morning.

Rates vary by the type of site you secure. Most campgrounds offer a range of options: tent sites, with or without electricity; RV sites with electricity and water; sites with electricity, water, and sewer. Waterfront sites or sites with boat dockage will be more costly. Extra people or vehicles at a site will incur additional per diem charges. All water is municipal, piped down to the Keys from Miami. Cable television and telephone hookups are noted when applicable. Back-in and pull-through dimensions vary. Call the campground if this is critical for your rig. Toll-free telephone numbers, when stated, are for reservation purposes only.

Rate ranges are based on a per diem stay during high season without the 11.5 percent state tax. (State park campground rates include this tax, however.) High season is considered December 15 through Easter. Some campgrounds also consider the summer months as high season. Weekly and monthly rates are usually available at a reduced cost; be sure to inquire when you make your reservation. Major credit cards are accepted unless noted to the contrary.

The Florida Keys

Upper Keys

John Pennekamp Coral Reef State Park
MM 102.5 Oceanside
Key Largo, FL
(305) 451–1202
www.dep.state.fl.us/parks
$

Aesthetically, the gravel sites at John Pennekamp Coral Reef State Park don't begin to compare with their waterfront siblings at the Keys' other two state parks, Bahia Honda and Long Key, but a canopy of mature buttonwoods shades most of the sites. The wide range of fabulous recreational opportunities within Pennekamp and its proximity to the nightlife in Key Largo more than make up for any lack of romantic oceanfront ambiance (see Parks in our Recreation chapter).

John Pennekamp Coral Reef State Park, like Bahia Honda State Park and Long Key State Park, follows a strictly regimented reservation policy (see the Making Reservations for State Park Campsites section in this chapter). If you have a guaranteed reservation at Pennekamp and you will be arriving after 5 P.M. you must call before 4 P.M. on the day of your arrival to obtain a site assignment and the combination to open the park's front gate. To cancel your reservation, you must call by 5 P.M. of the day before your scheduled arrival or you will be charged for one night's camping. The park opens at 8 A.M. and closes at sundown daily. You may stay a maximum of 14 days. The per-night camping fee includes all taxes and allows four people and one vehicle per campsite. Pets are not allowed in the campground. Intoxicants are forbidden anywhere in the park. Water and electric (30/50 amp) are available at all sites.

Key Largo Kampground and Marina
MM 101.5 Oceanside
Key Largo, FL
(305) 451–1431, (800) 526–7688
www.keylargo.org
$–$$

Croton and bougainvillea hedges separate the sites in this village-like campground laden with palm trees. Chickees line the arterial canal that connects the marina to the shallow oceanic bonefish flats beyond. About one-third of the condo campsites, with full hookups and free cable television, are available for overnighters. Some sites front the canal and have boat slips. Two beaches look out on Newport Bay, and a heated swimming pool and kiddie pool, shuffleboard, horseshoe pits, and volleyball add to the fun. John Pennekamp Coral Reef State Park is only a mile north of the 40-acre campground.

Rates are based on four people (two adults and two children younger than six) and one camping unit per site.

America Outdoors Camper Resorts
MM 97 Bayside
Key Largo, FL
(305) 852–8054
www.aokl.com
$$

Each of the sites at America Outdoors is carved out of a tropical hardwood hammock, two untouched acres of which have been set aside adjacent to the park as a nature preserve. The towering, lush vegetation, rarely found in campgrounds of

These elevated wood platforms are placed along interior bays and rivers of Everglades National Park, where no dry land exists. PHOTO: VICTORIA SHEARER

the Keys, creates private, shady campsites. The sparkling waters of Florida Bay complete the picture, offering lazy days and dazzling sunsets.

A sandy-bottom swim area extends into the bay, and you can launch your boat at the marina ramp and rent a slip at the T-dock. Or simply commandeer one of the rental water toys through the placid waters. Watch the sunset from the marina snack bar.

Hookups for air conditioning and electric heat are available at an additional charge at the roomy sites. Rates are based on two people and one vehicle per site, with no charge for children younger than six.

Fiesta Key Resort KOA Kampground
MM 70 Bayside
Long Key, FL
(305) 664–4922, (800) 562–7730
www.koa.com/where/fl/09250
$–$$$$

Surrounded by the warm waters of the Gulf of Mexico, which we call "bayside"

here in the Florida Keys, Fiesta Key KOA Kampground enjoys a tropical milieu and the famed Keys sunsets. Hot-pink oleander hedges lead to the 35-site tent village, and more than 300 campsites welcome RVs. Most of the sites are shaded with large palms or leafy trees and sport a cement patio.

Fiesta Key really does resemble a resort: Diversions are endless. A waterfront pub offers libations and relaxed dining. You will enjoy the Olympic-size, heated, freshwater swimming pool and two hot tubs. The children probably will prefer to camp out in the game room, on the playground, or the basketball court. On-premises rentals expand your horizons beyond the campground. Pontoon boats, runabouts, and center consoles take you over the calm Gulf waters. Fishing rods stand ready should you care to try your luck with a lure. A full marina provides a boat ramp and slips if you want to bring your own craft.

Rates are quoted for two people; children younger than six stay free.

Long Key State Park
MM 67.5 Oceanside
Long Key, FL
(305) 664–4815
www.dep.state.fl.us/parks
$

Every site is oceanfront when you camp at Long Key State Park. The sandy sites took quite a beating from Hurricanes Georges and Irene in recent years, destroying most of the vegetation, but you can't get closer to the ocean than this camping in the Florida Keys. Half the 60 sites offer water and electric, and all have picnic tables fronting the shallow saltwater flats. The paved road into the campground parallels the Overseas Highway on one side and the ocean on the other. Each deep site runs from the park road to the ocean.

Like John Pennekamp Coral Reef State Park and Bahia Honda State Park, Long Key State Park follows a strictly regimented reservation policy (see the Making Reservations for State Park Campsites section in this chapter). Rates are based on four people, one vehicle per site, and include all taxes. Only one camper and one small tent or two small tents are allowed per campsite.

The park opens at 8 A.M. and closes at sunset. Pets are not allowed in the camping areas, beaches or concession areas of the park.

Middle Keys

Knight's Key Park Campground & Marina
MM 47 Oceanside
Marathon, FL
(305) 743–4343, (800) 348–2267
$–$$

This family-oriented campground, started by three Kyle brothers more than three decades ago, occupies the land once called Knight's Key Junction at the foot of the Seven Mile Bridge. The tracks of Flagler's Railroad ended here. The train unloaded its cargo, which was stowed on ships heading to Key West or Cuba, and then Keys or Cuban cargo was placed aboard the train, which turned around and chugged back

north. The deepwater canal and swimming area, with waters 30 feet deep, remain from that bygone era when Knight's Key hummed with ship traffic.

Knight's Key Park Campground has a man-made beach, and, during the winter season, a stone aquarium near the canal is stocked with fish. From December 15 through March 30, the Kyle Inn, a pub-style restaurant with a Chicago-brick floor, provides meals, libation, bingo, cards, and billiards.

Unique to Knight's Key, you can dock your boat behind your camper at the harborside marina sites. Knight's Key maintains a pump and dump station but offers no sewer hookups. Electricity of 20-, 30- and 50-amp is available, but don't expect cable TV or telephone hookups.

Rates are based on two occupants. Minibikes and motorcycles are forbidden on park roads.

Lower Keys

Sunshine Key Camping Resort
MM 39 Bayside
Sunshine Key, FL
(305) 872–2217, (800) 852–0348
www.encorerv.com
$–$$$

Sunshine Key Camping Resort occupies an entire key, officially named Ohio Key. This bustling place, with nearly 400 sites, is more like a small Midwestern town than a camping resort in the Keys. The 75-acre Sunshine Key, with its winding sign-posted streets and myriad amenities, is friendly and family-oriented. The ocean-side portion of Sunshine Key has not been developed. It remains a tangle of mangroves, buttonwoods, and palm trees

Insiders' Tip
Camping and campfires are not permitted in National Wildlife Refuges.

that shields a feathered montage of wildlife popular with bird-watchers.

You will have to rise early to pack in all you can do in a day on Sunshine Key. The large marina, which even has a fishing pier, will shelter your boat, and the experts at the bait and tackle shop will put you on the fish. Tennis courts, a heated swimming pool, volleyball, horseshoes, and a full schedule of adult activities in the clubhouse keep things hopping. A game room, basketball courts, a playground, and watersports occupy the children.

Rates are based on two adults and their accompanying children younger than 12. Satellite television is free. Sunshine Key considers its high season November 15 through April 15. Maximum stay is six months plus one day.

Bahia Honda State Park
MM 37 Oceanside
Bahia Honda Key, FL
(305) 872–2353
www.dep.state.fl.us/parks
$

Claiming the Florida Keys' best natural beach (2½ miles long), Bahia Honda State Park offers campers three kinds of sites but no pull-through sites. The roomy sites at Buttonwood can accommodate large motor homes; Sandspur is limited to tents, vans, and pop-ups. Because these sites sit deep in a tropical hardwood hammock, the park is very selective as to which rigs are allowed to camp here. Only one car and one tent per site are permitted. All these sites have water, and more than half offer electricity. Bayside campsites, accessed by a road passing under the Bahia Honda Bridge, are restricted to tents or small pop-ups. The bridge provides only a 6-foot, 8-inch clearance. These campsites provide water but no electricity.

Three large cabins, each a heated and air-conditioned, two-bedroom duplex with a fully equipped kitchen, a full bathroom, and all linens, literally perch on the water near the Bayside campsites. You can throw a baited hook from your front porch, rock a little in the old rocker gracing the deck and catch your dinner without missing the sunset. Each cabin will sleep six, but you'll have to rough it without television or radio. No pets are allowed in the cabins, which must be reserved in person or by telephone up to 11 months in advance. A two-day deposit by credit card, check, or cash will secure the cabin reservation if it's received within 10 days of your making the reservation. The minimum stay is two nights; maximum, 14 nights. The rate per cabin, per night, including tax, is $125.15.

All campsites at Bahia Honda State Park provide a grill and picnic table. The park has a boat ramp, so you may bring your own craft and try your luck at catching a tarpon under the Bahia Honda Bridge, noted as one of the best tarpon fishing areas in the state (see our Fishing chapter). "You really don't even have to know what you are doing," counsels the assistant park manager. "Put a live mullet on the end of a line and the tarpon will bite."

Like John Pennekamp Coral Reef State Park and Long Key State Park, Bahia Honda State Park follows a strictly regimented reservation policy (see the Making Reservations for State Park Campsites section in this chapter). Rates are based on four-person occupancy and include all taxes. Maximum stay at a Bahia Honda campsite is 14 days. Pets are not allowed.

Bahia Honda State Park rents these spacious cabins at very reasonable prices. PHOTO: VICTORIA SHEARER

Big Pine Key Fishing Lodge
MM 33 Oceanside
Big Pine Key, FL
(305) 872–2351
$

The Big Pine Key Fishing Lodge abuts a natural oceanside inlet that was a byproduct of the dredging of Spanish Harbor Channel for Flagler's Railroad. The sites range from rustic grass or dirt tent sites without water or electricity to dockside sites with full hookups.

The boat basin, a part of the Big Pine Fishing Lodge since the late 1950s, accommodates small fishing boats up to 25 feet long for a per-foot daily charge. Ample fish-cleaning stations are provided so you can ready the spoils of the day for the frying pan. The Lodge has an oval swimming pool, sunken in a raised deck overlooking a peppering of statuesque coconut palms, all grown from seed.

Rates are based on one or two occupants with one vehicle and one camping unit. Children younger than six stay free. Air conditioning, phone outlets, and cable hookups are included in the camping fee. No dogs are allowed in the campground.

Sugarloaf Key Resort KOA Kampground
MM 20 Oceanside
Summerland Key, FL
(305) 745–3549, (800) 562–7731
www.thefloridakeys.com/koasugarloaf
$–$$$

Pelicans perched in mangroves near thatched chickees on a palm-speckled beach creates an island ambiance in this comprehensive KOA on Summerland Key. Nearly 200 gravel, grass, or dirt sites offer a choice of hookups but no pull-throughs are available. Optional cable hookup is available at an additional charge.

The facility offers what you have come to expect from a KOA Kampground—all the necessities plus the amenities of a resort. A full marina covers the gamut of boating and fishing needs. A large heated pool, hot tub, minigolf, horseshoes, and bicycle rentals offer landlubbers relaxing diversions. Volleyball, a game room, and a playground amuse the children. Social activities, crafts, and special events are scheduled during the winter season. Only 20 miles from Key West and near Looe Key National Marine Sanctuary, Sugarloaf Key

The first sight of the massive brick fortress of Fort Jefferson, guarding pristine Dry Tortugas, is breathtaking. PHOTO: WAYNE MOCCIA

KOA Kampground is close to all the action.

Rates are based on two occupants; children younger than six stay free. Some RV trailers are available for rent; call to inquire about amenities and pricing.

Bluewater Key RV Resort
MM 14 Oceanside
Sugarloaf Key, FL
(305) 745–2494, (800) 237–2266
www.bluewaterkey.com
$$$

As simple and elegant as a sophisticated ball gown, Bluewater Key RV Resort oozes class. The 80 spacious gravel sites feature metered utility hookups, including telephone and cable television. Uniquely angled toward the water and buffered with palms and shrubbery, each privately owned site has a stone patio with benches and a round cement table. No tents, popups or vans are allowed at Bluewater Key. All units must be self-contained RVs.

A clubhouse hosts table tennis or informal card games, and the freshwater swimming pool attracts sun worshipers from up North. Oceanside flats and deepwater canals surround the property, affording primo fishing for anglers. And if you want a little action at the end of your day of quiet solitude, you are but 14 miles

from the center of Key West. Need we say more?

Those reserving waterfront or canal sites may secure their small boats to the floating docks or bulkhead. The high season at Bluewater Key RV Resort is considered December 15 to April 15. Although the resort accepts reservations for one day or one week to a month or more depending upon availability, we suggest you book at least a year in advance if you'd like a waterfront spot. Bluewater Key RV Resort has an on-site manager and is protected from intrusion by a 24-hour, phone-operated security gate.

Boyd's Key West Campground
MM 5 Oceanside
6401 Maloney Avenue
Stock Island, FL
(305) 294–1465
www.gocampingamerica.com/boydskeywest
$–$$$

Although its brochures state a Key West address, Boyd's is actually on Stock Island, just outside the Key West city limits. Most of the level, shaded sites have cement patios. Bordering the ocean, Boyd's offers a boat ramp, a small marina, extensive dock space, and a heated swimming pool. The four bathhouses were renovated and updated in 2000. You can catch the city bus into Key West for unlimited diversions, hang out at Boyd's game room, or watch the large-screen television, which is tucked in a tiki hut near the pool.

Rates are based on two occupants and one camping unit per site. Small dogs are permitted in hard-shell campers only. Fifty-amp service and modem hookup is available.

Camping in the Beyond

If there is a little part of you that longs to forge through uncharted territory and live off the land (or the sea), you can fulfill your fantasies here. Everglades National Park and Dry Tortugas National Park, both daytrip excursions from the Florida Keys, offer unique camping experiences for the adventuresome spirits among you.

Everglades National Park

Canoe or commandeer a small motor craft into the backcountry wilderness of Everglades National Park. This 99-mile route, which is recommended for experienced canoeists only, connects Flamingo and Everglades City. The charted routing through such colorfully named spots as Darwin's Place, Camp Lonesome, Lostman's Five, and Graveyard Creek encompasses 47 primitive campsites of three basic types.

Chickees: These elevated, 10-by-12-foot wood platforms with roofs are placed along interior rivers and bays where no dry land exists. A design originally used by the Miccosukee Indians, these open-air structures allow the wind to blow through, keeping the insects away. A narrow walkway leads to a self-contained toilet. You will need to have a freestanding tent, because stakes and nails are not allowed.

Beach Sites: These are set on coastal beaches that have been built up through time from a conglomeration of fragmented shells. Campers are warned that Gulf waters can become extremely rough. Loggerhead sea turtles nest on Highland Beach and Cape Sable in the spring and

summer. If you see evidence of their nesting, refrain from lighting a campfire nearby. (Campfires are allowed at beach sites only.)

Primitive Ground Sites: These consist of mounds of earth just a few feet higher than the surrounding mangroves. Willy Willy, Camp Lonesome, and Canepatch are old Indian mound sites. Coastal aborigines, who lived here before the Seminole Indians, constructed mounds of shells or soil as dry dwelling sites amidst the mangroves. The ground sites, along interior bays and rivers, have a heavier preponderance of insects than either the beach sites or the chickees. Always be prepared for mosquitoes and tiny biting flies called no-see-ums, especially at sunrise and sunset. Mosquito season corresponds with the rainy season, April through October. We do not recommend you try to camp in the Everglades during these months.

You will need a permit (small fee in season) to camp in one of the backcountry sites. Apply in person at the Gulf Coast or Flamingo Visitor Center. Everglades National Park also offers camping in two in-park campgrounds for $14 per night. Seasonal reservations (November through April) can be made for these campsites by calling (800) 365-2267.

For more information on park or backcountry camping, contact the main park number at (305) 242-7700; the Gulf Coast Visitor Center, (941) 695-3311; or the Flamingo Visitor Center, (941) 695-2945. Canoes and kayaks may be rented at Flamingo Marina (941-695-3101), or in Everglades City (941-695-2591). The

Everglades National Park website is www.nps.gov/ever.

Dry Tortugas National Park

Roughing it takes on gargantuan proportions when you consider camping at Dry Tortugas National Park, but it's worth the effort, because this remote bit of Paradise has been preserved in a virginal state. You'll find the ten palm-shaded tent sites—available on a first-come, first-served basis—in a sandy area on Garden Key in front of Fort Jefferson. You must pack in all your supplies, including fresh water; only saltwater toilets, grills, and picnic tables are provided. There is no food, fresh water, electricity or medical assistance of any kind on the island.

You must take your chances on securing a campsite because reservations are not taken for the individual sites. (The park service says securing a site usually is not a problem.) Campsites accommodate up to eight people. You can reserve a group site for as many as 15 people, however, by contacting the park service, (305) 242-7700. The staff will send you a permit application, which you must mail to: Dry Tortugas National Park, Attn: Group Camping, P.O. Box 6208, Key West, FL 33041. The application requires the following information: name, address, day/night telephone number, group name, date of arrival/departure, number of people in group, primary activities (i.e., birding, snorkeling, etc.), and mode of transportation to the islands. If the site is available when you submit your completed application, a permit reserving the group site will be issued. You may stay up to 14 days at either individual or group sites, but keep in mind you must bring complete provisioning for the duration of your stay and pack out your trash. A small fee per person, per night must be paid upon arrival at Fort Jefferson.

You may have left the civilized world behind you in Key West, but the arena of natural splendor surrounding you in the Dry Tortugas is endless. Tour Fort Jefferson (self-guided), America's largest nineteenth-century coastal fort. The walls of the fort are 50 feet high and 8 feet thick. A white coral beach, nature-made not man-made, provides a tropical backdrop for doing nothing at all. But you can snorkel just 60 yards off the beach or dive the seemingly bottomless blue waters, which, preserved as a sanctuary, are filled with fearless battalions of finfish and squadrons of crawfish that are oblivious to your presence.

Bird-watching is superb. Sooty and noddy terns by the thousands gather in the Dry Tortugas from the Caribbean, nesting on nearby Bush Key. Single eggs are laid in depressions in the sand. Parent birds take turns shading them from the hot sun. The entire colony leaves when the babies are strong enough.

Getting to the Dry Tortugas presents a bit of a challenge—and expense. Seaplane is the fastest means of transportation to the Dry Tortugas, but it's also the most expensive. You can also reach the Dry Tortugas by sea. (See our Recreation chapter for information on the Yankee Fleet Ferry to Fort Jefferson.) The National Park Service provides a list of sanctioned transportation services to the Dry Tortugas, which means they are insured and bonded and they maintain good safety records. The park service cautions, however, that the criteria are stringent and the list is constantly monitored. Contact the park service, (305-242-7700) to get the current recommendations. Dry Tortugas National Park website is: www.nps.gov/drto.

The Dry Tortugas and Sandy Key provide two of the best natural beaches in the Florida Keys.

PHOTO: MARY MOCCIA

Making Reservations for State Park Campsites

Some of the most beautiful campsites in the Florida Keys nestle in hardwood hammocks or perch on oceanfront beaches in our three state parks. The per-dollar value of these sites cannot be beat, and demand out-steps supply in all seasons. The State of Florida has developed a highly structured procedure for the fair and equitable allocation of these coveted campsites. We hope this synopsis helps you snag a small patch of Paradise for your Florida Keys holiday.

Ninety percent of the sites at John Pennekamp Coral Reef State Park, Long Key State Park, and Bahia Honda State Park are available for advance reservation. Ten percent are allotted on a first-come, first-served basis. You must reserve a campsite no more than 11 months in advance in person or by telephone between the hours of 8 A.M. and sunset (phone numbers are listed below). If you plan to reserve your site via telephone, you may begin calling at 8 A.M. Expect the line to be constantly busy. Just keep hitting the redial button until you get through, and be diligent. If you are unlucky on your first try and your vacation plans allow, try calling again the next day, when available sites for 11 months forward will again be allocated for reservation. (Because all campers have the option of staying for 14 days, overlap may affect availability.)

Your reservation must be secured with a credit card number. If you do not have a credit card or choose not to use it, a check in the amount of one night's camping fee must be received within 10 days of the date you made your reservation. The low daily prices ($25.84 with electric and water, $23.69 without), pristine surroundings, and proximity to ocean and bay waters make the camping sites at these three state parks very desirable.

To reserve a campsite call:

John Pennekamp Coral Reef State Park
(305) 451–1202

Long Key State Park
(305) 664–4815

Bahia Honda State Park
(305) 872–2353

Cuts between mangrove islands lead from Gulf waters to the Atlantic. PHOTO: FLORIDA KEYS & KEY WEST TDC

Boating

The voice of the sea speaks to the soul, no more so than in the Florida Keys. Surrounded by the shimmering aquatic prisms of the Gulf of Mexico and the Atlantic Ocean, the Keys volunteer unlimited vistas for watery exploration. Our depths secret famed fishing grounds (see our Fishing chapter) and unparalleled dive sites (see our Diving and Snorkeling chapter). Cruisers the world over seek out our remote, pristine anchoring-out spots as well as our resort marinas (see our Cruising chapter). And peppering the Keys, from Key Largo to Key West, a proliferation of watersports facilities afford anyone visiting our shores the opportunity to get out on the water via canoe, sea kayak, water skis, personal watercraft, sailboards, even paddleboats (see our Recreation chapter). The waters surrounding the Florida Keys are protected as part of a marine sanctuary and so regulations concerning the use of personal watercraft are more stringent here than in other parts of Florida. For more information, contact the Sanctuary office at (305) 743-2437 or log on to www.fknms.nos.noaa.gov.

But the most popular means of wandering our aqueous acres is undoubtedly by boat. The waters encompassing the Florida Keys have been designated a National Marine Sanctuary since 1990, a marine zoning plan that imposes certain restrictions and responsibilities on all mariners so that our resources may be preserved for all time. (See the Florida Keys National Marine Sanctuary Regulation section of this chapter.) In this chapter we will introduce you to our waters, alert you to the rules of our hydrous highways and byways, and share some safety and navigational tips. We'll provide you with a primer of available public boat ramps, marine supply stores, boat sales and service businesses as well as motor and sailboat rentals, bareboat charters, and other sources to enhance your time on the water.

So follow our lighthouse beacon as we illuminate the joys and some of the hazards of boating in the waters of the Florida Keys. The Key West section gives you details of the boating scene in our southernmost city.

The Florida Keys

Bodies of Water

The waters of the Florida Keys conceal multiple habitats that sustain an impressive array of sea life not encountered anywhere else in the United States. Depths range from scant inches (which often disappear altogether at low tide) in the nearshore waters, the flats, and the backcountry of Florida Bay to the fathoms of the offshore waters of the deep-blue Atlantic. And buried at sea 4 to 5 miles from our shores runs the most extensive living coral reef track in North America

(see our Paradise Found, Fishing, Diving, and Cruising chapters for more information on these waters and the creatures dwelling within).

Flats, Backcountry, and Shallow Nearshore Waters

Perhaps the most complex of our waters are the shallows of the nearshore waters, those directly off both our coasts, which vary from a few inches to several feet in depth and sometimes stretch for a mile or more from shore. Called "skinny" waters by local captains, these "flats" of the Atlantic and backcountry waters of the Gulf of Mexico and Florida Bay (that portion of the Gulf bordered by the Upper

Keys and Everglades National Park) prove a challenge to navigate. Popular with anglers searching for bonefish, permit, tarpon, redfish, snook, and seatrout and inhabited by an array of barracudas, sharks, and lobsters, the shallow waters cover meadows of seagrass punctuated with patches of sand, which also function as the nursery waters for many offshore species.

As a boater in the Florida Keys, you should familiarize yourself with the necessary nautical charts before venturing off the dock. Learn to "read" the water (see the Aids to Navigation section in this chapter) because waters are littered with unmarked shoals. Nearshore waters are best traversed in a shallow-draft flatsboat or skiff, by dinghy, canoe, or sea kayak. Operators of personal watercraft should steer clear of the flats to avoid disturbing the aquatic life dwelling below.

If you do happen to run aground here, turn off your motor immediately; the rotating propeller will kill the seagrass. Usually all you need to do is get out of the boat to lighten the load and push the craft to deeper water. Then trim up your motor and proceed. If this doesn't work, wait until the tide rises a bit and try to push off the flat again.

Intracoastal Waterway

The primary navigable waterway in Florida Bay and the Gulf of Mexico is the Intracoastal Waterway. In the Keys it leads from Biscayne Bay at the mainland, under Jewfish Creek, and then parallels the Keys,

accommodating boats with drafts of up to four to six feet. The Intracoastal runs about two to three miles off the Gulf side of our islands, between shallow nearshore waters and the scattered mangrove islands that lie varying distances from the coast. The Intracoastal is well marked to about Big Pine Key where it meets the Big Spanish Channel and heads north into the Gulf of Mexico. (Red day markers should be kept to the starboard, or right, side of the vessel when traveling down the Keys in the Intracoastal Waterway.) From the Spanish Channel to Key West, boaters must pay close attention to nautical charts to navigate safe passage. Boaters will enter Key West through the well-marked Northwest Channel.

Patch Reefs, Hawk Channel, and the Barrier Reef

Between the nearshore waters of the Atlantic and the barrier reef some 4 to 5 miles offshore lies a smattering of patch reefs submerged at depths as shallow as 3 feet, with some even exposed at low tide. Surrounding waters vary in depth, but generally are much deeper than the flats and nearshore waters.

Hawk Channel—a safely navigable superhighway frequented by recreational boaters and cruisers—runs the length of the Florida Keys, bordering the reef at depths between 11 and 16 feet. Square red and triangular green day markers guide boaters through these waters; red markers should be kept to the starboard, or right, side of the vessel when traveling down the Keys in Hawk Channel.

Outside of this marked area, the waters are scattered with dive sites designated with anchor buoys and red-and-white flags, as well as marked and unmarked rocks and shoals. If red-and-white diver-down flags are displayed, boaters should steer clear. These flags indicate that a diver is beneath the water. Lighthouses now mark shallow reef areas, which, at one time, claimed ships that encountered bad weather or navigated carelessly close to the coral mountains.

Waters covering the coral reef can run as deep as 20 to 40 feet, but as history attests, depths can vary considerably. Always consult your nautical chart and "read" the water.

The Florida Straits

Outside the reef in the Florida Straits, the water depth of the Atlantic increases dramatically to as much as 80 feet, deepening further with distance from shore. Although on some days these waters are relatively calm, all offshore boaters should check wind and weather advisories before venturing out.

Creeks and Channels

The channels, or "cuts," between our islands often have extremely strong currents that make traveling between bridge pilings a bit dicey. Current continuously flows from the Gulf of Mexico into the Atlantic because sea level in the Gulf is slightly higher than that of the ocean. Exercise caution when boating in these waters.

Key West Harbor

The southernmost city's ports have traditionally been gracious, welcoming tall ships, steamships, ferries, barges, powerboats, and seaplanes. Pirates, wreckers, spongers, shippers, naval officers, and Cuban émigrés all have found shelter here in the midst of their work, play, and quest for worldly wealth and freedom.

Key West's port, the deepest in all the Florida Keys, has a main channel depth of about 33 feet; it is even deeper on the Atlantic side. Passenger cruise ships now include this island among their ports of call, and recreational cruisers often head for Key West's bustling harbor to prepare themselves and their boats for a Caribbean journey.

Like the rest of the Florida Keys, Key West is protective of its coral reefs and seagrass beds, and despite the fact that harbors run deep, waters in the backcountry are shallow everywhere. First-time and novice boaters often run aground here

and by Fleming Key and Sand Key west of the harbor.

Aids to Navigation

Nautical Charts

Always use nautical charts and a magnetic compass for navigation when boating in the waters of the Florida Keys. Use electronic means of navigation (GPS) only for confirmation of position. Be sure your vessel is equipped with a VHF marine radio.

The U.S. Coast Guard recommends you follow charts issued by the National Oceanic and Atmospheric Administration (NOAA). To secure nautical charts for the entire Florida Keys, you'll need to purchase a chart kit that includes charts for each section. You can also purchase NOAA charts individually. For instance, to navigate the waters surrounding Key West, the U.S. Coast Guard recommends you use navigational chart No. 11441 for the approaches to Key West Harbor and chart No. 11447 for the harbor itself.

Readily available in many marine supply stores throughout the Florida Keys and Key West (see store listings in this chapter), these charts are accurate based on the date marked on them. Store personnel will be able to help you secure the proper, up-to-date chart for the area you will be exploring. Be sure you know how to read the nautical charts before you set off.

Channel Markers

In most waters, boaters follow the adage: "red, right, return," meaning that the square red channel markers should be kept to the right, or starboard, side of the vessel when heading toward the port of origin. This jingle is confusing at best, for in the Florida Keys it does not appear to apply. Red markers should be kept to the starboard side of the vessel when heading down the Keys, from Key Largo to Key West, through Hawk Channel on the oceanside or the Intracoastal Waterway in the Gulf. Conversely, when traveling up the Keys, in either Hawk Channel or the

Intracoastal Waterway, triangular green markers should be kept to your starboard side; keep red markers on your vessel's port, or left, side.

When traversing creeks and cuts from oceanside to the Gulf, red markers should be kept on your starboard side, and when coming from the Gulf the opposite holds true. In any event, always consult your nautical chart to determine the channel of safe passage and the corresponding positioning of the navigational markers.

Tide Charts

It's important to determine mean low tides within the waters you plan to travel so that you do not run aground. In the Florida Keys tides typically rise and fall about 1 to 2 feet. During spring, autumn, and a full moon, tides tend to rise to the higher and lower ends of this scale. Boaters should, therefore, rely on a tide conversion chart. Most marinas, bait-and-tackle shops, and other businesses that cater to boaters can provide tide information for specific areas in conjunction with a current tide chart available from the U.S. Coast Guard.

"Reading" the Water

In the Florida Keys, visual navigation often means "reading" the water, that is, recognizing its potential depth by knowing which colors indicate safe passage and which connote danger. As water depth decreases, its underlying sea bottom is indicated by distinctive coloration. Be aware that readings may be difficult in narrow channels and in strong currents where the waters often are murky and restrict visibility. Wear polarized sunglasses to better distinguish one color from another.

The easiest way to remember what each water color signifies is to follow some poetic, but fundamental, guidance:

Brown, brown run aground. Reef formations and shallow seagrass beds close to the surface cause this color.

White, white you might. Sand bars and rubble bottoms may be in waters much shallower than you think.

Green, green nice and clean. The water is generally safely above reefs or seagrass beds, but larger boats with deeper drafts may hit bottom. If you are renting a boat, find out what the draft is.

Blue, blue cruise on through. Water is deepest, but changing tides may cause coral reefs to surface. Allow time to steer around them.

When You Need Help

Although the U.S. Coast Guard and the Florida Marine Patrol work closely together and will make sure you contact the proper party in any event, they do handle different aspects of our waters in the Florida Keys.

Florida Marine Patrol

The Florida Fish and Wildlife Conservation Commission's law enforcement arm is the Florida Marine Patrol. They deal with violations such as environmental crime, fish and crawfish bag limits, and illegal dumping. They also enforce boating safety laws, responding to reports of unsafe boating and wake violations as well as any perceived illegal activity on the water. You can reach the Florida Marine Patrol on a cellular telephone by dialing *FMP or on a regular telephone line at (800) DIAL FMP, (800) 342-5367, (305) 289-2320. The Marine Patrol vessels also monitor VHF channel 16.

U.S. Coast Guard

The U.S. Coast Guard maintains three bases in the Florida Keys and Key West. Their mission is to ensure maritime safety and handle life-threatening emergencies at sea, such as vessel collisions, drownings, onboard fires, or other accidents at sea. The Coast Guard monitors VHF channel 16 at all times. By cell phone, call *CG. If for some reason you do not have a radio or cellular telephone on board, flag a passing boat and ask someone on it to radio for assistance.

SeaTow

Run aground? Out of fuel? Motor problems? Instead of calling the Coast Guard, call SeaTow, a nationally recognized boater assistance service that maintains facilities the length of the Keys. Convey the details of your problem and what you think you need. Don't just ask for a tow if you have run out of gas or need only a minor repair. Describe your problem; the difference in cost between having gas delivered to your stranded boat and a multi-hour tow back to land could be a lot of money. SeaTow also will provide free advice, such as projected weather changes or directions in unfamiliar territory.

SeaTow can be reached on VHF channel 16 at sea by calling "SeaTow, SeaTow." By telephone the offices are: (305) 451-3330 in Key Largo; (305) 664-4493 in Islamorada; (305) 289-2055 in Marathon; (305) 872-2752 in the Lower Keys; and (305) 295-9912 in Key West. Or, consult their website: www.seatow.com.

Vessel Regulations and Equipment

Vessels must be equipped with Coast Guard-approved equipment, which varies according to the boat's size, location, and use (see the Required Equipment section in this chapter). All vessels must either be documented or registered (see below), and the appropriate paperwork must be carried on board.

Federal, state, and local law enforcement officials may hail your boat so they can come aboard and inspect it. Among their reasons for imposing civil penalties: improper use of a marine radio and misuse of calling the distress channel VHF 16; boating under the influence (a blood alcohol level of .10 percent or higher); and negligence. Negligence includes boating in a swimming area, speeding in the vicinity of other boats or in dangerous waters, bow riding, and gunwaling. Boaters without the required Coast Guard-approved equipment on board or with problematic boats that are considered hazardous may be directed back to port.

Vessel Registration

Whether or not you are a resident of the Florida Keys, your vessel must be registered in the State of Florida within 30 days of your arrival if one of our islands is its primary location. Registration renewals require your old registration form and a valid Florida driver's license, if you have one; for registering new boats, bring your manufacturer's statement of origin, dealer's sales tax statement, and bill of sale. If you are registering a used boat you have just purchased, you will need a title signed over to you and a bill of sale, one of which must be notarized, and the previous owner's registration if available.

Boats must be registered annually; only cash is accepted as payment. Excluded from registration requirements are rowboats and dinghies with less than 10 hp motors that are used exclusively as dinghies. All other boats may be registered any weekday between 8:30 A.M. and 4:30 P.M. at one of the following facilities:

Plantation Key Government Center, MM 88.7 Bayside, Plantation Key, (305) 852-7150. Head bayside on High Point Road and turn left into the Government Center parking lot. Boat registration is handled in the tax collector's office in the annex building.

Monroe County Tax Collector's Office, MM 47 Oceanside, Marathon, (305) 743-5585. The office is on the Overseas

Highway just past the Monroe County Sheriff's Department.

Harvey Government Center at Historic Truman School, 1200 Truman Avenue, Key West, (305) 294–8403. Follow the Overseas Highway until it becomes Truman Avenue. Proceed south on Truman until it intersects with White Street. The Harvey Government Center is on the corner of Truman and White. Head for the tax collector's office.

Required Equipment

The U.S. Coast Guard requires that vessels using gasoline for any reason be equipped with a ventilation system in proper working condition. With the exception of outboard motors, gasoline engines must also be equipped with a means of backfire flame control. In addition, Coast Guard-approved fire extinguishers are required for boats with inboard engines, closed or under-seat compartments with portable fuel tanks, and other characteristics. There are additional requirements for vessels of more than 39 feet and boats used for races, parades, and other specific purposes.

Personal flotation devices, night distress signals and navigation lights are other required equipment. Contact the U.S. Coast Guard at (305) 743–6778 or (305) 664–8078 for specific requirements for your size and style of boat.

Recommended Equipment

Regardless of your boat's size, location, and use, the U.S. Coast Guard recommends that you have the following equipment on board: VHF radio, visual distress signals, anchor and spare anchor, heaving line, fenders, first-aid kit, flashlight, mirror, searchlight, sunscreen and sunburn lotion, tool kit, ring buoy, whistle or horn, fuel tanks and spare fuel, chart and compass, boat hook, spare propeller, mooring line, food and water, binoculars, spare batteries, sunglasses (polarized to see water color variations better), marine hardware, extra clothing, spare parts, paddles, and a pump or bailer.

The Florida Keys National Marine Sanctuary Regulations

The Florida Keys fall within the boundaries of the Florida Keys National Marine Sanctuary, created by the federal government in 1990 to protect the resources of our marine ecosystem. And while, for the most part, visitors freely can swim, dive, snorkel, boat, fish, or recreate on our waters, there are some regulations, as of July 1997, to guide these activities. For a complete copy of the regulations and marine coordinates of the areas, contact the Sanctuary office (305–743–2437) or log onto their website: www.fknms.nos.noaa.gov.

Sanctuary-Wide Regulations

These mandates focus on habitat protection, striving to reduce threats to water quality and minimize human impact of delicate resources. The following are prohibited in our waters:

Removing, injuring, or possessing coral or live rock.

Discharging or depositing trash or other pollutants.

Dredging, drilling, prop dredging, altering, or abandoning any structure on the seabed.

Operating a vessel in such a manner as to strike or injure coral, seagrass, or organisms attached to the seabed.

Anchoring a vessel on living coral in water less than 40 feet deep when you can see the bottom. Anchoring on hardbottom surfaces is allowed.

Operating a vessel at more than idle speed within 100 yards of residential shorelines, stationary vessels, and navigational aids marking reefs.

Operating a vessel at more than idle speed within 100 feet of a diver-down flag.

Diving or snorkeling without a dive flag.

Operating a vessel in such a manner as to endanger life, limb, marine resources, or property.

Renting a houseboat enables you to explore our backcountry waters. PHOTO: SUZANNE TOBEY

Releasing exotic species.

Damaging or removing markers, mooring buoys, scientific equipment, boundary buoys, and trap buoys.

Moving, removing, injuring, or possessing historical resources.

Taking or possessing protected wildlife.

Using or possessing explosives or electrical charges.

Collecting marine life species—tropical fish, invertebrates, and plants—except as allowed by Florida Marine Life Rule (46-42 F.A.C.).

Marine Zoning Restrictions

The Sanctuary's 1997 marine zoning regulations focus protection on portions of sensitive habitats, while allowing public access in others. Only about 2 percent of the Sanctuary's waters fall into the five zoning categories. All sanctuary-wide regulations apply in the special zones as well as a number of additional rules and restrictions.

Western Sambos Ecological Reserve (ER)

All fishing activities, spearfishing, shell collecting, tropical fish collecting, lobstering, and other activities that result in the harvest of marine life by divers and snorkelers are prohibited. Direct physical contact with corals and anchoring on living or dead coral are also prohibited. Round yellow buoys mark the area.

Sanctuary Preservation Areas (SPA)

Eighteen small SPA zones protect popular shallow coral reefs. Spearfishing, shell collecting, tropical fish collecting, fishing, and other activities that result in the harvest of marine life by divers, snorkelers, and anglers are prohibited. Direct physical contact with corals and anchoring on living or dead coral is also prohibited. The 18 SPAs are located in portions of Alligator Reef, Carysfort/South Carysfort Reef, Cheeca Rocks, Coffins Patch, Conch Reef, Davis Reef, Dry Rocks, Grecian Rocks, Eastern Dry Rocks, Rock Key, Sand Key,

French Reef, Hen and Chickens, Looe Key, Molasses Reef, Newfound Harbor Key, Sombrero Key, and The Elbow.

Round yellow buoys mark the areas of restricted access.

Wildlife Management Areas (WMA)

The 27 Wildlife Management Areas are posted with one of the following restrictions: idle speed only/no wake, no motor, a buffer of no access, or limited closures. The WMAs include portions of Bay Keys, Boca Grande Key, Woman Key, Cayo Agua Keys, Cotton Key, Snake Creek, Cottrell Key, Little Mullet Key, Big Mullet Key, Crocodile Lake, East Harbor Key, Lower Harbor Keys, Eastern Lake Surprise, Horseshoe Key, Rodriguez Key, Dove Key, Tavernier Key, Marquesas Keys, Mud Keys, Pelican Shoal, Sawyer Keys, Snipe Keys, Tidal Flat South of Marvin Key, Upper Harbor Key, East Content Keys, West Content Keys, and Little Crane Key.

Existing Management Areas (EMA)

Sanctuary regulations complement those of existing management areas: Looe Key and Key Largo Management Areas; Great White Heron and Key West National Wildlife Refuges; and all the state parks and aquatic preserves. Operating a personal watercraft, airboat, or water skiing is prohibited in these waters.

Special Use Areas

Four areas are designated "research only" sites and may be accessed only by specifically authorized personnel with valid permits. They are closed to the general public. The areas are in the vicinity of Conch Reef, Tennessee Reef, Looe Key (patch reef), and Eastern Sambos Reef. Round yellow buoys mark the areas.

Public Boat Ramps

If you trailer your boat to the Florida Keys, you can launch it at any number of public ramps. Here is a list of boat launching sites maintained year round for your use. Parking is limited except at park sites.

Insiders' Tip

Before venturing into the Great White Heron National Wildlife Refuge, secure a Public Use Regulations Map from the Lower Keys Chamber of Commerce, MM 31 Oceanside, Big Pine Key, (305) 872-2411. Obey no-entry, no-motor, and idle-speed zones.

Upper Keys

MM 110 Bayside
Key Largo, FL

MM 92.5 Oceanside
Harry Harris County Park
Key Largo, FL
On weekends and holidays, nonresidents must pay a $5 admission fee to the park as well as $10 to launch a boat; parking is abundant.

MM 79 Bayside
Islamorada, FL

MM 71 Bayside
Islamorada, FL

Middle Keys

MM 54 Bayside
Marathon, FL

MM 48 Bayside
33rd Street
Marathon, FL

Lower Keys

MM 37 Oceanside
Bahia Honda State Recreation Area
A $5 admission fee to the park is required; parking is abundant.

MM 33 Bayside
Spanish Harbor Key

MM 27.5 Bayside
Little Torch Key

MM 22 Oceanside
Cudjoe Key

MM 10 Oceanside
Big Coppitt Key

Key West
MM 5
Stock Island

End of Rte. A1A on Smathers Beach

Marine Supply Stores

Marine supplies and NOAA charts recommended by the U.S. Coast Guard may be purchased at the following facilities.

Upper Keys

Boater's World Discount Marine Center
MM 105 Bayside
Key Largo, FL
(305) 451–0025

MM 50 Oceanside
3022 N. Roosevelt Boulevard
Marathon, FL
(305) 743–7707

Key Plaza
Key West, FL
(305) 295–9232
www.boatersworld.com

Boater's World carries a variety of items, including: marine paints, fenders, fishing and tackle supplies, hardware, electrical supplies, clothing, and shoes at discount prices.

Estes Watersports and Marina
MM 83.9 Bayside
Islamorada, FL
(305) 664–4745

For an outboard engine or a small boat, Estes stocks a complete selection of necessary parts and electrical supplies. In addition, Estes maintains a complete bait and

tackle shop for your fishing needs.

Middle Keys

Tugboats
MM 48.5 Oceanside
Marathon, FL
(305) 743–4585

Tugboats offers a comprehensive selection of marine supplies including electric, plumbing, and maintenance needs. Items such as pumps, steering wheels, paint, chairs, and rope are also available.

West Marine
MM 103.4 Bayside
Key Largo, FL
(305) 453–9050

MM 48.5 Oceanside
Marathon, FL
(305) 289–1009

725 Caroline Street
Key West, FL
(305) 295–0999
www.westmarine.com

West Marine is an expansive store that carries a variety of supplies for sailboats and powerboats. Hardware and electric, safety, plumbing, and maintenance needs can be met at West Marine.

Lower Keys

Keys Sea Center
MM 29.5 Oceanside
Big Pine Key, FL
(305) 872–2243, (877) 267–1088
www.keysseacenter.com

Keys Sea Center offers boat sales, services and supplies, including hardware, electric and maintenance needs.

Key West

Key West Marine Hardware Inc.
818 Caroline Street
Key West, FL
(305) 294–3425, (305) 294–3519

This is the place to go for every cleat, bolt, snap, or thingamajig your powerboat or sailboat requires, because Key West Marine Hardware has it all. You'll find the complete set of official NOAA nautical charts to the Keys and Caribbean waters along with cruising, fishing, and sailing publications of every description. The stock of fishing tackle is limited, but you really can dress your boat in style with all the add-on amenities offered here. You can also dress yourself. Key West Marine carries a large selection of stylish boating togs.

Boat Sales, Repairs, Fuel, and Storage

Facilities throughout the Florida Keys carry a wide variety of new and used boats. For boat owners, most of these sales centers provide all the necessary services, including local hauling, repairs, bottom painting, and fuel.

Upper Keys

Travis Boating Center
MM 106.2 Bayside
Key Largo, FL
(305) 451–3398
www.travisboatingcenter.com

Travis Boating Center carries Logic, Larson, Fishmaster, Evinrude, Johnson, and Mercury brands. The store offers a full-service repair department as well as mobile service. Travis Boating Center does not sell fuel but offers an in-water service area.

Plantation Key Boat Mart
MM 90, Bayside
Tavernier, FL
(305) 852–5424, (800) 539–2628
www.plantationboat.com

Plantation Key Boat Mart sells Mako, Silver King, and Hydrasport brand boats and is a Hurricane dealer. You will also be

able to buy Johnson and Evinrude engines here. Plantation Key Boat Mart maintains a full-service repair department.

Estes Watersports and Marina
MM 83.9 Bayside
Tavernier, FL
(305) 664–4745

Estes is the place to turn for repair service on all makes and models of outboard motors. Rack storage for boats of up to 22 feet in length is available, as well as a number of wet slips. You'll find a selection of used boats here. The facility offers 93 octane fuel.

Caribee Boat Sales
MM 90.3 Bayside
Tavernier, FL
(305) 852–2724

MM 81.5 Bayside
Islamorada, FL
(305) 664–3431
www.caribeeboats.com

Offshore anglers shop at Caribee for Grady Whites, Pursuits, and Contenders 20 to 36 feet in length. For fishing the backcountry, the facility carries 16- to 21-foot Hewes, Pathfinder, and Maverick

Insiders' Tip

BUI stands for "boating under the influence." In the state of Florida, BUI penalties include fines of up to $2,500, imprisonment of up to one year, non-paid public service work, and mandatory substance abuse counseling. If a drunken operator causes serious bodily injury or kills another person, the penalties increase.

boats as well as Boston Whalers. Indoor and outdoor storage is available, and certified mechanics are on duty seven days a week. Bottom painting and boat hauling are provided; Caribee carries 89 octane fuel and sells live bait, frozen bait, and ice. Mobile service is available.

Max's Marine & Boat Yard
MM 80.5 Bayside
Islamorada, FL
(305) 664–8884

An authorized dealer of Mercury Marine products, Max's carries Mariners and MerCruisers. This full-service boatyard and marina accommodates boats of up to 40 tons. Hauling and bottom painting is available, along with indoor and outdoor storage. Max's carries 93 octane fuel.

Middle Keys

The Boat House
MM 53.5 Oceanside
Marathon, FL
(305) 289–1323
www.theboathousefl.com

The Boat House offers full sales and service support for Yamaha and Johnson outboard engines as well as Parker, Ranger, and Century boats. It provides dry storage, inside and out, for vessels to a maximum of 33 feet.

Quality Yacht Service
MM 52 Bayside
10701 Fifth Avenue
Marathon, FL
(305) 743–2898

Quality Yacht Service offers marine fuel cleaning and tank cleaning for both diesel and gasoline engines. It provides mobile service.

Inflatable Boats of the Florida Keys
MM 48.5 Oceanside
Marathon, FL
(305) 743–7085, (888) 207–0011
www.keysinflatables.com

Buy, sell, or repair your inflatable boat here, for Inflatable Boats can take care of

your needs. The establishment offers Achilles, Caribe, Avon, and Hudson Bay as well as Tohatsu outboards and pre-owned boats. The shop also stocks parts, supplies, and accessories. You'll find life rafts here too.

Keys Boat Works Inc.
MM 48.5 Bayside
700 39th Street
Marathon, FL
(305) 743–5583

Keys Boat Works provides a comprehensive range of services for boats up to 67 feet in length and maintains 15-ton and 50-ton travel lifts. This full-service yard offers fiberglass work, carpentry, and Awlgrip topside painting. The six on-premises tenants contribute to the one-stop shopping for boat service: diesel mechanics, an electronics specialist, a yacht refinisher, sign painter, and fiberglasser. Keys Boat Works can store vessels up to 60 feet, either in or out of the water. The facility has a capacity for 180 boats.

Marathon Marina
MM 47.5 Oceanside
Marathon, FL
(305) 743–6575

This full-service boatyard offers the option of transient dockage at one of its 80 slips (dockage up to 110-feet length, 11-foot draft). You'll find fresh water, laundry, showers, bathroom facilities, and both 30- and 50-amp power. A ship's store is on the premises. The yard maintains a 50-ton travel lift and dry storage for up to

> ## Insiders' Tip
> Watchword for Keys boaters: "Steer clear of a standing bird with dry tail feathers." This water will be extremely shallow and you will run aground.

If you fancy yourself more Robinson Crusoe than Aristotle Onassis, try anchoring out. PHOTO: MARY MOCCIA

130 boats with 24-hour security. The Marathon Marina offers boat cleaning and detailing, preventive maintenance, bottom sanding and painting, wood work, plumbing and electrical services, fiberglass and epoxy work, and mechanics' services. The first marina on the Boot Key Channel (Marker No. 9), Marathon Marina maintains an easily accessible fuel dock. To reach the marina/boatyard, turn at 11th Street Oceanside.

Turn Key Marine
MM 47.5 Bayside
Marathon, FL
(305) 743-2502

Turn Key Marine is a sales and service dealer for Yamaha and Mercury outboard engines, Cobia, Action Craft boats, and Glacier Bay catamarans. A 12-ton boat lift facilitates vessel storage, both inside and outside. Bottom painting is also available here.

Lower Keys

Skeeter's Marine
MM 30.5 Bayside

Big Pine Key, FL
(305) 872-9040, (800) 771-2628
www.skeetersmarine.com

Skeeter's sells new boats manufactured by Angler, Stamas, Shamrock, Rampage, Hewes, and Talon Flats Boats. Full engine services are available here as well as mobile marine service to your boat. Skeeter's is a dealer for Mercury, Suzuki, Yamaha, and Yanmer engines. Hauling, dry storage, and bottom painting are also available.

Keys Sea Center
MM 29.5 Oceanside
Big Pine Key, FL
(305) 872-2243, (877) 267-1088
www.keysseacenter.com

Keys Sea Center carries new ProLines and Sea Pro/Citation and services Johnson, Evinrude, Mercury, OMC, and Force engines. Bottom painting and limited boat hauling are available. The facility carries 93 octane fuel and maintains a complete marine store with parts and accessories.

Tropical Marine Center Inc.
MM 19.5 Bayside
Crane Boulevard
Sugarloaf Key, FL
(305) 745–3663

Among the new boats available at Tropical Marine are Crest pontoons and Key Largo and McKee Craft boats. The facility also carries a varied selection of used vessels. A Johnson and Evinrude outboard engine dealer, Tropical Marine has a full-service department.

Key West

Andrew's Propeller Service
5600 3rd Avenue
Stock Island, FL
(305) 296–8887

Need a propeller for your boat? Come to Andrew's to find a large selection of new and rebuilt aluminum and bronze propellers—up to 64 inches in diameter. Andrew's also specializes in expert propeller repairs and shaft straightening.

Garrison Bight Marina
Garrison Bight Causeway
711 Eisenhower Drive
Key West, FL
(305) 294–3093
www.realpages.com/garrisonbight

This full-service marina offers both long- and short-term dry or in-water storage. Unleaded fuel may be purchased here, too; prices fluctuate according to the market. Garrison Bight Marina also rents powerboats (15 to 22 feet) by the hour, half-day, full day, or full week.

Island Propeller Service
5638 Third Avenue
Stock Island, FL
(305) 292–1846

You won't even need to take your boat out of the water to have its propeller fixed here. In addition to selling new and rebuilt equipment, the folks at Island Propeller can remove and replace your boat's propeller in or out of the water.

> ## Insiders' Tip
> All recreational boats with installed toilet facilities are required to have an operable Coast Guard-certified marine sanitation device on board.

Murray Marine
MM 5
Stock Island, FL
(305) 296–0364, Service (305) 296–9555

Stop here to buy a boat, dock it, fuel it, fix it, store it, buy stuff for it, and put it in the water. Offering a full-service marina, storage, fuel, a service department, engine sales, boat sales, a ramp, and a convenience store, Murray Marine defies easy categorization. This facility is an authorized dealer for Wellcraft, Bayliner, Robalo, and Action Craft skiffs, as well as being a Johnson and Mercury Outboards dealer.

Oceanside Marina
5950 Peninsula Avenue
Stock Island, FL
(305) 294–4676
www.oceansidemarina.com

Oceanside Marina is a kind of one-stop storage and service facility for boaters. Outside dry storage and inside storage is available. Oceanside sells fuel and has a mechanic on staff, a fully stocked tackle shop, a pump-out facility, and bathhouse.

Peninsular Marine Enterprises
6000 Peninsula Avenue
Stock Island, FL
(305) 296–8110

This combination boatyard and storage facility caters primarily to sailboats and large powerboats (30 feet or longer). Long-term storage on land is offered, but water storage is not available. There is no fork or ramp.

Purchase the nautical chart you need (see the Aids to Navigation section in this chapter) and bring it with you to the boat rental facility of your choice. Most facilities will provide you with an operational briefing and a nautical chart review before you set off. Some of these facilities require that you remain within a specific locale at all times; others base this decision on weather conditions.

Sunset Marina
5555 College Road
Stock Island, FL
(305) 296–7101

Long-term boat storage in the water or at the storage dock is available here. Sunset Marina is also a full-service marina, offering sales, service, and boating equipment.

Willett Marine
5950 Peninsula Avenue
Stock Island, FL
(305) 293–0110

Specializing in Yamaha outboard motors since 1983, Willett Marine sells Yamahas ranging from two horsepower to 250. The establishment will service your motor as well as do warranty work.

Powerboat Rentals

The following rental facilities offer U.S. Coast Guard–approved, safety-equipped vessels complete with VHF marine radios. Rental boat sizes vary from 15 to 27 feet, in a number of configurations: center consoles, bowriders, cuddy cabins, and pontoon boats. The boats feature options such as compasses, depth finders, Bimini or "T" tops, dry storage, swim ladders, and dive platforms. You can rent a powerboat for either a half-day or full day. Prices vary by size and age of the vessel, but expect to pay between $70 and $190 for a half-day and $100 to $295 for a full day. Call the establishments to inquire about specific boats offered, their features, and prices. (Prices are usually quoted without tax or gasoline.)

Upper Keys

Club Nautico
MM 100 Oceanside
at the Marina del Mar
Key Largo, FL
(305) 451–4120, (800) 628–8426

245 Front Street
at the Hilton Resort & Marina
Key West, FL
(305) 294–2225, (800) 628–8426
www.boatrent.com

Club Nautico rents 20- to 22-foot powerboats. Club Nautico members pay a lower rental fee. Club Nautico provides charts and local knowledge of the waters and suggests water-accessible-only sites to visit. Captains must have a minimum of two years of boating experience and complete a brief questionnaire of general information about boating. Boat use is resricted in shallow waters and mud flats, and boats must remain within a 15-mile radius of shore.

Estes Watersports and Marina
MM 83.9 Bayside
Islamorada, FL
(305) 664–4745

Estes rents 15- to 22-foot boats in several styles, including pontoon boats.

Robbie's Boat Rentals & Charters
MM 77.5 Bayside
Islamorada, FL
(305) 664–9814, (877) 853–0222
www.robbies.com

One of the Florida Keys' more interesting boat rental facilities, Robbie's is behind

Our sunsets take center stage in the twilight hours. PHOTO: MARY MOCCIA

the Hungry Tarpon Restaurant. Visitors come to Robbie's just to feed the many tarpon that lurk close to shore (see our Kidstuff chapter). Boat rentals, too, are popular, since Robbie's is only a half-mile from historic Indian Key (see our Attractions chapter). Robbie's rents boats from 14 feet to 27 feet in length.

Caloosa Cove Boat Rental
MM 73.5 Oceanside
Islamorada, FL
(305) 664–4455

Caloosa Cove rents 16-foot and 18-foot powerboats.

Middle Keys

Bud Boats Inc.
MM 48.5 Bayside
at the Buccaneer Resort
Marathon, FL
(305) 743–6316, (305) 743–5221,
(800) 633–2283

MM 31 Bayside, at Old Wooden Bridge
Fish Camp, Big Pine Key, FL
(305) 872–9165, (800) 633–2283
www.budboats.com

Bud Boats Inc. rents 17- to 25-foot powerboats.

Lower Keys

Dolphin Resort & Marina
MM 28.5 Oceanside
Little Torch Key, FL
(305) 872–2685, (800) 553–0308
www.dolphinresort.com

Dolphin Marina rents Angler powerboats that range in size from 18 to 22 feet. Built-in coolers are standard equipment. Boaters are given free nautical charts, and marina staff members review the charts and explain where you may and may not go. Weekly discounts and seasonal specials are available, so be sure to inquire when you reserve your vessel.

Cudjoe Gardens Marina
MM 21 Oceanside
Cudjoe Key, FL
(305) 745–2357, (877) 886–6621
www.cudjoegardensmarina.com

Cudjoe Gardens offers rental of 17- and 21-foot powerboats as well as 24-foot pontoon boats. Multiple-day rentals are discounted.

Key West

Key West Boat Rentals
617 Front Street, Key West, FL
(305) 294–2628, (800) 537–5068

You can rent Wahoos and Wellcrafts of 20- to 26-feet, and all recreational boats have Bimini tops. One 20-foot and two 17-foot Jet boats are also available for rent. Navigational charts are provided and reviewed, along with an overview of local waters and suggestions (based on weather conditions) of directions to take and places to see. A questionnaire and verbal review ensure that boaters are experienced.

Land's End Boat Rentals
At the foot of Caroline and Margaret Streets
Key West, FL
(305) 294–6447

Choose from rental boats of varying lengths and styles here. The options include a 23-foot Aquasport, two 20-foot Wellcrafts (one has a cabin, the other is open), a 17-foot Mako, and a 15-foot Jet boat. Land's End also has two sailboats available for rent: a 26-foot Pearson and a 25-foot Hunter. Guides are available for an additional charge, and sailing lessons are offered. The folks here are eager to make your day on the water a special one, so ask about customizing options.

Sailing

With an abundance of protected anchorages, harbors, and marinas and warm tropical waters, the Florida Keys are often described by sailors as the "American Caribbean." Our offshore barrier reef provides protection from swells. Our bayside is so sheltered that many skippers with low-draft boats (typically catamarans or small, monohull sailboats) can trim up their sails and guide their crafts through the Intracoastal Waterway. Catamarans and monohulls with drafts of 4 or 5 feet fare best along the sometimes shallow Intracoastal; monohulls with 6-foot drafts have difficulty getting out of bayside marinas. These boats may also run aground here. Most oceanside marinas and harbors typically run deep enough to accommodate virtually any type of sailboat. (See our Cruising chapter.)

Within the Florida Keys, local sailing clubs organize their own informal races. Sailing in the Florida Keys can include cruising, limited bareboat charters, and a combination of snorkeling, fishing, diving, or gunk-holing. Many head out simply to enjoy the sail. In order to sail the diverse waters of the Florida Keys, however, boaters must know a rig from a right-of-way.

Sailing Courses

Several facilities throughout our islands offer sailing courses for beginner through advanced levels, along with bareboat certification, and brush-up sessions. Prices vary greatly depending upon the duration and complexity of the courses and the number of people participating. Be sure to ask about all your options when you call to book your instruction.

International Sailing Center
MM 104.3 Bayside
Rick's Place
Key Largo, FL
(305) 451–3287

From basic sailing instruction through advanced race training, International Sailing Center shares their many years of expertise with Keys sailors and visitors from all over the country. Instruction commences on small monohulls and cata-

Insiders' Tip

Personal watercraft operators should refer to Marine Zoning Restrictions in the Florida Keys Marine Sanctuary section of this chapter.

Learn to sail at one of the Keys' sailing schools, or take a catamaran cruise to catch the last sunset rays.

PHOTO: VIVIENNE AFSHARI

marans. International Sailing Center is affiliated with the American Sailing Association and the U.S. Sailing Association. The center offers a full-day course for one to two people with boat and instructor or a 2½-day certification course, which includes instructional material, boat, instructor, and certification.

Offshore Sailing School
MM 61 Oceanside
Hawk's Cay Resort
Duck Key, FL

(305) 743–7000, (800) 221–4326
www.offshore-sailing.com

Earn your United States sailing certification aboard a Colgate-26 with a Learn to Sail course from Offshore Sailing School. The Offshore Sailing School, which has nine locations across the United States, is operated by Olympic and America's Cup sailor, Steve Colgate, and his wife, Doris. Colgate designed the vessel upon which you will learn to sail. (In 1999, this vessel design was chosen as the official U.S. Naval Academy training boat.)

No-wake zones are common throughout channels, harbors and marinas, and throughout protected waters of the Florida Keys.

Learn to Sail courses are offered at Hawk's Cay Resort and feature two options. The weekend course runs from Friday through Sunday. The weeklong course runs from Monday through Saturday. You'll have classroom instruction in the mornings and practice your skills on the water in the afternoons. The Learn to Sail course is the prelude to any advanced sailing courses.

Offshore Sailing School also offers a Liveaboard Cruise, where you can earn your cruising certification. Here, aboard a 48-foot Hunter with four private cabins, four students go on a six-day cruise to Key West and back, anchoring each night. You'll have drills and instruction daily, receiving hands-on experience in engine mechanics, advanced anchoring techniques, docking, meal preparation, going aground, radio skills, weather safety procedures, navigation, dinghy safety, and yacht handling. Your week of intensive learning culminates when you drop off your instructor and head out on your own for a 24-hour mini cruise. The Liveaboard program runs from Sunday through Saturday. The cost includes hotel accommodations at Hawk's Cay Resort for one night, the week's instruction, and all meals and beverages except two dinners (no alcoholic beverages provided). You must have basic sailing experience to participate.

If you haven't sailed before and want to do the Liveaboard Cruise you can sign up for the Fast Track to Cruising class. This 10-day experience includes a three-day Learn to Sail course, immediately followed by the Liveaboard experience. Fast Track runs from Friday through the following Saturday. Offshore Sailing School also offers a three-hour introduction to sailing course on the Colgate-26.

Banana Bay Sailing School
Banana Bay Resort
MM 49.5 Bayside
Marathon, FL
(305) 289-1433, (800) 484-8535, Ext. 1433
Banana Bay Sailing School offers a potpourri of options for sailing enthusiasts. Utilizing the azure waters of the Gulf of Mexico, the pros at Banana Bay will take you to sea aboard either 14½-foot day sailers or a 38-foot ketch. Sailing courses are offered for half days or full days. Packages, which include lodging at Banana Bay Resort, also are offered.

Both the basic courses (aboard a day sailer) and the bareboat courses (aboard the ketch) include classroom instruction and supervised hands-on sailing. The courses cover a range of topics: fundamentals of sailing, terminology, chart reading, sail theory, sail trim, points of sail, rules of the road, safety, seamanship, and knots. Half-day, brush-up courses and novice instruction are also available.

Southernmost Sailing
Oceanside Marina
5950 Maloney Avenue
Stock Island, FL
(305) 293-1883
www.keywest.com/sail

If you are interested in learning to sail, or if you would like a refresher course prior to chartering, Southernmost has instructors qualified to teach boaters of all sailing skill levels. Informal classes are customized to the student's needs and desires, from basic seamanship skills, such as knot-tying and navigation, to higher levels of sailing, such as learning to use a spinnaker. Brush-up skills may take anywhere from one to three days on the water to achieve, whereas those who know virtually nothing about the sport would be best served by a five-day program that includes three hours of formal schooling at the dock and four to five hours of sailing per day. Instructors recommend learning on the J-24, but all nonchartered boats are available. Prices are based on charter costs, and instructor fees are an additional cost. Reservations are recommended.

Bareboat Charters

If you already know how to sail or you prefer to explore our waters on your own, the Florida Keys also offers captained and bareboat charters for anywhere from two hours to several weeks. Prices vary depending upon the size of the vessel and the length of the bareboat excursion.

Treasure Harbor Marine Inc.
MM 86.5 Oceanside
Islamorada, FL
(305) 852–2458, (800) 352–2628
www.treasureharbor.com

Treasure Harbor maintains a fleet of 12 sloops and ketch rigs ranging in size from 19 to 47 feet by Cape Dory, Watkins, Hunter, and Morgan. Skilled sailors can charter any one of these boats on their own, and written and verbal "exams" will test your sailing experience. Professional captains will provide nautical charts, overviews of Florida Keys waters and suggestions of places to visit from John Pennekamp and the Everglades to Key West and the Bahamas. Skippers are available. A two-day minimum is required for all boats greater than 25 feet in length. Security deposits are required. Power trawler yachts are also available.

Treasure Harbor Marine also offers charters on an Antigua 37 catamaran or a 47-foot Marine Trader, which must be rented with an accompanying captain. Advance reservations for all vessels are suggested.

Southernmost Sailing
Oceanside Marina
5950 Maloney Avenue
Stock Island, FL
(305) 293–1883
www.keywest.com/sail

Southernmost Sailing maintains a fleet of 12 charter catamarans and monohull sailboats, including two Hunters, Ticon, Jeanneau, Corsair, Gemini, PDQ, Tobago, Beneteau, Morgan Out Island, and two J-24s. They range in size from 24 to 42 feet. Qualified sailing captains are permitted to sail virtually anywhere except Cuba, including Shark River, Florida's West Coast, the Marquesas, and the Dry Tortugas. A charter-boat captain is available at an additional cost.

If boats are not out on a multi-day charter, customers may rent them for a per diem cost or charter them with captain for the additional fee. All boats are equipped for cruising and have auxiliary engines that reduce fuel consumption.

Reservations are recommended. In the off-season, you probably won't have any trouble securing a boat as little as one week out. However, for high-season sailing, make your reservations at least three to six months in advance.

Sailing Clubs and Regattas

Avid sailors throughout our islands have formed sailing clubs, which sponsor casual regattas. These are not your upscale yacht clubs, but membership does have its privileges—discounted race entry fees and dinners, and the opportunity to meet enthusiastic individuals who share your interests.

Upper Keys Sailing Club
MM 100 Bayside
100 Ocean Bay Drive
Key Largo, FL
(305) 451–9972

Established in 1973, the Upper Keys Sailing Club is based in a club-owned house on the bay and is comprised of Upper Keys residents of all ages. Races on Buttonwood Bay are held on a regular basis. Spectators watch from clubhouse grounds. Two offshore races take place over a two-week period.

As a community service, members provide free two-day sailing seminars four times a year. Seminars combine two hours of classroom instruction with extensive time on the water aboard the club's 19-foot Flying Scots. Boaters with Sunfish and Hobie Cats are welcome. Membership requires a onetime initiation fee and annual dues.

Marathon Sailing Club
(305) 743-0448

The Marathon Sailing Club, a young, informal group, meets the second Wednesday of each month. Typically the club holds monthly regattas on courses around Marathon. The club's three major regattas each year attract sailors from all over the Keys: Marathon to Key West; a two-day Sombrero Cup race; and the bay-to-ocean race, a course running bayside from Marathon to Channel Five and then back oceanside. A Lady Skipper's trophy puts only women at the helm. Membership requires annual dues. Call Ridge Gardner for meeting locations and more information.

Key West Sailing Club
Garrison Bight Bridge
700 Palm Avenue
Garrison Bight Causeway
Key West, FL
(305) 292-5993

Key West Sailing Club is a private organization open to anyone for membership. The club itself is located at the base of the Garrison Bight Bridge. The club has 10 Sunfish boats and a 16-foot Hobie Cat. In addition, a sizeable fleet of privately owned JY15s is available for members to use on race days. The club sponsors monthly offshore races for boats 20 feet and larger; call for more information. During daylight-saving time, small boat (20 feet or less) races are held every Wednesday evening at 6 P.M. Group and private instruction is available for both adults and juniors (under 18). Dates and times of courses change seasonally; call for details.

Membership requires a onetime initiation fee and annual dues. The member-

Insiders' Tip

Pollution is against the law. The Federal Water Pollution Control Act prohibits the discharge of oil or hazardous substances that may be harmful to U.S. waters.

ship year begins in January, but dues are prorated so anyone who joins later doesn't pay for a full year. A membership entitles members to use club facilities seven days a week between 6 A.M. and midnight. Membership also grants possible dockage in a wet or dry slip; rates are based on boat length. Information on courses, boat races, and membership is available on the Club's information line listed above.

Sailmakers

Sail lofts throughout our islands will repair or replace your tattered sails; some even have on-staff riggers. You can satisfy your hardware and electrical needs as well.

Upper Keys
Calvert Sails
MM 81.5 Oceanside
200 Industrial Drive
Islamorada, FL
(305) 664-8056
www.calvertsails.com

You can count on Calvert Sails for fast repairs for any size sailboat. Calvert offers sails for performance boats and cruisers and specializes in multihull boats. Custom hardware supplies and services also are provided. The decades-old business, which began as a small, two-man operation of hand-designing and sewing sails, has since evolved into a state-of-the-art business that uses computers in design and manufacture.

Middle Keys

Abaco Sails
MM 53 Oceanside
Marathon, FL
(305) 743–0337

As long as your boat has a mast, Abaco can accommodate it. Sails here are made to order. A rigger on premises handles all wiring needs, and the facility carries mast and used boat hardware.

Quantum Florida Keys
MM 47.5 Oceanside
1025 11th Street at Marathon Marina
Marathon, FL
(305) 289–4388
www.quantumsails.com

A worldwide franchise with 33 locations, Quantum Florida Keys offers Grand Prix racing sails and Performance cruising sails, as well as sail repair. The business also performs complete canvas and cushion work and rigging.

Key West

Geslin Sailmakers
201 William Street
The Loft
Key West, FL
(305) 294–5854

Although primarily occupied with repairs on boat sails, awnings, and Biminis, this business will also repair "anything you can think of that has to do with boats and needles and thread." You can order a new sail here, and although the sail will be made outside the country (because it's cheaper), the measurements, weight, and material requests will be taken here. Geslin Sailmakers is located at Key West Seaport.

Meloy Sails
6000 Peninsula Avenue
Stock Island, FL
(305) 296–4351

Offering full-service work on sails and marine canvas, Meloy Sails will repair damaged sails or make new ones according to your specifications. Meloy is a UK sailmakers affiliate.

Royal Canvas Connection
5950 Peninsula Avenue
Stock Island, FL
(305) 295–0944

Opened as a two-man operation in 1996, Royal Canvas Connections now employs a half-dozen workers in its 2000-square-foot loft at Oceanside Marina and has a fully equipped mobile van that services the Lower Keys. Royal Canvas specializes in custom boat canvas, cushions, upholstery, and sail repairs. The folks here also design stainless steel and aluminum framework for Bimini tops, dodgers, and spray hoods, and have even been known to stitch up a tent or two for Renaissance festivals and awnings for homes and businesses. If it's anything to do with canvas, they'll make it.

Southard Sails and Awnings
326 Southard Street
Key West, FL
(305) 294–4492, (877) 294–4492

In addition to custom sails and all types of fabric awnings, hurricane shutters may also be purchased here. Hopefully you'll never need them.

Houseboat Rentals

Florida Keys houseboats provide all the comforts of home combined with a camplike experience. Whether you seek a weekend excursion or a gently rocking place to spend your vacation, these rentals may very well float your boat.

Insiders' Tip

If you see a red-and-white diver-down flag displayed while you are boating, stay at least 100 feet away. Divers or snorkelers are in these waters.

A flatsboat nearly flies across the skinny waters of the flats, home to bonefish, redfish, and other coveted creatures. PHOTO: MARY MOCCIA

**Houseboat Vacations of the
Florida Keys
MM 85.9 Bayside
Islamorada, FL
(305) 664–4009**

Houseboat Vacations of the Florida Keys offers six live-aboard vessels that range from a 40-foot-long craft that sleeps four adults to a 44-foot-long houseboat that accommodates eight. You must have some boating experience to rent one of these floating homes. Boaters must venture no further than 8 miles offshore along 25 miles of surrounding coastline in Florida Bay. You may not take the houseboats into the ocean. Each houseboat offers a full galley and air conditioning and features a gas grill on deck. There is a three-day minimum; weekly rentals are available. Call for current pricing.

Cruising

Put on that string bikini. Throw your necktie in the dumpster. And don't you dare bring your shoes. You are cruising the Florida Keys, and you must obey the dress code.

Regarded as America's out-islands by seasoned cruisers of motor and sailing yachts, the Florida Keys can justifiably boast about the sheltered harbors and easily navigated waters enveloping the serpentine stretch. Our waters are well marked; our charts, up to date; and the U.S. Coast Guard keeps channels dredged to the proper depth. The Atlantic's Hawk Channel runs along the ocean side of the Keys, protected by the only coral reef in the continental United States. The Intracoastal Waterway—called the Big Ditch in the North's inland waters—cuts through the causeway from the mainland at Jewfish Creek and then parallels the Keys through Florida Bay and the Gulf of Mexico. Keys' waters are most accessible to boats with drafts of up to $4\frac{1}{2}$ feet, but you can cruise the Keys with $5\frac{1}{2}$- to 6-foot drafts if you're careful.

If you covet first-class creature comforts, put into one of our comprehensive marinas and enjoy the perks of staying at a luxury resort. Do you relish seclusion? Anchor out on the leeward side of a remote uninhabited key. Or, take the best of both worlds and plan a combination of the two.

To help you plan your Keys cruising adventure, we guide you on a tour of our pre-eminent marinas and little-known anchoring-out destinations (in descending order from the Upper to Lower Keys). Be sure to read our Key West and Beyond section, where the junket continues.

The Florida Keys

Marinas

All marinas listed in this chapter take transient boaters, but we suggest you make reservations at least a month in advance during the popular winter season from December through March. Transient rates range between $1.75 and $3 per foot per day in high season and most marinas assign minimums. We will note any facilities whose charges are out of this range, such as the exclusive Little Palm Island. You may assume unless otherwise stated that all our recommended marinas supply hookups for both 30-amp and 50-amp service as well as fresh water. You'll find that provisioning is easy along the 120-mile stretch of the Florida Keys. Most marinas have ship's stores or are within walking distance of a convenience market.

The occasional exception is noted.

The marinas keep an active list of expert marine mechanics who are generally on call to handle any repair needs that might develop during your cruise. We highlight fuel dock facilities and availability of laundry, showers, and restrooms. We also point out restaurants and the hot spots for partying while ashore.

There are no restrictions against bringing children and pets unless specifically noted. Keep your pet on your vessel or on a leash at all times.

If you are a member of a private yacht club that belongs to the Florida Council of Yacht Clubs, the Marathon Yacht Club will reciprocally welcome you and your transient vessel. Contact the Marathon Yacht Club (305-743-6739) about availability of slips.

Dockmasters monitor VHF channel 16, but they will ask you to switch channels once you've established contact. So

Insiders' Tip

The Jewfish Creek drawbridge (11-foot clearance when closed) marks the point where the causeway of the 18-mile stretch from Florida City makes landfall on Key Largo. When traveling the Intracoastal Waterway be aware that the bridge opens only on the hour and on the half-hour Thursday through Sunday and on federal holidays. During the week you may seek passage on demand. A 1- to 2-knot current courses through Jewfish Creek. Note the direction to allow plenty of time if you have to wait for the bridge to open. Sailors take note: A mast taller than 80 feet will not be able to pass beneath cables near the bridge.

which lies within the underwater boundaries of John Pennekamp Coral Reef State Park and the Key Largo National Marine Sanctuary. All but a select few are usually booked far in advance from January through March, so plan ahead. The slips will accommodate vessels with a 14-foot beam, but depth at the mouth of the channel drops drastically at low tide, to about $4\frac{1}{2}$ feet, so exercise caution. You'll find no ship's store, but a short walk to the Overseas Highway will satisfy provisioning requirements. Marina Del Mar does not have its own fuel dock, so fuel your craft at Key Largo Harbor Marina in the channel. Laundry, shower, and restroom facilities are provided on the premises. Marina rates do not include water and electricity; a minimum daily charge will be levied. Marina Del Mar Resort (see our Accommodations chapter) has tennis courts, a swimming pool, and a hot tub for your use. Gorge yourself at the hotel's continental breakfast for a nominal charge. And don't miss Coconuts, a popular restaurant and percolating nightspot.

Dockmaster's directions: Via Hawk Channel, from up the Keys, follow Hawk Channel south of Mosquito Banks. Put marker Red No. 2 on your starboard and take a 350-degree heading to Marina Del Mar Resort Channel (a strip of land will be on your starboard). From Key West, take Hawk Channel past Rodriguez Key to marker No. 37. From marker No. 37 to marker Red No. 2 on your starboard, take 350 degrees from marker Red No. 2 to channel entrance.

Key Largo Harbor Marina
MM 100 Oceanside
100 Ocean Drive
Key Largo, FL
(305) 451–0045, (800) 843–5397, Ext. 4
www.holidayinnkeylargo.com

Associated with the Key Largo Holiday Inn and the Ramada Limited (see our Accommodations chapter), the Key Largo Harbor Marina shares the boat basin with Marina Del Mar. Hail the dockmaster on VHF channel 16, but he works on VHF

that you don't have to scribble instructions on the back of a napkin, we include dockmasters' directions for approaching the marinas, but be sure to read your charts closely.

Marina Del Mar
MM 100 Oceanside
527 Caribbean Drive
Key Largo, FL
(305) 451–4107, (800) 451–3483
www.marinadelmarkeylargo.com

Plan ahead if you want to stay at one of the 37 slips at Marina Del Mar marina,

channel 11. He advises you reserve your slip by August if you plan to come during the winter months. Most of the 45 slips have cable television and telephone hookups, and you may use the laundry facilities in the hotels. Modern restrooms and showers grace the premises.

You also have access to the hotels' three swimming pools, hot tub, playground, weight room, and tiki bar. And be sure to stop at Bogie's Cafe and visit the African Queen of movie fame docked nearby (see our Recreation chapter). On the east end, Key Largo Harbor's full-service boatyard, with a 60-ton travel lift, handles vessels up to 60 feet in length. A fuel dock supplies both diesel fuel and gasoline. Remember that the depth of the channel entrance is 4½ feet at low tide. The tide in the area varies 30 inches.

Dockmaster's directions: Via Hawk Channel, from the north, go to Mosquito Bank Light, Marker No. 35. Then turn west 270 degrees to marker Red No. 2. From Key West, when approaching Rodriguez Key, turn directly north on marker 37, 350 degrees, and look for the marker Red No. 2 about 1 mile north of the key. In either case, put marker Red No. 2 to your starboard side and take a 345-degree heading. Go past markers No. 4 and 6; go between markers 7 and 8; look for a lime-green house, which you should put on your starboard side. This puts you into the jetty. Proceed to the end of the canal and turn to port. Go to the turning basin. Slips will be on your starboard side in front of the Ramada Ltd.

Plantation Yacht Harbor Marina
MM 87 Bayside
Islamorada, FL
(305) 852–2381

You can grab a slip close to the Keys' fabled backcountry at the bayside Plantation Yacht Harbor, which is accessed from the Intracoastal Waterway or from the Atlantic via Snake Creek. This 90-slip marina can accommodate vessels up to 60 feet in length, drawing 5 feet. Mobile marine mechanics are on call to service needy vessels, and a fuel dock supplies both diesel fuel and gasoline. Plantation Yacht Harbor does not have a ship's store, but a 1-mile walk up the Overseas Highway will put you at a convenience store. You may use the on-site laundry, showers, and restroom facilities. Tennis courts, a swimming pool, and a small beach await your pleasure.

Dockmaster's directions: Via the Intracoastal Waterway, halfway between Intra-coastal Waterway markers No. 78 and No. 78A, which are about 2 miles apart, take an approximate heading of 150 degrees. (If you use binoculars, you can spot a miniature red-and-white-striped lighthouse at the entrance to the Plantation Yacht Harbor jetty.) If you come from Hawk Channel via Snake Creek, be careful at the headpins on both oceanside and bayside. There are low spots at low tide. And whatever you do, do not turn toward Plantation Yacht Harbor the minute you exit Snake Creek or you'll be left high and dry. Proceed north approximately 1 mile along the Intra-coastal and make your turn between markers No. 78 and No. 78A.

Holiday Isle Marina
MM 84 Oceanside
Islamorada, FL
(305) 664–2321, (800) 327–7070
www.holidayisle.com

Hold on to your rumrunner cocktail— Holiday Isle is where it's all happening. If you're lucky enough to snag one of the 19 transient slips at Holiday Isle Marina, you can party the night away. But first things first. Reserve your slip a couple of months in advance because this is a popular place. The on-premises Chevron offers all the essentials: gasoline, diesel fuel, and provisions. Mechanics are on call. Laundry, showers, and restrooms are available. Cable television hookup is free, but an additional charge is levied for telephone service.

Once you're settled in, graze the scene—Rip's for ribs and chicken, Horizon Restaurant on the rooftop for a more upscale meal, Wreck Bar for burgers and dogs, Raw Bar for seafood, Beach Bar for barbecue, Bimini Treats for eclectic outdoor noshing, and Kokomo's for libations and steel-drum music. Take time to shop at the Bimini Row's arty shops before things heat up in the evening. The Tiki Bar presents an afternoon Polynesian show, and live bands begin pulsating at nightfall and continue until the wee hours (see our Nightlife chapter).

Dockmaster's directions: Via Hawk Channel, at marker No. 40 take a 270-degree heading west, which takes you to the mouth of Whale Harbor Channel. The channel is well marked. Between Markers No. 1 and No. 2, the charts might show a 5-foot depth. Be aware that at dead low tide the actual depth drops to more like $4\frac{1}{2}$ feet. Take the channel to the split and then take a starboard tack. This brings you to the mouth of the basin, where you will see the Chevron sign.

Hawk's Cay Marina
MM 61 Oceanside
Duck Key, FL
(305) 743–7000, (800) 432–2242
www.hawkscay.com

Probably the best all-around marina in the Keys, Hawk's Cay offers a totally protected boat basin and all the amenities of its fine resort hotel (see our Accommodations and Restaurants chapters). Dock your boat at of one of the 50 full-service marina slips (5-foot draft), or if you come in a vessel less than 35 feet, you can dock it at one of 35 small-boat slips and stay at the hotel. These slips have no shore power, and you may not stay aboard your boat overnight. Rates will be the same as for the other transient slips, except there is no minimum.

Hawk's Cay maintains an extensive list of qualified marine mechanics in the area and has divers on call. The full-service ship's store sells everything, including groceries, fine wines, boating hardware, fishing tackle, clothing, and paperback books. It also offers video rentals. A full-service fuel dock pumps regular and premium gasoline and diesel fuel. Showers and restrooms are in the ship's store, and the marina is equipped with a pump-out station at the fuel dock. Laundry facilities are coin-operated. Cable television hookup is available at an extra fee.

Transient rates here are a hefty $3/foot (30-foot minimum) from December 1 through April 30, although off-season rates are less, and members of Boat US receive a 25 percent discount.

Dockmaster's directions: Via Hawk Channel, from up the Keys, find marker No. 44. Take an approximate 255-degree heading to the channel entrance. When approaching from Key West, find marker No. 45. Take an approximate 30-degree heading to the channel entrance. In either case, whatever you do, don't take the channel entrance that has only two markers; you'll run aground. The entrance, with eight markers, is on the south center of Duck Key. GPS latitude is 24°45.48; longitude is 80°54.40. You will see a small rock pile off the bow as you enter the channel. Turn to the starboard side, keeping the coral breakwater on the starboard side and the homes on your port side. Continue straight down the perimeter channel, remembering this is a no-wake zone. Continue straight to the main marina.

Faro Blanco Marina Bayside
MM 48.5 Bayside
Marathon, FL
(305) 743–9018, (800) 759–3276

The 95 slips at Faro Blanco Bayside surround the distinctive black, red, and white navigational lighthouse. This full-service marina covers the gamut: fuel dock, laundry, showers and restrooms, pump-out station, and ship's store. The marina accommodates vessels up to 125 feet, 7-foot draft. Dockage entitles you to all the amenities of this expansive resort, which spans both sides of the Overseas Highway (see our Accommodations chapter). Be sure to stop in for Angler's happy hour.

Dockmaster's directions: Via the Intracoastal Waterway from up the Keys, find

Rent a houseboat from the concessionaire at Flamingo in Everglades National Park and chart your own course into the Great Beyond. PHOTO: SUZANNE TOBEY

marker No. 17 just past Rachel Bank. Take an approximate heading of 182 degrees. From the Seven Mile Bridge find markers No. 19, 20 at Bethel Bank. Take an approximate heading of 132 degrees.

Faro Blanco Marina Oceanside
MM 48 Oceanside
Marathon, FL
(305) 743–9018, (800) 759–3276

Faro Blanco Oceanside, off Boot Key Channel, welcomes transient boaters to its 80 deep-dockage slips. Accommodating a 7-foot draft, the oceanside facility offers the same amenities as its bayside sister across the highway. Fuel, however, must be secured from one of the fuel docks in Boot Key Channel—Faro Blanco Oceanside does not have a fuel dock. Walk ¾ mile or dinghy to Faro Blanco Bayside for a swim, or a leisurely lunch at Angler's (see our Restaurants chapter).

Dockmaster's directions: Via Hawk Channel, come to the west end of Marathon and enter Boot Key Channel between marker No. 1 and No. 2. Look for marker Red No. 12.

Little Palm Island
MM 28.5 Oceanside
Little Torch Key, FL
(305) 872–2524, (800) 343–8567
www.littlepalmisland.com

Arriving at Little Palm Island by sea, you will be certain you missed your tack and landed in Fiji, because this exquisite jewel is more reminiscent of the South Seas than South Florida. Little Palm Island, the westernmost of the Newfound Harbor Keys, lies 4 nautical miles due north from Looe Key Light. And, while the average bank account strains at the tariffs charged for villa accommodations on the island (see our Accommodations chapter), staying at the marina is a real deal, even though it is the most expensive marina in the Florida Keys. As marina guests you're invited to use all the recreational facilities: sailboards, day sailers, fishing gear, canoes, snorkeling gear, beach, lagoonal swimming pool, and the sauna.

Little Palm's marina, though small, maintains eight slips on Newfound Harbor for boats up to 60 feet, 5½-foot draft and 4 slips on the ocean side for boats under 35 feet, 4-foot draft. The front dock or Sunset Dock can accommodate two deep-draft vessels—one up to 135-foot length, 18-foot draft, one up to 70 feet, 6-foot draft. The controlling depth coming into the harbor is 6 feet, but the dockmaster will help you navigate around the tides. The dockmaster monitors VHF channels 9 and 16 at all times. Dockhands are available to assist with lines. Hookup for one 50-amp service is included in dockage fees; additional connections depend upon availability. Boats docked at the T-dock enjoy 100-amp service.

Because you're staying on an out-island, offshore from the contiguous Keys and their more plentiful water supply, you will be allowed only one gallon of water per foot per day. However, the resort offers you use of guest showers and bathrooms in the quarterdeck and a laundry facility during your stay, so this water conservation is not a hardship.

Little Palm Island's renowned gourmet restaurant welcomes you for breakfast, lunch, and dinner. You may choose to cook aboard your vessel, but be advised that you're prohibited from consuming your own food or beverages in island public areas. Children younger than 16 are not permitted at Little Palm Island nor are villa guests allowed to bring pets. Little Palm does accommodate pets of overnight marina guests, but you must keep them on a leash and walk them only in designated areas. In keeping with the tranquil ambiance of the island, motorized personal watercraft also are banned. Transient rates are a whopping $7/foot ($350 minimum) at both the slip docks and the Sunset Dock. Discounts are offered to members of Boat US.

Dockmaster's directions: Little Palm Island, at the entrance to Newfound Harbor, is called Munson Island on the charts and is marked by Channel marker Red No. 2. Call the dockmaster on VHF channel 9 when you approach marker Red No. 2 so he can have the dockhands on deck. When

cruising from the north, take care to avoid the coral heads, which run parallel to the Newfound Harbor Keys approximately a half-mile offshore. Use GPS latitude 24°37.11; longitude 81°24.42.

Anchoring Out

Fancy yourself more Robinson Crusoe than Aristotle Onassis? Then you'll discover that anchoring out in the pristine waters lacing the Florida Keys approaches nirvana. From the northernmost keys of Biscayne Bay to Loggerhead Key at the end of the line, remote havens remain unspoiled, many reachable only by boat. Ibis, white pelicans, and bald eagles winter among select out-islands, and whole condominiums of cormorants take over the scrub of tiny mangrove islets. Gulf waters simmer with snapper, redfish, lobster, and stone crabs. The Atlantic Ocean sparkles with the glory of the living coral reef beneath. So pack up and push off for an Insiders' bareboat cruise of the Florida Keys, from tip to toe.

Elliott Key

On the eastern side of Biscayne Bay, the island of Elliott Key, which has the ranger station for Biscayne National Park, guards a complex ecosystem from the ocean's battering winds. Anchor on the leeward side of Elliott Key just off the pretty little beach north of Coon Point. This anchorage—good in northeast to east to southeast winds—is usually accessed via the Intracoastal Waterway.

A strong current rushes through the shallow channel between Sands Key and Elliott Key, and small-boat traffic is heavy on weekends. Although the fishing and diving here are first rate, take care. At the southern tip of Elliott Key, Caesar Creek—named for notorious pirate Black Caesar, who dipped in to stay out of sight in the 1600s—offers dicey passage to Hawk Channel for boats carefully clearing a 4-foot draft at high tide. The more forgiving Angelfish Creek, farther south at the north end of Key Largo, is the favored route from Biscayne Bay to the ocean in this wild and deserted area. Angelfish Creek is the Intracoastal Waterway's last outlet to the ocean until after Snake Creek Drawbridge for large boats or those heading for Hawk Channel.

Pumpkin Key

Safe anchorage surrounds Pumpkin Key, making this island an ideal choice for winds coming from any direction. Be sure to test your anchorage because Pumpkin Key's waters cover a grassy sea bottom. Nearby Angelfish Creek—filled with grouper, snapper, and angelfish—almost guarantees dinner. Scoot out the creek to take advantage of the diving at John Pennekamp Coral Reef State Park. Approachable from Hawk Channel or the Intracoastal, this area remains virginal even though it rests in the shadow of Key Largo.

Blackwater Sound

As you anchor in the placid ebony waters of Blackwater Sound, the twinkling lights of Key Largo remind you that civilization is but a dinghy ride away. Have dinner at the Italian Fisherman or sample the local color at the Caribbean Club, Humphrey Bogart's famous bar from moviedom (see our Restaurants and Nightlife chapters). Anchor along the southeast shoreline of Blackwater Sound for a protected anchorage in east to southeast winds. The Cross

Key Canal, which connects Blackwater Sound to Largo Sound, passes under a fixed bridge at the Overseas Highway in Key Largo. If your boat clears 14 feet safely, traverse the canal to dive or snorkel in John Pennekamp Coral Reef State Park.

Tarpon Basin

Enter Tarpon Basin through Dusenbury Creek or Grouper Creek. Both passages teem with snapper and grouper. Dinghy from this protected anchorage to The Quay restaurant (see our Restaurants chapter).

Largo Sound (John Pennekamp Coral Reef State Park)

John Pennekamp Coral Reef State Park and the adjacent Key Largo National Marine Sanctuary encompass the ocean floor under Hawk Channel from Broad Creek to Molasses Reef. Exit the Intracoastal Waterway at Angelfish Creek and enter Hawk Channel to proceed to Largo Sound. Enter Largo Sound through South Sound Creek. Park staff supervises this anchorage, which is completely sheltered in any weather. Call on VHF channel 16 to reserve a mandatory mooring buoy in the southwest portion of the Sound; anchoring is prohibited. A nominal fee for the moorings entitles boaters full use of park facilities and its pump-out station.

The reefs of John Pennekamp Coral Reef State Park shine brighter than others in the Keys. The bulk of Key Largo's landmass has inhibited development of the erosive channels that cut between the other Keys, preserving shallower waters. More sun filters through the shallow water, causing the coral to flourish. Much of this reef breaks the surface of the water during low tide.

Butternut Key and Bottle Key

Don't worry. Those baby sharks you see in the waters surrounding Butternut Key won't hurt you. The skittish infants leave this nursery area when they reach two to three feet in length. Prevailing winds will determine anchorage sites near these

becomes an island beach. And, if you'd just like to commune with nature, the forested northeast section of Upper Matecumbe Key hosts a rookery for good birdwatching. Note: There is a no-motor zone on the tidal flat.

Lignumvitae Key

Government-owned Lignumvitae Key stands among the tallest of the Keys, at 17 to 18 feet above sea level. A virgin hammock sprinkled with lignum vitae trees re-creates the feeling of the Keys of yesteryear, before mahogany forests were cut and sold to Bahamian shipbuilders. From 1919 to 1953, the Matheson family, of chemical company notoriety, owned the island, where they built a large home and extensive gardens of rare plantings.

Hug the northwest side of the island for good anchorage in east to southeast winds. Dinghy to the Lignumvitae Key dock for guided tours conducted by the State Park Service. You can also dinghy through Indian Key Channel to historic Indian Key (see our Attractions chapter). Nearby Shell Key almost disappears at high tide, so exercise caution. Pods of playful dolphins romp in Lignumvitae Basin, and a sighting of lumbering sea turtles is not unusual. But be sure to bait a hook—fishing is prolific.

Matecumbe Bight

If winds are not good for anchoring near Lignumvitae, Matecumbe Bight provides good holding ground, except in a north wind. Two miles south, Channel Five—east of Long Key—offers a good crossover between Florida Bay and Hawk Channel for large sailboats. Strong currents run in the channel beneath the bridge, which is a fixed span with a 65-foot overhead clearance.

Long Key Bight

Anchor in Long Key Bight, which is accessed via Hawk Channel oceanside or through Channel Five from the Intracoastal Waterway. Bordering Long Key State Park—a 300-acre wilderness area

islands, which offer good holding ground. On the Florida Bay side of Tavernier, Butternut Key and Bottle Key showcase voluminous bird life. Roseate spoonbills breed on Bottle Key, feeding upon the tiny killifishes of the flats. A pond on the island attracts mallard ducks in the winter. And amid this gunk-holers' paradise, the elusive bald eagle rewards the patient observer with a fleeting appearance.

Cotton Key

Approach Cotton Key from the Intracoastal Waterway. This anchorage, protected from north to southeast winds, offers the best nightlife in the Keys north of Key West. Take your dinghy around the entire island of Upper Matecumbe and the community of Islamorada. Catch the action at Papa Joe's, the Lorelei, or Atlantic's Edge at Cheeca Lodge (see our Restaurants chapter). Check out the fishing charters at Bud n' Mary's Marina (see our Fishing chapter). Stop in at the Islamorada Fish Company and take ready-to-eat stone crabs back to your boat for a private sunset celebration (see our Seafood Markets and Specialty Foods chapter). Dinghy through Whale Harbor Channel to the Islamorada Sand Bar, which at low tide

with a good campground, tables, and grills—the Bight is protected yet open. Dinghy through Zane Grey Creek for good gunk-holing. Legendary author Zane Grey angled at the former Long Key Fishing Club during the days of Flagler's Railroad. Beach-comb for washed-up treasure on the southeast shores of Long Key.

Boot Key Harbor

Boot Key Harbor in Marathon serves as a good, safe port in a bad blow, but, crowded with liveaboards, it is a bit like anchoring out in Times Square. Enter this fully protected harbor from Sister's Creek or at the western entrance near the beginning of the Seven Mile Bridge.

Note: Moser Channel goes under the hump of the Seven Mile Bridge, creating a 65-foot clearance. The draw-span of the old bridge has been removed, but the rest remains. A portion on the Marathon end now functions as the driveway to Pigeon Key (see our Attractions chapter). A stretch on the Bahia Honda end is maintained for bridge fishing and is referred to locally as the "longest fishing pier in the world." The Moser Channel and the Bahia Honda Channel (with 20-foot clearance) are the last crossover spots in the Keys. You must decide at Marathon if you will travel the Atlantic route or via the Gulf to Key West. If you need fuel, note that the marina at Sunshine Key is the last bayside marina until Key West.

Big Spanish Channel Area

Leave all traces of civilization behind and head out the Big Spanish Channel toward the out-islands. Proceed with care, for this remote sprinkling of tiny keys is part of the Great White Heron National Wildlife Refuge. Before venturing into this back-country area, secure a Public Use Regulations Map from the Lower Keys Chamber of Commerce (305–872–2411, 800–872–3722). Obey no-entry, no-motor and idle-speed zones. Get your Florida Bird Guide out of the cabin and count the species. Then, treat yourself to a swim with the dolphins, which travel in pods throughout these Gulf waters.

Little Spanish Key

The western side of Little Spanish Key provides the best protection from northeast to southeast winds. Explore the surrounding clear waters by dinghy where the endangered green turtles, which weigh between 150 and 450 pounds, have been spotted feeding on seagrass. Catch your limit in snapper and share your bounty with the friendly pelicans.

Newfound Harbor

Newfound Harbor—formed by the Newfound Harbor Keys and the southern extension of Big Pine Key—stars as the premier oceanside harbor between Marathon and Key West. Dinghy to exquisite Little Palm Island, the setting for the film PT-109, the story of John F. Kennedy's Pacific experience during World War II (see the Marinas listing in this chapter). Newfound Harbor lies within easy reach of Looe Key National Marine Sanctuary, a spur and groove coral reef ecosystem popular with divers and snorkelers.

Key West and Beyond

Welcome to the ultimate cruising destination: Key West. Full of history and histrionics, this vibrant, intoxicating port pumps the adrenaline, pushes the envelope, and provides a rowdy good time for all. And when you signal a turn back into the slow lane again, dust off your charts and head out to the wild beyond of the Dry Tortugas, the end of the line.

Marinas

All of our suggested marinas take transient boaters, but the multiplicity of celebrated special events in Key West dictates that you prudently reserve a slip as far in advance as possible. You may assume unless otherwise stated that all our recommended marinas supply hookups for both

Faro Blanco's coveted transient slips surround the distinctive black, red, and white navigational lighthouse. PHOTO: MARY MOCCIA

30-amp and 50-amp service as well as fresh water. Transient rates range from $2 to $2.75 per foot per day in high season, sometimes higher during holidays, mini-lobster season, and Fantasy Fest. Some marinas impose a minimum charge. Key West offers extensive self-provisioning facilities ranging from supermarkets to gourmet take-out shops (see our Seafood Markets and Specialty Foods chapter). The city also supports a variety of good marine mechanics, which the marina dockmasters will contact on your behalf should the need arise.

Our directions for approaching the marinas will help you find your way, but be sure to hail the dockmaster on VHF channel 16 and read your charts closely.

A&B Marina
700 Front Street
Key West, FL
(305) 294–2535, (800) 223–8352
www.abmarina.com

A&B Marina is situated in the heart of Old Town, right in the middle of all the action. Most of its 50 transient slips will accommodate vessels with up to 7-foot drafts. Cable television hookup is included in dockage fees. A&B maintains a diesel fuel dock.

A $3.5 million renovation of the marina, completed in 2000, gave A&B quite a face-lift. They've added a convenience store, air-conditioned shower facilities, a laundry room, a 24-hour (10 months of the year) bar and grill, and the Commodore Waterfront Steakhouse. A&B Lobster House, upstairs, has been feeding hungry cruisers for nearly 50 years, and still welcomes one and all. And people-watching is great from the dockside bar.

Dockmaster's directions: From the Atlantic, come in the main ship channel, which is marked S.E. Channel on the charts, to markers No. 24 and No. 25. From the Gulf, take the N.W. Channel until it intersects with the main ship channel. Take a port turn to markers No. 24 and No. 25. From either direction, turn east between markers No. 24 and No. 25 and proceed about one-eighth mile to Marker Red No. 4. Take a starboard turn around Red No. 4, and you are 400 feet off the dock.

The Galleon International Marina
619 Front Street
Key West, FL
(305) 292–1292, (800) 662–7462
www.galleonresort.com

Cruisers love the Galleon, probably the most popular of Key West's marinas. The carbonated excitement of Duval Street pulsates only a few blocks away, but the ambiance at the Galleon remains unhurried and genteel. The 91 dockage slips will accommodate vessels up to 150 feet, 9-foot drafts. One 30-amp or one 50-amp service is included in the daily dockage rate, but you can secure another for an additional fee. Cable and telephone hookups are available for a minimal charge. Fuel is available in Key West Bight or at Conch Harbor Marina.

The Galleon indulges you with all the amenities and then some: shower and restroom facilities, a laundry, pump-out station, deli, swimming pool, tiki bar, private beach, fitness center, sauna, patio, and picnic tables. And if that is not enough, book an afternoon of snorkeling at the on-premises dive shop or plan a fishing expedition with one of the charter boats at the dock. Rent a moped or bicycle and explore Key West, or just kick back and relax on the sun deck.

Pets are welcome in the marina but not on the adjoining resort property.

Dockmaster's directions: Follow the main ship channel, NOAA Chart No. 11441, to marker No. 24, then call the dockmaster on VHF 16. He will guide you to marker Red No. 4 at the east end of the breakwater and into the entrance to the marina.

Key West Hilton Resort and Marina
245 Front Street
Key West, FL
(305) 292–4375
www.keywestresort.hilton.com

The Key West Hilton Resort and Marina offers transients all the perks of its lavish property: pool, hot tub, and weight room as well as Bistro 245 restaurant and Latitudes restaurant on Sunset Key (see our Accommodations and Restaurants chapters). About one-quarter of the marinas dock space is available to transients. The south basin offers floating slips that accommodate vessels with 30-foot drafts; the north basin's 600 feet of rigid dock space handles craft with 15-foot drafts or less.

Make reservations up to six months in advance to dock at the Key West Hilton Resort and Marina. Only one block off famed Duval Street, its location can't be beat and it fills up quickly. In addition to daily transient rates, an additional power fee is levied. Cable television hookup is included in the dockage fee, and the requisite laundry, shower, and restroom requirements are supplied on the premises. Fuel may be obtained a half-mile up the channel at Key West Bight.

The Key West Hilton Resort and Marina owns the private offshore Sunset Key. Guests of the hotel or marina may take a daytrip to the island and enjoy its pristine beach, away from the fray of Key West.

Dockmaster's directions: From the south, come up the main cruise-ship channel. At marker Red No. 14 hail the dockmaster on VHF 16. You will be a half-mile from the marina, which is the first break in the sea wall. From the north, come down the N.W. Channel. At marker Green No. 17, hail the dockmaster on VHF 16. The marina will be a half-mile dead ahead. On most charts the marina is listed as Pier B. The dockmaster urges you to hail the marina at the specified markers so he can be on hand to assist your dockage.

Key West Yacht Club
Garrison Bight
Key West, FL
(305) 296-3446

Although Key West Yacht Club is a private club, provisions in its charter with the City of Key West mandate that visiting yachts may make transient dockage. The club allots three of its 66 slips to visiting transients each day. You may make reservations up to 30 days in advance. The marina accommodates vessels with a maximum depth of 6 feet. Be advised: overhead high-tension power lines have a safety clearance of 50 feet. The ship's store offers limited provisions, and there are no on-site laundry facilities, but a supermarket and coin-operated laundry require only a short jaunt on foot. Restrooms and showers are provided.

Dockmaster's directions: Enter Garrison Bight. Steer a straight course to marker Green No. 25, and leave Green No. 25 to port. After passing Green No. 25, turn to port 45 degrees and aim for the blue and white gas station across the street from the sea wall. When you are approximately 40 feet off the sea wall, take another port turn and just point your bow at the starboard side of the marina.

Oceanside Marina
MM 5
5950 Peninsula Avenue
Stock Island, FL
(305) 294-4676
www.oceansidemarina.com

This top-drawer marina, occupying a finger of Stock Island, offers a Key West alternative for peace and solitude, for it is tucked far away from the fray. Its 106 slips will accommodate vessels up to 150 feet in length with 12-foot maximum drafts. Access to the marina is directly from Hawk Channel. Reservations are suggested 30 days in advance during the winter season. Gas- and diesel-qualified marine mechanics work on the premises. Oceanside provides all the essentials: gas and diesel fuel dock, ship's store and tackle shop, laundry, showers and restrooms, and free cable hookups. An additional charge is levied for telephone hookup. Your pet is welcome if kept on a leash.

Dockmaster's directions: Proceed to latitude 24°32.5 north; longitude 81°43.9 west for the outer marker, which is marker Red No. 2 at the entrance to Safe Harbor Channel.

Anchoring Out

The highway may stop in Key West, but the path to adventure continues into the sunset. The Dry Tortugas, the brightest gems in the necklace, mark the real end of

Anchoring out in the pristine waters lacing the Florida Keys approaches nirvana. PHOTO: MARY MOCCIA

the line in the Florida Keys. Once you leave Key West Harbor, you join the ranks of the swashbucklers who have abandoned the safety of civilization to explore the vast unknown.

Be sure you know the range and capabilities of your craft because only self-sufficient cruising vessels can make the 140-nautical-mile trek to the Dry Tortugas and back. There is no fuel, fresh water, provisioning, or facilities of any kind once you leave Key West. Unpredictable foul weather could keep you trapped at sea for days, so make sure you are fueled for 200 miles, and stock the larder for extenuating circumstances.

Key West

If you want to anchor out in busy Key West Harbor, look for a spot west of Fleming Key in about 10 to 15 feet of water. You'll find less current, good holding ground, and less fishing vessel traffic than around Wisteria Island. The municipal dinghy dock at the foot of Simonton Street is the only official place to land your dinghy, but you might want to arrange secured short-term dockage for your dinghy from one of the marina dockmasters.

Boca Grande Key

A string of shoals and keys snakes west from Key West, offering unparalleled diving and fishing opportunities. Beyond Man and Woman Keys—popular snorkeling spots—Boca Grande Key offers a good day anchorage on the northwestern side with a beautiful white sand beach. The current is too swift to anchor overnight, but snorkel the small wreck visible just north of the island. Be alert to the constantly shifting shoals around the entrance channel. Note also that this island is a turtle nesting ground—all or parts of it are off limits during specific times of the year, and fines are possible.

Marquesas Keys

About 24 miles from Key West, a broken collar of low-lying, beach-belted islands form the Marquesas Keys. If you pass Mooney Harbor Key on your way into the inner sanctum, watch for coral heads about 1,100 yards offshore. Prevailing winds will determine at which side to anchor, but you should be able to achieve a protected anchorage. Many a ship crashed on the coral heads in this area, leaving interesting wrecks, but check with the Coast Guard before you dive, because the U.S. Navy has been known to use the area

Cruise ships dock at Mallory Square in Key West several times a week. PHOTO: JANET WARE

west of the Marquesas as a bombing and strafing range. Explore the big rookery of frigate birds or take aim with a little spearfishing. Note: A 300-foot no-motor zone is established around the three smallest islands, a 300-foot no-access buffer zone is established around one mangrove island, and an idle speed only/no-wake zone is established in the southwest tidal creek. This pit-stop on the way to the Dry Tortugas rates as an end point in itself.

Dry Tortugas

Open water stretches like a hallucination from the Marquesas to our southernmost national park, the Dry Tortugas. Ponce de Leon named these islands the Tortugas—Spanish for turtles—in 1513, presumably because the waters teemed with sea turtles, which he consumed as fresh meat. Lack of fresh water rendered the islands dry.

The first sight of the massive brick fortress of Fort Jefferson, the colorful history of which began in 1846, is breathtaking (see our Attractions chapter). The best deep anchorage is usually directly in front of the entrance to the fort on the southeast side of Garden Key, but, depending upon the weather, you may want to check with the ranger first.

Unparalleled diving exists in these unsullied waters. Colors appear more brilliant because the waters are clearer than those bordering the inhabited Keys. The entire area is a no-take zone, so don't be alarmed if you spot a prehistoric-size lobster or jewfish. Be sure to snorkel the underwater nature trail. From your dinghy, watch for the nesting sooty and noddy terns in their Bush Key sanctuary (landing is forbidden).

Loggerhead Key

Just beyond Garden Key dozes Loggerhead Key, called the prettiest beach in the Keys by those in the know. A good day anchorage with a legion of interesting coral, this is literally the end of the line for the Florida Keys. Nothing but 900 miles of water lies between this point and the Mexican coast. Hope you remembered to fuel up in Key West!

Insiders' Tip

Never anchor on a reef. Your anchor will destroy the living coral. Drop anchor only in sandy areas. A sandy sea bottom appears white. Use mooring buoys wherever offered.

Fishing

Angling in the Florida Keys approaches a religion to many. The very essence of the Keys is embodied in gleaming packages of skin and scales, for a day fishing the cerulean waters that lap our islands creates a sensory memory not quickly forgotten. Long after the last bait is cast, tales of captured prizes or the ones that got away evoke visions of the sun, the sea, and the smell of the salt air.

Anglers fish here with an intensity rarely seen anywhere else in the United States...the world even. Eavesdrop on a conversation anywhere in the Keys, and someone will be talking about fishing. As you drive down the Overseas Highway and look out at our acres of shimmering waters, you will feel an overwhelming urge to join in the battle of power and wits—fish against angler—that makes the Keys so special.

The Florida Keys has more than 1,000 species of fish; most are edible, all are interesting. Six of them—bonefish, permit, tarpon, redfish, snook, and sailfish—have earned game-fish status, meaning they may not be sold. To pursue these and other species, you will need a saltwater fishing license (see the Fishing Licenses section in this chapter). You must obey catch and season restrictions and size limits. These regulations change often. Ask for an up-to-date listing when you purchase your fishing license.

The Florida Keys falls within the boundaries of the Florida Keys National Marine Sanctuary, created by the federal government in 1990, to protect the resources of our marine ecosystem. And while, for the most part, visitors freely swim, dive, snorkel, boat, fish, or recreate on our waters, some regulations took effect in July 1997, to guide these activities. Refer to our Boating chapter for information on these regulations, before you venture into our waters. For a complete copy of the regulations and marine coordinates of the areas, contact the Sanctuary office, (305-743-2437) or check their website, www.fknms.nos.noaa.gov.

Catch-and-Release Ethics

Preserve our natural resources. "A fish is too valuable to be caught only once," the U.S. Department of Commerce, the National Oceanic and Atmospheric Administration, and the National Marine Fisheries Service maintain. We agree. The spirit behind the catch-and-release policy is to enjoy the hunt and the score, but take a photograph of the fish home with you, not the quarry itself. Taxidermists do not need the actual fish to prepare a mount for you; they only need the approximate measurements. Take home only those food fish you plan to eat.

To properly release a fish, keep the fish in the water and handle it very little whenever possible. Dislodge the hook quickly with a hookout tool, backing the hook out the opposite way it went in. If the hook can't be removed quickly, cut the leader close to the mouth. Hold the fish by the bottom jaw or lip—not the gills—with a wet hand or glove so that you don't damage its mucous or scales. Have your photo taken with the fish. Cradle the tired fish, rocking it back and forth in the water until it is able to swim away under its own power. This increases the oxygen flow through its gills, reviving the fish and thereby augmenting its chances for survival against a barracuda or shark.

Where to Fish

To introduce you to our complex watery ecosystem and the species of fish dwelling

257

Those two magic words every Keys angler likes to hear: "Fish on." PHOTO: MARY MOCCIA

therein, we have divided fishing destinations into four distinct sections: the flats, the backcountry, the bluewater, and the bridges.

The Flats

The continental shelf is nature's gift to the Florida Keys. Stretching from the shoreline like a layer of rippled fudge on a marble slab, it lingers for many shallow miles before plunging to the depths of the bluewater. In the Keys, we rather reverently call this area the flats. Waters ranging from mere inches to several feet in depth cover most of the flats, but some areas completely surface during low tide, exposing themselves to the air and intense sunlight. Changing winds, tides, temperatures, and barometric pressure ensure that conditions in the flats fluctuate constantly.

An unenlightened observer might think the flats uninteresting, for most of this watery acreage is covered with dense turtle grass, shell-less sand, or muddy muck. But, far from being a wasteland, the flats are the feeding grounds and nursery for a city of marine families whose members inspire dramatic tales of daring and

conquest from every person who has ever baited a hook here.

The 4,000 square miles of flats—from Key Biscayne to Key West and beyond—yield a trio of prize game fish—bonefish, permit, and tarpon—which, when caught in one day, we refer to as the Grand Slam. And keeping company in the same habitat are the bonus fish—barracuda and shark—that regularly accommodate anglers with exciting runs and fights. Fishing the flats is really a combination of angling and hunting, for you must first see and stalk the fish before you ever cast the waters. The hunt for bonefish, permit, and tarpon requires patience and unique angling skills, but most essentially, you must be at the right place at the right time.

We cannot even begin to teach you how to fish for these formidable fighters of the flats, in this chapter. You should hire a professional guide, for which there is no substitute—at least while you are a novice. Guides know the local waters well and keep detailed records of where to find fish under every condition, saving you precious hours and money in the pursuit of your mission (see the Guides and Charters section of this chapter). But we will introduce you to the exciting species you will encounter on our flats, relate their personalities, tattle about their habits, and point you in the right direction so you can learn all you wish to know and share in the angling experience of a lifetime: fishing the flats in the Florida Keys.

First in the see-stalk-cast sequence so important in fishing the skinny waters of the flats is the visible interpretation of the watery hallucination under the surface. To see the fish of the flats, you must have polarized sunglasses to cut the sun's glare so you can concentrate on looking through your reflection on the top of the water, to the shallow bottom. Under the water, fish often look like bluish shadows, or they may appear as indistinct shadings that simply look different than the waters surrounding them.

Most waters of the flats in the Keys are fished from a shallow-draft skiff, or flatsboat, although you can wade out from shore in many areas, if you prefer. Never motor onto a flat; the fish can hear the engine noise and spook easily. Use an electric trolling motor or, better yet, pole in, using a push pole. A push pole is a fiberglass or graphite dowel, 16- to 20-feet long with a V-crotch on one end, for traversing the soft bottom of the flats and a straight end on the other, for staking out. Using it requires body power and coordination and more than a little practice. A flatsboat has a raised poling platform that enables the poler or guide a height advantage to more readily distinguish the fish from its shadowy surroundings, in preparation for an accurate cast.

At the turn of the tide, the fish begin to move into the flats, grazing like sheep in a pasture. Guides know where the fish congregate during an incoming (flood) tide and an outgoing (ebb) tide. While it may prove dangerous for the fish to come up on the flats—they expose themselves to predators—the concentration of food is too enticing for them to resist. The fish prefer feeding during the low, incoming tide; the food is still easy to find, but they won't risk becoming stranded on the flats.

Bonefish: Phantom of the Flats

A sighting of the glistening forked tail of the Gray Ghost—alias of the famed bonefish (*Albula vulpes*) haunting our flats—has been known to elevate the blood pressure of even the most seasoned Keys angler to celestial heights. This much-respected, skittish silver bullet is considered the worthiest of all opponents, a wily, suspicious street fighter, here one moment, gone the next. The bonefish's superior eyesight, acute hearing, keen sense of smell, and boundless speed routinely befuddle anglers, some of whom dedicate their lives to thwarting the fish's Houdini-like escape attempts.

You can spot a bonefish three ways: tailing, mudding, or cruising. When the slender, silvery bonefish feeds, it looks like a washerwoman leaning over to get her laundry out of the basket—head down, bottom up. The fork of the tail will break the surface of the water—a tailing fish. The bonefish feeds into the current because its food source is delivered in the drift. As the fish puts its mouth down into the sand and silt, routing around on the bottom of the flats, looking for shrimps, crabs, and other crustaceans, the water clouds up. This is called "making a mud." As the mudding bonefish continues feeding, the current takes the cloudy water away so he can see his prey once again. Bonefish require water temperatures of 70 degrees and higher for feeding on the flats.

Spotting a cruising fish takes some practice. Look for "nervous water." The bonefish pushes a head wake as it swims, which sometimes shows as an inconsistency on the surface of the water. On other occasions, a mere movement by the fish underwater will cause the surface water to appear altered. Most of the time that the bonefish is cruising, however, it is swimming in deeper water; you will have to spot it. The back and sides of the bonefish are so silvery they act as a mirror. The fish swims right on the bottom of the flats in 8 or more inches of water. The sun shining through the water causes the bottom to reflect off the sides of the fish. So if you think you have seen a ripple of weeds, the image may actually be a bonefish.

The best bait for bonefishing is live shrimp. A guide with an experienced eye will put you on the fish by calling out directions like the hands of a clock. The bow of the boat will always be 12 o'clock. You will be instructed by the guide to look in a direction—for instance, 2 o'clock—and, at a specified distance, to spot the bonefish in preparation for a cast. The cast is the most crucial part of successfully hooking a bonefish. You should be able to cast 30 feet quickly and accurately. A cast that places the bait too close to the fish will spook it and cause the bonefish to dart away at breakneck speed. If the bait is cast too far away, the fish won't find it at all. The bait should land 2 to 3 feet in front of the fish and be allowed to drift to the ocean floor.

Many times the bonefish will smell the bait prior to seeing it because the fish is down current of the bait and swimming into the current. The bonefish begins to dart back and forth and goes in circles, looking for the scented prey. Once the fish locates the source of the scent, it tends to suck in the bait. You, the angler, must make sure there is no slack in the line and that your rod tip is low to the water. Then firmly but gently lift up to set the hook. Hold on tight and raise your rod straight up in the air, holding your arms as high above your head as possible. Once the fish realizes something is wrong—that it's hooked—it will peel away in an electrifying run, taking out 100 to 150 yards of line in a heartbeat. This whole process—from sighting to hooking—explodes in adrenaline-pumping nanoseconds. Ten to 30 minutes later, after the bonefish makes several pulse-pounding sprints, you can reel in the tired fish to the side of the skiff, where the guide will photograph both victor and spoils. Then quickly release the bonefish so that it may rest up and thrill another angler on yet another day (see the previous section in this chapter on Catch-and-Release Ethics).

Bonefishing is a major playing card of the fishing deck we so lavishly deal here in the Florida Keys. Bonefish usually range in size from 5 to 10 pounds, but the size of this fish deceptively belies its strength. A 5-pound bonefish fights like a 20-pound wannabe. The Keys are the only place in the continental United States where an angler can fish for bonefish. Locals boast that the Keys have the biggest and best-educated bonefish this side of the Gulf Stream. Expect bonefish to grace our flats during April, May, June, September, October, and occasionally into November. Cool weather and cold fronts push them into deeper waters from December through March. The hot weather of July and August drives them to cooler, deeper waters as well, although some will stay all year.

Permit: Ultimate Flats Challenge

Though sharing the same waters as the bonefish and stalked in the same manner, the permit (*Trachinotus falcatus*) proves to be a more elusive catch. Spooky, skittish, and stubborn, this finicky eater, which can take out line like a long-distance runner, is so difficult to catch that most anglers never even see one. Three or four times the size of a bonefish—averaging 20 to 30 pounds—the silvery, platter-shaped permit forages in the safety of slightly deeper

Insiders' Tip

Dispose of your garbage back at the boat dock. Be careful that trash does not blow out of the boat. Do not leave anything behind that cannot be immediately consumed by the ecosystem.

waters, not risking exposure of its iridescent blue-green back. Its sickle-shaped, black-tipped tail pokes out of the water as it feeds on bottom-dwelling crabs and shrimps, often tipping off its location. The permit's shell-crushing jaws, rubbery and strong, can exert 3,000 pounds of pressure per square inch, enabling it to masticate small clams and crustaceans and dash many an angler's expectations.

The permit will tail or mud like a bonefish. In fact, both fish have been known to rub their snouts so raw from repeatedly routing around in the mud, looking for food that they caricature W.C. Fields. But, unlike a bonefish, the permit is often spotted lazily cruising near the surface of the water. Many times its wispy black dorsal fin will break the water, looking like a drifting piece of weed.

The best days to find permit are those glorious, cloudless sunny smiles from Mother Nature, cooled by a slight ocean breeze. Schools of permit will graze the top of the flats and near rocky shorelines in higher tides and poke around in basins and channels during low tides, searching for a meal of small crabs and crustaceans. They often hover above submerged objects such as lobster pots. If you pass over an area littered with sea urchins, be on the lookout for permit searching for gourmet fixings.

Not easily duped, a tailing permit will make you forget all about a bonefish because, if you manage to hook one, you've got a street brawl on your hands that could last an hour or more. When hooked, the permit instinctively heads for deeper water. In the transition zone between the flats and the bluewater, the permit will try to cut the line by weaving through coral heads, sea fans, and sponges. The fish will pause in its run to bang its head on the bottom or rub its mouth in the sand to try to dislodge the hook. If you manage to follow the permit through this obstacle course, you may actually catch it a quarter-mile from where you hooked it.

Tarpon: the Silver King

It is little wonder that the tarpon (*Megalops atlanticus*) is dubbed the silver king, for it wins nine out of every ten encounters with an angler. The tarpon's lung-like gas bladder allows it to take a gulp of atmospheric air from time to time, enabling the fish to thrive in oxygen-depleted water. This magnificent superhero of the sea, ranging in size from 50 to 200 pounds, will break the surface and "roll" with a silvery splash as it steals an oxygen jolt and powers on for an intensified fight. The tarpon frequents the deeper flats of 4 to 8 feet or hangs out in the rapidly moving waters of channels, or under one of the many bridges in the Keys. Live mullet, pinfish, and crabs will entice this hungry but lazy despot, who faces into the current, effortlessly waiting for

The magnificent tarpon wins nine out of every ten encounters with an angler, but not this time.

PHOTO: MELANIE WINTER

baitfish to be dragged into its mouth. The tarpon's toothless lower jaw protrudes from its head like an overdeveloped underbite, filled with bony plate that crushes its intended dinner.

The successful angler will use heavy tackle and a needle-sharp hook. Hold the rod with the tip at 12 o'clock and wait. When the fish strikes and eats the bait, let the rod tip drop with the pressure, giving minimal resistance. When the rod is parallel to the water and the line is tight, set the hook through the bony structure with a series of short, very strong jabs. Once hooked, the stunned fish runs and leaps repeatedly, with reckless abandon, entering the water head first, tail first, sideways, belly-flopped, or upside down, an Olympian confounding its rod-clutching judge. It is important to have a quick release anchor when fishing for tarpon because, once the action starts, you must be on your way, chasing the cavorting fish. (See the Close-up: Local Secrets to Tight Lines in this chapter.) Be prepared to duke it out, for it is often a standoff as to who tires first, the angler or the tarpon.

Exciting to catch on light tackle is the schooling baby tarpon, which at up to 50 pounds, sprints and practices its aerobatics like its older siblings. Look for baby tarpon in channels and in harbors.

Tarpon season generally begins in April and continues until mid-July. Because the tarpon is primarily a nocturnal feeder, the best fishing is at daybreak and dusk or during the night.

This magnificent creature grows very slowly, not reaching maturity until it is at least 13 years old. Since the tarpon is not

an edible fish, some people consider killing it akin to murder.

If you want a simulated mount of your catch, take an estimate of the length and girth for the taxidermist, take a photograph with your prize, and release the fish quickly and carefully. If you insist on keeping and killing a tarpon, a $50 tarpon tag is required.

Barracuda: the Tiger of the Flats

Look for the barracuda (*Sphyraena barracuda*), which packs a wallop of a fight, anywhere the water is about 2 feet deep, especially grassy bottom areas. This toothy, intelligent predator has keen eyesight and moves swiftly. The barracuda's inquisitive nature causes it to make investigative passes by your boat, where it is oft tempted to sample your baited offerings intended for other species. Pilchards make good bait for catching barracuda. Cut off part of the tail fin of a pilchard before baiting the hook. This injury causes the bait to swim erratically, attracting the insatiable barracuda. When casting to a barracuda, your bait should land at least 10 feet beyond the fish and be retrieved across its line of sight. A cast that lands the bait too close—five feet or less—will frighten the 'cuda into deep water. If you are using artificial baits such as a tube lure, be sure to retrieve the bait briskly to pique the barracuda's interest.

Humans eat barracuda in some tropical areas but not in the Keys. The flesh is sometimes toxic, and it is not worth the risk. You are better off quickly releasing the fish so that it might fight another round.

Sharks

Several shark species (order *selachii*) roam our flats looking for a free meal. Sand sharks and nurse sharks are relatively docile, but bonnetheads and blacktip sharks readily will take a shrimp or crab intended for a bonefish or permit, putting up a determined fight. If you happen to catch a shark, wear heavy gloves and cut the leader with pliers. The shark will swim away and will be able to work the hook loose from its mouth. Digestive acids and salt water will corrode the hook in mere days, causing the fish no permanent harm.

The Backcountry

When Mother Nature bestowed the prolific oceanside saltwater flats on the Florida Keys, she didn't stop at our rocky isles. As the Gulf of Mexico meets mainland Florida, a lively ecosystem flourishes in a body of water known as Florida Bay. Hundreds of tiny uninhabited keys dot the watery landscape, referred to locally as the backcountry. Loosely bordered by the Keys—from Largo to Long—and Everglades National Park, backcountry waters offer a diverse habitat of seagrass or mud flats, mangrove islets, and sandy basins. The southernmost outpost of the Everglades National Park is at Flamingo, which maintains a marina, boat rentals, houseboats, and guide services.

You'll usually be able to find snappers, sheepshead, ladyfish, and the occasional shark along the grass-bed shorelines, the open bays, and in the small creeks flowing out of the Everglades. And the silver king, the mighty tarpon, frequents backcountry creeks and channels, flats, and basins and is rumored to be particularly partial to the Sandy Key Basin in the summer months. But beckoning anglers to these skinny waters is another sporting trio—redfish, snook, and spotted seatrout—which when caught in one day is boasted far and wide as the Backcountry Grand Slam.

Redfish, a.k.a. Red Drum

The coppery redfish, or red drum (*Sciaenops oceallatus*), all but disappeared in the 1980s from overfishing, but conservation measures by the State of Florida and the federal government caused a rebirth. This fast-growing fish migrates offshore to spawn when it reaches about 30 inches (four years). It is a protected species in federal waters. Regulations open a scant 9-inch window for anglers to keep one captured redfish per day, which must measure between 18 and 27 inches. All redfish measuring less than 18 inches or more than 27 inches must be released always. Because it grows so rapidly, the redfish is exposed to harvest for only one year of its life.

As with fishing for bonefish or permit, you will look for redfish on an incoming tide, when they will be routing for crabs on the shoals and flats. As the water gets higher, the fish work their way up on the flats. You will want to use a shallow-draft boat with a push pole or electric trolling motor and be prepared with polarized sunglasses for enhanced vision in spotting a tailing fish. You'll hear experienced anglers say, "A tailing red is a feeding red." The reddish, squared-off profile of the redfish's tail can be spotted from several hundred feet. When the fish is really hungry, you may see its entire tail exposed, even the shady eyelike spot at the base. Cruising redfish will push a head wake similar to that of a bonefish.

Although a redfish isn't nearly as easily spooked as a bonefish, you should still stay as far away from the fish as possible while still casting a right-on winner. Live shrimps or crabs will entice the fish, which, with poor eyesight, hits most any bait coming its way. The hooked redfish often sticks around and puts up a hard fight. Attracted to its discomfort, other redfish swim to the scene of the accident. You can often catch another redfish if you can get another baited hook into the water fast enough. The redfish is highly coveted for eating, put on the culinary map by New Orleans' Chef Prudhomme and his famed Cajun blackening process.

The backcountry of the Florida Keys is one of the only places in the world where you can fish for redfish year round, although they prefer cooler waters. It is illegal, however, to buy or sell our native redfish, and they must be kept whole until you reach shore. You are forbidden to gig, spear, or snatch the red drum.

Snook

The second member of the Backcountry Grand Slam, the snook (*Centropomus undecimalis*) likes to tuck against the shady mangrove shorelines to feed on baitfish that congregate in the maze of gnarled roots. A falling tide will force the baitfish out of their rooted cages and into deeper holes where the snook can get at them. But the baitfish aren't the only ones getting snookered. This cagey, sought-after game fish, once hooked, has buffaloed many an angler, vanishing back into the mangroves and snapping its tenuous connection to the rod-wielder like a brittle string. If you win the battle of the bushes or find the snook pushing water in the open or at the mouth of a creek, you still haven't won the war. Once hooked, the snook thrashes about violently, trying to dislodge the barbed intruder. Its hard, abrasive mouth and knife-sharp gill covers can dispense with your line in a flash.

This silvery, long-bodied fish—thickened around the middle like a middle-aged spinster—faces its foes with a depressed snout and a protruding lower jaw. A distinctive lateral, black racing stripe extends the length of its body, all the way to its divided dorsal fin. The snook is unable to tolerate waters lower than 60 degrees. And while some anglers feel snook is the best tasting fish in the Keys, Florida law mandates you may not fish for snook from December 15 through January 31, nor in the months of June, July, and August. The fish must measure between 18 inches and 34 inches. Limits are two snook per person, per day. Snook may not be bought or sold, and you must purchase a $2.50 snook stamp for your saltwater fishing license in order to fish for them.

Spotted Seatrout, a.k.a. Spotted Weakfish

Even though this backcountry prize is called a weakfish, it can be a challenging catch. The weakfish moniker derives from its clan's easily torn mouth membranes. The spotted seatrout (*Cynoscion nebulosus*)—actually a member of the fine-flavored drum family—nevertheless, resembles a trout, with shimmering iridescent tones of silver, green, blue, and bronze.

The seatrout's lower jaw, unlike a true trout's, projects upward, and a pair of good-size canine teeth protrudes from the upper jaw. These predatory, opportunistic feeders enjoy a smorgasbord of offerings but are particularly fond of live shrimp. The seatrout makes a distinctive splash and popping sound when it feeds on a drift of shrimp. These weakfish are easily spotted in the shallow backcountry waters, popular with light tackle enthusiasts who enjoy the stalk-and-cast challenge.

Seatrout prefer temperatures between 60 and 70 degrees. They must measure at least 12 inches. The catch is limited to four fish per person, per day. They are highly ranked as a table food because they are so delicately flavored, but the flesh spoils rapidly. Ice it quickly, and fillet the fish immediately upon returning to shore.

The Bluewater

The Gulf Stream, or Florida Current, moves through the Florida Straits south of Key West and flows northward, along the entire coast of Florida, at about four knots. This tropical river, 25 to 40 miles wide, maintains warm-water temperatures, hosting a piscatorial bounty from the prolific Caribbean that constantly restocks the waters of the Keys. The bluewater encompasses deep water from the reef to the edge of the Gulf Stream and is particularly prolific at the humps, which are underwater hills rising from the sea floor. The Islamorada Hump is 13 miles offshore from Islamorada. The West Hump lies 23 miles offshore from Marathon and rises from a depth of 1,100 feet to 480 feet below the surface.

Bluewater fishing is synonymous with offshore fishing here in the Keys. To an angler, it means big game: tuna, billfish, dolphin, cobia, wahoo, and kingfish. Also offshore, at the edge of the coral reef and the nearshore patch reefs, you will find a palette of bottom fish, snappers, and groupers coveted more for their table value than their fighting prowess, and a grab bag of bonus fish—some good to eat, all fun to catch.

Until you are experienced in our waters, you will need a guide. To troll for big game fish in the bluewater, you should book a private charter, which will put you on the fish and supply everything you need, including the professional expertise of the captain and mate, who know when to hold 'em . . . and when to fold 'em. These charters usually accommodate six anglers and though pricey—$750 to $900 per day plus tips—provide the most instruction and individual attention. You can divide the cost with five other anglers or join with another party and split the tab (see the Guides and Charters section of this chapter).

Alternately, sign on to a party boat, or head boat, which usually accommodates 50 or more anglers. These boats usually take anglers to the reef for bottom fishing, where you can drop a line and try your luck for snapper, grouper, and even kingfish and some of their sidekicks. Mates on deck untangle lines, answer questions, and even bait your hook. And although it is a little bit like taking the bus during rush hour instead of a limousine, at $30 to $40 per day—rods, tackle, and bait included—a party boat remains the most economical means of fishing offshore.

Billfish: Blue Marlin, White Marlin, Sailfish

Before you head out to the bluewater to hunt for sailfish and marlins, you might want to have a cardiac work-up and check your blood pressure because, if your trolled bait takes a hit, it will prove a battle of endurance.

The cobalt-blue marlin (*Makaira nigricans*), largest of the Atlantic marlins, migrates away from the equator in warmer months, enigmatically gracing the Keys waters on its way northward. Females of the species often reach trophy proportions—1,000 pounds or more—but

> ## Insiders' Tip
> When you see a boat being propelled by someone pushing it with a pole, please give that boat wide berth. These anglers are stalking game fish in the shallows of the flats. The sound of an engine will frighten all the fish.

males rarely exceed 300 pounds. Tuna and bonito provide the mainstay of the blue marlin's diet, but some blue marlins have been found with young swordfish in their stomachs. Anglers trolling ballyhoo or mullet have the chance of latching onto a blue marlin, especially in tuna-infested waters. A fighting blue marlin creates a specter of primitive beauty: A creature the size of a baby elephant plunges to the depths then soars in gravity-defying splendor, only to hammer the water once again and shoot off in a torpedolike run.

Less often caught in our waters is the white marlin (*Tetrapturus albidus*), which is much smaller than the blue, averaging 50 to 60 pounds and rarely exceeding 150 pounds. Both marlins use their swordlike bills to stun fast-moving fish, which they then consume. Unlike other members of its family, the dorsal and anal fins of the white marlin are rounded, not sharply pointed. The upper portion of its body is a brilliant green-blue, abruptly changing to silvery white on the sides and underslung with a white belly. White marlin will strike trolled live bait, feathers, and lures, hitting hard and running fast with repetitive jumps. The white marlin begins its southward migration as the waters of the North Atlantic cool in the autumn.

A shimmering dorsal fin, fanned much higher than the depth of its streamlined steel-blue body, distinguishes the sailfish (*Istiophorus platyperus*) from its billed brethren. Fronted with a long, slender bill, this graceful creature—averaging 7 feet long and 40 pounds in Florida waters—is meant to be captured and released but stuffed no more. Probably the most popular mount of all time—the flaunted mark of the been-there, done-that crowd—the sailfish, at least in the Florida Keys, is generally allowed to entertain, take a bow, and go back to the dressing room until the next show. Taxidermists now stock fiberglass blanks, so you need only phone in the prized measurements to receive your representative mount.

The migration of the sailfish coincides with that of the snowbirds, those Northerners who spend the frigid months in the balmy Florida Keys. In late autumn and early winter, the sailfish leave the Caribbean and Gulf waters and head up the Gulf Stream to the Keys. A fast-growing fish—4 to 5 feet in one year—the sailfish seldom lives more than five years. Feeding on the surface or at mid-depths on small fish and squid, the sailfish also is amenable to trolled appetizers of outrigger-mounted, live mullet, or ballyhoo that will wiggle, dive, and skip behind the boat like rats after the Pied Piper. The sailfish, swimming at up to 50 knots, will give you a run for your money, alternating dramatic runs and explosions from the depths with catapults through the air. The sailfish delights novice and expert alike. The inexperienced angler can glory in the pursuit with heavy tackle, while the seasoned veteran can lighten up, creating a new challenge. Both will savor the conquest.

Florida law allows you to keep one billfish per day and mandates size limitations. Sailfish must be at least 63 inches; blue marlin, 99 inches; and white marlin, 66 inches. We recommend, however, that you follow the ethical considerations of catch-and-release, recording your conquest on film instead.

Blackfin Tuna

Highly sought by anglers and blue marlin alike, the blackfin tuna (*Thunnus atlanticus*) is set apart from the other six tunas of North America by its totally black finlets. Rarely exceeding 50 pounds, this member of the mackerel family is not as prized as the giant bluefin of North Atlantic waters, but Keys anglers still relish a substantial battle and the bonus of great eating. Primarily a surface feeder, the blackfin terrorizes baitfish from below, causing them to streak to the surface and skitter out of the water like skipping stones, a move that attracts seabirds. A sighting of diving gulls will tip off the presence of tuna at the feed bag. Blackfin tuna are partial to a chumming of live pilchards but will also attack feathers and lures trolled at high speeds. Tuna fishing on the humps is usually good in the spring months.

Dolphin: Schoolies, Slammers, and Bulls

Anyone who has ever seen a rainbow of schooling dolphin (*Coryphaena hippurus*) knows the fish's identity crisis is unfounded. Nothing about this prismatic fish suggests the mammal sharing its name. The dolphin fish resembles a Tech-

Second only to billfish and tuna, the dolphin fish are prized by bluewater anglers.

PHOTO: FLORIDA KEYS & KEY WEST TDC

surface feeders, attracted to the small fish and other tasty morsels associated with floating debris or patches of drifting sargassum weed. Flying fish, plentiful in the Gulf Stream waters, form a large portion of their preferred diet. A school of dolphin will actually attack a trolled bait of small, whole mullet or ballyhoo, streaking from a distance in a me-first effort like school boys to the lunch gong. It is not unusual for three or four rods to be hit at one time, an all-hands-on-deck effort that approaches a marathon. And, as long as you keep one hooked dolphin in the water, alongside the boat, its buddies will hang around and wait their turn for a freshly baited hook.

Dolphin are a rapidly growing fish, living up to five years. The young are called schoolies, generally in the 5- to 15-pound range. Slammers make an angler salivate, as they each weigh 25 pounds and more, and an attacking school can get your heart pumping. Doing battle with the heavyweight, the bull dolphin, quite often happens by accident while you are trolling for some other species. But the bull can hold his own in any arena. Dolphin season is generally considered to be from March until August, but the fish tend to stay around all year.

nicolor cartoon. Its bright green, blue, and yellow wedgelike body looks like the fish just crashed into a paint cabinet, and its high, blunt, pugnacious forehead and Mohawk-style dorsal fin evoke a rowdy, in-your-face persona not wholly undeserved. Once out of the water, however, the brilliant hues ebb like a fading photograph, tingeing sweet victory with fleeting regret.

Second only to billfish and tuna, dolphin are prized by bluewater anglers. Frantic fights follow lightning strikes, and the dolphin often throws in some aerobatics besides. This unruly fighter rates as a delicacy at the table as well, celebrated as moist white-fleshed dolphin fillets in the Keys and South Florida, but marketed as mahi-mahi elsewhere. Dolphin fish are

Cobia: the Crab Eater

The cobia (*Rachycentron canadum*) the orphan of the piscatory world, enjoys no close relatives and is in a family by itself. Excellent on the table or on the troll, the adult cobia is a favorite bonus fish, often caught during a day in the bluewater looking for sailfish. Particularly partial to crabs, the cobia also feeds on shrimp, squid, and small fish. The young cobia is found often in the flats of nearshore bays and inlets around the mangroves and around buoys, pilings, and wrecks.

Wahoo

A fine-eating bonus fish, generally caught by fortunate accident while trolling for

Wahoo—a fine-eating bonus fish—is generally caught by accident while trolling for billfish.

PHOTO: LOUISE SKIDMORE

sailfish or kingfish, the wahoo (*Acanthocybium solandri*) is far from an also-ran. One of the fastest fish in the ocean, the wahoo is a bona fide member of the mackerel family, similar in many ways to the Spanish mackerel. Its long, beak-like snout and slender silver-and-blue-striped body contribute to its prowess as a speed swimmer, for when hooked, the wahoo runs swiftly, cutting and weaving like a tailback heading for a touchdown. This loner rarely travels in schools. Wahoo season is in May, but the fish are here year round.

Kingfish, a.k.a. King Mackerel

Here in the Florida Keys, we call the king mackerel—which goes by assorted aliases in other parts of the country—the kingfish. At the turn of the nineteenth century, kingfish was the most popular catch off the Keys. Sailfish, then unrevered, were considered pests because they crashed the kingfish bait. The streamlined kingfish (*Scomberomorus cavalla*) travels in large schools, migrating up and down the coast in search of warm waters. Kingfish commonly frequent the waters of the Keys during the winter months, heading north in the spring.

Kings can be caught by drift fishing, where anglers cut the boat's engines and drift, fishing over the schools. Alternately, you can troll for kingfish with whole mullet or ballyhoo. Some captains prefer to anchor and chum, lacing the slick from time to time with live pilchards. Any method you use, a wire leader is essential when angling for kingfish because the fish displays razor-sharp teeth it is not reticent to use. Kingfish caught in our waters commonly weigh in at about 20 pounds, although the fish have been recorded reaching upwards of 40 pounds. The kingfish is a good sport fish and also makes a fine meal.

Amberjack

When all else fails in the bluewater, you can always find a deep hole and battle an amberjack (*Seriola dumerili*). This powerful, bottom-plunging fish—nicknamed AJ—guarantees a good brawl. Bringing in an amberjack is like pulling up a Volkswagen Beetle with light tackle.

The Reef Elite: Grouper, Snapper, and the Mackerels

Inhabiting the edge of the barrier reef that extends the length of the Florida Keys and in the smaller patch reefs closer in to shore, several finned species noteworthy for their food value coexist with the brightly painted tropicals and other coral-dwelling creatures. Like a well-branched family tree, these fish encompass many clans, all entertaining to catch and most delectable to eat. Startled anglers have even brought in permit while fishing the wrecks along the reef line. The brooding presence of the barracuda is always a strong possibility on the reef because the 'cuda is partial to raw snapper "stew" or grouper "tartare" when given the opportunity. It thinks nothing of stealing half the hooked fish in one mighty chomp, leaving the angler nothing but a lifeless head.

You will need a boat at least 20 feet long to head out to the reef, some 4 to 5 miles offshore. But with a compass, your NOAA charts, a GPS, tackle, chunked bait, and some information gathered locally at the nearest bait and tackle shop, you should be able to find a hot spot on your own. Then all you need to do is fillet the captives, find a recipe, and fry up the spoils.

More than 50 species of grouper are found in the Florida waters, but three stand out in waters of the Florida Keys. The black grouper (*Mycteroperca bonaci*) has been known to reach 50 pounds and 3 feet in length. Distinguished from other grouper by the black blotches and brassy spots mottling its olive or gray body, the black grouper is, nonetheless, often confused with the gag grouper. Large, adult black groupers are found on the rocky bottom in deep water, although the youth hang out close to shore.

The aforementioned gag grouper (*Mycteroperca microlepis*) reaches a length and proportion similar to that of the black grouper, but its body is a uniform gray color with dark wormlike markings on its sides. The red grouper (*Epinephelus morio*), so named because of its brownish-red pigmentation and scarlet-orange mouth lining, lives on rocky bottoms at medium depths. This makes it an accessible catch for anglers using small boats and light tackle.

All groupers are hermaphrodites, meaning they possess both male and female reproductive organs. The young are females that change into males as they mature. Fond of small fish and squid, groupers can be enticed to hit chunked ballyhoo, mullet, and pilchards as well as shrimp. You will need a stout rod, a heavy leader, and a heavy sinker because the grouper will head for the rocks once it comprehends the insult of the hook. The ensuing fight is not for the fainthearted. You will have to horse the fish out of the rocks and corals, where the grouper will make every attempt to cut your line.

The snapper family is a popular bunch in the Florida Keys. The prolific cousins—all pleasurable to eat, delightful to catch, and kaleidoscopic to see—confuse Northerners with their dissimilarity. Snappers travel in schools and like to feed at night. Most common on the Keys table is probably the sweet, delicate yellowtail snapper (*Ocyurus chrysurus*), which usually ranges from 12 to 16 inches in length. Big yellowtails, called flags, approach 5 to 6 pounds and 20 inches in length and are prevalent from late summer through October. The yellowtail's back and upper sides shade from olive to bluish with yellow spots. A prominent yellow stripe begins at the yellowtail's mouth and runs mid-laterally to its deeply forked tail, which, as you would expect, is a deep, brilliant yellow. The yellowtail is skittish, line-shy, and tends to stay way behind the boat. The fish's small mouth won't accommodate the hooks most commonly used in the pursuit of the other snappers. Successful anglers use light line, no leaders, and small hooks buried in the bait (see our Close-up, Recipe for Yellowtail Chum Balls, in this chapter).

The mangrove snapper, or gray snapper (*Lutjanus griseus*), though often haunting the coral reef, also can be found inshore in mangrove habitats. Grayish in color with a red tinge along the sides, the mangrove snapper displays two conspicuous canine teeth at the front of the upper jaw. The mangrove is easier to catch than the yellowtail or the mutton snapper. Live shrimp and cut bait, added to a small hook, will induce these good fighters to strike. Anglers enjoy taking the mangroves on light tackle.

The brightly colored mutton snapper (*Lutanus analis*) shades from olive-green to red, with a bright blue line extending from under its eye to its tail. A black spot below the dorsal fin marks its side like an unwanted birthmark. Mutton snappers are most often caught in blue holes, so called because the water color of these deep coral potholes appears bluer than the surrounding waters. You will also find muttons in channels and creeks and occasionally even on a bonefish flat. The fish range in weight from 5 to 20 pounds. Mutton snappers are rumored to be shy and easily spooked by a bait that is cast too closely, but they love live pilchards. Usually caught in cloudy, churned up water, the muttons provide a fierce confrontation.

Ergonomically designed for speed, the torpedo-shaped Spanish mackerel (*Scomberomorus maculatus*) distinguishes itself from the king and the cero with a series of irregular, buttercup-yellow spots on its stripeless sides, which look like the freckles on the Little Rascals. Cherished by light-tackle enthusiasts, the Spanish mackerel averages less than 2 pounds, 20 inches in length. Its razorlike teeth dictate you carefully consider your choice in terminal tackle, for slashing your line rates at the top of the Spanish mackerel's getaway tactics. Spanish mackerel migrate into Florida Bay in February.

Larger than its Spanish cousin, the cero mackerel (*Scomberomorous regalis*) displays yellow spots above and below a bronze stripe that runs down its silvery sides, from the pectoral fin to the base of its tail. The cero is the local in our visiting mackerel lineup, not straying far from the waters of South Florida and the Keys, where it feeds on small fish and squid. The cero makes excellent table fare when consumed fresh, but fillets do not freeze well.

You may encounter the tripletail (*Lobotes surinamensis*) if you fish around

Mutton snappers are members of the reef elite, inhabiting the edge of the barrier reef. PHOTO: LOUISE SKIDMORE

wrecks, buoys, or sunken debris. Nick-named the buoy fish, the tripletail has been known to reach 40 pounds and a length of 3 feet. The fish's dorsal and anal fins are so long that they resemble two more tails, hence the name tripletail. The tripletail is a mottled palette of black, brown, and yellow, looking like an autumn leaf. Young tripletails, which like to stay close to shore in bays and estuaries, often are spotted floating on their sides at the surface, mimicking a leaf on the water. The tripletail will put up a valiant fight, and, though not seen on a restaurant menu, it will make a tasty dinner. You must catch tripletail with a hook and line only, no snatch hooks.

The Bridges

The bridges of the Florida Keys attract fighting game fish and flavorful food fish like magnets draw paper clips. The State of Florida replaced many of the original bridges of the Overseas Highway with wider, heavier spans in the late 1970s and '80s, subsequently fitting many of the old bridges, no longer used for automobile traffic, for use as fishing piers. These bridges are marked with brown and white signage depicting a fish, line, and hook. (Many of the old bridge structures have been closed because lack of maintenance has left them unsafe. Be sure to fish only from those bearing the county signage.) The fishing bridges offer the general public free fishing access to many of the same species that frequent more far-flung areas of our waters. Parking is provided at the fishing-pier bridges. The Seven Mile Bridge, the Long Key Bridge, and the Bahia Honda Bridge have been designated historical monuments.

The waters beneath the bridges host a lively population of tarpon, mangrove snappers, snook, baby groupers, and yel-lowtails (See the flats, backcountry and bluewater sections of this chapter for information on these fish.). Grunts (*Haemulon plumieri*) also are commonly caught at the bridges. Though little respected in other Keys' waters, this small,

bluish-gray fish is, nevertheless, fun to catch and makes a tasty meal. The grunt's name is derived from the sounds escaping the fish's bright orange mouth when it is captured. This grunting sound is actually the grinding of the pharyngeal teeth, which produces an audible noise ampli-fied by the air bladder.

Night fishing is popular from the bridge piers, too. An outgoing tide with a moderate flow inspires the fish to con-tinue feeding after dark. Baitfish and crus-taceans, a temptation too great for many of the finned predators to pass up, are fun-neled through the pilings and out to sea.

Stop in at one of the local bait and tackle shops to get rigged out for bridge fishing. The local fishing experts working in these shops are encyclopedias of knowl-edge and will be able to guide you as to times, tides, and tackle. Locals recom-mend you use stout tackle when fishing from one of our bridges. You'll not only have to retrieve your catch while battling a heavy current, but you also must lift it a great distance to the top of the bridge.

Live shrimp, cut bait, or live pinfish will attract attention from at least one of the species lurking below. You will need to keep your shrimp alive while fishing from the bridge. Put the shrimp on ice in a 5-gallon bucket with an aerator or in a large Styrofoam cooler with an aerator. You can also lower a chum bag (filled with a block of chum available at all bait shops) into the water. Tie a couple of dive weights to a long rope, lower the chum bag down the surface of a piling on the down-current side of the bridge, and tie it off to the rail-ing. Then fish the slick. The chum will drift with the current, attracting sharks and any finfish in the neighborhood.

You will need sinkers on your line in order for your baited hook to drop to the bottom because a swift current pulses under the bridges. Don't launch your cast away from the bridge. Drop your bait straight down, near a piling or down cur-rent, at the shore side of the bridge. Rub-ble from past construction sometimes piled here creates a current break allowing the fish a place to rest, feed, or hide in the swirls or eddies. Don't forget to buy a fishing license.

Fishing Licenses

Florida law states you must possess a saltwater fishing license if you attempt to take or possess marine fish for noncommercial purposes. This includes finfish and such invertebrate species as snails, whelks, clams, scallops, shrimps, crabs, lobsters, sea stars, sea urchins, and sea cucumbers.

Exempt from this law are individuals younger than 16 and Florida residents 65 and older. You are also exempt if you are a Florida resident and a member of the U.S. Armed Forces not stationed in Florida and home on leave for 30 or fewer days, with valid orders in your possession.

Florida residents who are fishing in salt water or for a saltwater species in fresh water, from land, or from a structure fixed to land need not purchase a license. Land is defined as "the area of ground located within the geographic boundaries of the state of Florida that extends to a water depth of 4 feet." This includes any structure permanently fixed to land such as a pier, bridge, dock or floating dock, or jetty. If you use a vessel to reach ground, however, you must have a license. And if you are wading in more than 4 feet of water or have broken the surface of the water wearing a facemask, you also must have one.

You are not required to have a license when you fish with one of our licensed captains on a charter holding a valid vessel saltwater fishing license or if you are fishing from a pier that has been issued a pier saltwater fishing license. Other, more

obscure exemptions also apply. Check the summary of fishing regulations issued with your saltwater fishing license.

A Florida saltwater fishing license is available from most bait and tackle shops and from any Monroe County tax collector's office. You can also obtain a license over the telephone by dialing (888) 347-4356. Residents and nonresidents pay differing amounts for this license. The state defines a resident as: anyone who has lived in Florida continuously for at least six months; anyone who has established a domicile in Florida and can provide evidence of such by law; any member of the U.S. Armed Forces who is stationed in Florida; any student enrolled in a college or university in Florida; or an alien who can prove residency status.

Residents pay $13.50 for one year and $61.50 for five years. Applications for the five-year license may be obtained from the tax collector's office. Nonresidents must pay $6.50 for a three-day license, $16.50 for seven days, and $31.50 for one year. This price includes $1.50 tax collector processing fee. Fifty cents more is charged if you purchase your license at a location other than the tax collector's office. If you wish to take snook or lobster, you must add the appropriate stamp to your Florida saltwater fishing license. Each stamp costs $2.50.

Florida residents may purchase a lifetime saltwater fishing license. If you are between the ages of 13 and 64, the cost is $301.50; for those younger than 13, rates are less. Lifetime licenses are available at the county tax collector's office. No snook or crawfish stamps are required. If you are a Florida resident and are certified as totally and permanently disabled, you are entitled to receive, without charge from the county tax collector, a permanent saltwater fishing license.

The penalty for fishing without the required license or stamps is $50 plus the cost of purchasing the proper documentation. A $50 tarpon tag is required if you insist upon keeping and therefore killing a tarpon instead of releasing it (see the

Catch-and-Release Ethics section in this chapter).

Tournaments

If you're an angler who would like to compete against your peers instead of just yourself, the Florida Keys offers a plethora of exciting tournaments encompassing most of the finned species enriching our waters. These tournaments, scheduled year round, from Key Largo to Key West, award prizes, cash, or trophies in a variety of categories ranging from heaviest or longest to most caught and released in a specified time period.

Generally, the tournaments fit into one of three categories, although some tournaments have multiple divisions. The billfish tournaments—white marlin, blue marlin, and sailfish—are the most prestigious and the most expensive, with entry fees per boat of four anglers of $450 and higher. Billfish tournaments are catch-and-release events. Proof of the catch usually requires a photograph and a sample of the leader, which will be tested for chafing. Scoring follows an intricate point system. A catch of a white marlin, a blue marlin, and a sailfish in one day—not your average day, even in the Keys—constitutes a slam.

Dolphin tournaments are more family-type competitions. Generally, the fee per angler is about $50. Anglers use their own boats without guides, and if the dolphin exceeds pre-specified poundage, it may be brought in and weighed. Anglers can keep the fish, which are excellent eating.

Flats tournaments—tarpon, bonefish, and permit—are always catch-and-release, usually scored by a point system. A catch on a fly rod scores more points than one retrieved on light tackle. The fish must be measured, a photo must be taken, and the process must be witnessed. We recommend you book one year in advance for tarpon tournaments.

Some of our tournaments are restricted to a specific category of angler—women only or juniors only, for instance—or to a particular type of tackle, such as light tackle or fly rods. Others award a mixed bag of catches ranging from game fish to groupers to grunts. Many of the tournaments donate at least a portion of their proceeds to a charitable organization.

In the following section, we introduce you to a sampling of the most important fishing tournaments held annually in the Keys. For a complete listing, call Florida Keys Fishing Tournament Administrator Christina Sharpe at (305) 872-2233 or check the website www.fla-keys.com and follow the fishing icons.

Cheeca Lodge Presidential Sailfish Tournament
Islamorada, FL
(305) 664-4651
www.cheeca.com

This important tournament, held in mid-January, was named the Presidential back when former president George Bush fished our Islamorada waters. The name still holds, for it's one of the most popular tournaments of the season. Anglers (four per boat) fish for two full days in search of the most sailfish, which are caught and released. Anglers follow the honor system as to what constitutes a catch. Any disputes are handled with a lie detector test—no kidding! This is the only billfish tournament in the Keys with an outboard division, which affords any angler with a boat the chance to compete, no charter required. Cash prizes and trophies are awarded the winners. Contact person is Julie Olsen.

Ladies Tarpon Tournament
Marathon, FL
(305) 743-6139
www.worldclassangler.com

The waters under the Seven Mile Bridge and the Bahia Honda bridge are invaded by tarpon-seeking women each year in late April or early May in this ladies-only tarpon tournament. The number of tarpon caught and released in the two-day tournament determines the winners of a cache of rods and reels, trophies, and an assortment of jewelry. Points are awarded

Angling in the Florida Keys approaches a religion to many, especially during one of our many fishing tournaments. PHOTO: MARY MOCCIA

for catches on 12-pound test and 30-pound test. Dave Navarro is the contact person.

Texaco Key West Classic
Key West, FL
(305) 294–4042

Big money can be won in this late-April tournament, which holds a large pot spread over a variety of categories. The major targets are blue or white marlin, sailfish, tarpon, and permit, all catch-and-release except for fun-fish. All boats registered in other divisions can participate in the fun-fish categories, which award cash prizes for the heaviest dolphin, tuna, and wahoo weighing in at more than 20 pounds. Proceeds benefit the National Mental Health Association. Contact Findlay Sinclair for more information.

Key West & Lower Keys Fishing Tournament
Key West, FL
(305) 745–3332, (800) 970–9056

This unusual tournament must have been designed for the angler who just can't fish

enough. It lasts seven months, from April to late November, and encompasses a potpourri of divisions and species. Both charters and individuals can register for the tournament and also participate in a two-day kickoff tournament-within-a-tournament, which in itself awards cash prizes. Anglers weigh their food-fish catches or record their releases at participating marinas and are awarded citations for their efforts. At the grand finale of the tournament, the tabulated results are announced, and all prizes are presented. Contact person is Capt. Linda Luizza.

Coconuts Dolphin Tournament
Key Largo, FL
(305) 453–9794

The largest dolphin tournament in the Florida Keys, Coconuts Dolphin Tournament at Marina Del Mar in mid-May regularly hosts more than 700 anglers. This three-day tournament, which awards cash prizes, runs from 8 A.M. to 3 P.M. each day. You can book a charter to fish the tournament or use your own boat. The director says there has been no proven advantage to having a charter. Scoring is determined by weight of the fish. Since this is a food-fish tournament, anglers may bring in all dolphin of more than 10 pounds. Mohammad Motamedi is the contact person.

Don Hawley Invitational Tarpon Tournament
Islamorada, FL
(903) 450-4450

The oldest tarpon-on-fly tournament in the Keys and the first all-release tournament, the Don Hawley event is a five-day fishing extravaganza of all-fly, all-tarpon, and all-release. Anglers are awarded 1,000 points for a catch-and-release on 12-pound tippet, 750 points on 16-pound. Winners amassing the most points secure original Keys art by such notables as Al Barnes, Bill Elliott, and Kendall Van Sant. Proceeds of the tournament benefit the nonprofit Don Hawley Foundation, which supports the study of tarpon fishery and preservation in the Florida Keys and provides assistance to guides and their families in time of need. The tournament is held in early June. Eddie Miller is the person to call for information.

Women's World Invitational Fly Championships—Tarpon Series
Islamorada, FL
(305) 664-2080

This ladies-only, three-day, tarpon catch-and-release tournament is limited to 30 anglers, one per boat. The tarpon must be taken on fly only and measure at least 4 feet. Touching the leader is a catch in this release tournament. Regulation measuring sticks and the honor system determine size of the catch. Winners are awarded original artwork of the Keys, crystal trophies, and an assortment of rods and reels. This nonprofit tournament, held in mid-June, awards a scholarship to a local high school student who will pursue studies in environmental or marine science, thereby giving back the gift of knowledge to the Keys. There is usually a waiting list for this tournament, so contact Suzan Baker or Diane Harbaugh as soon as possible.

Mercury S.L.A.M. Tournament
Key West, FL
(305) 664-2002
www.redbone.org

First in the Celebrity Tournament Series each year is the S.L.A.M. (Southernmost Light-tackle Anglers Masters) event in early September, directed by Gary Ellis, for the benefit of cystic fibrosis research (see the Baybone and Redbone tournament events). Participants in this two-day fishing event angle to score a grand slam: the catch and release of a bonefish, permit, and tarpon in two days. Points are awarded for each release in categories of fly, spin/plug, and general bait. Each release is photographed against a measuring device.

Like the other two tournaments in this series, the S.L.A.M. awards original art and sculpture to its winners. Anglers can fish as a two-person team or one angler can opt to fish with a celebrity. The contact person is Gary Ellis.

Little Palm Island Grand Slam
Little Torch Key, FL
(305) 664-2002
www.redbone.org

This small and select two-day tournament in late August or early September, with a kickoff and awards banquet at the elite Little Palm Island, is a catch-and-release event in search of the elusive grand slam: tarpon, bonefish, and permit in two days. Winners of the 30-boat event (two anglers per boat) receive original paintings, limited-edition prints, and pieces of sculpture. Proceeds of this tournament, like the Celebrity Tournament Series, benefit research by the Cystic Fibrosis Foundation. Contact Gary Ellis for more details.

Women's World Invitational Fly Championships—Bonefish Series
Islamorada, FL
(305) 664-5423

This late-September event, open to both men and women, cashes in on the growing popularity of saltwater fly-fishing.

Though sharing the same waters as the bonefish and stalked in the same manner, the permit proves to be a more elusive catch. PHOTO: VICTORIA SHEARER

Participants will be fishing for bonefish, on fly only. Photographs and regulation measuring sticks will provide proof of the catch in this release tournament. Prizes include original art pieces, fine crystal, and tackle. The director will book you a guide if desired. A portion of the proceeds benefits environmental scholarship funds. Contact Sue Moret for more information.

Mercury Baybone
Key Largo, FL
(305) 664–2002
www.redbone.org

Event No. 2 in the Celebrity Tournament Series, the prestigious catch-and-release Baybone tournament in late September or early October, run by Gary Ellis, benefits

cystic fibrosis research. Ellis is particularly interested in this worthy cause because his daughter, Nicole, has cystic fibrosis. The Celebrity Tournament Series, which includes the Redbone and the Mercury S.L.A.M., donates 100 percent of its proceeds to the Cystic Fibrosis Foundation for research. The stalked catch for the Baybone is bonefish and permit, which are photographed against a measuring device and released. Points are awarded for catches on fly, spin/plug, or general bait; nothing heavier than 12-pound test may be used in all divisions. An intricate point system determines the winners, who receive original paintings and sculptures as prizes. Anglers can fish as a two-person team or one angler can be paired with a celebrity.

Mercury Cheeca/Redbone
Islamorada, FL
(305) 664–2002
www.redbone.org

Third in the Celebrity Tournament Series and co-sponsored by Cheeca Lodge, the prestigious Redbone (first held in 1988), attracts anglers in competitive search for bonefish and redfish, in early November. Also benefiting cystic fibrosis research, the Redbone follows the rules and regulations of the other two tournaments in the series. Many anglers try to fish all three tournaments. The grand champion of the series wins a gold Rolex Yachtmaster watch. Again, Gary Ellis is the one to call for more on this tourney.

George Bush/Cheeca Lodge
Bonefish Tournament
Islamorada, FL
(305) 664–4651
www.cheeca.com

Perhaps the most prestigious of all tournaments in the Florida Keys is the George Bush/Cheeca Lodge Bonefish Tournament, held in autumn. The former president, George Bush, himself competes in this event. (He came in second in 1999.) Preceded by a kickoff meeting, two days of intense fishing are followed by an awards banquet at Cheeca Lodge. Fifty boats participate, two anglers per boat. Other than those included in the most-catches category, bonefish must weigh at least 8 pounds to qualify. All must be released. Trophies are awarded to winners. Proceeds benefit a variety of Keys environmental groups. Contact Julie Olsen for more information.

Guides and Charters

Nearly 1,000 charter captains and guides—be it flats, bluewater, or backcountry—do business in the Florida Keys. Our guides are the most knowledgeable in the world—licensed captains who maintain safe, government-regulated watercraft. Hiring a guide allows the first-time visitor or the novice angler an opportunity to learn how to fish the waters of the Florida Keys and catch its bounty without having to spend too much time learning about the fish's habits. And guides will be your best teachers, for they usually have a lifetime of experience. Once you fish our waters, however, you will be the "hooked" species, for this unforgettable angling experience is addictive.

Book a guide as soon as you know when you are coming to the Keys because the guides here book up quickly, especially during certain times of the year. If you hope to fish our waters with a guide during tarpon season, especially the months of May and June, plan a year ahead. Holidays such as Christmas and New Year's book up quickly also. Traditionally, the months of August through November are a bit slower. You may be able to wing it during those months, but we wouldn't advise it. Even if you don't take a charter trip, stop at a fishing marina about 4 P.M. and check out the catch of the day.

Bluewater or offshore fishing charters can accommodate six anglers. The captain guides the vessel to his or her favorite hot spots, which are anywhere from 6 to 26 miles offshore and usually closely guarded secrets. Often he will stop on his bluewater trek so the mate can throw a cast net for live bait. The mate will rig the baits, ready the outriggers, and cast the baited hooks for you. Big game fish are usually stalked by trolling, as are dolphin. You need do nothing but relax, soak in the sea air, and wait for the call, "Fish on!" Then the action is up to you.

Bluewater charter boats range in size from 35 to 50 feet. Each generally has an enclosed cabin and a head (toilet) on board. Everything you need for a day's fishing is provided except your refreshments, lunch, and any personal items you may need. Expect a half-day charter to cost $450 to $600. A full day will run anywhere from $750 to $900, depending upon the size of the boat. It is customary to tip the mate 10 to 15 percent cash if you have had a good day.

Guides for flats fishing or backcountry angling usually take a maximum of two anglers per boat. The guide will pole the skiff or flats boat through the skinny water, attentively looking for fish from atop the poling platform. This sight fishing dictates both guide and anglers stand alert, all senses engaged. The angler, whether fly fishing or spin casting, casts to the desired location directed by the guide.

Flatsboats measure 16 to 18 feet. They are not outfitted with any shading devices, nor do they have a head. Be aware, you may have to use rather primitive facilities. Many of the guides will dip into shore for a pit stop, but others will not, so inquire before you leave the dock. All fly or spin rods, reels, tackle, and bait are provided. Some guides even tie their own flies, providing special furry or feathery creations proven to entice the fish. A half-day flats or backcountry guide will charge between

Insiders' Tip
Remove litter and leftover bait from piers, bridges, and other fishing sites.

Spotting a cruising bonefish in the flats takes some practice and a knowledgeable guide.

PHOTO: FLORIDA KEYS & KEY WEST TDC

$275 and $350. A full day will cost between $375 and $450. Night tarpon fishing runs about $400. It is customary to tip the guide 10 to 15 percent in cash if you were happy with the excursion.

When booking a charter, inquire about penalties for canceling your reservations. No-shows frequently will be charged the full price.

Always bring sunscreen, polarized sunglasses, a hat with a long bill lined with dark fabric to cut the glare, and motion-sickness pills (even if you've never needed them before). Anglers are responsible for providing their own lunches and refreshments. Keys tradition is to bring lunch for the captain and mate on a bluewater charter or for the guide on a flats trip.

Many guides are known only on a word-of-mouth basis, but we have compiled a source list of fishing marinas and outfitters you may call to secure an offshore charter or flats or backcountry guide. The chambers of commerce in Key Largo, Islamorada, Marathon, the Lower Keys, and Key West also act as referral sources (see subsequent listings).

Perhaps even more than the rest of the Keys, you'll need a guide to find the fish in the waters surrounding Key West. A busy harbor for centuries, Key West's marinas and bights are a bustling maze to the uninitiated. Many of the more than 60 charter boats in the Key West fleet dock at the City Marina at Garrison Bight, which is accessed on Palm Avenue, just off N. Roosevelt Boulevard. This marina is locally referred to as Charter Boat Row. From 7 to 7:30 A.M. and 3:30 to 5 P.M. the captains are available at their vessels, to take direct bookings. You can meet them and their crews, see the offshore vessels, and save money to boot. Booking a charter directly with the captain instead of a charter agency nets you a sizable discount.

Some guides are willing to captain your private vessel at a much-reduced charter rate. If this interests you, inquire when you call one of these booking sources. Often hotels maintain a source list of guides or charter captains they will recommend. Inquire when you reserve your accommodations.

Offshore and Backcountry Guide Booking Sources

Establishments acting as booking services will determine your needs and book your flats/backcountry guide or bluewater/offshore charter directly. They usually require a deposit of $100 to $200 and accept credit cards. Cancellation policies vary and change from year to year, so be sure to inquire about procedures and penalties before you book your charter. The top guides in the Florida Keys book out of the establishments listed below. Be sure to log onto their websites to find out more information on the guides they represent.

Upper Keys

Holiday Isle Marina
MM 84 Oceanside
Islamorada, FL
(305) 664-2321, (800) 327-7070
www.holidayisle.com

Whale Harbor Dock & Marina
MM 81.9 Oceanside
Islamorada, FL
(305) 664-4511

Sandy Moret's Florida Keys Outfitters
MM 81.9 Bayside
Islamorada, FL
(305) 664-5423
www.floridakeysoutfitters.com

World Wide Sportsman Inc.
MM 81.5 Bayside
Islamorada, FL
(305) 664-4615, (800) 327-2880
www.worldwidesportsman.com

Besides booking your guide, World Wide Sportsman acts as a full-service travel agency. It also can arrange your hotel and rental car.

Bud n' Mary's Fishing Marina
MM 79.8 Oceanside
Islamorada, FL
(305) 664–2461, (800) 742–7945
www.budnmarys.com

Papa Joe's Marina
MM 79.7 Bayside
Islamorada, FL
(305) 664–5005, (800) 539–8326
www.papajoesmarina.com

Middle Keys

Hawk's Cay Marina
MM 61 Oceanside
Duck Key, FL
(305) 743–9000
www.hawkscay.com

Key Colony Beach Marina
MM 54 Oceanside
Key Colony Beach Causeway
Key Colony Beach, FL
(305) 289–1310
www.keycolonybeachmarina.com

Captain Hook's Marina
MM 53 Oceanside
Marathon, FL
(305) 743–2444
www.captainhooks.com

World Class Angler
MM 50 Bayside
Marathon, FL
(305) 743–6139
www.worldclassangler.com

Lower Keys

Strike Zone Charters
MM 29.5 Bayside
Big Pine Key, FL
(305) 872–9863, (800) 654–9560
www.strikezonecharter.com

Sea Boots Outfitters
MM 30 Bayside
Big Pine Key, FL
(305) 745–1530, (800) 238–1746
www.seaboots.com

Key West

In addition to the limited number of fishing marinas and outfitters booking guides or charters, Key West's fishing excursions are put together by charter agencies operated out of booths peppering Mallory Square, Duval, and other major streets of Key West. You also can book party boats at these booths.

Oceanside Marina
5950 Peninsula Avenue
Stock Island, FL
(305) 294–4676
www.oceansidemarina.com

The Saltwater Angler
Hilton Resort & Marina
243 Front Street
Key West, FL
(305) 296–0700, (800) 223–1629
www.saltwaterangler.com

Chambers of Commerce

Key Largo Chamber of Commerce &
Florida Keys Visitors Center
MM 106 Bayside
Key Largo, FL
(305) 451–1414, (800) 822–1088
www.keylargo.org

This chamber will provide names of guides who either belong to the Key Largo Chamber of Commerce or those from other areas of the Keys who pay a fee to the Florida Keys Visitors Center for representation.

Islamorada Chamber of Commerce
MM 82.5 Bayside
Islamorada, FL
(305) 664–4503, (800) 322–5397
www.islamoradachamber.com

This chamber maintains an active list of guides in the Islamorada area.

Greater Marathon Chamber of Commerce
MM 53.5 Bayside
Marathon, FL
(305) 743–5417, (800) 262–7284
www.floridakeysmarathon.com

Upon request, this chamber will send you a list of guides belonging to the Marathon Guides Association. (The list is also posted on their web page.) The list specifies the guide's name, address, telephone number, type of fishing (i.e., bluewater or flats), fishing specialties (spin or fly), and size and make of boat. If you don't have time to wait for this list by mail, the chamber will provide several selections over the telephone. The Visitor's Center maintains a reservation line at (877) 934–FISH.

Lower Keys Chamber of Commerce
MM 31 Oceanside
Big Pine Key, FL
(305) 872–2411, (800) 872–3722
www.lowerkeyschamber.com

The Lower Keys chamber goes beyond its membership list to refer you to a wide range of guides and captains in the area.

Key West Chamber of Commerce
Mallory Square
Key West, FL
(305) 294–2587, (800) 648–6269
www.fla-keys.com

The staff at the Key West Chamber of Commerce will mail you a list of guides or captains who are chamber members.

Party Boats

Party boats, sometimes called head boats, offer a relatively inexpensive way to fish the waters of the Keys. Half-day excursions average about $27 per adult, $20 per child. Some party boats offer only an all-day option, which averages about $48. Evening fishing trips, generally lasting four to five hours, cost between $30 and $35.

The party boats, U.S. Coast Guard–inspected and certified vessels, generally hold 50 passengers or more, but most average no more than 25 to 30 anglers. Party boats take anglers out to the reef where they anchor or drift and bottom fish for more than 40 species of fish. Spring and summer seasons sport a plethora of groupers, snappers, dolphin

> ## Insiders' Tip
> In the accessible Gulf waters near Key West and beyond, more than 30 wrecks, such as the *Luchenbach* and the *Gunvor*, harbor legions of fish within their graveyard decks and holds.

fish, and yellowtails, while kingfish and cobia are more apt to make an appearance in the winter months. Porgies, grunts, and some species of snappers and groupers show up all year. Occasionally even a sailfish or a big shark has been caught from a party boat here.

The party boat offers rod and reel rental at a nominal fee per trip. This includes your terminal tackle—hook, line, and sinker—and all bait. If you bring your own fishing gear, bait is included in the excursion fee. You do not need a fishing license on a party boat. While most party boat information mentions your license is included in the excursion fee, this actually is only a temporary license, good for the duration of your fishing trip only. Two or more mates will be working the boat, helping you bait hooks, confiding fishing tips, and untangling the inevitable crossed lines.

Most of the party boats have seats around the periphery of the lower deck and a shaded sun deck up top. You are advised to wear shorts rather than swimsuits and durable sneakers or deck shoes, not thongs or sandals. Remember, there will be a lot of anglers and many flying hooks on the boat. Put some sturdy cloth between your skin and that accidental snag. Most captains recommend bringing a lightweight long-sleeved shirt for protection against the sun and a jacket to ward off cool breezes. Bring sunglasses, sunscreen, a hat, and motion sickness pills (many people who never suffered from

Local Secrets for Tight Lines

- Break off the fanned out portion of a shrimp's tail before baiting your hook. This immediately releases a scent into the water.

- Wet your hands before you handle any fish you catch. When you touch a fish you inadvertently knock off scales and remove the slime layer that protects its skin from microorganisms in the water.

- Bow to the silver king. Whenever a tarpon jumps, lower the rod tip, releasing the pressure from the line when the fish is out of the water. Many hooks have been pulled and lines broken when the angler forgets to release the pressure.

- As soon as a bonefish takes out line, tearing off from the flat, put your rod and your arms as high in the air as possible to keep the line out of the water. This keeps the line from breaking on small mangrove shoots or coral ledges of the deeper water.

- When fishing for bonefish, don't use oils, lotions, or repellents on your fingers. A keen sense of smell allows the bonefish to discern this odor on your bait. Instead, apply the liquid to the back of one hand and rub it on the back of the other.

- To catch a barracuda: When the barracuda strikes, point the rod tip toward the fish and put a little slack in the line. Let the fish pull against the line, then set the hook with a gentle snap.

- An injured or dying fish will have red, bloodshot eyes. Many game fish will prey on the weak or injured in their midst, so use an artificial lure with red eyes.

- When handling a tarpon, wear wetted gloves. The gloves protect your hands from the tarpon's sharp gill plates and keep the line from cutting your fingers if the powerful fish leaps to escape your grasp. Wet the gloves so as not to injure the fish's scales.

- Don't try to stop a bonefish when it's running. Attempting to reel while the fish is taking out line will only put a severe twist in your line, weakening the strength of the line. When the fish slows down and stops taking out line, begin your retrieve using a pump-and-reel action.

- Look for large stingrays. Redfish, bonefish, and permit will follow the stingray as it stirs up the mud on the bottom, hoping for an uncovered morsel or two.

- Noise originating from above the water frightens bonefish. Remember: no loud talking, don't slam the cooler lid, and don't stumble over the anchor.

- Use a quick-release anchor when fishing for tarpon in the current beneath our bridges. Attach your anchor line to a float buoy. Then attach your boat to the float buoy with a snap hook. When you hook a tarpon, start your motor, unsnap the anchor line from the boat and go with the fish. After you have caught and released the fish, return and pick up the float and re-hook your boat to the anchor line. This allows you fast access to the chase and the ability to return to the exact same hot spot.

seasickness before find drifting in the swells causes them mal de mer). Also bring a fishing rag or towel to wipe your hands on during the day.

After you land a fish, a mate will help you take it off the hook and will check the species to make sure it is not one of those protected by law, such as Nassau grouper. The mate then will measure the fish to ensure it meets the required size limit, tag it with your name, and place it on ice. At the end of the fishing trip, you may reclaim your catch. The mate will clean your fish, usually for tips. Party boats with a set cleaning-fee policy will be noted in the descriptions. Mates work for tips aboard party boats, the standard tip being 10 to 15 percent if you had a good day and if the mate was helpful.

The following party boats may be booked for day or evening charters. It is always a good idea to arrive at the docks 30 minutes before departure to stow your gear on the boat and secure a good position on deck. All boats have restrooms on board. Most have an enclosed cabin and offer a limited snack bar, beer, and soda. Exceptions will be noted.

In all cases, you are allowed to bring your own cooler filled with lunch and refreshments. All party boats recommended in this section take credit cards unless otherwise stated. Children's rates for youngsters 12 and younger are often available.

Upper Keys

Sailor's Choice
Holiday Inn Marina
MM 100 Oceanside
Key Largo, FL
(305) 451–1802

Sailor's Choice, a 65-foot, aluminum, custom-built craft with an air-conditioned lounge, offers plenty of shade and seating for anglers on its daily fishing excursions. Children are welcome on both day and evening trips. During the day, they can easily see the big fish in the water and seabirds, porpoises, and sea turtles.

The two daily excursions are from 9 A.M. to 1 P.M. and 1:30 to 5:30 P.M.

Captain Michael
Holiday Isle Resort
MM 84.5 Oceanside
Islamorada, FL
(305) 664–8070, (877) 664–9814
www.robbies.com

If you just can't get enough fishing, the *Captain Michael* offers a money-saving option: Fish the morning excursion, and go out again in the afternoon at a reduced price. Rates for children younger than five, who will only be "assisting" Mom and Dad, are further reduced. The 65-foot *Captain Michael*, with spacious decks and an air-conditioned cabin, is available for private charters, sunset cruises, and wedding receptions.

Daily trips are from 9:30 A.M. to 1:30 P.M. and 1:45 to 5:45 P.M. The evening excursion is from 7:30 P.M. to 12:30 A.M.

Miss Tradewinds
Whale Harbor Marina
MM 83.5 Oceanside
Islamorada, FL
(305) 664–8341 (dock), (305) 664–4511 (office)
www.misstradewinds.com

Docked at Whale Harbor Marina since 1973, *Miss Tradewinds* makes a quick 30-minute trip to the reef so you can maximize a full three hours of fishing time. The captains of *Miss Tradewinds*, each with more than 15 years experience fishing the Keys' waters, offer you a great advantage.

Two daily excursions are available, from 9:30 A.M. to 1:30 P.M. and 1:45 to 5:30 P.M. The evening trip takes place from 7:30 P.M. to 12:30 A.M.

Gulf Lady
Bud n' Mary's Marina
MM 79.8 Oceanside
Islamorada, FL
(305) 664–2461, (800) 742–7945
www.budnmarys.com

Mates are stationed at the bow and at the stern of the *Gulf Lady* and the captain also

A knowledgeable guide and mate can put you on the fish in the bluewaters of the Atlantic.

PHOTO: VIVIENNE AFSHARI

works the boat, so you'll get plenty of assistance on this fishing trip. If you bring your own tackle, the captain recommends you have both 12-pound and 20-pound test. This 65-foot vessel also is available for private fishing charters and wedding receptions.

Daily trips are from 9:30 A.M. to 4:30 P.M.

Middle Keys

Marathon Lady
Marathon Lady Dock
at the Vaca Cut Bridge
MM 53 Oceanside
Marathon, FL
(305) 743-5580

Children fish for significantly reduced rates aboard the *Marathon Lady*. Inquire when you make your reservations. If you rent a rod and reel for the excursion, your tackle is included, but if you prefer to bring your own gear, terminal tackle is available for a nominal fee. The mates will clean your catch for 25 cents per fish. A cooler with lunch and refreshments is allowed on all-day winter excursions. However, on summer evening excursions, which replace the all-day winter ventures, the captain prefers you bring your refreshments in a plastic bag; the crew will put them on ice for you.

From October through May, daily trips are conducted from 8:30 A.M. to 12:30 P.M. and from 1:30 P.M. to 5:30 P.M. From June through August, daily trips run from 8:30 A.M. to 12:30 P.M. and from 6:30 P.M. to midnight. *Marathon Lady* does not run during the month of September.

Key West

Key West party boats are docked at Charter Boat Row on Palm Avenue off N. Roosevelt. You can call the numbers listed to make reservations, book a space at one of the booths on Duval Street and in the Mallory Square area, or simply come down to the docks and make arrangements directly with the captain. Vessels usually operate at far less than maximum capacity during most seasons, so finding a spot should not present a problem.

Can't Miss
Charter Boat Row
City Marina
Garrison Bight, FL
(305) 296-3751

The excursion fee with the *Can't Miss* includes your rod, reel, terminal tackle, and bait. Senior citizens and members of

> ### Insiders' Tip
>
> Commercial shrimping is big business in Key West bluewaters, and the bonito and tuna like to follow these boats, scavenging the smorgasbord the shrimpers leave behind.

the military services receive a discount on the all-inclusive fishing excursion fee. The on-board snack bar serves a selection of sandwiches and other refreshments. Mates will clean your fish, but negotiate the fee before they begin. The *Can't Miss* is available for sunset charters and private trips to the Dry Tortugas. Daily excursions are from noon to 5 P.M. Evening outings, June through August only, run from 6:30 P.M. to 1 A.M.

Capt. John's Greyhound V
Charter Boat Row
City Marina
Garrison Bight, FL
(305) 296-5139

Daily trips are from 11 A.M. to 4 P.M. Passengers who would like to ride along and use the sun deck instead of fishing may do so for a lesser charge.

In July and August, two excursions are offered daily: 8:30 A.M. to 1 P.M. and 3 P.M. to 8 P.M. The party boat does not operate in the month of September. Mates charge a nominal fee to clean your fish.

Gulf Stream III
Charter Boat Row
City Marina
Garrison Bight, FL
(305) 296-8494

The *Gulf Stream III* provides a full-service lunch counter offering sandwiches, beer, and soda. Ever prepared, the crew will provide free motion-sickness pills if the need arises. The mates will clean your catch for 30 cents apiece.

Patience is the key word when fishing the protected waters of Everglades National Park.

PHOTO: VICTORIA SHEARER

Daily excursions, September through June, are from 9:30 A.M. to 4:30 P.M. Evening outings are conducted in July and August only, from 6:30 P.M. to 1 A.M. Sunbathers may come along on this party boat for half price.

Tortuga
Conch Harbor Marina
951 Caroline Street
Key West, FL
(305) 292–1189

Prices on the *Tortuga* include rod and reel as well as bait. Two excursions leave daily, 9 A.M. to 1 P.M. and 2 to 6 P.M. In June, July, and August, an evening trip leaves at 7 P.M., returning at midnight.

Outfitters

Upper Keys

Sandy Moret's Florida Keys Outfitters
MM 81.9 Bayside
Islamorada, FL
(305) 664–5423
www.floridakeysoutfitters.com

The focus here is on fly-fishing, and this outfitter's personnel rank as some of the most experienced in the sport. You'll find Orvis, Sage, G. Loomis, and Scott fly rods and Tibor and Abel fly reels, plus a wide selection of flies and fly-tying materials. In addition to Columbia, Sage, Patagonia, and Orvis clothing, Florida Keys Outfitters sells Teva sandals and Sebago and Columbia boat shoes. An angling art gallery features originals and prints by Millard Wells, Al Barnes, Don Ray, Tim Borsky, C.D. Clark, and Kendall Van Sant.

World Wide Sportsman Inc.
MM 81.5 Bayside
Islamorada, FL
(305) 664–4615, (800) 327–2880
www.worldwidesportsman.com

Anglers will discover nirvana at World Wide Sportsman, a 29,000-square-foot super store in Islamorada (see our Shopping chapter). Owned by Johnny Morris of Bass Pro Shops, World Wide is stocked to the rafters with a wide assortment of fishing tackle, including Billy Pate, Tibor, Penn, Sage, Daiwa, Shimano, Orvis, and many more. You'll find fly-tying materials and a huge assortment of flies here. A rod and reel repair center is on premises. ExOfficio, Woolrich, Bimini Bay, Sportif, Tarponwear, and Columbia fishing clothes for both men and women are just a few of the many brands offered.

The facility also features a full-service marina of 40 to 50 slips, accommodating boats up to 42 feet in length. Many of the area guides launch from these facilities. The marina offers a fuel dock (both gas and diesel) as well as frozen, live, and fresh bait. All things considered, this fishing emporium is every angler's dream store.

Bonefish Bob's
MM 81 Bayside
Islamorada, FL
(305) 664–9420
www.bonefishbob.com

This unique outfitter carries all kinds of tackle but specializes in fly-fishing gear and collectibles. Bob stocks Thomas & Thomas and Winston rods and Penn, Abel, Sea Master, and Lamson reels. You can find a nifty fly-tying table and all the supplies here too. Bob sells more than 400 used rods and maintains a collection of antique fishing memorabilia, including everything from old books to bamboo poles. Expert advice is free for the asking, and the owner gives free fly-casting lessons on the lawn out back.

Middle Keys

World Class Angler
MM 50 Bayside
Marathon, FL
(305) 743–6139
www.worldclassangler.com

World Class Angler sells anything and everything you'll need for saltwater fishing, stocking 37 brand names of reels, rods, and fishing gear. The facility specializes in the tarpon worm lure, a must-have if you are lucky enough to witness the annual worm hatch in our waters. The tarpon worm hatches at night for two nights in a row, and then in two weeks another worm hatch takes place. No one can predict exactly when the hatchings will happen, usually in June, but the tarpon go wild over the worms. So, we are told, do the anglers.

Lower Keys

Sea Boots Outfitters
MM 29.9 Bayside
Big Pine Key, FL
(305) 872–9005, (800) 238–1746
www.seaboots.com

This friendly, family-owned and operated outfitter is a Pro Fly Shop with a complete assortment of flies, including the famous Lefty Deceiver for tarpon, designed by famous angler Lefty Kreh. You'll find G. Loomis and Star spin or fly rods, Penn reels, and Islander fly reels as well as a selection of Columbia, Kahala, and Rum Reggae fishing togs and Sebago deck shoes. Sea Boots sells Scientific Angler Mastery Series fly line. You'll also find the Sportsman Collection of Florida Keys fishing videos here, so you don't have to wait for that Saturday morning television show.

Insiders' Tip

The most famous bluewater angler in Key West's collective consciousness remains Ernest Hemingway, who augmented his famous writing with a passion for fishing these waters. Photographs of Hemingway with his prized, monster-size tarpon and sailfish cause many a covetous angler to turn green with envy.

Key West

The Saltwater Angler
Hilton Resort & Marina
243 Front Street
Key West, FL
(305) 296–0700, (800) 223–1629
www.saltwaterangler.com

The Saltwater Angler specializes in fly tackle. Look for Sage, G. Loomis, Billy Pate, Orvis, and Scott rods and Orvis, Lamson, Sage, Tibor, Loop, Fin-Nor, Sea Master, and Abel reels. The store also stocks a full assortment of flies and fly-tying materials. You can also select from a complete line of top-brand fishing apparel by ExOfficio, Orvis, Patagonia, and Columbia. Books and artwork with an angling theme round out their offerings.

Fly-Fishing Schools

Sandy Moret's Florida Keys
Fly Fishing School
MM 81.9 Bayside
Islamorada, FL
(305) 664–5423
www.floridakeysoutfitters.com

Founded and directed by veteran saltwater fly fisherman Sandy Moret, this school brings freshwater fly anglers back to school in droves to learn saltwater fly-

fishing skills and techniques. Moret, who also owns and operates Florida Keys Outfitters, is a three-time grand champion of the Gold Cup Tarpon Tournament. With more than a dozen fly rod grand slams and four world records to his credit, he has assembled an outstanding team of world-renowned anglers to teach both novices and veterans the tricks of the trade. Working on a rotating basis, the staff includes Chico Fernandez, Flip Pallot, Steve Huff, Tim Klein, Craig Brewer, Rick Ruoff, and Steve Rajeff.

Contact Sandy Moret's Florida Keys Fly Fishing School for specific program information, schedules, and prices. The school schedule typically offers three options, including introductory and advanced level saltwater fly-fishing instruction and guided fly-fishing sessions in area waters.

Island Fly Fishing Academy
MM 61
Hawk's Cay Resort
Duck Key, FL
(305) 743–7000, Ext. 3570, (888) 809–7305
www.hawkscay.com

Students at Island Fly Fishing Academy are taught how to fly fish in the ocean on the very first day of instruction. Offering weekend courses for both beginners and experienced fly-fishing anglers, a team of expert saltwater fly-fishing instructors teach students the basics, as well as ocean casting, fly-tying, boating etiquette, and specifics of our sensitive ecosystem. The program features at least four hours of on-the-water instruction a day and culminates with a half-day guided fly-fishing excursion.

Contact the Academy for specific program information, schedules, and prices. Lunch and all fishing equipment are provided.

Instructors at Sandy Moret's Fishing School manipulate a "stuffed" bonefish to explain how to spot a tailing fish. PHOTO: BILL BEARDSLEY

Recipe for Yellowtail Chum Balls

Take one bag of good quality chum (packed from a commercial fish market in clear plastic, not a box). Allow chum to defrost overnight. Drain liquid. In a large container, mix chum with an equal portion of fine-grained mason's sand. Add flour, oatmeal, and glass minnows. Mix together well and form into solidly packed 2-inch balls (much like you would a snowball). Add more flour to the mixture if the balls do not hold together. Bait a hook (size 4 to size 1) with 1-inch, cut-up pieces of ballyhoo or mackerel. Bury the hook and bait inside the chum ball. Your hook should be tied directly to the line—no leader, no swivels, no double lines, and no sinkers. The weight of the chum ball will carry your bait to the bottom.

Open the bail on your reel or set your reel to free-spool and drop your baited hook in the water. As it goes down to the bottom, bits of the chum ball will break off. When it hits the bottom, the chum ball will break up completely, freeing your baited hook. The cloud of swirling chum will attract the yellowtails. Keep your line in free-spool until the yellowtail grabs the bait and peels off line. Close the bail and set the hook. The rest is history.

Yellowtail snappers travel in schools and like to feed at night. PHOTO: WAYNE MOCCIA

Snorkeling in our crystal clear waters nets a bonanza of underwater sea life sightings.
PHOTO: FLORIDA KEYS & KEY WEST TDC

Diving and Snorkeling

The greatest treasure of the Florida Keys, the most extensive living coral reef system in North America, lies approximately six miles offshore beneath the sea, hidden but not yet lost (see our Paradise Found chapter).

Ranking as the third-largest reef system and one of the most popular dive destinations in the world, the Florida Keys' reef runs 192 miles from Virginia Key in Biscayne Bay all the way to the Dry Tortugas in the Gulf of Mexico. A fragile symbiotic city of sea creatures crowds our reef—fishes, sponges, jellyfish, anemones, worms, snails, crabs, lobsters, rays, turtles, and, of course, both soft and stony corals—sometimes mixing it up with sunken bounty of a different kind: shipwrecks of yesteryear.

Although our coral reef appears sturdy and, indeed, has proved intractable to the many unfortunate wooden-hulled vessels it has so callously pierced throughout the centuries, this toothsome barrier is actually made up of colonies of tiny living animals. These coral polyps secrete calcium carbonate, developing so slowly it can take years for some species to grow just one inch. The careless toss of an anchor can destroy decades of coral growth in just seconds. Even the gentle touch of a finger can kill the delicate organisms instantly. When polyps are damaged or killed, the entire colony becomes exposed to the spread of algae or disease, and the reef is at risk.

To protect and preserve our marine ecosystem, Congress established the Florida Keys National Marine Sanctuary in 1990, signed into law by former president George Bush. Extending on both sides of the Florida Keys, the 2,800-square-nautical-mile sanctuary is the second-largest marine sanctuary in the United States (see our Paradise Found chapter). The sanctuary encompasses two of the very best diving areas in the reef chain of the Keys: the Key Largo National Marine Sanctuary, established in 1975, which in turn envelops John Pennekamp Coral Reef State Park; and the Looe Key National Marine Sanctuary, formed in 1981. The proliferation of marine life, corals, and finfish is incomparable anywhere on this continent.

The State of Florida adjusted its offshore boundaries from seven miles to three miles. This means many of the underwater dive and snorkel sites that used to be referred to as John Pennekamp Coral Reef State Park are now actually part of the Key Largo National Marine Sanctuary. Many dive operators and much promotional literature still refer to diving and snorkeling in Pennekamp Park. The actual boundaries of the park are much smaller than they used to be. To clear up the confusion remember: Key Largo National Marine Sanctuary encompasses the waters of John Pennekamp Coral Reef State Park, but Pennekamp is not synonymous with the sanctuary.

In this chapter we provide you with a rundown of great reef and wreck dives and snorkel adventures from Key Largo to the Dry Tortugas. Our reefs are not within swimming distance of the shore, so you will need to make your way by boat. If you plan to venture out on your own craft or in a rental boat, be sure to stop at a dive center or marine supply store and purchase a nautical map that denotes the exact coordinates for dive and snorkel sites (see our listings in this chapter). Motor to the reef only if you know the waters, are an experienced boat handler, and can read the nautical charts well. You are financially liable for damage to the reef, so always anchor only at mooring buoys when provided or on sandy areas of the sea bottom. Florida law dictates you fly the diver-down flag, which is red with a diagonal white stripe, to warn other boaters that divers are underwater within 100 feet of your craft.

Probably the most popular and hassle-free way to dive or snorkel in the Florida Keys is to go out with a dive charter. Most reputable dive centers in the Keys belong to the Keys Association of Dive Operators, which sets standards of safety and professionalism. Crews are trained in CPR, first aid, and handling dive emergencies. Emergency oxygen supplies are kept on board. The dive captains, who must be licensed by the U.S. Coast Guard, judge weather conditions and water visibility each day and select the best sites suited to your experience level. Often their coveted knowledge of little-visited patch reefs and wrecks affords you an experience you could not duplicate on your own. We offer you a guide to dive centers, noting the comprehensive services ranging from instruction and underwater excursions to equipment rentals and sales.

In the Florida Keys, usually neither the crew nor the dive master accompanies divers in the water. Divers spread out across a shallow reef, two by two, swimming in a buddy system. The dive master stays on board and watches everyone from the boat. You must prove your experience level by showing current dive certification and your dive log before you may go out on a dive charter. If you have not made a comparable dive within the past six months, you must hire an instructor to accompany you in the water. Be sure you are comfortable with the sea conditions and that they are consistent with your level of expertise. If this is your first dive, alert the crew so they can help you.

Whether you dive on your own or go out to the reef with a charter, you should be aware of the strong current of the outgoing tidal flow and in the Gulf Stream. It is easy to overlook the current in the fascination of your dive until, low on both energy and air, you must swim against it to get back to the boat. Begin your dive by swimming into the current. To determine the direction of the current, watch the flow of your bubbles or lie back into a float position and see which way the current carries you.

Be careful around bridges. The tremendous energy of the tides passing through the pilings of our bridges creates coral outcroppings that would not normally be so close to shore. Divers and snorkelers without boat transportation to the patch reefs or the Gulf waters like to take advantage of this underwater terrain to look for lobsters. Be forewarned: It is very dangerous to dive or snorkel under and around our bridges. The currents are swift and the tidal pull is strong. Boat traffic is often heavy. If you do decide to dive or snorkel here be sure to carry a diver-down flag with you on a float, and follow the buddy system. The best and safest time to tackle these turbulent waters is just before slack tide, during slack tide, and immediately following slack tide. The time of this cycle varies with wind, the height of the tide, and the phase of the moon.

With the privilege of diving and snorkeling in our waters comes responsibility. We sprinkle Insiders' Tips throughout this chapter because we know you also would like to preserve our fin-tastic coral reefs for all time.

For the most part, visitors freely can swim, dive, snorkel, boat, fish, or recreate on our waters, but there are some Florida Keys National Marine Sanctuary regulations that took effect in July 1997 to guide these activities. Refer to our Boating chapter for information on these regulations before you venture into our waters. For a complete copy of the regulations and marine coordinates of the areas, contact the Sanctuary office (305-743-2437) or log onto their website: www.fknms.nos.noaa.gov.

Whether you'd like to spend a few hours, days, weeks, or a lifetime exploring our coral reefs and wrecks, you'll find in this chapter all you need to know to "get wet," as divers like to say, in the Florida Keys.

In Emergencies

Divers in the Florida Keys are in good hands in the face of a recompression emergency. The Florida Keys Hyperbaric Center (305–853–1603) is located at Mariners Hospital in the Upper Keys (see our Healthcare chapter).

Dive shop personnel, instructors, dive masters, and boat captains have joined with members of the local EMS, U.S. Coast Guard, Marine Patrol, NOAA, Monroe County Sheriff's office, and the Florida State Highway Patrol to develop a coordinated evacuation program to get injured divers off the water and to the hyperbaric chamber quickly. In case of a decompression injury, call 911 and get the victim to the nearest emergency room as rapidly as possible.

The Keys to the Reef

Most diving and snorkeling takes place on the barrier reefs of the Florida Keys. These linear or semicircular reefs, larger than the inner patch reefs, have claimed a graveyard of sailing vessels, many laden with gold and silver and other precious cargo. Salvaged by wreckers for centuries, the remains of these wrecks entice experienced divers, some of whom still hope to discover a treasure trove. Lighthouses were erected on the shallower, more treacherous sections of the barrier reef during the 19th century as an aid to navigation. They now also mark popular dive and snorkel destinations.

The coral reef system of the Florida Keys is distinctively known as a spur-and-groove system. Long ridges of coral, called spurs, are divided by sand channels, or grooves, that merge with the adjoining reef flat, a coral rubble ridge on the inshore edge of the reef. The ridges of elkhorn coral thrive in heavy surf, often growing several inches a year. The spurs extend 100 yards or more, with shallower extremities sometimes awash at low tide while the seaward ends stand submerged in 30 to 40 feet of water. Small caves and tunnels wind through to the interior of the reef, home to myriad species of marine plants and animals. The white grooves separating the spurs are covered with coarse limestone sand, a composite of coral and mollusk shell fragments and plates from green calcareous algae. The wave action passing between the spurs of coral creates furrows in the sand floor of the grooves.

Generally, the shallower the reef, the brighter the colors of the corals, because strong sunlight is a prerequisite for reef growth. Legions of fish sway back and forth keeping time with the rhythm of the waves. While deep dives yield fascinating discoveries for those with advanced skills—such as long-lost torpedoed ships—sport divers will not be disappointed with the plethora of sea life within 60 feet of the surface. Night dives reveal the swing shift of the aquatic community. While the parrotfish may find a cave, secrete a mucous balloon around itself, and sleep the night through, sparkling corals blossom once the sun sets, and other species come out of hiding to forage for food.

Supplementing our coral barrier and the broken bodies of reef-wrecked ships, artificial reefs have been sunk to create underwater habitats for sea creatures large and small. The Florida Keys Artificial Reef Association, a nonprofit corporation of Keys residents, banded together in 1980 to capitalize on putting to use the many large pieces of concrete that became available during the removal of some of the old Keys bridges. More than 35,000 tons of rubble were deep-sixed throughout the Keys' waters between 1981 and 1987, creating acres of artificial reefs. In recent years, steel-hull vessels up to 350-feet long have been scuttled in stable sandy-bottom areas, amassing new communities of fish and invertebrates and easing the stress and strain on the coral reef by creating new fishing and diving sites. You'll find a comprehensive list of the artificial reef locations at the Florida Fish and Wildlife Conservation Commission website: www. state.fl.us/fwc/marine.

The reef harbors myriad species of tropical fish. PHOTO: WAYNE MOCCIA

Always use a mooring buoy if one is available. The large blue-and-white plastic floats are drilled directly into the sea bottom and installed with heavy chains or concrete bases. They are available on a first-come, first-served basis, but, if you are a small craft, it is courteous to tie off with other similar boats, allowing larger vessels use of the mooring buoys. Approach the buoy from downwind against the current. Secure your boat to the pickup lines using a length of your own rope. Snap shackles provide quick and easy pickup and release. Large boats are advised to give out extra line to ensure a horizontal pull on the buoy. If no mooring buoys have been provided, anchor only in a sandy area downwind of a patch reef, so that your boat's anchor and chain do not drag or grate on nearby corals.

Safety Tips for Divers

Always display the red-and-white diver-down flag while you are scuba diving or snorkeling. Approaching boats must stay 100 yards from this flag or vessel and slow down to idle speed. Be sure to stay within 100 yards of your diver-down flag when you are diving or snorkeling.

Be careful of fire or false corals of the genus *Millepora*. These tan or golden-brown platelike vertical growths topped with white are very smooth and lack the well-defined cups of true stony corals. If you brush against the toxic fire corals, you will feel an intense, though short-lived, sting, which usually causes a painful welt. Wear a thin-skin jumpsuit when you dive, even in the summer months, for protection.

Float a line with a buoy behind your boat when diving in waters where there is a strong current. If you surface from your dive behind your boat, grab the line so the current does not carry you farther away. You can pull yourself into the boat, saving air and energy.

Always dive with a buddy and keep track of each other. Always have an octopus (extra mouthpiece connected to your air tank) as part of your dive gear. If your buddy's air runs out, you will have to share your air until you both can get to the surface.

Snorkelers, be sure to wear a float vest so you don't have to stand on the coral to make any necessary adjustments to your gear. Divers, wear only the minimum weight you need to maintain neutral buoyancy so you do not have contact with the ocean floor. Areas that appear lifeless may, in fact, be supporting new growth.

Dive Sites

In the Florida Keys part of this section, we highlight 20 of the better-known and most enchanting dive and snorkel sites, listed in descending order from the top of the Keys in the Key Largo National Marine Sanctuary to the Looe Key National Marine Sanctuary in the Lower Keys.

In Key West, our coral reef system heads west into the sunset as it swings by Cayo Hueso into the untamed and isolated but charted waters leading to the Marquesas and the Dry Tortugas. (The half-day dive excursions based in Key West do not venture as far as these outer, uninhabited Keys. You will have to charter private overnight dive excursions or travel the distance in your own motor or sailing yacht if you wish to explore these waters; see our Cruising chapter.) In the Key West and Beyond part of this section, we highlight 19 of the most interesting dive and snorkel sites from Key West to the Dry Tortugas National Park.

Upper Keys

Carysfort Reef

Situated at the extreme end of Key Largo National Marine Sanctuary, Carysfort Reef appeals to both novice and intermediate divers. British vessel H.M.S. *Carysfort* ran aground here in 1770. The reef, now marked by the 100-foot steel Carysfort Lighthouse, undulates between 35 and 70 feet. Lush staghorn corals, which look like bumpy deer antlers, and masses of plate coral, which overlap each other like roofing tiles, cascade down the 30-foot drop to the sandy bottom. Schools of algae-grazing blue tang and pin-striped grunts circulate among the coral heads of a secondary reef.

The H.M.S. *Winchester*, a British man-of-war built in 1693, hit the reef in 1695 after most of her crew died of the plague while en route from Jamaica to England. The wreck, discovered in 1938, was cleaned out by salvagers in the 1950s. It rests southeast of Carysfort Light in 28 feet of water.

The Elbow

Aptly named, The Elbow looks like a flexed arm as it makes a dogleg turn to the right. Prismatic damselfish and angelfish, so tame they will swim up and look you in the eye, belie this graveyard of sunken cargo ships, the bones of which litter the ocean floor. The 191-foot *Tonawanda*, built in 1863 in Philadelphia, ended its short career as a tug and transport vessel in 1866 when it stranded on the reef. The c. 1877 passenger/cargo steamer *City of Washington*, cut down and sold as a barge, piled up on the Elbow Reef in 1917 as it was towed by the *Edgar F. Luchenbach*. Dynamited so it would not impede navigation, the barge's scattered remains rest near the *Tonawanda* in about 20 feet of water covered with purple sea fans and mustard-hued fire coral trees. The unidentified Civil War Wreck, now nothing more than wooden beams held together by iron pins, sits in 25 feet of water. A search of the area may yield a sighting of an old Spanish cannon, probably thrown overboard to lighten the load when one of the ships ran aground. The Elbow, marked by a 36-foot light tower, provides good diving for the novice. Depths at this spur-and-groove reef range between 12 and 35 feet and currents vary.

Christ of the Deep Statue

Perhaps one of the most famous underwater photographs of all time is of the Christ of the Deep Statue, which stands silhouetted against the sapphire-blue ocean waters bordering Key Largo Dry Rocks. This 9-foot figure of Christ, arms upraised and looking toward the heavens, was donated to the Underwater Society of America by Egidi Cressi, an Italian industrialist and diving equipment manufacturer. Designed by Italian sculptor Guido Galletti and cast in Italy, the statue is a bronze duplicate of the Christ of the Abysses, which stands underwater off Genoa. Surrounded by a flotilla of nonchalant skates and rays, the statue's left hand appears to be pointing to the massive brain corals peppering the adjoining ocean floor. With depths ranging from shallow to 25 feet, snorkeling is outstanding. Schools of electric-blue neon gobies congregate in cleaning stations, waiting to service other fish who wish to be rid of skin parasites. A slow offer of an outstretched arm may net you a goby-cleaned hand.

Grecian Rocks

This crescent-shaped patch reef, which ranges in depth from shallow to 35 feet, ranks as a favorite among snorkelers and novice divers. Colonies of branched elkhorn corals, resembling the racks of bull moose or elk, provide a dramatic backdrop for the curious cruising barracudas, which often unnerve divers by following them about the reef but rarely cause a problem. Colossal star corals dot the area, which is populated by a rainbow palette of Spanish hogfish and a scattering of protected queen conch. An old Spanish cannon reportedly is concealed in one of the more luminous of the star coral, placed there some time ago by rangers of John Pennekamp Coral Reef State Park. Look for a small patch reef near Grecian Rocks where old cannons and fused cannonballs litter the landscape. At low tide this reef rises out of the water.

Benwood Wreck

The English-built freighter *Benwood*, en route from Tampa to Halifax and Liverpool in 1942 with a cargo of phosphate rock, attempted to elude German U-boats early in World War II by running without lights. Unfortunately, the American freighter *Robert C. Tuttle* also took a darkened route. In their ultimate collision, the American ship ripped the *Benwood's* starboard side open like a can opener. As it limped along a fire broke out on deck and attracted a German U-boat, which finished her off with two torpedo hits. A memorable first wreck for novice divers, the bow of the ship remains in about 50 feet of water, while the stern rests in but 25 feet. It lies in line with the offshore reef about 1½ miles north of French Reef.

French Reef

Even novice divers can negotiate the caves at French Reef. Swim through the 3- to 4-foot limestone ledge openings or just peer in for a glance at the vermilion-painted blackbar soldierfish, who often swim upside down, mistakenly orienting themselves to the cave ceilings. Limestone ledges, adorned with tub sponges, extend from the shallows to depths in excess of 35 feet. Follow the mooring buoys for the best route. A mountainous star coral marks Christmas Tree Cave where, if you swim through the two-entrance passage, trapped air bubbles incandescently flicker in the cave's low light. Hourglass Cave sports a shapely column of limestone that divides the space in half, and White Sand Bottom Cave, a large swim-through cavern, shelters a potpourri of groupers, dog snappers, moray eels, and copper-colored glassy sweepers.

White Bank Dry Rocks

A garden of soft corals welcomes snorkelers and novice divers to these patch-reef twins. With calm waters and depths ranging from shallow to 25 feet, White Bank Dry Rocks extends north and south along Hawk Channel at the southern end of Key Largo National Marine Sanctuary. You will feel as if you are swimming in a giant aquarium, for the lacy sea fans, feathery sea plumes, and branching sea whips create surreal staging for the fluttering schools

of sophisticated black and yellow French angelfish. Bring an underwater camera.

Molasses Reef

Shallow coral ridges of this well-developed spur-and-groove reef radiate from the 45-foot light tower that marks Molasses Reef. Mooring buoys bob in deeper water, about 35 feet. Just off the eastern edge of the tower lies a single windlass, all that remains of the so-called Winch Wreck, or Windlass Wreck. Look for Christmas tree worms among the masses of star coral. The conical whorls, resembling maroon and orange pine trees, are actually worms that reside in living coral. If you slowly move a finger toward these faux flowers, they will sense your presence within a half-inch and disappear like Houdini into their coral-encased tube homes.

USCG *Bibb* and USCG *Duane*

Advanced divers will relish the exploration of the two U.S. Coast Guard cutters sunk as artificial reefs 100 yards apart near Molasses Reef. Both these vessels, c. mid-1930s, saw action in World War II and the

The U.S. Coast Guard cutter Duane *is sunk as an artificial reef near Molasses Reef and is fascinating to explore.* PHOTO: FLORIDA KEYS & KEY WEST TDC

Vietnam War. Both did search and rescue in their later peacetime years and were decommissioned in 1985. A consortium of dive shops and the Monroe County Tourist Development Council bought the cutters, which were subsequently stripped of armament, hatches and masts, then cleaned. In 1987 the Army Corps of Engineers sank the 327-foot vessels on consecutive days. The *Bibb* rests on her side in 130 feet of water with her upper portions accessible at 90 feet. The upright *Duane* sits in more than 100 feet of water, but you can see the wheelhouse at 80 feet and the crow's nest in 60 feet of water.

Pickles Reef

Pickles Reef got its name from the coral-encrusted barrels strewn about the ocean floor near the remnants of a cargo ship, called the Pickles Wreck, that carried them to their demise. The kegs are said to resemble pickle barrels, hence the name of the reef, but more likely were filled with building mortar bound for burgeoning construction in Key West. Look for the distinctively marked flamingo tongue snails, which attach themselves to swaying purple sea fans, grazing for algae. Flamboyantly extended around the outside of the flamingo tongue's glossy cream-colored shell is a bright orange mantle with black-ringed leopard-like spots. Don't be tempted to collect these unusual creatures, for the colorful mantle is withdrawn upon death. With depths between 10 and 25 feet and a moderate current, Pickles Reef is a good dive for novice to intermediate skill levels.

Conch Reef

Dive charters usually anchor in about 60 feet of water at Conch Reef, but the area actually offers something for everyone. With depths ranging from shallow to 100 feet and currents varying from moderate to strong, beginners as well as intermediate and advanced divers will be entranced here. The shallow section, festive with swirling schools of small tropicals, extends for a mile along the outer reef line. Conch Wall steeply drops from 60 to 100 feet, where sea rods, whips, fans, and plumes of the gorgonian family's deepwater branch congregate with an agglomeration of vaselike convoluted barrel sponges. The coral of Conch Reef was nearly decimated by heavy harvesting in bygone eras; dead stumps of pillar corals can still be seen.

Hens and Chickens

A brood of large star-coral heads surrounds a 35-foot U.S. Navy light tower within seven feet of the water's surface on this inshore patch reef, bringing to mind a mother hen and her chicks. Less than three miles from shore, this easily accessed 20-foot-deep reef remains popular with novice divers. Plumes, fans, and candelabra soft corals intermingle with skeletons of the coral graveyard (almost 80 percent of the reef died in 1970 after an unusually cold winter). Jailhouse-striped sheepsheads mingle with shy notch-tailed grunts and the more curious stout-bodied groupers, but don't be tempted; spearfishing is not allowed here. Remains of the Brick Barge, a modern casualty, and an old steel barge torpedoed during World War II lie among the coral heads.

Eagle

In 1985 an electrical fire disabled the 287-foot *Aaron K*, a freighter that carried scrap paper between Miami and South America. Declared a total loss, it was sold to the Monroe County Tourist Council and a group of local dive shops and then scuttled for use as an artificial reef. The vessel was renamed the *Eagle* after the Eagle Tire Company, which provided much of the funding for the project. A must-do for advanced divers, the *Eagle* landed on her starboard side in 120-foot waters, though her upper portions lurk within 65 feet of the surface. Densely packed polarized schools of silversides flow and drift within her interior. The tiny fork-tailed fish will detour around divers swimming through the school.

Diving for Lobster

Umm, umm good. Lobster.

Now, you Easterners may conjure up scarlet visions of the mighty Maines, but when we say lobster here in the Florida Keys, a totally different creature comes to mind. Equally delectable and much in demand, the Florida lobster, or spiny lobster, is actually a crustacean whose relatives include crabs, shrimp, and crawfish. Unlike its Down East cousin, the Florida lobster is clawless. Ten spiderlike legs support its spiny head and hard-shell body, and radar-like antennae make up for bugged eyes and weak eyesight. But its best defense, and most coveted by hungry humans, remains its powerful tail muscle, which propels the lobster backward at breakneck speed.

Diving for lobster is a popular sport in the waters of the Florida Keys. Like any other hunt, you will need to understand your intended prey, for self-preservation will be their only consideration. Nocturnal feeders, spiny lobsters hide underwater in crevices, between rocks, in caves, under artificial reefs, near dock pilings, or in dead coral outcroppings during the day. They are not easy to spot. They occasionally peek out from their protective holes, but most often only a single antenna will be visible. The good news is that a whole gang may be hiding out together.

So how do you catch these potentially tasty morsels locals call "bugs"? We have found a few basic tools—and tricks—help swing the scales in our favor. You will need a pair of heavy-duty dive gloves, for the two large horns on the lobster's head and the sharp spines of his whipping tail can draw blood. To store your captive prizes, get an easy-to-open mesh game bag that has a fastener that you can hook to your weight belt. Be sure this bag does not drag over the reef, which would damage coral and other marine life. A probe, or "tickle stick," which is a long metal or fiberglass rod with a short, 90-degree bend on one end, allows you to wisely restrain from poking your arm into a crevice or hole in order to coax out a lobster. That hole could just as easily house a moray eel as a lobster. (This toothsome green eel has been known to clamp its enormous mouth firmly and painfully into many an unsuspecting diver's arm.) And, finally, a lobster net is a must if you hope to capture the tickled lobster.

Florida law mandates lobster hunters carry a device to measure the carapace of each lobster. (The carapace is that portion of the lobster shell beginning between the eyes and extending to the hard-end segment just before the tail.) The carapace should measure at least 3 inches, otherwise the lobster —deemed a "short"—must be

Sport diving for lobster is popular in Florida Keys' waters.
PHOTO: WAYNE MOCCIA

returned to the sea. The measuring device is most often made of plastic or metal and can be attached to a string and secured to your game bag. Measure the lobster before you put it in your bag; do not bring it to the boat to be measured.

To recreationally harvest lobsters in the Florida Keys, you must possess a valid Florida saltwater fishing license with a current crawfish stamp (see our Fishing chapter).

Look for lobsters in the patch reefs on the oceanside. Patch reefs can usually be found by using the NOAA navigational charts. Look for relatively shallow areas (15 to 20 feet) surrounded by deeper water (25 to 30 feet). If your boat is equipped with a chart recorder, use this device to detect bottom contours and the presence of fish. Look for irregular bottom areas, which will usually mean coral outcroppings and sponges. When you find the suspected patch reefs, check them out with a quick dive to the bottom before anchoring your boat. You will need to scuba dive for lobsters in the patch reefs.

Alternately look for lobster "holes" in the shallow gulfside waters and, wearing mask, fins and snorkel, free-dive for the crustaceans—a one-breath challenge for sure. These areas will appear as patches of brightness in the turtle grass floor as you skim across the water in your skiff. Sandy sea bottom looks bright also, so you must slow to idle speed and look for a hunk of coral. It helps to throw a buoy marker at this spot (connect a dive weight to a Styrofoam buoy with a length of line), because these coral outcroppings are few and far between. Send a dive scout over the side to bird dog the outcropping for antennae, and with a little luck, the hunt will begin.

You have displayed your diver-down flag. You're equipped. You're psyched. You're under water. Now what? Stay cool and calm. Move slowly. These crusty crustaceans are a wily group. When frightened, the lobster will contract its powerful tail and propel itself like a bullet backward to the far recesses of its shelter or deep into the seagrass. Tickle your way to victory. Slowly slide your tickle stick behind the lobster and tap his tail. Bothered from behind, the lobster is persuaded to slowly leave his shelter to investigate. Once the lobster is out of the hole, place the net behind (yes, behind!) the lobster with the rim firmly resting on the sandy bottom if possible. Tap the lobster's head with the tickle stick. This time, irritated, the lobster will propel backward into your net. Quickly slam your net down on the sea floor so the lobster cannot escape. Then secure the net closed with your other hand. The lobster may thrash and become tangled in the net.

Holding the netted lobster firmly with one hand, measure the carapace. Carefully remove the lobster from the net. If the lobster is a short, release it to be captured another day. If it is legal size, place it securely in your game bag, tail first. One thrust of the vigorous tail could negate all your efforts. Also, be careful not to release any other "bugs" you have already bagged. If you see a dark spot or reddish-orange nodules under the tail, this lobster is an egg-bearing female. By Florida law you must release her.

Place your captured lobsters in the saltwater-filled bait well of your boat or store them on ice in a cooler with a lid. Do not wring the tails from the lobsters until you get back to shore. It is against Florida law to separate the tail from the body while on Florida waters. Once on dry land you may pull the tails, which by law must measure more than 5½ inches. There is negligible meat in the body of the Florida spiny lobster, so it may be discarded unless you want to boil it to make lobster stock. After wringing the tail, break an antenna from the severed body of the crawfish. Insert the antenna, larger end first, into the underside base of the tail and then pull it out. The spiny thorns of the antenna will snag the intestinal tract, which will be removed with the antenna. If you wish to freeze the lobster tails, place several in a small plastic zipper bag, fill the bag with fresh water, and place the bags in the freezer for up to six months.

We think the best way to cook Florida lobster tail is on the grill. First, with a sharp knife or kitchen scissors, butterfly the tail by cutting through the outer shell and meat. Spread the tail open and sprinkle with melted butter, salt, pepper, and onion powder or garlic powder if desired. Place the tail on a double-thick piece of aluminum foil and fold the foil envelope-style, sealing tightly. Grill over hot coals for 15 to 20 minutes or until the shell is bright red and the meat is no longer translucent. Serve grilled lobster tail with clarified butter or a slice of Key lime.

Sport Lobster Season

Sport lobster season takes on festival proportions in the Florida Keys, but the competition is keen. Previewing the official opening of lobster season, the last consecutive Wednesday and Thursday in July are a designated sport season in the state and federal waters for the nonprofessional spiny lobster hunter. Every motel, hotel, and campground in the Florida Keys is filled beyond capacity. Divers are allotted six lobsters per person per day; sunrise to sunset is considered a day. Diving at night is not permitted. John Pennekamp Coral Reef State Park is closed to lobstering during the sport season. Contact the Florida Keys National Marine Sanctuary (305–743–2437) or their website, www.fknms.nos.noaa.gov, for more information on sport lobster season rules and restrictions.

Sport lobster season takes on festival proportions in the Florida Keys, and competition is keen.
PHOTO: LOUISE SKIDMORE

Regular Lobster Season

Regular season, which is when commercial lobstermen begin putting out their traps, commences in early August and ends in late March. Rules differ slightly in state and federal waters. The bag limit in state waters is six lobsters per person per day, or 24 per boat, whichever is greater. State waters surround the Florida Keys out to 3 miles oceanside and 9 miles on the Gulf. You may dive for lobster at night in state waters during regular lobster season.

Areas of John Pennekamp Coral Reef State Park restricted from lobstering include Turtle Rocks, Basin Hills North, Mosquito Bank North, Three Sisters North, Higdon's Reef, Basin Hills East, Mosquito Bank Southeast, Three Sisters South, Cannon Patch, and Basin Hills South. Lobstering is prohibited year round in Everglades National Park, Biscayne Bay/Card Sound Spiny Lobster Sanctuary, and Dry Tortugas National Park. Three areas of the Florida Keys National Marine Sanctuary are no-take areas, marked by 30-inch-diameter round yellow boundary buoys: Sanctuary Preservation Areas (SPAs), Special-use

Research Only Areas, and Ecological Reserves. See the Sanctuary's website for more information: www.fknms.nos.noaa.gov.

Those waters beyond the state limits are deemed federal waters; see a NOAA chart for the official boundary lines. The bag limit in federal waters is six lobsters per person per day, or six per person per trip when the trip is longer than one day. The per-boat quota does not apply in federal waters. You may not combine the federal bag limit with the state bag limit.

Words to the Wise

- Always display your diver-down flag when you are diving or snorkeling for lobster.
- Be careful not to damage coral while you are harvesting lobster.
- Anchor in the sand or use a mooring buoy.
- Use an official NOAA navigational chart when navigating our waters.
- Do not molest, damage or take lobster from traps. It is a felony offense in Florida.
- You may not use spears, hooks or wire snares to capture or dismember lobsters.

Middle Keys

Alligator Reef

Launched in 1820 in Boston, the USS *Alligator* hunted pirates in Florida as part of the West Indies Squadron. A 136-foot light tower now marks her namesake, Alligator Reef, which claimed the copper- and bronze-fitted warship in 1825. The Navy stripped the ship's valuables and blew her up. The *Alligator* rests offshore from the 8- to 40-foot-deep reef, now a bordello of brilliant tropicals, corals, and shells.

Coffins Patch

Gargantuan grooved brain corals join staghorns and toxic fire corals at Coffins

Patch, a 1½-mile reef popular with Middle Keys divers. A drift of yellow-finned French grunts and festive angelfish join an escort of mutton snappers, each distinctively branded with a black spot below the rear dorsal fin, as they guard the remains of the Spanish galleon *Ignacio*, which spewed a cargo of coins across the ocean floor in 1733.

Thunderbolt

In 1986 the artificial reef committee bought the *Thunderbolt*, a 188-foot cable-laying workboat, from a Miami River boatyard. The vessel was cleaned and her hatches removed. It then was towed south of Coffins Patch, where it was sunk as an artificial reef. Sitting majestically upright in 115 feet of water, the *Thunderbolt's* bronze propellers, cable-laying spool and wheelhouse are still recognizable. A stainless steel cable leads from the wreck to a permanent underwater buoy. Current is strong at this wreck. Clip a line to the eye on the buoy and walk down the line. This dive is suitable for those with advanced certification.

Delta Shoals

This shallow 10- to 20-foot shoal claimed many an unsuspecting ship through the centuries. Perhaps the most colorful history is that of an old vessel that ran aground in the 1850s. The ship yielded no treasure, but recovery of unique relics and elephant tusks led to the name Ivory Wreck. Among the wreckage were leg irons and brass bowls, leading historians to believe this was a slave ship from Africa.

Sombrero Key

A 142-foot lighthouse tower marks this living marine museum. Coral chasms, ridges, and portals support a proliferation of fuzzy, feathery, or hairy gorgonians as well as a salad bowl of leafy lettuce coral. A battalion of toothy barracudas swims reconnaissance, but don't be alarmed. You are too big to be considered tasty.

Lower Keys

Looe Key National Marine Sanctuary

In 1744 Capt. Ashby Utting ran the 124-foot British frigate H.M.S. *Looe* hard aground on the 5-square-mile Y-shaped reef now bearing her name. Remains of the ship are interred between two fingers of living coral about 200 yards from the marker in 25 feet of water. The ballast and the anchor remain camouflaged with centuries of vigorous coral growth. Preserved as a national marine sanctuary since 1981, the 5- to 35-foot-deep waters surrounding Looe Key protect the diverse marine communities from fishing, lobstering, or artifact collecting, all forbidden.

The sanctuary, like Key Largo National Marine Sanctuary in the Upper Keys, offers interesting dives for novice, intermediate, and advanced divers alike. The spur-and-groove formations of Looe Key National Marine Sanctuary are the best developed in the Keys, and you can observe a complete coral reef ecosystem within the sanctuary's boundaries (see the Paradise Found chapter).

Take a laminated reef-creature guide sheet (readily available in dive shops) on your dive to identify the senses-boggling array of sea life at Looe Key. Look for some of these interesting species: The yellowhead jawfish excavates a hole in the sand with his mouth and retreats, tail-first, at the first sign of danger. The wary cottonwick sports a bold black stripe from snout to tail. The prehistoric-looking red lizardfish rests camouflaged on rocks and coral. The occasional blue-spotted peacock flounder changes color, chameleon-like, to match its surroundings. Commercial dive charters provide excursions to Looe Key from Big Pine Key, Little Torch Key, and Ramrod Key.

The *Adolphus Busch*

Scuttled in 1998 between Looe Key and American Shoal, this 210-foot freighter is the first new artificial reef sunk in the waters of the Florida Keys in a decade. Named after the scions of the brewing industry, the *Adolphus Busch* sits upright in 100 feet of water. A tower comes within 40 feet of the surface and can be penetrated. *Adolphus Busch* is rapidly becoming a thriving tenement of fish and marine organisms.

Key West

Eastern Sambo

An underwater ridge at 60 feet dropping off sharply to the sand line at 87 feet goes by the name of Eastern Drop-off in this immensely popular reef area southeast of Key West. Reddish-brown honeycomb plate corals encrust the sloping reef face while boulder corals pepper the base at the outer margin of the reef. The Hook, a long spur-and-groove canyon, extends south from the Eastern Sambo reef marker. Look for cruising tarpon during the summer months. West of Eastern Sambo is a site commonly referred to as No. 28 Marker, where sea turtles and nurse sharks make their rounds of the elkhorn coral.

Middle Sambo

Coral heads and soft corals cover the sand beneath the 30- to 40-foot depths of Middle Sambo. You won't be alone as you observe the prolific lobsters haunting this area, especially in the summer months. Look for squadrons of tarpon and snook.

Western Sambo

Mooring buoys mark this popular reef area with a variety of dives to 40 feet. Fields of branch coral stretch into the blue infinity while mountains of sheet, boulder, star, and pillar corals cover the dramatic drop from 28 to 40 feet. Small yellow stingrays, which are actually covered with dark spots and can pale and darken protectively when the environment dictates, lie on the bottom with their stout, venomous tails buried in the sand. In the protected mid-reef area of the Cut, goggle-eyed blennies mill about with a colony of yellowhead jawfish, retreating tail-first into their sand holes when frightened.

A half-mile south of Western Sambo, the remains of the *Aquanaut*, a 50-foot wooden tugboat owned by Chet Alexan-der, was scuttled in 75 feet of water as an artificial reef. Scattered about amid drifts of mahogany snappers and nocturnal glasseyes, the wreck is alive with spiderlike yellow arrow crabs.

Cayman Salvager

The 187-foot-long, steel-hulled buoy tender *Cayman Salvager*, built in 1936, originally sank at the Key West docks in the 1970s. Refloated and innards removed, it went back down under in 1985 for use as an artificial reef, coming to rest on her side. Hurricane-force waves later righted her and it now sits in 90 feet of water on a sandy bottom. Look for the fabled 200-pound jewfish and 6-foot moray eel residing in her open hold.

Joe's Tug

Sitting upright in 60 feet of water, *Joe's Tug*, a 75-foot steel-hulled tugboat, was scuttled as an artificial reef in 1989. The boat rests inshore from the *Cayman Salvager* on a bed of coral. This is one of the most popular wreck dives in the Key West circuit. Look for Elvis, the resident jewfish who hangs out at the tug with yet another large moray eel.

Eastern Dry Rocks

Shells, conchs and the ballast stones, cannonballs, and rigging of disintegrating wrecks litter the rubble zone, coral fingers, and sand canyons of Eastern Dry Rocks. With depths between 5 and 35 feet and only light current, this dive is suited to novices.

Rock Key

Twenty-foot cracks barely as wide as a single diver distinguish Rock Key from nearby cousins at Eastern Dry Rocks. A 19th-century ship carrying building tiles from Barcelona went aground on Rock Key, scattering her bounty about the ocean floor. Tiles carrying the Barcelona imprint are reportedly still occasionally recovered.

Starfish blanket the ocean floor. PHOTO: FLORIDA KEYS & KEY WEST TDC

Stargazer

Billed as the "world's largest underwater sculptured reef," Stargazer stands 22 feet below the surface, 5 miles off Key West between Rock Key and Sand Key. The creation of artist Ann Lorraine Labriola, Stargazer mimics a primitive navigational instrument, its giant steel sections—ranging between 2,000 and 8,000 pounds—emblazoned with constellation symbols and emblems. A "mystery chart" sends divers on an underwater treasure hunt with a series of puzzles that require a certain amount of celestial knowledge to solve.

Sand Key

Originally called Cays Arena by early Spanish settlers, Sand Key, 6 miles south of Key West, is partially awash at low tide. Topped by a distinctive 110-foot red iron lighthouse, Sand Key's shape, comprised of shells and ground coral, changes with each hurricane and tropical storm. Sand Key shines as a good all-weather dive and, with depths ranging to 65 feet, appeals to all skill levels. The shallows of the leeward side provide good snorkeling, with elkhorn corals and artifacts from the old brick lighthouse that was destroyed in 1846. In spring and summer, the Gulf Stream movement over the shallows provides great visibility and vibrant colors. You can easily reach Sand Key on your own in a 17- to 18-foot boat on a calm day.

Ten-Fathom Bar

Advanced divers peruse a gallery of deep dives on the western end of the outer reef system, which is nearly 4 miles long. The southern edge, Fennel Ridge, begins at about 60 feet deep, giving the site its name, then plunges to the sand line, undulating between 90 and 120 feet. Encrusted telegraph cables at 45 to 55 feet, apparently snaking a line to Havana, cut across the eastern end of the Ten-Fathom Bar, competing with man-size sponges and dramatic black coral. Near the cable, Eye of the Needle sports a plateau of coral spurs. Deep, undercut ledges shelter the spotted, white-bellied porcupinefish. Divers can swim under a ledge and up through a broad "eye" to the top of the plateau. Depths max out at 120 feet, but you'll see much more between 40 and 80

This brain coral looms like an underwater mountain. PHOTO: WAYNE MOCCIA

feet. Be prepared for a sea squadron of fin-driven tropicals to shadow your every move.

Western Dry Rocks

Experts will love the unusual marine life at Western Dry Rocks. Novices and snorkelers will, too, because this site ranges in depth from 5 to 120 feet, averaging 30 feet with lots of light. Coral fingers with defined gullies and coral formations laced with cracks and caves showcase species normally found more in the Bahamas than in the Keys. The deep-dwelling candy basslets hide themselves away at 90 feet, while their more gregarious cousins, the orangeback bass, hang out in the open. The dusky longsnout butterflyfish prefer dark recesses, though they will sometimes curiously peer out to see what's happening. Sharks have been wit-

nessed regularly enough to prompt advice against spearfishing.

Alexander's Wreck

Commercial salvor Chet Alexander bought a 328-foot destroyer escort from the U.S. Navy at the bargain price of $2,000 and sank her (still sporting her deck guns) in about 40 feet of water west of Cottrell Key as an artificial reef in 1972. Though the current fluctuates from moderate to strong, the relatively shallow depths here allow conscientious novices a chance to swim among fascinating sea creatures: The bodies of the prison-bar-striped spadefish resemble the spade figures in a deck of playing cards. Zebra-striped sheepshead are so curious that if you remain stationary they may come over to investigate. The flashy metallic gold- and silver-striped porkfish is apparently the victim of a cruel creator—two bold, black, diagonal bands slash across its glittery head.

Cottrell Key

A snorkeler's paradise at 3 to 15 feet, Cottrell Key, on the Gulf side, saves the day for divers when the weather is foul on the Atlantic. The grassy banks of the adjoining lakes protect the reef in east-southeast to southwest winds. Ledges and solution holes run for several miles amid intermittent coral heads and swaying gorgonians. The pits, crevices, and coral caves hold great treasures: encrusting orange sponges, which look like spilled cake batter; lustrously mottled cowries camouflaged by their extended mantles; the Florida horse conchs, which will venture out of their long conical spire if you wait patiently; and the spindle-shaped freckled tulip snails.

And Beyond

The Shipwrecks of Smith Shoal

Between June and August 1942, four large ships met their demise near Smith Shoals, apparent unwary victims of American military mines. USS *Sturtevent*, a 314-foot-long four-stack destroyer, was only two hours out of port escorting a convoy when two consecutive explosions ripped her apart. It rests in 65 feet of water. The 3,000-ton American freighter *Edward Luchenbach*, en route from Jamaica to New Orleans with a cargo of tin, zinc, and tungsten, joined the *Sturtevent* after hitting the same mine field. The Bosiljka also made a navigational misstep, succumbing to an American mine as it carried her pharmaceutical cargo from New Orleans to Key West. Groupers, jewfish, snappers, and cobias populate the sunken 277-foot Norwegian ship *Gunvor*, taken by a mine on her way to Trinidad from Mobile, Alabama. The wreckage is scattered in 60 feet of water.

Marquesas Keys

This group of 10 mangrove islands surrounded by shallow waters has alternately been called the remains of a prehistoric meteor crater and an atoll. The ring of keys was named for the Marquis de Cadierata, commander of the 1622 Spanish fleet that included the wrecks Atocha and Santa Margarita. The wrecks were partially salvaged until 1630 by the Spanish, who enticed slave divers to search the remains, promising freedom to the first diver to recover a bar of silver from the site. Mel Fisher rediscovered the ships in 1985. Fisher, the famous 20th-century salvor, found a mother lode of treasure in the holds. The islands evidence little human influence, for they remain uninhabited. Clusters of coral heads shrouded in grouper and snapper mark the southern edge of the islands. Twenty-five miles from Key West, the Marquesas appeal to divers cruising in their motor yachts or on an overnight charter or to hale and hearty daytrippers. West of the Marquesas several wrecks dot the suboceanic landscape. Exercise caution before diving, however, because the U.S. Navy has been known to use them as bombing and strafing targets from time to time. Before you strap on your tanks, check your radio for a Coast Guard bulletin regarding this area.

Northwind

The *Northwind*, a large metal tugboat belonging to Mel Fisher's Treasure Salvors Inc., tragically sank in 1975 while working on the *Atocha* project. Said to have a malfunctioning fuel valve and a leaky bulkhead, the *Northwind* capsized while at anchor, taking Fisher's son and daughter-

> ## Insiders' Tip
> Purchase a NOAA nautical chart—which notates the exact coordinates for dive and snorkel sites—at a dive center or marine supply store before you try to find dive locations in your own vessel.

in-law to a watery grave. The vessel lies on her side in 40 feet of water 3.5 miles southwest of the Marquesas.

Cosgrove Shoal

A 50-foot skeletal lighthouse marks the northern edge of the Gulf Stream, 6 miles south of the western Marquesas. This rocky bank runs for miles, a prehistoric dead reef where caves and ledges support gardens and forests and social clubs of marine fin and flora. A contingent of giant barracudas patrols the shallows, and black coral grows up from the depths, which extend beyond recreational diving capacities. Be sure to take the strong outgoing tide into consideration before you dive here.

Marquesas Rock

Moderate to strong currents and depths to 120 feet dictate that this dive is only suited to advanced skill levels. A can-buoy marks the rocky plateau of Marquesas Rock, the cracks and crevices of which reveal a potpourri of sea life. A school of jacks, apparently attracted by your bubbles, may make a swing past. Saucer-eyed reddish squirrelfish, with elongated rear dorsal fins resembling squirrel tails, mind

their own business in the shaded bottom crevices. Occasional sightings of sailfish, sperm whales, and white sharks have been reported. Keep in mind that when diving at Marquesas Rock you are 30 miles from the nearest assistance.

Dry Tortugas National Park

The end of the line in the Florida Keys, the Dry Tortugas lie some 60 miles beyond Key West. Small boats are discouraged from making the trip, because strong tidal currents flowing against prevailing winds between Rebecca Shoals and the reef of the Tortugas can be treacherous. There is no fuel, fresh water, or facilities offering provisions, nor will you find any emergency assistance. Nonetheless, if your vessel is self-sufficient, if you are with a charter out of Key West, or you have traveled to the Dry Tortugas by seaplane or ferry to camp on Garden Key (see our Recreation and Campgrounds chapters), you are in for the treat of a lifetime.

The eight-island chain is guarded as our southernmost national park. All living creatures below are protected from collection or capture, so a virtual mega-aquarium exists beneath the sea. The constant Gulf Stream current cleanses the waters, allowing visibility of 80 to 100 feet over the 100-square-mile living coral reef. Just off the beach on the west side of Loggerhead Key slumbers a snorkelers' paradise. About a mile offshore lies the remains of a 300-foot, steel-hulled French wreck. Divers report that a monster-size jewfish estimated to be 150 years old resides under the wreck. Other wrecks are littered about the ocean floor, claimed by the reef over centuries past.

Dive Centers

As you drive down the Overseas Highway from Key Largo to Key West, you will notice banner-size, red-and-white, diver-down flags heralding one dive shop after another. More than 100 such establishments are listed in the phone book alone.

To help you navigate this minefield of choices, we supply you with the best ammunition: information.

Many of the dive operations offer the same basic services and will take you to similar, if not the same, spots. But each also differs in many ways. Snorkelers and divers often are taken to the reef in the same excursion, for the varied depths of our spur-and-groove reefs can be experienced with multiple levels of expertise. Snorkel-only trips also are an option. The size of dive excursions varies greatly, ranging from 20 individuals or more to a small-boat group called a six-pack.

Dive rates are based on a two-tank, two-site daylight dive. The excursion plus tanks and weights ranges from $50 to $65. Excursion plus a full-gear package—generally including two tanks, buoyancy compensator, weight belt, regulator, octopus breathing device, gauges, and occasionally mask, fins, and snorkel—ranges from $65 to $90. A wet suit (only needed in the winter months) will cost between $10 and $15 extra. Always ask exactly what is included if you need a full-gear package. All our recommended dive centers make a one-tank, night-dive excursion on request unless otherwise specified.

Snorkel-only rates, which oftentimes include equipment, run between $25 and $35. Children usually are offered a reduced fare. Bubble Watchers, those who'd like to come along for the ride and watch their companions dive or snorkel, will pay between $15 and $25. You may assume that snorkelers and Bubble Watchers can accompany divers unless otherwise stated.

Virtually all of our listed dive centers offer optional dive packages, either for multiple days of diving or for hotel/dive combinations. If you plan to dive on several days of your holiday, you will save money with a package, but you will be limited to diving with one exclusive dive center.

You may assume, unless otherwise noted, all featured dive centers rent full equipment and maintain a retail dive shop where you can purchase equipment, accessories, and underwater camera housings if needed. You may also count on the fact that all recommended dive centers offer a one-day "let's give it a try" resort course (it ranges between $150 and $175) and a basic open-water certification course ($350 to $425). These courses are based on participation of two or more people. Private courses also are available at a considerably higher fee. Many of our recommended dive centers offer a wide selection of PADI, NAUI, and other advanced classes.

The nine-foot figure of Christ, arms raised and looking toward the heavens, was donated to the Underwater Society of America by Egidi Cressi, an Italian diving equipment manufacturer. PHOTO: FLORIDA KEYS & KEY WEST TDC

Hermit crabs take over abandoned conch shells and call them home. PHOTO: WAYNE MOCCIA

You will be required to show your certification card and logbook, and you must wear a buoyancy compensator and a submersible pressure gauge. Snorkels are required equipment for all divers. To dive deeper than 60 feet, considered a deep dive, you must hold advanced certification or a logbook entry showing dives to equivalent depths within the last six months. If you cannot meet these specifications, you will be required to be accompanied by an instructor or guide, which often requires an additional fee that can vary between $30 and $40. You must wear an octopus (an emergency breathing device to share air with your dive buddy) or carry spare air for a deep dive, and you must be equipped with a depth gauge or a timing device. You do not need advanced certification to participate in a night dive, but you must own or rent a dive light and carry a Cylume stick as a backup lighting system.

All dive centers request you check in at least 30 minutes prior to the excursion's departure. Allow even more time if you are renting a full-gear package. We list the dive centers in descending order from Key Largo through the Lower Keys to Key West.

Upper Keys

Captain Slate's Atlantis Dive Center
MM 106.5 Oceanside
51 Garden Cove Drive
Key Largo, FL
(305) 451–1325, (800) 331–3483
www.pennekamp.com/atlantis

You can watch Captain Slate feed bait fish to a barracuda, mouth to mouth and see him cuddle with a moray eel on the weekly Friday morning "Creature Feature" dive trip with Captain Slate's Atlantis Dive Center, when the captain himself performs these fearless feats underwater. Divers from all skill levels enjoy outings with the Atlantis Dive Center. Snorkelers can make a snorkel-only excursion to one destination aboard a glass-bottom boat at 9:30 A.M., 12:30 P.M., and 3:30 P.M., or they can accompany divers to two reef locations. Snorkeling rates here include mask, fins, snorkel, and safety vest. Dive departure times at Captain Slate's are 8:30 A.M. and 1 P.M.

A special feature of Captain Slate's is the custom underwater wedding package. Divers are married in front of the Christ of the Deep Statue at Key Largo Dry Rocks. Vows are made via underwater slates as guest-divers watch the ceremony from the ocean floor and guest-snorkelers view the proceedings from overhead. Guest-land-lubbers are accommodated in the glass-bottom boat, where the perspective varies yet again. Videos and still-photography of the blessed event are also available.

Sharky's Dive Center
MM 100 Oceanside
Key Largo, FL
(305) 451–5533, (800) 935–3483

Sharky's high-speed catamaran transcends the waters covering dive sites from Carysfort Reef at the north end of Key Largo National Marine Sanctuary to the Eagle in Islamorada. If desired, Sharky's will design a custom, three-tank dive trip for you, consisting of one deep dive and two shallower ones. Dives depart from the Holiday Inn Marina at 8:30 A.M. and 1 P.M.

Snorkelers head out to the shallower reefs of the sanctuary at 9:30 A.M., 12:30, and 3:30 P.M. daily.

Kelly's on the Bay and
Aqua-Nuts Dive Center
MM 104.2 Bayside
Key Largo, FL
(305) 451–1622, (800) 226–0415
www.kellysonthebay.com
www.aqua-nuts.com

At Kelly's on the Bay, you can literally step off the boat and fall into bed, because this dive operation is a complete waterfront resort. Aqua-Nuts takes divers to all the popular reefs in Key Largo National Marine Sanctuary and John Pennekamp Coral Reef State Park, including Christ of the Deep Statue, the wreck of the *Benwood*, Molasses Reef, The Elbow, the *Duane*, and even to Conch Reef. And unlike most dive shops, you can rent its gear without booking onto one of its

charters—a real plus if you are venturing out on your own. Dive and snorkel departures are at 8:30 A.M. and 1 P.M. Night dives are regularly offered on Tuesdays, Fridays, and Saturdays, and other times upon request.

Amy Slate's Amoray Dive Resort
MM 104.2 Bayside
Key Largo, FL
(305) 451–3595, (800) 426–6729
www.amoray.com

From this resort, you can hop out of bed onto the deck and take off for a scuba excursion. The Amoray Dive Resort's villa lodging options, complete with hot tub and pool, cater to your every diving whim (see our Accommodations chapter). Amoray's catamaran will whisk you to the reefs of the Key Largo National Marine Sanctuary for a two-tank dive. Dive and snorkel departures are at 8:30 A.M. and 1 P.M. Night dives are regularly scheduled on Thursdays and Saturdays.

Silent World Dive Center Inc.
MM 103.2 Bayside
Key Largo, FL
(305) 451–3252, (800) 966–3483
www.pennekamp.com/sw

Silent World regularly visits The Elbow, Key Largo Dry Rocks, the Benwood, French Reef, Carysfort Reef, and other popular sites within Key Largo National Marine Sanctuary. Dive and snorkel departures are at 9 A.M. and 1 P.M.

John Pennekamp Coral Reef State Park
Boat Rentals & Dive Center
MM 102.5 Oceanside
Key Largo, FL
(305) 451–6322, (877) 538–7348
www.johnpennekamp.com

Pennekamp State Park Dive Center prides itself on being the "only authorized dive center" in John Pennekamp Coral Reef State Park, although all the Key Largo dive centers advertise themselves as diving Pennekamp State Park. The only dive center actually situated inside Pennekamp's grounds, this company's scuba shuttles

keling time at Molasses Reef, White Bank Dry Rocks, Grecian Rocks, Key Largo Dry Rocks, or Cannon Patch. Departures are 9 A.M., noon, and 3 P.M. There is a $5 charge for equipment.

Another option is a four-hour sail and snorkel aboard a 38-foot catamaran, which leaves daily at 9 A.M. and 1:30 P.M. If you feel like staying close to shore, you can rent mask, fins, and snorkel for $10 and paddle around in the water off Cannon Beach, where, yes, there really are a couple of sunken cannons and ancient anchors.

regularly visit such novice sport dives as Molasses Reef, French Reef, Christmas Tree Cove, the wreck of the *Benwood,* and the Christ of the Deep Statue. All dives are less than 60 feet, and certification requirements are stringent. If you have not dived in the past two years, you must hire a guide. If you have not dived in three years, you will have to take a review course. Dive departures are at 9:30 A.M. and 1:30 P.M. Pennekamp does not offer night dives.

It pays to call ahead as you may be able to take advantage of Pennekamp's occasional telephone specials. Discount coupons are available at the Key Largo Chamber of Commerce, MM 106. Snorkelers are not routinely taken with divers at this operation (see Coral Reef Park Company below), but members of your party who don't dive may go on the dive shuttles and snorkel above you.

Coral Reef Park Company
MM 102.5 Oceanside
John Pennekamp Coral Reef State Park
Key Largo, FL
(305) 451–1621
www.johnpennekamp.com

Snorkel-only excursions in John Pennekamp Coral Reef State Park leave the docks three times daily. The shallow-reef sites vary, depending upon where the least current, least wave action and best visibility conditions exist. The snorkel trip lasts 2½ hours, with 1½ hours of actual snor-

Ocean Divers
MM 100 Oceanside
522 Caribbean Drive
Key Largo, FL
(305) 451–1113, (800) 451–1113
www.oceandivers.com

Each day of diving with Ocean Divers brings a different adventure, because this company tries to maintain a rotating schedule of set dive sites if conditions allow. Visiting the popular sites within the Key Largo National Marine Sanctuary, Ocean Divers slips into Eagle Ray Alley and Fire Coral Cave at Molasses Reef, Christmas Tree and Hourglass Caves at French Reef, and between the stands of the rare day-feeding pillar coral. Advanced divers can visit the *Bibb* and the *Duane.* Regular dive and snorkel departures are at 8 A.M. and 1 P.M. Night dives are regularly offered on Tuesdays, Thursdays, and Saturdays, and other times upon request.

Ocean Divers is adjacent to Marina Del Mar Resort. It maintains two dive shops. The second is American Diving Headquarters, MM 105.5, Bayside, Key Largo, (305) 451–0037, (877) 451–0037, www.americandiving.com.

Tavernier Dive Center
MM 90.7 Oceanside
Tavernier, FL
(305) 852–4007, (800) 787–9797
www.tavernierdivecenter.com

Tavernier Dive Center will take you as far north as French Reef and all the way south to the wreck of the *Eagle* or to Alligator Reef. While the center caters to all skill levels, if you want a three-tank dive or an all-day charter, this outfit will accommodate you. A two-tank dive with Nitrox tanks and weights is $70. Regular departures are 9 A.M. and 1 P.M. daily. Snorkelers may accompany divers to reef destinations.

Florida Keys Dive Center
MM 90.5 Oceanside
Tavernier, FL
(305) 852–4599, (800) 433–8946
www.floridakeysdivectr.com

The Florida Keys Dive Center offers two-location reef dives between Key Largo and Islamorada as well as combo wreck/reef dives. A dive to the 100-foot-deep *Duane* is followed by a shallower dive at Molasses or Pickles Reef; an excursion to the *Eagle* is followed by a trip to Crocker or Davis Reef. Departures are 8:30 A.M. and 1 P.M.

Florida Keys Dive Center will video your adventure or arrange for Nikonos or video rentals if you want a do-it-yourself setup. The center offers a discount diving package with accommodations at Ocean Point Suites (see our Accommodations chapter).

Lady Cyana Divers
MM 85.9 Bayside
Islamorada, FL
(305) 664–8717, (800) 221–8717
www.ladycyana.com

Cyana first dove beneath the Aegean Sea in the fifth century B.C. to cut the anchor lines of the invading Persian fleet. Today you are in good hands, too, when you join a dive excursion with Lady Cyana. The friendly staff knows the dive sites within the 6-mile stretch of reef off Islamorada so well you can get wet for 10 days and never be taken to the same location twice. Lady Cyana offers you either a two-reef dive or a wreck and a reef, visiting Pickles, Davis, and Alligator reefs as well as the *Eagle* and the *Duane*.

To dive a wreck with Lady Cyana Divers, you must have made a 70-foot unsupervised wreck dive or an equivalent saltwater dive within the past year, or you will be required to hire a guide. Departures are 8:30 A.M. and 1 P.M. Snorkelers may go out on the dive boat, although when the excursion is to a wreck and a reef, they will only be able to snorkel during the second dive. The water at the wreck is too deep to see anything.

Middle Keys

Tilden Scuba Center
MM 61 Oceanside
Hawk's Cay Resort
Duck Key, FL
(888) 443–6393
www.divingathawkscay.com

Long known as a topnotch dive center in the Florida Keys, Tilden's heads to such reef locations as Coffins Patch, Porkfish Reef, and Shark Harbor, and takes advanced divers on guided excursions to the *Thunderbolt* and the *Adelaide Baker* wreck. Since no other dive boats operate for 20 miles on either side of Duck Key, Tilden's reports that these Middle Keys reef tracts are very healthy. Tilden Scuba Center operates the largest dive vessel in the Middle Keys—licensed to carry 40 passengers—but limits its excursions to 24 divers and snorkelers.

Divers find a multitude of corals at our barrier reef.
PHOTO: WAYNE MOCCIA

Abyss Dive Center
MM 54 Oceanside
Marathon, FL
(305) 743–2126, (800) 457–0134
www.abyssdive.com

The Abyss Dive Center in Marathon subscribes to the less-is-more theory of diving, which guarantees lots of personal attention. The company takes a maximum of six divers or snorkelers to 48 sites spread over the reefs at Sombrero Key, Coffins Patch, Yellow Rocks, and Delta Shoals. Abyss will take you to the *Thunderbolt* if your certs are current or your dive experience warrants, or you can hire an instructor and explore the wreck with a guide. Departures are at 8:30 A.M. and 12:30 P.M.

The Diving Site
MM 53.5 Oceanside
Marathon, FL
(305) 289–1021, (800) 634–3935
www.divingsite.com

The Diving Site finds plenty of good dives for novices and intermediate divers alike, including Yellow Rocks, Coffins Patch, Delta Shoals, and Sombrero Reef. If you would like to dive the *Thunderbolt* with The Diving Site, you will need to show advanced certification or three logged dives of 100 feet or greater. If that is not in the cards, don't despair. You can hire an experienced instructor to guide you through the fascinating wreck. Divers and snorkelers depart at 8:30 A.M. and 1 P.M. On Wednesday and Saturday afternoons, The Diving Site offers a shark dive, where you can mingle and interact with a group of nurse sharks.

Hall's Diving Center
MM 48.5 Bayside
Marathon, FL
(305) 743–5929, (800) 331–4255
www.hallsdiving.com

If you are an advanced certified diver or have an 80-foot dive under your weight belt, head out to the *Thunderbolt* with Hall's. Divers of other skill levels will enjoy diving the Middle Keys' 25- to 90-

foot reef specialties, from Looe Key to Coffins Patch and especially around Sombrero Reef. Dive excursions depart at 9:30 A.M. and 1:30 P.M. Snorkelers may accompany divers at shallow reef locations.

In addition to standard equipment, a deluxe full-gear package, featuring top-of-the-line Nitrox clean gear, is available. Hall's also rents and provides certification in the use of a re-breather. Or you can rent mask, fins, and snorkel and explore the shallow Gulf waters or the Atlantic Ocean off Sombrero Beach with a buddy.

Hall's Diving Center, a popular Marathon dive center for decades, offers multiple-day dive/lodging packages in conjunction with Faro Blanco Marine Resort.

Lower Keys

Underseas Inc.
MM 30.5 Oceanside
Big Pine Key, FL
(305) 872–2700, (800) 446–5663
www.keysdirectory.com/underseas

> ## Insiders' Tip
> Shipworms, or teredo worms, are sea animals that have decimated the wood-timbered sunken ships off the Florida Keys. Shipworms (actually bivalves) resemble tiny clams when they are young and swim about freely. They attach to wood and bore downward and inward with their two clamlike shells, tunneling as much as three-quarters of an inch per day. Shipworms have been known to honeycomb timbers within six months.

North America's only underwater barrier reef beckons divers from all over the world. PHOTO: WAYNE MOCCIA

In the Lower Keys, when you've said Looe Key National Marine Sanctuary, you've said it all. And when you need a dive center, Underseas will take you there. With depths to satisfy all levels from snorkelers and novice divers to those with advanced skills, Looe Key is endlessly fascinating. Departures are at 9 A.M. and 1:30 P.M.

Strike Zone Charters
MM 29.5 Bayside
Big Pine Key, FL
(305) 872–9863, (800) 654–9560
www.strikezonecharter.com

Docked out back and ready to transport you to the Looe Key National Marine Sanctuary for a spectacular two-tank dive, Strike Zone Charter's glass-bottomed catamarans depart at 9:30 A.M. and 1:30 P.M. Strike Zone now also visits the Keys' newest artificial reef, the *Adolphus Busch.*

Looe Key Reef Resort & Dive Center
MM 27.5 Oceanside
Ramrod Key, FL
(305) 872–2215, (800) 942–5397
www.diveflakeys.com

The friendly crew at Looe Key Reef Resort whisks you off to the Looe Key National Marine Sanctuary, where you will visit three sites with at least an hour bottom time at each location. On Wednesday and Saturday, divers visit two reef sites plus the wreck of the *Adolphus Busch.* The other days divers will visit three reef sites. Snorkelers may accompany divers. The excursion runs from 10 A.M. to 3 P.M.

Looe Key Reef Resort and Dive Center offers dive/lodging packages at its adjoining motel. The dive boat leaves from its mooring directly behind the motel so schlepping your gear is not a burden here.

Key West

Captain's Corner Dive Center
125 Anne Street
Key West, FL
(305) 296–8865, (305) 296–8918
www.captainscorner.com

Captain's Corner Dive Center's reef and snorkel excursions leave at 9:30 A.M. and 1:30 P.M. Wreck and reef dives and double wreck dives are available by special arrangement.

Spearfishing

One of the oldest methods for securing food from the sea was with a spear. Originally, this weapon was used at the water's surface while the hunter stood near or on the shore. Today divers equipped with scuba gear and spear guns spearfish under water, which equalizes the suboceanic playing field.

The 3-foot to 6-foot stainless steel shaft of the spear gun is operated with a system of rubber slings. At the end of the arrow is a sharp barb. You must first commence the hunt. Swim very quietly and peer over every rock and ridge of the outer edges of the reef until you find the fish. Reef fish are territorial, seldom found far from their habitual hiding place. (Mutton snapper and black grouper are considered prizes.) Move slowly and carefully as you stalk the fish until it is in range. Lead the fish like you would if you were hunting with a rifle and try to hit its head. Be sure not to spearfish near any other divers.

Man and barracuda swim side by side.
PHOTO: WAYNE MOCCIA

Once you spear a fish, it thrashes about and causes justified commotion. Blood will be released into the surrounding waters and may attract sharks cruising the area. Be alert to their presence. While they will be after the injured fish, not you, the sharks may not readily make the distinction.

Be sure to check The Florida Keys National Marine Sanctuary section of our Boating chapter for restrictions before spearfishing in our waters.

The fish in our waters know the rules. Do you? You may not spearfish:

• Within 100 yards of a public swimming beach, a commercial or public fishing pier, or any part of a bridge from which public fishing is allowed.

• Within 100 feet of any part of an above-surface jetty, unless the final 500 yards of the jetty extend more than 1,500 yards from shore.

• In state waters (from shore to 3 miles out) from Long Key Bridge north to the Dade County line.

• In Key Largo National Marine Sanctuary, Looe Key National Marine Sanctuary, Everglades National Park, Dry Tortugas National Park, or in any body of water under the jurisdiction of the DEP's Division of Recreation and Parks.

• Without a valid Florida saltwater fishing license.

• For redfish (red drum), jewfish, billfish (all species), shark, spotted eagle ray, sturgeon, bonefish, Nassau grouper, pompano, tarpon, spotted sea trout, African pompano, permit, Manta ray, snook, weakfish, tripletail, blue crab, stone crab, and lobster.

• For families of ornamental reef fish: puffers, parrotfish, angelfish, trunkfish, squirrelfish, trumpetfish, surgeonfish, butterflyfish, cornetfish, damselfish, pipefish, porcupinefish, or seahorse.

During daylight-saving-time months you can dive the twilight wreck and reef dive on Tuesdays, Thursdays, and Saturdays. First you dive a wreck, then watch the sunset from the deck of the boat. After dark, experience the after-hours sea life during a reef dive. Captain's Corner always has instructors in the water with you, so you can sign on even if you are a novice diver. Snorkelers and riders who would like to accompany diving members of their party for the twilight dive may come at no charge.

Dive Key West Inc.
3128 N. Roosevelt Boulevard
Key West, FL
(305) 296–3823, (800) 426–0707
www.divekeywest.com

Dive Key West offers "reef du jour," customizing the schedule based on diver demand and weather conditions. It concentrates on the 30-foot reef lines where the light is better and the colors are more brilliant, allowing you more bottom time. The inner reefs have large stands of coral

Insiders' Tip

The Florida Keys National Marine Sanctuary has devised a Shipwreck Trail that directs you to nine historic shipwreck sites along our coral reef. Underwater site guides for each of the wrecks are available at local dive shops. The guides provide shipwreck and mooring-buoy positions, history of the wrecked ships, a site map, and information on marine organisms you may encounter on your adventure.

and a high concentration of tropical fish, while at the outer reefs you will see less coral, more big sea fans, sponges, and larger finfish. For your two-dive combo you can choose between a wreck and a reef or two reefs. Dive Key West visits the wrecks of the *Cayman Salvager*, *Joe's Tug* and the *Alexander*, which, at 90 feet, 60 feet, and 30 feet, respectively, offer a skill level for everyone. Regular departures are at 9 A.M. and 2 P.M.

If you do not have the skill level for the wreck dive of your choice, you may hire an instructor to accompany you. Snorkelers will be custom-fitted with gear at no extra charge, and free instruction is available. Night dives, scheduled upon request, are always accompanied by an instructor. Departure times for the night dive vary by daylight-saving time.

Key West Diving Society
MM 4.5 Oceanside
Stock Island, FL
(305) 292–3221
www.keywestdivingsociety.com

Catering to small groups, Key West Diving Society semi-customizes their dive excursions between two reef sites or a wreck and a reef. They visit such popular sites as *Joe's Tug*, *Cayman Salvager* and the Western Sambos. Departures are at 9 A.M. and 2 P.M. Snorkelers may accompany divers on reef dives.

The Key West Diving Society offers technical divers the opportunity to book private charters to the *Wilkes-Barre* wreck or the Curb. All dive masters at KWDS have a specialty, so you can arrange special-interest dives such as spearfishing, lobstering, photography, and more.

Lost Reef Adventures
261 Margaret Street
Land's End Marina
Key West, FL
(305) 296–9737, (800) 952–2749
www.keywest.com/lostreef.html

Lost Reef Adventures customizes its dive trips one day before departure based upon the skill levels and dive site desires

The spiny blowfish fascinates a Keys diver. PHOTO: WAYNE MOCCIA

divers to hold advanced certification or equivalent experience. Monday mornings the boat goes to the wreck of the *Alexander*, whose shallower depths invite exploration by those of all experience levels. These dives depart at 9 A.M.

Subtropic offers trips to two reefs in the afternoons for those who are less experienced. These reef/reef trips (and the reef-dive portion of the morning wreck/reef excursions) visit the Sambos, Rock Key, Sand Key, and the Dry Rocks. Departure is at 2 P.M. Snorkelers are welcome on the afternoon reef/reef diving excursions or they may opt for a snorkel-only trip, which is offered daily at 9 A.M. and 1 P.M. Night dives are offered regularly on Wednesdays and Saturdays.

Situated at the far end of Garrison Bight Marina, Subtropic Dive Center also has a large selection of spear guns and offers special spearfishing courses and charters for $79, which includes tanks, weights, and spear gun. Spearfishing excursions require a four-person minimum and visibility must be 20 feet or better.

of interested divers. Excursions visit the celebrated *Joe's Tug, Cayman Salvager* and *Alexander* wreck sites and reefs from Western Sambo to the Western Dry Rocks. The wreck/reef trip leaves at 8:30 A.M. The reef/reef dive and snorkel excursions depart at 9 A.M. and 1:30 P.M. Lost Reef offers night pilgrimages seasonally. First you can pay homage to the sun as it sinks into the water; then you will take the plunge for a one-tank twilight dive.

Subtropic Dive Center
1605 N. Roosevelt Boulevard
Key West, FL
(305) 296–9914, (800) 853–3483
www.subtropic.com

Mornings find Subtropic's dive boat exploring a wreck and a reef. Wednesday, Friday, and Sunday, they visit *Joe's Tug* and Tuesday, Thursday, and Saturday, the *Cayman Salvager*. These wreck dives require

Insiders' Tip

Please do not try to feed the fish from your hand. This changes the natural behavior and diet of the fish.

Recreation

If you want to scuba dive, fish, sail, or motor in our abundant waters, see the related chapters in this book. For a plethora of other stimulating diversions, read on. We show you where the action is—from sky diving, parasailing, and watersports to sunset cruises, gunk-holing eco-tours, and bicycling. You'll find out about our beaches and public parks in this chapter. And, if the weather isn't fine—which is rare—or you would just like to stay indoors, look here, too, for billiards, bowling, bingo, and movie theaters.

We give you an idea of the price range for each of your recreational choices in the preface to each category. Look for fee information for those one-of-a-kind activities within the write-up. Recreation facilities are organized by category from Key Largo to Key West.

Air Tours and Sky Diving

Lower Keys

Fantasy Dan's Airplane Rides
MM 17 Bayside
Lower Sugarloaf Airport
Sugarloaf Key, FL
(305) 745–2217

Fantasy Dan takes passengers in his Cessna 182 on 10- to 45-minute flights, 500 feet over the Florida Keys. Excursions, which cover areas from the Seven Mile Bridge to Key West, operate from 9 A.M. to sunset. Air tours, which accommodate three people, range in price from $50 to $180. Call in advance or stop by the airport. To reach Lower Sugarloaf Airport, turn toward the bay at the paved road bordering the west end of Sugarloaf Lodge.

Skydive Key West
MM 17 Bayside
Lower Sugarloaf Airport
Sugarloaf Key, FL
(305) 745–4386, (800) 968–5867
www.skydivekeywest.com

Try tandem skydiving from 10,000 feet over the Lower Keys and Key West with Skydive Key West. First-timers are welcome. Allow one hour per person for this venture, including training and the jump.

Soft landings are provided on Lower Sugarloaf Key. Skydive expeditions aboard a Cessna 182 depart Sugarloaf Airport between 10 A.M. and sunset seven days a week. Skydivers are advised not to scuba dive for 24 hours before their jump. Videos and photographs are available for purchase as souvenirs. Jumps are by reservation only and you must be at least 18 years of age to take the plunge. Book several days in advance during the winter season. Expect to spend between $200 and $300 for this adventure.

Key West

Seaplanes of Key West
Key West International Airport
3471 S. Roosevelt Boulevard
Key West, FL
(305) 294–0709, (800) 950–2359,
(800) 950–2FLY
www.seaplanesofkeywest.com

There is simply no faster, easier, more incredible way to reach Dry Tortugas National Park—70 miles due west over open water from Key West—than via seaplane. With Seaplanes of Key West, everyone on board gets a window seat for the 45-minute flight to Fort Jefferson. In addition to navigating the skies, your pilot will point out the sights as you glide just 500 feet above the emerald waters of the Gulf of Mexico. Along the way, you're likely to spot sea turtles, rays, dolphins, and a shipwreck or two.

Seaplanes of Key West offers half-day (morning or afternoon) and full-day trips to Fort Jefferson. The half-day trip encompasses 4 hours (45 minutes of flying time each way, plus at least 2¼ hours on the island). Half-day round-trip fares are $179 for adults and $129 for children ages 7 through 12; kids 6 and younger fly for $99 each. The full-day trip takes eight hours, at least six of which are spent on the island. Full-day round-trip fares are $305 for adults, $225 for children ages 7 through 12, and $170 for children 6 and younger. In either case, children under age 2 fly free. Fare includes soft drinks and snorkeling equipment, but if you want lunch, you'll have to pack your own.

A drop-off/pickup service is provided for campers at a cost of $329 for adults, $235 for children 7 through 12, and $179 for children 6 and younger. Campers must carry everything, including water, into and out of the park; the extra charge covers the cost of transporting their gear. Weight allowance is restricted to 40 pounds per camper; no dive tanks are permitted.

A maximum of nine passengers can be accommodated per plane trip, and reservations are required. Allow plenty of lead time for reservations, especially during high season.

Beaches and Public Parks

"Life's A Beach," the T-shirts say, but first-time visitors to the Keys who expect to find soft, white, endless sand along the ocean are bound to be disappointed. The coral reef protects the Keys from the pounding surf that grinds other shorelines into sand, and so most of ours must be carted in by the truckload. Nevertheless, if stretching out in the sand tops your recreational must-do list, humans and nature have teamed up here to bring you a stretch or two. Some of our parks and beaches, as designated, charge admission fees, and most have specific hours of accessibility.

Keys beaches do not maintain lifeguard stations. Riptides are rare here, but jellyfish are not. Swim at your own risk and never venture out alone or after dark.

Upper Keys

John Pennekamp Coral Reef State Park
MM 102.5 Oceanside
Key Largo, FL
(305) 451–1202
www.dep.state.fl.us/parks

Well known to divers and snorkelers as the first underwater state park in the United States, John Pennekamp also serves a wide palette of diversions within its land-based boundaries. You can explore most of the fascinating habitats of the Florida Keys here (see our Paradise Found chapter). Enjoy campfire programs, guided walks, and canoe trips. The park offers a nature trail, beaches, picnic areas, campsites (see our Campgrounds chapter), restrooms, showers, and watersports concessions (see listings in this chapter) where you can rent any equipment you might desire, from scuba gear to sailboats.

Expect to pay a nominal admission fee per person and per vehicle. The park is open from 8 A.M. to sunset.

Friendship Park
MM 101 Oceanside
Key Largo, FL

This park sports a playground, a Little League field, swings, and a basketball court. It's perfect for those lazy afternoons with children in tow, and it's especially inviting for picnics. The park is open from 8 A.M. until dusk or when a Little League game is scheduled. Admission is free.

Harry Harris Park
MM 92.5 Oceanside
Tavernier, FL
(305) 852–7161

Bring the kids along to Harry Harris, where a small beach fronts a tidal pool protected by a stone jetty. You'll find a playground, ball field, volleyball net, in-

Babes of all ages love the sandy shores of Sombrero Beach in Marathon. PHOTO: VIVIENNE AFSHARI

line skating park, and picnic grounds. Restrooms are available. To reach the park, follow signs leading toward the coast along the oceanside by mile marker 92.5 (Burton Drive). Stay on Burton Drive about two miles and follow the signs to the left. Admission is free, except on weekends and federal holidays when nonresidents (persons residing outside Monroe County) must pay a per person admission fee as well as a docking fee to use the boat ramp. The park is open from 8 A.M. to sunset.

Islamorada Village of Islands
Plantation Yacht Harbor
MM 87 Bayside
Islamorada, FL
(305) 852–2381, Ext. 502

Shortly after Islamorada incorporated in 1998, the new city bought Plantation Yacht Harbor Resort and converted its grounds into a city park. The bayside beach and watersports concession are open to the general public, offering numerous opportunities for sunning, swimming, snorkeling, and other water-based activities. You also can rent kayaks, clearbottom boats, and paddleboats here. Lounge chairs are available for rent, and restrooms are on the premises. To aid in the upkeep of the park, the City of Islamorada charges a small admission fee. Monroe County residents receive a 50 percent discount. Use of the pool, which has a capacity of only 30, is restricted to Islamorada residents and their guests.

Holiday Isle Resort & Marina
MM 84 Oceanside
Islamorada, FL
(305) 664–2321
www.holidayisle.com

Holiday Isle Resort offers two beaches with watersports concessions, volleyball, and limitless grazing and quaffing at numerous lively tiki bars and waterfront grills. Lounge chairs are available for rent. Body watching and mingling top the list of pastimes at this singles favorite. Restrooms are dubbed "Kokomo Toilets." This beach extravaganza is open to the general public.

Beach Behind the Library
MM 81.5 Bayside
Islamorada, FL

This stretch of beach has no more official name than its general location, but it does offer a playground, restrooms, and showers. There is no admission charge.

Indian Key Beach
MM 78 Oceanside
Islamorada, FL

Although there isn't much of a beach here, a swimming area and boat access are available. Admission is free.

Anne's Beach
MM 73.5 Oceanside
Islamorada, FL

At low tide, tiny Anne's Beach holds enough sand to accommodate several blankets, but it attracts sun worshipers by the dozens. Swimming waters are shallow. Parking is limited. To find Anne's Beach, slow down along the Overseas Highway southwest of Caloosa Cove Resort and look toward the ocean for a small parking lot. Blink and you'll miss it. There is no charge.

Long Key State Park
MM 67.5 Oceanside
Long Key, FL
(305) 664–4815
www.dep.state.fl.us/parks

A long, narrow sand spit makes up the "beach" at this state park, which is fronted by a shallow-water flat. Rent a canoe and enjoy the calm, easily accessible waters while you bird-watch and fish in ideal conditions. The picnic area is equipped with charcoal grills. Long Key State Park offers superb oceanfront campsites (see our Campgrounds chapter), restrooms, and shower facilities. Expect to pay a nominal admission fee per person and per vehicle. Long Key State Park is open from 8 A.M. to sunset.

Middle Keys

Sombrero Beach
MM 50 Oceanside
Sombrero Beach Road
Marathon, FL

This spacious, popular public beach offers a picnic area, playground, and sweeping views of the Atlantic. Swimming waters run deep off Sombrero Beach. Restrooms are available. Marathon Chamber of Commerce, along with volunteer organizations, work to keep this gem of a beach in pristine condition. There is no admission charge, and parking is plentiful.

Marathon Community Park
MM 49 Oceanside
Marathon, FL

The city of Marathon boasts a new 14.8-acre public park, which offers two softball fields, four tennis courts, a playground, picnic area, three basketball courts that are also used as a roller-hockey rink, a jogging path, a pavilion, and restrooms. City officials say it is only phase one of the park project. Phase two, still in the planning stages, will add 8.9 more acres and include a band shell and more playgrounds.

Lower Keys
Little Duck Key Beach
MM 39 Oceanside
Little Duck Key, FL

With restrooms and picnic shelters, this beach makes for an ideal lunch spot. The small beach provides a swimming area but no lifeguards. Open from 8 A.M. until dusk, the beach is free to the public. And don't be confused by the name. This beach is on Little Duck Key, not Duck Key. You will find it on the left side of the Overseas Highway, just this side of Bahia Honda, as you are traveling south toward Key West.

Bahia Honda State Park
MM 37 Oceanside
Bahia Honda, FL
(305) 872–2353
www.dep.state.fl.us/parks

Across the Seven Mile Bridge from Marathon, Bahia Honda State Park sparkles like a diamond and boasts the best natural beach in all of the Florida Keys. Narrow roads wind through the mangrove thickets, many of which have been fitted as campsites (see our Campgrounds chapter). Tarpon fishing beneath the Bahia Honda Bridge attracts seasoned anglers and novices alike, and the park has its own marina with boat ramps and overnight dockage.

At the dive shop in the concession building, you can rent snorkeling equipment or book a trip to Looe Key National Marine Sanctuary. Groceries, marine supplies, and souvenirs are sold here, too.

Bahia Honda offers picnic facilities, restrooms, guided nature walks, and charter boat excursions. Expect to pay a nominal admission fee per person and per vehicle. The park is open 8 A.M. to sunset.

Key West
Higgs Beach and Rest Beach
Atlantic Boulevard
Key West, FL

These twin beaches are so close together they are often mistaken for each other. Higgs Beach offers a playground, picnic tables, and nearby tennis courts. It is between White and Reynolds Streets on Atlantic Boulevard. The beach is open sunrise to 11 P.M. Admission is free.

Rest Beach is smaller than Higgs Beach and is dwarfed by the massive White Street Pier. This pier is a favorite with anglers and dog walkers and is sometimes called the "unfinished road to Cuba." Rest Beach has the same hours as Higgs Beach. Right across the street is an extensive playground called Astro City, a favorite with the kids.

Smathers Beach
S. Roosevelt Boulevard
Key West, FL

Across from Key West International Airport, Smathers is a long strip of sand that bustles with food vendors, watersports concessions, and beautiful bods in itsy-bitsy, teeny-weeny suits. Smathers underwent extensive renovation in spring 2000 so now, or at least until the next hurricane blows through, it looks like what you'd expect a Florida beach to look like.

Admission here is free, but bring plenty of quarters for the streetside parking meters (you'll need one per hour). If you don't mind carting your beach gear a few extra yards, free parking is available on the far side of S. Roosevelt. The beach is open sunrise to 11 P.M.

Fort Zachary Taylor
Truman Annex at the end of Southard Street
Key West, FL

Look to the left of the brick fort for a pleasant, although rocky, beach with picnic

From fire eaters to furniture jugglers, you'll rarely see the same routine two nights in a row at the Mallory Square sunset celebration. PHOTO: FLORIDA KEYS & KEY WEST TDC

tables and barbecue grills. The locals call this place "Fort Zach"; this is where they come in droves to sunbathe and snorkel. The water is clear and deep, and you're likely to see many colorful fish congregating around the limestone-boulder breakwater islands constructed just offshore. When it gets too hot on the beach, head for the shade—there's plenty of it available under the lofty pine trees in the picnic area. The beach area is open 8 A.M. to sunset (see the Key West section of our Attractions chapter for admission charges and other activities here).

Dog Beach
Waddell and the ocean
Key West, FL

Tucked next to Louie's Backyard Restaurant is this tiny little beach, a favorite with locals mainly for one reason: It's the only beach in Key West where dogs are allowed.

Bayview Park
Truman Avenue and Jose Marti Drive
Key West, FL

You will definitely notice Bayview Park if you are driving into Key West on North Roosevelt Boulevard, which becomes Truman Avenue. On your left as the road narrows and you head into Old Town, Bayview Park is one of the only green spots still left in Key West. Look for the gazebo. Several picnic tables are strewn throughout the park and come highly recommended for a shady afternoon lunch.

Bicycling

You'll be able to get a "wheel" deal when you rent a bike and cycle the Keys. Rentals are offered by the day (9 A.M. to 5 P.M.), 24 hours, multiple days, week, or month. The one-speed cycles, which we call beach cruisers, average about $6 to $7 for 8 hours or $8 to $10 for a 24-hour rental. Weekly rentals are range from $35 to $45. Tandem bikes are available at some Key West establishments for about $15 per day. Most of these establishments sell parts and new bicycles, do repairs, and rent helmets and other gear. Remember, Florida state law requires helmets for cyclists younger than 16.

Upper Keys

Among the best places to bike the Upper Keys are Harry Harris Park, where bicycle lanes are provided, and on the bicycle paths in the median and along the oceanside of the Overseas Highway in Key Largo. Down the Keys, you may safely cycle through Islamorada's Old Highway, which borders the Overseas Highway on the oceanside. A bike path on the bayside finishes a tour through Upper Matecumbe Key and on through Lower Matecumbe Key, thereby making it possible to safely cycle from about mile marker 90 to approximately mile marker 72.

Equipment Locker Sport & Bicycle
MM 101.4 Oceanside
Key Largo, FL
(305) 453–0140

MM 53 Bayside
Marathon, FL
(305) 289–1670

Equipment Locker rents beach cruisers by the 24-hour period or by the week. The store also offers 21-speed mountain bikes. Here, too, you can rent in-line skates with complete gear, knee boards, water skis, or towable tubes.

Tavernier Bicycle and Hobbies
MM 92 Bayside
Tavernier, FL
(305) 852–2859

Tavernier Bicycle and Hobbies rents cruisers (one-speed bicycles) for men, women, and children by the day, week, or month. Per-day prices decrease with multiple-day rentals.

Middle Keys

There are few bicycle paths in the Middle Keys. In Marathon, you'll need to cycle on the old Seven Mile Bridge to Pigeon Key (a good 2-mile-plus jaunt), use the Key Colony Beach bicycle lane (turn onto the Key Colony Causeway at mile marker 53.5 to get to Key Colony), or pedal along the relatively traffic-free streets of the Sombrero residential area (turn onto Sombrero Beach Road, MM 50, next to Kmart).

Key Colony Beach Marina
MM 53.5 Oceanside
589 Sixth Street
Key Colony Beach, FL
(305) 289–1310

Rent bikes by the day, week, or month. You'll find the marina on the Key Colony Beach Causeway on the left side.

Lower Keys

The Lower Keys span 30 miles, but toward the end of the Keys you will have the best luck finding rental bikes on Stock Island and Key West (see section below).

Big Pine Bicycle Center
MM 31 Bayside
Big Pine, FL
(305) 872–0130

This is the best source for bicycle rentals in the upper portion of the Lower Keys.

Key West

Adventure Scooter & Bicycle Rentals
Key Plaza Shopping Center
2900 N. Roosevelt Boulevard
Key West, FL
(305) 293–9933

Adventure has seven locations in Key West and offers conch cruisers with locks and adjustable padded seats.

The Bicycle Center
523 Truman Avenue
Key West, FL
(305) 294–4556

The Bicycle Center offers single-speed bicycles with coaster brakes, locks, and baskets.

The Bike Shop
1110 Truman Avenue
Key West, FL
(305) 294–1073

The Bike Shop rents one-speed cruisers with baskets and locks.

Canoeing the backcountry waters attracts anglers and gunk-holers alike. PHOTO: VICTORIA SHEARER

Conch Bike Express
3340 N. Roosevelt Boulevard
Key West, FL
(305) 294–4318

Strictly a delivery service, Conch Bike rents one-speed cruisers with baskets, locks, and lights. Trikes, tandems, and kids' bikes are also available. Pickup, delivery, and road service from 9 A.M. to 5 P.M. daily are free with your bike rental.

Island Bicycles
929 Truman Avenue
Key West, FL
(305) 292–9707

Island Bicycles offers a full selection of bicycles for sale and rent, including one-speed cruisers and adult trikes. Repairs and accessories are also available here.

Moped Hospital
601 Truman Avenue
Key West, FL
(305) 296–3344

Moped Hospital rents single-speed bicycles with coaster brakes, baskets, and locks by the hour, day, and week.

Paradise Rentals Inc.
105 Whitehead Street
(305) 292–6441

430 Duval Street
Key West, FL
(305) 293–1112

Paradise Rentals Inc. offers daily and weekly cruiser rentals.

SUN-N-FUN Rentals
925 Duval Street
Key West, FL
(305) 295–6686, (866) 295–6686

In addition to single-speed bicycles, SUN-N-FUN rents multi-speed bikes, from single-speed cruisers to 18- to 21-speed mountain bikes, tandem bikes, electric bikes, and electric cars. Rent bicycles by the hour (with a two hour minimum). Delivery is available to cruise ships, hotels, and guesthouses.

TJ's Fudge Cycle
MM 5 Oceanside
5704 Maloney Avenue
Stock Island, FL
(305) 294–7090

TJ's bills itself as "the sweet ride." In addition to rentals, TJ's has the largest cycle showroom in the Keys, plus a complete repair shop.

Billiards, Bingo, and Bowling

Yes, we do occasionally have inclement weather here in the Keys, but we never let rainy days and Mondays get us down. In addition to the three indoor leisure pastimes described in this section, the Florida Keys has a busy bridge league schedule. For dates, times, and locations of weekly games with the American Contract Bridge League, see our Retirement chapter. Please note that indoor activities like bingo may not be offered year round and specific times may change. It is always a good idea to phone ahead before venturing out.

Upper Keys

St. Justin Martyr Catholic Church Bingo
MM 105.5 Bayside
Key Largo, FL
(305) 451–1316
Doors open Tuesday night at 6 P.M.; early birds begin at 7 P.M.; and regular bingo is at 7:30 P.M.

Key Largo Lion's Club Bingo
MM 99 Oceanside
232 Homestead Avenue
Key Largo, FL
(305) 451–1271
Public bingo is held Thursdays at 7 P.M. and Sundays at 11:30 A.M.

Elks Lodge BPOE 1872 Bingo
MM 92.5 Bayside
Tavernier, FL
(305) 852–5615
Friday nights at the Elks Lodge feature bingo at 7 P.M.

Fish Bowl
MM 83.2 Bayside
Islamorada, FL
(305) 664–9357

Extensively renovated in 2000, the Fish Bowl—the only bowling alley in the Keys—offers 12 bowling lanes, glow bowling, billiards, an arcade room, and a snack bar.

Middle Keys

Loyal Order of Moose Lodge 1058 Bingo
MM 54 Bayside
Marathon, FL
(305) 743–6062
Monday night bingo begins at 7 P.M.; Thursday matinee games start at 1 P.M.

Disabled American Veterans
Chapter 122 Bingo
MM 52 Bayside
Marathon, FL
(305) 743–4705
You'll find another Friday night game here. Bingo is at 7 P.M.

Elks Club BPOE 2139 Bingo
MM 51.5 Oceanside
Marathon, FL
(305) 743–2652
The Elks Club holds bingo on Sundays from 2 to 5 P.M.

Gary's Pub & Billiards
MM 49 Oceanside
Marathon, FL
(305) 743–0622
Visitors and residents alike revel in Gary's, the upscale billiard parlor with a long, mahogany bar that is a welcome addition to the Marathon recreational scene. Brass-trimmed overhead lights dimly illuminate the nine coin-operated pool tables. A jukebox, dart boards, and video and pinball machines in the back entertain those not playing pool. Some 25 television sets dot the interior. Sunday afternoons feature billiard tournaments (see our Nightlife chapter).

American Legion Post 154 Bingo
MM 48.5 Oceanside
Marathon, FL
(305) 743–4783
Bingo is held each Wednesday at 7 P.M.

San Pablo Catholic Church Bingo
MM 53.5 Oceanside
670 122nd Street
Marathon, FL
(305) 289–0636

Tuesday night is bingo night at San Pablo, January through April. Games are played from 7 to 10 P.M. Proceeds go toward college scholarships for local students.

Lower Keys

Boondocks
MM 27.5 Bayside
Ramrod Key, FL
(305) 872–4094

You'll find two billiard tables at this popular Lower Keys watering hole and restaurant (see our Restaurants and Nightlife chapters).

Loyal Order of Moose Lodge 1585 Bingo
MM 28.5 Bayside
21 Wilder Road
Big Pine Key, FL
(305) 872–4063

The only year-round bingo in the Lower Keys, these Monday and Thursday night games begin at 6 P.M. However, they are open only to members and their guests.

Key West

Down Under Sports Bar
1970 N. Roosevelt Boulevard
Key West, FL
(305) 294–1970

This sports bar features two billiard tables, darts, pinball machines, video games, and a half-dozen televisions that offer satellite programming. Play billiards at Down Under free of charge.

Stick and Stein Sports Rock Cafe
Key Plaza Shopping Center
2922 N. Roosevelt Boulevard
Key West, FL
(305) 296–3352

At Stick and Stein, 13 billiard tables are set around four bars with sports playing on 70 large- and small-screen televisions. Billiards is free with a food or beverage

purchase from 11 A.M. to 4 P.M. (unlimited number of players). After 4 P.M., you pay an hourly fee. (See our Nightlife chapter.)

Boat Excursions, Sunset Cruises, and Gambling Junkets

Our crowning glory rests in our encompassing waters. Explore the backcountry and the waters of the Everglades National Park on group gunk-holing eco-tour expeditions (see our Paradise Found chapter) or take a glass-bottom boat trip to the reef to view the fascinating creatures residing there. Relax aboard a sunset cocktail cruise or fire up for a casino cruise.

Snorkeling-only trips range between $30 and $45 per person. (See our Diving and Snorkeling chapter for charters that take both divers and snorkelers to the reef.) Glass-bottom boat rides cost between $15 and $20. Plan on paying about $20 per hour for a guided gunk-holing eco-tour jaunt, as these are generally small, intimate excursions. Private eco-tour charters are priced per boat, usually two to three people, and range from $150 to $225 per half day. Sunset and sailing cruises range from $25 to $35 per adult, depending on the size of the vessel and length of the cruise. In most cases, children's rates are less.

Upper Keys

John Pennekamp Coral Reef State Park
MM 102.5 Oceanside
Key Largo, FL
(305) 451–1621

Pennekamp's glass-bottom catamaran, the *Spirit of Pennekamp*, carries as many as 150 people on 2½ hour tours of the reef. Tours are offered three times daily. The 38-foot catamaran, *Salsa*, departs the park marina twice daily.

Everglades Safari Tours
MM 102 Bayside
Dolphin Cove
Key Largo, FL
(305) 853–5161, (888) 224–6044

Venture 17 miles into the waters of the Everglades National Park, in and around mangrove and bird rookery islands (see our Paradise Found chapter) aboard a 23-foot pontoon boat. Tours are limited to six passengers and depart twice daily. A 1½ hour champagne sunset cruise for up to 28 passengers departs aboard the paddle-wheeler *Bay Princess*; times vary depending on the whim of the setting sun. And then there's the Crocodile Tour, a nighttime adventure that takes you in search of the elusive Florida saltwater crocodile.

African Queen
MM 100 Oceanside
Holiday Inn Docks
Key Largo, FL
(305) 451-4655

Board the legendary *African Queen*—featured in the Humphrey Bogart and Katharine Hepburn movie of the same name—in Key Largo for daily one-hour cruises and sunset or charter excursions during the autumn and winter months. In summer, the boat goes on tour.

Quicksilver Catamaran
MM 100 Oceanside, Holiday Inn Docks,
Key Largo, FL
(305) 451-0105

Sails through the sanctuary waters of John Pennekamp Coral Reef State Park are offered three times daily—morning, afternoon, and sunset—aboard the 50-foot catamaran, *Quicksilver*. Discounts and family rates are available on snorkel/sunset sail combinations. Private and group charters also can be arranged. Gear rental is extra.

Key Largo Princess Glass Bottom Boat
MM 100 Oceanside
Holiday Inn Docks
Key Largo, FL
(305) 451-4655

This princess carries passengers on narrated two-hour tours that drift above the reef. A full bar is on board, and guests can buy hot dogs and snacks. *Key Largo Princess* tours are offered three times daily. Family rates and private charters are available. The boat is wheelchair-accessible.

The legendary African Queen, *featured in the classic Bogart/Hepburn movie of the same name, will take you on a one-hour cruise on the waters of Key Largo.* PHOTO: FLORIDA KEYS & KEY WEST TDC

SunCruz Casino
MM 100 Oceanside
Holiday Inn
Key Largo, FL
(305) 451–0000

Sports betting, blackjack, slot machines, dice, roulette, and video poker are among the many diversions on board *SunCruz Casino*. A full bar and a la carte sandwich menu satisfy hungers of another kind; a welcome-aboard cocktail and hors d'oeuvres are served to all free of charge. Guests at Key Largo's Holiday Inn, Ramada, or Marriott sail for free, as often as they desire. The general public may board the more than 100-foot vessel's gambling sails for a small admission fee. On Wednesdays, Saturdays, and Sundays, the first trip is at 2 P.M. Every other day, trips begin at 5 P.M. The actual casino is moored each day 3 miles offshore in federal waters. Water taxis take guests to and from the casino vessel every two hours.

Caribbean Watersports
MM 97 Bayside
Westin Beach Resort
Key Largo, FL
(305) 852–4707, (800) 223–6728

Cheeca Lodge
MM 82 Oceanside
Islamorada, FL
(305) 664–9547, (888) 732–7333
www.enviro-tours.com

Glide through the Everglades with Caribbean Watersports' two-hour guided Hobie Sailing Safaris and explore uninhabited mangrove islands all along Florida Bay. Environmental gunk-holing tours (see our Paradise Found chapter) at both locations provide the same guided ride in a 17-foot rigid inflatable Zodiac that has a fiberglass hull, stabilizing inflatable side pontoons, and a quiet electric trolling motor. Enviro-tours depart about every two hours beginning at 9:15 A.M. daily. Tours are limited to six people; you must call ahead to reserve a spot.

Freya Sailing Cruises
MM 81.9 Bayside
Lorelei Restaurant and Marina
Islamorada, FL
(305) 664–8582

The two-masted, 63-foot schooner *Freya* makes sunset trips through the bay daily from mid-November through April. (The boat operates out of East Dennis on Cape Cod during the rest of the year.) Passengers bring their own coolers, food, and beverages. The *Freya* accommodates a maximum of 35 passengers. Advance reservations are suggested.

Bud n' Mary's Glass-Bottom Boat
MM 79.5 Oceanside
Islamorada, FL
(305) 664–2211
www.budnmarys.com

Sightseers and snorkelers aboard this glass-bottom boat stop at two locations along the reef. Depending upon weather conditions, the three-hour trip departs daily at 1:30 P.M. If you plan to go, call at 10:30 A.M. to confirm that the trip is scheduled.

Middle Keys

Hawk's Cay Resort and Marina
MM 61 Oceanside
Duck Key, FL
(305) 743–7000

Sail aboard the 40-foot custom sailing catamaran *Horizon* at up to 20 knots or sign on for a more leisurely sunset cruise. Board the *Osprey*, a glass-bottom boat, on one of the twice-daily narrated trips to the reef. Or rent a sea kayak for a self-guided eco-tour of the out-islands near Duck Key. All these excursions may be booked at Hawk's Cay.

Many other water-related activities are available at Hawk's Cay, including chartered fishing excursions to the backcountry or the reef. For those with other interests, many other amusements are available, including personal watercraft and small-boat rentals, water skiing, pontoon party barge rentals, and parasailing.

Skimmer Charters
MM 61 Oceanside
Duck Key, FL
(305) 743–7436

This is the only private gunk-holing charter that will whisk you away at 35 knots into the backcountry waters of Florida Bay to the Arsnicker Keys, 7 miles northwest of Lower Matecumbe, to see the fabulous white pelicans. These ultimate snowbirds winter in the Keys from November until about the end of March. The flock often numbers 500 or more around the tiny islets of the Arsnicker. Captain Joe Winter stealthily poles his flatsboat through the shallows so as not to alert the birds to your presence. Bring your camera! A *Skimmer* gunk-holing charter for two people costs $200 for three hours. Captain Winter is also an expert flats fishing guide, specializing in bonefish, permit, tarpon, redfish, snook, and other backcountry species. Four hours of guided fishing costs $275. You can combine the bird-watching gunk-holing excursion with some guided backcountry fishing if you like.

Spirit Catamaran Charters
MM 47.5 Oceanside
56223 Ocean Drive
Marathon, FL
(305) 289–0614

Insiders' Tip
Frequent and even application of your sunscreen is every bit as important as its SPF. Do not venture into the hot, intense Florida sunshine without sunscreen protection, and if you get wet, be sure to reapply it.

A 40-foot catamaran named *Spirit* takes passengers snorkeling to popular Middle Keys reefs twice a day, makes family charter cruises to Pigeon Key, offers marine biology tours with classrooms of children, and sets off for a daily sunset cruise at the end of the day. Call in advance to make reservations.

Safari Charters
MM 49.5 Bayside
Banana Bay Resort
Marathon, FL
(305) 289–1433

A conjunctive business with Banana Bay Sailing School (see our Boating chapter), Safari Charters offers an array of adventures on the water. You can enjoy a daytime snorkel trip aboard the large sailboat or, in the evening, join the vessel as it sails off for a sunset cruise. Safari Charters also rents an assortment of do-it-yourself watercraft, including ocean kayaks and day sailers.

Lower Keys

Strike Zone Charters Island Excursion
MM 29.5 Bayside
Big Pine Key, FL
(305) 872–9863, (800) 654–9560
www.strikezonecharter.com

This five-hour, backcountry out-island excursion, which includes a fish cookout on a secluded island, will entice your entire family (see our Kidstuff chapter for more details and see our Diving and Snorkeling chapter for Strike Zone's underwater offerings).

Key West

A Key West Reef Trip
MM 5.5 Oceanside
Safe Harbor Marina
6810 Front Street
Stock Island, FL
(305) 292–1345
www.reefchief.com

Board a classic, wood sailing schooner for dive and snorkel trips to Sambo Reef or for leisurely day, sunset, and evening sails.

Sailing lessons and music cruises are also available on the 65-foot schooner *Reef Chief*, a classic Chesapeake Bay–style schooner. Ask about special activities such as full moon sails, Sunworship Sundays, Turtle Watch Tuesdays, and wild dolphin watching.

Adventure Charters
MM 5.5 Oceanside
Safe Harbor Marina
6810 Front Street
Stock Island, FL
(305) 296–0362, (888) 817–0841
www.keywestadventures.com

Looking for an alternative to the traditional party boat/booze cruise? Captain Tom of Adventure Charters offers half-day snorkel cruises, half-day backcountry nature excursions, and full-day backcountry adventures that combine kayaking, snorkeling, fishing, and beachcombing through tidal streams and along mangrove islands that are unreachable by larger boats. To find Adventure Charters, turn at MacDonald Avenue near Chico's Cantina.

Appledore **Charter Windjammer**
201 William Street
Key West, FL
(305) 296–9992

Daily snorkel trips aboard this 85-foot, oak-framed, pine schooner head for the reef. The excursion includes a full lunch, a fruit platter, snacks, and beverages, plus beer and wine for after-snorkeling libation. Gear is provided, and passengers need only bring towels and sunscreen. A nightly sail-only excursion includes beer and wine (champagne during sunset).

During the high season, the *Appledore* fills up quickly; call with a credit card to confirm reservations in advance. The *Appledore*, which has circumnavigated the world, summers in Maine and is in Key West October through May.

Danger Charters
Hilton Resort & Marina
231 Front Street
Key West, FL
(305) 296–3272, (305) 744–8476
www.dangercharters.com

Don't let the moniker fool you: *Danger* and *Danger Cay* are the names of the two Chesapeake Bay Skip Jack sailboats, not any situation you will encounter on this adventurous charter. Up to six people board the skipjack and right away owner and Captain Wayne Fox assigns one of his new crew as first mate. The fun begins as the new mate learns the intricacies of tending to a sailboat and tacking into the wind. The boat soon travels to the backcountry, where the crew disembarks into three double kayaks and journeys through the mangrove islands. Then the sailboat moves to another location where snorkeling gear is donned. Finally, after much adventure, the boat sails back home. Excursions last about five hours. Full-day trips, sunset cruises, and specialized bird-watching trips are also available. Call for details and pricing.

Discovery **Glass Bottom Boat**
Key West Historic Seaport
Key West, FL
(305) 293–0099, (800) 262–0099
www.discoveryunderseatours.com

This 78-foot, 124-passenger, triple-decker vessel makes three trips daily to Eastern Dry Rocks. Cruise times vary depending on the season. A 45-minute excursion through the harbor and out to the reef includes a narration of Key West history. Once the vessel arrives at the reef, passengers head downstairs beneath the water line where windows provide the main viewing and glass-bottom wells at the stern add to the visual feast. All trips, with the exception of *Discovery's* sunset cruise, are two hours long. At sunset, the captain cruises slowly by Mallory Square on his 2-

Naturalists guide visitors through the wonders of our ecosystem. PHOTO: VICTORIA SHEARER

hour and 20-minute itinerary so that passengers can view the unusual live entertainment from the ocean-side (see our Attractions chapter).

Fury Catamarans
201 Front Street
Key West, FL
(305) 294–8899, (800) 994–8898
www.furycat.com

Climb aboard one of Fury's 65-foot catamarans for a sail by day or night. Fury offers two three-hour trips to the reef daily for snorkeling—one in the morning, one in the afternoon—plus a two-hour champagne sunset sail each evening. You can buy separate tickets for day snorkeling or sunset sailing, or purchase a combination snorkeling/sunset sail ticket. Fury also offers snuba excursions. (Snuba, a cross between scuba diving and snorkeling, involves a cylinder of compressed air attached to a raft and connected to two 20-foot-long regulator hoses that participants use for breathing.) Beer, white wine, sodas, and snorkeling/snuba gear are included in the price of your ticket. In addition, Fury offers parasailing as well as a land/sea excursion package that includes a trip to the reef and a tour of Key West aboard either the Conch Tour Train or Old Town Trolley.

Liberty Fleet of Tall Ships
Hilton Resort and Marina
245 Front Street
Key West, FL
(305) 292–0332
www.libertyfleet.com

The 80-passenger schooner *Liberty* now resides full-time in Key West, offering two-hour morning, afternoon, and sunset sails year round. Sunset sails include complimentary beer, wine, and champagne. Passengers are invited to participate in hands-on sailing, but it's perfectly okay if you just want to sit back and let the captain do all the work.

The 125-foot, 115-passenger *Liberty Clipper* plies the waters off the Florida Keys and Dry Tortugas from November through May. On Tuesday, Thursday, and Sunday nights, passengers can dine on Hard Rock Cafe's Caribbean-style barbecue aboard the *Liberty Clipper* while they listen to reggae music and watch the sun sink into the Gulf. During the summer months, the *Liberty Clipper* offers a variety of adventure cruises along the Atlantic coast. Check the website for details.

Mangrove Mistress Eco-Charters
Murray Marine
MM 5
Stock Island, FL
(305) 745–8886
www.floridakeys.net/mangrovemistress

Gunk-hole within the Great White Heron Natural Wildlife Refuge aboard the 30-foot river cruiser *Mangrove Mistress*, a 1930s-style, smooth-riding wood craft. Snorkel gear is onboard, including equipment for children. Captain Lynda Schuh guarantees "no seasickness" on the two half-day trips she offers daily. If a half-day cruise is too long, try a serene sunset or sunrise voyage through the mangroves. Customized charters and full-day cruises are also available.

Mosquito Coast Island Outfitters
1107 Duval Street
Key West, FL
(305) 294–7178

Full-day kayak trips depart Key West by van for Geiger Key or Sugarloaf Key where guided backcountry tours include a narration of the trees, birds, fish, coral, sponges, seagrass, and sea creatures (see our Paradise Found chapter). Single and double kayaks are available; half the trip is devoted to snorkeling. Gear, snacks, and bottled water are included in the fee. Children are welcome but must be at least nine years old to participate. Tours leave Key West at 8:45 A.M. and return at 3 P.M.

PT-728 Cruise
Key West Historic Seaport
Key West, FL
(305) 295–5544

If you ever wanted to follow in the footsteps of John F. Kennedy, hop aboard this authentic World War II torpedo boat for a one-hour narrated tour of Key West Harbor. You'll learn about U.S. Navy missions in Key West waters over the past 100 years, including pirate encounters, World Wars I and II, and the Cuban Missile Crisis. The captain will also re-create a simulated torpedo run. Operated by the Historic Naval Ship Association, *PT-728* departs every hour, beginning at noon. The last tour leaves at 6 P.M. Price is $30 per person; $40 per person for the sunset excursion.

Sebago Catamarans
328 Simonton Street
Key West, FL
(305) 292–4768, (800) 507–9955
www.keywestsebago.com

Head out to the reef for a snorkeling/sailing adventure aboard Sebago's 60-foot catamaran or cruise Key West harbor at sunset. Complimentary drinks are served on both excursions. Sebago also offers parasailing as well as a six-hour "Island Ting" trip that includes kayaking, snorkeling, and sailing, plus a luncheon buffet. Call for details.

> ## Insiders' Tip
>
> If you plan to make frequent visits with friends and family to John Pennekamp, Bahia Honda, Fort Zachary Taylor, or any of the 47 state parks in Florida, consider purchasing an annual pass. The pass allows unlimited park access for up to eight people per vehicle for one year from the date of purchase. You need not be a Florida resident to buy one.

The Schooner *Wolf*
Key West Historic Seaport
Key West, FL
(305) 296–9653, (877) 296–9653
www.schoonerwolf.com

This 74-foot steel-hull schooner—flagship of the Conch Republic—offers nightly two-hour sunset sails, which include beer, wine, champagne, and nonalcoholic beverages and feature a guitarist who strums sea chants and Jimmy Buffett music. Other offerings include day sails at 11 A.M. and 2 P.M. Kids always sail for half the adult price, plus they get a cool pirate hat and pirate puzzle to take home. And everyone gets in on the act when the captain suddenly announces that his treasure is missing. It's either help with the search or walk the plank! The folks at the Schooner Wolf recommend advance reservations for all sails.

Stars & Stripes Catamaran Tours
Key West Historic Seaport
Key West, FL
(305) 294–7877, (800) 634–6369
www.adventurekeywest.com

The 53-foot catamaran *Gold Coast* is equipped to carry as many as 44 passengers but typically takes smaller groups. Sandwiches, salads, and beverages are included in the per-person price for the all-day cruise. The sunset cruise offers beer, wine, mimosas, and nonalcoholic beverages. If you take the all-day excursion, you can get a sizable discount on the sunset cruise for another night of your visit.

Sunny Days Catamaran
Key West Historic Seaport
Key West, FL
(305) 292–6100 (ferry)
(305) 296–5556 (reef cruises)
(800) 236–7937
www.sunnydayskeywest.com

Sunny Days could once boast of having the only "high-speed catamaran service" to Dry Tortugas National Park. Although that's no longer true, with the launching of its *Fast Cat II* in May 1999, Sunny Days does continue to have the fastest ferry service. The 100-passenger, high-speed *Fast Cat II* makes the voyage from Key West to Fort Jefferson in just under two hours. As a result of the time saved, passengers aboard *Fast Cat II* can get in a little extra snorkeling at Garden Key or even squeeze in a snorkeling side trip to the Windjammer wreck (there's an extra $10 charge per person for the side trip).

Fast Cat II leaves from its berth at the foot of Elizabeth Street at 8 A.M. and returns by 5:30 P.M. daily. The day-trip fare for adults is $85, $80 for seniors and military, and $55 for children. A continental breakfast and lunch are included in the fare, along with snorkeling gear and instruction and a guided tour of Fort Jefferson. Campers pay an extra $35 to accommodate their gear, plus $3 per person, per night.

In addition to its daily run to Fort Jefferson, Sunny Days also offers twice-daily catamaran cruises aboard their original *Fast Cat* to the reef for snorkeling, a combination snorkeling/sunset cruise, and a champagne sunset cruise. Prices vary depending on the length of the cruise and the time of day.

Vegas West Casino Cruises
245 Front Street
Key West, FL
(305) 295–7775

Traditionally, gambling cruises don't fare so well in Key West. Apparently, there are too many other activities to keep tourists occupied. However, Vegas West may be the exception to that rule; it celebrated its two-year anniversary of operation in February 2001.

One of the reasons for this cruise line's success may well be its prices. Evening cruises aboard the good ship *Rendezvous* cost only $9. Day cruises are even cheaper, $7, and the Sunday all-day cruise includes a buffet lunch. The catch, of course, is that you are supposed to gamble while aboard and that does cost money. You'll find plenty of opportunities to take your chances—slots, blackjack, roulette, and stud poker during the day, plus dice games at night.

Day cruises leave the Hilton Pier on Tuesdays, Thursdays, and Sundays at noon and return at 4 P.M. Evening cruises are daily from 6:30 to 11 P.M. (11:30 P.M. Fridays and Saturdays). Phone ahead for reservations.

Western Union
202 William Street
Key West, FL
(305) 292–9830
www.schoonerwesternunion.com

A sail aboard the 130-foot schooner *Western Union* is truly a voyage back in time. Built and berthed in Key West, the *Western Union* was launched off Simonton Beach in 1939 as a working schooner. Until 1974, it sailed the Caribbean and South Atlantic, logging more than 30,000 miles and maintaining thousands of feet of communications cables for the Western Union Company. In 1997, it returned to Key West to begin its second career as a passenger vessel.

From its slip next to Schooner Wharf Bar at the foot of William Street, the *Western Union* offers two-hour afternoon sails and sunset and starlight cruises; it is also available for private charters and other seafaring adventures. The sunset sails include music and complimentary beer, wine, and champagne.

Schooner *America*
Key West Historic Seaport
Key West, FL
(305) 292–7787
www.schooneramerica.com

In 1851, the original schooner *America* defeated all challengers in the 100 Guinea Cup Race in England. The cup was brought to the United States and subsequently renamed America's Cup in the ship's honor. Now, you can sail on the *America* yourself—not the original, of course, but a $4 million facsimile—which resides in Key West during the winter months. *America* offers two-hour day sails.

Yankee Fleet Ferry to Fort Jefferson and Dry Tortugas National Park
Key West Historic Seaport
Margaret Street
Key West, FL
(305) 294–7009, (800) 926–5332
www.yankeefleet.com

A voyage to Dry Tortugas National Park, 70 miles west of Key West, requires a full day. But, if you have the time, be sure to include the adventure in your itinerary. Not only is this a spectacular ride back in history, it's a chance to experience what the Florida Keys are truly all about.

Ponce de Leon named the seven islands *Las Tortugas* (The Turtles) in 1513. The word "Dry" was later incorporated into the title to let seafarers know that there is no fresh water available here. You'll be able to take a tour of the massive and historical Fort Jefferson on Garden Key and enjoy calm seas, pristine natural sand beaches, and some of the best snorkeling anywhere. The protected waters surrounding the Tortugas sparkle with all the sea creatures of the coral reef, plus a few shipwreck remains. And because this area has been designated a "no take zone," the creatures you see get a chance to grow larger than those you might otherwise encounter. Do remember, however, that there is no food, fresh water, electricity, or medical assistance at Fort Jefferson.

The Yankee ferry service used to offer a slow boat to the Tortugas, but no more. The *Yankee Freedom II*, a 100-passenger, high-speed catamaran, took the place of the old ferry in March 1999 and now passengers are "whisked" from Key West to Fort Jefferson in less than 2½ hours. *Yankee Freedom II* departs promptly at 8 A.M. and returns at 5:30 P.M. daily. The day-trip fare is $95 for adults; $85 for senior citizens, military, and students with identification; and $60 for children 16 and younger. Fare includes round-trip transportation; snorkeling gear; en route commentary by a naturalist/historian; a 45-minute guided tour of Fort Jefferson; continental breakfast of bagels, doughnuts, cold cereal and juice; and lunch consisting of cold salads and a make-your-own sandwich bar. Coffee, iced tea, and water are complimentary; you can buy sodas, beer, wine, and mixed drinks on board. Passengers are not permitted to carry alcohol to the Dry Tortugas.

Only campers staying the night on Garden Key may bring large coolers (see our Campgrounds chapter). Campers pay slightly higher fees for passage aboard *Yankee Freedom II* to accommodate their gear: adults, $109, and children 16 and younger, $79.

Golf and Tennis

Putters and players drive the Keys links, and racketeers of all ages love our courts. Read on and be on the ball. Court time will cost between $5 and $15 per hour, per person, depending upon the facility. Greens fees are reasonably priced at the public course in Marathon, but very, very pricey at the public course in Key West. If you belong to a country club back home, be sure to contact Sombrero Country Club to see about reciprocal privileges.

Upper Keys

Islamorada Tennis Club
MM 76.8 Bayside
Islamorada, FL
(305) 664-5340

This facility maintains four clay and two hard courts, five of which are lit for extended play into the evening hours. Private lessons, clinics, round robins, and tournaments are offered to the general public, and Islamorada Tennis Club will arrange games at all levels. A pro shop and boutique are on premises. Same-day racket stringing is available.

Middle Keys

Duck Key Tennis Garden
MM 61 Oceanside
Hawk's Cay Resort
Duck Key, FL
(305) 743-7000

Hawk's Cay offers a wide range of organized tennis to both hotel guests and the general public. Regular events include clinics, round robins, stroke of the day, and assorted drill sessions. Clay courts are lit. You can rent courts by the hour. Ball machine rental and private lessons are also available by reservation.

Key Colony Beach Golf and Tennis
MM 53.5 Oceanside
Eighth Street
Key Colony Beach, FL
(305) 289-1533

Greens fees at Key Colony Beach's nine-hole, par 3 public course are a real deal ($7.50 for nine holes at press time). And you can rent clubs and a pull cart for just a couple of dollars more. Tee times are not required. The course is open 7:30 A.M. to sunset. Key Colony Beach Golf Course is the only public course in the Keys outside Key West.

Tennis players can enjoy the two lit hard courts, which are open from 8 A.M. to 9 P.M.

To find the golf course, turn toward the ocean onto Key Colony Beach Causeway at the traffic light at MM 53.5.

Wonderlin Tennis
MM 50 Oceanside
Sombrero Resort Lighthouse and Marina
Sombrero Boulevard
Marathon, FL
(305) 743-2250, Ext. 526

Marathon's favorite pro, Tim Wonderlin, together with Sombrero Resort, offers a tennis package that is difficult to beat. A $5-per-day guest fee entitles you to unlimited tennis and pool privileges at the resort; you can also purchase a seasonal membership. The four hard courts are lit so play commences at 7 A.M. and can continue until 10 P.M. During the high season (November 15 through April 15), Wonderlin offers morning two-hour special clinics and organized round-robin play: women's day, men's day, or mixed doubles. Expect to pay an additional charge

With a wingspan of ten feet, white pelicans—winter visitors to the Florida Keys—can be found on a gunk-holing expedition to Little Arsnicker or Sandy Keys. PHOTO: MARY MOCCIA

for these events. Private lessons may be scheduled.

Sombrero Country Club
MM 50 Oceanside
Sombrero Boulevard
Marathon, FL
(305) 743–2551

Members of Golf Association country clubs in the United States may obtain reciprocal golfing privileges at the private Sombrero Country Club by following a specific procedure; call for details. Monthly memberships are also available for nonmembers who do not own property in Monroe County.

Key West

Bayview Park Tennis
1310 Truman Avenue
Key West, FL
(305) 294–1346

The tennis courts at Bayview Park are open to all on a first-come, first-served basis. Reservations are neither required nor accepted. There are no court fees, and courts are lit until 10 P.M.

Key West Golf Club
MM 5 Bayside
Stock Island, FL
(305) 294–5232

The only public 18-hole course in the Keys, this par 70 course designed by Rees Jones offers a clubhouse, pro shop, and lessons. Greens fees are a whopping $125 in high season but about a third less in the off-season. For late afternoon golfers, special "twilight" fees are available after 2:30 P.M. Monroe County residents receive discounts, but you must reside here year round to qualify. Call for details.

Key West Tennis Too
811 Seminole Avenue
Key West, FL
(305) 296–3029

Affiliated with the Wyndham Casa Marina Resort and Beach House and adjacent to it, Key West Tennis Too utilizes the hotel's three hard-surface courts. Tournament lights make nighttime play possible. A pro offers lessons by appointment, you can rent a ball machine, and a complete pro shop carries top-brand rackets and offers in-house stringing. Guests of the Wyndham Casa Marina or Reach Resort play for about half the court fees that the public pays. Tennis clinics are held daily.

Watersports

Pick your pleasure and make a splash—parasailing, waterskiing, and kayaking. You'll find personal watercraft and paddleboat rentals in this section. For a rundown of scuba diving/snorkeling trips to the reef, see our Diving and Snorkeling chapter. Parasailing ranges in cost from $35 to $45, depending on length of the ride and height achieved. Kayaks range from as much as $10 per hour to only $35 per day. Personal watercraft single seaters cost anywhere from $30 to $45 per half-hour, $60 to $65 per hour. Two-seaters cost approximately $45 per half-hour, $80 per hour. Count on spending about $15 to rent a paddleboat.

Upper Keys
Florida Bay Outfitters
MM 104 Bayside
Key Largo, FL
(305) 451–3018
www.kayakfloridakeys.com
FBO offers a wide selection of kayaks, canoes, and camping supplies and provides basic lessons for using such equipment as paddle floats, spray skirts, and bilge pumps. The company offers guided and self-guided tours through the fascinating waters of Florida Bay and the Everglades National Park. Guided tours include virtually all areas of the Florida Keys: through North Sound Creek, Lignumvitae Key and Indian Key, Great White Heron Refuge, John Pennekamp Coral Reef State Park, and Everglades National Park. Prices vary, based on degree of difficulty and length of excursion. Florida Bay Outfitters is open 9 A.M. to 6 P.M. seven days a week from October 1 through June 30 (closed on some holidays). From July through September, the shop is closed on Tuesdays and Wednesdays. Check the website for a complete description of tour options and reservation policies.

It's a Dive Watersports
MM 103.8 Bayside
Marriott Key Largo Bay Beach Resort
Key Largo, FL
(305) 453–9881, (800) 809–9881
www.marriottkeylargo.com
It's a Dive offers personal watercraft and kayak rentals. Parasailing, waterskiing, and scuba instruction are available, and snorkeling trips aboard a glass-bottom boat depart twice daily.

Coral Reef Park Company
MM 102.5 Oceanside
John Pennekamp Coral Reef State Park
Key Largo, FL
(305) 451–1621
www.johnpennekamp.com
Coral Reef Park Company rents snorkeling equipment at Pennekamp Park for unguided exploration of the nearshore Pennekamp waters off Cannon Beach, or you can sign on with one of the snorkeling tours to the reef (see our Diving and Snorkeling chapter for details). Rent canoes, kayaks, or Spyaks here and paddle the mangrove water trails. Small boats also are available for hire.

Caribbean Watersports
Westin Beach Resort
MM 97 Bayside
Key Largo, FL
(305) 852–4707, (800) 223–6728
Cheeca Lodge
MM 82 Oceanside
Islamorada, FL
(305) 664–9547, (888) 732–7333
www.caribbeanwatersports.com
Caribbean Watersports maintains watersports concessions, otherwise known as beach huts, at two Upper Keys resorts. Both carry Hobie Cats and sailboats and provide a refresher course or an overview of how to sail before you head out on the water. You'll find parasailing (try the

Insiders' Tip

If you plan to explore the backcountry or go on a guided eco-tour, first read our Paradise Found chapter for a gunk-holing primer of the fascinating creatures you will discover.

tandem flight with a friend) every hour; snorkeling trips twice daily; snuba dive excursions (instead of wearing a tank, you are tethered to a topside oxygen tank with a 27-foot hose), for which you must take a one-hour lesson. Caribbean Watersports offers kayak, sailboard, and five-passenger Jamaican bobsled (long, inflated pontoon-style kayaks pulled by powerboats) rentals. You'll find personal watercraft at the Westin facility and waterskiing at the Cheeca, which also has a full dive center. For all these watersports, call ahead for reservations.

Splash Watersport Rentals
MM 84.5 Oceanside
Pelican Cove
Islamorada, FL
(305) 664–8892
www.pcove.com/splash

On the beach at Pelican Cove, Splash rents personal watercraft and 16-foot skiffs for round-trip visits to the Sand Bar (a popular snorkeling and swimming site). A reef boat takes snorkelers on excursions, and 16-mile, guided, personal watercraft tours depart before sunset and head through the backcountry.

Holiday Isle Watersports
MM 84 Oceanside
Holiday Isle Resort
Islamorada, FL
(305) 664–5390, (800) 327–7070
www.holidayisle.com

Raft, kayak, and sailboard rentals are at the southwest end of Holiday Isle's beach.

Personal watercraft are available by the half-hour or hour, and parasailing trips lead adventurers 300, 600, and 1,000 feet in the air. Takeoffs and landings are smooth and dry from specially designed winch boats. You can also enjoy eco-tours aboard personal watercraft.

A1A Watersports
MM 82.5 Oceanside, behind Day's Inn
Islamorada, FL
(305) 664–8182

Rent personal watercraft from A1A at half-hour and hourly increments, but rent your kayak by the day or week. A1A also offers a guided, two-hour, 26-mile sunset Wave Venture or Raider tour around the islands, harbors, and mangroves. Tours must be arranged in advance, and the shop recommends reservations for holiday watercraft rentals.

Pier 68
MM 68 Bayside
Long Key, FL
(305) 664–9393

You can't possibly miss the bright yellow and red building next to Lime Tree Bay Resort. Here, personal watercraft, Hobie Cats, and day-sailers are available for half- and full-day rentals. If a powerboat is more your style, you can get that here, too.

Middle Keys

Hawk's Cay Resort and Marina
MM 61 Oceanside
Duck Key, FL
(305) 743–7000
www.hawkscay.com

The watersports facility at Hawk's Cay offers parasailing, pontoon or center-console boat rentals, personal watercraft, and kayak rentals, as well as water ski and wakeboard rentals and instruction. A sailing school is also on the premises.

Rick's Watercraft Rentals Inc.
MM 49.5 Bayside
Banana Bay Resort
Marathon, FL
(305) 743–2450, (800) 694–6848
www.rickswatercraft.com

Rent a personal watercraft from Rick's for a half-hour or hour. Try the two-seater Yamaha IIIs, or rent your own 20-, 22-, or 23-foot boat for the day.

Seven Mile Marina
MM 47.5 Bayside
Marathon, FL
(305) 289–9849

At the Seven Mile Marina, personal watercraft are available for rent by the half-hour, hour, half-day, or full day. Riders must remain within sight of the dockmaster.

Lower Keys

Big Pine Kayak Adventures
MM 31 Bayside
Old Wooden Bridge Fishing Camp
No Name Key, FL
MM 28.5 Bayside
Parmer's Place
Little Torch Key, FL
(305) 872–2896, (877) 595–2925
www.keyskayaktours.com

Kayak tours through the Lower Keys backcountry waters of the Great White Heron Refuge make for superb gunk-holing (see our Paradise Found chapter). Skiff tours take up to four people and their kayaks deeper into the backcountry waters. Custom back country tours can also be arranged, and guided eco-tours on sit-atop kayaks are an option. If you prefer to head out on your own, you'll be given operational and chart instructions and suggestions of where to explore. Paddle on over to the Sandbar Restaurant (see our Restaurants chapter) for lunch, a mere 10 minutes away. Kayak reservations are required.

Key West

Island Watersports
245 Front Street
Hilton Resort and Marina
Key West, FL
(305) 296–1754
www.island-watersports.com

Personal watercraft and jet boats are available for rental by the half-hour or hour.

This business also boasts the largest riding area in Key West. If you like, wet suits and goggles are also offered. The 1½- to 2-hour guided tour aboard a personal watercraft is a great way to see the island.

Key West Boat Rentals
617 Front Street
Key West, FL
(305) 294–2628, (888) 288–8395
www.keywestboat.com

Rent personal watercraft by the half-hour and hour here. Backcountry jet boat tours are available. Prices for these custom tours are based on where you want to go and how long your excursion is. You can also arrange for a 22-mile, 1½ hour, personal watercraft guided tour—a good value because you get an extra half-hour, plus a guide, for the same price as a one-hour PWC rental only.

Key West Water Sports Inc.
714 Seminole Street
Wyndham's Casa Marina Resort and
Beach House
Key West, FL
(305) 294–2192

A wide variety of watersports gear is ready and waiting for you here. Feel like a lazy afternoon just drifting? Try a Sun Cat floating lounge chair. Or maybe a Sea Peeper—a two-person glass bottom boat—is more your style. Key West Water Sports is also home to high performance short boards and quality sailboarding equipment. If you've never tried the sport before, climb aboard the Cat Surfer—the folks here guarantee that anyone can learn to sailboard on this baby. For the rest of you, Hobie Cats, personal watercraft, baby-seat bikes, double-seater scooters, waterskiing, and parasailing are also available.

Land's End Boat Rentals
Key West Historic Seaport
Key West, FL
(305) 294–6447

Rent all sorts of boats from this place, including sailboats, powerboats, and jet boats. Rentals are available by the hour, half-day, full day, and week. Take advantage of the guided island tours or just take some sailing lessons.

Parawest Watersports Inc.
700 Front Street
Key West, FL
(305) 292–5199

This enterprise prides itself on offering more free falls and dips than any other excursionist in Key West. Regular rides of 8 to 10 minutes include heights of 300 feet with one free fall and one dip; longer, higher rides of 10 to 12 minutes reach 600 feet and include several free falls and dips. Most parasailing is done behind Christmas Tree Island and Sunset Key. Single and double personal watercrafts also are available for rent. Individuals who rent personal watercraft must remain within a limited riding area.

Sunset Watersports
Smathers Beach
Key West, FL
(305) 296–2554

This outfit offers something for everyone. Parasailing, Hobie Cats, kayaks, and sailboards are all provided on Smathers Beach. For an all-inclusive daytrip, take the "Do It All." From the Key West Seaport, a 44-foot catamaran takes you out about 3 miles to a shallow wreck. From there, take turns exploring with personal watercraft, waterskiing, and just about anything else they can imagine.

Tropical Sailboats
Higgs Beach
Key West, FL
(305) 296–0423
Smathers Beach
Key West, FL
(305) 296–4185

Two locations provide an extensive list of watersports rentals. Choose from Hobie Cats, sailboards, kayaks, rafts, and snorkeling equipment. Both locations offer free instruction, and both are authorized

Hobie Cat dealers. Rentals are available by the hour or half-day.

Let's Go to the Movies

Cinema buffs can screen the latest flicks here. The theaters offer matinees on Saturdays and Sundays and sometimes on weekdays at a reduced ticket price.

Upper Keys

Tavernier Towne Twin Cinema
MM 91.5 Bayside
Tavernier Towne Shopping Center
Tavernier, FL
(305) 853–7003

This twin cinema offers Hollywood's latest creations twice nightly, with matinees on weekends. Monday through Thursday, moviegoers who are 65 and older benefit from discounted rates.

Middle Keys

Marathon Community Cinema
MM 50 Oceanside
Marathon, FL
(305) 743–0288

This is no average movie theater. Owned and operated by the Marathon Community Theater, the cinema is small and intimate, although the screen is large. Seating is informally arranged in comfy barrel chairs around cocktail-style tables. A single movie is shown twice nightly. Matinees are offered on Saturdays and Sundays. The theater is tucked behind Marathon Liquors & Deli.

Key West

Regal Cinema 6
Searstown Shopping Center
3338 Roosevelt Boulevard
Key West, FL
(305) 294–0000

Six movies run concurrently at the Florida Keys' only multiplex cinema. All tickets for shows before 6 P.M. are discounted. Listening devices for the hearing impaired are available here as well.

Cinema Shores
Atlantic Shores Resort
510 South Street
Key West, FL
(305) 296–2491

Enjoy a movie under the stars every Thursday night (weather permitting), beginning at 9 P.M. Atlantic Shores Resort shows a new feature each week, downstairs from the pool in the parking lot area. Call for details. Recent offerings have included adult-oriented short subjects, foreign films, and popular feature flicks you may have missed on the big screen. Ticket prices include popcorn. Cocktails are available for purchase. In case of rain, the film is usually postponed until Friday night.

Physical Fitness

Upper Keys

Body Balance Fitness Center
Tradewinds Plaza Shopping Center
MM 101.4 Oceanside
Key Largo, FL
(305) 451–5761

At Body Balance you'll find Nautilus equipment, free weights, and cardiovascular equipment such as NordicTrack, LifeStep, and LifeCycle. Aerobics and karate are offered here, and a pro shop carries weight-training accessories. Personal trainers are available, and the center offers a wellness program that works in conjunction with local physicians. Body composition testing provides body-fat analysis. Vitamins and vitamin supplements are sold on premises.

Middle Keys

Nick's Fitness Express
Town Square Mall
MM 53 Bayside
Marathon, FL
(305) 743–7618

Patrons work out in this full-service gym with free weights and weight machines, and cardiovascular equipment including treadmills, step machines, and stationary

bikes. Weight management, body-fat testing, and certified personal trainers are other features here. Open Monday through Saturday 6 A.M. to 9 P.M. and Sunday 9 A.M. to 5 P.M., Nick's offers daily rates in addition to weekly or monthly options.

Keys Fitness Center
MM 49.5 Oceanside
Marathon, FL
(305) 289–0788
www.keysfitnesscenter.com

Offering state-of-the-art fitness equipment by Paramount, Life Fitness, and Nautilus, Keys Fitness Center also sports a separate free-weights room for the serious workout addict. The facilities offer private showers and a relaxing sauna. Personal trainers are bilingual. Keys Fitness Center is open daily from 6 A.M. to 9 P.M.

Lower Keys

Sugarloaf Sports and Leisure Club
MM 19.5
Bad George Road
Sugarloaf Key, FL
(305) 745–3577
www.sugarloafclub.com

Whether you want to work out hard with free weights or just kick back and take it easy poolside with a refreshing drink, you'll find the means to do it at this combination fitness center and social club. With its outdoor swimming pool, Jacuzzi,

Insiders' Tip
Many recreational activities are available just outside the Keys. For instance, KeysGate Community offers a golf course that is open to the public, and NASCAR racing is in nearby Homestead.

fully equipped weight room, tennis and volleyball courts, restaurant, and health center, Sugarloaf Sports and Leisure Club truly has something for everyone. Families, couples, singles, even kids feel equally welcome here.

The club's Fitness Center, opened in spring 2000, offers the opportunity for a complete workout, from cardiovascular equipment to weight training machines and free weights, plus a Precor Elliptical Trainer. Licensed professionals, including acupuncture physician and massage therapists, are available for consultations, and aerobics classes are taught both in the water and on dry land. Lunch and dinner are served at the club's restaurant, Sneaky Pete's, and catering is available for social events or meetings. In addition, the club hosts frequent theme parties for members, which feature food, live music, and special activities for kids.

Sugarloaf Sport and Leisure is open Tuesday through Sunday. Memberships are available at a variety of levels, including annual, semi-annual, and monthly. A daily membership, which entitles you to full use of all club facilities, is also available.

The club is tucked about a mile off U.S. Hwy. 1. To reach it, turn at Sugarloaf Middle School (MM 19.5), then follow Crane Boulevard to Bad George Road.

Key West

Body Zone South
2740 N. Roosevelt Boulevard
Overseas Market
Key West, FL
(305) 292–2930

Key West's largest gym offers something for everyone. A full range of exercise equipment is available, including Nautilus equipment, treadmills, stationary bikes, stair climbers, and plenty of free weights. Exercise programs come in all shapes and sizes, from those for children to seniors and from low impact to hard core. Personal training and massage are available. The juice bar and play care for children are both convenient services.

Club Body Tech
1075 Duval Street
Key West, FL
(305) 292–9683

Some of the most high-tech equipment in the fitness industry, including the David 900 Series machines, is available at Club Body Tech. Stationary bikes, stair climbers, and free weights also are available. The center offers classes in aerobics, step, abdominals, and back and leg. Check here, too, for personal training and massage services.

Coffee Mill Cultural Center
916 Pohalski Street
Key West, FL
(305) 296–9982

This local center promotes good health. It's the home of the Key West Dance Theatre and also offers many workout opportunities. Get ready for some yoga meditation in the morning, or opt for aerobics, dance, Pilates, or martial arts. Classes are held daily and visitors are welcome. Attend a single class or sign up for a month's worth.

Iron Bodies Nutrition Center and Gym
1010 Truman Avenue
Key West, FL
(305) 296–3250

If you're in the market for a low-impact, highly social fitness experience, you won't find it here. Iron Bodies is a no-nonsense, get-down-to-business, sweat-and-burn kind of gym. Think no pain no gain, and you've got the picture. In addition to a full range of Nautilus equipment and more than 10,000 pounds of iron, this place also features a full boxing ring, plus all the accouterments—gloves, speed bags, jump ropes, etc.—that pugilist training requires. The gym's Bubba Boxing team practices here five days a week.

Iron Bodies opens at 6 A.M. daily (Sundays, too!). Memberships are available in a variety of terms and price ranges. But beware: Apply only if you're serious about your workouts. Casual exercisers won't feel comfortable here.

Paradise Health and Fitness
1706 N. Roosevelt Boulevard
Key West, FL
(305) 294–4120

If you've ever feared walking into a health club because you think everyone else will be perfectly toned and attired in the most fashionable exercise togs, fear no more. At Paradise Health and Fitness, all your lumps, bumps, and comfy old clothes are welcome.

In addition to a full circuit weight room featuring Hoist equipment, Paradise offers a wide range of group classes, including yoga, tai chi, cardio kick-boxing, toning, low-impact, and step, for all ages and fitness levels. If you'd like some individual attention, Paradise has five personal trainers on staff to assist you; they even make home visits if you're so inclined.

Short- or long-term memberships as well as daily rates are available.

Yoga College of Key West
812 Southard Street
Key West, FL
(305) 292–1854

This is the real thing and is not for wimps—yoga with an attitude. Renowned yoga experts often give seminars here, expounding upon what they call "Rambo Yoga." Classes are held daily; call for details.

Just Plain Fun

Skateboard Park
Corner of Flagler Avenue and Kennedy Drive
behind the fire station
Key West, FL
(305) 292–2899

At last, something new for Key West kids to do. Built by the City of Key West and operated by the YMCA, the yet-to-be-officially-named Skateboard Park offers thrills and spills aplenty. It opened to great fanfare in July 2000 and is currently available to in-line skaters and skateboarders only; no BMX bikes allowed.

Hours vary depending on the season, with longer hours over summer, weekends, and school vacation periods. Y members under 18 pay $3 for a two-hour session on the ramps; the price jumps to $5 if you're over 18. Tourists not interested in joining the local Y can still use the park, but it costs a little more—$10 per session. Pads and helmets are required; if you don't have your own, you may rent them for $1. The Y requires release forms, signed by parents, for all skaters/skateboarders under the age of 18.

Even if you don't plan to skate, do stop by and watch. The ramps make for amazing acrobatic feats. You won't believe what some of these kids can do!

Enjoy some fun in the sun gunk-holing by dinghy in shallow nearshore waters. PHOTO: VICTORIA SHEARER

This 90-foot light tower, built in 1847, affords visitors a bird's-eye view of Key West.

Attractions

Our landmass is but a drizzle of frosting across our seas, but this yummy confection of coral yields some tantalizing attractions. Don't wait for a rainy day (you might not have one) to explore our historic sites, out islands, museums, nature preserves, and marine research centers.

We've organized the attractions described in this chapter by mile marker in descending order down the Keys, beginning in Key Largo. In our Key West section, we offer several categories of attractions scattered throughout our southernmost city. Many are free or charge a nominal amount for admission. You'll find the majority of our most popular land-based diversions bordering the Overseas Highway, for our string of islands is not very wide.

And don't miss this chapter's final section, "And Beyond . . .," where we reveal the hidden treasures of our three nearby national parks—Biscayne, Everglades, and the Dry Tortugas.

So put on your sandals, grab your hat, and look for those car keys. Dally with us on an Insiders' tour of Paradise's distractions.

The Florida Keys

Upper Keys

Dolphin Cove
MM 101.9 Bayside
Key Largo, FL
(305) 451–4060, (877) 365–2683
www.dolphinscove.com

Dolphin Cove, situated on a five-acre lagoon in Key Largo, offers an in-water encounter with bottle-nosed dolphins in addition to a myriad of other water activities. The dolphin program is offered three times daily from mid-December until early March. During the remaining months the encounter is offered on Saturday and Sunday only. Participants must be age 7 and older and, if under age 18, must be accompanied by an adult. The encounter is preceded by a 30-minute boat ride in the waters of the backcountry, where you will receive an orientation briefing about the dolphins and about the interactions you will experience. Pricing for 2001 was $150 per person but is subject to change for 2002. Inquire before you book your encounter.

Dolphin Cove also offers guided ecological tours of the Everglades National Park backcountry waters and Florida Bay, where you'll learn the mysteries of the mangrove habitat and probably encounter many of the species of birds and sealife discussed in our Paradise Found chapter. Other interesting trips into Florida Bay are offered on request, such as guided snorkel trips, kayak tours, sunset cruises, and even a private nighttime crocodile search in the nearshore waters of the Everglades. Call Dolphin Cove to arrange one of these customized trips.

Dolphins Plus Inc.
MM 100 Oceanside
Ocean Bay Drive
Key Largo, FL
(305) 451–1993, (866) 860–7946
www.dolphinsplus.com

This marine mammal research and education facility offers you the opportunity to learn the fascinating habits and lifestyles of the bottle-nosed dolphin and enter its world for a compatible swim. Offered twice daily (9 A.M. and 1:45 P.M.) the 2½-hour natural swim teaches you all about dolphins, including their social pod structure, communication methods, and anatomy. You'll learn how to conduct yourself in the water for your 30-minute swim with the dolphins. Participants must be comfortable in water over their heads and know how to use a mask, fins, and snorkel. Participants who do not wish to swim are also welcome. Individuals 8 and older may swim with the dolphins, but a participating adult must accompany those younger than 13. Participants ages 13 to 17 may swim alone but must be accompanied by an observing parent or guardian. Cost of the full environmental education program, including the dolphin swim, is $100. Two 30-minute back-to-back swims cost $175.

Dolphins Plus also offers a two-hour, structured interaction program where you can be in the water and involved directly with the dolphins. After an educational briefing, you will experience a structured water session encompassing platform behaviors and in-water behaviors. Interaction varies in each session, depending on the dolphin and the instructor. Three sessions for the structured orientation program are offered daily: 8:30 A.M, 1 P.M., and 3:15 P.M. Participants must be age 7 or older, and a participating parent or guardian must accompany anyone younger than age 13. Cost of this program is $150 per participant. Pregnant women may not participate in either program.

Nonswimmer admission for both programs is $10 for ages 8 to adult and $5 for ages 7 to 17; children younger than 7 are admitted at no charge. A combo swim—natural swim and structured swim in one day—costs $210. Participants in all programs must call for reservations. Directions to Dolphins Plus are complicated. Call the center or check the website for detailed instructions.

Florida Keys Wild Bird Center
MM 93.6 Bayside
Tavernier, FL
(305) 852–4486, (888) 826–3811
www.florida-keys.fl.us/flkeyswildbird.htm

Dedicated to the rescue, rehabilitation, and release of ill, injured, and orphaned wild birds, the Florida Keys Wild Bird Center will fascinate visitors of all ages. Artificial environmental hazards such as entanglement with anglers' lines or fishhooks also can render the birds injured and helpless. This rapid-care aviary treats the wounds, supervises the convalescence, and releases the birds back into the wild. Meanwhile, you may walk along a boardwalk path through the birds' natural habitats, which have been discreetly caged with wire enclosures. Signage and brochures provide environmental education of Keys habitats.

The Wild Bird Center is open seven days a week during daylight hours. The center is funded by public donations, there are no admission fees. Look for the Florida Keys Wild Bird Center signs as you drive down the Keys.

Windley Key Fossil Reef State Geologic Site
MM 85.5 Bayside
Windley Key, FL
(305) 664–2540

Quarried long ago by workers building Flagler's railroad extension, the fossilized coral reef that forms the bedrock of the Keys (see our Paradise Found chapter) is exposed here for all to see. Borrow the in-house trail guide, which interprets what you'll discover on Windley Key's four trails, such as fossilized imprints of ancient shells and marine organisms still embedded in the coral quarry walls.

The state site is open Thursday through Monday from 8 A.M. to 5 P.M. Admission charge is $1.50 per person for self-guided tours or $2.50 for one-hour guided tours, which are offered at 10 A.M. and 2 P.M.

Theater of the Sea
MM 84.5 Oceanside
Islamorada, FL
(305) 664–2431
www.theaterofthesea.com

With continuous performances offered daily from 9:30 A.M. to 4 P.M., Theater of the Sea is the Florida Keys' showiest marine entertainment facility. The natural saltwater lagoons, created by excavations for Flagler's railroad, are home to a potpourri of popular marine creatures: dolphins, stingrays, sharks, sea turtles, game fish, and more. Call for current rates.

Special programs are offered for an additional fee, which includes park and show admission. The Trainer-for-a-Day program, open to those 10 and older, allows you to assist the trainers in feeding and caring for the dolphins and sea lions. You'll learn about nutrition and food preparation behind the scenes, then interact with the mammals in this three-hour session, but you will not swim with the dolphins or sea lions. Trainer-for-a-Day sessions, at 9:30 A.M. and 1:30 P.M., cost $75 per person.

The Swim with the Dolphins program is available three times a day—9:30 A.M., noon, and 1:30 P.M. for $110. Swim with the Sea Lions sessions are offered at noon and 2 P.M. for $75. Minimum age for both programs is five years. (Children ages five to seven must have a parent or legal guardian swim with them.) The programs include 30 minutes of instruction and 30 minutes in the water snorkeling and swimming with the dolphins or the sea lions. The swim with the Stingrays pro-

gram includes 15 minutes of instruction and 30 minutes in the water snorkeling with the stingrays, sea turtles, and other marine life. Swimmers must be age five or older to participate. (Minors must be accompanied by a parent or legal guardian in the swim area.) These sessions are offered at 11:15 A.M., 1:30 P.M., or 3:45 P.M. The program costs $35 per person.

Participants in the special swim programs must be competent swimmers, must not be pregnant, and must speak and understand English. Call for reservations.

Pioneer Cemetery
MM 82 Oceanside
Cheeca Lodge
Islamorada, FL

Their gravestones defiled in the hurricane of 1935, the founding fathers and mothers of Islamorada—the Parkers, Pinders, and Russells—still rest in the Pioneer Cemetery, now a part of the extensive grounds of Cheeca Lodge. A schoolhouse and the Methodist church, both destroyed in the hurricane, once bordered the cemetery. The angel statue marking the grave of Etta Dolores Pinder was found on the highway, miraculously intact except for a broken arm and wing. In 1989 Cheeca Lodge and University of Miami historian Josephine Johnson researched the cemetery, leading to the designation of the Pioneer Cemetery as a historic site by the Historical Association of Southern Florida. A plaque at the cemetery gate commemorates the event. You'll find the tiny Pioneer Cemetery surrounded by a white picket fence near the beach on the Cheeca Lodge grounds. The cemetery is open for free viewing by the general public.

Hurricane Monument
MM 81.6 Oceanside
Islamorada, FL

Honoring the hundreds of residents and railroad workers in Islamorada who lost their lives in the Labor Day hurricane of 1935, this monument depicts the fury of nature's elements with a bas-relief of high seas and wind-battered palm trees. Carved

Key West Architecture

The mix of Key West architecture, like the cultural melting pot of the nineteenth century, is duplicated nowhere else in the world. Self-taught craftsmen, working from their own designs, built many of the nearly 3,000 frame structures in historic Old Town. These ship carpenters and sea captains drew upon their knowledge of wooden vessels to construct their new homes. They were primarily influenced by the structural techniques of their homeland, the Bahamas. Several houses were actually dismantled in the Bahamas and transported to Key West, where they were reassembled.

Two-story Conch houses, with columns supporting roof overhangs on both levels, are the predominant architectural style of Old Town. PHOTO: JANET WARE

The climate of Key West and the Bahamas is similar, so every attempt was made to capture breezes and keep the houses cool. Houses had to be built to withstand the hot sun, heavy rains, and hurricanes. Builders used hand-hewn wood instead of plaster because plaster cracks and decays in high wind and humidity. Dade County pine, when available, was imported from the Upper Keys and Pensacola. It was preferred because the heavy resin content made it dense and impenetrable to termites. But much of the time wood from wrecked ships or the cargo salvaged from them was used. Nails were scarce because they were handmade and expensive, so wooden pins held the timbers together.

Most of the houses were built on wooden posts or coral rock piers for protection from high tides and storm waters. Roofs were designed to shed heavy water, with gutters and downspouts carrying the runoff to cisterns, where it was collected for later use. The roofs featured scuppers, or scuttles, which are openings that allow the hot air from the upper stories or attics to escape. Window and door openings were protected from the sun by louvered wood blinds. Wide covered verandas protected windows and doors from rain. And the houses were trimmed with intricately carved wood molding that has come to be known as gingerbread.

The nineteenth-century Key West homes preserved today through ongoing restoration efforts are unique architectural mutations we call Conch houses, after the original Bahamian settlers who first designed them. These styles are often referred to as Classic Revival, Victorian, or Queen Anne.

The so-called eyebrow house is easy to spot because the sloping front roofline all but covers the upper story windows, like bushy eyebrows over glassy orbs.

The two-story Conch temple has distinctive columns supporting roof overhangs on both levels.

The simple shotgun houses are so called because the interior rooms are lined up, one behind the other, with a hallway extending the length of the house from front to back. Hence, a bullet shot from the front door would hit no wall at all before it reached the back of the house. Most shotgun houses were built in the 1800s by cigar factories to house their workers.

You'll find other elaborate frame structures laden with capitals and pediments, porches and bay windows, gingerbread and other decorations borrowed from styles throughout the ages, as distinctively individual as their owners and defying easy classification.

For a good, thorough look at the architecture of Key West, get a copy of *The Houses of Key West* by Alex Caemmerer (available at Key West bookstores). Caemmerer describes the architectural styles in detail, inside and out, and gives addresses of classic examples of these private homes so all you need to do is put on your walking shoes and stroll back in time down the streets of Key West's historic district.

Shotgun houses are so called because the rooms are lined up from front to back along a single hallway. Hence, a bullet shot from the front door to the back would hit no wall. PHOTO: JANET WARE

The road to restoration and preservation of Key West's charming architecture is paved with official actions at several levels of government. In 1965 the city of Key West established the Old Island Restoration Commission; its mission was to preserve the historic buildings in Old Town. The U.S. Congress passed the National Historic Preservation Act in 1966, creating a National Register of historic buildings, sites, and districts. The Florida legislature created the Historic Key West Preservation Board of Trustees in 1972 to specifically deal with Key West. In 1986 the Historic Architectural Review Commission (HARC) assumed responsibility for the ongoing restoration and preservation of Key West's historic areas and does so to this day.

out of local coral limestone, the Hurricane Monument may be viewed just off the Overseas Highway.

Indian Key State Historical Site
MM 77.5 Oceanside
Indian Key, FL
(305) 664-2540

A colorful history paints Indian Key, a 10-acre, oceanside island about .75 mile offshore from Lower Matecumbe Key. Now uninhabited, this tiny key has yielded archeological evidence of prehistoric Native American cultures. Once visited by Spaniards and pirates alike, the island was purchased in 1831 by Jacob Housman, who established a thriving settlement. Indian Key became the Dade County seat in 1836. Physician Henry Perrine sat out the Second Seminole War here, which proved a misguided decision, for Indians attacked the island in 1840, and he lost his life after all. Fires destroyed all the structures except for the foundations. Although some people returned after the assault, by the early 1900s the key supported only burgeoning vegetation.

Indian Key is accessible only by boat. Limited private dockage is available for small boats, but the site has no restrooms or picnic facilities. The historic site is open from 8 A.M. to sundown. Ranger-led tours at 9 A.M. and 1 P.M. are $1 per person.

Robbie's Marina, MM 77.5 Bayside, (305-664-9814), offers the only regularly scheduled tour transportation to the island. Tours depart Thursday through Monday to Indian Key and Lignumvitae Key (see the following write-up). No tours are given on Indian Key on Tuesdays and Wednesdays, but the island is open to those with their own transportation. The boat shuttle to Indian Key departs Robbie's docks at 8:30 A.M. and 12:30 P.M. The launch will carry you to Lignumvitae Key at 9:30 A.M. or 1:30 P.M. Cost for either excursion is $15 for adults, $10 for children. Admission to the islands is included in this price. If you'd like to visit both islands—one in the morning, one in the afternoon—the cost is $25. Reservations

are preferred. And while you are waiting for the boat, buy a cup of bait and feed the tarpon that come around the docks regularly.

Lignumvitae State Botanical Site
MM 77.5 Bayside
Lignumvitae Key, FL
(305) 664-2540

Named after the lignum vitae tree, Lignumvitae Key—our highest island at 17 feet above sea level—supports one of the best examples of a virgin hardwood hammock in the Florida Keys (see the Hardwood Hammock section in our Paradise Found chapter). Also on the island is the 1919 home of the Matheson family, of chemical company notoriety, who owned the island for many decades. The stilt-style home sports two storm hatches—bedroom and porch—so doors would not be blown off their hinges in a bad blow. The screened porch enabled the Mathesons to leave via the hatch, keeping the mosquitoes at bay.

One-hour ranger-guided walks at 10 A.M. and 2 P.M. allow visitors to tour the house and the hardwood hammock. Cost is $1 per person (children 6 and under tour for free). You may not enter the hammock unless accompanied by a ranger. Park officials suggest you come equipped with mosquito repellent and sturdy shoes. Like Indian Key, Lignumvitae Key may be accessed only by boat, and limited private dockage for small crafts is available (see previous write-up for information on Robbie's Marina, which offers transportation to the key). Lignumvitae Key is closed Tuesdays and Wednesdays.

Middle Keys

The Dolphin Connection
Hawk's Cay Resort
MM 61 Oceanside
Duck Key, FL
(888) 814-9174
www.hawkscay.com

Dolphin Connection's Dolphin Discovery provides an interactive, 25-minute, in-water encounter with the most famous of our Florida Keys marine creatures, bottle-nosed dolphins. You will not actually swim with the Connection's dolphins, but you'll get to know them up-close and personal. You'll be able to touch, feed, pet, and play with them from the security of a submerged platform (great for nonswimmers or those people with physical limitations).

After a short classroom orientation reviewing dolphin and people etiquette, you will sit in the water on a shallow platform where the trainer will familiarize you with the dolphin's anatomy. Trainers enlighten participants about the dolphins and their marine environment as well as the Florida Keys' ecosystem. From the submerged platform you will move to the deep area, standing in water three feet deep. Here you will play games with the dolphins, which will jump, splash, and fetch and thoroughly entrance you. (Other special guidelines apply.)

The 45-minute Dolphin Discovery program is open to participants who are 4 feet, 6 inches or taller. The encounters are held at 10 A.M. and 1, 2:30, and 4 P.M. There is a maximum of six people per program, with the intimate ratio of three people to one trainer and one dolphin. Cost is $90 for Hawk's Cay Resort guests, $100 for the general public.

Adults who do not wish to get wet in the Discovery program can participate in Dockside Dolphins, as can pregnant women, who are not allowed to join in the in-water Dolphin Discovery. Dockside Dolphins is a 30-minute, behind-the-scenes look at dolphin training sessions. Participants learn how the professionals at Dolphin Connection train the dolphins and then, from the dock, take part in an actual training procedure. You'll be able to feel, feed, and pet the dolphins but not have to get into the water. Adults and children love this experience (children five and younger must be accompanied by a paying adult). Dockside Dolphins is offered at 11:30 A.M. daily. Hawk's Cay Resort guests pay $40, the general public pays $45.

Kids have a ball as participants in the unique 30-minute Dolphin Detectives program. From the dry docks, the children learn how to be dolphin trainers. (Children five and younger must be accompanied by a paying adult.) The kids learn the trainer's hand signals and get to try them out on the playful dolphins during a supervised training session. The participants are taught how to feed the dolphins—touching, weighing, and preparing those fish the mammals like so much. Dolphin Detectives kicks off every day at 11:30 A.M. Cost is $40 for resort guests; $45 for the general public. Advance reservations are required for all programs. Bookings are accepted up to three months in advance.

Dolphin Research Center
MM 59 Bayside
Grassy Key, FL
(305) 289–1121, (305) 289–0002, reservations
www.dolphins.org

Look for the giant statue of a dolphin and her calf that heralds the Grassy Key home of the Dolphin Research Center. Once the lodging for Flipper, the famed television star of yesteryear, the Dolphin Research Center offers a variety of fascinating encounters with these smart marine mammals.

One-hour, narrated walking tours introduce you to the dolphins in their natural environments, where you'll witness their training sessions. Walking tours are offered five times daily (10 and 11 A.M. and 12:30, 2, and 3:30 P.M.) and require no reservations. Admission for adults is $12.50; senior citizens, $10; and kids ages 4 to 12, $7.50. Children younger than 4 are admitted free with a paying adult.

The half-day Dolphin Encounter enables you to learn how people interact with the dolphins. You'll attend a workshop, take the walking tour, and then spend 20 minutes in the water with two dolphins and up to five other people. The ratio of people to dolphins is never more

At Hawk's Cay Resort's Dolphin Encounters you can get in the water and get up-close-and-personal with the friendly mammals. PHOTO: HAWK'S CAY RESORT

than 3-to-1. Children ages 5 to 12 must be accompanied in the water by a paying adult. Life jackets will be supplied to participants of all ages who desire them. This program is very popular, and access is limited. For reservations, you must call on the first or 15th day of the month preceding the month you'd like to swim. (For example, call October 1 if you'd like to reserve a dolphin swim from November 1 to November 14; call October 15 if you'd like a reservation from November 15 to the end of the month). Cost is $125 per person regardless of age.

In the Dolphin Splash program you can meet the dolphins in the water without swimming. Participants stand on a submerged platform, waist-deep in water, and the dolphins swim up to say hello. You'll receive 30 minutes of instruction, enjoy 10 minutes in the water, and then take one of the guided walking tours. Make reservations following the same procedures as Dolphin Encounter. For Dolphin Splash, however, a few spots are saved every day for walk-ins, so you might get lucky. Participants must be at least 44

inches tall; children below this height must be held in the arms of a parent or guardian. Cost is $70 per person. Children younger than age 3 are admitted free. A participating adult must accompany children younger than age 13.

You can immerse yourself in a dolphin world and earn college credit at the one-week DolphinLab, a series of dolphin behavior seminars and hands-on encounters. You'll live on-premises in the center's dormitory and enjoy side trips to Key West and snorkeling at Looe Key National Marine Sanctuary. Cost is $1,125. Summer programs for middle school, junior high, and teens are also available. Call for more information.

Museums of Crane Point
MM 50.5 Bayside
Marathon, FL
(305) 743-9100

The small, interesting Museum of Natural History and the adjoining Florida Keys Children's Museum (see our Kidstuff chapter) sit on the skirt of the Crane Point hammock, which covers a bit of history in itself. The museum houses a potpourri of Keys icons and exhibits. Creatures of the reef have been authentically re-created in tropical splendor and are accompanied by an audio of the sounds of the deep. You'll see the inhabitants of the Pinelands habitat—slash pines, red mangroves, silver buttonwood, Key deer, and miniature raccoons; ancient shipwreck memorabilia; shells of giant sea turtles; tree snails of the tropics; even a stuffed osprey, great white heron, egret, frigatebird, and the like.

Between the two museum structures, a fish-filled lagoon attracts fin fanciers, and the wild bird rescue flight cage fascinates bird lovers of all ages. You'll see a Caribbean-style sailing canoe, paddled here in 1989 by three Guatemalan refugees, and an authentic Cuban freedom raft. Children enjoy the outdoor osprey nest exhibit, in which they really get a bird's-eye view of the museum. They can climb right up into the nest. Guided tours of the museum are offered weekdays from December through April at 10 A.M. and 1:30 P.M.

After you tour the exhibits, traipse down the nature trails that loop through Crane Point hammock, which is named for the Cranes, who owned the property until the early 1970s. The Cranes protected the area from development and preserved the forested land as a good example of our rare hardwood hammock habitat (see our Paradise Found chapter). A ¼-mile boardwalk trail, which leads through a mangrove habitat, was created in 2000.

The museum provides a self-guided tour pamphlet that also lists some of the unusual tropical hardwoods you'll see along the nature trails. The Adderley House walk, about a half-mile long, leads to the restored Bahamian-style house built around 1905 by George Adderley, a black Bahamian settler of the Middle Keys. The concrete-like walls of the one-room structure are constructed from ground shells.

Crane Point is open Monday through Saturday from 9 A.M. to 5 P.M. and Sundays from noon to 5 P.M. One admission charge allows access to both trails and museums: Cost for adults is $7.50; ages 65 and older, $6; and students, $4. Children age 6 and younger get in free.

Pigeon Key National Historic Site
Old Seven Mile Bridge, Bayside
Pigeon Key, FL
(305) 289–0025, (305) 743–5999 (gift shop)
www.pigeonkey.org

Though undoubtedly Pigeon Key was known to Native Americans and Bahamian fishermen in the early days of the Keys, it was Henry Flagler's East Coast Railroad Extension that put the tiny key on the historical map. And it is the volunteer-staffed Pigeon Key Foundation that keeps it there. The island is connected to the mainland by a bridge that was originally built for the railroad and which served as a construction and maintenance site for the railroad from 1908 to 1935. The hurricane of 1935 flooded Pigeon Key and caused so much damage to the railroad that the company decided not to rebuild (see our Historical Evolution chapter). When the Seven Mile Bridge was built over the railroad spans in the late 1930s, Pigeon Key became headquarters for the Bridge and Toll District.

Over the ensuing decades the key was used as a fishing camp, a U.S. Navy site, a park, and a marine biology center for the University of Miami. In 1982 the new Seven Mile Bridge was constructed, bypassing Pigeon Key from auto traffic. The Pigeon Key Foundation, a nonprofit local organization with the stated mission "to preserve the history and environment of the Florida Keys" was established in 1993, securing a long-term lease to the island from Monroe County.

Pigeon Key is a living testament to the Florida Keys of 1912 to 1940. The foundation has restored eight of the 5.3-acre island village's buildings dating from the early 1900s. Automobiles are not allowed on the Old Seven Mile Bridge. A trolley shuttle leaves every day on the hour from 10 A.M. to 4 P.M. from the Pigeon Key Visitors

Center, which occupies a quaint, old railway car that still rests on Flagler's tracks at MM 47 Oceanside, Knight's Key. Once on the island, the trolley driver conducts a 20-minute guided tour of Pigeon Key. You may return on any shuttle you wish; the last one leaves the island at 5 P.M.

Visitor's fees, which include shuttle service, are $7.50 per person ($5 for children 12 and younger). Residents of Monroe County pay only $6. You can get out to Pigeon Key under your own steam, if you'd rather. The 2 miles of renovated bridge make for a good workout via walking, jogging, in-line skating, or biking. Stop by the visitors center (open daily 10 A.M. to 4 P.M.) to purchase tickets before your trek through history. Pigeon Key hosts a number of festivals and special events each year, which require a separate admission charge (see our Annual Events chapter).

Lower Keys

**National Key Deer Refuge and
Watson Nature Trail
MM 30.5 Bayside
Key Deer Boulevard
Big Pine Key, FL
(305) 872–2239**

The National Key Deer Refuge protects the pineland habitat frequented by the Key deer, a small species—not much larger than a German shepherd—that is found nowhere else in the world (see our Paradise Found chapter). Some areas of the refuge, which encompasses a large portion of Big Pine Key, are off limits to visitors and are so marked. National Wildlife Refuge signs, depicting a flying bird, mark the boundaries of the refuge, which is open for daytime public access on designated trails.

You can find the ⅔-mile Watson Nature Trail 1.3 miles north of the intersection of Key Deer and Watson Boulevards. The trail winds throughout the pineland habitat of the refuge (see our Paradise Found chapter). The short Mannillo Trail, ⅕ mile, traverses pine rockland and freshwater wetland habitats.

The Key deer are protected by law—even feeding them is a misdemeanor offense. Road kill remains a primary hazard to the Key deer. Speed limits on U.S. Highway 1 through Big Pine Key are reduced to 45 mph during the day and 35 mph at night and are strictly enforced. The best time to look for Key deer is early in the morning or at dusk.

You can sometimes spot Key deer beside U.S. 1, but you are more likely to see them along the back roads and especially on No Name Key, where there are fewer human inhabitants. To reach No Name Key, turn right at the intersection of Key Deer and Watson Boulevards. The road will take you through a residential neighborhood and over a cement bridge to No Name Key, ending abruptly at a pile of boulders. In between the bridge and the boulders, drive slowly and keep your eyes peeled.

**The Blue Hole
MM 30.5 Bayside
Key Deer Boulevard
Big Pine Key, FL
(305) 872–2239**

You may wonder why all those cars are parked on the side of Key Deer Boulevard, for from the roadside the area looks like an uninhabited stand of slash pines. Park your vehicle and join the crowd. A few steps into the thatched palm understory you'll see a large, water-filled barrow pit, known as The Blue Hole. Inhabiting this incongruous water hole are a couple of resident alligators, the only known 'gators in the Keys. If you're lucky, you may catch a glimpse of one of these illusive reptiles.

Ducks and wading birds stay out of the alligators' path. The Blue Hole is 1.25 miles north of the intersection of Key Deer and Watson Boulevards.

**Perky Bat Tower
MM 17 Bayside
Sugarloaf Key, FL**

Richter Perky may have had bats in his belfry in 1929 when he decided to build this Sugarloaf Key tower, but such are dreams that lay the foundations for legends. Perky believed that the uniquely designed, louvered pine tower, when laced with the proper bait, would attract a Keys population of mosquito-loving bats, thus solving his insect-infestation problem. Alas, the nocturnal flyers bypassed his offering, and Perky had to go back to the drawing board. The structure has withstood the tests of time and the elements, however. Perhaps Perky should have called it a hurricane shelter.

To find Perky Bat Tower, turn right (bayside) at the Sugarloaf Airport sign just beyond Sugarloaf Lodge when heading down the Keys. When the road forks, bear to the right. No admission is charged

Key West

Key West's historic Old Town district is perfect for a leisurely stroll to take in the history and eccentricity of this tiny island. How about visiting an aquarium, a cemetery, or a garden? Or maybe a tour of haunted houses or an old wrecker's house filled with antiques? We've checked out all the high points for you, including a few "only in Key West" attractions guaranteed to keep you entertained.

Key West attractions have been divided into three categories: Historic Homes and Museums, One of a Kind, and Guided and Self-Guided Tours. Within each category, attractions are listed in alphabetical order. The prices cited below are the advertised admission fees; they may or may not include sales tax.

Historic Homes and Museums

Audubon House & Tropical Gardens
205 Whitehead Street
Key West, FL
(305) 294–2116, (877) 281–2473
www.audubonhouse.com

It was 12 years before the house was built, but in 1832 John James Audubon did spend time on the grounds of John Geiger's huge garden. Legend has it that Audubon sketched the white-crowned

pigeon and the geiger tree he found in the garden here. During his stay in the Keys, Audubon produced 18 sketches of native wildlife. Original lithographs of these drawings are on display at the Audubon House. The house and environs, however, are more reminiscent of the family of Capt. John Geiger, a wrecker who built the house and lived here with his family. Set your own tour pace with a free pair of headphones and a tape that brings the house alive.

Audubon House is open daily from 9:30 A.M. to 5 P.M., but last entry is at 4:30 P.M. Admission for adults is $8.50; senior citizens, $7.50; students, $5; children ages 6 through 12, $3.50; and children younger than 6, free.

Curry Mansion
511 Caroline Street
Key West, FL
(305) 294–5349, (800) 253–3466
www.currymansion.com

This imposing home evokes images of an opulent, old Key West, although the three-story Conch house now serves as the focal point for a bed-and-breakfast inn and a museum. Built in 1905 by Milton Curry, Florida's first homegrown millionaire, the inn's public rooms display a selection of antiques and memorabilia. Poke around in the attic, and you'll find an 1899 billiards table among the old dresses and luggage. From the attic you can climb the widow's walk for a panoramic view of Key West Harbor. Self-guided tours are available daily from 10 A.M. to 5 P.M. Admission is $5 for adults and $1 for children 12 and younger. See our Accommodations chapter for information on overnight stays in the adjacent buildings.

Duval Street Wrecker's Museum—
The Oldest House
322 Duval Street
Key West, FL
(305) 294–9502

Withstanding every storm since 1835, the former Watlington House has rightly earned its Key West nickname as the oldest house in the city. Capt. Watlington bought the house in 1839, and it was family-occupied for the next 130 years. Donated to the State of Florida in 1974, it is now the Wrecker's Museum, housing nautical photos and memorabilia from the Key West wrecking era, including an authentic wrecking (some prefer to call it salvaging) license. Highlights are a shipwreck display, which shows the location of many a wreck on local reefs; an antique dollhouse that even has a miniature Key West mural; and the detached cookhouse kitchen, separated from the main structure to safeguard against fires.

The Wrecker's Museum is open from 10 A.M. to 4 P.M. daily. The tours are self-guided, but a docent is always available on-premises to answer questions. Admission is $5 for adults and teens; children 12 and younger are admitted for $1.

East Martello Museum
3501 S. Roosevelt Boulevard
Key West, FL
(305) 296-3913
www.kwahs.com

This enchanting, artifact-filled former fort will bring you up to speed on Key West history. Built during the Civil War, the brick fortress was never completely finished because the circular Martello design became antiquated before it was ever armed. Operated today as a museum and gallery by the Key West Art and Historical Society, the 8-foot-thick walls support pictures, artifacts and historical documents. Featured in the small gallery are the charming wood carvings of Key West's Mario Sanchez and the funky welded sculptures by the late Stanley Papio of Key Largo, fabricated from bedsprings, toilet fixtures, and other so-called "junk." You can climb the citadel to the lookout tower for an unobstructed view of the Atlantic coast.

East Martello Museum is open daily from 9:30 A.M. to 5 P.M., but the last admission is at 4:15 P.M. Cost is $6 for adults and $4 for students; kids younger than 6 get in free. Adults may purchase a combination ticket that allows admission to this museum, the Key West Lighthouse Museum, and the Key West Museum of Art and History at the Custom House (see descriptions later in this chapter). Visits to all three facilities need not be made on the same day.

Harry Truman's Little White House Museum
111 Front Street
Key West, FL
(305) 294-9911
www.trumanlittlewhitehouse.com

Ordered by his doctor to retreat to a stress-free climate and recover from a lingering cold, President Harry S Truman came to Key West for the first time in 1946. Like so many others, he was instantly smitten with the island and spent 11 working vacations in the commandant's quarters, dubbed the Little White House. Built in 1890, the house was renovated for its famed visitor in 1948. Opened to the general public as a museum dedicated to "Give 'Em Hell Harry" in 1991, the home has once again been restored to its 1948 splendor. You'll be able to view Truman's Winter White House as it looked when he spent his 175 working vacation days here. The family quarters, poker porch, dining room, and living room (complete with Truman's piano) are open to the public.

The guided tour takes you into the rooms and lives of Harry and Bess. The Exhibition Room displays a permanent collection of photographs of Presidents Eisenhower and Kennedy. Eisenhower spent two weeks here recuperating from his second heart attack, and Kennedy held a summit meeting here before the Bay of Pigs action. Jimmy Carter visited with his family in 1996. A 10-minute video recounts the history of the home, and a collection of presidential memorabilia is on display in the museum gift shop.

Guided tours are conducted daily between 9 A.M. and 5 P.M., with the last tour beginning at 4:30. Admission is $8 for adults and teens and $4 for children ages 4 through 12. Children younger than age 4 are admitted free.

President Harry Truman spent eleven working vacations in the Navy's Commander's Quarters (later dubbed the Little White House) in Key West. PHOTO: JANET WARE

Hemingway Home and Museum
907 Whitehead Street
Key West, FL
(305) 294–1136
www.hemingwayhome.com

Once the home of Key West's most famous writer, Ernest Hemingway, the Hemingway Home and Museum ranks at the top of any must-do list and is Key West's most popular attraction. Built by wrecker Asa Tift in 1851, the home took on historic significance when Ernest and Pauline Hemingway moved in. Pauline spearheaded extensive remodeling, redecorating, and refurnishing and fitted her backyard with the island's first swimming pool. Hemingway wrote several of his most celebrated works, including *For Whom the Bell Tolls*, *Death in the Afternoon*, *The Green Hills of Africa*, and *To Have and Have Not*, from his pool house office out back. The Hemingways lived in this Key West home from 1931 to 1939.

Guided tours lasting approximately 45 minutes are offered every 10 minutes from 9 A.M. to 5 P.M. daily. Admission is $8 for adults and teens and $5 for children ages 6 through 12; children younger than 6 enter free. Be sure to look for the infamous six-toed cats!

Heritage House Museum and Robert Frost Cottage
410 Caroline Street
Key West, FL
(305) 296–3573
www.heritagehousemuseum.org

The memorabilia in the Heritage House Museum pays tribute to Jessie Porter, a cultured, well-traveled woman at the center of Key West society in the mid-1900s. Visitors to the house included Tallulah Bankhead, Thornton Wilder, Gloria Swanson, Tennessee Williams, Pauline Hemingway, and, of course, regular visitor Robert Frost, who stayed in the small cottage in the rear garden when he wintered in Key West, which he did off and on from 1945 through 1960. Visitors are invited to make themselves at home in the comfortable original surroundings and even to play the antique piano.

Tours of Heritage House are offered Monday through Saturday from 10 A.M. to

Once home of Key West's most famous writer, Ernest Hemingway, the Hemingway Home and Museum ranks at the top of any must-do list as a popular attraction. PHOTO: FLORIDA KEYS & KEY WEST TDC

5 P.M. and on Sunday from 11 A.M. to 4 P.M. The last tour begins a half-hour before closing. Heritage House is generally closed the first two weeks of September, and in summer, hours may be shortened; in either case, it is best to phone ahead. Admission is $6 for adults, $5 for senior citizens and $1 for students ages 12 to 18 visiting with their families. Children younger than 12 get in free.

Key West Lighthouse Museum
938 Whitehead Street
Key West, FL
(305) 294–0012
www.kwahs.com

This 1847 structure, inland on a Key West street just across from the Hemingway Home, affords visitors a bird's-eye view of Key West from atop its 90-foot light tower (88 steps to the top). Why a lighthouse so far from the water? It was positioned here to avoid the fate of its predecessor on Whitehead Point, which toppled in a hurricane the previous year. The keeper's quarters houses maritime memorabilia and a gift shop.

The lighthouse museum is open daily for self-guided tours from 9:30 A.M. to 5 P.M.; last admission is at 4:30 P.M. Admission for adults and teens is $8. Students with ID are admitted for $4, and children under 6 are free. Adults may purchase a combination ticket for admission to this museum, the East Martello Museum and the Key West Art and History Museum at the Custom House (see descriptions elsewhere in this chapter).

Mel Fisher Maritime Heritage Society
and Museum
200 Greene Street
Key West, FL
(305) 294–2633
www.melfisher.org

For 16 years, "today's the day" was the hope of treasure salvor Mel Fisher, who finally struck pay dirt on July 20, 1985. Finding the *Nuestra Señora de Atocha*, which Fisher estimated to be worth $400 million, ensured his legacy as treasure hunter extraordinaire. Heavy gold chains, jeweled crosses, and bars of silver and gold are among the artifacts on display at the permanent first-floor exhibit. Hefting a gold bar worth more than $18,000 is a highlight. The second-floor exhibit changes frequently—call for details. A museum shop offers a variety of pirate and nautical gifts.

The museum is open daily from 9:30 A.M. to 5:30 P.M. Admission for adults and teens is $6.75; students, $5; children ages 6 to 12, $3; and children younger than 6 are admitted free. AARP, AAA, and student discounts are available.

San Carlos Institute
516 Duval Street
Key West, FL
(305) 294–3887

Founded in 1871 by Cuban exiles, the San Carlos Institute was established to preserve the language and traditions of the Cuban people. Dubbed "La Casa Cuba" by legendary poet and patriot Jose Marti, the Institute helped unite the exiled Cuban community. The present building was completed in 1924 and operated as an integrated school until the mid-1970s, when deteriorating conditions necessitated its closing. With the perseverance of the Hispanic Affairs Commission, a state agency headed by Rafael Penalver, restoration of the San Carlos was completed and the Institute reopened on January 3, 1992, 100 years to the day after Jose Marti's first visit in the late nineteenth century. Today the San Carlos Institute is a museum, library, school, art gallery, theater, and conference center. The Institute is open Tuesday through Saturday from 11 A.M. to 5 P.M. and Sunday from 11 A.M. to 4 P.M. Admission is free.

West Martello Tower Joe Allen Garden Center
Atlantic Boulevard and White Street
Key West, FL
(305) 294–3210

Built in 1862, the West Martello Tower, like the other forts on the island, was never involved in an actual war. It was,

including quotes from Psalms and Genesis. If you would find such references offensive, consider skipping this attraction.

A Key Encounter is open daily except Saturday from 11 A.M. to 5 P.M. with showings every 30 minutes. Admission is $5 for adults and $3 for students. Children 12 and under are admitted free with an adult.

Flagler Station Over-Sea Railway Historeum
901 Caroline Street
Key West, FL
(305) 295–3562
www.flaglerstation.net

Our southernmost city can literally trace its beginnings as a tourist destination to the vision of one man—Henry Morrison Flagler—and his Key West Extension of the Florida East Coast Railroad. Flagler made his money in oil, but he made his name by building a railroad as well as luxury hotels along the east coast of Florida from Jacksonville to Miami. In 1905, at the age of 75, Flagler proposed his most daring venture to date—he instructed his engineers to extend the Florida East Coast Railroad 130 miles out to sea to Key West.

This museum, part of which is housed in an actual Florida East Coast Railroad car, celebrates Flagler's magnificent obsession which took eight years, $30 million and the loss of hundreds of lives to complete. Costumed "historytellers" and video footage help re-create the day in January 1912 that the Key West Extension, also known as the Over-Sea Railway, opened to great fanfare with a frail Henry Flagler himself aboard the first train to arrive in Key West. You'll see photos and memorabilia from that momentous occasion, as well as a film titled "The Day the Train Arrived," which includes eyewitness accounts from people who were actually there and who made the trip by rail on the Key West Extension. There's an entire display devoted to the building of the Seven Mile Bridge, an amazing engineering feat even by today's standards, as well as photos and video recollections of the devastat-

however, used for target practice by the U.S. Navy, which accounts for its somewhat shabby condition. Today the tower is also the Joe Allen Garden Center, and the Key West Garden Club operates here. Use the self-guided tour to spot local flora, including a Key lime tree, or just find an inviting spot to relax.

West Martello is open Tuesdays through Saturdays in season from 9:30 A.M. until 3:15 P.M. The schedule may vary in summer; call for more information. Admission is free, but note that shirt and shoes are required.

One of A Kind

A Key Encounter
Clinton Square Market
291 Front Street
Key West, FL
(305) 292–2070
www.akey.org

When your feet get weary and you need a break, head up to the second floor of Clinton Square Market for a 20-minute, triple-screen movie showcasing the natural habitats of the Florida Keys and the flora, fauna, and marine creatures dwelling therein. The narrated feature, which is set to music, is a great way to get a glimpse of what's beneath the surrounding waters without getting wet. The 23-foot skin of an anaconda that ate a woman, along with a tape-recorded account of this terrifying story, are highlights here, too. A word of caution, however. While the cinematography is exquisite, the underlying narration is heavily laden with creationist references,

ing hurricane of 1935 that took out the Over-Sea Railway.

Flagler Station is open daily from 9 A.M. to 6 P.M. Tickets are $5 for adults and $2.50 for children 12 and under. There are no senior discounts.

Fort Zachary Taylor State Historic Site
Truman Annex at Southard Street
Key West, FL
(305) 292–6713
www.forttaylor.com

Although not fully completed until 1866, this Key West military bastion served the Union well during the Civil War, when it guarded against Confederate blockade runners. So impressive were its defenses, the fort was never attacked. It saw continuous usage by the military until the federal government deeded the structure to the State of Florida for use as a historic site. The Florida Park Service opened Fort Zachary Taylor to the public in 1985.

Today, however, much of the fort is again closed to public exploration, this time because the structure has succumbed to the ravages of time. The park service secured a $1.25 million grant, used to restore the north curtain, which is where the guns were mounted. As portions of the fort are structurally repaired, they will be reopened. At present, only the parade ground, the south curtain observation deck and the north curtain can be toured. The museum is also closed for repairs and will remain so indefinitely. Exhibits have been transferred to East Martello Museum (see earlier listing) until the restoration is complete. You may wander on your own or, if you prefer, guided tours of the fort are available twice daily at 12 noon and 2 P.M. There is no additional charge for the tour beyond your admission fee to the park.

The surrounding park offers a beach for fishing, swimming, or snorkeling, as well as picnic areas equipped with tables and grills, outside showers, snack bar, and restroom facilities. It also offers one of the best, unobstructed views of the sunset.

Admission charges are uniquely computed: It's $1.50 if you are walking or riding a bicycle or scooter, $2.50 if you drive in alone. Cars with passengers are charged $5. The car, driver, and one passenger are included in this fee; 50 cents is charged for each additional passenger. Fort Zachary Taylor is open daily from 8 A.M. to sunset. Hang on to your ticket stub; you may leave the park and return at any time throughout the same day by simply showing your ticket to the booth attendant. Hint: Lots of people leave the beach in the afternoon, then return here to watch the sunset away from the craziness going on down at Mallory Square (see description later in this chapter).

Key West AIDS Memorial
Foot of White Street and Atlantic Boulevard
Key West, FL

Key West has been especially hard-hit by the AIDS epidemic; more than a thousand here have died. The names of many of those victims are inscribed on this memorial which consists of flat granite slabs embedded in the walkway approaching White Street Pier.

Built with private funds and dedicated on World AIDS Day, December 1, 1997, the memorial has room for 1,500 names. At the unveiling, it contained 730. New names are engraved annually and dedicated in a ceremony that takes place each December on World AIDS Day. Members of a volunteer group—Friends of the Key West AIDS Memorial—maintain and protect this site.

Key West Aquarium
1 Whitehead Street at Mallory Square
Key West, FL
(305) 296–2051, (800) 868–7482
www.keywestaquarium.com

Key West's oldest tourist attraction (built in 1934) and still one of the most fascinating our southernmost city has to offer, the Key West Aquarium affords you a diver's-eye view of the marine creatures of our encompassing waters. Stroll at your leisure alongside the back-lit tanks recreating our coral reefs, but don't miss the guided tours (11 A.M. and 1, 3 and 4:30 P.M. daily) when you'll witness the feeding of the species. You'll marvel at the feeding frenzy of the sharks and sawtooths; the nurse sharks and stingrays flipping and splashing for their rations; and the tarpon, barracudas, game fish, and sea turtles recognizing the hands that feed them in the outdoor Atlantic Shores Exhibit, created to look like a mangrove lagoon.

A highlight for kids is the "touch tank" just inside the front door. Here, they can reach in and grab hold of horseshoe crabs, hermit crabs, conch, sea cucumbers, and many other creatures that populate the waters surrounding Key West. Be sure to bring your camera—you'll want to capture the expression on your child's face when the horseshoe crab in his or her hand suddenly flexes its legs.

The aquarium is open daily from 10 A.M. to 6 P.M. Admission for adults and teens is $8; children ages 4 to 12, $4; children age 3 and younger, free. Discounts are available. Adults holding a trolley, train, or cruise ship coupon may enter for $7. Do hang on to your tickets. Should you forget to pack your camera, you can use those tiny slips of paper to re-enter the following day at no additional charge.

Key West Botanical Gardens
Botanical Garden Way and College Road
Stock Island, FL

Follow College Road, then turn right just past Bayshore Manor, to find this little-known slice of serenity tucked between the Aqueduct Authority plant and the Key West Golf Course. Maintained by volunteers from the Key West Botanical Garden Society and funded by donations, this 11-acre garden represents the last undeveloped native hardwood hammock in the environs of Key West. Despite its proximity to U.S. Highway 1 and a busy public golf course, the garden is surprisingly peaceful—home to numerous birds, butterflies, and other native creatures. On any given day, you're apt to see a turtle

sunning itself on a log or an egret searching for food in Desbiens Pond.

The Gardens took an especially hard hit from Hurricane Georges in 1998 and as a result, where there was once dense shade, there is now bright sunlight; some areas remain inaccessible still due to fallen limbs. Botanists predict that it will be many years before the Gardens return to their pre-storm state. Nevertheless, this remains a pleasant place to spend a quiet hour and marvel at what Key West once looked like before we humans arrived.

The Gardens are open daily from 8 A.M. to sunset; the gates are locked at 8 P.M. in summer. There is no admission fee, but donations are welcomed.

Key West City Cemetery
Bordered by Angela, Frances, and
Olivia Streets, and Windsor Lane
Key West, FL
(305) 292–8177

Built in 1847 after the horrific hurricane the year before washed out the sand sanctuary at the island's southernmost point, Key West City Cemetery, right in the center of town, adds a human element to the history of Key West. The marble monuments of the wealthy were shipped to the island; local markers were generally produced from brick or coral-based cement. Carved with symbols and prosaic sayings, such as "I told you I was sick" and "Devoted fan of Julio Iglesias," the gravestones are a living legacy for those lying beneath. Some of the tombs are "bunked," or stacked, because digging in the coral rock proved difficult and seawater percolates just under the surface.

The Historic Florida Keys Foundation makes it easy to explore the Key West City Cemetery. The organization's self-guided tour pamphlet lists graves of 42 of Key West's most prominent or notorious deceased citizens, with brief personality profiles and a translation of the meaning of the carved symbols on the gravestones. Pick up a free Historic Key West City Cemetery Self-guided Tour pamphlet in the Florida Room at the Monroe County

Located "dead" center in Old Town, the Key West City Cemetery reflects the quirky character of the southernmost city better than any history lesson. PHOTO: JANET WARE

Public Library, 700 Fleming Street, or at the Key West Chamber of Commerce, Mallory Square.

If you'd like a little help with your meandering, an hour-long guided tour of the cemetery is available every Tuesday and Thursday, courtesy of the Historic Florida Keys Foundation. Tours leave at 9:30 A.M. from the cemetery's main gate, which is located at the corner of Margaret and Angela Streets. No reservations are required; however, a donation of $10 is requested. For information, phone (305) 292-6718.

Historic preservationist Sharon Wells also conducts cemetery tours by reserva-tion only (see the "Guided and Self-Guided Tours" Section of this chapter). Tour times and prices vary. Call (305) 294-8380 for information.

Key West Historic Memorial Sculpture Garden
Mallory Square
Key West, FL
(305) 294-4142
www.historictours.com

Located on Key West's original shoreline just behind Mallory Square, this tiny fenced-in "garden" pays homage to three dozen men and women whose lives and deeds have had tremendous impact on the southernmost city. Here you will find the stories and likenesses of such former influential citizens as wreckers Asa Tift and Capt. John Geiger; Charles Toppino and Sons, who took part in almost every major construction project from Marathon to Key West; Ernest Hemingway, writer; Harry Truman, former United States president; railroad magnate Henry Flagler; and Sister Louise Gabriel whose Grotto to Our Lady of Lourdes is said to have protected Key West from hurricanes for more than 75 years.

All of the bronze busts, as well as the imposing wreckers sculpture that is the centerpiece of the Garden, are the works of sculptor James Mastin of Coral Gables, Florida.

As you wander through the garden, be sure to look down, too—the walkways are paved with commemorative bricks purchased by individuals and families in remembrance of their friends and relatives. Monies derived from the sale of these bricks help support construction and maintenance of the Garden. The Sculpture Garden is open daily during daylight hours; there is no admission charge.

Key West Historic Seaport and HarborWalk Along the Gulf of Mexico from Front Street to Margaret Street
Key West, FL
(305) 293–8309
www.keywestseaport.com

Formerly known as Key West Bight, this once-seedy piece of prime waterfront real estate was where shrimpers, spongers, and turtle traders came to unload their daily catch, tell tall tales of the sea, quaff a few brews, and just generally hang out. With the relocation of the shrimp boats to Stock Island and the demise of sponging and turtle hunting, this area has undergone a complete metamorphosis. In January 1999 it was officially opened as the Key West Historic Seaport and Harbor-Walk.

Tall ships still tie up here, but so do million-dollar yachts. Trendy shops, restaurants, and raw bars now line a pristine wooden boardwalk that follows the bend of the coastline here from the foot of Front Street to the foot of Margaret Street. Despite gentrification, this remains a busy, working marina. Vessels bound for the Dry Tortugas leave from here as do many of the snorkel and sunset cruises and fishing charters (see our Recreation chapter for details). You can even still catch an occasional glimpse of the old Key West in places like Turtle Kraals, a turtle-cannery-turned-restaurant, and Schooner Wharf Bar.

The Seaport area bustles with activity on a daily basis; it's also home to numerous special events throughout the year. For a complete listing of Seaport shops, services, activities, and attractions, pick up a free copy of the Historic Seaport Log. This quarterly publication can usually be found at several locations along the Har-borWalk, at the Key West Chamber of Commerce on Mallory Square and at stores throughout Key West. Look for it wherever you see stacks of free weekly newspapers.

The Key West Museum of Art and History at the Custom House
281 Front Street
Key West, FL
(305) 295–6616
www.kwahs.com

Even if it contained no exhibits, this lovely building just off Mallory Square where Front and Whitehead Streets come together, would be worth a stop. With its 20-foot ceilings, arched windows, 12 fireplaces, and magnificently restored staircase, the structure itself is a work of art. Designed by the renowned architect Henry Hobson Richardson and completed in 1891 at a cost of less than $110,000, the building required 917,000 bricks from New York, iron from Pennsylvania,

Recently returned from another in a series of beauty treatments, "Sponge Man" is now a permanent fixture at the Key West Historic Seaport.
PHOTO: JANET WARE

dozens of masons from Massachusetts, and more than 100 carpenters, plasterers and other skilled construction workers from throughout the United States. Although it was officially called the U.S. Custom House, this structure also housed the U.S. Postal Service and the U.S. District Court. Here, in the second-floor courtroom, the official inquiry into what caused the sinking of the USS *Maine* was conducted. The Custom House served the city well for four decades, but as government needs changed and the various agencies moved to larger quarters elsewhere on the island, the building was deemed "superfluous property" and abandoned in the 1960s. Fortunately, it was not targeted for demolition. It is, in fact, today on the National Register of Historic Places and remains one of the finest examples of Richardsonian/Romanesque Revival architecture in existence.

For close to 30 years, the Custom House stood empty and forlorn. In 1990, the Key West Art and Historical Society acquired the building and began a restoration that would take nine years and nearly $9 million to complete. It was finally reopened to the public as a museum of national stature in August 1999.

Inside you will find seven galleries and a gift shop. Exhibits of artwork and historical artifacts change periodically; however, those on the second floor traditionally focus on the history of Key West. Be sure to continue up the stairs to the third floor. There are no exhibit galleries here, but the works of folk artist Mario Sanchez, which line the walls between the closed office doors, are worth the climb. There's a great view from the arched window overlooking Sunset Key and the harbor here, too.

The museum is open daily from 9 A.M. to 6 P.M. Admission is $8 for adults; $4 for students (age 7 to 17); children under 6, free. Adults may purchase a combination ticket that allows admission to this museum as well as to the East Martello Museum and the Key West Lighthouse Museum (see descriptions elsewhere in this chapter).

Key West Shipwreck Historeum
1 Whitehead Street
Mallory Square
Key West, FL
(305) 292-8990
www.keywestshipwreckhistoreum.com

Relive the days of wreckers, lumpers, and divers at the Shipwreck Historeum—part museum, part theater—where actors, video footage, and interactive presentations re-create vestiges of Key West's once-lucrative wrecking industry. During the 1800s about 100 ships passed by the port of Key West daily, many running aground on the reef. Asa Tift, a nineteenth-century wrecker and the original owner of what would one day become the Hemingway Home, tells his story of salvaging the

Key West's wrecking days are recreated at the Shipwreck Historeum. PHOTO: JANET WARE

goods of the SS *Isaac Allerton*, which was downed by a hurricane (see our Kidstuff chapter).

Catch daily shows every 30 minutes from 9:45 A.M. to 4:45 P.M. Admission for adults and teens is $8; children ages 4 to 12, $4; children younger than 4, free.

Mallory Square Sunset Celebration
1 Whitehead Street
Key West, FL
(305) 292–7700
www.sunsetcelebration.org

A do-not-miss event during any visit to Key West is the famous (perhaps infamous) sunset celebration. Buskers and

Buskers, street players, vaudevillians, and carny wannabes strut their stuff every day at the Mallory Square sunset celebration in Key West.
PHOTO: FLORIDA KEYS & KEY WEST TDC

street players, vaudevillians and carny wannabes strut their stuff every day as the sun sinks into the Gulf of Mexico over Sunset Key off Mallory Square. Beverage and nosh vendors hawk refreshments while the entertainers compete for your attention. From fire eaters to furniture jugglers, tightrope walkers to sword swallowers, you'll rarely see the same routine two nights in a row. A foot bridge links Mallory Square to the pier at the adjacent Hilton Resort and Marina where the likes of Speedbump the pot-bellied pig, and Dominique's high-flying cats delight the crowd.

This daily event, a Key West tradition since 1984, is free to all, but pack your pocket with small bills because the performers play for tips. The fun starts approximately one hour before sunset at Mallory. Check page three of the morning *Key West Citizen* for daily sunset times.

Mile Marker 0
Corner of Whitehead and Fleming Streets
Key West, FL

Key West is truly the last resort and here's the proof: the official green-and-white mile marker 0 signifying the end of U.S. Highway 1 is posted at this corner. Have someone snap a picture of you in front of the sign that reads "End – U.S. 1." It will make a wonderful reminder of that very moment you finally arrived at the end of your road…that's providing some souvenir hunter hasn't made off with the sign, which happens with great regularity. Tampering with highway signs (including those enticing green mile markers) is against the law, by the way. If you must own one, replicas of Mile Marker 0 are available for purchase in many Key West shops.

Nancy Forrester's Secret Garden
1 Free School Lane
Key West, FL
(305) 294–0015

The garden isn't a secret anymore, because Nancy Forrester's arboreal and botanical prowess has become legendary.

A knowledgeable expert on specimen palms and tropical plants, Forrester has created a garden rain forest that offers a welcome respite from the flesh-pressing masses churning up and down Duval Street. Examine the panoply of exotic vegetation or bring a picnic lunch and just sit a spell. Outdoor tables and chairs are peppered about the garden.

The garden is open for self-guided tours daily from 10 A.M. to 5 P.M. during the winter season. During summer, call for hours of operation. Admission is $6 for all, including children. In-depth, personalized horticultural tours are also offered with advanced reservations. Call for information and fees. The Secret Garden is at the end of Free School Lane, behind the wooden gate. Free School Lane is off the 500 block of Simonton Street between Fleming and Southard Streets.

Ripley's Believe It or Not! Odditorium
527 Duval Street
Key West, FL
(305) 293-9694, (800) 998-4418
www.entcon.com/ripleys/rkwhome

Robert L. Ripley was no accidental tourist. This adventurer knew exactly what he was doing when he traveled the world amassing unusual artifacts, real and imagined, now displayed in "odditoriums" around the world. So, believe it or not, Ripley's Key West even displays a few Keys-style "artifacts" you won't find in the other odditoriums. Be brave as you encounter a monster-size hammerhead shark.

Ripley's is open daily from 9 A.M. to 11 P.M. Admission charge for adults and teens is $11.95; children ages 4 to 12 pay $8.95; children younger than 4 are admitted free.

The Southernmost Point
Corner of Whitehead and South Streets
Key West, FL

Look for the traffic jam at the Atlantic end of Whitehead Street and you'll see the giant red, white, green, and yellow marker buoy that designates the southernmost point of the continental United States.

And standing in front of it, in the street, blocking traffic trying to turn left onto South Street, preen a never-ending stream of Key West visitors, trying to capture the moment they stood closer to Cuba than anyone else in the country. Call it touristy, even tacky, if you like, but the crowds seem to love it.

Wildlife Rescue of the Florida Keys
Atlantic Boulevard and White Street
Key West, FL
(305) 294-1441, (888) 826-3811

On the grounds of McCoy Indigenous Park, a large, quiet park full of rare and native species of flora, lies Wildlife Rescue of the Florida Keys. Since 1993, Wildlife Rescue has released more than 2,000 healed animals back into the wild. At any given time, approximately 100 animals, ranging from sea birds to raccoons to chickens, are recovering here; you can see them during visiting hours. Wildlife Rescue will rescue animals anywhere from the Seven Mile Bridge to the Dry Tortugas.

The Park is open daily from sun-up to sundown. Visiting hours at Wildlife Rescue are 9 A.M. to 5 P.M. daily. Admission is free, but donations are appreciated, and volunteers are always needed.

Guided and Self-Guided Tours
Conch Tour Train
301 Front Street at Mallory Square
Key West, FL
Key West Welcome Center
3840 N. Roosevelt Boulevard
Key West, FL
(305) 294-5161
www.conchtraintour.com

Some folks might think a narrated motor tour spells tourist with a capital T, but the quirky little Conch Tour Train is a great way to garner an overview of Key West in the shaded comfort of a canopied tram. You'll pass by most of the attractions we've written up in this chapter, sometimes twice, because in tiny Key West the train weaves a circuitous route that often changes from one hour to the next

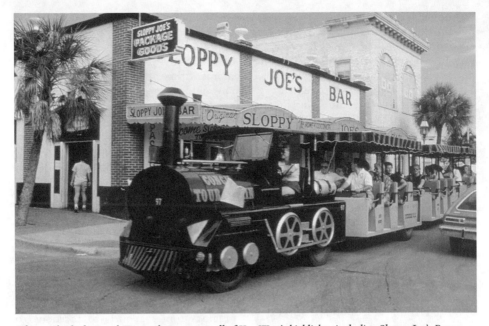

The quirky little Conch Tour takes you past all of Key West's highlights, including Sloppy Joe's Bar.
PHOTO: FLORIDA KEYS & KEY WEST TDC

depending on road construction and special events that necessitate street closures. Regardless of the path, you're sure to enjoy the ride as your guide recounts fact and legend, tall tales, and sad stories about life in Key West.

Tours start at Mallory Square from 9 A.M. to 4:30 P.M. If you're driving into town, you can park free of charge at the Key West Welcome Center, 3840 N. Roosevelt. A shuttle bus will deliver you directly to the train depot at Mallory. Tickets for adults and teens are $19; children ages 4 to 12, $10; children younger than 4 ride free. The tour lasts 90 minutes, with one 10-minute rest break at the Conch Tour Train ticket station, 501 Front Street. Train passengers can also get off at Land's End Village at the foot of Margaret Street to explore the Historic Seaport area on foot, then reboard another train to complete the tour.

Ghost Tours of Key West
Key West, FL
(305) 293–8009, (305) 294–9255
www.hauntedtours.com

Love a good ghost story? Key West's No. 1 haunted attraction, Ghost Tours, offers you the chance to get an in-depth introduction to the most famous ghosts of our island. Highlights include a visit to the city's original hanging tree. Tales of Robert, a haunted doll said to have been possessed by an evil spirit, intensify the mystery. Disbelief and awe surround the deeds of the German count who dug up the body of his true love, dressed her in a bridal gown, and serenaded her for seven years. Narrated by a spooky, caped, lantern-bearing guide, this 1-mile tour wends its way through Key West after dark and lasts about 90 minutes.

Tours leave nightly at 8 P.M. from the lobby of the Holiday Inn La Concha, 430 Duval Street. Plan to arrive approximately 15 minutes in advance to purchase your tickets and do bring cash or travelers checks; no credit cards are accepted. Groups of six or more may purchase tickets in advance in the lobby of the La Concha Hotel. Ticket prices are $18 for adults and $10 for children 12 and younger, but look for the Ghost Tour flyers around town that entitle you to a $3 discount on each adult ticket (up to six people). You will need to make reservations for this popular tour. Space is limited so book early by phoning the number shown above.

Key West Nature Bike Tour
(305) 294–1882

Join local character Lloyd Mager on his two-hour, two-wheeled tour of Key West's lesser-known spots. Highlights of this easy-to-ride tour include tasting many local species of flora, including mangoes, tamarind fruit, Key limes, and whatever else may be in season. You'll see a sand palm so large it is hard to fathom. Call the number above for information about the next scheduled tour time and day. Reservations are not required; just show up at the Moped Hospital, 601 Truman Avenue, at the appointed time. The tour costs $20, plus $3 for a bike if you don't bring your own.

Old Town Trolley Tours
Key West Welcome Center
3840 N. Roosevelt Avenue
Key West, FL
(305) 296–6688
www.trolleytours.com

Join the Old Town Trolley Tour for an informative, convenient entry into Key West. The trolley stops at most major hotels, handy if you're staying in the southernmost city. Daytrippers will appreciate the free parking at the Key West Welcome Center where you can pick up the tour. The trolleys depart every 30 minutes, and, best of all, you can get off at any of the 14 stops and reboard the same day, whenever you like. All along the way the tour guide will treat you to a Key West history lesson, full of anecdotes and legends.

Old Town Trolley Tours run daily from 9 A.M. to 4:30 P.M. Ticket cost per day for adults and teens is $19; children ages 4 through 12 pay $10; for children younger than 4, it's free.

Pelican Path
Old Island Restoration Foundation
Key West, FL
(305) 294–9501

Visitors who like to wander on their own should be sure to first pick up a copy of the Pelican Path brochure at the Chamber of Commerce on Mallory Square. This handy compact walking guide and map offers a short history of Key West as well as a suggested route that will take you past 50 of our most prominent historic structures. Most of the buildings described in this brochure are now private homes and guesthouses. Those that are open for touring are highlighted in yellow. Don't be surprised, however, if you can't spot those yellow and blue Pelican signs described in the brochure as path markers; many of them have disappeared over the years. Even so, the Pelican Path remains relatively easy to follow and is a great way to get acquainted with island history.

Sharon Wells' Walking and Biking Guide
(305) 294–8380
www.seekeywest.com

Historic preservationist Sharon Wells makes it easy for you to explore and enjoy Key West at your own pace with this superbly organized, information-packed guide. In addition to 10 self-guided tours, complete with maps and descriptions of the important structures you will see along the way, this 64-page booklet contains suggestions for nature treks in and around Key West. Best of all, it's free.

You'll find copies of Sharon Wells' Walking and Biking Guide at more than 200 locations in and around Key West, including the Key West Public Library, 700 Fleming Street; and the Key West Chamber of Commerce, Mallory Square. Up the Keys you'll find the guide at the chambers of commerce in Big Pine Key, mile marker 30.5 Oceanside; Marathon, mile marker 53.5 Bayside; Islamorada, mile marker 82.5 Bayside; and Key Largo, mile marker 106 Bayside.

If you'd rather not go it alone, Wells also offers personally guided tours called Island City Strolls. These include a 90-minute architectural stroll, which winds through the historic neighborhoods of Old Town, a 90-minute cemetery stroll, and two bike tours—The "Island Trek" through Key West's historic neighborhoods and the "Literary Landmarks Trail," leading past the homes of famous Key West writers. Upon request, Sharon can also put together a personalized tour for individuals or groups. Space is limited on all guided tours and reservations are required. Call for prices and tour times.

Trails of Margaritaville
(305) 292–2040

For Jimmy Buffett fans, known as Parrotheads, a trip to Key West is akin to a religious pilgrimage. Thousands of them "phlock" here annually to buy Buffett paraphernalia, down a few margaritas and visit the venues where their hero played and sang before he went big-time. This 90-minute tour gives them all an officially sanctioned peek at the places and legends of Buffett's 1970s salad days in Key West.

The guides, attired in full Parrothead regalia—Hawaiian shirts, parrot hats, etc.—lead you past the former site of Howie's Lounge, the compound on Ann Street where Buffett once lived, and Shrimpboat Sound, the studio where he still records, spinning yarns about Buffett and Key West in general all along the route. The tour ends, you guessed it, at Margaritaville Cafe on Duval Street.

If you are an inveterate Parrothead, you probably won't learn anything new on this tour—you've read it all before—but you will at least see the places you've heard about. If you're not a Parrothead, you may not understand the fans' fascination with Buffett, but you'll

still find this tour fun, even if it does mean that you have to walk around town with a silly-looking shark fin hat on your head.

The tour departs daily at 4 P.M., appropriately, from Captain Tony's Saloon, 428 Greene Street, Key West. In case you don't know it, Buffett played for Captain Tony back in the '70s and immortalized this former Key West mayor in his song "Last Mango in Paris." Tour tickets are $18 for adults, $15 for locals with ID, and $10 for children. Bring cash or travelers checks; no credit cards accepted. Reservations are required. And if you have a Margaritaville passport, bring it along, too; these folks will stamp it for you.

For Jimmy Buffet fans, a visit to Key West is akin to a pilgrimage. The "Trails of Margaritaville" walking tour takes you past this site. PHOTO: JANET WARE

And Beyond . . .

Biscayne National Park
National Park Service Main Visitor Center
Convoy Point, FL
(305) 230-7275

Only 4 percent of Biscayne National Park's 181,500 acres are above water, consisting of about 45 tiny keys and a mangrove shoreline. The crystalline depths shelter the northern portion of the Florida Keys' barrier reef and all the marine life lurking in the submerged coral nooks and crannies. Biscayne's complex ecosystem, like that of the Florida Keys, extends from the mangrove-lined shoreline to the Gulf Stream. The northernmost of the Florida Keys protects the waters of Biscayne Bay from the pounding surf of the Atlantic.

The best time to visit Biscayne National Park is from mid-December to mid-April. Unless you have your own boat, you will have to explore the park's waters by concessionaire-run cruises. You'll find glass-bottom boats that will take you on a reef cruise or for a snorkeling or diving excursion. More than 200 species of fish, as well as spiny lobsters, crabs, shrimp, sponges, sea turtles, and other marine life, will be visible as you pass from the nursery grounds of the turtle grass at 4 to 10 feet to the deeper waters of the reef. Some of the excursions visit Adams Key, Elliott Key, and Boca Chita Key where picnic facilities, restrooms, and nature trails have been established for visitors.

Visitors may also enjoy swimming, water skiing, fishing, and bird-watching. Canoes are available for rent. Biscayne National Park is open year round. There are no entrance fees, but concessionaire boat trips levy a charge. From Homestead, take SW 328th Street to the park entrance.

Everglades National Park
National Park Service Main Visitor Center
FL Highway 9336
Florida City, FL
(305) 242-7700

The largest remaining subtropical wilderness in North America and one of the world's richest biological preserves, Everglades National Park encompasses the eight ecosystems of the Everglades within its 1.5 million acres. Endlessly fascinating, the Everglades is so much more than the ubiquitous alligator that quickly comes to mind. From the acres of sawgrass prairie to the pinelands, the hardwood hammocks, and the mangrove-lined inland waterways, the Everglades supports a fascinating array of organisms at all levels of the food chain.

Ranger-led activities emanate from the various visitor centers of Everglades National Park, located at the southern tip of the 100-mile-long stretch of the Everglades. Three centers are accessible from the main entrance: Main Visitor Center, at the park's main entrance near Florida City; Royal Palm, off the main park road a few miles inside the main entrance; Flamingo, on the main park road at Florida Bay. Other centers include Shark Valley, at the north end of the park on U.S. Highway 41; and Gulf Coast Ranger Station, at Everglades City on Florida Highway 29 at the northwest entrance.

You'll find naturalist-led hikes and talks, guided canoe trips, and evening programs under the stars. Also available are tram tours and scenic, narrated boat tours into the backcountry waterways of Whitewater Bay or the Gulf waters of Florida Bay. Available for rent are motorboats, canoes, kayaks, bicycles, even houseboats. Fishing is good in the waters of Everglades National Park, and bird-watching is unparalleled, for the 'glades is home to the multi-specied heron, egret, and ibis families as well as wood storks, ospreys, bald

Insiders' Tip

What about alligators? With the exception of the 'gators relocated to the Blue Hole in Big Pine Key, you won't find these critters in the Keys since they are freshwater dwellers. To find an alligator in the wild, you'll have to visit Everglades National Park.

eagles, snail kites, and more. The Anhinga Trail at the Royal Palm Visitors Center teems with wading birds and alligators in January and February. Bring your camera.

The best time to visit Everglades National Park is the dry season, mid-December through mid-April, when mosquitoes are minimal. Many park activities are curtailed during the rainy season. Entrance fee is $10 per car, per week (seven-day period); $8 if you enter at Shark Valley. From Florida City take Florida Highway 9336 and follow signs to the Main Visitor Center.

Dry Tortugas National Park
National Park Service
(305) 242–7700

Visit Dry Tortugas National Park, the end of the line in the Florida Keys, for a spectacular ride back in history. Accessible only by boat or seaplane (see our Cruising, Camping, and Recreation chapters for transportation options), the Dry Tortugas, 70 miles west of Key West, harbor a rich history and an even more prolific underworld.

Ponce de Leon named the seven islands in 1513, presumably for the multitude of sea turtles (tortugas) and the lack of fresh water (dry) on these keys. You'll be able to take a self-guided tour of Fort Jefferson on Garden Key, America's largest nineteenth-century coastal fort, which was started in 1846 but never completed. The walls are 50 feet high and 8 feet thick. For years, the fort operated as a military prison. Fort Jefferson's most famous inmate was Dr. Samuel Mudd, who was convicted of conspiracy after he set the broken leg of President Lincoln's assassin, John Wilkes Booth.

The protected waters surrounding the Tortugas sparkle with all the sea creatures of the coral reef as well as a good many shipwreck remains. With natural sand beaches and calm seas, snorkeling and swimming are a must. All the waters of the Dry Tortugas National Park are designated a no-take zone, so you may see fish and lobsters of gargantuan proportions.

There is no food, fresh water, electricity, or medical assistance at Fort Jefferson. Saltwater toilets, grills, and picnic tables are provided. No lodging exists out here in the beyond, but you may camp on Garden Key if you pack in and pack out all water and supplies (see our Camping chapter). Campers pay slightly more than daytrippers for passage to Fort Jefferson, mostly to cover the cost of transporting the gear they must carry in and out.

Insiders' Tip

See the Camping in the Beyond section in our Campgrounds chapter for private charter transportation to the Dry Tortugas.

Passport to Adventure

A visit to several Key West attractions can be a costly venture. However, Historic Tours of America—the folks who run the Conch Train and Old Town Trolley tours, plus a host of other Key West attractions—now offer a passport program that lets you enjoy as many as 11 diversions in the southernmost city for one convenient price.

Passports are available at three levels. The barebones Island Passport ($48.50 per person), covers admissions to: The Key West Aquarium, Flagler Station Historeum, Hemingway House, Key West Shipwreck Historeum, Bone Island Shuttle, Conch Tour Train or Old Town Trolley, and the Truman Little White House, plus shopping discounts. With the middle-of-the-road Paradise Passport ($74.50 per person), you get all of the Island Passport attractions, plus admission to the Key West Museum of Art and History at the Custom House and lunch or dinner at El Meson de Pepe Cuban restaurant (see our Restaurants chapter). The top-of-the line Key West Passport ($94.50 per person) entitles you to enjoy all the attractions covered by the Island and Paradise Passports, plus a daysail aboard the Schooner Western Union (see our Recreation chapter).

Passports may be purchased with a credit card on-line (www.keywestpassports.com) or at any of the attractions that accept them. For information, check the website or phone (800) 717–7790.

A word of caution: Don't be tempted simply by the promise of a good deal. These passports can be moneysavers, but only if you intended to visit all those attractions in the first place. Do your math before you buy.

Kids and parents alike enjoy this pirate slide at Hawk's Cay Resort. PHOTO: HAWK'S CAY RESORT

Kidstuff

Get ready, get set, go!

It's time to explore the alphabet soup of things to do in the Florida Keys and Key West, especially for kids. But we have to warn you. Your parents will want to come along.

We deviate from our usual geographic arrangement in this chapter, but all the attractions we list include addresses and phone numbers. Look to related chapters for a comprehensive listing of hours of operation, admission costs, and websites.

Tell Mom and Dad if they want to find out more details of our ABCs (and 1, 2, 3s in Key West), they can look in our Recreation and Attractions chapters, where they'll find lots more fun things to do.

The Florida Keys

Fun From A to Z

A is for . . .

affectionate sea lions that may try to kiss you at Theater of the Sea, MM 84.5 Oceanside, Islamorada, (305) 664-2431—so be prepared. You can pet the sharks in the touch tank and touch the dolphins in another tank. In the main lagoon, created by excavations for Henry Flagler's railroad (see our Historical Evolution chapter), the dolphins put on quite a show. Watch them walk on their tails and jump high in the air. You'll see tropical fish and game fish, stingrays, and sea turtles. There is even a boat ride through the lagoon. (For more on Theater of the Sea, see our Attractions chapter.)

B is for . . .

baiting a hook. Go fishing on one of our group party boats (see our Fishing chapter for complete information). You may catch the prismatic dolphin fish, which has a blunt forehead like Bart Simpson's. Or reel in some yellowtail snappers; they really have yellow tails. Almost certainly you'll catch grunts. They make a funny grunting sound when you take them out of the water. Keep a lookout for the playful mammal dolphins and sea turtles.

C is for . . .

climbing into the osprey nest exhibit at the Florida Keys Children's Museum at Crane Point, MM 50.5 Oceanside, Marathon, (305) 743-9100. You'll really get a bird's-eye view because you'll be 3 feet off the ground. You can dress up in pirate clothes and hop aboard a pirate ship or play in a thatched chickee sandbox built by the Miccosukee Indians. You'll find a real Cuban freedom raft, a fishpond where you can feed the fish, a touch tank full of hermit and horseshoe crabs, and a huge seashell exhibit. Don't miss looking for

Insiders' Tip

If little feet have a difficult time keeping up while touring Key West, take a pedal cab or rent bicycles for the day. (See our Getting Here, Getting Around chapter.)

the resident wild iguanas. (For more, see our Attractions chapter.)

D is for . . .

"Don't touch!" If you touch the sap of the poisonwood tree when you walk through the nature trails at Crane Point, MM 50.5 Oceanside, Marathon, (305) 743-9100, it will make you itch like poison ivy does. This tropical Keys forest is full of interesting sinkholes, red mangroves, thatch palms, and lots of cool lizards, land crabs, and birds. One fee covers admission to the hammock and the Florida Keys Children's Museum. And you'll enjoy the adjoining Museum of Natural History too. (See our Attractions chapter.)

E is for . . .

examining the fossilized imprints of ancient shells and marine organisms you'll find in the coral quarry walls of Windley Key Fossil Reef Geologic Site, MM 85.5 Bayside, Windley Key, (305) 664-2540. If you bring a paper and crayon, you can make a crayon rubbing. (See our Attractions chapter for more on the museum.)

F is for . . .

feeding the giant tarpon that swim in the waters at Robbie's Marina, MM 77.5 Bayside, Islamorada, (305) 664-9814, (877) 664-8498. You can purchase a cup of bait fish, the tarpon's favorite snack, at the marina. These giant "silver kings" will swim in a frenzy before your very eyes, jockeying to be first in line when you throw the fish in the water.

G is for . . .

grabbing some rays at the beach. Play in the sand or look for crabs and crustaceans at Sombrero Beach in Marathon, MM 50 Oceanside, Sombrero Beach Road, which even has picnic tables so you can make a day of it. There is no admission fee. Bahia Honda State Park, MM 37 Oceanside, has two beaches. A small one near the concession stand at the south end of the park is calm, sheltered, and roped off for safety. The other, the Sandspur, is much longer. You can wade in the soft sand through waters that vary from several inches to 3 feet deep looking for sea creatures and washed up treasure. (See our Recreation chapter for more on beach options.)

H is for . . .

hopping aboard a glass-bottom boat for a 5.5-hour ecological tour of the Lower Keys backcountry with Strike Zone Charters, MM 29.5 Bayside, Big Pine Key, (305) 872-9863, (800) 654-9560. You'll learn the history of the Key deer and the tiny out-islands, the hurricanes, the wreckers, and the Indians. You'll see bald eagle nesting sites, great white herons, egrets, and dolphins feeding in the wild. You can snorkel and fish a little too. And to top it all off, you'll enjoy a fish cookout picnic on a private island. (See our Recreation chapter for more information.)

I is for . . .

investigating the Blue Hole—but don't feed the alligators. This freshwater sinkhole at MM 30.5 Bayside, Key Deer Boulevard, Big Pine Key, is home to a couple of curious 'gators, and they'll swim almost up to the viewing platform. Keep your puppy on a leash because its barking will ring the alligator's dinner bell. You'll see turtles in the Blue Hole, and Key deer come 'round at dusk. There is no admission charge.

Buy a bucket of bait and feed the giant tarpon at Robbie's Marina. PHOTO: MARY MOCCIA

J is for . . .

jumping into a good book. Visit one of our Keys public libraries: Key Largo, MM 101.4 Oceanside, Tradewinds Shopping Center, (305) 451–2396; Islamorada, MM 81.5 Bayside, across from the Hurricane Monument, (305) 664–4645; Marathon, MM 48.5 Oceanside, next to Fisherman's Hospital, (305) 743–5156; Big Pine, MM 31 Bayside, 213 Key Deer Blvd., (305) 289–6303; Key West, 700 Fleming Street, (305) 292–3595.

K is for . . .

kicking your finned feet as you practice snorkeling in the shallow waters of the protective U-shaped jetty called The Horseshoe, MM 35 Bayside, just over the Bahia Honda Bridge as you head down the Keys (see Insiders' Tip in our Diving and Snorkeling chapter). You'll see a natural aquarium of colorful tropical fish with no danger from sharks or barracudas 'cause they can't get in. It's free.

L is for . . .

looking a great white heron in the eye at the Florida Keys Wild Bird Center, MM

93.6 Bayside, Tavernier, (305) 852–4486, (888) 826–3811. Although some of the birds you'll see are permanent residents at the shelter because they can't exist in the wild anymore, others are recovering from injuries and will leave the center once healed. All the birds live in natural habitats that have been enclosed by huge wire cages. You can even go into the pelican cage by yourself. (See our Attractions chapter for more on the center.)

M is for . . .

meeting friendly dolphins up close and personal at the Dolphin Research Center, MM 59 Bayside, Grassy Key, (305) 289–1121. The dolphins' behavior trainers will put them through learning exercises in the saltwater lagoon. You can swim with dolphins in the Dolphin Encounter if you are between 5 and 12 years old and your mom or dad goes with you. (See our Attractions chapter for more information.)

N is for . . .

navigating your way through marked mangrove trails or the Largo Sound of John Pennekamp Coral Reef State Park,

Children discover the friendly Keys bottle-nosed dolphin at the Dolphin Research Center.

PHOTO: DOLPHIN RESEARCH CENTER

MM 102.5 Oceanside, Key Largo, (305) 451-1621, in a two person Spyak rented from Coral Reef Park Company. Take a grown-up with you and then paddle the glass-bottom kayak and spy on all the neat fish and sea creatures that are under the water. (For more information, see our Recreation chapter.)

O is for . . .

observing the catch of the day when you visit one of our fishing marina docks between 3:30 and 4 P.M. (see our Fishing chapter). That's when the charter boats come back in from offshore, and if their luck held, so will yours. You'll see giant dolphin, tuna, snapper, wahoo, grouper, and cobia. But you probably won't see sailfish and marlin because, since they aren't good to eat, we prefer to release them back into the ocean so they may continue to live. This is free fun.

P is for . . .

paddling your very own kayak through the mangrove creeks and backcountry of Florida Bay. If you are at least 10 years old, Mom and Dad can accompany you on a Sit-on-Top or in an enclosed cockpit kayak called a Keowee II. The staff at Florida Bay Outfitters, MM 104 Bayside, Key Largo, (305) 451-3018, will provide you with a life jacket, paddle, paddlefloater, and chart. You and your family can go off on your own or take a guided family tour. (See our Recreation chapter.)

Q is for . . .

qualifying as a super sleuth when you participate in the Dolphin Connection's Dolphin Detectives Program. If you are at least 5 years old, you can learn how to be a dolphin trainer. You'll get your hands all fishy preparing the dolphin's food. And you might get splashed as you supervise a dolphin training session from the dry docks. You'll find Dolphin Connection at Hawk's Cay Resort, MM 61 Oceanside, (888) 814-9174. (See our Attractions chapter.)

R is for...

riding out Watson Boulevard in Big Pine Key and crossing the bridge to No Name Key. If you come just as the sun is setting, you'll probably see our miniature Key deer—they're only 3 feet tall—wandering along the roadside. To get to No Name Key, go to MM 31 Bayside. Turn right on Key Deer Boulevard, then right on Watson and over the bridge. This is a free ride.

S is for...

swimming in the tidal pool at Key Largo's Harry Harris Park, MM 92.5 Oceanside, (305) 852-7161, if you get tired of swinging or playing on the slide. This state park has a small beach collared by a stone jetty so the waters are always calm. When the tide goes out, you can look for sea creatures. (For more information, see our Recreation chapter.)

T is for...

taking in a movie matinee. Visit one of the Keys cinemas: Tavernier Towne Twin Cinema in the Tavernier Mall, MM 91 Bayside, Tavernier, (305) 853-7003; Marathon Community Cinema, MM 50 Oceanside, Marathon, (305) 743-0288; or Regal Cinema 6, Searstown Shopping Center, 3338 Roosevelt Blvd., Key West, (305) 294-0000.

U is for...

unlocking the mysteries of a hardwood hammock on a nature walk with a naturalist on Lignumvitae Key, (305) 664-2540. You'll have to take a boat trip from Robbie's Marina, MM 77.5 Bayside, Islamorada, (305) 664-9814, for Lignumvitae is out in Florida Bay. This is the way all the Keys looked long ago. You'll see the red bark of the gumbo limbo tree, called the "tourist tree" because the bark peels like a sunburned vacationer. You'll also encounter leafy trees with unusual names

> ## Insiders' Tip
> Don't let your kids miss the sunset celebration at Key West's Mallory Square pier. As the sun sinks into the water, performers on land eat fire, juggle coconuts, play music, and entertain everyone. And it's free.

like mastic, strangler fig, and pigeon plum. The lignum vitae tree (its name means "wood of life") grows very slowly. (See our Attractions chapter for more information.)

V is for...

viewing the fascinating undersea world through the glass bottom of the Osprey. You can see everything a snorkeler sees without ever getting wet. And the boat's captain will narrate some fascinating tales as he takes you out to the coral reef. You'll find the Osprey at MM 61 Oceanside, Hawk's Cay Marina, Duck Key, (305) 743-7000.

W is for...

watching pottery being made by hand at Bluewater Potters in Treasure Village, MM 86.7 Oceanside, Islamorada, (305) 853-0616. Treasure Village is a castle-like shopping village with a gigantic lobster statue out front. Or pull Mom and Dad into Rudy's Kids Club (305-853-1265) for an alligator T-shirt or one of their unusual environmental toys. You can climb a short stairway to the top of the castle building, where you can get a bird's-eye view of the Overseas Highway.

X is for...

relaXing by watching a video from Blockbuster Video, MM 100 Oceanside, Key Largo, (305) 451-1313; MM 91 Bayside, Tavernier, (305) 852-0202; and MM 50

Nothing like a splash in the pool to put smiles on kids' faces. PHOTO: CHEECA LODGE

Bayside, Marathon, (305) 743–3034. You can also rent game machines here.

Y is for . . .

"Yow!" That's what you'll say when you see a shark really close up. Stop at Captain Hook's Marina, MM 53.1 Oceanside, Marathon, (305) 743–2444, and look at their 48,000-gallon outdoor aquarium. Every day at 4 P.M. you can watch the sharks—and lots of other big fish, too—receive their evening meal. Keep your fingers out of the tank so you don't become dessert. It's free fun.

Z is for . . .

zipping across the old Seven Mile Bridge to Pigeon Key in an old-time trolley car. Or you can walk, jog, or ride a bicycle to this 5-acre history-rich island. Pigeon Key was the construction camp for workers building Henry Flagler's Railroad. Now the preserved early-nineteenth-century buildings are listed on the National Register, and you can see them and take an island tour with a volunteer. Catch the trolley shuttle at the Visitors Center, MM 47 Oceanside, Knight's Key, (305) 743–5999. (See our Attractions chapter for more information.)

Kid-Friendly Resorts

Several of our premier resorts in the Florida Keys offer special organized programs for children, ensuring that you, Mom, and Dad have some time to pursue your own interests or just unwind and relax with a good book by the swimming pool. You will find more information about these hotels in our Accommodations chapter.

The Fun Factory
Westin Beach Resort Key Largo
MM 97 Bayside
Key Largo, FL
(305) 852–5553, (800) 539–5274
www.kidsfunfactory.com
www.keylargoresort.com

Kids are special at The Fun Factory. If you are staying at the Westin or are a local resident with a membership to use the hotel grounds, your children can really take advantage of some interesting activities.

The children have sessions in the swimming pool and take walks along a nature trail and to the pier in search of bird and animal life. They snorkel at the beach or build sand castles. Lunch is provided for morning and all-day sessions. The day's activities revolve around a different theme every day, such as Bug Out, Natural Wonders, Larger Than Life, Arctic Explorers, or Lost Treasure. Beading and coconut crafts, hat making, spin art, sand art, hand painting, toy boat modeling, and puppet creation—all keep little fingers busy.

The all-day session at The Fun Factory runs from 9 A.M. to 4 P.M. The cost, which includes lunch, is $40 per child. A half-day session, from 9 A.M. to 1 P.M. or 1 to 4 P.M., is $22. Children between the ages of 3 and 11 are eligible.

On Friday and Saturday nights, The Fun Factory offers kids theme activities and frees up Mom and Dad to enjoy a romantic dinner alone. Kids enjoy a special pool party complete with waterfall basketball, volleyball, water balloons, and splash contests. The evening activities run from 5:30 to 8:30 P.M. Cost is $22 per child.

Babysitting service is available through the hotel for $15 per hour (up to two children). All sitters are bonded and well screened.

Camp Cheeca
Cheeca Lodge
MM 82 Oceanside
Islamorada, FL
(305) 664–4651, (800) 327–2888
www.cheeca.com

Camp Cheeca maintains an environmental focus through its never-ending selection of children's activities. From sailboarding to sewing, nutrition to cooking, exercise to massage and facials, the kids learn while they have fun. In the summer, Everglades Alert teaches them about the endangered ecosystems of the Everglades National Park and about Florida's trees and plants. The winter season brings Earth Alert, when the children learn how to protect species all over the world.

The kids make recycled art: Pencil holders formed from Styrofoam meat trays and paper towel or toilet paper cardboard rolls are finished off with glue and sand for a stucco effect. Or the participants may braid plastic grocery bags into a rug. Nature art classes result in weavings of palm fronds, painted coconuts, or sand sculptures. And the Cheeca Challenge, team problem-solving initiatives, prove that everyone is important, even the little people, as the children work together to achieve a common goal.

The mysteries of the coral reef unfold in a classroom-like setting. Then the children learn to snorkel in the swimming pool and finally are taken out to the reef itself or under the oceanfront pier, where they experience the undersea wonders firsthand. The children even cast a few lines, displaying the environmentally sound practice of catch-and-release fishing.

Insiders' Tip
Take the kids fishing on one of the Keys' party boats. See our Fishing chapter.

Camp Cheeca operates daily except Monday during holiday periods throughout the high season (the last three weeks of December, the first two weeks of January, and the end of February through April). From June to Labor Day the camp is open from Monday through Sunday (Sunday is a half-day). During the rest of the year Camp Cheeca is open on weekends. Children ages 6 to 12 are invited to participate if they are guests of the hotel or if their families are members of the Cheeca Club (a membership fee is required to use hotel facilities). A full-day session, 9 A.M. to 4 P.M., costs $26. Half-days (9 A.M. to noon or 1 to 4 P.M.) are $15. Cheeca Club members pay a lower rate. A half-day morning session will replace the all-day session if fewer than four children sign up.

Friday nights are special at Cheeca Lodge. This Kids Night Out provides videos and popcorn from 7 to 9 P.M. for $10 per child. Children ages four and up are welcome to attend. All quoted prices for Camp Cheeca are subject to change.

Little Pirates Club and Island Adventure Club
Hawk's Cay Resort and Marina
MM 61 Oceanside
Duck Key, FL
(305) 743–7000, (800) 443–6393
www.hawkscay.com
Little Pirates Club, for children ages 3 to 5, and Island Adventures Club, for kids 6 to 12, are day camps offering ever-changing nature-oriented activities organized around a different theme every day. Housed in Hawk's Cay Indies Club, a multimillion dollar recreation and fitness center, the Little Pirates Club and the Island Adventures Club enjoy some state-of-the-art recreation equipment of their own.

A special pool is outfitted with a pirate ship, slides, and water cannons. A treehouse playground—complete with a rock-climbing wall, S-curve, wave and rocket slides, a bridge, and a tire swing—beckons the adventurous.

Little Pirates meet Monday through Saturday from 9:30 A.M. to 1 P.M. to do such fun activities as paint-the-counselor, yo-yo

fishing, and building sand castles. Cost is $30 per child, which includes lunch. The older kids in Island Adventure Club create tie-died fish-print shirts, fish at the marina, go on bicycle scavenger hunts, play the Duck Map Adventure game, or a game of paint wars. A full day, which includes lunch, runs from 9:30 A.M. to 4 P.M. and is $40 per child. The half-day session is $30.

The Kid's Night Out program allows Mom and Day a night out, too. On Wednesday, Friday, and Saturday nights, the children are treated to an evening of thematic fun. Jungle Adventure Night, A Night at the Ball Park, and Camp Out are a few of the offerings, which typically include island games, crafts, dinner, and a movie. Kid's Night Out is open to children ages 6 to 12 and runs from 7 P.M. to 10 P.M. Cost is $30 per child.

Key West

Calling all kids. Come and join the countdown of the Top 5 things to do in Key West. We know you won't want to miss a single one.

No. 5
Step back in time as you explore the Civil War-era fort at East Martello Museum and Gallery, 3501 S. Roosevelt Boulevard, (305) 296–3913. The brick walls are 8 feet thick, and you can climb the winding steps right to the top of the tall citadel. Explore the restored life-size dollhouse that used to belong to native Key West Conch Edna Wolkowsky. Go inside, it has chairs, tables, and cabinets and is filled with dolls and toys. And you'll see some pretty neat junk-art sculptures outside in the courtyard. (For more on the museum, see our Attractions chapter.)

No. 4
Climb the 88 steps to the top balcony of the Key West Lighthouse, 938 Whitehead Street (305–294–0012) which was built in 1847. You'll have a sweeping view over Key West and its surrounding waters from the

Kids learn the joy of camping at Hawk's Cay Resort's Little Pirates Club. PHOTO: HAWK'S CAY RESORT

top of this 90-foot tower. Its three red sector panels used to signal dangerous approaches to the Key West harbor. A photoelectric cell lights up in the tower when daylight fades, and the light can be seen for several miles out at sea. Be sure to visit the Lighthouse Keeper's Quarters, too, and look at the museum full of lighthouse memorabilia. (See our Attractions chapter.)

No. 3

At the Mel Fisher Maritime Heritage Society and Museum, 200 Greene Street, (305) 294–2633, you'll see all kinds of gold and silver treasure recovered from the ancient ship *Atocha*, which sank off the Marquesas in 1622. Every 30 minutes a documentary movie shows how Mel Fisher searched for the fortune, a task that took nearly 20 years. Examine gold coins, bars of silver, gold chains, and giant emeralds. Upstairs, the museum showcases maritime exhibits that change every six months. You can get a special guide at the front desk and if you can successfully identify the objects in the exhibit you might be awarded a small prize. Be sure to visit the Discovery Room, which has 160 drawers for you to open.

Each drawer secrets maritime artifacts that will teach you about shipwrecks and treasure salving. (For more information on the museum see our Attractions chapter.)

No. 2

Deep in a dark cistern, a foot below sea level, you'll meet a 175-year-old wrecker named Asa Tift at the Key West Shipwreck Historeum, 1 Whitehead Street at Mallory Square, (305) 292–8990, (800) 868–7482. Surrounded by thick ropes, jugs, rigging, and cannonballs, he'll tell all about the wreck of the *Isaac Allerton*, the richest Key West shipwreck of all. This funny little man (really an actor) asks if you'd like to hire on as a lumper or a wrecker or, if you can hold your breath a long time, as a diver to help salvage the cargo off the wreck. You'll see a video about old Key West, then Mr. Tift will personally invite you to the upper deck of the "ship," where you can see all kinds of interesting things he has salvaged. Each exhibit has headphones you can put on to hear recorded messages chock-full of information. Don't miss the laser mannequin, Capt. Philip Philpot—you'll swear he's real. Climb up to the top

Life's a beach when you are a kid in the Florida Keys. PHOTO: FLORIDA KEYS & KEY WEST TDC

around the aquarium, and look at all the saltwater species of brightly colored tropical fish, blooming corals, and sea fans. Look for the giant green moray eel. Go outside to the Atlantic Shores exhibit, re-created to give you the experience of a Florida Keys mangrove habitat. You'll see huge tarpon, snook, jacks, and sea turtles swimming in the crystal-clear water. If you don't get a chance to snorkel or dive in the ocean waters of our coral reef, this is the next best thing. The aquarium is open daily from 10 A.M. to 6 P.M. (See our Attractions chapter.)

Kid-Friendly Resorts

Wyndham Kids Club
Casa Marina Resort and Beach House
1500 Reynolds Street
Key West, FL
(305) 296–3535, (800) 626–0777
www.wyndham.com/casamarinaresort
Wyndham Reach Resort
1435 Simonton Street
Key West, FL
(305) 296–5000, (800) 874–4118
www.reachresort.com

Under the Wyndham umbrella, both the Casa Marina Resort and the Reach Resort now offer a sparkling new Kids Club. Children age 4 to12 are invited to partake in an array of fun activities, such as arts and crafts, sand castle building, swimming, and movies. Wyndham Kids Club operates Thursday through Sunday. Sessions are available from 9 A.M. to noon or 1 to 5 P.M. Cost is $25. An all-day program is also available, running from 9 A.M. to 5 P.M. This program is $35. Children participating in the all-day program receive a T-shirt, duffle bag, and a personal diary in which to record their vacation memories.

of the lookout tower and do as Asa Tift tells you: Shout "Wreck ashore!" (See our Attractions chapter for more information.)

No. 1

This is it. The place where you'll meet all the fish and sea creatures we tell you about in our Diving and Fishing chapters: The Key West Aquarium, 1 Whitehead Street at Mallory Square, (305) 296–2051, (800) 868–7482. Be sure not to miss the guided tours—11 A.M. and 1, 3, and 4:30 P.M.—because you'll be able to watch the feeding sessions of the stingrays, sharks, sawfish, and barracudas. A splash from the eager stingray may even get your shirt wet. You'll get the chance to pet the tail of a nurse shark. The tour guide will show you the touch tank, where you can handle the hermit crabs, horse conchs, horseshoe crabs, sea cucumbers, pencil urchins, and common starfish. The guide will pick up a queen conch and let its slimy brown body slither out of its pretty pink shell. Walk

Annual Events

No one knows how to throw a party better than residents of the Florida Keys. Come dress with us in period attire as we relive eras of our past. Or join locals and folks from all over the world in a challenging road race on a bridge spanning miles of open sea.

We also have boat parades, bikini contests, battle reenactments, and our own unplugged, underwater concert. Or try your angling skills in one of our many fishing tournaments (see our Fishing chapter for an expanded listing). Immerse yourself in Florida Keys arts and culture at our historic observances, music festivals, or arts and crafts fairs.

And my, how we love to eat. From Key Largo to Key West, food festivals abound. These events provide an inexpensive means of sampling incredibly fresh seafood and menu items from leading local restaurants.

The following selection of festivals and events is a sampling of what we offer annually in the Florida Keys, organized by month, from Key Largo to Key West. Additional events occur sporadically from year to year. Dates and locations often change from year to year, and admission prices vary. Call the local chambers of commerce for details: Key Largo, MM 106 Bayside, (305) 451-1414, (800) 822-1088; Islamorada, MM 82.5 Bayside, (305) 664-4503, (800) 322-5397; Marathon, MM 53.5 Bayside, (305) 743-5417, (800) 262-7284; Lower Keys, MM 31 Oceanside, (305) 872-2411, (800) 872-3722; Key West, Old Mallory Square, (305) 294-2587, (800) 527-8539. You can pick up the annual "Attractions & Events" brochure at any of these chambers. You also will find annual event information on the official website of the Monroe County Tourist Development Council: www.fla-keys.com.

January

Holiday Isle Special Events
MM 84 Oceanside
Islamorada, FL
(305) 664-2321
www.holidayisle.com

Holiday Isle, the party magnet of the Keys (see our Nightlife chapter), sponsors special-theme events, competitions, tournaments, and festivals several times each month. Events vary from year to year, but all have something in common: They are great fun! For detailed information on what's happening, call the Holiday Isle special events coordinator at the number listed above, or check their website.

Cheeca Lodge Presidential Sailfish Tournament
MM 82 Oceanside
Cheeca Lodge
Islamorada, FL
(305) 664-4651
www.cheeca.com

One of the most popular sailfish tournaments of the season, the Presidential received its name back when George H.W. Bush was president and came to fish our Islamorada waters. Cash prizes and trophies are awarded in this catch-and-release tournament. See our Fishing chapter for details.

Even 10-foot seas don't dampen the enthusiasm of these anglers as they seek tournament sailfish.
PHOTO: VICTORIA SHEARER

Florida Keys Renaissance Faire
Marathon, FL
(305) 743-5417, (305) 743-4386

How gallantly we begin the year, stepping into the medieval era as professional performers portray members of the royal court. You'll enjoy jousting, a living chess match, and an ever-changing montage of Renaissance entertainment. Medieval rides and games are on-site for the enjoyment of young and old alike. Enticing aromas fill the air, and master craftspeople hawk their wares in the Market Lanes. Music from the Shire's Minstrels resounds throughout the fair grounds. Expect to pay an admission fee. Call for prices.

Pigeon Key Music Festivals
Pigeon Key, FL
(305) 289-0025

Following on the heels of its successful music festivals in the past few years, Pigeon Key now hosts two to three concerts per year—from January through March—featuring a wide variety of music. Call for admission prices.

Annual House and Garden Tours
Various Key West sites
(305) 294-9501

Olde Island Restoration, a nonprofit organization that encourages preservation of Key West's many historic structures, sponsors this popular tour to show off some of the city's finest private properties. Typically, the event features five or six privately owned homes every year. Tours explore shotgun-style cottages, Conch-style mansions, and everything in between (see our Architecture Close-up in the Attractions chapter).

The tours are self-guided, but participants may meet at the Olde Island Restoration offices along Mallory Square and then embark on a Conch Train bound for the tour site. Home tours typically are held in the evening on three weekends in January, February, and March. Scheduled dates vary from year to year. There is an admission fee.

GMC Yukon Yachting Race Week
Waters off Key West
(781) 639-9545

Sailors from throughout the world flock to Key West the second week in January for this event, the biggest annual regatta in America. More than 300 sailboats compete for no money, just glory and prestige. America's Cup teams use this event for training and to scope out the competition. Everyone who's anyone in sailing is sure to be here. The event lasts five days, with races beginning each day at around 10 A.M. Spectating is free.

Key West Craft Show
Whitehead and Caroline Streets
Key West, FL
(305) 294–1241

Key West ends the month of January with a weekend-long exhibit of original crafts. Among the one-of-a-kind items offered for sale, you'll find handmade jewelry, leather goods, wood carvings, kitchen accessories, and beach and lounge chairs. Exhibitors come from throughout the United States. The craft show takes place in the street—on Whitehead Street between Eaton and Greene and along Caroline Street in Truman Annex. Admission is free.

You never know what you'll get into at the Florida Keys Renaissance Faire in Marathon. PHOTO: ANDY NEWMAN

Key West Literary Seminar
San Carlos Institute
516 Duval Street
Key West, FL
(888) 293–9291

In 1981 Key West author David Kaufelt and a group of his colleagues capitalized on Key West's literary reputation by bringing writers from throughout the world together to discuss their works. Since then, the Key West Literary Seminar has blossomed into a highly respected, annual theme event featuring such prominent panelists that the seminar sells out months in advance.

Not all attendees are writers. Some are professors; others are plumbers. They travel the world over for this event because they share a common interest or hobby: writing and reading. Past themes have included "American Writers in the Natural World," which addressed all forms of nature writing and featured Annie Dillard, Jim Harrison, and Peter Matthiessen. A journalism seminar brought together the likes of David Halberstam, Anna Quindlen, and Louis Harris. Pulitzer Prize winner Frank McCourt, author of *Angela's Ashes*, led an all-star cast of writers in discussions focusing on "The Memoir". Other topics covered by the Key West Literary Seminar have included literature in film and travel, new directions in American theater, and children's literature.

Key West's San Carlos Institute, 516 Duval Street, serves as the home base for these sessions. Writing workshops, tours of legendary local authors' homes, and cocktail parties also are offered to seminar participants. Included in the core seminar price, these parties offer the opportunity to mingle with panel guests. Workshops and tours cost an additional fee. The four-day event is typically held during the second week of January. Call for information on registration and workshop fees, but reserve early. These events are typically sold out nine to ten months in advance.

February

Florida Keys Outdoor Art Show
Key Colony Beach Park
W. Ocean Drive
Key Colony Beach, FL
(305) 743–5417, (800) 262–7284

In addition to the works of artists throughout the country, local high school students display their talents at this intimate showing. Bronze, stone, and metal sculptures, oil paintings, watercolors, and other fine arts and crafts are among the items featured. Judging is held for the work of high school students only. Food, beverages, and live entertainment are offered throughout the weekend, and a raffle drawing affords you the chance to win some of the work on display. Admission is free.

Pigeon Key Art Festival
Pigeon Key
Marathon, FL
(305) 289–0025
www.pigeonkey.org

More than 700 artists from throughout the country apply to display their works in this annual show, but only 70 are selected by the judges to participate, so you can be assured of the highest quality work. The Festival is generally scheduled for the first weekend in February, on the shores of Pigeon Key. At weekend's close, judges bestow awards for the best artwork in categories such as watercolor, oil and acrylic painting, jewelry, photography, sculpture, glass, pottery, and graphics. Live entertainment features the music of steel-drum bands, jazz groups, classical ensembles, and country-and-western performers. Local restaurants sell food, and raffle drawings include original artwork donated by each participating artist.

Getting to this festival by your choice of water taxi, trolley, or Pigeon Key choo-choo is half the fun, and transportation is included in the admission price. All proceeds are donated to the Pigeon Key Foundation for restoration of the island (see our Attractions chapter). Artists pay entry fees, and half the show's work has a Florida theme.

Old Island Days Art Festival
Whitehead Street
Key West, FL
(305) 294–1241

If you appreciate art, your heart is bound to beat faster at the sight of several blocks of exhibits by talented local artists. Inspired by this southernmost city, they take this opportunity to showcase their vivid creations. Virtually all artistic mediums are represented in this pre-juried, weekend-long show, including oil, watercolor, and acrylic paintings; graphics; wood, metal, and stone sculptures; glasswork; and photography. Judges provide merit awards within each category. Old Island Days Art Festival exhibits line Whitehead Street from Greene Street to Caroline and into Truman Annex. No charge for browsing.

March

The Original Marathon Seafood Festival
Marathon, FL
(305) 743–5417

Sponsored by the Marathon Chamber of Commerce and Organized Fishermen of Florida (OFF), The Original Marathon Seafood Festival features thousands of pounds of fish, including cobia ceviche, golden crabs, conch fritters, Florida lobster,

Insiders' Tip

Dates, locations, and some admission fees for events tend to vary from year to year. Events may sometimes even be canceled without notice. Word to the wise: Call in advance to confirm all details before venturing out.

and a raw bar. Landlubbers can munch on hot dogs, hamburgers, and ethnic dishes.

Pick up some of the distributed educational literature on the commercial fishing industry, and check out the Mid Keys Marine Association's festival flea market with new and discontinued marine items at below-retail prices. Rides, games, vendors, raffles, and live entertainment mean fun for the entire family. There is an admission fee.

Key West Garden Club Flower Show
West Martello Tower
Atlantic Boulevard and White Street
Key West, FL
(305) 294-3210
Established in 1949 by former Key West politician Joe Allen, the Garden Club organizes monthly educational seminars for the public. Plant-swapping sessions also are popular. The group holds a pre-juried show every other year (the next is scheduled for 2003). (The Orchid Society has a show at West Martello Tower on the alternate years.) Held at the Joe Allen West Martello Tower, home of the Key West Garden Club, the show features some 800 entries of floral arrangements, potted plants, palms, rare tropical flowers, and hybrids. Judges from garden clubs throughout the state of Florida award ribbons and prizes in several categories. The Flower Show is typically held during the spring, not necessarily always in March. There are admission costs.

Conch Shell Blowing Contest
Sunset Pier
Ocean Key House
Duval Street
Key West, FL
(305) 294-9501
Feel free to toot your own horn. The Conch Shell Blowing Contest offers adults and children the opportunity to sound off. Prizes are awarded to the loudest, the funniest, and the most-entertaining conch shell blowers in several divisions. This one-day, springtime event takes place on the waterfront and on various dates each year, but usually in March or April. Participation is free.

Heritage Days
Ft. Zachary Taylor State Historic Site
Truman Annex at Southard Street
Key West, FL
(305) 292-6713
www.forttaylor.com
This annual festival and Civil War re-enactment celebrates the unique history of Fort Zachary Taylor. Against all odds, the fort remained a Union stronghold throughout the Civil War, despite the fact that Florida had seceded from the Union. Costumed re-enactors—soldiers and their families alike—stage military drills and demonstrate everyday life in a Civil War-era fort. Heritage Days is typically held the first weekend in March. The event is free with admission to Fort Zach (see our Attractions chapter).

April

Taste of Islamorada
Islamorada, FL
(305) 664-4503, (800) 322-5397
Islamorada's most popular restaurants all come together for this annual Chamber of Commerce fund-raiser that lets you cast your "palate ballot" for the best appetizer, entree, dessert, low-calorie, and vegetarian selections. Booths at the event allow visitors to sample a variety of unlimited cuisines from 15 to 20 fine dining establishments, all for one minimal cover charge. If you have never dined at Islamorada's local restaurants, this is a wonderfully inexpensive opportunity to try out several. Live entertainment and raffle prizes make this a popular family event. Locations change annually. Expect to pay an admission fee.

Earth Day at Cheeca Lodge
MM 82 Oceanside
Islamorada, FL
(305) 664-4651, (800) 327-2888
Every year, Cheeca Lodge puts on quite a spectacle in honor of Mother Earth. The big draw here is the land-based aerial dis-

play, where revelers put together the words "Earth Day" in huge letters made out of sand. Other events include fishing tournaments, cooking demonstrations, costume contests, live entertainment, and barbecues. Open to the public, Cheeca Lodge's Earth Day celebration raises funds for environmental causes. Admission is free.

Seven Mile Bridge Run
Marathon, FL
(305) 743–8513

Men and women from all over the world flock to this seven-mile roadway, which spans the open water between Marathon and Bahia Honda. In the wee morning hours, these spirited individuals participate in the most scenic competition of its kind: a run across one of the world's longest bridges. Organized by the Marathon Runners Club, sponsored by a number of Florida Keys businesses, and designed to raise money for local schools and youth groups, the run is said to be the only one in the world held completely over and surrounded by water. Post-race prizes are awarded in various categories, and runners gather for what is likely the world's largest early morning celebratory bash. Usually, the run is held on the second Saturday in April and begins on the Marathon end of the Seven Mile Bridge. Expect to pay an entry fee. Spaces are lim-

Insiders' Tip

The Seven Mile Bridge Run closes the Seven Mile Bridge on a Saturday morning for approximately two hours. If you need to be somewhere at a certain time that day and your route requires a trip across the bridge, make sure you're on the desired side before 7:30 A.M.

ited, so if you plan to run, reserve your spot early.

Conch Republic Independence Celebration
Various Key West sites
(305) 296–0213
www.conchrepublic.com

Key West has always been marked by an independent spirit, and this 10-day festival exalts it. It officially commemorates the city's attempt to secede from the United States on April 23, 1982, after the U.S. Border Patrol established roadblocks at the end of the mainland to screen for drugs and illegal aliens. Independent Key Westers rebelled, creating their own flag and attempting to secede from the United States.

The secession fizzled, of course, but locals here find the brief attempt at independence a reason to party nevertheless. Around this same time every year, officials of the fictitious Conch Republic—secretary general, prime ministers, navy, air force, and all—host a picnic, fashion show, buffet, and a pirate's ball. Events also include Conch cruiser car shows, the Red Ribbon Bed Race down Duval Street, and what has been dubbed "the world's longest parade"—spectators lining the route simply join in the fun as the floats pass by.

One final word on emancipation in the southernmost city: Duck! During the Great Battle of the Conch Republic, all forms of food whiz through the air and ultimately find their marks on participants and spectators. The battle engages the Conchs and the U.S. Coast Guard in a water fight held at sea just off Mallory Square. Conch Republic Celebration events are held all over the island and on the water.

A Taste of Key West
Higgs Beach
White Street at Atlantic Boulevard
Key West, FL
(305) 296–6196

"So many restaurants, so little time," is the lament we often hear from visitors to

Key West. Our tiny island boasts well over 100 eateries, and on an average visit, you simply can't try them all. But if you're lucky enough to be here in late April/early May, you may have the chance to sample the best of the best on one night, at one location.

A Taste of Key West, which benefits AIDS Help Inc., brings together chefs and their favorite dishes from many of Key West's finest restaurants. There is no admission charge, but you must buy tickets to eat. Each ticket costs $1, and the individual restaurants set the number of tickets you will need to sample their wares. For three tickets, you can nosh on a salad or a dessert; entrees typically cost four or five tickets. In addition to cash, be sure to bring your appetite—the portions are always generous.

The date for this annual event changes from one year to the next, but it is always held outdoors and typically on a Monday or Tuesday night in late April or early May.

Texaco Key West Classic
Various Key West sites
(305) 294–4042
This tournament spreads a huge pot of prize money over a variety of categories—blue or white marlin, sailfish, tarpon, and permit. Proceeds benefit the National Mental Health Association. See our Fishing chapter for details.

May

Key West Songwriters Fest
Waterfront Playhouse
Mallory Square
Key West, FL
(305) 745–9988
You may not recognize the names of the performers at this annual event, but if you're a country music fan, you'll almost certainly know their songs. This festival, launched in 1996, brings some of the country's foremost performing songwriters to the Key West stage.

Past performers have included Billy Dean, whose "Somewhere in My Broken Heart" earned a Grammy nomination and Academy of Country Music Song of the Year honors; Gretchen Peters, whose "Independence Day," sung by Martina McBride, won a Country Music Association Song of the Year Award; and Mark Selby and Tia Sellers, whose roster of hits includes the Dixie Chicks' 1999 Grammy winner "There's Your Trouble."

The four-day festival includes two nights of intimate concerts by all the songwriters in the round at Waterfront Playhouse plus free daytime shows by selected performers at numerous venues around Key West. You can pick up tickets for the Friday and Saturday night concerts in advance and at the door. There are no reserved seats, so plan to arrive early for the best choice.

Annual Key West Minimal Regatta
Schooner Wharf Bar
202 William Street
Key West, FL
(305) 292–9520
Putting together a boat with as few supplies as possible is the goal at the Minimal Regatta, which is held every year at the Schooner Wharf Bar. Contestants must create a floatable object (a "boat") from such materials as glue, nails, and a couple of boards. The boat that floats the farthest wins. Food and drinks are available at the bar. Come early and register even earlier for this memorable event. The Regatta is free to watch, but you have to pay an entry fee if you want to participate.

June

Don Hawley Invitational Tarpon Tournament
Islamorada, FL
(903) 450–4450
This Don Hawley event is the Keys' oldest tarpon-on-fly tournament and the original all-release event. Proceeds benefit the nonprofit Don Hawley Foundation, which supports the study of tarpon fishery and preservation in the Florida Keys. See our Fishing chapter for details. Eddie Miller is the contact.

Swim Around Key West
Waters off Key West
(305) 872-2668, (305) 923-1070

Call early for information on this great event, which started more than 20 years ago. The swim was originally scheduled to take place on the Fourth of July, but as the organizers seek the best tides and currents, the actual date may vary. The event may even be canceled altogether (as it was in 2000), depending on water quality conditions. The swim usually lasts six hours or more, so plan well if you want to participate. Swim Around participation is free, but you need to register in advance. Entrants must, obviously, be competent swimmers, but there are no other restrictions.

July

Fourth of July Parade
Overseas Highway
Key Largo, FL
(305) 852-3216

From Mardi Gras to Native American, this old-fashioned, community-oriented parade goes the distance, from MM 98 to MM 105. The Overseas Highway is closed during the hour-long parade, which begins at 10 A.M., except when the holiday falls on a Sunday, in which case the parade begins at 1 P.M. All are welcome to participate. Award plaques are presented to the best floats in seven categories, including most beautiful, best use of theme, and best use of natural materials. A barbecue at the Elks Lodge traditionally follows. The parade is free. Admission price to the barbecue varies.

Fourth of July Fireworks
Bayside
Key Largo, FL
(305) 664-2266

View this 30-minute fireworks display from land or, if you are a boater, by sea. Funded by local merchants, the show typically begins at 9 P.M. The best coastal viewing spots are the Caribbean Club, Señor Frijoles, Sundowners, and Marriott

Key Largo Bay Beach Resort. Some of these facilities host barbecues with live entertainment. Admission is free, but you must be a patron to enjoy the view from a private business. Food and drinks are sold separately.

Star Spangled Event
Sombrero Beach
MM 50 Oceanside
Marathon, FL
(305) 743-5417

On July 4, follow a parade to the beach, where fireworks decorate the sky, and enjoy all-American hot dogs, hamburgers, and fish sandwiches. Live entertainment is provided; games are available for the kids, and an afternoon volleyball tournament welcomes last-minute sign-ups. Many people see the fireworks display from the decks of their boats, anchoring offshore for the extravaganza. The traffic jam at sea rivals the one on land. No admission or entry fee is required. Food and games are priced individually.

Underwater Music Festival
MM 31 Oceanside
Big Pine Key, FL
(305) 872-0100

Whether you dive, snorkel, or merely swim, here is an unplugged series of concerts that beats music videos finsdown. Enjoy six hours of prerecorded, commercial-free music—from Beethoven to the Beatles to the humpback whale song—in synchronicity with tropical fish swimming across the reefs of the Looe Key National Marine Sanctuary. Dance the day away underwater, and look out for surprises such as mermaids and the Keys' very own Snorkeling Elvises. Typically, the music fest runs from mid-morning to mid-afternoon and is broadcast live on WWUS/US 1 radio, 104.1 FM (see our Media chapter). Landlubbers and those who have danced up an appetite can enjoy this same music plus a variety of foods, arts and crafts, and family games at the Lower Keys Chamber of Commerce, MM 31 Oceanside. Admission to both the concert and the food festival, usually held the second Saturday in July, is free. See our Diving chapter for a list of dive and snorkel charters that will take you to the reef.

July 4th VNA/Hospice Picnic
Wyndham Casa Marina Resort
and Beach House
1500 Reynolds Street
Key West, FL
(305) 294–8812

The whole town turns out for this old-fashioned beachside picnic to benefit the Visiting Nurses Association/Hospice of the Florida Keys. You'll find plenty of hot dogs, hamburgers, watermelon, and fun for all, plus special activities for the kids, continuous live entertainment, and a raffle. The picnic begins around 5 P.M., but because the beach at the Casa is one of the best places to view the fireworks, you'll probably want to come early and stick around until well after dark. Admission is charged for the picnic.

July 4th Fireworks
White Street Pier
White Street and Atlantic Boulevard
Key West, FL
(305) 294–2587

The Key West Rotary Club sponsors this pyrotechnic extravaganza every July 4th beginning at 9 P.M. and lasting approximately 30 minutes. Best viewing spots are Higgs Beach and the Wyndham Casa

Marina. There is no admission charge; the fireworks are funded strictly by donations.

Reef Awareness Week
Reef Relief
201 William Street
Key West, FL
(305) 294–3100
www.reefrelief.org

Reef Relief is one of the best known and largest of the organizations with the sole purpose of protecting North America's only living coral reef. And when these folks throw a party, they invite everyone. This week-long event offers all sorts of information to those who want to learn about the coral reef. Visit the art auction and poetry readings, or become a member of this worthy organization during the kickoff week. For more information, call Reef Relief, or visit the organization's retail store at the address above. Admission is usually free, but some events may carry an entry fee.

Hemingway Days Festival
Hemingway Home and Museum
907 Whitehead Street
Key West, FL
(305) 296–2388
www.hemingwaydays.com

Celebrate the legendary author's birthday with residents of the old man's former hometown by the sea. Tours of the Hemingway Home and Museum are offered, along with a street fair, short story competition, and a Hemingway look-alike contest at what was one of his favorite haunts, Sloppy Joe's (see our Nightlife chapter). This week-long event centers on the author's July 21 birthday. Fees for some events are required. Call for more information.

Battle of the Bars
Schooner Wharf Bar
202 William Street
Key West, FL
(305) 292–9520

This annual fundraiser for Big Brothers/Big Sisters pits some of Key West's most legendary bartenders (also barbacks, bouncers, and servers) against one another in a series of contests requiring skill, dexterity, and just plain chutzpah. Teams of seven, dividing up their responsibilities, make the perfect margarita, walk an obstacle course to a customer who will drink it, recycle the bottles, tap a keg of Key West Lager, and serve the beer to team members—sometimes even bribing the judges along the way. It's all in good fun and all for a great cause. Past events have netted $10,000 or more for Big Brothers/Big Sisters.

September

Florida Keys Poker Run
Miami through Key West
(305) 294-3032

With so many magnificent bridges, the Florida Keys is extremely popular with motorcycle riders. For this event, more than 10,000 motorcyclists ride from Miami to Key West, stopping at various points within our islands to pick up playing cards. At the end of the ride, the player with the best poker hand wins, and all enjoy live bands, field events, and runs-within-a-run on Duval Street. Bikers can also get their machines blessed before returning home. Entry is free; each poker hand costs a nominal fee.

Mercury S.L.A.M. Tournament
Key West, FL
(305) 664-2002
www.redbone.org

First of the annual Celebrity Tournament Series is the Southernmost Light-Tackle Anglers Masters (S.L.A.M). Anglers try to score a Grand Slam by catching and releasing a bonefish, permit, and tarpon in one day. Proceeds benefit the Cystic Fibrosis Foundation. See our Fishing chapter for details or contact Gary Ellis at the number listed above.

WomenFest Key West
Various Key West sites
(305) 296-2491

They are women; hear them roar. Each week after Labor Day, thousands of women from all over the country gather in Key West for a bit of female bonding. They include women from diverse races, religions, professions, and sexual preferences; motto is "Free to Be You with Me in Key West." Atlantic Shores Resort serves as the headquarters for this seven-day celebration, which includes women-only watersports, cocktail comedies, and concerts. Organizers host wine-tasting dinners, parties, and picnics, and women ship off together on sunset sails.

Many events are free, including the "Sisters for Brothers" blood drive to compensate for the gay male population not being permitted to donate blood. Discounted party passes are available for groups of events that come at a cost such as the Old Town Trolley Tour that highlights infamous Key West women.

Gay male and female guesthouses and mainstream hotels provide accommodations, and some of the island's "all-boys" houses (see our Accommodations chapter) become all-women for this week instead.

October

Mercury Baybone Tournament
Westin Beach Resort
Key Largo, FL
(305) 664-2002
www.redbone.org

Event No. 2 in the Celebrity Tournament Series (see our Key West's September section for the first event) is a catch-and-release tournament in pursuit of bonefish and permit. Proceeds benefit the Cystic Fibrosis Foundation. See our Fishing chapter or contact Gary Ellis at the number above for more information.

Octoberfright
Pigeon Key
Marathon, FL
(305) 289-0025
www.pigeonkey.org

Pigeon Key becomes a "haunted island" on the third weekend in October. Come celebrate the sunset as you wait for the ghosts and goblins to make their appearances after dark. Lots of food and fun for the whole family, plus no admission charge.

Fantasy Fest
Various Key West sites
(305) 296–0202

This is Key West's biggest party of the year—a citywide celebration similar to Mardi Gras in New Orleans (see our Close-up in this chapter).

Goombay Festival
Petronia Street
Key West, FL
(305) 293–8305

Designed to showcase the cultural customs of the city's Bahamian community through food, music, and crafts, this grassroots affair has grown to include African, Filipino, and Latin traditions, too. Food booths dish up typical festival fare such as gyros, sausages, peppers, and Thai selections, but tucked among them are the treasures of this event: Jamaican-jerk chicken and pork, Bahamian cracked conch, conch salad, fried fish, and pigeon

peas and rice, all highly seasoned. Dance in the streets to the music of African and steel drummers or calypso bands. Stop by the simulated Nassau straw market to see straw hats and fruit baskets being woven.

The festival stretches from the corner of Petronia at Duval down to Emma Street and now encompasses many of the streets that make up a good share of the neighborhood known as Bahama Village. Held the first weekend of Fantasy Fest (see our Close-Up in this chapter), Goombay sets the stage for an even wider segment of society to flaunt their heritage. There is no admission charge.

Key West Theatre Festival
Various Key West sites
(305) 295–9278

Emerging playwrights rarely are offered the chance to see their work produced, but the Key West Theatre Festival provides one such opportunity. Throughout the year, members of the nonprofit organization, Theatre Key West, receive hundreds of scripts. For this 10-day festival, they and more than 100 community members pool their talents to produce

Hemingway wannabes get fired up for the annual look-alike contest at Sloppy Joe's Bar in Key West.
PHOTO: JANET WARE

about five of them. The festival features script readings, seminars on writing and acting, and public presentations in theaters throughout the islands (see our Arts and Culture chapter).

Events are priced individually and take place at a variety of locations. The Key West Theatre Festival is typically held during the first two weeks of October.

November

Island Jubilee
Harry Harris Park
MM 92.5 Oceanside
Tavernier, FL
(305) 451-1414

This two-day festival has been voted best of the Upper Keys. Held in conjunction with the Miss Island Jubilee Pageant, the Island Jubilee Talent Quest, and the Island Jubilee Cook-Off, the festival features arts-and-crafts displays and food booths, games for kids, and local entertainment performed by professional bands and talent quest winners. The cook-off culminates in prizes for the best recipes in the categories of professional, amateur, and haute cuisine entrees, appetizers, and desserts. Even if you do not enter the contest, you can take part in a post-judging, public tasting. Admission

costs $3 (free for children younger than 12). Food, beverages, rides, and games require additional fees.

George Bush/Cheeca Lodge
Bonefish Tournament
MM 82 Oceanside
Islamorada, FL
(305) 664-4651
www.cheeca.com

Former president George H.W. Bush himself participates in this, the most prestigious of all our tournaments. All bonefish must be released. Winners are awarded trophies. See our Fishing chapter for details.

Mercury Cheeca/Redbone Tournament
Islamorada, FL
(305) 664-2002
www.redbone.org

Third in the Celebrity Tournament Series is the Redbone, the competitive search for bonefish and redfish. Proceeds in this tournament also benefit the Cystic Fibrosis Foundation. For more information, check out our Fishing chapter or contact Gary Ellis at the number listed above.

Sky Dive Marathon
Marathon Airport
MM 52 Bayside
Marathon, FL
(305) 743-5417

More than 150 skydivers from throughout the United States participate in this two-day event, typically held in November on the grounds of the Marathon Airport. Weekend activities include skydiving demonstrations and an air show. There is no admission fee. Food and beverages are available for purchase.

Cuban American Heritage Festival
Various locations around Key West
(305) 295-9665

With so many Key West residents claiming Cuban roots, this was an event just waiting to happen. Launched in 1999, this now-annual, five-day festival celebrates Key West's Cuban heritage. Events include a street fair, two-day fishing tournament, cigar dinners, guided tours highlighting Key West links to its nearest neighbor, salsa bands, and a domino tournament. Perhaps the highlight, however, is a coast-to-coast conga line stretching down Duval Street from the Atlantic to the Gulf. Everyone—Cuban or otherwise—is invited to participate.

On the more serious side, a three-day symposium at San Carlos Institute, 516 Duval St., examines Cuba, then and now. Most festival events, including the symposium, are free.

Offshore Power Boat Race Week
Waters off Key West
(305) 296–6166

Just as Key West begins to recover from Fantasy Fest, the big boats roar into town to compete in a week's worth of offshore races that culminate in the naming of the world's champ. These are no little, put-put motorboats; they are high-performance ocean racers costing more than $1 million each and boasting speeds of 125 to 150 miles per hour. Close to 50,000 fans line the waterfront to view the competition, which generally takes place the second week of November. There's no charge to watch, and the best viewing spots are along Mallory Square and at the harborside hotels—the Pier House, Ocean Key House, Hyatt, and Hilton. Even if you're not a particular fan of powerboats, these are something to see.

Cayo Carnival
East Martello Museum
3501 S. Roosevelt Boulevard
Key West, FL
(305) 294–3100

This annual party to benefit Reef Relief is like a mini Taste of Key West. Your ticket (discounted if purchased in advance) entitles you to dance the night away to more than half a dozen local bands and sample the food and drink offered by some of Key West's finest restaurants. The party always takes place on the Saturday night of the weekend before Thanksgiving in the gardens at East Martello Museum; for many Key Westers, Cayo Carnival marks the start of the holiday season.

Parking on-site is limited, but free transportation is available from several locations around town, including the Key West Welcome Center, Key West High School, and Reef Relief.

December

Christmas Boat Parade
Bayside
Key Largo, FL
(305) 664–2266

Deck the boats with boughs of holly . . . Come watch a festive parade of between 30 and 50 lighted boats glow its way through Blackwater Sound. Prizes are awarded in various categories. At recent events, we've spotted Santa Claus catching a sailfish and Frosty the Snowman waterskiing. As with the Fourth of July Fireworks, the best coastal viewing locations are the Caribbean Club, Señor Frijoles, Sundowners, and Marriott Key Largo Bay Beach Resort. Some of these facilities host barbecues with live entertainment. Admission is free, but you must be a patron at any of these facilities to enjoy the view.

Fantasy Fest

Kookier than Carnival and merrier than Mardi Gras, Fantasy Fest is Key West's own decadent decibel of dreamy delight.

Fantasy Fest was originally conceived as a way to boost tourism in an otherwise soft season. It succeeded—and how! Today, more than two decades after its conception, this event more than doubles the island's population for one week in October, culminating with the arrival of some 70,000 revelers on Duval Street for the Saturday night parade.

Fantasy Fest is a nine-day adult Halloween celebration that commences on a Friday night with the Royal Coronation Ball, where the King and Queen of Fantasy Fest are crowned. The competition is open to all, and campaigning for the titles begins as early as late August. The winners are the ones who "buy" the most votes (translation: They raise the most money for AIDS Help Inc.). The closer it gets to Fantasy Fest, the fiercer the competition becomes and the more creative the candidates must become at finding sponsors and venues for their fund-raising efforts.

Contributions are accepted right up to the last minute when the final tally takes place at the Coronation Ball. The man and woman—or man and man-in-drag—are dubbed "royalty" only after emerging from a field of entrants whose votes have been bought and sold and bought and sold all over again. The King and Queen receive regal robes, crowns, and scepters and preside over all official Fantasy Fest events. While it's considered quite a coup to be named King or Queen, the real winners in all of this are the people served by AIDS Help Inc.

The competition doesn't end with the race for King and Queen. It continues over the weekend as captains seek the winner's cup in the Fantasy Yacht Race's Victory at Sea. On Masked Monday, fines are imposed on anyone (including any unsuspecting tourist) who does not comply with the loony law of the land: You must be masked to meander Duval Street, or the Mask Rangers will make an example of you.

Each year, Fantasy Fest features a new theme, which is emblazoned on posters and T-shirts promoting the events—all of which are for sale, of course. In keeping with Key West's penchant for parties, a poster-signing celebration is held on Masked Monday. The following night, you can enjoy a preview of some courageous/outrageous costumes at the Masked Madness and Headdress Ball. Then on Wednesday, be sure to enter your pet (and yourself) in the Pet Masquerade and Parade. No species is excluded.

At Fantasy Fest, designers vie for the most beguiling masquerade creations.

PHOTO: FLORIDA KEYS & KEY WEST TDC

Key Colony Beach Boat Parade
MM 53.5 Oceanside
Key Colony Beach, FL
(305) 289–1212

A more intimate, equally spectacular version of the Key Largo boat parade, this one is held along the landmark canals of Key Colony Beach. Admission is free.

Boot Key Harbor Christmas Boat Parade
Marathon, FL
(305) 743–4011

Sponsored by the Marathon Power Squadron, this parade begins at sundown on the first Saturday in December. The best public viewing areas include Faro Blanco Marina, Boot Key Harbor Bridge, and the Dockside Lounge on Sombrero Road, where judging ceremonies are held immediately following the parade.

Trees Around the World
Marathon Garden Club
MM 50 Bayside
Marathon, FL
(305) 743–4971

This annual display by the Marathon Garden Club features more than a dozen Christmas trees, each decorated in the traditional style of a different country. Expect to pay an admission fee.

Christmas by the Sea
Various Key West sites
(305) 292–9520

Lighted boat parades are common throughout our islands, and Key West is no exception. In addition to the magical entourage of skiffs, schooners, and cruisers, viewers may enjoy the pre-parade sunset activities at Mallory Square. The boat parade begins at Schooner Wharf Bar at the foot of William Street, but you can get the best view from Mallory Square and the pier beside the Hilton Resort and Marina. The boat parade is typically held on the third Saturday in December. Participation is free, but call Schooner Wharf (305-292-9520) to reserve your spot.

Christmas by the Sea also includes a traditional land parade, complete with floats, marching bands, and Santa Claus riding atop a fire truck. Unlike most parades in Key West, which begin and end on Duval Street, the route for this one follows Truman Avenue (U.S. Highway 1) instead. The Christmas street parade is sponsored by the city of Key West and is usually scheduled for the first Saturday night in December.

On the first weekend in December, the Key West Historic Seaport becomes a pirate stronghold. Events include tall ship sea battles, sunset pirate sails, a living history re-enactment, and nonstop entertainment.

Other Christmas events in Key West include the annual Christmas concert at St. Paul's Episcopal Church, 401 Duval Street, on the Sunday night immediately preceding Christmas, and the lighting of the nation's southernmost Christmas tree on the first Saturday afternoon in December. The tree, and accompanying carolers, are carried by Conch Train from the Christmas tree lot at the old Harris School, 812 Southard Street, to the Southernmost Point at the foot of Whitehead.

New Year's Eve on Duval Street
Key West, FL
(305) 295–3230 (fireworks)
(305) 294–5717 (conch shell)
(305) 294–4737 (high heel)

Times Square has nothing on us when it comes to knowing how to ring in a new year. We close off the street and, in typical Key West style, party outdoors 'til the bars close down at 4 A.M. So come New Year's Eve, grab your hat and horn and head for Duval to watch the conch shell drop from the top of Sloppy Joe's Bar at the stroke of midnight (or the red high heel at Bourbon Street Pub). Just don't wear your best silks and satins for this celebration because it will be raining champagne for sure! Round out your New Year's revelry with an "ooh" and an "ah" as you watch the fireworks explode over Key West Harbor.

Arts and Culture

Creative juices flow freely in the Florida Keys. Is it the sunshine? Or maybe the profusion of riotous colors everywhere you look? Perhaps our pervasive nothing-is-impossible, sky's-the-limit attitude is a contributing factor. Or maybe it's the fact that when you're in the Keys, you take the time to smell the bougainvillea.

Key West is the cultural center of the Florida Keys. This scintillating port has long attracted free spirits and adventurers—wreckers, sailors, spongers, shrimpers, and pirates—who played an enormous role in Key West's settlement and development. An enigmatic quality inherent in the essence of Key West draws fertile minds and searching souls to its inner sanctum like moths to a flame. From Ernest Hemingway to earnestly trying, Key West has hosted for a time the famous, the infamous, and the obscure.

Join us for an Insiders' look at the arts, from Key Largo to Key West, some traditional, others not so. Enjoy our music, theater, and dance while you are here and tour our myriad galleries. Or, if your timing is right, catch an arts festival, literary seminar, or theater gala for a creative night out. Be sure to check our Annual Events chapter for descriptions of special arts festivals and events.

Arts Organizations

The Monroe Council of the Arts Corp. is considered the official arts organization of the Florida Keys. Regional organizations offer members the opportunity to network and showcase their talents. Arts organizations are organized alphabetically.

Florida Keys Art Guild
P.O. Box 501382
Marathon, FL
(305) 743–7577

Anyone interested in the arts is invited to attend the monthly meetings of the Florida Keys Art Guild, where speakers and technique demonstrations bring the world of the arts to life. The group meets the second Tuesday of the month at the Faro Blanco Conference Center, 15th Street, Marathon. Members of the guild are artists in a variety of media as well as the creators of fine crafts. The group holds five shows between November and April at venues in Marathon.

> ## Insiders' Tip
> Anyone can borrow paperbacks from the Monroe County Library, no card required. Take out as many as you like and keep them as long as you like. Access is strictly on the honor system.

Lower Keys Artists Network
MM 30.5 Bayside
221 Key Deer Boulevard
Big Pine Key, FL
(305) 872–1828
wwww.theartistsinparadise.com

Formed in 1994, the Lower Keys Artists Network has about 50 members, and anyone in the Lower Keys interested in art is welcome to join. Meetings are held from December to May at Artists in Paradise, a

Creative juices flow here like no place on earth. PHOTO: VICTORIA SHEARER

co-op gallery in Big Pine. Members assist in judging student art competitions and work with the public library to provide arts and crafts programs for children. The group raises funds for art scholarships through corporate sponsorships. Lower Keys Artists Network also provides demonstrations and seminars on all forms of art, including watercolor, wood sculpture, food sculpture, stained glass, and etching.

Monroe Council of the Arts Corp.
5100 College Road
Key West, FL
(305) 294–4406
www.keysarts.com, www.keysarts.org

The Monroe Council of the Arts was incorporated in February 1997 and acts as the "chamber of commerce" of arts throughout the Keys. The Council's stated mission is "to connect artists and arts organizations with each other, with local audiences, and with the important tourism economy." They maintain an artist registry and two websites on which you'll find complete, year-round listings of the arts and entertainment events in the Keys. In addition, they get the cultural

word out to the public via a weekly calendar in five local newspapers and a quarterly brochure of events.

One of the Council's most prominent projects is the ongoing "Art in Public Places" program, in which the group displays the works of local artists in changing exhibits at such places as the Key West airport.

The Arts Council both writes and provides grants that benefit individual artists, arts organizations, schools, and libraries. It is supported by Monroe County and private donations and has several hundred members throughout the Florida Keys. A referral and support service, the Arts Council provides thousands of artists throughout the Keys with a means of political clout.

Purple Isle Art Guild
159 Harbor Drive
Tavernier, FL
(305) 853–0718

Purple Isle Art Guild encourages art in the Upper Keys and welcomes artists at all levels of experience, from beginning amateurs to professionals. The guild holds an annual multimedia exhibit that includes mixed-media presentations, photography, sculpture, and watercolor, oil, and acrylic paintings. Participation in the show is open to members only, each of whom are allowed to submit three pieces of their work. Purple Isle Art Guild meets the third Thursday of the month at Burton Memorial Methodist Church, MM 93, Tavernier. The meeting, open to the public, features a speaker and a demonstration.

Each year the guild offers a three- to four-day workshop taught by a well-known artist, such as watercolorist Janet Walsh. A paint-out group called the Brown Baggers meets every Wednesday and paints together, usually outdoors, sharing ideas and expertise. Membership in the Purple Isle Art Guild includes a monthly newsletter and discount excursions to Miami museums and art shows such as the Coconut Grove Art Festival.

South Florida Center for the Arts
(305) 453-4224

After Hurricane Andrew tore through South Miami and Dade County in 1992, the South Dade Center for the Arts moved to Key Largo and established itself as the South Florida Center for the Arts (SFCA). A private, nonprofit organization, SFCA provides a community concert series and some years offers jazz and chamber music programs as well as concerts for children.

Local fund-raisers support Arts for Youth, which encourages young audiences to participate in the arts. Members also provide workshops, plays, and arts programs in local schools. Between its arts and concert association members, this organization has approximately 350 members, many of whom reside in the Upper Keys.

Performing Arts

Theater

Tickets range in price from $15 to $40, depending upon the theater and production.

Insiders' Tip

The theaters in Key West are small and tickets sell out quickly, but do check with the box office. A few single seats may be available at the last minute.

Key Players
(305) 453-0997

Established in 1979, the Key Players community group was the dream of former Key Largo School principal Ed Caputo, who was interested in the arts and influential in getting a group of friends together to produce plays. The first production of Caputo and friends was *Curse You, Jack Dalton*, an old-fashioned melodrama. Soon after, the group formed the nonprofit corporation, Key Players, whose membership has since grown from 30 to nearly 100. The group puts on three productions annually, in the fall, winter, and spring. The group also produces and directs area school-age children in a Key Players Kids production each year.

Toward summer's end, Key Players holds an open house, a free play, or musical review to express appreciation to the community for its support throughout the year. Shows are held in local school auditoriums. All community members are welcome to audition for productions and to join the Key Players. Members often wear a variety of hats, including set and costume design and publicity. A seven-member board of directors handles financing.

Marathon Community Theatre
MM 50 Oceanside
Marathon, FL
(305) 743-0994

Providing topnotch live theatrical entertainment to locals and visitors for decades, the Marathon Community Theatre annually stages three productions, such as *Educating Rita, Ravenscroft,* and *Applause!,* which each run Thursdays through Saturdays for a month. Productions utilize full sets and full costuming, and actors hail from all over the Keys, from Key Largo to Key West. The group also hosts other productions, ranging from art shows and concerts to the Lovewell Foundation's summer theatre program for children.

Red Barn Theatre
319 Duval Street (rear)
Key West, FL
(305) 296–9911
www.redbarntheatre.com

Quaint and charming, the restored carriage house that houses the Red Barn Theatre has stood in the shadows of one of Key West's oldest houses, now the Key West Women's Club, for more than 50 years. Up from its humble beginnings as an animal stable, the building hosted the Key West Community Players for a time and also was the venue for puppet shows and piano concerts. Lovingly restored in 1980, the 88-seat structure shines with professional regional theater at its finest. And because of its size and layout, there isn't a bad seat in the house.

The Red Barn Theatre does five or six shows each year, including original comedies, musicals, and dramas by published writers. Its season runs from late November through June. Past productions have included *I Love You You're Perfect, Now Change, Down Mt. Morgan, The Vagina Monologues,* and *The Bathroom Plays* by Key West's own, the late Shel Silverstein. Full sets, costumes, and orchestrated scores are featured.

Tennessee Williams Fine Arts Center
5901 W. College Road
Stock Island, FL
(305) 296–1520
www.keywesttheater.org

The Tennessee Williams Fine Arts Center (TWFAC) opened in January 1980 on the campus of Florida Keys Community College with the world premiere of Tennessee Williams' unpublished play, *Will Mr. Merriwether Return From Memphis?* Named after one of Key West's most illustrious writers, this 478-seat, air-conditioned theater features a thrust stage extending 8 feet in front of the curtain line, a fly system, and a state-of-the-art lighting and sound system.

The Tennessee Williams Fine Arts Center produces a full season of dance, theater, chamber music, and shows by nationally known performing artists. It is also home to the Key West Symphony Orchestra (see separate listing later in this chapter). In-house productions involve amateur actors from the community and feature students working toward associate of science degrees in acting and theater production. Professional touring companies bring a wave of nationally and internationally recognized artists to the Florida Keys. The St. Petersburg Ballet of Russia has appeared here, as have the Irish Rovers and singer Cleo Laine with Johnny Dankworth. Chamber music concerts are sprinkled throughout the copious performance calendar of the Tennessee Williams Fine Arts Center, which runs from late November through April.

Most of the productions are held in the evening, but some events offer matinees on weekends as well. The Florida Keys Community College Chorus, which is coed, performs here three times each year, including early December and mid- to late March. (The chorus also offers a concert under the stars at Fort Zachary Taylor Historical Site in April.)

Waterfront Playhouse
Mallory Square
Key West, FL
(305) 294–5015

Community theater at its finest shines from an unlikely thespian arena on the waterfront. Once the site of Porter's warehouse, the physical structure served as an icehouse in the 1880s, storing blocks of ice cut from New England ponds and brought to Key West as ships' ballast. The Waterfront Playhouse restored the old warehouse into the present theater, infusing the crumbly stone walls with enduring creativity and talent.

The Waterfront Playhouse, dedicated to expanding knowledge of dramatic works to the general public, presents a variety of musicals, comedies, dramas, and mysteries each season. Past productions have included *The Pinchpenny Phantom of the Opera, The Sunshine Boys, Six Degrees of Separation,* and Terrence McNally's *Lips Together, Teeth Apart.* The community thespians also offer a children's theater workshop in the summer and other participatory theater experiences to Key West school children throughout the year.

The performance season is from November through April.

Participatory Theater

Theatre des Seances
Porter Mansion
429 Caroline Street
Key West, FL
(305) 292–2040
www.historichaunting.com

You say you don't believe in ghosts? This re-creation of a turn-of-the-century seance might just change your mind. The adventure begins at 7 and 9 P.M. each night in the sitting room of the old Porter Mansion, one of Key West's oldest houses, at the corner of Duval and Caroline Streets. First, you'll learn about some of this city's more bizarre tales of house hauntings and grave robbers, then you'll take a few psychic tests to be sure you and your companions on this journey are prepared to meet the spirits.

Once your host determines that all in your group are receptive, you'll be ushered into the seance parlor, where you'll take your seat around a large, antique dining room table for the main event. Once the candles are extinguished, the real fun begins. Every presentation is unique, and success depends on the energy and focus of the group. Past groups are said to have experienced some strange, not easily explained phenomena. It's a little scary, but a lot of fun; a real Key West experience for the not so faint of heart.

Reservations are required. Book early because seances are limited to 13 participants per interactive production.

Cinema

Key West Film Society
P.O. Box 1283
Key West, FL 33040
(305) 294–5857
www.keywestfilm.org

Key West has had a long and colorful history with film. More than 20 feature films and television series have been shot here. Perhaps that is one reason why local audiences hunger for cinematic fare that is a cut above what is generally available at traditional theatrical venues like Regal Cinemas (see our Recreation chapter).

The Key West Film Society (KWFS) was formed in 1999 to address that hunger. The Society's goal is to offer the most interesting, provocative, and artistic of the available independent, foreign, and alternative films. Some become available to the Society only after they have exhausted their theatrical lives and are transferred to 16-mm format; others are made available sooner, as promotional screenings from the studio's publicity department. In either case, the KWFS has been able to bring films to Key West audiences that they might otherwise not have seen. Past offerings have included the award-winning *Life Is Beautiful, Requiem for a Dream, Shadow of the Vampire, Angela's Ashes,* and *Magnolia.*

The films are generally shown on Sundays at 8 P.M. at San Carlos Institute, 516 Duval Street. Tickets are $5 for KWFS members, $8 for nonmembers. Check the website for membership information and a schedule of coming attractions.

Music

The Middle Keys Concert Association, Inc.
Every year since 1969, the Middle Keys Concert Association has brought live

concert artists to the Florida Keys for the cultural enrichment of our residents and visitors. Four to six concerts are held annually at Marathon venues, quite often San Pablo Catholic Church (MM 53.5 Oceanside). A well-balanced season of offerings includes classical and semiclassical music, encompassing voice, strings, brass, and organ.

You may purchase a subscription to all concerts or buy tickets at the door. Children are admitted for free. Pick up a current brochure at the Marathon Chamber of Commerce, MM 53.5 Bayside, (305) 743–5417 or (800) 262–7284.

Key West Symphony Orchestra
1119 Varela Street
Key West, FL
(305) 292–1774

On a laid-back island like Key West, where Duval Street rocks until 4 A.M. with the beat of calypso and socca, blues and Buffett wannabes, you might not expect to find many hard-core classical music fans. But they are here all right. And in enough numbers, it seems, to support a symphony orchestra.

Thanks to the enthusiasm, not to mention the untiring fundraising efforts, of a small but dedicated corps of classical music fans, the Key West Symphony Orchestra made its debut in fall 1998. Under the musical direction of native Key Wester Sebrina Maria Alfonso, the orchestra plays to standing room only at the Tennessee Williams Fine Arts Center on three weekends between November and April. The critically acclaimed symphony consists of more than 40 classical musicians, many of whom are from major metropolitan symphonies throughout the U.S., who come together to perform under the baton of conductor Alfonso. In addition to a regular concert series, selected members of the orchestra also participate in community outreach programs, taking their music directly into the Monroe County Schools and participating in question-and-answer sessions at a variety of fundraising events.

Performances by the Key West Symphony Orchestra take place on consecutive Friday and Saturday evenings in November, February, and April at the Tennessee Williams Fine Arts Center on the campus of Florida Keys Community College. Tickets are generally priced at around $35 per concert and may be purchased at the TWFAC box office.

Art Galleries

Unique galleries dot the Florida Keys, often tucked amid commercial shops in a strip mall or gracing a freestanding building off the beaten track. In Key West, galleries abound along Duval Street, and you'll also find small lofts and garrets secreted off the beaten track down narrow lanes. Come along for a gallery crawl through the high spots of the Florida Keys' art scene, from Key Largo to Key West. The Florida Keys section is organized by descending mile marker. Listings are alphabetical in the Key West section.

The Florida Keys

The Gallery at Kona Kai
MM 97.8 Bayside
Key Largo, FL
(305) 852–7200, (800) 365–7829
www.konakairesort.com

The Gallery at Kona Kai secrets away a small yet exquisite changing exhibit of fine art treasures. The gallery showcases prominent South Florida artists such as Clyde Butcher, who is known for his hauntingly surreal black-and-white photography of the Everglades and Big Cypress National Preserve. Also featured are Gregory Sobran, a watercolorist who chronicles quintessential scenes of the Keys in a spectrum of pastel hues; John David Hawver, who captures the ebb and flow of Keys' waters in a symbiosis of line and color; and Bari Cook, who uses strong color and bold style in her paintings of flora and South Florida people.

In 2000, Kona Kai Gallery partnered with a Paris gallery, so they now also represent some fine contemporary French artists whose works in oils and bronze sculptures feature interpretations of flower fields of the French countryside, landscapes of Provence, and depictions of the French people.

Rain Barrel Village of Artists and Craftspeople
MM 86.7 Bayside
Islamorada, FL
(305) 852-3084

The Rain Barrel Village of Artists and Craftspeople is a garden complex of creativity. The 2000-square-foot front galley, Rum River Gallery, is owned and operated by Carol Cutshall, Rain Barrel's founder and proprietor for more than 20 years. At the entrance to the "village," this mixed media galley features an array of paintings, sculpture, woodwork, and decorative glass, including delicate blown creations by Michael Robinson. More than 100 artists from all over the United States are represented here. You'll find an eclectic assortment of art and craft creations, including whimsical ceramics and an expansive wind chime collection.

Joan Purcell's Sunshine Art Gallery (305-852-3960) features the etcher/lithographer's oil paintings of fanciful tropical marine life, which she creates on slabs of ancient coral. Two coats of resin make the coral creations shimmer like the sea.

The resident potter at Rain Barrel is Nancy Jefferson of Jefferson Clay Creations (305-852-6911). She handcrafts creative vases and dinnerware in the shape of our Keys tropical fish and also works in the medium of raku. Her crystalline-glazed vases are striking. Jefferson Clay Creations also offers classes.

The commanding sculptures of Bill Campbell, Leon Kula, and Fernando Rodriguez dominate the floor space of the Rain Barrel Sculpture Gallery (305-852-8935). From fired copper to winged driftwood sculptures, talent oozes from every corner of the expansive room.

Also with galleries in Rain Barrel are artists Dan Lawler and John David

Hawver (305-664-8037), and a silk flower studio called Silk Flower Creations (305-853-5123), where you can find one-of-a-kind custom silk arrangements. At Stained Glass of the Florida Keys (305-852-1174), Marlen Mesa specializes in custom-designed stained glass art, from decorative boxes to intricate windows. She also gives classes teaching her craft.

Jeweler Dwayne King works on his designs right on the premises of King's Treasure Jewelry (305-852-9797). You'll also find shipwreck coin jewelry as well as a fascinating selection of silver charms. And if you feel like a bite to eat, stop in at Garden Cafe (see listing in our Seafood Markets and Specialty Foods chapter).

Rain Barrel Village of Artists and Craftspeople is open seven days a week from 9 A.M. to 5 P.M.

Bluewater Potters
MM 86.7 Oceanside, at Treasure Village
Islamorada, FL
(305) 853-0616

High-fire stoneware and functional pottery set the theme for Bluewater Potters. Husband-and-wife owners, Corky and Kim Wagner, demonstrate their work right on the premises. The couple creates collaborative pieces: He manages the throwing, and she does the hand-building. The Wagner's inventory includes everything from spoon rests to full dinnerware and architectural pieces. Some work is brought in by outside artists. Among the pieces offered are wine goblets and baking dishes. All glazes are oven, microwave, and dishwasher safe. Custom dinnerware is a specialty of the Wagners.

Art Lovers Inc.
MM 86.7 Oceanside, at Treasure Village
Islamorada, FL
(305) 852–1120
www.artloversusa.com

More than 50 artists and sculptors from the Keys, South Florida, and other parts of the United States are represented at Art Lovers. The creations span all media. Most of the originals and signed lithographs, such as those by locally known artists Jeannine Bean and Kathleen Denis, depict tropical subjects. Don Ray, Dan Goad, Sandy Kay, Robert Pierce, and others are also featured.

Art Lovers' sculpture gallery showcases the work of the renowned Kendall VanSant. Works by a talented stable of other artists—in the media of wood, bronze, copper, and stone—reflect Florida Keys history and wildlife. Art Lovers also sells a wide selection of artists' supplies.

Redbone Art Gallery
MM 82 Oceanside
200 Industrial Drive
Islamorada, FL
(305) 664–2002
www.redbone.org

The Ellis family of Islamorada began this nonprofit organization as a means of raising funds for research for cystic fibrosis, a disease that afflicts their daughter. Each year the Ellises hold a trilogy of celebrity backcountry fishing tournaments in order to raise these funds (see the Tournaments section of our Fishing chapter), and their art gallery defrays the cost of office expenses.

The gallery sports a variety of saltwater and marine art and sculptures from local artists and others noted for their works related to sport fishing, such as Don Ray, Diane Peebles, James Harris, Jeanne Dobie, and C. D. Clarke. Redbone Art Gallery exclusively showcases the original watercolors of Chet Reneson in South Florida.

The Gallery at Morada Bay
MM 81.6 Bayside
Islamorada, FL
(305) 664–3650

Upscale crafts bedazzle the browser here at this enticing gallery, situated on the lushly landscaped grounds of the restaurant Morada Bay. Offered here is a selection of the metal hollowware plates and candlesticks of Thomas Markusen, whose work graces the White House. You'll also find handcrafted paper shades by Galbraith & Paul and Correia glass, as well as blown creations from Rogers Glassworks and brightly colored paperweights and perfume bottles by a variety of American artists. The Gallery also features porcelain tableware by Dan Levy as well as sculptured glass by artists Kaleb Nichols and Val Surjah.

Wyland Gallery
MM 80.9 Oceanside
Islamorada, FL
(305) 517–2625, (888) 323–9797
www.wyland.com

What more fitting location for Wyland's new gallery than Islamorada, "Sportfishing Capital of the World." Situated in the Galleria, this dramatically striking gallery showcases Wyland's fine art and collectibles, testament to his commitment to saving our oceans and creatures dwelling within. (You can see one of Wyland's famous whaling wall murals adorning the Kmart building in Marathon.) The works of other artists are also displayed. Wyland Gallery is closed Mondays and Tuesdays.

Bougainvillea House Gallery
MM 53.5 Bayside
Marathon, FL
(305) 743–0808

A varied group of talented Marathon artists showcase their works at the Bougainvillea House Gallery, a charming cooperative gallery. Fronted by an enormous hot-pink bougainvillea "tree" that intertwines through the roof of the wooden front porch, Bougainvillea House Gallery features reasonably priced prints, original watercolors, acrylics, mixed media, sculpture, decorative baskets, hand-sculpted glass, jewelry, and ceramics by local artists.

Kennedy Studios
MM 48 Oceanside
Marathon, FL
(305) 743–2040, (877) 539–2787
www.flkeysart.com

Kennedy Studios frames the Keys, thanks to the steady, creative hand of owner Diane Busch. Custom framing of any and all objets d'art is the specialty of this studio, which resembles the chain—established by watercolorist Robert and oil painter Michele Kennedy—in name only. Works by both Kennedys are included in the collection here, including limited edition prints of Pigeon Key, the Seven-Mile Grill, and the Faro Blanco lighthouse. Also displayed are original works by such local artists as Lynn Voit, Eileen Seitz, Christi Mathews, Millard Wells (A.W.S.), and wildlife artist Dan "Spider" Warren.

In addition to custom framing, Kennedy Studios provides creative matting for needle arts and shadow boxes. The studio also does museum and conservation framing. Folks come back year after year just to hear Busch's Quaker parrot, Sonny, imitate her infectious laughter and do its Wheel-of-Fortune routine.

Artists in Paradise
MM 30.5 Bayside
221 Key Deer Boulevard
Big Pine Key, FL
(305) 872–1828
www.theartistsinparadise.com

Artists in Paradise is a cooperative gallery in Big Pine run by those artists from the Lower Keys Artists Network who use the gallery to display their work (see the listing in this chapter). More than thirty artists presently show works done in a variety of media: sculpture, oils, watercolors, acrylic, pen and ink, pottery, copper, and stained glass. The gallery is open from 10 A.M. to 6 P.M. daily.

Key West

Blue Dolphin Gallery
914 Duval Street
Key West, FL
(305) 294–0071

This inviting little shop is filled with hand-cut metal sculptures by Haitian artists that will serve as delightful reminders of your Keys vacation when you display them back home. Also, look for Trip Harrison's scenes of Key West as well as the enticing fish prints and sculptures by Don Ray.

Florida Keys Community College
5901 W. College Road
Stock Island, FL
(305) 296–9081
www.firn.edu/fkcc

Florida Keys Community College stages four art shows a year in the Library Gallery. Invitational shows are held in October and February, and the Florida Artist series is showcased in January and February. Student work is exhibited during the month of April.

The Gallery on Greene
606 Greene Street
Key West, FL
(305) 294–1669
www.galleryongreene.com

Think you can't afford fine art? Think again. This gallery prides itself on displaying original art priced for every pocketbook—from $10 to $25,000! Among the

Insiders' Tip
The works of local artists are displayed at the Key West airport on a rotating basis. Even if you aren't flying, stop by for the cultural experience.

offerings here are works by former part-time Key West resident the late Jeff Mac-Nelly (he drew the cartoon strip "Shoe"), critically-acclaimed, abstract-expressionist Kim Northrup, and Henry La Cagnina, the last survivor of 12 artists brought to Key West in the 1930s by the WPA. This gallery also supports working artists. You can usually expect to find at least one artist-in-residence, bent over his or her work, in a corner of the gallery.

Gamefish Gallery and Outfitters
608 Greene Street
Key West, FL
(305) 294–7111

This gallery offers primarily prints and artwork of big game fish and wildlife. A souvenir from here is perfect for the fishing aficionado or the sports enthusiast. Choose from large framed original oil paintings, small prints, or sports-themed gear, including hats, shirts, belts, and shoes. Shipping is available.

Gingerbread Square Gallery
1207 Duval Street
Key West, FL
(305) 296–8900
www.gingerbreadsquaregallery.com

Billed as Key West's oldest private art gallery, established in 1974, Gingerbread Square Gallery on upper Duval features sculptures, art glass, one-person shows, and ongoing presentations of the highly acclaimed works of Key West's favorite artists. Sal Salinero's oils depict the treasures of the rain forest. John Kiraly's fanciful paintings capture the spirit of locales real and imagined, and George Carey's photo-realistic acrylics depict Key West, then and now.

Glass Reunions
825 Duval Street
Key West, FL
(305) 294–1720

Glass is the business here, and you can get it in almost any form or color imaginable. Lamps, vases, and mirror wall hangings all showcase the talents of the various artists. For the traditionalist, a wide selection of stained-glass art is available.

Guild Hall Gallery
614 Duval Street
Key West, FL
(305) 296–6076

More than 20 local artists display their work here, presented in a vast array of mediums. Most of the pieces focus on island life, with a definite Bahamian and Caribbean influence thrown in. Head upstairs for more unusual, and larger, works of art. This is Key West's original artists' co-op.

Haitian Art Company
600 Frances Street
Key West, FL
(305) 296–8932
www.haitian-arts-co.com

Bold, wild colors and primitive designs mark the artistic offerings of Haiti, displayed in the multiple rooms of Haitian Art Company. The intricate paisley-style designs often weave an image of a serpent or wild animal within the overall picture. The work of Haiti is a study of form and color not readily encountered in this country. All pieces are originals. This gallery is tucked in a residential neighborhood at the corner of Frances and Southard Streets, way off Duval, but it's definitely worth the walk.

Hands On
1206 Duval Street
Key West, FL
(305) 296–7399

The loom in the front of this attractive shop says it all. Here you will find the ever-changing, always-exquisite creations of owner Ellen Steiniger. Her hand-woven scarves, jackets, and shawls are as beautiful to see as they are enjoyable to wear. Shop here, too, for handcrafted earrings, bracelets, and beads to accessorize your wearable art as well as an array of other fine American-made crafts.

Restored to its original grandeur, Key West's Custom House reopened in 1999 as an art and history museum of national stature. PHOTO: JANET WARE

Harrison Gallery
825 White Street
Key West, FL
(305) 294–0609

Sculptor Helen Harrison and her husband Ben, a musician and author, have operated this charming gallery since 1986. In addition to Helen's own work, ever-changing exhibitions highlight local artists. Open daily, but please ring the bell.

Helio Gallery Store
814 Fleming Street
Key West, FL
(305) 294–7901
www.heliographics.com

The emphasis here is on wearable, functional art, all of which is produced locally. Hand-screened throw pillows, pottery, tapestries, glassware, botanical prints, and T-shirts celebrate a passion for the tropics. Much of what you see is one-of-a-kind, and many of the works on display are simply that—display. The artist-owners specialize in custom work specific to the individual client and since one of the three owners is always on-site, usually creating

her work, feel free to discuss your own particular needs. Shipping is available.

Island Arts
1128 Duval Street
Key West, FL
(305) 292–9909
www.island-arts.com

This co-op of local artists fashions itself after a Caribbean bazaar, and many of the items herein illuminate just how fertile the imagination can be. Welded sculptures created out of scrap iron, metal junk, old screws, and tools turn up as a rooster, ostrich, duck, or dinosaur. Paper Smash is sculpted recycled paper made into snakes, pelicans, fish, and manatees. You'll also find a potpourri of hand-painted tiles, stained-glass pieces, and ceramics, all with an island theme.

Joy Gallery
1124-B Duval Street
Key West, FL
(305) 296–3039

A little sign that hangs amid the surreal paintings of out-of-body experiences by

Lucie Bilodeau in the Joy Gallery reads: "Warning—The purchase of fine art is not necessarily a logical decision." Bilodeau's brooding pieces are joined by limited editions by Irma Quigley and Gretchen Williams.

Karen Laake Studios
421 Simonton Street
Key West, FL
(305) 296–0648

This tiny shop, located a block off Duval Street, is not only a gallery, it is a working studio. Meet the artist herself while you browse through her works that capture the essence of Key West in acrylics. Also on display are paintings by guest artists from Key West and the Bahamas.

Kennedy Gallery
1000 Duval Street
Key West, FL
(305) 296–0060
www.kennedystudios.net

This gallery of Kennedy originals deserves mention, for it should not be confused with the bevy of Kennedy Studios franchises that sell prints across the nation as well as down Duval Street a few blocks. The Kennedy Gallery, like its siblings in Provincetown, Boston, and Nassau, features originals by Michele Richard Kennedy, Robert Kennedy, and other celebrated artists from Key West and around the world.

Key West Art Center
301 Front Street
Key West, FL
(305) 294–1241

You can duck out of the teeming crowds of tourists at Mallory Square for a serene perusal of the pastels, watercolors, and oils of local Key West artists at this spacious two-story gallery. Catch your breath and see Key West from the locals' perspective.

Kokopelli Contemporary Gallery
824 Duval Street
Key West, FL
(305) 292–4144

If you'd rather hang your favorite art around your neck than on your walls, be sure to visit this gallery, where hand-crafted jewelry is the focus. You'll find everything from sterling silver and amethyst earrings to rings crafted from 14k gold and black opals. Most of the offerings are one-of-a-kind, and the artists hail from throughout the United States.

Lucky Street Gallery
1120 White Street
Key West, FL
(305) 294–3973

Contemporary fine art of the cutting-edge variety is the focus here. Sculptures by John Martini and the works of artists Roberta Marks, Susan Rodgers, Lincoln Perry, and others are featured. New shows are staged approximately every two weeks.

Mary O'Shea's Glass Garden
213 Simonton Street
Key West, FL
(305) 293–8822

The ancient Egyptians get credit for discovering glass fusion 5,000 years ago, but Mary O'Shea is the artist who brought it to Key West. Her gallery, opened in 1999, features a profusion of original and colorful sculpture, masks, bowls, plates, and jewelry—all made from fused glass and each taking three days to complete.

Each piece of glass must be cut and layered to form a double thickness, then melted in a kiln. The piece is then cooled for a day, melted again, transposed, and formed into the desired shape. The resulting pieces are not only beautiful, but are durable, dishwasher and microwave safe. Don't be afraid to touch and don't hesitate to ask Mary about custom designs.

Studio A
1210 Duval Street
Key West, FL
(305) 294–0005

To browse this gallery is to take a photographic journey of South Florida and beyond. Here you will find the exquisite works of renowned photographer Alan S. Maltz. You may be familiar with his work from his books *Key West Color* and *Miami City of Dreams*. Shop here for limited edition prints of these as well as other photographs that capture the essence of the Keys' natural beauty and unusual light.

Threelegged Dog Gallery
1102 White Street
Key West, FL
(305) 294-3535
www.threeleggeddoggallery.com

This artist-owned studio and gallery features original works by Rick Worth as well as exhibits by other local artists. Worth is perhaps best known for his "Conch Cruisers," cars painted with a variety of vibrant colors and designs. One of the more unusual vehicles is the mosaic VW Beetle with the three-legged dog on top. It is usually parked in front of this gallery.

The Wave Gallery
1205-B Truman Avenue
Key West, FL
(305) 296-7688

Barbara Grob is the owner of this way, way off-Duval Street gallery. You may not recognize her name, but chances are, you've seen her work around town—the steel gecko sculptures for which she is justly famous. She opened this tiny shop in April 2000 to display her own work as well as that of about a dozen other artists, including ceramist Corey Lewis, glass fuser Mary O'Shea, and Mark Weld, a water-color artist from New York. Most of the art for sale here is priced between $95 and $1000, but Grob hopes to eventually expand her offerings to include works priced as low as $15.

Wild Side Gallery
Clinton Square Market
291 Front Street
Key West, FL
(305) 296-7800

From carved wood walking sticks to ceramics, jewelry, and watercolors, all objets d'art in this interesting and afford-

Insiders' Tip

See our Annual Events chapter for information on special concerts and art shows throughout the Florida Keys.

able gallery depict some element of nature. Artists and craftspeople represented here are from all over the United States.

Wings of Imagination, The Butterfly Gallery
1108-C Duval Street
Key West, FL
(305) 296-2988, (800) 839-4647

The Butterfly Boutique
Clinton Square Market
291 Front Street
Key West, FL
(305) 296-2922, (800) 839-4647

Art really does imitate life in the case of these two galleries. Raised in butterfly farms and imported from the continents of South America, Africa, and Southeast Asia, the butterflies live out their 10-day life cycle and are then shipped to the Key West production studio, where they are arranged in geometric compositions and preserved in acrylic cases. Don't miss this fruition of Sam Trophia's childhood dream, capturing the everlasting beauty of the "flowers of the sky."

Woodenhead Gallery
907 Caroline Street (rear)
Key West, FL
(305) 294-3935

No truer words could be used to describe this unimposing gallery than those on the sign out front, which reads "Definitely not Duval." There's no glitz, no glamour, and no watercolors of gingerbread houses here, just nonconformist works reflecting real-life Key West by real-life starving

Art Behind Bars

Art doesn't always imitate life. Sometimes it can be used to reshape one.

That is the premise underlying Art Behind Bars, an unusual rehabilitation program for female inmates that originated at the Monroe County Detention Center on Stock Island and is now widely imitated elsewhere.

Art Behind Bars is the brainchild of Key West artist Lynne Vantriglia, who came up with the idea after visiting the jail as a volunteer for the state attorney's office. She realized that while the male inmates had plenty of opportunities for productive work and recreation, the females did not. A firm believer in the therapeutic value of art, Lynne created Art Behind Bars, a program she hoped would bring joy and purpose to the lives of incarcerated women.

Art Behind Bars gives female inmates with good conduct the opportunity to express themselves creatively while they learn new skills and develop a sense of community service. The inmates get together with Lynne and her corps of volunteers for two hours each week at the Detention Center to create their art—everything from hand-painted T-shirts and birdhouses to masks, quilts, Valentine cards, and Christmas ornaments.

When it comes to media and artistic expression, the ladies have free rein. Only three rules apply: all supplies must be returned to the shelves at the end of each session, floors and uniforms must be kept paint-free, and no one is allowed to duck out early to avoid cleaning up.

And what happens to the art that is created in these sessions? Why, it's for sale, of course. The paintings are displayed in galleries all around Key West. Works from Art Behind Bars often go on the auction block to raise funds for various charitable causes, too. And, now, in a joint venture with Jimmy Buffett's Margaritaville, the birdhouses and other painted wooden items are being sold in Margaritaville stores in Orlando, New Orleans, and Charleston. Some are also on permanent display in the Detention Center lobby, at the Monroe County Sheriff's headquarters, and at the Key West branch of the Monroe County Public Library.

The inmates realize no direct profit from the sale of their work. A share of the proceeds is pumped back into the program to purchase supplies. The rest goes directly to charity. Organizations like AIDS Help, Hospice/Visiting Nurses Association, Wesley House (childcare center), Habitat for Humanity, Toys for Tots, and SafePort, a drug rehabilitation community for women, have benefited from Art Behind Bars. The women have created two panels for the national AIDS quilt and hand-painted more than 700 T-shirts for needy kids.

Since its inception in June 1994, Art Behind Bars has earned kudos from criminal justice authorities and generated thousands of dollars for charity. Today, the program serves as a model for correctional institutions throughout Florida. Best of all, however, Art Behind Bars has accomplished exactly what Lynne Vantriglia hoped it would. The more than one thousand incarcerated women who have participated in Art Behind Bars leave the Monroe County Detention Center with higher self-esteem and a better-than-average chance of making it on the outside.

artists, most of whom hold day jobs just to make ends meet. The emphasis here is on art for art's sake. The shows are not juried, and the doors are wide open to artistic expression of all kinds. Special exhibits, like the annual Valentine's Day *Ars Eroticus* show, are sometimes controversial.

Wyland Galleries
102 Duval Street
(305) 294–5240, (888) 292–4998
719 Duval Street
(305) 292–9711, (888) 292–4998

The first East Coast display venues of Wyland, the world's leading marine life artist, these two Key West galleries display a wide range of the environmental artist's work. His world-renowned, life-size whaling wall murals, one of which adorns the Kmart building in Marathon and another the Waterfront Market building at the Key West Historic Seaport, reflect Wyland's unshakable commitment to saving the earth's oceans and thereby its marine creatures. Also displayed are several paintings from the "above and below" series, for which Wyland collaborated with other talented artists to create a scene looking beneath and above the sea concurrently.

Zbyszek Art Gallery
519 Fleming Street
Key West, FL
(305) 295–9085

Billed as the "home of the piano dog," this gallery features the works of Zbyszek and Tippi Koziol. Here you'll find paintings, toys, wood sculptures, painted furniture, and wearable art in vibrant colors and whimsical designs. This is not for every taste, but definitely fun to own and worth a look.

Shopping

Stretched along our 100 miles of Overseas Highway is every diversion imaginable for the serious (and not so serious) shopper. Scuba aficionados find nirvana here, reveling in state-of-the-gear offerings from our plethora of dive shops (see our Diving and Snorkeling chapter). Anglers, who may readily concede that you might be able to be too thin or too rich, staunchly maintain that you can never have too many fishing rods or an excess of tackle (see our Fishing chapter). And boaters, who all know that a vessel is really a floating hole into which you pour money, find a virtual smorgasbord of shopping options guaranteed to fertilize their needs exponentially (see our Boating chapter).

But what about the rest of us, free spirits who like to see the ocean through the rim of a glass, preferably while lying prone by the swimming pool in the shade of a coconut palm? We know we don't require much in the way of clothing here in the Keys' tropicality, just a suit (small and stringy), shoes (light and strappy), and a hat (woven and floppy), but we have pent up shopping desires, too.

So here is the ultimate road map to the shops. We describe our favorite shops in geographic order by mile marker, from Key Largo to Key West. Our Key West section is divided into four sections. Best of Duval is organized by numerical address, from upper Duval (oceanside) to lower Duval (gulfside), so you can stroll the street and take in all the shops. Off Duval, the not to be missed shops on surrounding streets, is organized in alphabetical order. Lastly, we give you information on noteworthy shops Way Off Duval and in New Town. Be sure to scope out our Arts and Culture chapter for descriptions of galleries selling creative works, many by local artists. And turn to our Seafood Markets and Specialty Foods chapter to find piscatory treasures and other palate pleasers.

Upper Keys

Divers Outlet
MM 106 Bayside
Key Largo, FL
(305) 451–0815, (800) 348–3872
www.DiversOutlet.com

For a virtual supermarket of dive gear at discount prices, stop at Divers Outlet. They advertise the "world's largest selection and lowest prices—guaranteed." Looks like the choice is up to you.

Island Smoke Shop
MM 103.5 Bayside
Pink Plaza
Key Largo, FL
(305) 453–4014, (800) 680–9701
www.islandsmokeshop.com

The Island Smoke Shop offers a full line of cigars, lighters, and accessories and has one of the largest selections of pipes in South Florida as well as some wonderful house blends of tobacco. The shop also exclusively sells El Originale cigars, voted best in the United States by both *Smoke* and *Cigar Aficionado* magazines. On Saturdays, Island Smoke Shop has live cigar-rolling demonstrations; the rollers come down from Miami. You can order by mail here.

The Gift House
MM 102.3 Oceanside
Key Largo, FL
(305) 451–0650
www.TheGiftHouseKeyLargo.com

Full of tropical treasures as well as the dessert and coffee bar for The Fish House next door (see our Restaurants chapter), The Gift House is loaded with hand-crafted gifts, gourmet mustards and sauces, garden sculptures, Keysy place-mats, and works by local artists. A brick path leads from the restaurant to this clever combo shop, where you'll surely be tempted by such creations as "chocolate nemesis," "carmel apple granny," or "torta tiramisu with kahlua."

The Sandal Factory
MM 102 Bayside
Key Largo, FL
(305) 453–9644

MM 82 Oceanside
Islamorada, FL
(305) 664–9700

These sandal outlets allow you to fit yourself. Pick from a copious sea of ladies' sandals—strappy, sport, and utilitarian. Men and children can be accommodated here, too. You won't find every style in every size, but you can choose from hundreds of designs.

Equipment Locker Sport & Bicycle
MM 101.4 Oceanside
Tradewinds Shopping Center
Key Largo, FL
(305) 453–0140

MM 53 Bayside
Marathon, FL
(305) 289–1670

You'll find a great selection of bicycles and related biking gear here as well as exercise equipment and the gamut of necessities for every sport from hoops, to weight lifting, to in-line skating. Top-brand athletic shoes line the walls.

Steve & Co.
MM 101.4 Oceanside
Tradewinds Shopping Center
Key Largo, FL
(305) 451–5646

Offering a wide selection of men and women's casualwear, Steve & Co. is the place to go if you need to dress up, Keys style. Look for racks and racks of tropical print shirts, de rigueur here for a night on the town. You'll also find top brands of shorts and knit shirts, including Kahala, Sportif, Weekenders, Rum Reggae, Hook & Tackle, and Tori Richard.

The Book Nook
MM 99.6 Oceanside, Waldorf Plaza
Key Largo
(305) 451–1468

If reading rates a spot in your Florida Keys vacation, The Book Nook packs a multitude of bestsellers, popular paper-backs, children's books, and specialty publications into a compact space. The shop, with friendly and helpful personnel, also carries national and international daily newspapers.

World Watersports
MM 99.6 Oceanside
Key Largo, FL
(305) 451–0118, (800) 243–8938
www.worldwatersports.com

A grand watersports emporium, World Watersports offers everything from men's, women's, and children's clothing—swim-suits, strappy dresses, shorts, shirts, and shoes—to dive gear, kayaks, boat towables, surfboards, wakeboards, snorkeling and scuba gear, underwater photography equipment, and videos and books about the fascinating undersea world. As their business card boasts, this is the place to come for "everything you need to get wet!"

Elsie's Kingdom
MM 99.5 Oceanside
Key Largo, FL
(305) 451–3772

Head to Elsie's if crafting is your passion. Bountiful supplies of beads, bangles, rib-bons, baskets, and fabric painting necessi-ties are just the beginning. You'll be able to fuel your imagination here for sure.

Arteffects
MM 98.5 Bayside
Key Largo, FL
(305) 852–5933

Almost like an outdoor mini-museum, Arteffects warrants a look-see. You'll see a changing rota of fascinating creatures that at any one time might include a concrete pig, cowpoke, bull, giraffe, camel, dolphin, mermaid, crane, cherub, elephant, even possibly a pharaoh or a selection of Buddhas. Arteffects features merchandise from Southeast Asia, Africa, and Central and South America.

Anthony's Women's Apparel
MM 98.2, in the median
Key Largo, FL
(305) 852–4515

MM 82 Bayside
Islamorada, FL
(305) 664–3530

MM 50.5 Bayside
Gulfside Village
Marathon, FL
(305) 743–5855

At Anthony's, you can expect to find a constantly changing array of reasonably priced, casual attire in petite, junior, and misses sizes, by such manufacturers as Liz Sport and Ocean Pacific. The shops offer a wide variety of swimsuits and cover-ups as well as a decent selection of lingerie and nightwear. Anthony's sales are not to be missed.

Island Feet and Fashion
MM 92 Bayside
Tavernier, FL
(305) 852–5691

Island Feet and Fashion decks out your tootsies in style with a wide selection of sandals, boat shoes, sneakers, sport sandals, and flip-flops. You'll also find top brands of sport clothing here as well as a selection of hats, handbags, and lingerie.

Bensons Camera
MM 90.2 Bayside
Tavernier, FL
(305) 852–0106, (305) 852–1902

You can't miss Bensons' screaming yellow building, bayside in Tavernier. Expect to find all the major brands of cameras, equipment, and supplies at Bensons, including Nikon, Cannon, Pentax, Olympus, and Leica. Bensons also sells Sony camcorders, televisions, and VCRs as well as binoculars and both video and still underwater photo equipment. The only lab in the Florida Keys that processes APS film, Bensons also will develop your 35 mm or 120 film in one hour. You can purchase either amateur or professional Kodak or Fuji film here.

Cover to Cover Books
MM 90.1 Oceanside
Tavernier, FL
(305) 852–1415

You can lose yourself for hours in this nifty book shop. Situated in a pale gray building surrounded by lush landscaping, on the old road just off the Overseas Highway, Cover to Cover stocks more than 35,000 titles, including a good Florida collection. The selection of children's books and educational games is outstanding. Sprinkled throughout the shop are gift items, specialty wrapping papers, and even some interesting jewelry. Stop and sip a spell at Cover to Cover's coffee bar.

Island Hammocks
MM 89.2 Bayside
Tavernier, FL
(305) 852–9222, (888) 252–5299

You can really lie around in style, lazin' in the Florida Keys' sun, if you pick up a hammock from this colorful store. Chock-a-block with try-'em-out samples of styles by Hatteras Hammocks, Nicamaka, Pawleys Island, and more. Island Hammocks also stocks frames, ropes, fasteners, and hammock accessories.

Gerry Droney Tropical Gardens
MM 88.7 Bayside
Tavernier, FL
(305) 852–4715

A riot of orchids, bromeliads, anthuriums, gingers, and other exotic tropical plants greets you as you wander through Gerry Droney's Tropical Gardens. This is tropical browsing at its finest. You'll find pots galore of every shape, size, and color as well as a full line of insecticides, fertilizers, and soil additives. Even if you eventually have to hop a plane for home, stop in here to see how Paradise blooms.

Anna Banana
MM 86.7 Oceanside
Islamorada, FL
(305) 853–1200

Anna Banana offers draped Moroccan cottons and elegantly long casual linen dresses amid their tropical ladies' fashions. Plus sizes are available here. Look for funky costume jewelry to finish off your ensemble. Anna Banana also offers a good selection of the Harmony Kingdom collectibles.

Blue Marlin Jewelry
MM 86.7 Oceanside
Islamorada, FL
(305) 664–8004, (888) 826–4424
www.bluemarlinjewelry.com

Discover gold in this interesting jewelry shop. Blue Marlin sports a great selection of gold charms, depicting most of the species of our ecosystem. Especially striking are the black coral fish. Many pieces are also offered in sterling silver.

The Rain Barrel Village of Artists & Craftspeople
MM 86.7 Bayside
Islamorada, FL
(305) 852–3084

A lush, tropical hideaway greets you in this artisan village as artists and crafters work in retail shops that are peppered beneath the gumbo limbos and amid the bougainvillea. Refer to our Arts and Culture chapter for a rundown of the galleries and studios at The Rain Barrel.

Expressions Sun N' Swimwear
MM 86.7 Oceanside
Islamorada, FL
(305) 852–1155

MM 81.5 Oceanside
Islamorada, FL
(305) 664–0081

Ladies, tropicalize your wardrobe at Expressions, which offers the wonderful Caribbean prints by Jams in a variety of comfortable styles. You'll find swimsuits and floppy hats as well as cover-ups—everything you need for a sojourn, Keys style. Men can dress down as well, finding their favorite tropical brands here.

Treasure Village
MM 86.7 Oceanside
Islamorada, FL
(305) 852–0511

From the road, Treasure Village does evoke memories of a pirate's castle, but inside the portals, a charming boardwalk fronts a potpourri of interesting shops. In the center of the square, tropical plantings shade picnic tables and lounge chairs, and island steel-drum music lilts from every corner. Island Body and Sol (305-853-0929) is a wonderfully scented little shop where you'll find all manner of lotions, salves, oils, balms, and aromatherapy to pamper your body (and soul). Bahama Bob's Flotsam & Jetsam (305-853-0259) features handmade creations of wood and leather, such as cutting boards, toys, utensils, sculptures, even wooden combs and switch plates decorated with frogs, geckos, and turtles.

You'll find clothing for ladies and tots at P.J. Max Caribbean Clothing (305-852-2082). Rudy's Kids Club (305-853-1265) is the place where your little ones will discover clothes, books, toys, games, puzzles, and even pint-size furniture—all with an environmental theme. At Treasure Harbor Trading Co. (305-852-0511), a treasure trove of men's and women's clothing and T-shirts mingles with an eclectic array of costume jewelry, books, and Keys memorabilia. Entry to this store is just beyond Big Betsy, known as the world's largest lobster. You'll be able to spot Big Betsy from the highway.

You'll find unusual, hand-carved, and custom-made candles at Ziggy's Candles (305-853-5382). Caribbean Furnishings (305-852-0828) displays one-of-a-kind tropically colored furniture made from Ponderosa pine as well as brightly hued dishes and creative sculptures.

Evoking memories of a pirate's castle, Treasure Village secrets a cache of treasure-filled shops.
PHOTO: MARY MOCCIA

If you feel a bit hungry, stop in at the Treasure Village Cafe (305-852-1911). And refer to our Arts and Culture chapter for information on Bluewater Potters and Art Lovers Gallery.

Somewhere in Time Spanish Treasure
MM 82.8 Oceanside
Islamorada, FL
(305) 664-9699
www.shopfloridakeys.com/treasure

Step into Somewhere in Time and you'll find a tiny shop chock-full of shipwreck treasure—coins, jewelry, bits of pottery, bottles, cannons, guns, and other collectibles. Although it's set up like a museum, most of the treasure is for sale.

Latitude 25
MM 82.7 Bayside
Islamorada, FL
(305) 664-4421

A step inside this low-lighted, paneled emporium evokes a big-game feeling.

Massive mounted tarpon, blue marlin, swordfish, and jewfish adorn the walls. Latitude 25 offers upscale, popular brands of men's and women's sport togs, such as Tommy Bahama, as well as accessories and gift items. The simple, sophisticated ladies' sundresses, tops, and shorts are made of exquisitely soft cottons in muted wear-anywhere colors. You'll also find a small children's department.

Down to Earth
MM 82.5 Oceanside
Islamorada, FL
(305) 664-9828

Poke around in this cute little shop on a rainy, or even sunny, day. Down to Earth stocks an eclectic selection of decorative items for the home as well as some neat gift items, such as coconut candles. You'll also find a good selection of aromatherapy items.

Garden of Eden
MM 82.3 Oceanside
Islamorada, FL
(305) 664–5558

Have you noticed those manatee mailboxes along the Overseas Highway? Well this is the place to find them. Garden of Eden is filled with silk flowers and arrangements, including orchids, bromeliads, and many other faux tropicals. Look for the handcarved bottle stoppers; the caricatures are a riot and sure to remind you of someone back home.

Island Silver & Spice
MM 82 Oceanside
Islamorada, FL
(305) 664–2715, (305) 664–2714

Billed as the Keys' department store, Island Silver & Spice offers a quality sampling of many things. The men's department is tucked away in the rear of the store, allowing the much larger ladies' section to predominate. Dressing rooms, looking like tiny pastel conch houses, are sprinkled throughout the store. Fine jewelry is offered as well as a limited selection of shoes, children's clothing, books, and games. The peach-and-green building also houses an eclectic assortment of gourmet kitchen items, bath and household accessories, and an upstairs bargain corner.

Angelika
MM 81.9 Oceanside
Islamorada, FL
(305) 664–9008

Upmarket ladies' fashions with an old-fashioned twist, natural fabrics, and whimsical designs mark the merchandise at Angelika's. Look for Angelika's great hats, and don't miss the Judybags, a fantastic array of hand-created dress purses by Judy Adler.

Justine's Jewelry
MM 81.9 Bayside
Islamorada, FL
(305) 664–5120, (800) 211–5120
www.justinesjewelry.com

Justine's small shop holds a mother lode of silver treasure inside. You'll find a good selection of creative sterling silver jewelry, many inlaid with turquoise and other semiprecious stones. The one-of-a-kind pieces are strikingly unusual.

Sunny Exposures
MM 81.9 Bayside
Islamorada, FL
(305) 664–8445, (800) 725–0801

See suits, suits, and more suits here—for surf and sun, not the office. Ladies' swimsuits of every style and description, for every imaginable body type, join ranks with cover-ups, lotions, and sunglasses. Sunny Exposures even carries some men's and kids' suits.

World Wide Sportsman Inc.
MM 81.5 Bayside
Islamorada, FL
(305) 664–4615, (800) 327–2880
www.worldwidesportsman.com

Don't miss a stop at World Wide Sportsman, the massive fishing emporium that is an Islamorada must-see. Housed in a former in-and-out storage building renovated with an old-fashioned, exposed-brick exterior and surrounded by native trees and shrubs, World Wide showcases the exact replica of Hemingway's 42-foot ship, the *Pilar*. Visitors can climb aboard and examine Hemingway's chair and even his typewriter. Rumor has it that he wrote at least one novel while fishing on the *Pilar*. A 6,000-gallon, saltwater aquarium presents the creatures of our reef, including baby tarpon, bonefish, and redfish. A small art gallery upstairs features works of local artists.

Memorabilia aside, World Wide is stocked to the rafters with a wide assortment of fishing tackle (see the Outfitters section in our Fishing chapter), and a full line of men's and women's technical clothing is offered, including ExOfficio, Woolrich, Sportif, Columbia, and much more.

If your stamina runs out before your money does, sit a spell in one of the rocking chairs lining the back porch and watch the action on the Gulf of Mexico. Or pop up to the Zane Grey Bar; sink into a leather chair; look at the vintage fishing photos of Grey and his cronies; and sip a tall, cool one. Even if you don't like to fish, World Wide Sportsman is one place you won't want to pass by.

Middle Keys

All That Glitters
MM 61 Oceanside
Duck Key, FL
(305) 743–0058

All That Glitters is a jewelry store specializing in custom-made items. You'll see a large collection of treasure-coin jewelry as well. All That Glitters buys coins directly from the divers who explore the ancient wrecks that litter our reefs. This is the place to take any jewelry that needs fixing (even many of the area jewelers send items here to be repaired).

Bayshore Clothing and Small World
MM 54 Bayside
Quay Village
Marathon, FL
(305) 743–8430

Expanded three-fold in 2000, Bayshore caters to men's and women's tropical garment needs, a guaranteed attitude adjustment from the busy work-a-day world up north. The little people's shop beckons parents and especially grandparents with a cute selection of swimsuits, warm-weather togs, and toys. You'll even find a pint-size grass skirt, halter-top, and floral lei. An extensive selection of interactive cloth books are especially clever.

The Enchanted Elephant
MM 54 Bayside
Quay Village
Marathon, FL
(305) 289–0646

Full of interesting tropical gift items and mementos, The Enchanted Elephant also features an interesting array of fun stuff for your feline, at the bequest, no doubt, of the owner's resident kitty. Customized

mailboxes get a tropical brushstroke here, and look for enameled parrot, turtle, or fish hairbrushes.

Key Bana Resort Apparel
MM 53.5 Oceanside
Key Colony Beach Causeway
Marathon, FL
(305) 289–1161

Ladies, you are sure to find a new swimsuit or tropical cotton item here that you can't pass up. And Key Bana has a roomful of shorts and shirts for men too. It gives them something to do as you browse.

D'Asign Source
MM 52.7 Bayside
Marathon, FL
(305) 743–7130
www.dasignsource.com

This wonderful home furnishing and design center oozes with class. You'll find the very latest and very best in materials, fixtures, finishes, and designs for home remodeling, building, and furnishing. Even if you aren't in the market for a home makeover, make way to D'Asign Source's mega store, completed in 2001. Browsing the 25,000-square-foot showroom is an inspiration.

My Gift Cottage
MM 52.5 Bayside
Marathon, FL
(305) 289–9911, (877) 252–4438
www.mygiftcottage.com

This nifty shop is chockablock with interesting stuff—all very reasonably priced. Picture frames, wind chimes, mobiles, and memorabilia compete with household accessories and decorative items, all-in-all creating a bazaarlike hodgepodge of curiosities. Be sure to allow enough time to poke around for a while.

Island Junction
MM 51.5 Oceanside
Marathon, FL
(305) 743–2580, (800) 255–4803

World Wide Sportsman Inc., the massive Islamorada fishing emporium, is stocked to the rafters with fishing tackle and memorabilia. PHOTO: MARY MOCCIA

You will not want to leave our islands without trying one of the famed Key West Aloe products you will find at Island Junction. The lotions, sun creams, and shampoos are super.

Wicker Web
MM 51.5 Oceanside
Marathon, FL
(305) 743–3696
Across from the Marathon Airport runway, in the Southwind Building, you'll discover the Wicker Web, three showrooms chock-full of tropically inspired items for every room in your house. You'll find a wide selection of baskets, wall hangings, wicker items, lamps, plasticware, and bath accessories.

P & J Antiques
MM 51.2 Oceanside
Marathon, FL
(305) 743–0136
P & J Antiques displays collectible glassware and antique items in a cozy little warren, perfect for those who like to rummage through the spoils of antiquity. This shop is open in high season.

Beachcomber Gifts and Jewelers
MM 50.5 Bayside
Gulfside Village
Marathon, FL
(305) 743–2245
Beachcomber's showcases more than just fine jewelry. You'll find a good selection of hostess gifts and an extensive Swarovski collection of cut-crystal figurines. Also a Hallmark shop, Beachcomber's offers plenty of cards, wraps, ribbons, and what-nots, in addition to some mighty fine display-case chocolates.

Driftwood Designs
MM 50.5 Bayside
Gulfside Village
Marathon, FL
(305) 743–7591
Driftwood's claim of being "The Definitive Gift Store" is well deserved. Browsing the eclectic selection of bronze and fine-art sculptures, jewelry, wearable art, and

pottery is like exploring a museum but more fun, because you can actually purchase the curiosities. This smorgasbord of merchandise is upmarket and fascinating.

Food for Thought
MM 50.5 Bayside
Gulfside Village
Marathon, FL
(305) 743–3297

Food for Thought is really two shops in one: half books and magazines, half health foods (see our Seafood Markets and Specialty Foods chapter). You can fuel your mind and your body at the same time. Custom orders are the norm here.

Marathon Men's Shop
MM 50.5 Bayside
Gulfside Village
Marathon, FL
(305) 743–5657
www.shopfloridakeys.com/marathonmensshop

Perhaps the oldest men's clothing establishment in Marathon, this men's shop features such classic sport brands as Hook & Tackle and Sperry. This is the place in the Middle Keys to rent a tuxedo for your next formal affair.

The Port Hole
MM 50.5 Bayside
Gulfside Village
Marathon, FL
(305) 743–3552

Don't miss The Port Hole, an upmarket ladies' clothing boutique guaranteed to pry open your pocketbook. Jean and her crew keep even more temptations in the back room, so be sure to clue them in to your tastes, and they'll dress you in style. This is one of the few shops around where the clerks pamper you with service while you're in the dressing room, exchanging sizes and styles, replacing the clothes on the hangers, and suggesting smart accessories. The Port Hole sells Judybags, too.

Lazy Lizard
MM 50.3 Bayside
Marathon, FL
(305) 743–5001

Full of cool cottons, fun aprons, Keys jewelry, stationery, cards, and glassware, Lazy Lizard is a shop for all occasions. This is the place to find a campy touch of the Keys for your memory box.

Keyker's Boutique & Gallery
MM 50.3 Oceanside
67 53rd Street
Marathon, FL
(305) 743–0107

Keyker and other local clothing designers create custom island clothing for women and children, unusual yet flattering styles using exquisitely fine cottons. You'll find them displayed at this co-operative establishment, along with interesting jewelry, accessories, craft items, and paintings.

Patio & Home Furniture Art Gallery
Furniture Gallery Gulfside
MM 50 Bayside
Gulfside Village
Marathon, FL
(305) 289–2038

Furniture Art Gallery
MM 49.6 Oceanside
Marathon, FL
(305) 743–2740

Casual Furniture Gallery
MM 48.6 Bayside
Marathon, FL
(305) 743–2776
www.patiohome.com

The Furniture Gallery Gulfside is the first of three stores that make up the sprawling Patio & Home Furniture Art Gallery. The Gallery crams a warehouse full of bargains in its spacious, good-deal shop. Sometimes we stroll through the enormous Furniture Art Gallery just to see what wild new things they've added to the collection. Besides offering the most complete selection of quality furniture in the Keys, the Furniture Art Gallery peppers the showroom with accessories that range from the sublime to the outrageous. You have to see it to believe it. You'll find a wide range of Oriental antiques and artifacts here as well.

The Casual Furniture Gallery is the third of the trio of furniture stores. This large showroom stocks all the name brands in outdoor and casual furniture and has a way-out selection of only-in-the-Keys accessories.

Inspiring Soles
MM 50 Oceanside
Marathon, FL
(305) 743–0770
Inspiring Soles displays the best selection of upscale men's and women's brand-name shoes in the Middle Keys. You'll find lots of strappy sandals, clogs, boat shoes, and dress footwear here, in a wide variety of styles and sizes.

Paradise Ltd.
MM 49.6 Oceanside
Marathon, FL
(305) 289–9090
Stop at Paradise before you go to Sombrero Beach, because the tiny boutique is chockful of swimsuits, coverups, and sandals, plus a good smattering of Keys-specific reading material.

Marathon Discount Book Center
MM 48.2 Oceanside
Marathon, FL
(305) 289–2066
Marathon Discount Book Center offers all books at 10 to 90 percent off retail prices. Selling primarily publisher's overstock, the store also offers best sellers, local interest books, and books on tape. The staff also will place special orders.

Pigeon Key Foundation Gift Shop
MM 47 Oceanside
Pigeon Key Visitors Center
Marathon, FL
(305) 743–5999
Look for the old railway car, still sitting on the tracks of Flagler's railroad at MM 47 Oceanside. Hidden unassumingly inside resides the Pigeon Key Visitors Center Gift Shop, a potpourri of Keys memorabilia and gift items. The gift shop, like everything on Pigeon Key, is run by a contingent of loyal volunteers, and all proceeds go to the Pigeon Key Foundation.

Lower Keys

Little Palm Island Gift Shop
MM 28.5 Oceanside
Little Torch Key, FL
(305) 872–2524
Stop at this mainland substation of the Little Palm Island and visit the gift shop. You'll find interesting glassware, sculptures, and handpainted plates, in addition to upscale clothing and straw hats. If you go out to Little Palm Island itself, for lunch or dinner or to stay the night, don't miss the island shop. The tropical ambiance will tempt you to discard your shorts and don an island caftan.

Seacloud Orchids and Tropicals
MM 10
Big Coppitt, FL
(305) 294–3639
Words cannot describe this glorious shop. If you like plants, you will love this place. In addition to a good selection of orchids, you'll find other tropical plants, flowers, trees, and beautiful, one-of-a-kind containers. The staff is very friendly and knowledgeable. You'll find it difficult to leave without adopting a piece of our Keys flora.

Key West

For shoppers, Key West lives up to its reputation as Paradise. Colorful, funky, one-of-a-kind shops abound on our fair island. To aid your search and purchase mission, we have taken the best of Key West—a little of this, a little of that—and presented it in a simple format. Our shop 'til you drop tour of Key West begins on Duval Street with the Best of Duval section. Other little treasures are tucked in and about the narrow, quiet streets of Old Town, and although sometimes tough to find, they are definitely worth the search. We've categorized them as Off Duval. And finally, we lead you to Way Off Duval, for some interesting offerings, with a mention of New Town, where you'll find the major retail chains, which stock all the basics for living in Paradise. The Best of Duval is arranged by numerical address order, from the Atlantic to the Gulf. Off Duval is organized alphabetically. If your tastes lean more toward original artwork and handcrafted jewelry, be sure to check the Art Galleries section of our Arts & Culture chapter for additional shopping suggestions.

Best of Duval

The Chicken Store
1229 Duval Street
Key West, FL
(305) 294–0070
www.TheChickenStore.com

Only in a place like Key West, where chickens still roam free, could there be a store like this one. Here, tucked among the fine art, crafts, and world-exclusive T-shirts celebrating the gypsy chickens of Key West, you'll find the real thing. Caged roosters, hens, and chicks—some wounded, some orphans, some simply deemed neighborhood nuisances—reside in this tiny shop while they recoup (no pun intended),

recover, and await relocation. Take home a brochure that tells the Key West chicken story (a 25-cent donation is appreciated) or even a live souvenir—not the bird itself but a fresh, fertilized egg and a miniature incubator to help you hatch it.

L. Valladares and Son
1200 Duval Street
Key West, FL
(305) 296–5032

Billing itself as "Key West's Oldest Newsstand," L. Valladares offers a wide selection of regional and national newspapers and magazines. You'll also find an array of works by Key West authors.

Key West Havana Cigar Company
1117 Duval Street
Key West, FL
(305) 296–1977

Make your selection from among the many brands of quality, handcrafted cigars, and accessories in this small shop that doubles as the front entry of the Speakeasy Inn. A prompt mail-order service is available, so you can readily send cigars to the folks back home.

City Zoo
1108 Duval Street
Key West, FL
(305) 292–1711, (305) 292–9563

Get your animal memorabilia here. Faux animals of all shapes and sizes abound, unbridled in this fetching little store. If an adorable little stuffed frog doesn't tickle your fancy, then perhaps a tropical fish mobile will. You'll find plenty for the children on your shopping list.

Country Conch
1108 Duval Street
Key West, FL
(305) 294–1452

It was only a matter of time before the country craze in decorating that swept the Midwest a few years back made its way to Key West. Shop here for household accessories that say "country" with a South Florida flair. Wicker and muted tropical prints abound, along with the ubiquitous chickens, manatees, dolphins, and conch shells.

Abaco Gold
1102 Duval Street
Key West, FL
(305) 294–7796

418 Front Street
Key West, FL
(305) 296–0086

A honeymoon voyage to the Abaco Islands prompted owners John and Angela to dub their stores "Abaco Gold." The jewelry line here is exclusive—like no other in the Florida Keys or elsewhere for that matter. Abaco Gold specializes in unique, nautical designs featuring mermaids, dolphins, and tropical themes. If you love jewelry, you'll love these stores.

Eye! Eye! Eye!
1102 Duval Street
Key West, FL
(305) 292–7909

Connie and her experienced staff have the best selection of frames this side of Miami. Choose from Oliver Peoples, LA Eye Works, Giorgio Armani, Gucci, Maui Jim, and others. This is a super place for sunglasses as well as small repairs.

Nannie Mixsells
1102 Duval Street
Key West, FL
(305) 293–0015

This store calls itself a "purveyor of the unique for body and abode." We'd call that an understatement. This charming shop with its whimsical atmosphere has everything from vintage style clothing to mango potpourri. You'll find one-of-a-kind glassware as well as lovely picture frames and jewelry here, too.

Fletcher on Duval Island Furniture
1024 Duval Street
Key West, FL
(305) 294–2032

Decorate your home with the fine-crafted furniture offered by Fletcher. The specialty here is coral keystone, wrought into strange and wonderful forms. Coffee tables with end stands of this intricate rock hold a glass top in place. Choose from a variety of artistic pedestals, fireplace mantels, and much more. Be prepared to spend a considerable amount—art like this doesn't come cheap.

Creative Generations
1024 Duval Street (rear)
Key West, FL
(305) 294–0448

If wandering the art galleries of Key West has you itching to make a little art of your own, you'll want to stop here first. Creative Generations is stocked to the gills with everything you need to get started. Sketchbooks, charcoal, paints, pencils, brushes, palettes, canvas, and easels—it's all waiting for you here.

Pro Photo
1020 Duval Street
Key West, FL
(305) 294–9908

335 Duval Street
Key West, FL
(305) 294–9331, (800) 864–1350

There's no excuse for being camera-shy in Key West—not when you have two Pro Photo locations to choose from. These folks have everything you need to capture your vacation for posterity—film, batteries, even disposable cameras, in the event you forgot to pack your own. And just in case you can't wait until you get home to see how it all turned out, drop your film for processing here, too. You can have it back in as little as one hour.

Tikal Trading Company
910 Duval Street
Key West, FL
(305) 293–0033

129 Duval Street
Key West, FL
(305) 296–4463

Two locations hold a vast store of women's apparel. Artfully displayed flowery dresses, perfect for the warm climate of the islands, invite passersby to step inside. The same prints and styles are available in several sizes, suitable for both mothers and daughters.

Blue Heron Books
826 Duval Street
Key West, FL
(305) 296–3508

This cozy little neighborhood bookstore is the perfect place to while away an hour or so. The on-site selection is limited, focusing mainly on classic titles and good beach reads, but if you don't see something you want, ask. The staff is especially friendly and eager to help. You'll find a great little Florida interest section here, plus cards, journals, and a few shelves of used books. Browsing is encouraged; feel free to curl up in one of several comfortable chairs while you peruse your selections. Oh, and don't forget to pet the resident kitty.

Pandemonium
825 Duval Street
Key West, FL
(305) 294–0351

Music from the 1950s will help you toe-tap your way through Pandemonium, a funky, eclectic shop featuring imaginative crafts and objets d'art created from recycled items. Pick out a travel-log journal covered with an old automobile license plate—from the state of your choice. Or perhaps you'd like a tin man sculpted from an old typewriter or a horse made from used rubber tires. You'll find an airplane whose prop is fashioned from beer cans, a leather belt adorned with beer-bottle caps, and even a chenille dress, every bit as soft as grandma's bedspread, from which it was probably made.

The Official Conch Republic Store
817 Duval Street
Key West, FL
(305) 296–1976

Ever since Key West attempted to secede from the union over a dispute with the Border Patrol in 1982, we've been flaunting our independence in grand and glorious style. Now you can, too. This store is filled with all manner of items to commemorate the founding of our republic. Take home a flag, license plate, banner, or T-shirt, then display them proudly to show your support.

Cuba! Cuba!
814 Duval Street
Key West, FL
(305) 295–9442

Get a little *"Libre!"* in your life with this quaint little shop that espouses a passion for all things Cuban. Art is very much a part of the selection, evidenced by nostalgic wood carvings, depicting a typical Cuban kitchen. Cookbooks and authentic jams and marmalades line the shelves, and guitars and maracas are just begging to be played. A selection of cigars is also on display.

Towels of Key West
806 Duval Street
Key West, FL
(305) 292–1120, (305) 294–1929

Towels in all shapes, sizes, and budgets fill this simple store. Get the best-selling, colorful print terry robe, or immerse yourself in a big, warm, oversized, colorful towel.

Conch Republic Trading Co.
725 Duval Street
Key West, FL
(305) 292–9002

If you loved the ambiance of the original Banana Republic stores before they went upscale, you'll no doubt find Conch Republic Trading Co. (formerly known as H.T. Chittum & Co.) equally charming. Not to be confused with The Official Conch Republic Store (see description in this section), this shop is short on politics but long on style. Here you'll find some of the finest clothing labels in the country—Tommy Bahama, Sigrid Olsen, Lilly Pulitzer, Timberland, Lacoste, Sportif, Reyn Spooner, and Holland Bros. leather goods to name just a few.

Key West's famed Duval Street attracts visitors from the world over. PHOTO: FLORIDA KEYS & KEY WEST TDC

In Touch of Key West, Inc.
715 Duval Street
Key West, FL
(305) 292–7293

This quirky little shop is a great place to find cards, unusual stationery, wrapping paper, gifts, and hilarious, though not necessarily tasteful, T-shirts. The bins near the cash register hold novelties like rubber spiders and wind-up ladybugs—the kind of toys you remember shopping for at the dime store if you're old enough to remember the dime store, that is. Share these with your kids, but keep them away from the greeting card section. These birthday cards wouldn't pass muster at Hallmark. They are most definitely for adults, both straight and gay; some are quite graphic.

Island Shoe Box
712-A Duval Street
Key West, FL
(305) 294–7420

Yes, even in Paradise, some occasions may require you to wear real shoes. And this is the place to find them. Island Shoe Box stocks hundreds of styles for men, women, and children—everything from traditional oxfords to high-heeled pumps as well as a complete array of sandals.

Open Minded
703 Duval Street
Key West, FL
(305) 295–9595

Tiffany lamps of all shapes and vivid colors perch daintily in the front display window of this unusual store. Part New Age and part boutique, Open Minded caters to those who wish to decorate their lives and homes in an otherworldly manner. Colorful wall hangings, chimes, and women's apparel co-mingle with incense, Tarot cards, and colorful serenity.

Worldwide Flags
626 Duval Street
Key West, FL
(305) 292–9301

Sometimes the name says it all. Flags it is, and if you are French, Dutch, or even Lithuanian, you'll find a flag to rouse your patriotism. You'll find vast quantities of official flags from many countries and all 50 states here, but don't forget a Conch Republic flag or a Key West rainbow flag. Or just take home a colorful windsock.

White House-Black Market
621 Duval Street
Key West, FL
(305) 292–7740

You'll have no trouble deciding on the right color for your next new outfit here, because you have only one choice—black or white. Every dress, skirt, shirt, or pair of trousers in this shop is either solid black or solid white. There are simply no shades of gray. It's an unusual concept—particularly in a climate where pastels and bright prints rule—but it certainly takes the guesswork out of buying.

Island Style
620 Duval Street
Key West, FL
(305) 292–7800

This shop is aptly named, for everything displayed inside has that certain look about it, that thing we call "island style." Shop here for accessories that will give your home the look of the islands no matter where you might reside—brightly colored coasters, glassware, swizzle sticks, placemats, napkins and napkin rings, candlesticks, tableware, potholders, decorative tiles, etc. Before you know it, you'll be humming "Jamaica Farewell" while you unload your dishwasher back in Cleveland or Detroit.

ACA Joe
617 Duval Street
Key West, FL
(305) 294–1570

Need some cargo shorts? A pair of deck shoes? A lightweight jacket for your sunset cruise? ACA Joe has a wide assortment of cool, comfortable cotton clothing for men and women as well as shoes that are perfect for boating and beachcombing. You'll find a nice selection of tropical print camp shirts here, too—tasteful

enough to wear even when you return home.

Hot Hats
613 Duval Street
Key West, FL
(305) 294–1333

If you're heading out into the midday sun, you'd best wear a hat. And you're sure to find a flattering one at this shop devoted entirely to headgear, including everything from canvas caps to straw boaters. There's even a rack full of multicolored baseball caps with propellers for catching those island breezes in a whimsical way.

Birkenstock of Old Town
610 Duval Street
Key West, FL
(305) 294–8318

With sandals being essential apparel for island life, it makes good sense for Birkenstock to have a large, full-service store right in the middle of it all. Although Birkenstocks don't come cheap, the shoes are exceptionally durable and comfortable. Rare is the local who doesn't own at least one pair. Count on paying upwards of $50 for yours, but do watch the sale rack here. You can sometimes get a pretty good deal on discontinued styles.

Lido
532 Duval Street
Key West, FL
(305) 294–5300

If those enticing, pseudo paper lanterns or art deco desk lamps in the display window aren't enough to whet your appetite, then your tastes may be a little too traditional for this store. Inside you'll find an eclectic array of goods to spruce up your body and your abode—shirts, shorts, lamps, glassware, gifts, and accessories that combine the best of East Coast kitsch and South Beach style.

Environmental Circus
518 Duval Street
Key West, FL
(305) 294–6055

A Deadhead's delight lies within this cozy store, filled to the brim with tie-dyed T-shirts, essential oils, lava lamps, dyed wall hangings, and smoking accessories.

The Coach Store
517 Duval Street
Key West, FL
(305) 292-2708

If you're a fan of Coach products, you no longer have to make the trek to Miami to find them. Great-looking, discounted leather items—everything from belts, handbags, and portfolios to wallets, key cases, and luggage, all in the inimitable Coach style—await you here.

Sunlion Jewelry
513 Duval Street
Key West, FL
(305) 296-8457

You'll know you've struck treasure when you see the gold and gemstone bracelets, necklaces, earrings, and rings designed on-premises, by Fantasy Fest's official jeweler. Conch pearls and treasure coins also are among the elegant trinkets here.

Get Wet
509 Duval Street
Key West, FL
(305) 294-7738

Funny name for a shoe store, but then again this place was never meant to be one; it just evolved that way. Get Wet opened originally as a Dive Shop. You can still book a snorkel or scuba trip here, and you can still buy wet suits, masks, flippers, weights, water shoes, bathing suits, and beach bags. But you'll also find sunglasses, T-shirts, tank tops, Hawaiian shirts, shorts, cover-ups, and dresses—from casual beachwear to cocktail frocks—and, of course, shoes. Pumps, platforms, flats, flip-flops, strappy sandals—you name it, they've got it. If the airlines lose your luggage on the way to Key West, better head directly here. With such an array of merchandise, you could outfit yourself quite adequately until your bag shows up.

Bath and Body Works
505 Duval Street
Key West, FL
(305) 295-0464

Big barrels full of goodies and sales clerks in red checked aprons make you feel as though you've wandered into a country kitchen, but this is no store full of pantry provisions. This is a place to pick up the goods for pampering yourself. It's chock full of soaps, lotions, and bath oils, loofahs, and back massagers, plus all manner of baskets to present them in. This is a great place to buy souvenirs and gifts for friends.

Banana Republic
501 Duval Street
Key West, FL
(305) 293-0087

That sleek, open and oh-so-Banana Republic style awaits you inside this, the most recent addition of national brands to the Duval Street scene. This clothing chain maintains a certain look in every store, and the Key West outlet is no exception. A friendly staff will help you shop here for classic—albeit pricey—men's and women's clothing.

Fast Buck Freddie's
500 Duval Street
Key West, FL
(305) 294-2007

If there weren't literally hundreds of stores to explore in Key West and you never reached the bottom of your pockets, Fast Buck Freddie's, at the southeast corner of Duval and Fleming, would be your one-stop shop. FBF's carries men's and women's clothing in metropolitan and tropical styles. Just around the bend from the mega-store's clothing section are imported items from around the world, such as clocks, candle holders, picture frames, and some of the most unusual home furnishings you'll see anywhere. Look to Freddie's kitchenware department for an extensive selection of cookbooks, gourmet kitchen accessories, herbs, flavored oils, and Godiva chocolates. And be sure to check out the unusual toys, novelty items, and greeting cards in the back of the store. But beware—some may be X-rated.

See our listing later in this chapter for Half Buck Freddie's, Fast Buck Freddie's discount store.

Margaritaville Store
500 Duval Street
Key West, FL
(305) 296–3070
www.margaritaville.com/keywest

Everything here is tuned to one thing—the works of Key West's favorite son, Jimmy Buffett. All his albums are available here, along with tons of shirts, books, photos, and other Parrothead paraphernalia. Spend some time perusing the walls—they're packed with photos and memorabilia related to events in the life of the man from Margaritaville. This place is a must-stop for Buffett fans old and new.

Bird in Hand
430 Duval Street
Key West, FL
(305) 292–8969

Relocated once again—this time from Simonton Street to Duval—this shop is one of Key West's oldest and most respected establishments. Here you'll find local, handmade jewelry (both fine and costume), collectibles (including Lladro and Hummel pieces), and a wide selection of local and imported gifts.

Earthbound Trading Co.
400 Duval Street
Key West, FL
(305) 292–8604

Semiprecious stones and minerals fill this shop, in more forms than you would think possible. Big pieces of lovely purple amethyst and golden citrine are offered in their natural forms, but you could also opt for a marble chess set, wood-carved animals, beautiful sliced opaque rock chimes, bead jewelry, or agate bookends. This is a great place to buy a toe ring, too!

Shades of Key West
335 Duval Street
Key West, FL
(305) 294–0519

306 Front Street
Key West, FL
(305) 294–0329

Protect your eyes from the intense tropical sunlight with a wide selection of brand-name sunglasses, including Oakley, Ray-Ban, Vuarnet, Armani, Arnet, and Hobie. These are not your drugstore variety sunglasses—everything's top quality.

Sweet Mischief
335 Duval Street
Key West, FL
(305) 296–0777

There's nothing secret about the stock at this store. Sweet Mischief is crammed to the gills with the silkiest, sexiest lingerie imaginable. Shop here for briefs and bikinis, bras and bustiers, teddies, camisoles, negligees, swimwear, cocktail dresses, and evening gowns. And if you're in the market for a pair of red patent leather platform pumps with three-inch heels, this is the place to find them.

Hair Wraps of Key West
310 Duval Street
Key West, FL
(305) 293–1133

If you want to make a real statement or you just want to get your hair done in a new way, head over to Hair Wraps in the courtyard of the Garden Cafe. Tons of beads are available, and these folks have just about any color or detail you'd like.

Key West Candle Company, Inc.
310 Duval Street
Key West, FL
(305) 296–8447

Candles galore abound in this small store, tucked in the back of the courtyard of the Garden Cafe. All candles are made on the premises, and, if you are lucky, you just might happen upon the candle maker at work.

This little wedge of a store is packed at Christmastime with gift buyers looking for that perfect Key West memento. Favorites include ornaments of snorkeling Santas, Christmas dolphins, and anything of an island nature.

Off Duval

Assortment, Inc.
514 Fleming Street
Key West, FL
(305) 294-4066

This chic men's clothing store, just a few steps off Duval Street, carries the latest in men's casual fashions with a dressy flair. Handsome jackets, shirts, slacks, and shoes are tastefully displayed. Polo by Ralph Lauren, Wilke-Rodrigues, and Cole-Haan shoes are just a few of the lines you'll find here. Assortment, Inc. also offers great-looking gifts and accessories for that special guy in your life.

Becky Thatcher Designs
425 Eaton Street
Key West, FL
(305) 296-0886

If one-of-a-kind jewelry creations from unusual gemstones such as tourmaline, boulder opal, fancy sapphire, tanzanite, sugalite, and chrysocolla pique your interest, visit Becky Thatcher Designs. Set in gold or silver, the gemstones join with shells and ancient beads from around the world, creating what Becky calls "picture" necklaces and earrings that capture the essence of spirit and individuality.

Besame Mucho
315 Petronia Street
Key West, FL
(305) 294-1928

Step into this tastefully decorated shop, and you will feel as though you have stepped back in time. Ceiling fans stir the air, and the CD playing softly in the background is reminiscent of Old Havana. The shelves are filled with items that look as though they belong on a movie set, circa 1940. Here you'll find an assortment of picture frames, desk accessories, tableware,

Tropical Wave
310 Duval Street
Key West, FL
(305) 292-7543

It would be easy to miss this shop, which is tucked deep in the corner behind Garden Cafe, but don't. Inside, you'll find a nice selection of casual resort wear and dresses, plus a wall filled with handmade, hand-painted shoes. You're sure to find at least one pair in colors that will complement your outfit.

Neptune Designs
301 Duval Street
Key West, FL
(305) 294-8131

Most of the jewelry filling this shop is of an oceanic nature and is wrought in gold or silver. Leaping silver dolphin necklaces frolic with golden, gliding sea turtles on a black background. Noah's Ark figurines are on display—tiny ships decked with all manner of wildlife.

Biker's Image
121 Duval Street
Key West, FL
(305) 292-1328

Get your Harley tuned up, and race over to Biker's Image, where you can splurge on your fantasies with leather, Harley T-shirts, helmets, smoking accessories, and just about anything that complements the biker lifestyle.

The Partridge Christmas Shop
120 Duval Street
Key West, FL
(305) 294-6001

lucky tokens, tropical cards and books, baskets, Tahitian bath oils—in short, what the owners lovingly refer to as "essential island provisions."

Blue
718 Caroline Street
Key West, FL
(305) 292–5172

Shop here for classic linen skirts, tops, jackets, pants, and dresses that will look just as appropriate on Fifth Avenue as they do on Duval. Be sure to check out the accessories here, too. The bead jewelry is handmade, and the colors are a perfect complement to the easy-fitting, understated styles.

Caribbean Adventures Sport, Game & Toy Co.
408 Greene Street
Key West, FL
(305) 296–5666

Walk past the picket fence and up the steps to this tiny shop, just brimming with toys, puppets, and stuffed animals. You'll find a whole wall of beach toys— squirt guns, Frisbees, inflatables, and the like—plus the largest selection of puzzles in the Keys. Whether you're a kid or just a kid at heart, you'll find plenty to amuse you here.

The China Clipper
333 Simonton Street
Key West, FL
(305) 294–2136
www.chinaclipper.com

Need inspiration for your interiors? Head to The China Clipper, where quality Oriental furnishings, accessories, and artwork are the bill of fare.

Clinton Square Market
291 Front Street
Key West, FL
(305) 296–6825

Enclosed within Clinton Square, you'll find a number of shops worth stopping in to see. Island Jewelry (305-296-0699) combines local design with native elements, such as sea turtles, dolphins, and manatees. All are carved or emblazoned in 14- and 18-karat gold and sterling silver. Native Colors, Inc. (305-292-2302) features gifts and home accessories, while Club West (305-294-3864) and Summersalt Resort Wear (305-294-4940) offer tropical clothing and souvenirs. Wings of Imagination (305-296-2922) is a shop devoted to butterflies. And for feline fanciers, there's The Blue Cat (305-293-9339), fully stocked with all manner of cat-related merchandise.

Colombian Emeralds International
400 Front Street
Key West, FL
(305) 292–2223

Diamonds may be a girl's best friend, but the emeralds, rubies, sapphires, garnets, tanzanite, and other colored gemstones available here make pretty good buddies, too. This company, which began in St. Thomas, has duty-free stores throughout the Caribbean. The Key West outlet, catering to cruise ship passengers and locals alike, is one of only two in the U.S. (the other is in Alaska). Shop here for elegant gold and silver jewelry, gemstones, watches, and the one-of-a-kind Key West Hook bracelets designed by in-house jeweler Mitchell Ousley. Available in gold or silver, these bracelets feature a single W and a key-shaped latch. The eight bands on each represent the island's dimensions—2 by 4 miles.

Commodore Antiques
500 Simonton Street
Key West, FL
(305) 296–3973

The address reads Simonton Street, but the door of this dusty little shop is actually on the corner of Fleming and Simonton Streets. The goods are mostly furniture, glassware, and small, silver accent items. "Do not touch" signs abound here, and much of the merchandise is encased behind glass. Still, if you're into antiques, it's worth a quick look-see.

Commotion
800 Caroline Street
Key West, FL
(305) 292–3364

Stylish island separates that are as fun to wear as they are practical to own await you here. These natural, washable linen and flax fabrics will help you keep your cool—a definite must in the Florida Keys. Best of all, unlike some island designs that look out of place outside the tropics, these will look just as great when you get back home.

Duck and Dolphin Antiques
601 Fleming Street
Key West, FL
(305) 295–0499

This elegant shop—reminiscent of the antique shops we've seen in Europe—is filled with ornate furnishings and accent pieces that can only be called trés chic. You'll find everything from a grand piano to a crystal chandelier. No secondhand goods here. These items are in mint condition, with price tags to match.

Fabric World
613 Simonton Street
Key West, FL
(305) 294–1773

Founded in 1970, Key West's only shop devoted solely to fabrics is like a box of crayons—plain on the outside, a riot of color within. The owners have hand-picked all of the fabrics, including more than 200 bolts of upholstery materials and the tropical fish prints for which this shop is justly famous. Patterns, sewing notions, and decorator trims are also available. This is a must-shop for anyone who sews.

Flaming Maggie's Books, Art & Coffee
830 Fleming Street
Key West, FL
(305) 294–3931

A large selection of works by local writers is available here as well as one of the island's best selections of gay and lesbian literature. The store, which used to be Caroline Street Books, is housed in the former site of Maskerville. Enjoy some fresh-ground coffee while you browse.

From the Ruins
219 Whitehead Street
Key West, FL
(305) 293–0897

No one—and we do mean no one—should pass up the opportunity to experience From the Ruins, where one-of-a-kind handmade garments and accessories make for a mellifluous museum. Wear your heart on your sleeve with a handbag crafted in the form of your favorite dog breed, or pick up an intricate, hand-blown glass vase. Be sure to bring a full wallet—these one-of-a-kind artifacts have one-of-a-kind prices. Look for the cozy cottage with a white picket fence and welcoming front porch.

Gaspara's Toy Box
218 Whitehead Street
Key West, FL
(305) 296–2611

If you have little ones on your gift list, this tiny shop is a must-stop. The stock includes unusual T-shirts, wooden puzzles, games, and a complete menagerie of stuffed animals in a variety of sizes.

Gecko Roamin'
316 Simonton Street
Key West, FL
(305) 293–9988

Geckos are to Key West as squirrels are to the Midwest. You can't walk a block in Old Town without having at least one of these engaging little reptiles scurry across the sidewalk in front of your feet. Geckos are not only cute and harmless, in some cultures they are considered good luck. This shop celebrates the gecko by hand-screening the little lizard on original fashions made from hand-dyed cotton and linen fabrics. Choose from sheaths, jumpers, cover-ups, jackets, and pants in muted colors with coordinating shells and shirts. Then select a piece of handcrafted jewelry to complement your outfit.

Global Nomad
830 Caroline Street
Key West, FL
(305) 294–2410

Looking for something to wear that is a little less traditional, a lot more exotic? This could be your place. Global Nomad features clothing and jewelry from the Far East, India, and Africa. Select a free-flowing, floor-length caftan, then accessorize with bangle bracelets and a jingling silver anklet.

Half Buck Freddie's
726 Caroline Street
Key West, FL
(305) 294–2007

Slightly dated, overstocked, or slow-moving merchandise from Fast Buck Freddie's (see earlier listing in this section) never dies. It simply ends up across Duval and down a few blocks, at Half Buck Freddie's on Caroline. Everything here, from clothing to calendars to kitchen gadgets, was once on sale at Freddie's. Now it's moved out and marked down 50 percent from its original price. The stock changes regularly, and the hours are limited. Shop for bargains here Thursdays through Sundays only. Half Buck Freddie's does not have a phone number. The number listed above is for Fast Buck Freddie's; the folks there can answer all your questions.

Heatwave Swimwear
403 Greene Street
Key West, FL
(305) 296–0292

One of South Florida's best bikini shops, Heatwave carries a variety of styles and sizes with a Caribbean flair.

Island Vibrations
418 Eaton Street
Key West, FL
(305) 292–7675

Anyone who wants to enjoy hemp as an ecologically sound source of raw material

for paper, clothing, and other products will feel at home here, where everything—from T-shirts and rugs to stationery and soap is made from hemp. Books extolling the virtues of marijuana use for medicinal purposes as well as rolling papers, pipes, and alternative (all legal) smoking products are also available.

Kalypso
609 Whitehead Street
Key West, FL
(305) 296–0977

This open-air gallery of paintings, sculpture, furniture, and jewelry abounds with bold colors and island styles. The artwear—hand-stenciled skirts, pants, and tops made from natural fibers—are especially attractive, practical and fun.

Key West Aloe
524 Front Street
Key West, FL
(305) 294–5592
www.keywestaloe.com

Step into the Key West Aloe on Front Street for a showroom of the only perfumes, skin-care products, and cosmetics to boast a "made in Key West" label. Then be sure to visit the factory outlet store at 540 Greene Street for discounts on these items and to take a free tour of the laboratory where the products are made.

Key West Hand Print Fabrics and Fashions
201 Simonton Street
Key West, FL
(305) 294–9535, (800) 866–0333
www.keywestfashions.com

At Key West Hand Print Fabrics and Fashions, silk-screeners and seamstresses create brightly-colored men's and women's fashions from more than 3,000 original designs. Copyrighted Key West prints adorn men's shirts and neckties as well as various ladies' fashions and accessories, all ready to wear for your next outing. The prints are also sold by the yard; be sure to ask for a label to sew inside your own personal creations.

Key West Hemp Co.
201 William Street
Key West, FL
(305) 293–1888
www.kwhempco.com

Were it not for the sign on the door, you'd never know that the classic blazers, slacks, dresses, shorts, and shirts hanging in this shop are made from hemp. But then so is everything else here, including shoes, socks, soap, shampoos, lotions, and paper products.

Key West Island Bookstore
513 Fleming Street
Key West, FL
(305) 294–2904

Doubled in size in 1999, this shop sells everything from the classics to the best-sellers, along with topical nonfiction and the works of Florida Keys and Key West writers—often at below-market prices. This store is especially supportive of Florida authors and often hosts book-signing events that generate lots of local excitement and a party atmosphere. Carl Hiaasen, James Hall, Jimmy Buffett, Philip Caputo, James Dickey, and Thomas McGuane have all signed books here. Be sure to check the rare book room in the back. You probably won't find a first-edition Hemingway on the shelves, but then again you might.

Key West Kite Company
409 Greene Street
Key West, FL
(305) 296–2535
www.shopfloridakeys.com/kites

The Key West Kite Company is just waiting to make windy days wondrous with flags, banners, and flying tours. The first kite store to set up shop in all of Florida, Key West Kites offers everything from handmade to high-performance sport kites. There's a great selection of yo-yos here, too, plus juggling supplies and instructions.

Key West Winery, Inc.
103 Simonton Street
Key West, FL
(305) 292–1717

This is wine like you've never tasted before. Not one variety is made from grapes! These wines live up to Key West's tropical image—laid back, funky, and packed with pizzazz. All the wines are made from a potpourri of fruits, such as Eleganta, a semi-sweet red raspberry variety that won a silver medal at the Indiana International Wine Competition in 1999. Also medal winners: Hot Sun, a dry white wine with a slight tomato taste and a hint of peppers; Orange Sunshine: a semi-sweet wine made from 100 percent fresh-squeezed Florida orange juice; and 40 Karats: a buttery semi-dry white wine similar to a Chardonnay, but, 100 percent carrot and much more flavorful. You'll find many, many more interesting fruit wines here, and best of all, you can stop in and taste as many wines as you want, seven days a week.

Kino Sandals
107 Fitzpatrick Street
Key West, FL
(305) 294–5044

Whatever you do in Key West, do not miss Kino Sandals. Tucked in the corner of Kino Plaza, across from the Key West Cigar Factory, this factory offers handmade leather footwear for less than $10. Now that's something to wiggle your toes about.

Local Color
276 Margaret Street
Key West Historic Seaport
Key West, FL
(305) 292–3635

425 Greene Street
Key West, FL
(305) 296–0151

The Margaret Street shop is where locals and tourists alike come to purchase the colorful, comfortable clothing that fits the Key West lifestyle. In addition to casual apparel for men and women, you'll find fun hats, handbags, and costume jewelry to complete your island look. The Greene Street location is the place to shop for inexpensive, fun jewelry to adorn your neck, ears, wrists, fingers, even ankles and toes.

Marsha Crafts Antiques
536 Fleming Street
Key West, FL
(305) 296–8106

It won't take but a few minutes of your time to check out the stock at this tiny shop. There's not a lot of it, but if you're looking for an unusual gift, you might just find it here. The art deco picture frames—like the ones that used to grace many a piano or dressing table in the '20s and '30s—are especially nice.

Maskerville
309 Petronia Street
Key West, FL
(305) 292–3699

The business of Maskerville is original, handcrafted, feathered masks, lampshades, and dusters. These incredibly intricate, incredibly beautiful creations are not to be believed. Maskerville is open intermittently depending on whether the owners are in town or off presenting their work at art shows throughout the country. You can bet they will be back well before Fantasy Fest, however, as their feathered creations take center stage at the various balls and other masked events that highlight this week of revelry.

Mustard Seed
527 Fleming Street
Key West, FL
(305) 293–8734

For wearable crafts and gifts, Mustard Seed (formerly Island Needlework) carries original handmade accessories, including belts and handbags, as well as needlepoint canvases and the yarns to complete them. Patterns for cross-stitching Key West sights like the Hemingway House and the Southernmost House are available here too.

Native Material
605 Whitehead Street
Key West, FL
(305) 296–0466

Handcrafted goods and natural fibers from Central and South America are the centerpiece for this tiny shop that is actually an open-air marketplace. Shop for colorful handbags, hammocks, baskets, and other home accessories.

90 Miles to Cuba
616 Greene Street
Key West, FL
(305) 292–1333

Everything about this shop says Old Key West. Tucked among the used books, secondhand lamps, recycled costume jewelry, and picture postcards, you'll find reproductions of old magazine covers (we spotted a *Life* cover of Ernest Hemingway from the 1940s for $7) and enlargements of postcards depicting the Florida Keys in the 1930s and 1940s—perfect for framing and hanging on a wall back home. Be on the lookout, too, for old Key West street signs. Some of the lesser known Old Town lanes go for around $80.

Noah's Ark
416 Fleming Street
Key West, FL
(305) 294–2757

Noah's Ark is an animal-theme gift shop in a Conch house more than 100 years old. This fetching store showcases room after room of collectibles, stuffed animals, clothing, and housewares that cover hundreds of species.

Pelican Poop Shop
314 Simonton Street
Key West, FL
(305) 292–9955

This eclectic collection of artwork, which is housed in what was once a Ford dealership, includes originals from all over the Caribbean. If you're in the market for a life-size, stone, Mayan deer dancer or a Haitian oil drum sculpture, this is the place to come. You'll browse to the tropical sounds of Harry Belafonte's "Matilda," and, if you buy $10 in merchandise or pay a $2 fee, you can tour the private Casa Antigua gardens out back, linked forever to Ernest Hemingway by a quirky twist of fate. He completed *A Farewell to Arms* here while awaiting delivery on his new Ford back in 1928.

Long after Hemingway left Key West, this building became a hotel, then later the island's largest brothel, and its first drag club. Today it is home to City Commissioner Tom Oosterhoudt and his mother Mary Ann Worth. On your visit to the gardens, you will hear Tom himself recount the colorful history of the building in a six-minute audio presentation.

Perkins & Son Chandlery
901 Fleming Street
Key West, FL
(305) 294–7635

Perkins can supply everything you need to set out to sea or add a nautical theme to your home: brasswork, ships' clocks, models, charts, and books, plus jackets, shorts, hats, and foul-weather gear. Allow plenty of time just to browse; this shop is stuffed from floor to ceiling. Many of the antiques are for display purposes only and not for sale. However, if you see something you like, ask. Some sales are negotiable.

Pretty Marsh
218 Whitehead Street
Key West, FL
(305) 295–8777

Look up to spot this shop, which is located at the top of the stairs, on the second level of Galleon Square. This combination interior design shop and gallery features the work of owner/artist Russell D'Alessio, who captures island and coastal life from two perspectives—Key West and Bar Harbor, Maine. An outstanding collection of pillows, pottery, baskets, and other home accessories awaits you here.

Queen Losha
423 Simonton Street
Key West, FL
(305) 294–0094
www.queenlosha.com

For all things African, this is the place. Queen Losha stocks a wide array of handcrafted, African baskets and bags, clay and wood masks, hand-painted fabrics, batiks, and potato prints and carvings, including traditional fertility dolls from the Ashanti tribes and handmade wooden chess sets from Kenya.

Reef Relief Environmental Center & Store
Key West Historic Seaport,
end of William Street
Key West, FL
(305) 294–3100
www.reefrelief.org

You can learn about our fragile coral reef here at the Reef Relief Environmental Center. Continuous videos, displays, and

You are closer to Havana than you are to Miami when you are in Key West. PHOTO: JANET WARE

free information will heighten your awareness of what you can do to protect North America's only living coral reef. Merchandise on sale includes coral reef books, educational products for both adults and children, and informational videos.

The Restaurant Store
313 Margaret Street
Key West, FL
(305) 294-7994

The Restaurant Store is chock-full of kitchen and cooking gear to feed 5 or 50. You'll discover state-of-the-art utensils, pots and pans, and accessories for culinary aficionados and chefs alike.

Sam's Treasure Chest
518 Fleming Street
Key West, FL
(305) 296-5907

Talk about truth in advertising! The sign in the window here reads "We buy junk and sell antiques." Step inside and you'll find everything from old costume jewelry and hats to worn out baskets and battered license plates. The prices are reasonable, and the stock here changes regularly, so our advice is to shop early and often.

Scrubs of Key West
720 Caroline Street
Key West, FL
(305) 295-7232
www.scrubskeywest.com

Scrubs are not necessarily just for surgeons anymore. Nor do the loose-fitting shirts and drawstring pants have to be hospital green. Scrubs of Key West stitches them up in all manner of tropical prints—fish, palm trees, lizards, and the like. And although plenty of local doctors, nurses, dentists, and hygienists shop here, non-medical types have discovered that this is a great place to buy casual wear and gifts—like soft fabric handbags, keychains, and eyeglass cases.

Sign of Sandford
328 Simonton Street
Key West, FL
(305) 296-7493

This store specializes in wholesale fabrics but also offers a selection of wearable art created by designer Sandford Birdsey, for retail sale.

Swingin Gators
218 Whitehead Street
Key West, FL
(305) 292-1188

The sturdy hammocks you'll find hanging all over this shop give new meaning to the phrase "laid-back life." Go ahead, try one out for size and comfort. With so many styles to choose from—single, double, even chair-like hammocks you can suspend from the ceiling—there's sure to be one to suit your taste and budget.

Timmy Tuxedo's
812 Fleming Street
Key West, FL
(305) 294–8897

Believe it or not, we islanders occasionally have to go formal. But that doesn't necessarily mean black tie. At this, the only formal wear outlet in Key West, the ties and cummerbunds are just as likely to be tropical prints. Tuxedos, dinner jackets, and all the accompaniments are available for rent or sale here, in a wide array of sizes and styles.

The T-Shirt Factory
316 Simonton Street
Key West, FL
(305) 292–2060

No trip to Key West would be complete without the purchase of at least one T-shirt to commemorate the event. Key West is loaded with T-shirt shops, but most of them carry exactly the same styles. So you can purchase your shirt on Duval and risk looking like everyone else, or you can come here and find a shirt that's truly unique. These tees are handscreened on site using vivid colors, water-based inks, and designs supplied by local artists. You'll find a wide variety of sizes and styles here, including traditional tees, long-sleeved tees, tanks, crop tees, as well as beach cover-ups and sweats for kids and adults. The average T-shirt price is around $15, design included.

Whitfield Jack Jewelry Genius
200 Elizabeth Street
Key West, FL
(305) 294–7092
www.jewelrygenius.com

Were it not for the cases of jewelry lining the walls of Whitfield Jack, you likely wouldn't realize you are inside a store at all. Set inside a simulated tropical garden, Whitfield Jack jewelers carries original 14-karat designs.

Way Off Duval
Bargain Books and Newsstand
1028 Truman Avenue
Key West, FL
(305) 294–7446

South Florida's largest retailer of pre-read books is right here on our tiny island. Wander through room after slightly dusty room of fiction, sci-fi, romance, and other literature. A couple of cats may find your lap a cozy spot to take a nap as you peruse a favorite title from one of the comfortable chairs strewn throughout. If you love books and you love a bargain, you won't be disappointed. But be prepared to spend some time here. Half the fun of finding your bargain book is in the search for it.

Insiders' Tip
Some Duval Street T-shirt shops advertise bargain prices to reel you inside, then hook you with extra charges once you take the bait. Be aware, and do not let yourself be overcharged for such additions as special designs. By city ordinance, all T-shirt shops are required to post a list of prices inside the store. Be sure to confirm the total price before consenting to a purchase. If you feel you have been overcharged by any store, call Key West Code Enforcement at (305) 292-8191.

Insiders' Tip

See our Fishing chapter
for the lowdown on
angling outfitters.

find something you might have worn in a previous life—like to your senior prom or your first wedding. You're also likely to unearth some practical finds—a pair of khaki shorts, a leather purse, a cotton sundress. Half the fun of this shop is in the looking.

Consigning Adults
802 White Street
Key West, FL
(305) 294–2125

This is the designer boutique of Key West consignment shops. These folks are very picky about what they will take on consignment, and the prices reflect that. The merchandise is clean, pressed, and artfully displayed. You'll see men's and women's clothing with labels from Ralph Lauren and Liz Claiborne as well as shoes from Ferragamo, Bellini, and Allan Edmonds. Prices are steeper than other consignment shops, but bargains still abound. You can pick up a tuxedo or a three-piece suit here for about $50; a pair of Ferragamo shoes was priced at $20.

In One Era
1118 White Street
Key West, FL
(305) 293–0208

Don't carry too large a bag on your shoulder here unless you want to buy what you break. The shop is crowded with furniture, and the shelves and counters overflow with many breakable antiques and collectibles. You'll find a nice selection of old jewelry, postcards, buttons, bottles, cigar boxes, and cookie jars. Plan to spend some time here just browsing.

The Little Consignment Shop
Around the Corner
1102 Truman Avenue
Key West, FL
(305) 294–3327

The clothing sold here is not just used; it's pre-loved. At least that's what the sign says, and we believe it. Pick your way through the racks of dresses, suits, shirts, slacks, shorts, and shoes. You are sure to

Records and Rogues
1018 Truman Avenue
Key West, FL
(305) 296–4115

Who said that second-hand applies only to furniture, books, and clothes? Certainly not Records and Rogues, where the specialty is music. With shelf after shelf of used CDs, priced from $2 to $10, plus new selections at reasonable prices, this is Key West's largest discount music store. Take your old CDs and trade them for credit, or just find that old record your collection has been lacking. Afraid to take a chance on a used CD? Not to worry. These are all guaranteed. And if you find you don't like your selection once you get it home, you can bring it back and trade it for something else.

Victoria Lesser Design Statement
1011 Truman Avenue
Key West, FL
(305) 292–0101

Get some stylish clothes made to order or buy them straight off the rack. Designer Victoria Lesser is affectionately called "Pajama Mama" by Bill Cosby, because she designed all the pajamas he wore on his popular television show. She has designed clothes for many others, including Barbara Mandrell, The Bee Gees, Sophia Loren, Aerosmith, and Goldie Hawn.

Waldenbooks
2212 N. Roosevelt Boulevard
Key West, FL
(305) 294–5419

Not surprisingly, this is Key West's largest bookstore and, perhaps, its most visible. It's a stand-alone shop on U.S. Hwy. 1 with plenty of free parking. On the inside, the store looks much like every other Waldenbooks you've ever been in with a notable exception: Right up front, there's a huge display of titles by Key West authors as well as an impressive array of books on a variety of Florida-related subjects. In addition to several guides to Key West and Florida Keys' attractions, you'll find island cookbooks, maps, history tomes, and nature guides to help you identify our native flora and fauna. You'll also find especially helpful clerks here as well as frequent book signings/sales, the proceeds of which are often earmarked for local charities.

Best of New Town

The New Town area along N. Roosevelt Boulevard is often overlooked by shoppers enamored with the funky shops of Old Town. But this is where the locals shop. A series of strip malls or plazas—Kennedy, Key, Luani, Overseas Market, Searstown—are within blocks of each other and feature the staples of everyday life as offered by major retail chain stores.

Retirement

If we are to believe Noah Webster, retirement means "withdrawing from active life." Not so in the Florida Keys. Our retirees are anything but retiring. Each year, about the time Jack Frost starts whistling up North, the influx of snowbirds to our sun-kissed islands begins, and the collective pulse of our communities quickens.

Unlike other retirement areas in Florida, our seniors usually don't keep to themselves in pre-planned communities. You'll find them living in residential neighborhoods and condominiums, RV parks, and mobile-home villages. Our seniors contribute an added dimension to our communities. They form a much-needed core of volunteers for many of our public services, including the county libraries, local hospitals, and area schools.

The American Association of Retired Persons (AARP) accepts individuals 50 and older into membership, which means the first wave of baby-boomers have already reached "senior" status and some are taking the Florida Keys by storm. These prime-of-lifers have taken a career course detour, leaving that corporate 9-to-5 (or, more likely, 9-to-9) grind to venture off the track into uncharted territory.

Regardless of age, the retirees in the Florida Keys remain youthful. Our warm tropical climate is kind to old bones (young ones, too!). The pace of our lifestyle moves to a different drummer . . . well, more of a reggae beat. Some people even feel we live longer down here . . . and they're in their 90s. Our energetic retirees enjoy fishing and scuba diving, golf and tennis, boating, and bridge. They are active in myriad special-interest organizations the length and breadth of the Keys. Many pursue artistic hobbies long put on the back burner while the rest of their lives simmered. Some go back to school, developing new skills and honing others.

At the heart of the retirement community in the Florida Keys are the senior citizen centers, which serve as cohesive units of companionship and support to retirees of all ages and circumstances. The centers were constructed and are maintained as a joint venture between Monroe County and the local chapters of AARP. The county nutrition sites are in the centers (see Nutrition Services later in this chapter). Membership in AARP is not a prerequisite for most activities of the senior citizen centers, but anyone age 50 or older may pick up an application to AARP at any of the centers. Because our seniors participate in activities based all throughout the Keys, we have organized this chapter by interest group, incorporating all areas of the Keys from Key Largo to Key West.

Senior Citizen Centers

**Upper Keys AARP Senior
Citizens Center
MM 88.7 Bayside
Plantation Key, FL
(305) 852–7132**

This active group of seniors in the Upper Keys has a series of fund-raisers, such as its annual rummage sale, to raise money for 12 to 15 community organizations, including the fire department, the ambulance corps, and the local Red Cross chapter. Each Christmas, members also serve refreshments at the Santa Claus party at the Theater of the Sea. Besides monthly meetings, this Upper Keys group enjoys bingo on Sunday evenings; members donate the money raised to Hospice. During the winter season, when the ranks swell by some 60 to 75 percent, Spanish classes are offered at the center. Puzzles, crafts, and cards are favorite impromptu activities.

Many of the retirees in the Upper Keys are active in conservation and preservation organizations, fraternal organizations, the Monroe County Fine Arts Council and the Key Players (see our Arts and Culture chapter), and human service groups such as Hospice and the Domestic Abuse Shelter.

The center is next to the Sheriff's Substation.

**Middle Keys AARP Senior
Citizens Center
MM 48.8 Bayside
535 33rd Street
Marathon, FL
(305) 743-4008**

This lively bunch in the Middle Keys maintains a whirlwind of activities, especially during the winter season, such as bridge, crafts, weekly bingo on Tuesday afternoons, and regular exercise sessions. A balanced meal is served at the center every weekday at noon. The seniors trip the light fantastic with special events, such as the Valentine Sweetheart Dance and the St. Patrick's Day party. They charter buses and go on special excursions to the Monkey Jungle or Everglades National Park, to Homestead or Miami, even an overnight to Busch Gardens in Tampa. The trips usually cost a nominal fee and include entrance fees and dinner.

The center offers Arrive Alive instruction for seniors several times throughout the year. Arrive Alive is a bookwork driving course that when passed nets the senior citizen a discount on auto insurance. The crafting groups hold boutiques in October, November, and December, where they display and sell their creations. The seniors have a series of yard sales throughout the year to make money to maintain the center. Volunteers also go to the elementary schools several times a week and, like grandparents, assist children in reading or math, or just talk to the child and give a hug when needed.

The Marathon Senior Citizens Center has a large lending library. It also has free income tax preparation when that dreaded time rolls around. Free flu shots and blood-pressure checks are available on a regular basis.

The center is near the Marathon Yacht Club.

**Lower Keys AARP Senior
Citizens Center
MM 31 Bayside
380 Key Deer Boulevard
Big Pine Key, FL
(305) 872-3990**

Not to be outdone by the other Keys centers, the seniors in the Lower Keys boogie in a bevy of activities like their compatriots up the Keys. The winter season finds them country line-dancing and exercising, taking French lessons, and attending classes in hatha-yoga. Every month the center shows a classic movie, Sunday afternoons are reserved for bingo, and the second Tuesday evening of every month is a combination potluck and bingo night. The group has an active barbershop quartet and a serious chess club. Two times each month seniors can get free blood-pressure checks.

The Lower Keys Senior Citizens Center, which is right behind the Big Pine Key firehouse, is open every day for card playing and puzzle-making. The seniors sponsor 55 Alive driving classes (much like the group in the Middle Keys) as well as computer instruction. Every Friday night during the winter season the center holds a dance, playing recorded Big Band music.

**AARP Senior Citizens Center
Harvey Government Building
1016 Georgia Street
Key West, FL
(305) 292-3565**

The seniors in Key West often go their own way, we are told, so not as many organized activities emanate from this center as from others in the rest of the Keys. The seniors are active in the Key West Garden Club, the Art and Historical Society, the Maritime History Society, the Key West Yacht Club (see our Cruising chapter), the Power Squadron, and

Upper Keys Campus
MM 89.9 Oceanside
Coral Shores High School
Tavernier, FL
(305) 852-8007, (305) 852-2737
www.firn.edu/fkcc

Seniors and retirees particularly enjoy the computer classes offered at this branch of Florida Keys Community College. They also sign up for such classes as conversational Spanish, watercolor painting, beginning drawing, creative writing, and American and English literature.

Middle Keys Campus
MM 50 Oceanside
900 Sombrero Beach Road
Marathon, FL
(305) 743-2133, (305) 743-0749
www.firn.edu/fkcc

The Middle Keys branch of FKCC offers general-interest classes in foreign language and computer science as well as some more unusual fare, such as nature walks, tours of the Everglades, conservation classes, and photography instruction.

Florida Keys Community College
5901 W. College Road
Stock Island, FL
(305) 296-9081, ext. 495 or 496
www.firn.edu/fkcc

The main campus of the Florida Keys Community College offers many more classes of interest to seniors than the other branches up the Keys. The fee structure remains the same, however. Art classes in ceramics, stained glass, jewelry making, lettering and calligraphy, drawing, wheel throwing, print making, photography, graphic arts, painting, and sculpture will intrigue the artistically inclined. New courses in computerized photography and graphic arts are also offered. Many foreign languages are available, and the selection of literature courses includes one on Florida Keys writers and literature. Seniors can try their hands at creative writing and dabble in the natural sciences with marine data collection, marine archaeology, and the cul-

fraternal organizations such as Moose and Elk. More than 50 seniors regularly come to the center for the county-supplied hot meal each day (see "Nutrition Services" in this chapter), staying to play bingo or cards afterward. Bridge is popular at the center, too. The center is located at the corner of Truman Avenue and White Street.

College Courses

The Florida Keys Community College offers a selection of courses of interest to seniors. Classes cost $50.90 per credit hour (for Florida residents) with a one-time $15 application fee. Those students from out of state must pay a higher fee. There is no tuition break for senior citizens. The academic year is divided into three terms. The fall class session runs from August through December. The spring term is January to May. Summer classes are held from the beginning of May through mid-August. (See our Key West section in this chapter for courses at the main campus of FKCC.) Class offerings change often, so call the college branch of your choice for a course catalog and the most recent class schedule.

ture and environment of the Florida Everglades. Vocational courses include marine propulsion technology (good for those with boats to repair) and electronic engineering technology (to fix VCRs, etc.).

FKCC has a beautiful swimming pool and offers classes in water aerobics and fitness swimming. Seniors can take classes as non-degree-seeking students or work toward an Associate of Arts or Associate of Science degree.

Lifelong learning doesn't necessarily mean that you must enroll in a degree program or semester-long course. FKCC also offers a variety of continuing education workshops, seminars, and classes devoted to a single subject such as stock-market investment, custom rod-making, accessing the Internet, or bookbinding. These classes may meet for a single session or several weeks depending on the complexity of the subject matter. For additional information and a list of upcoming classes, contact the FKCC Continuing Education Department at (305) 296–9081, ext. 233.

Public Libraries

The four Monroe County libraries outside Key West are popular reading-room destinations with seniors in the Keys. They all maintain ever-growing large-print collections and a wide selection of current magazines. In addition, most of the libraries have a burgeoning number of videotapes and books-on-tape that may be checked out. Card catalogs in each of the libraries list all the materials in the system. Your local library will be able to get information from other branches for you upon request. The Key West library maintains a well-stocked Florida History Room that provides a fascinating look back through the centuries in Key West and all of the Keys. Volumes of old photographs are housed here.

The libraries also host special events, such as lectures and film screenings, throughout the year. The library system has a strong volunteer program as well.

The Monroe County library system includes the following branches: Key Largo, (305) 451–2396, MM 101.4 Oceanside, Tradewinds Shopping Center, Key Largo; Islamorada, (305) 664–4645, MM 81.5 Bayside, Islamorada; Marathon, (305) 743–5156, MM 48.5 Oceanside, next to Fishermen's Hospital, Marathon; Big Pine, (305) 872–0992, MM 31 Bayside, 213 Key Deer Boulevard, Big Pine Key; and Key West, (305) 292–3595, 700 Fleming St., Key West.

Special-Interest Activities

It is not uncommon here in the Florida Keys to hear a senior citizen complain, "Since I've retired, I've never been so busy in my life!" Seniors get involved in civic clubs and fraternal organizations such as the Elks, Eagles, Moose, and Shriners. They work with human-service organizations such as Big Brothers/Big Sisters, Florida Keys Children's Shelter, Domestic Abuse Shelter, and the AIDS Prevention Center. Retirees donate valuable time to the Monroe Fine Arts Council, the American Cancer Society, and Guardian Ad Litem. And they participate in activities helping the Florida Keys themselves such as Reef Relief, Florida Keys Wild Bird Rehabilitation Center, Friends of the Everglades, and the Nature Conservancy's Bay Watch (see our Paradise Found chapter).

Contact the chamber of commerce in your area for a complete listing of the special-interest organizations of the Florida Keys. Area chambers include those in Key Largo, (305) 451–1414, (800) 822–1088; Islamorada, (305) 664–4503, (800) 322–5397; Marathon, (305) 743–5417, (800) 262–7284; Lower Keys, (305) 872–2411, (800) 872–3722; and Key West, (305) 294–2587, (800) 527–8539.

Garden Clubs

Some of the most popular organizations in the Florida Keys are its garden clubs, perhaps because we have so many days of glorious sunshine or because our subtropical climate fosters the growth of such

Gardening is a favorite pastime in the Keys; garden clubs are popular in Key Largo, Marathon, and Key West. PHOTO: VICTORIA SHEARER

exotic flowering foliage and palms. But our planting medium is unyielding coral rock that must be pick-axed into a hole where we place dirt imported from the mainland. To complicate matters further, a bulging cupboard of insects hangs around all year long, feasting on the fruits of our labors. And we must pay for irrigation watering by the ounce!

Membership in garden clubs in the Florida Keys is open to all interested parties.

Upper Keys Garden Club
MM 94 Bayside
Key Largo, FL
(305) 852–8629

Built about 1960, the Frances Tracy Garden Center (next to the Red Cross Building) hosts members of the Upper Keys Garden Club on the third Tuesday of every month. The group often hears a lecturer speak on some phase of subtropical horticulture. In the fall the group holds a Plant Ramble sale as a fund-raiser and, in January, sponsors a garden walk through six lovely private gardens of the Upper Keys. In March or April, depending upon when Easter falls, the Garden Club has an accredited flower show, which is judged by professional judges in the categories of artistic (flower arranging) and horticulture (plants).

The Upper Keys Garden Club is affiliated with the Florida Federation of State Garden Clubs and the National Council of State Garden Clubs. The club passes a donation basket at each meeting in support of the Florida Keys Wild Bird Rehabilitation Center (see our Attractions chapter). Members also support the community's landscaping needs by donating plants and labor in landscaping the Coast Guard Station, Coral Shores High School, and Plantation Key Elementary School.

The Upper Keys Garden Club helps a fledgling group of junior gardeners at Key Largo Elementary School with money and shared talents. Junior gardeners, under the instruction of the school's horticul-ture teacher, participate in the Garden Club's annual flower show.

Marathon Garden Club
MM 50 Bayside
Marathon, FL
(305) 743–4971

The Marathon Garden Club was organized in March 1955, when the Keys were in desperate need of beautification. Beginning as a small grass-roots group that held meetings in each other's homes, the ranks have burgeoned to almost 200. Much of the lovely landscaping gracing public areas of Marathon is the work of the Marathon Garden Club. You'll notice the group's creative handiwork at the American Legion, the chamber of commerce building, the firehouse, Fishermen's Hospital, the public library, the Key Colony Causeway, along the Overseas Highway, and at Marathon High School.

Since the 1970s the group has sponsored successful house tours, plant and craft fairs, and flower shows. In 1990 the Marathon Garden Club started a conservation program called Save the Queen Conch. A state environmental grant of $8,700 was given to the club to help enforce fines and educate the public by erecting signs on water and land, warning about taking the endangered conch. The club was recognized for its efforts with the Governor's Environmental Education Award in 1992. The same year, the club purchased the William B. Bradley building and adjoining nursery property for use as the Marathon Garden Club Center. An addition now augments the original structure with a 40-by-60-foot meeting room.

In December, the Marathon Garden Club stages its annual Christmas Around the World display: more than a dozen Christmas trees, each decorated in the traditional ornaments of a different country. In addition to the general public, the club has hosted more than 900 Monroe County school children at this exhibit. Garden club members also take their

Good food, good company, great sunset—it doesn't get any better than this. PHOTO: VICTORIA SHEARER

collective expertise into the Monroe County schools, where they teach the children about plants and trees as well as flower arranging.

The Marathon Garden Club meets the third Friday of each month from October through May. The public is invited. The gift shop, which offers a changing rota of unusual specialty gift items, is open year-round from Monday through Saturday, 10 A.M. to 2 P.M.

Key West Garden Club
West Martello Tower
Atlantic Boulevard and White Street
Key West, FL
(305) 294-3210

The Key West Garden Club maintains the gardens of West Martello Tower, an old Civil War fort at Higgs Beach on Atlantic Boulevard. The Garden Club meets once a month for a short business meeting followed by a presentation by a guest speaker, often a visiting horticulturist. These events are open to the general public. Twice a year the group holds a plant

sale at its West Martello Tower headquarters. You can walk away with beautiful plants at bargain prices and a wealth of free gardening tips and information to boot. Every March the Key West Garden Club sponsors a garden tour during which the general public can visit five private gardens in Key West. (See our Annual Events chapter for details.)

American Contract Bridge League

Duplicate bridge passes muster as the game of choice among those addicts of the sport. "If there's a game in town, we'll find it," says one duplicate player. There are seven regular weekly games of duplicate bridge in the Florida Keys between Key Largo and Marathon, plus four more in Key West (see details in the Key West section of this chapter). The play is recognized by the National American Contract Bridge League, and you can earn Life Master's points. The games are open to all. If you don't have a partner, don't worry, the director will pair you with a partner for the day's game. Play costs about $3.

It is best to call the director before the day of play to make sure the schedule has not been changed. The groups are listed here by location.

Bank of America, MM 100 Oceanside, Key Largo. Play is year-round on Mondays at 1 P.M. Director is Lucy McGraw (305-451-2302).

Bank of America, MM 100 Oceanside, Key Largo. Play is year-round on Tuesday evenings at 7 P.M. and Fridays at 1 P.M. Director is Carol Duffy (305-852-5369).

San Pablo Catholic Church, MM 53.5 Oceanside, 550 122nd Street, Marathon. Play is year-round on Thursdays at 12:30 P.M. Director is Sally Whitman (305-743-7154).

Kirk of the Keys, MM 51 Oceanside, Marathon. Play is on Mondays and Wednesdays at 12:30 P.M. with director Richard Foley (305-743-3296) and on Fridays at 10:30 A.M. with director Joy Thomas (305-743-1992).

Senior Center, Harvey Government Building, 1016 Georgia St., Key West. Play is on Tuesdays, Thursdays, and Sundays at 1:30 P.M. and on Wednesdays at 6 P.M. Director is Suzy Park (305-292-6318).

Golf and Tennis

Two of the most popular sports among seniors are golf and tennis. See our Recreation chapter for information on facilities in the Florida Keys.

Quilter's Club

Next to avid gardeners, bridge fanatics, loyal golfers, and tireless tennis players, quilters rank as a group prepared to go the distance. We've never known a quilter who could pass up a fabric store or a quilt shop, and it is a hobby that has burgeoned across the nation.

Totally hooked on quilting in the Florida Keys are the members of the Quilter's Club, who come from all over the Keys, and even South Florida, to attend meetings at the Key Largo Library every Friday at 10 A.M. The group does not jury any bodies of work, but participants have a popular show-and-tell of projects in

process. Each month members also hold a themed fabric exchange of 6-inch squares and a "block of the month" drawing.

Every other year the Quilter's Club has a quilt show on National Quilting Day in March, complete with national advertising. It draws a worldwide audience, we're told. Contact the Key Largo Public Library (305-451-2396) for more information and to be sure the meeting is on for a particular week. The quilters sometimes get bumped by another organization that needs the meeting space.

Senior Services

Monroe County Social Services

The Florida Keys offers senior citizens a wide range of services through the Monroe County Social Services Agency, whose main administrative offices are in Key West. We have listed the branch office locations in the Upper and Middle Keys below and the contact numbers of each department in the individual descriptions. Note that services in the Middle Keys also include Big Pine Key, which ordinarily is included with the Lower Keys throughout the book. The rest of the Lower Keys are handled from the offices in Key West.

Alternately, you can call the Elder Help Line (800-273-2044), and describe your problem or need; you will be referred to the proper agency. Monroe County Social Services office locations include: in the Upper Keys, Plantation Key Government Center Annex, MM 88.8 Bayside, Tavernier; in the Middle Keys, Marathon Government Annex, MM 50.5 Oceanside, 490 63rd Street, Suite 190, Marathon; and, in the Lower Keys, Public Service Building, Wing III, 5100 College Road, Key West.

Welfare Department
Upper Keys (305) 852-7125
Middle Keys (305) 289-6016
Lower Keys, Key West (305) 292-4408

Monroe County, which encompasses the Florida Keys, has the highest cost of living

Tennis is a favorite pastime among Keys' seniors.
PHOTO: VICTORIA SHEARER

of any county in the State of Florida. Yet no adjustment is made in eligibility requirements for aid for senior citizens, who are usually managing on fixed incomes. This county agency works with seniors on a case-by-case basis as an interim assistance agency, helping solve unexpected crises that put them at temporary financial risk. The agency also aids seniors in matters of lost checks, robbery, and fraud; provides equipment loans of wheelchairs and walkers; and helps out with short-term medical needs such as prescriptions, eyeglasses, and hearing aids. This help is designed to restore the individuals to self-sufficient status or to refer them to the appropriate state or fed-

eral agencies for more long-term support. Documentation of need is required to qualify for assistance.

Senior Community Service Employment Program (SCSEP)
Upper Keys (305) 852–1469, Ext. 6328
Middle Keys (305) 289–6328
Lower Keys, Key West (305) 292–4593

The Senior Community Service Employment Program (SCSEP) is a national program funded by Title V of the Older Americans Act. It provides temporary work experience and training for persons 55 and older who meet financial and eligibility guidelines. Most seniors living on Social Security payments alone will qualify. The training occurs at governmental and nonprofit community service agencies. Jobs include library aides, nutrition site aides, senior citizen center receptionists, or aides in the Social Security office, Job Service office, or Red Cross office. The employment prepares candidates for jobs in the private sector.

In-Home Services
Upper Keys (305) 852–7154
Middle Keys (305) 289–6324
Lower Keys, Key West (305) 292–4583

In-Home Services networks information and referrals between the private and public sector for family members, friends, and other agencies seeking services on behalf of impaired elderly persons. Participants must be at least age 60. The program is designed so the elderly may maintain quality of life while remaining in their homes.

The information and referral telephone line (800–273–2044) is staffed by case managers from 8 A.M. to 5 P.M., Monday through Friday. They will specifically target the needed assistance and refer the caller to the resources available. Case management provides a social worker to support and help those requiring assistance.

Chore services for impaired elderly who can no longer accomplish the tasks for themselves are available. These include yard work, heavy-duty cleaning services, and small minor household repairs. Homemaking support with light housekeeping, meal preparation and planning, shopping, laundry tasks, and other essential errands assist clients in need. Personal care, in-home respite aides will help with bathing, dressing and other personal needs, providing relief for caregivers. A fee schedule assessment based on the person's income will determine what or if he/she will have to pay for these services.

Nutrition Services
Upper Keys (305) 852–7133
Middle Keys (305) 743–3346
Lower Keys (305) 292–4523
Key West (305) 294–0708, (305) 295–5166

Funded by the Older Americans Act of 1960 and the Alliance for Aging for Miami-Dade and Monroe Counties, and aided with a 10 percent cash match by the Monroe County Board of Commissioners, seniors 60 and older may take advantage of many county nutrition programs. Homebound persons can receive a daily hot meal from Meals on Wheels. Other congregate sites throughout the Keys offer a low-cost, noontime, complete balanced meal. The midday repast is supplemented with instruction on nutrition, hygiene, healthcare concerns, and hurricane preparedness, and the group also participates in card games and organized activities.

One help to seniors is the ongoing registration for special telephones that Bell-South supplies to the hearing-impaired elderly of the Florida Keys. The sound of these telephones is enhanced, and the numbers are extra large. All seniors are eligible for one of these free telephones. Call one of the congregate centers (see earlier listings) and request an application form for a telephone for the hearing-impaired. Telephones will be delivered to the homebound. All customers of BellSouth pay a few cents per month, probably without even knowing it, to provide this service to the elderly.

The midday congregate meals for the Upper, Middle, and Lower Keys are held at the respective AARP Senior Citizens Centers. The congregate centers and Nutrition Services contacts in Key West are Douglas Community Center, 800 Emma Street, (305) 294–0708, and the AARP Senior Citizens Center, Old Truman School Cafeteria, 1016 Georgia Street, (305) 294–7646.

Transportation Program
Upper Keys (305) 852–7148
Middle Keys (305) 289–6052
Lower Keys, Key West (305) 292–4424

Monroe County maintains eight minibuses throughout the Keys, providing transportation for individuals 60 and older or those physically challenged or transportation-disadvantaged (those who don't or can't have a driver's license for some reason). Travelers must be able to get to the bus unassisted, but the vehicle has a wheelchair lift to aid entry. The bus picks up and drops off at your door between 8:15 A.M. and 5 P.M. (last pickup is 4:30 P.M.). Seniors must call for bus service 24 hours in advance, no later than 3 P.M. The route is figured every day, based on the pickup times and locations requested. Riders must allow plenty of

Insiders' Tip
Be sure to inquire about senior citizen discounts wherever you go in the Florida Keys. You may find admission costs reduced or waived at some of our tourist attractions as well as state and national parks. Some restaurants have early bird specials or offer discounts to seniors.

time to get to their appointments and should expect that actual pickup may be 30 minutes before or after requested pickup time.

Each of the eight buses has a set territory: The Lower Keys circuit is considered Key West to Big Pine Key. The Middle Keys territory is between Sugarloaf Key and Marathon. The two Upper Keys routes travel between Marathon and MM72 and between MM 72 and MM 112 at the county line on the 18-mile stretch. Fees are figured on a sliding scale based on mileage. Inquire about the cost of your transport when you make your reservation. The dispatcher will compute the mileage between your pick-up point and your destination.

Grandparents host a buried treasure hunt on an uninhabited mangrove island. PHOTO: DICK ADLER

Assisted-Living Facility

Bayshore Manor
MM 4
5200 College Road
Stock Island, FL
(305) 294–4966

Bayshore Manor is the oldest assisted-living facility in Monroe County and the only such facility in the State of Florida owned and operated by county government. It is staffed on a 24-hour basis by State Certified Nursing Assistants and is licensed to provide full residential care for up to 16 clients.

In addition to full-time residents, Bayshore Manor also operates the only respite/daytime program in Monroe County for elderly residents who either require constant nonmedical attention at home because of mental, emotional, or physical limitations or simply because their families are concerned about them remaining at home alone during the day. This program provides daily group activities such as field trips, arts and crafts, music, games, and simple calisthenics plus a daily hot lunch. This service is available seven days a week.

Additionally, bed space permitting, short-term admissions for up to 30 days are available for caregivers who require longer periods of time away from the person in their care. Residents live in private rooms equipped with a color television. The facility is centrally air-conditioned, and meals are served in a communal dining room. In addition to assistance with activities of daily living, Bayshore Manor provides a full laundry service.

The monthly fee for residential service is based upon the client's ability to pay, and the admission procedure is a joint process involving both the Bayshore Manor director and the Monroe County Social Services Department's social workers.

Healthcare

In case you need healthcare while you're here, this chapter offers a synopsis of options, listed by category in descending mile-marker order from Key Largo to Key West, then alphabetically in Key West.

We have included information on healthcare options, ranging from full-service hospitals and specialty care-providers for patients in need of cancer or dialysis treatments to physical therapy clinics and mental health services. And don't miss the information on veterinary-care options. We care about Spot and Fluffy, too!

Please be reminded, however, that this is not intended to be a comprehensive listing of all possible health services. The Florida Keys and Key West are served by physicians in nearly every specialty as well as by osteopaths, chiropractors, podiatrists, dentists, and optometrists. So if, while visiting our islands, you should develop a sudden toothache from downing one too many frozen coladas or drop a contact lens somewhere in the sand, don't despair. One of our many healthcare providers will be available to help you, even on short notice. Ask your hotel concierge for a referral to the appropriate specialist or consult the Yellow Pages.

And should your situation call for medical expertise that is not available in the Florida Keys, rest assured that you will still be able to receive state-of-the-art treatment in a timely manner. The University of Miami's renowned Jackson Memorial Medical Center as well as other mainland hospitals and trauma facilities are just a helicopter ride away.

Acute-Care Centers

Upper Keys

Keys Rapid Care Center
MM 101.4 Oceanside
Tradewinds Shopping Center
Key Largo, FL
(305) 453–0666

Immediate care for cuts, insect bites, allergies, minor emergencies, and illnesses is available for children and adults at this readily accessible clinic located at the Tradewinds Shopping Center between Publix and Kmart. Medical specialties here include family practice, pediatrics, gynecology, and dermatology. The center is open Monday through Saturday. Appointments are appreciated but not necessary; walk-ins and tourists are welcome. A second clinic, offering in-house laboratory services and X

rays, is located across from Mariners Hospital, at MM 91.4 in Tavernier.

Associates in Orthopaedics
and Sports Medicine
MM 100.3
Key Largo, FL
(305) 451–0361

13357 Overseas Highway
Marathon, FL
(305) 743–2182

At these two full-service orthopaedic and sports medicine facilities, physicians perform both surgical and nonsurgical intervention on orthopaedic problems. Other services available include arthroscopic surgery, joint replacement, and hand and spine surgery. X-ray facilities are on the premises, and minor surgical procedures are performed in the office. The centers are open during regular business hours.

Kessler.RMS Physical Rehabilitation Center
MM 100 Bayside
Key Largo, FL
(305) 453–0409

MM 49.5 Oceanside
Marathon, FL
(305) 743–1881

33 Ships Way
Big Pine Key, FL
(305) 872–2720

3156 Northside Drive
Key West, FL
(305) 292–1805

Kessler.RMS maintains a network of therapists throughout the Florida Keys, specializing in physical, speech, and occupational therapy. Some locations also offer orthopedist, family physician, and internist referrals.

Fresenius Medical Care
MM 92.2 Bayside
Tavernier, FL
(305) 852–0255

Originally opened to patients in June 1997, as Vivra Renal Care, this kidney care center provides those in need of dialysis an opportunity to receive treatment close to home instead of traveling to Home-

stead on the mainland, about 40 to 50 miles away. Based in Massachusetts, FMC is a for-profit corporation providing dialysis services nationwide.

Mariners Hospital
MM 91.5 Bayside
Tavernier, FL
(305) 852–4418

Mariners Hospital, established as a nine-bed physicians' clinic in 1959, today is a state-of-the-art hospital facility, completed at the end of 1998. Among the services provided here are 24-hour emergency care, surgery (including outpatient), respiratory therapy, pulmonary rehabilitation, cardiac rehabilitation, and radiology (including MRI, CT scans, and mammography). Mariners maintains a sleep diagnostic center, laboratory, and pharmacy and has a hyperbaric, or decompression, chamber (see our Diving and Snorkeling chapter). Mariners has a helicopter pad for transfer of severe cases to mainland hospitals.

The hospital is an affiliate of Baptist Health Systems of South Florida, a non-profit organization. Mariners Hospital also maintains and operates a state-of-the-art physical therapy center in a separate location at MM 100.3 Bayside, Key Largo, (305) 451–4398.

Middle Keys

Fishermen's Hospital
MM 48.7 Oceanside
Marathon, FL
(305) 743–5533

The medical staff at this 58-bed facility offers cardiology, cardiac rehabilitation, family practice, general surgery, gynecology, oncology, internal medicine, neurology, pathology, radiology, rheumatology, and plastic/reconstructive surgery. A CT scanner, known as a helical scanner, provides three-dimensional images with extraordinary clarity. Emergency service and same-day surgery also are available.

A helicopter pad allows for emergency chopper services, and a hyperbaric emergency response team is on call for divers. Fishermen's Overnight Guest program provides testing and pre-surgery (the

Emergency Numbers

While we sincerely hope you won't ever need to use the following telephone numbers, it is a good idea to keep this information in a convenient place.

Police, fire, or rescue emergencies	911
Florida Poison Information Center	(800) 282–3171
U.S. Coast Guard Marine and Air Emergency	(305) 295–9700 CG, VH channel 16
Florida Marine Patrol	(305) 289–2320 (800) DIAL-FMP; (800) 342–5367
Florida Highway Patrol	(800) 240–0453 FHP (statewide cell phone number)
Monroe County Emergency Management	(305) 289–6018 (800) 427–8340 (hurricane preparedness)

night prior to surgery) room and board. Also licensed to provide home healthcare, Fishermen's accepts most forms of insurance. Other offerings include a certified diabetes educator and nutritional support services. Fishermen's Hospital also offers physical therapy services at two separate locations: at MM 54, across from the Quay on Marathon Key, and at the Big Pine Key Plaza at MM 29.7. For information on either of these physical therapy centers, phone (305) 289-9950. This hospital is a for-profit organization.

Lower Keys

**Big Pine Medical and
Minor Emergency Center
MM 30 Oceanside
Big Pine Key, FL
(305) 872–3321**

This emergency care center, conveniently located clinic on Big Pine Key, treats minor illnesses and emergencies (broken bones, cuts, insect bites, etc.). Although appointments are encouraged, walk-ins are wel-

come. The clinic is generally open Monday through Friday, from 8 A.M. to 5 P.M. and some Saturday mornings. However, hours may vary with the season and patient demand, so it is best to phone ahead.

Key West

**The Clinic Urgent Care Center
1503 Government Road
(corner of Flagler Avenue and 7th Street)
Key West, FL
(305) 295–7550**

Not feeling so hot? Need to see a doctor in a hurry? This is the place to go. No appointment is ever necessary and the staff here promises that you will be in and out within one hour.

Treatment for minor illnesses and injuries is available seven days a week, from 8 A.M. to 6 P.M., and credit cards are accepted. Some local insurance plans may also be accepted. However, this facility is strictly designed for urgent care; it is not meant to serve as a replacement for your family doctor.

Sometimes serenity is as close as a garden hammock of tropical foliage. PHOTO: VICTORIA SHEARER

Fresenius Medical Care
1122 Key Plaza Shopping Center
N. Roosevelt Boulevard
Key West, FL
(305) 294–8453

This facility offers dialysis for kidney patients who would otherwise have to travel to the Upper Keys or Homestead. FMC is open during regular business hours and on Saturdays as well.

Keys Cancer Center
5900 Junior College Road
Stock Island, FL
(305) 296–0021

External and internal radiation therapy for all types of cancer, including breast, skin, prostate, lung, and AIDS-related malignancies, is provided at the Keys Cancer Center. Patients are generally referred by other physicians, but walk-ins are always welcome. The center also offers state-of-the-art seed implants for prostate cancer.

The Keys Cancer Center is open Monday through Friday, from 8 A.M. to 4:30 P.M. The staff actively works to educate and promote cancer awareness within the community, sponsoring screenings and working closely with cancer support groups.

Lower Florida Keys Health System
5900 Junior College Road
Stock Island, FL
(305) 294–5531

This accredited primary-care hospital is the only hospital in the Florida Keys to offer maternity services. Lower Florida Keys Health System maintains 169 beds, a 24-hour emergency room, a clinical lab, and a heliport. Added services include pediatrics, inpatient and outpatient psychotherapy, physical therapy, radiation therapy, chemotherapy, and cardiovascular and ambulatory care. The hospital offers substance-abuse assistance and comprehensive wellness programs.

Navy Branch Clinic
Corner of U.S. Hwy. 1 and A1A
at the foot of Cow Key Bridge
Key West, FL
(305) 293–4570

Completed in January 2000, at a cost of $20 million, the Navy Branch Clinic at the site of the former Navy Hospital provides a full range of outpatient medical and dental services to active duty personnel and qualifying veterans. Approximately 26,000 patients are treated here annually. This state-of-the-art facility is the first in the U.S. military to use digital technology.

Mobile Medical Care

Rural Health Network Medi-Van
(305) 872–5522
Inaugurated in September 1999, to address Monroe County residents' need for affordable and accessible health care, this fully equipped RV travels up and down the Keys to provide free medical services to folks who are uninsured and might not otherwise seek primary care treatment. A combined effort of the Monroe County Health Department, the United Way, the three Keys hospitals, and the Florida Keys Area Health Education Center in conjunction with the University of Miami, this mobile medical service starts in Key Largo on Monday and finishes on Friday in Key West.

The van is equipped like a doctor's office with two small examination rooms and a cab that doubles as a triage area and is staffed by a registered nurse and a nurse practitioner as well as nursing and medical students. In addition, the medical

Insiders' Tip

Don't try to acquire your Florida tan in a single day. The sun burns hotter here than it does up north, so ease into our sunshine gradually. And always, always use some form of sunscreen.

director (a physician) is available from 10 A.M. to 7 P.M. for consultation. Patients needing care beyond the scope of the Medi-Van staff may be referred to specialists and area hospitals.

Appointments are available and walk-ins are welcome. The Medi-Van's services are free of charge, but donations are appreciated.

Home-Health Services

Hospice of the Florida Keys/
Visiting Nurse Association
MM 92 Oceanside
Tavernier, FL
(305) 852–7887

MM 50.5 Oceanside
Marathon, FL
(305) 743–9048

1319 William Street
Key West, FL
(305) 294–8812
Hospice provides care for terminally ill patients with six months or less to live. Services are provided in private homes and nursing homes throughout the Keys by a staff of registered nurses, patient-care managers, and social workers. Certified nursing assistants tend to personal needs such as bathing, grooming, and bedding. All home-care patients must be referred to the agency by a physician. Comfort Care, which is private-duty nursing care, is also available. Hospice's purpose is to ensure patients' comfort so that the last days of their lives are quality ones.

Within this same nonprofit organization, the Visiting Nurse Association provides more aggressive home care for patients still undergoing various treatments or who need blood tests or care for wounds. This service also is provided upon a physician's request. Both Hospice and VNA are on call 24 hours a day, seven days a week. Medicare and Medicaid are accepted.

Nursing Homes

Upper Keys

Comprehensive Care Center of Plantation Key
MM 88.5 Bayside
48 High Point Road
Tavernier, FL
(305) 852–3021

Comprehensive Care is a 120-bed facility specializing in long- and short-term convalescent care and physical and occupational therapy. This center, Marathon Manor, and Comprehensive Care Center of Key West (see subsequent listings) are under the same ownership.

Middle Keys

Marathon Manor
MM 50 Bayside
320 Sombrero Beach Road
Marathon, FL
(305) 743–4466

A long-term, skilled-care facility, Marathon Manor also responds to a variety of medical needs, including IV therapy, short-term rehabilitation, and physical and occupational therapy. The facility maintains 120 beds and a day-care center for community children.

Lower Keys and Key West

Comprehensive Care Center of Key West
5860 W. Junior College Road
Stock Island, FL
(305) 296–2459

The 120-bed Comprehensive Care Center provides skilled and acute care as well as

physical, speech, and occupational therapy. Psychologists are on staff.

Mental-Health Services

Upper Keys

The Counseling Associates
Nationsbank Building
Suite 205
MM 99.5 Oceanside
Key Largo, FL
(305) 453–9522

Fishermen's Hospital Medical Complex
MM 48 Oceanside
Marathon, FL
(305) 743–4748

A multidisciplinary staff, which includes a psychiatrist, psychologists, and social workers, has been providing comprehensive counseling and evaluation services for individuals, couples, and families since 1989. Their specialties include stress management and marital counseling, hypnotherapy, psychiatric medication management, and evaluations related to learning disabilities, attention-deficit disorder, and child custody issues.

The Guidance Clinic of the Upper Keys
MM 92.5 Bayside
Tavernier, FL
(305) 853–3284

Two psychiatrists and a psychologist provide comprehensive mental health care at this outpatient clinic. Available services include individual and group psychotherapy, marital and family therapy, and parental and child guidance. Substance abuse counseling is also available. Clinic hours are by appointment, Monday through Friday, from 8 A.M. to 5 P.M.

Middle Keys

The Guidance Clinic of the Middle Keys
MM 49 Oceanside
3000 41st Street
Marathon, FL
(305) 289–6150

This mental health facility offers primarily inpatient treatment for substance

Crisis Intervention and Help Lines

Abuse Registry (800) 96–ABUSE; (800) 962–2873

AIDS Help Inc. (305) 296–6196

AIDS Hotline for Counseling and Information (800) 590–2437

Alcoholics Anonymous Key Largo, (305) 852–6186
Islamorada, (305) 664–8683
Marathon, (305) 743–3262
Lower Keys and Key West, (305) 296–8654

Alcohol Treatment Center, 24-hour Helpline (800) 711–6402

Codependents Anonymous (800) 672–2632

Consumer Helpline (800) 435–7352

Crisis Intervention 24-hour Helpline (305) 296–4357; (800) 273–4558

Drug Helpline (800) DRUGHELP; (800) 378–4435

Elder Helpline (800) 273–4558

Florida Council on Compulsive Gambling (800) 426–7711

Hospice of the Florida Keys Upper Keys, (305) 852–7887
Middle Keys, (305) 743–9048
Lower Keys, (305) 294–8812

Insurance Consumer Hotline (800) 342–2762

Missing Children Information Clearing House (888) FL–MISSING
(888) 356–5774

Narcotics Abuse 24-hour Helpline (800) 234–0420

Narcotics Anonymous Islamorada, (305) 664–2270
Key West, (305) 296–7999; (800) 711–6375

Overeaters Anonymous (305) 293–0070

Teenline (24-hour crisis intervention) (305) 292–8440; (800) 273–4558

abuse and mental illness. Other programs include day treatment, job coaching, case management, medication management, a detox unit, a crisis stabilization unit, and a residential program. The staff consists of a psychiatrist and several qualified and licensed care providers.

Lower Keys and Key West

Care Center For Mental Health
1205 Fourth Street
Key West, FL
(305) 292–6843

This traditional outpatient community mental health center offers psychiatric diagnosis, treatment, evaluation and testing; psychological services; substance-abuse treatment services; 24-hour emergency services for those in imminent danger; crisis services during business hours on a walk-in basis; and acupuncture service.

Alternative Healthcare

Many of the people who reside full-time in the Florida Keys are laid-back types who were drawn to our islands by a desire to pursue a less-than-conventional lifestyle. In many cases, their approach to healthcare is as nontraditional as their approach to life.

The Florida Keys, and Key West in particular, boast a wealth of options in the alternative healthcare category. These include everything from yoga classes and massage therapy on the beach to acupuncture, homeopathic medicine, organic foods, and herbal remedies. For a complete list of alternative healthcare options/practitioners throughout the Florida Keys, consult the local Yellow Pages under the following categories: Acupuncture, Health Clubs, Health and Diet Food Products, and Massage Therapists.

Veterinary Services

Your four-legged friends and "family" sometimes need healthcare, too. These pet clinics cater to their needs from the top of the Keys to Key West.

Upper Keys

Animal Care Clinic
MM 100.6 Bayside
Key Largo, FL
(305) 453–0044

Boarding and grooming are small parts of the operation at Animal Care Clinic. The clinic maintains oxygen-intensive critical-care units and offers surgery, lab testing, X rays, EKG, and ultrasound dentistry, as well as emergency on-call service, 24 hours a day, seven days a week.

Upper Keys Veterinary Clinic
MM 87 Oceanside
Islamorada, FL
(305) 852–3665

This clinic provides comprehensive services for all types of animals, including dogs, cats, birds, reptiles, ferrets, and exotics. Twenty-four hour emergency care is offered seven days a week. Boarding is provided for clients.

Middle Keys

Marathon Veterinary Hospital
MM 52.5 Oceanside
Marathon, FL
(305) 743–7099, (800) 832–7694

Marathon Veterinary Clinic is small, but the vets here offer full services, including 24-hour emergency care, for dogs, cats, and all exotics.

Animal Hospital of the Keys
MM 52.5 Bayside
Marathon, FL
(305) 743–3647, (305) 743–2287

This veterinary hospital offers a full range of services, including 24-hour emergency care and boarding. (Note that the last four digits of their telephone numbers respectively spell "dogs" and "cats.")

Lower Keys

Cruz Animal Hospital
MM 27 Bayside
Ramrod Key, FL
(305) 872–2559

A variety of medical services for virtually all pets, plus 24-hour emergency service is available at Cruz Animal Hospital.

The Vetmobile
(305) 872–7997

This mobile service based in Big Pine Key is available for veterinary house calls by appointment.

Doc Syn's Veterinary Care
MM 22.7 Bayside
Cudjoe Key, FL
(305) 744–0074

At Doc Syn's, the motto is "we treat your pets as if they were our own." The facility offers complete medical and surgical care for dogs, cats, birds, ferrets, and reptiles.

Key West

All Animal Clinic and Hospital
5505 Fifth Avenue
Stock Island, FL
(305) 294–5255

This clinic offers medicine, surgery, dentistry, an in-house laboratory, X rays, and emergency care. They offer house calls by appointment and also have an air-conditioned boarding facility.

Animal Hospital of Olde Key West
and Stock Island
6150 Second Street
Stock Island, FL
(305) 296–5227

Veterinary services for dogs, cats, birds, and small exotics are provided in a modern, full-service facility that offers a yearly healthcare plan. A complete boarding facility is also on the premises. Twenty-four-hour emergency service is also available.

Cross Animal Clinic
928 Truman Avenue
Key West, FL
(305) 294–9551

Cross Animal Hospital offers full-service care, including vaccinations, worm testing, cat boarding, and drop-off service. Evening and weekend hours are available.

Lower Keys Animal Hospital
3122 Flagler Avenue
Key West, FL
(305) 294–6335

This facility treats small exotics but mostly sees cats and dogs. The staff offers regular checkups, surgery, dentistry, X rays, vaccinations, and general medical treatment for pets.

Insiders' Tip

To avoid sunburn, use a sunscreen with a protection factor (SPF) of at least 15. Apply your first coat about 30 minutes before going outside, then reapply approximately every two hours—more often if you are in the water.

Education and Childcare

The Florida Keys and Key West are served by public and private schools, preschools, and a community college. Thanks to a visiting institute and college degree programs at the Boca Chica Naval Air Station in the Lower Keys, students can earn bachelor's, master's, and even doctoral degrees without ever leaving our islands. In addition, several institutions of higher education in Miami are within commuting distance.

Following the information on education options is a comprehensive look at the childcare scene in the Florida Keys and Key West. We explore traditional childcare services along with other handy (sometimes vacation-saving) options such as drop-in care, babysitting, sick-child and respite care, family childcare homes, and public after-school programs.

Education

The Florida Keys

Public Schools

The Monroe County School District oversees schools from Key Largo to Key West, including three high schools. Some elementary and middle schools within our county occupy the same building; other middle and high schools share facilities.

Upper Keys students attend Coral Shores High School in Tavernier or Key Largo Elementary and Middle School or Plantation Elementary and Middle School in Tavernier. The site for a new Upper Keys high school has been chosen, but construction has not started.

Students in the Middle Keys are taught at Switlik Elementary School and Marathon Middle and High School.

Lower Keys elementary-age students are taught at Big Pine Neighborhood School or the new Sugarloaf Elementary/Middle School, a $16 million dollar, state-of-the-art campus opened to students in winter 2000. High school students may choose between Key West High School and Marathon High School.

Key West elementary schools are Glynn Archer on White Street, Gerald Adams on W. College Road, Poinciana on 14th Street, and Sigsbee on Felton Road. Grades six through eight are at Horace O'Bryant Middle School on Leon Street, and grades nine through twelve are at Key West High School on Flagler Avenue.

The school system, which operates on a school year that runs from late August through early June, offers computer technology and other innovative programs, including a television production lab and theatrical program at Key Largo School and a mentoring program and a welcome package for new students at Coral Shores High School in Tavernier. Dropout prevention programs and college credit courses taught in high school are other special programs.

An elected board headed by an elected superintendent, who oversees five district representatives, governs our public schools. Board members serve four-year terms. School funding comes from Monroe County property taxes.

Private Schools

Private schools typically offer smaller student-teacher ratios and a variety of learning curricula. The following list includes private schools operating in the Florida Keys and Key West.

Montessori Island School
MM 92.3 Oceanside
Tavernier, FL
(305) 852–3438

Montessori schools across the country work on the principle of self-pacing for children. This Montessori school, established in 1996, works on the same idea of purposeful action. The school provides education for preschool through elementary children with Montessori-certified teachers. Year-round programs are available.

Island Christian School
MM 83.4 Bayside
Islamorada, FL
(305) 664–2781

14 125th Street Bayside
Marathon, FL
(305) 743–2200

Established in 1974 by a group of parents from Island Community Church, Island Christian began with 54 students. As grade levels were added and the school became accredited, enrollment increased to 300. Island Christian today teaches pre-kindergarten through high school level students in a traditional college preparatory curriculum that incorporates the Abeka and Bob Jones Christian teachings. The average class size is 18. The school offers a full interscholastic sports program to junior and senior high school students. Each elementary-level class has computers, and junior and senior high levels have computer labs. Some creative senior scheduling is allotted to allow hands-on experience as teacher aides.

Marathon Lutheran School
MM 53.3 Bayside
325 122nd Street
Marathon, FL
(305) 289–0700

A service of Martin Luther Chapel and the Lutheran Church Missouri Synod, a national Lutheran organization, Marathon Lutheran School offers education from kindergarten through 6th grade. Using the School of Tomorrow PACE program, Marathon Lutheran offers its students the opportunity to learn at their own speeds with several class levels combined. Established in 1987, the school requires students to attend weekly chapel service and take religion classes. Music and karate instruction also are offered here, and students work on computers at least once a day. The school year at Marathon Lutheran is the same as that of public schools.

Vineyard Christian School
MM 30 Bayside
100 County Road
Big Pine Key, FL
(305) 872–3404

Within Vineyard Christian Church, this 11-year-old school serves kindergarten pupils beginning at age three (age five is typical for other schools) and has classes through 6th grade, with a total enrollment of approximately 90 students. Grade levels are combined for classroom instruction. Students are taught using the traditional Christian-based Abeka curriculum, which incorporates Bible study into the basic reading, writing, and arithmetic textbook education. All students receive computer training, and additional computer instruction and gymnastics are offered as extracurricular activities. Weekly chapel attendance is required. The school is behind the Coca-Cola Building.

Higher Education

The Union Institute
Venture Centre
16853 N.E. Second Avenue
Suite 102
North Miami Beach, FL
(305) 653–7141, (800) 486–7141
www.tui.edu

Since 1994, The Union Institute has acted as a remote adult-education facility that offers bachelor's and doctoral degrees to Florida Keys residents via self-directed independent study. Fully accredited by the Commission on Institutions of Higher Education of the North Central Association of Colleges and Schools and licensed by the State Board of Independent Colleges and Universities, The Union Institute was founded in 1963. Classwork is accomplished via computer. Courses of study include criminal justice, hotel management, social work, psychology, public administration, maritime archaeology, multicultural studies, coastal resource management, and more. Financial aid is available.

Additional Educational Opportunities

Residents and visitors to the Florida Keys may participate in a number of hands-on educational opportunities listed below.

MarineLab Marine Resources
Development Foundation
51 Shoreland Drive
Key Largo, FL
(305) 451–1139
www.mrdf.org

Offering students an in-depth introduction to the ecology of the Keys, the non-profit Marine Resources Development Foundation provides customized programs for students. Learn about sea life in the Emerald Lagoon or explore the MarineLab Undersea Laboratory. Customized programs can include scuba certification, coral reef ecology, mangrove ecology, or a trip to the Everglades. Teacher workshops are also offered.

Outward Bound Florida Sea Program
MM 32 Oceanside
Big Pine Key, FL
(305) 872–4102, (800) 643–4462

Based in Rockland, Maine, the nonprofit Outward Bound educational organization offers wilderness courses for middle school students through adults. Other adventures are tailored to women, families, and educators. Probably the most publicized of all Outward Bound excursions are those within the organization's Career/Life Renewal program, whereby adults at various crossroads in their lives are rewarded by teamwork and the ability to meet physical challenges.

The organization was founded in 1941 with the belief that action and thought should not be separated from educational experiences. Its 44 schools throughout the world offer days of sailing, mountain climbing, kayaking, dogsledding, and other outdoor activities coupled with community service work. The goal is to help students develop self-esteem, self-reliance, and concern for others and the world around them. Outward Bound's Lower Keys program includes sailing, snorkeling, swimming, and natural history instruction. Classes are held here from November through May.

> ## Insiders' Tip
>
> The University of Miami, Florida International University, and Barry University, all well-known institutions of higher education, are within driving distance of the Upper Keys. All of these universities offer student housing. For commuters, Miami-Dade Community College is also nearby.

For course information and a complete catalog of Outward Bound programs in South Florida and elsewhere, call the toll-free number listed above.

Seacamp Association
MM 30 Oceanside
Newfound Harbor Road and
1300 Big Pine Avenue
Big Pine Key, FL
(305) 872–2205, (305) 872–2331
This scuba and marine science camp for children ages 12 through 17 has been in Big Pine Key for more than 30 years. Children from all over the world sign up for Seacamp's 18-day program to experience scuba diving, sailing, snorkeling, and sailboarding. Marine science classes teach about such subjects as exploring the seas, animal behavior, and Keys critters. Scuba certification is available.

The camp operates from June through August and offers a day camp in summer for resident children ages 10 through 14. In addition, Seacamp is affiliated with the Newfound Harbor Marine Institute, which hosts three-day winter field trips for teachers and students from 4th grade through high school.

Key West

Public Schools

Key West has four elementary schools, a middle school, and a high school. See the discussion of Monroe County's public school system in The Florida Keys section of this chapter for additional information.

Private Schools

Grace Lutheran School
2713 Flagler Avenue
Key West, FL
(305) 296–8262
Established in 1952 and designed for pre-kindergarten three-year-olds through 2nd graders, Grace Lutheran offers computers and teaches Spanish in all but pre-

kindergarten level classes. During "God Time," students learn about Christian ideals and how to live them. The school maintains an active parent-teacher group.

Mary Immaculate Star of the Sea
700 Truman Avenue
Key West, FL
(305) 294–1031
Mary Immaculate follows a pre-kindergarten through 8th grade curriculum outlined by the Archdiocese of Miami, including religious instruction. The school's mission is to provide opportunities for all Lower Keys families to experience a Catholic education. Within a Christian environment, the instructors foster spiritual, academic, and social development. Class sizes average 15 to 25 students.

Montessori Children's School of Key West
1221 Varela Street
Key West, FL
(305) 294–5302
Montessori is designed to support a child's need for purposeful action. Here teachers guide students without unnecessary interference—all furnishings are child-size, and photos are hung at a child's viewing level. Allowed freedom within certain guidelines, Montessori children work at their own pace on their own projects. Classes are mixed in age (ages three through five and grades one through three study together). The idea is to foster learning by example and learning to share. A director and assistant director are assigned to each class of about 28 students. The school also offers summer day-care programs.

Higher Education

Florida Keys Community College
5901 W. College Road
Key West, FL
(305) 296–9081
www.firn.edu/fkcc
When Florida Keys Community College (FKCC) began operation in fall 1965, it became the first institution of higher

Tennessee Williams Fine Arts Center (see our Arts and Culture chapter). Its marine environmental technology and dive programs are especially popular. Certificate programs are offered at FKCC in business data processing, marine propulsion technology, small business management, addiction studies, and more. Vocational training is also available for law enforcement and correctional officers. In 1995, FKCC opened the Mario F. Mitchell Aquatic Safety Center for dive technology and a state-of-the-art oceanfront pool.

Through FKCC's dual enrollment/dual credit program, students in the Monroe County School District can begin earning college credit in high school. Distance learning is provided through telecourses that air on cable Channel 5.

In addition to its main campus on Stock Island, Florida Keys Community College also offers a limited number of classes at two other Keys locations: The Middle Keys Center at 900 Sombrero Beach Road, MM 50, Marathon, (305) 743-2133; and the Upper Keys Center at MM 90, Tavernier, (305) 852-8007.

Troy State University Florida Region
718 Forrestal Street
Boca Chica Naval Air Station
Key West, FL
(305) 293-2987
www.troyst.edu

Established by the Alabama legislature in 1887 as Troy State Normal School, this university began as a normal, or teachers', college. Troy State grew steadily, earning university status in 1967. The institution serves civilian citizens throughout the United States and military personnel here and abroad. With its main campus and three sites in Alabama, 10 sites in Florida, and 40 more around the world, Troy State has graduated more than 75,000 students.

In the Florida Keys and Key West, the university offers graduate degree programs in counseling and psychology and

education in the Florida Keys. FKCC was established through funding provided to Monroe County by the Florida state legislature after parents and teachers had expressed concerns over the lack of a college in the Keys. Today the school boasts an enrollment of more than 6,000 and offers Associates of Science and Arts degree programs in such fields as business administration, computer programming and analysis, nursing, multimedia technology, and marine environmental technology. Credits earned at FKCC may be transferred to other institutions of higher learning for application toward a bachelor's degree.

FKCC's performing and visual arts programs are enhanced by the college's

in management. Many of these programs consist of weekend-intensive courses or evening classes and may be completed within one year.

Saint Leo College–Key West Center
718-A Hornet Street
Boca Chica Naval Air Station
Key West, FL
(305) 293–2847
www.saintleo.edu

Saint Leo College offers the only regionally accredited bachelor's degree program in the Florida Keys. Located in Key West since 1975, Saint Leo is a private college that offers Associate of Arts and Bachelor of Arts degrees in business administration, criminology, human services, and/or human resource administration. Situated at the Naval Air Station, Saint Leo College is open to all civilian and military personnel and their families in the Florida Keys. Classes are designed for the working adult.

Additional Educational Opportunities

San Carlos Institute
516 Duval Street
Key West, FL
(305) 294–3887

In keeping with its century-old mission of promoting Cuban culture and democratic ideals, the historic San Carlos Institute offers Spanish language classes for adults in two terms: winter and summer. Taught by native speakers, these eight-week sessions are available at three levels: beginner, intermediate I, and intermediate II.

Childcare

Gone are the days of Ward and June, Ozzie and Harriet, and Lucy and Ricky, those televised icons of the '50s nuclear family. In their TV Land, Pop went to the office while Mom stayed home with the children. Nowadays, when fathers go off to work, most mothers are right behind them on their way to jobs; grandparents

work, too. Childcare has become a necessity, and the Florida Keys' scenario differs little from this national norm.

The problem of finding good, competent childcare is compounded here by a shortage of available providers at any cost. According to the National Association for the Education of Young Children, childcare is the fourth-largest item in the family budget after food, housing, and taxes. Infant care (birth to age one) and weekend and evening care are in particularly short supply in Monroe County, which encompasses the Keys.

Day-to-day childcare in the county generally falls into two categories: center-based care and family childcare homes.

In this section, we describe qualities you should seek in childcare providers and provide information on resources, types of childcare programs, and contacts for centers that serve the Florida Keys and Key West.

Resources

Wesley House Community Child Care
Coordinating Agency
1011 Virginia Street
Key West, FL
(305) 292–7150
www.wesleyhouse.org

With offices in Key West and serving all of the Florida Keys, Wesley House assists families in making the best of a difficult situation. The Wesley House Resource & Referral Network is perhaps the most important resource in the Keys for parents looking for appropriate, quality childcare. (Wesley House is a national division agency of the United Methodist Church and a United Way of Monroe County agency.) WHR&R acts as a link between families and the childcare services they seek. It can recommend affordable childcare for children up to 5 years old and after-school and summer care for children up to 12 years old.

Other assistance comes in the forms of subsidized childcare and scholarships and help in obtaining legal aid, medical aid, food stamps, and other services. The network conducts classes for parents in money management, parenting skills, nutrition, and handling everyday pressures. It provides personal help for families with at-risk children, assisting them in filling out paperwork to meet eligibility requirements. Wesley House also offers transportation to and from childcare centers for children in at-risk situations.

Wesley House will provide referrals for families needing sick care or in-home nursing specialists. Some childcare centers will offer drop-in care. Wesley House can make recommendations in this area as well.

Types of Programs

This section describes the center- and home-based childcare options available to parents in Monroe County.

ChildCare/Preschool Centers

The minimum state licensing requirements dictate that a childcare center must hold a valid license from the Health and Rehabilitative Services Department of the State of Florida. The license must be posted in a conspicuous place within the center.

The center must adhere to the number of children for which it is licensed, and it must maintain the minimum staff-to-child ratio for each age level: Younger than

1, one teacher for every 4 children; age 1, 1 to 6; age 2, 1 to 11; age 3, 1 to 15; age 4, 1 to 20; and age 5, 1 to 25. We stress that this is the minimum ratio. It may not be sufficient to give your child the level of care you desire.

Licensing standards mandate health and safety requirements and staff training requirements. These include: child abuse and neglect training, a 20-hour childcare training course, a 10-hour specialized training module, and eight hours of in-service training annually. In addition, there must be one CPR- and first aid–certified person on site during business hours. Some centers are prepared to accept infants; others are not.

Some childcare centers are exempt from HRS licensing. They are accredited and monitored by religious agencies, the school board, or the military. Care provider to child ratio, quality of care, and training standards vary and may be lesser or greater than that of licensed centers.

Unfortunately, no childcare centers are open weekends or evenings in the Keys.

Contact Wesley House for a list of HRS-licensed and license-exempt childcare/preschool centers in the Florida Keys and Key West.

Family Childcare Homes

Family childcare is considered by the State of Florida to encompass home-based childcare with five or fewer preschool-age children from more than one family unrelated to the caregiver. Any preschool children living in the home must be included in the maximum number of children allowed. The adult who provides the childcare is usually referred to as a family childcare home operator.

Some counties in Florida require that family childcare homes be licensed. Monroe Country, which includes the Florida Keys, requires only registration with the Department of Health and Rehabilitative Services. Every adult in the household must be screened. Registration requires no on-site inspection of the home for minimum health, safety, and sanitation standards, however. Nor is there a requirement that the family childcare operator have CPR or first-aid training.

Military programs are exempt from this registration (see military-certified programs in this chapter). They have their own accreditation procedures and are available only to family members of military personnel.

Wesley House actively recruits for and offers a three-hour course covering basic health and safety issues to persons who wish to operate registered family childcare homes.

Public After-School Programs

Many public schools in the Florida Keys and Key West run their own after-hours programs for school-age children from 2:15 to 5:30 P.M. and also on school holidays and summer weekdays. Most schools charge for this service. Contacts at the schools are: Key Largo Elementary School, MM 104.8, Key Largo, (305) 451-5571; Plantation Key School, 100 Lake Rd., Tavernier, (305) 853-3281; Switlik Elementary, MM 48.8 Bayside, 33rd St., Marathon, (305) 289-2490; Big Pine Key Neighborhood School, Palomino Horse Trail, Big Pine Key, (305) 872-1266; Sugarloaf Elementary/Middle School, 255 Crane Rd., Sugarloaf Key, (305) 745-3282; Poinciana Elementary School, 1212 14th St., Key West, (305) 293-1630; Sigsbee Elementary, Sigsbee Naval Base, Key West, (305) 294-1861 (military families only); Gerald Adams Elementary School, 5855 College Rd., Key West, (305) 293-1609.

Babysitting

Personal knowledge of the person you choose to care for your child in your absence is the best of all possible worlds,

but it isn't always a reality. If you are a visitor to the Florida Keys or Key West or a newly relocated resident, you may have to take a leap of faith and entrust your child to someone you do not know. Therefore, you should check references. For referrals, contact Wesley House (see listing under Resources) or ask the concierge at your hotel.

You can also contact local chambers of commerce, which often keep lists of local residents who babysit: Key Largo, (305) 451-1414, (800) 822-1088; Islamorada, (305) 664-4503, (800) 322-5397; Marathon, (305) 743-5417, (800) 262-7284; Lower Keys, (305) 872-2411, (800) 872-3722; and Key West, (305) 294-2587, (800) 527-8539. Be sure to ask by what criteria these referrals have been checked for more insight as to who best suits your needs.

Media

Even after Henry Flagler's extension of the Florida East Coast Railroad provided Florida Keys residents access to the mainland, communications on our islands were limited. In order to receive local news and news outside the South Florida area, residents relied on radio broadcasts from Miami, sporadic postal service, and what was probably their most effective and timely means of dispatch: word-of-mouth or what is jokingly referred to as "the Conch telegraph."

Today, two dailies and a contingent of weeklies and free papers tie the Keys together. Both AM and FM radio stations are still restricted by wattage, and residents must subscribe to satellite or cable service to get television reception.

Newspapers

In addition to home delivery, our newspapers are often sold in curbside vending racks, grocery stores, pharmacies, convenience stores, and bookstores. A handful of shops carry national and international newspapers. Because the Florida Keys is considered a remote distribution site, some national newspapers, such as *The New York Times*, are sold at a higher newsstand price. A rule of thumb: Get to the newsstand early. The farther you travel from the mainland, the more quickly the out-of-town papers sell out.

Dailies

The Key West Citizen
3420 Northside Drive
Key West, FL
(305) 294-6641
www.keysnews.com

In 1904 a small, weekly newspaper known as *The Citizen* appeared on the newspaper scene in Key West; it was later consolidated with the 1899 *Inter-Ocean* to form *The Key West Citizen*. Cooke Communications now owns *The Key West Citizen*, along with *Solares Hill*, the *Free Press Community Newspapers*, and Florida Keys News Service.

The Citizen shares editorial coverage and classified advertisements with its sister publications and features a significant amount of syndicated material and lifestyles coverage.

The *Citizen's* editorial focus is primarily on features. "Paradise," a tabloid appearing in Thursday's edition, is a comprehensive compendium of what's currently happening in the theaters and at the clubs and galleries around town. Free copies of "Paradise" are available at newsstands, hotels, guesthouses, restaurants, and other businesses throughout Key West. *The Citizen* also publishes "The Menu," a free quarterly guide containing menus from several area restaurants.

The Citizen is published every day except Saturday. If you happen to be in the Keys on April 1, be sure to grab a copy of the April Fool's edition. The front page is almost believable and always a hoot!

The Miami Herald
1 Herald Plaza
Miami, FL
(800) 437-2535

619 Eaton Street
Key West, FL
(800) 294-5131 (newsroom)
www.miamiherald.com

The largest-circulation daily newspaper in the Southeastern United States, this Pulitzer Prize–winner has maintained Key West correspondents for decades and now has a bureau in the southernmost city, Key West. *The Miami Herald* features crisp writing and tends to favor features over hard news except when issues are pressing.

Herald humor columnist and Pulitzer Prize winner Dave Barry is popular in the Keys as he is most everywhere else. His column is syndicated nationally.

The *Herald* is widely available throughout the Keys.

Weeklies and Biweeklies

Florida Keys Keynoter
MM 48.6 Oceanside
Marathon, FL
(305) 743–5551

Key West Keynoter
2720A N. Roosevelt Boulevard
Key West, FL
(305) 296–6989
www.keynoter.com

The *Florida Keys Keynoter* is owned by Knight-Ridder Publishing and is considered *The Miami Herald's* sister newspaper. The *Keynoter* is Monroe County's second-oldest publication. With a weekly television news program and now a separate Key West edition (inaugurated in June 2000), the twice-weekly *Keynoter* offers comprehensive local coverage of the Florida Keys. Known for its in-depth coverage of the Keys' political scene, once weekly the *Keynoter* also features "L'Attitudes," an arts and entertainment section that includes complete television listings

for the area, special features, and upcoming Keys events.

This tabloid-style newspaper is published each Wednesday and Saturday and is widely available in shops, newsstands, and curbside racks throughout the Keys.

Free Press Community Newspapers
MM 81.5 Oceanside
Islamorada, FL
(305) 664–2266, (800) 926–8412

MM 52 Oceanside
Marathon, FL
(305) 743–8766

Formerly known as *The Islamorada Free Press*, this group of weekly tabloid newspapers has grown to include five separate editions, each serving a segment of the Florida Keys population, from Ocean Reef to Big Pine Key. Owned by Cooke Communications since August 2000, the *Free Press Community Newspapers* cover local news and sports in each area. The newspapers are published each Wednesday and available free in grocery and convenience stores as well as in curbside racks from Homestead to Big Coppitt Key.

The Lower Keys Barometer
MM 30.3 Oceanside
Big Pine Key, FL
(305) 872–0106

Keith Monti and his wife, Diane, started this newspaper in 1995, to provide strictly Lower Keys coverage. *The Lower Keys Barometer*, published Thursdays, combines columns and local news in an op-ed format and reflects Monti's self-proclaimed citizen's rights philosophies. This free newspaper is distributed to restaurants, hotels, shops, convenience stores, supermarkets, and pharmacies between Duck Key and Key West.

The Reporter
MM 91.6 Oceanside
Tavernier, FL
(305) 852–3216

When *The Reporter* began in the early 1900s, the newspaper, which was based in

Key Largo, was mimeographed. As the publication grew, its owners bought what was at the time a top-of-the-line printing press—a monumental event in Keys publishing, since few newspapers were actually printed in this stretch of Monroe County. (Even today, newspapers are sent down the Keys to Key West or up to Miami-Dade County for printing.) *The Reporter* is now published by Knight-Ridder, which also publishes *The Miami Herald* and the *Florida Keys Keynoter*.

Published each Thursday, this tabloid packages community news from south Miami-Dade County to Marathon in a traditional black-and-white format and is available in stores throughout the Upper Keys.

Key West

Celebrate Key West
1075 Duval Street
Key West, FL
(305) 295–8292
www.celebratekeywest.com

Celebrate Key West caters to the gay and lesbian population of Key West. Offering various community features along with gay-perspective editorials and stances on issues, *Celebrate Key West* provides a welcome alternative forum in Key West publishing. Of particular interest is a pull-out section listing gay-owned and gay-friendly businesses in and around

Key West. This free paper is distributed throughout Key West each Friday.

El Faro
2311 Fogarty Avenue
Key West, FL
(305) 296–3719

El Faro editor and publisher Jose Cabaleiro was working in the accounting department of a company in Cuba that printed Spanish versions of *Reader's Digest*, *Time*, and *Life* magazines when the Castro regime confiscated the business. Cabaleiro fled to Venezuela. In 1962 he moved to the United States, and in 1971, he established *El Faro* newspaper.

Published on the 15th and 30th of each month, this free Spanish/English newspaper covers social and political issues affecting residents of Monroe and Miami-Dade Counties.

The Island News
3140 A Northside Drive
Key West, FL
(305) 296–1566
www.islandnews-kw.com

Island News was established in 1996 with a specific mission: Be the locals' hometown weekly paper. The focus is a broad one, covering aspects such as lifestyles, health, education, sports, and community news. Free copies of *The Island News* are distributed across Key West on Fridays.

Key West The Newspaper
422 Fleming Street
Key West, FL
(305) 292–2108

Since its debut in January 1994, *Key West The Newspaper* has found its niche in the realm of politics and entertainment. While the paper boasts a hearty entertainment section full of live music listings, reviews, and local color, it is perhaps best known for its investigative reporting. This free weekly is distributed every Friday morning in Key West and Stock Island.

Solares Hill
1201 White Street
Key West, FL
(305) 294–3602
www.solareshill.com

Founded in 1971, the free weekly *Solares Hill* ceased its independent status in 1998 when it was acquired by the publishers of the *Key West Citizen* and the *Free Press Community Newspapers*. Although the newspaper's former slogan "the straight truth plainly stated" has been replaced with the words "the way a newspaper should be," its focus remains primarily on politics and business, along with a smattering of restaurant, theater, and book reviews. Distributed free of charge on Fridays from Key West to Big Pine Key, *Solares Hill* covers the Lower Keys and Key West exclusively.

Radio

Radio reception in the Florida Keys is heavily influenced by factors such as weather and distance from the transmitter. We have therefore grouped stations according to the areas where your chances for clear reception are the best. Clear skies and sunshine will optimize good reception; luckily, we have plenty of both most of the time.

Upper Keys

WKLG Star 102.1 FM: Hits from the '70s through the '90s, traffic and weather reports, and syndicated news.

WFKZ SUN 103.1 FM: Pop/contemporary music with a mix of oldies, live local news, daily live fishing reports, weather, and tide information.

WKEZ 96.9 FM: Contemporary adult music/easy listening.

WCTH 100.3 FM: Country music with fishing reports, community calendar, news, and sports.

Middle Keys

WAVK Wave 105.5 FM: Adult contemporary music from the '60s to today, local talk shows, news, daily fishing and dive reports.

WGMX 94.3 FM: Adult contemporary music/soft hits from the '70s to today.

WFFG 1300 AM: All-talk sports (Miami Dolphins, Miami Heat, NASCAR), news, and commentary 24 hours a day.

WKYZ 101.3 FM: Classic rock, covering the Keys from Key Largo to Key West.

Lower Keys

WWUS (US 1 Radio) 104.1 FM: Oldies music, reggae, and Jimmy Buffett, daily fishing reports, on-air flea market, morning magazine (interviews), and live local news.

Insiders' Tip

A gasoline-powered generator nicknamed "Zippy" became a hero for residents of the Florida Keys during and immediately following Hurricane Georges in September 1998. When the power went out from Key Largo to Key West, Zippy kept WWUS (US 1 Radio), Big Pine Key, on the air throughout the storm, providing the only link residents of the Keys had to one another and to reports coming out of the National Hurricane Center in Miami. Zippy helped US 1 Radio earn national recognition for its storm coverage in the form of the Edward R. Murrow Award, the Pulitzer Prize of broadcasting.

WPIK PIK'n 102.5 FM: Continuous country music.

Key West

WAIL 99.5 FM: Classic rock.

WCNK Conch 98.7 FM: Smooth jazz.

WEOW 92.7 FM: Top 40 hits.

WIIS Island 107 FM: Adult-alternative music, local news and weather, fishing reports, and tide and wind information.

WKIZ 1500 AM: Spanish-language music and news.

WKEY Key 93.5 FM: Soft adult contemporary music, weather and tide information, daily stock reports, health tips, and cultural and community calendars. Special programs feature classical, jazz, and Latin music.

WKWF 1600 AM: All sports radio; home of the Key West Conchs.

WSKP 107.9 FM: Spanish language/ music.

Television

On July 1, 1999, Monroe County ceased its subsidy of the translator that supplied network programming at no cost to residents of the Florida Keys. Consequently, residents must now pay for cable television service in order to receive network channels. Our cable provider is AT&T Broadband—(305) 743-5575 in Marathon, (305) 852-2288 in Key Largo, and (305) 296-6572 in Key West.

In addition to national programming, local-origination programming is offered on Channels 5 and 16. This public-service programming includes live coverage of city commission and local political meetings, as well as real estate listings, a dating service, and local interest shows on a variety of topics such as healthcare and fishing. *The Florida Keys Keynoter* airs a news-related talk show with interviews and commentary on Wednesday evenings. Channel 5 also offers interesting and informative infommercials during the day and evening, highlighting many of the Keys' attractions found in this book.

Satellite communication is an alternative to cable service. Check the Yellow Pages for companies offering satellite dishes and service.

Worship

The Florida Keys owes much of its religious history to the Conchs, the group of seafaring settlers who emigrated from the Bahamas.

Some of the Conchs were the descendants of members of the Eleutherian Society, who left England in 1649 and 1650 to seek religious freedom. Others were descendants of loyalists who fled the Carolinas and Georgia during the American Revolution to settle in the Bahamas, which was then still controlled by England. They settled primarily in Key West, bringing with them devout religious beliefs, mostly Methodist.

Until 1881, local lay preachers filled the ministerial needs of the sparsely populated Florida Keys (except for Key West). Settlements were scattered and rustic, their inhabitants farming the unyielding coral rock with attempts at growing pineapples, tomatoes, limes, and melons. Many worked the sea as fishermen, harvesting a bounty more prolific. Two Key West ministers began making rounds of the Keys communities by boat, holding services for the next six years anywhere they could find a welcoming group of worshipers.

St. Paul's Episcopal Church is a stately historic structure in Key West. PHOTO: VICTORIA SHEARER

The main Upper Keys settlements in the late 1800s were Tavernier at the southern end of Key Largo; Planter, a mile north of Tavernier; Rock Harbor (present-day Key Largo); Newport, between Rock Harbor and Tarpon Basin; and Basin Hills, at the northern end of Key Largo. The first actual building outside Key West dedicated solely for worship services was built at Newport in 1885. Then a church was built in 1886 in Tavernier, named Barnett's Chapel in honor of its pastor. By 1887, a minister from the Florida Methodist Conference traveled a month-long circuit of the Upper Keys, visiting Basin Hills, Newport, Tavernier, and Matecumbe.

Plantation Key Methodists built their own church in 1899, and other congregations began assembling in private homes.

After the turn of the century, with the advent of Flagler's East Coast Railroad Extension, the population of the Keys above Key West began to grow, and this growth spawned churches of diverse denominations. After World War II, the Florida Keys saw a further boom in population (see our Historical Evolution chapter), which spurred the construction of more churches. Unfortunately, the devastating hurricanes of 1935 and 1960 wiped

According to legend, this grotto at St. Mary Star of the Sea has protected Key West from bearing the full brunt of a hurricane since 1922. PHOTO: VICTORIA SHEARER

out the physical church structures of the Middle and Upper Keys. None of the church buildings on these islands approach the age and stature of those of Key West, but vigorous and devout congregations welcome visitors and new parishioners.

Consult the Yellow Pages of the local telephone directory for times and locations of worship services. Some of the churches offer childcare during selected services or prayer groups. If this is of interest to you, call the church directly to inquire about arrangements.

Key West

Earliest worship in Key West took place in the old courthouse on Jackson Square, where English-speaking persons would gather and hold nondenominational services. If a clergyman happened to be on the island for any reason, a service would be held and would be well attended by the devout of all faiths. When a group sharing the same beliefs became large enough, members splintered off and built a church of their own.

The first settlers to arrive were Bahamians who followed the Church of England's Anglican teachings. They were seafarers, descendants from the religious dissenters who had left England more than 100 years before. They brought deeply religious convictions with them to the Keys. In March 1831, a movement started to bring a clergyman to the island of Key West on a permanent basis. It was

Insiders' Tip

To appreciate the 128 stained-glass windows that grace Key West's St. Paul's Episcopal Church, 401 Duval Street, you must step inside the sanctuary. The windows are concealed from the outside by a sturdy, plastic-like material that protects them from breaking. Without this protection, church members would have to cover each window with plywood in the event of a hurricane.

Insiders' Tip

The coral rock grotto built in 1922 at Key West's St. Mary Star of the Sea's Convent of Mary Immaculate holds a legend. A destructive hurricane passed over the island in 1919, leaving death and property damage strewn in its wake. Sister Louis Gabriel envisioned the grotto as a shrine dedicated to protecting Key West from hurricanes. Since then, whenever a hurricane threatens, islanders flock to the grotto to say prayers and light candles. So far, their faith has worked. Key West narrowly missed the hurricanes of 1935 and 1960 that hit the rest of the Keys. And although the island took a direct hit from Hurricane Georges in 1998, many believe there were no deaths or serious injuries and only minimal property damage because of the grotto.

stipulated, interestingly enough, that he would not be required to stay any portion of August or September that he found disagreeable. These happen to be the most hurricane-prone months in the Florida Keys.

From the Bahamian root of religious conviction sprang a proliferation of church denominations in Key West, some of which still meet for worship today. Many churches in Key West are historically or architecturally significant: St. Paul's Episcopal Church, 401 Duval Street; First United Methodist (Old Stone) Church, 600 Eaton Street; St. Mary Star of the Sea, 1010 Windsor Lane; and Cornish Memorial A.M.E. (African Methodist Episcopal) Zion Church, 702 Whitehead Street.

For a complete listing of worship services in Key West each week, see the Friday edition of *The Key West Citizen*.

Index

About the Author

Victoria Shearer

Victoria Shearer traversed more than the Atlantic Ocean when she settled in Paradise in 1993. Yin met yang. After traipsing through the British Isles, the European continent, the Middle East, and the Far East from a two-year temporary base in gray, cloudy London in the early '90s, she relocated to the Florida Keys. Far from the culture shock she expected, life in the islands was immediately enchanting to her. No stranger to the wonders of the world, Vicki found that the Keys reign in a class by themselves.

A University of Wisconsin graduate, Vicki taught school briefly, then worked in advertising. In the late 1980s, she was a copy editor for *The COOK'S Magazine*. Her passions for travel and food were further kindled during the period she spent overseas. A member of the Society of American Travel Writers, she now writes on these topics for newspapers and magazines across the nation. Besides this and previous editions of *Insiders' Guide to the Florida Keys and Key West*, she is also the author of the recently published travel guide, *Walking Places in New England*.

Writing from her home on Duck Key, Vicki shares the bounty of the Keys with her husband, Bob, and her visiting adult

The thrills of the great beyond lure Vicki and Bob Shearer from the Florida Keys to Anchorage, where they are poised to take a seaplane. PHOTO: VICTORIA SHEARER

children and grandchildren—Kristen, John, and Christopher, and Brian, Lisa, Bethany, and Bobby.